ALBERTA

BRITISH COLUMBIA

MANITOBA

NEW BRUNSWICK

Guide to Canada

NEWFOUNDLAND

NORTHWEST TERRITORIES

NOVA SCOTIA

By LEN HILTS

Foreword by Dan Wallace
Former Director,
Canadian Government
Office of Tourism

ONTARIO

PRINCE EDWARD ISLAND

QUEBEC

SASKATCHEWAN

THE YUKON

RAND McNALLY & COMPANY Chicago • New York • San Francisco

TRAVEL INFORMATION

THE KEY TO THE ENJOYMENT of any trip is knowing what to do and what to see in each area you visit. There is nothing more disappointing than to pass through a place, only to learn later that you missed an exciting attraction or interesting side trip. The purpose of this guide is to introduce you to these special treats, but Canada is such a vast land of varied attractions that, of necessity, some could not be included or are described briefly. However, the problem is easily solved because the nation has the best organized tourist service in the world, and you can be well informed down to the smallest detail long before you leave home.

Before you begin your travels write to the Canadian Government Office of Tourism for the information you want. The headquarters are in Ottawa and there are branch offices throughout the United States. (See addresses below.)

The provincial travel bureaus are also extremely helpful. A letter to any of these agencies, indicating where you expect to visit, will bring a quick supply of brochures and pamphlets. You'll find the travel bureaus particularly useful when you need information of a changing nature—for example, the time and place of special events or the seasons and regulations for hunting and fishing.

In Canada you will find offices of tourist information located conveniently in every city and most towns. During the summer months some metropolitan centers, such as Toronto and Montreal, establish information kiosks at a number of places throughout their cities.

You can mail inquiries to the Canadian Government Office of Tourism at 150 Kent St., Ottawa, Ontario, KIA OH6, or to any of the offices listed below.

CALIFORNIA
510 W. Sixth St.
Los Angeles, Cal. 90014

Suite 1160, Alcoa Building
One Maritime Plaza
San Francisco, Cal. 94111

DISTRICT OF COLUMBIA
1771 N Street N.W.
Washington, D.C. 20036

GEORGIA
260 Peachtree St. N.W.
Atlanta, Ga., 30303

ILLINOIS
332 S. Michigan Ave.
Chicago, Ill. 60604

MASSACHUSETTS
Sixth Floor
500 Boylston St.
Boston, Mass. 02116

MICHIGAN
1900 First Federal Building
1001 Woodward Ave.
Detroit, Mich. 48226

MINNESOTA
Chamber of Commerce Building
15 S. Fifth St.
Minneapolis, Minn. 55402

NEW YORK
Room 1030
1251 Avenue of the Americas
New York, N.Y. 10020

Suite 3550
One Marine Midland Center
Buffalo, N.Y. 14203

OHIO
Tenth Floor
55 Public Square
Cleveland, Ohio 44113

PENNSYLVANIA
Suite 1810
3 Benjamin Franklin Pkwy.
Philadelphia, Pa. 19102

TEXAS
Suite 1600
2001 Bryan Tower
Dallas, Tex. 75201

WASHINGTON
Suite 1616
600 Stewart St.
Seattle, Wash. 98101

Canadian provincial travel bureaus:

ALBERTA
Travel Alberta
10065 Jasper Ave., Capital Square
Edmonton, Alberta T5J 0H4

BRITISH COLUMBIA
Department of Travel Industry
Parliament Buildings
Victoria, British Columbia

MANITOBA
Manitoba Government Travel
200 Vaughan St.
Winnipeg, Manitoba R3C 1P5

NEW BRUNSWICK
Department of Tourism
Promotion & Development Branch
PO Box 12345
Fredericton, New Brunswick E3B 5C3

NEWFOUNDLAND & LABRADOR
Tourist Services Division
Confederation Building
St. John's, Newfoundland A1C 5T7

NOVA SCOTIA
Department of Tourism
PO Box 130
Halifax, Nova Scotia B3J 2R5

ONTARIO
Ontario Travel
Queen's Park
Toronto, Ontario M7A 2E5

PRINCE EDWARD ISLAND
Tourism Services
PO Box 940
Charlottetown, Prince Edward Island C1A 7M5

QUEBEC
Department of Tourism, Fish, & Game
Tourism Branch
150 E. Saint-Cyrille Blvd.
Quebec City, Quebec G1R 4Y3

SASKATCHEWAN
SaskTravel
1825 Lorne St.
Regina, Saskatchewan S4P 3N1

YUKON TERRITORY
Division of Tourism
PO Box 2703
Whitehorse, Yukon Territory Y1A 2C6

NORTHWEST TERRITORIES
TravelArctic
Yellowknife, Northwest Territories X1A 2L9

Photographs courtesy of the
Canadian Government Office of Tourism

Guide to Canada *was formerly entitled* Explore Canada

Library of Congress Catalog Number: 76-44095
Printed in United States of America

PREFACE

THIS IS THE FIFTH EDITION of Rand McNally's *Guide to Canada*. Although the format of the book has been retained because readers have found that it suits their needs, all entries have been checked and revised when needed, and new attractions have been added.

With the book in hand, you should be able to plan your trip and enlarge your vacationing pleasure. It makes little difference where you want to go or what you want to do, because the high spots in all the provinces and territories are explored throughout the pages.

Canada is indeed an interesting place to visit for you, the exploring tourist, whether you are a Canadian taking a long-awaited holiday or a visitor from the United States or some other country bound on enjoying the delights of a land you haven't seen before.

Canada is a wonderful place to vacation because, first of all, you find gracious hospitality everywhere you go. Travelers from Toronto, for example, who stop in the pretty fishing villages along the Sunshine Coast of British Columbia, or who follow the spectacular Cabot Trail around Nova Scotia's Cape Breton Island, are treated as honored guests—not just because they're Canadian, and not because they're tourists, but because they're there. The latch string is always out, and residents want visitors to enjoy themselves.

I found this same welcome extended to all tourists, whereever I went during the preparation of this book—and it cheered me. This attitude is certainly not typical of many of the tourist-oriented countries of the world, where the traveler has become an important source of revenue, an impersonal commodity, not unlike a load of wheat, to be processed profitably and rapidly.

Second, Canada is a magnificent place for the exploring traveler because of the amazing variety of attractions, natural and otherwise, it has to offer. Looming mountains, wild and placid rivers, wide golden plains, fjords and bays, colorful villages and urbane metropolitan areas, cool lakes—the list is endless. Just about the only scenic phenomenon Canada lacks is a great desert, and this deficiency has yet to affect my travel enjoyment in this vast land.

This book attempts to capture the scope of Canada, past and present, and to catalog its wonders. You might consider it as a kind of shopping guide through which to browse when planning your next holiday. I have tried to find the interesting places—some of them tucked into out-of-the-way spots—and to list where you could be intrigued. You'll find all kinds of things to do, from panning for gold on the banks of the Fraser to shopping for cheese on the Ile D'Orleans.

Though I tried very hard to include all of the good places, I know there are many others that you will find. But that is the real delight of travel—for each of us to discover unique spots that become special experiences. With this in mind, use this book as a sampler and let it lead you to places that attract you. Then, once on the site, you should find dozens of things to see and do that I was not able to cover.

Canada's amazing network of tourist information services should be a big help to you. Wherever you go, you'll find an office, a store, a stand, or a kiosk conveniently at hand, staffed by smiling people with stacks of literature and maps waiting to give you a hand. The Government Office of Tourism in Ottawa sets the pace for these operations. The provinces do a fine job in their own areas, and the cities and town are equally capable.

I have found that the people who staff these places take a particular delight in ferreting out answers to difficult and improbable questions. In Nova Scotia, I decided I wanted to take a picture of a lobsterman at work. Five minutes after I asked, the pretty lady behind the information desk had me on my way to a place where I could find my man.

It seems to me that Canada offers a remarkably large number of opportunities for "dinner-table conversation," unusual trips guaranteed to provide an exchange of memories at the dinner table for years after you take them. The train ride from The Pas to Churchill would fall into this classification, and so would a sojourn up the Alaska Highway or a visit to the site of Vinland on the northern tip of Newfoundland.

In putting this book together and in making revisions, I have had tremendous help from people in all branches of Canada's travel industry. I had to ask thousands of questions to verify the statements in the copy, because, although I travel throughout Canada from Victoria to St. Johns, changes take place between my visits. New events are scheduled. Interesting attractions open their doors. Wonderfully cooperative persons in the Canadian Government Office of Tourism in Ottawa and in each of the provincial travel bureaus have taken the time to find answers to my questions and to suggest new ideas. Without their help and enthusiastic cooperation, the revisions would not have been possible. Although there isn't room to mention them by name, my deepest thanks to all of them.

Len Hilts

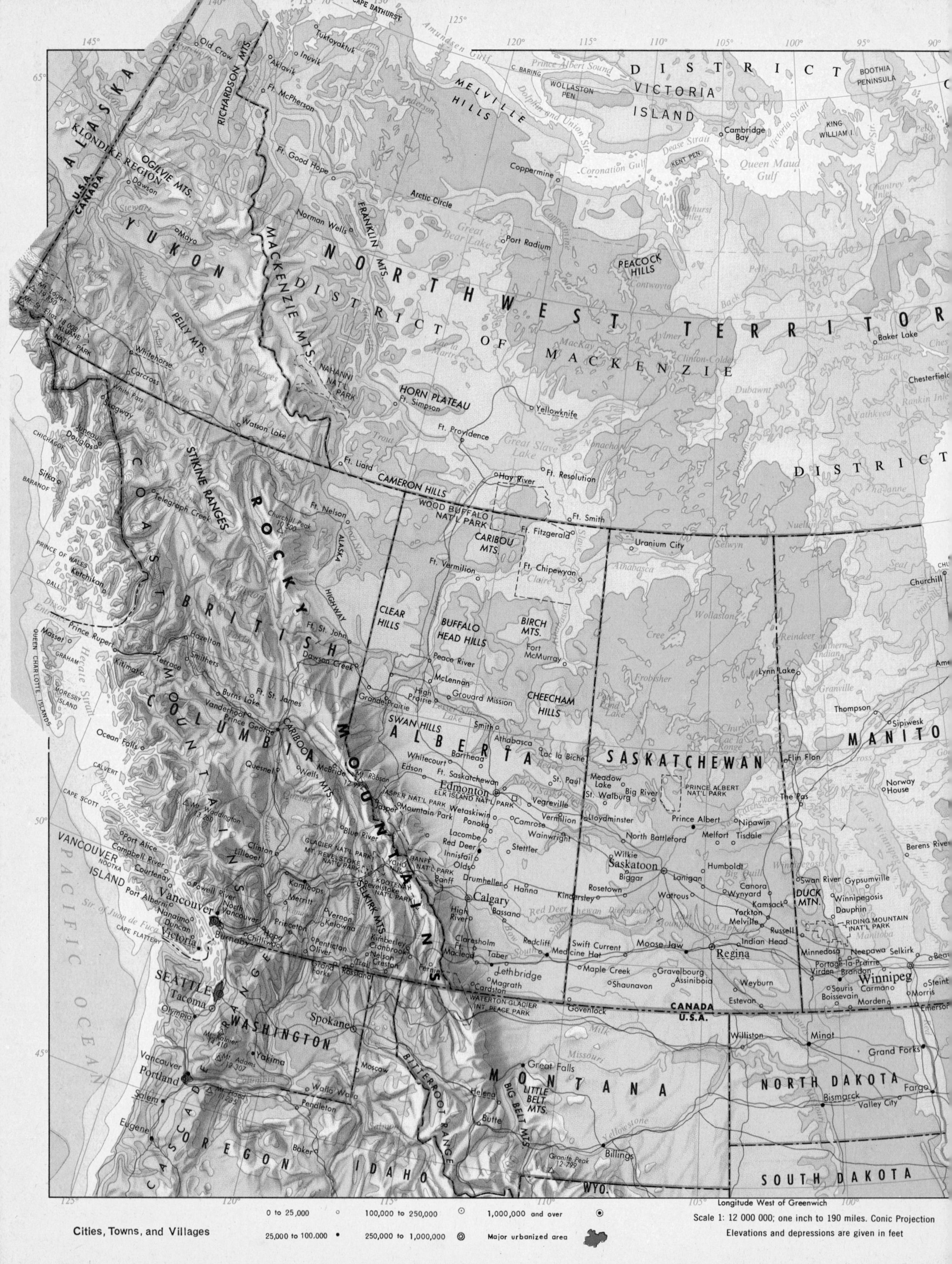

NORTHWEST TERRITORIES
DISTRICT OF MACKENZIE
DISTRICT
VICTORIA ISLAND
YUKON
ALASKA
BRITISH COLUMBIA
ALBERTA
SASKATCHEWAN
MANITO
WASHINGTON
OREGON
IDAHO
MONTANA
NORTH DAKOTA
SOUTH DAKOTA
WYO.
PACIFIC OCEAN
ROCKY MOUNTAINS
COAST MOUNTAINS
CASCADE RANGE
MACKENZIE MTS.
RICHARDSON MTS.
OGILVIE MTS.
KLONDIKE REGION
PELLY MTS.
FRANKLIN MTS.
MELVILLE HILLS
STIKINE RANGES
CARIBOO MTS.
SELKIRK MTS.
BITTERROOT RANGE
BIG BELT MTS.
LITTLE BELT MTS.
HORN PLATEAU
CAMERON HILLS
CARIBOU MTS.
CLEAR HILLS
BUFFALO HEAD HILLS
BIRCH MTS.
CHEECHAM HILLS
SWAN HILLS
PEACOCK HILLS
DUCK MTN.
NAHANNI NAT'L PARK
WOOD BUFFALO NAT'L PARK
PRINCE ALBERT NAT'L PARK
JASPER NAT'L PARK
ELK ISLAND NAT'L PARK
GLACIER NAT'L PARK
MT. REVELSTOKE NAT'L PARK
BANFF NAT'L PARK
KOOTENAY NAT'L PARK
YOHO
RIDING MOUNTAIN NAT'L PARK
WATERTON-GLACIER INT. PEACE PARK
KLUANE NAT'L PARK
ALASKA HIGHWAY
Arctic Circle
U.S.A. CANADA
CANADA U.S.A.
CAPE BATHURST
C. BARING
WOLLASTON PEN.
BOOTHIA PENINSULA
KING WILLIAM I.
KENT PEN.
Amundsen Gulf
Prince Albert Sound
Dolphin and Union Str.
Coronation Gulf
Queen Maud Gulf
Dease Strait
Victoria Strait
Great Bear Lake
Great Slave Lake
Lake Athabasca
Reindeer Lake
Lake Winnipeg
Hecate Strait
Str. of Juan de Fuca
QUEEN CHARLOTTE ISLANDS
MORESBY ISLAND
GRAHAM
VANCOUVER ISLAND
PRINCE OF WALES
BARANOF
CHICHAGOF
CAPE SCOTT
CAPE FLATTERY
Mt. Logan 19,850
Mt. St. Elias 18,008
Mt. Waddington 13,260
Mt. Robson 12,972
Churchill Peak 10,500
Mt. Rainier 14,410
Mt. Adams 12,307
Mt. Hood 11,235
Granite Peak 12,799
Old Crow
Tuktoyaktuk
Inuvik
Aklavik
Ft. McPherson
Ft. Good Hope
Norman Wells
Coppermine
Port Radium
Cambridge Bay
Dawson
Mayo
Whitehorse
Carcross
Skagway
Juneau
Douglas
Sitka
Watson Lake
Ft. Simpson
Ft. Providence
Yellowknife
Ft. Liard
Hay River
Ft. Resolution
Ft. Smith
Ft. Fitzgerald
Ft. Chipewyan
Uranium City
Baker Lake
Chesterfield
Churchill
Ft. Nelson
Telegraph Creek
Ketchikan
Ft. Vermilion
Ft. St. John
Fort McMurray
Peace River
Dawson Creek
McLennan
High Prairie
Grouard Mission
Grande Prairie
Prince Rupert
Masset
Hazelton
Smithers
Terrace
Kitimat
Burns Lake
Ft. St. James
Vanderhoof
Prince George
Ocean Falls
Quesnel
Wells
McBride
Smith
Athabasca
Lac la Biche
Barrhead
Whitecourt
Edson
Ft. Saskatchewan
Edmonton
Jasper
Mountain Park
Wetaskiwin
Ponoka
Vegreville
Vermilion
Camrose
Wainwright
Lloydminster
St. Paul
Meadow Lake
St. Walburg
Big River
Prince Albert
Nipawin
Melfort
Tisdale
North Battleford
Lynn Lake
Thompson
Sipiwesk
Flin Flon
The Pas
Norway House
Berens River
Blue River
Clinton
Lillooet
Port Alice
Campbell River
Courtenay
Powell River
Port Alberni
Nanaimo
Duncan
Victoria
Vancouver
North Vancouver
Burnaby
Chilliwack
Hope
Kamloops
Revelstoke
Merritt
Princeton
Vernon
Kelowna
Penticton
Oliver
Trail
Nelson
Creston
Rossland
Grand Forks
Kimberley
Cranbrook
Fernie
Golden
Banff
Lacombe
Red Deer
Innisfail
Olds
Drumheller
Stettler
Hanna
Calgary
High River
Bassano
Claresholm
Ft. Macleod
Taber
Lethbridge
Magrath
Cardston
Redcliff
Medicine Hat
Kindersley
Rosetown
Wilkie
Biggar
Saskatoon
Humboldt
Lanigan
Watrous
Swift Current
Maple Creek
Shaunavon
Gravelbourg
Assiniboia
Moose Jaw
Regina
Indian Head
Weyburn
Estevan
Canora
Wynyard
Kamsack
Yorkton
Melville
Russell
Swan River
Gypsumville
Winnipegosis
Dauphin
Minnedosa
Neepawa
Selkirk
Portage-la-Prairie
Brandon
Virden
Winnipeg
Souris
Boissevain
Carman
Morden
Morris
Emerson
Steinbach
Govenlock
Seattle
Tacoma
Olympia
Spokane
Yakima
Vancouver
Portland
Salem
Eugene
Walla Walla
Pendleton
Baker
Moscow
Great Falls
Helena
Butte
Billings
Williston
Minot
Grand Forks
Bismarck
Valley City
Fargo
Missouri
Yellowstone
Milk
Columbia
Longitude West of Greenwich
Cities, Towns, and Villages
0 to 25,000
25,000 to 100,000
100,000 to 250,000
250,000 to 1,000,000
1,000,000 and over
Major urbanized area
Scale 1: 12 000 000; one inch to 190 miles. Conic Projection
Elevations and depressions are given in feet

Longitude West of Greenwich
Same scale as main map
QUEBEC
NEWFOUNDLAND
ATLANTIC OCEAN
HUDSON BAY
All islands within bays and straits lie within Northwest Territories.
FRANKLIN
KEEWATIN
BAFFIN ISLAND
PENINSULE D'UNGAVA
QUEBEC
LABRADOR
ONTARIO
NEW BRUNSWICK
NOVA SCOTIA
MAINE
NEW YORK
PENNSYLVANIA
MICHIGAN
WISCONSIN
ATLANTIC OCEAN
Relief
Meters
Feet
3050 10 000
1525 5000
610 2000
305 1000
152.5 500
Sea Level
0 0
152.5 500
1525 5000
3050 10 000
A-520200-76
COPYRIGHT BY RAND McNALLY & COMPANY
MADE IN U.S.A.
0 25 50 75 100 200 300 400 500 Miles
0 100 200 400 600 800 Kilometers

FOREWORD 

"TRAVEL" HAS NOW COME a long way from its ancient sense of "travail" (hard work). In time, money, and trouble, it now costs relatively less than ever before to roam this globe and explore new worlds and old.

This excellent and eminently useful book edited by Len Hilts is an "Open Sesame!" to Canada. Mr. Hilts has researched his subject carefully—without being overwhelmed by the immensity, the complexity, and the magic of his subject. And what a country it is! In size, second only to the U.S.S.R., it is sparsely populated with 22 million people. It is a land of immense distances—in many ways different from the United States and yet in many ways its twin: in scenic vistas, with lively cities, and yet with placid, rural areas and vast wilderness solitudes.

Canada and the United States, as close neighbors, each year exchange many millions of visitors. More important, we exchange ideas and form friendships. Travel is, preeminently, the best sort of people-to-people communication ever devised. People by the millions are on the move in North America, indeed, all over the world. In their pilgrimage to discover other peoples, other places, they are gaining new insight into the inner universe of their own personalities. The impact of mass travel on the world's future has yet to be assessed. While we are all "members of one humanity," the jet plane has also made us neighbors—for (given airports nearby) none of us is more than one day's jet journey from each of the three billion people that share this planet with us. Hopefully, as we move around more freely, and increase the number of our friends and the depth of our understanding of their problems and aspirations, we will be forced to the conclusion that friendship should encircle this globe and peace should be granted dominion over us all.

In no part of this world is travel more active—or understanding deeper and more enduring—than across the 5,000 mile United States–Canada border. No one guidebook can open Canada and all its marvels and mysteries to the visitor—or even to Canadians who have lived here all their lives. But Mr. Hilts has made a splendid beginning. His book can be your faithful companion as you set out to learn more about Canada. It can "go with you and be your guide" as you go adventuring to find out more about Canada, Canadians, and—not least important—by the relaxed and tranquil pace of your travelling, to learn more about yourself.

Canada is a land so immense it takes three oceans and the Great Lakes to encompass it: it reaches, in depth, halfway from the North Pole to the Equator; and it is seven time zones wide. While it cherishes the language and cultures of its two founding races, Canada is a mosaic of many customs and many languages, and annual festivals recall their rich flavor and gaiety. In his historical notes, Mr. Hilts recreates the excitement of "old . . . far-off things and battles long ago." He talks of the handicrafts characteristic of each region, he notes "not-to-be-missed" events so his reader can attend at least *some* of them, and his detailed accounts of places of special significance ensure that a traveller in Canada knows what to see, what to do, where to go.

In short, Len Hilts has done a yeoman job in compiling this book about Canada. I believe that his *Guide to Canada* will help you get more from your travels in our country—and persuade you to range more widely in your exploring, to feel the dynamism of the citizens of this New World as they roll, with hope and high hearts, into the exciting early years of their Second Century of Confederation.

One thing is sure: you will be greeted everywhere in our country with relaxed and unassuming hospitality. The mat is out whether it says "Welcome," "Bienvenue," or both! And for your venturing across our land Canadians of both languages and of all origins agree on the words and the sincere, heartfelt good wish: "Bon Voyage!"

Dan Wallace
Former Director
Canadian Government Office of Tourism
Ottawa, Canada

CONTENTS

Travel Information ii
Preface iii
Foreword vi
Canadian Facts 4

PACIFIC & ROCKIES · 6
British Columbia 9
Alberta 19
The Cities:
Vancouver 23
Victoria 25
Edmonton 27
Calgary 29

GREAT PLAINS · 30
Saskatchewan 33
Manitoba 38
The Cities:
Winnipeg 42
Regina 43

HEARTLAND · 46
Ontario 51
The Cities:
Toronto 58
Ottawa 59
Hamilton 61

LA BELLE PROVINCE · 62
Quebec 65
The Cities:
Quebec City 71
Montreal 72

MARITIMES · 74
New Brunswick 78
Prince Edward Island 80
Nova Scotia 80
Newfoundland 82
The Cities:
Saint John 83
Halifax 84
St. John's 85

WILDERNESS · 86
Yukon Territory 88
Northwest Territories 89

PARKS · 92
Camping 104
Hunting & Fishing 150
Weather 161
Transportation 162
Boat Trips 164
Shopping 166
Accommodations & Restaurants 168
Border Crossing 181
Index 182

MAPS

Physical–Political iv–v
Highway 2–3
British Columbia 10
Alberta 18
Vancouver 23
Victoria 26
Edmonton 27
Calgary 27
Saskatchewan 34
Manitoba 39
Winnipeg 42
Regina 43
Ontario 50
Toronto 58
Ottawa 59
Hamilton 59
Quebec 67
Quebec City 71
Montreal 71
Atlantic Provinces 79
Saint John 83
Halifax 83
St. John's 83
Yukon–Northwest Territories 91
Alberta campgrounds 106
British Columbia campgrounds 111
Manitoba campgrounds 114
Atlantic Provinces campgrounds 115
Ontario campgrounds 118
Quebec campgrounds 119
Saskatchewan campgrounds 122

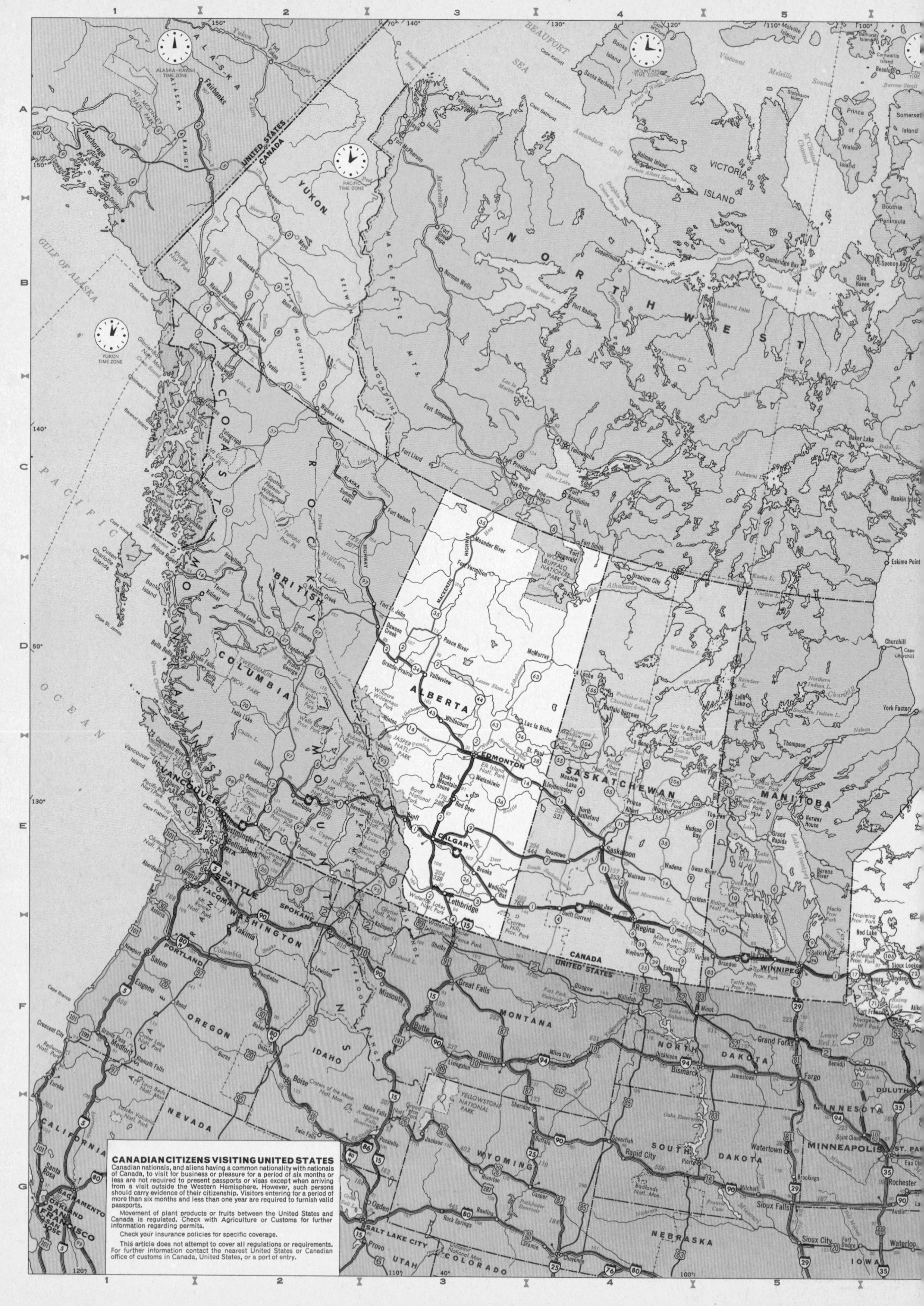

CANADIAN CITIZENS VISITING UNITED STATES

Canadian nationals, and aliens having a common nationality with nationals of Canada, to visit for business or pleasure for a period of six months or less are not required to present passports or visas except when arriving from a visit outside the Western Hemisphere. However, such persons should carry evidence of their citizenship. Visitors entering for a period of more than six months and less than one year are required to furnish valid passports.

Movement of plant products or fruits between the United States and Canada is regulated. Check with Agriculture or Customs for further information regarding permits.

Check your insurance policies for specific coverage.

This article does not attempt to cover all regulations or requirements. For further information contact the nearest United States or Canadian office of customs in Canada, United States, or a port of entry.

NOTE: RED FIGURES ON THIS CHART INDICATE KILOMETERS. BLUE FIGURES INDICATE MILES.
For example the distance between Montreal and Vancouver is 2960 miles or 4765 kilometers.

	CHICAGO	EDMONTON	FREDERICTON	HALIFAX	HAMILTON	LONDON	MONCTON	MONTREAL	NEW YORK, NY.	NIAGARA FALLS	NORTH BAY	OTTAWA	QUEBEC
CALGARY	1602 / 2578	178 / 286	2828 / 4550	3120 / 5021	2055 / 3308	1982 / 3189	2953 / 4753	2269 / 3652	2404 / 3869	2098 / 3377	1937 / 3116	2166 / 3487	2414 / 3885
CHICAGO		1628 / 2619	1448 / 3941	1630 / 2623	457 / 735	384 / 618	1463 / 2354	828 / 1333	802 / 1290	500 / 805	660 / 1072	713 / 1147	989 / 1592
EDMONTON			2858 / 4600	3150 / 5068	2085 / 3357	2012 / 3239	2983 / 4802	2320 / 3735	2430 / 3912	2251 / 3624	1967 / 3165	2196 / 3535	2484 / 3999
FREDERICTON				292 / 470	913 / 1469	954 / 1535	125 / 201	538 / 866	646 / 1039	956 / 1538	891 / 1434	662 / 1065	374 / 602
HALIFAX					1205 / 1938	1246 / 2005	167 / 269	830 / 1336	929 / 1495	1248 / 2008	1183 / 1903	954 / 1535	666 / 1072
HAMILTON						73 / 117	1038 / 1670	375 / 604	437 / 703	43 / 69	241 / 388	288 / 463	539 / 867
LONDON							1079 / 1736	416 / 669	510 / 821	116 / 187	282 / 454	329 / 529	580 / 933
MONCTON								663 / 1067	762 / 1226	1081 / 1739	1016 / 1635	787 / 1266	499 / 803
MONTREAL									378 / 608	418 / 672	853 / 568	124 / 199	161 / 259
NEW YORK, NY.										394 / 634	678 / 1091	467 / 751	518 / 834
NIAGARA FALLS											284 / 457	331 / 533	582 / 936
NORTH BAY												299 / 368	517 / 832
OTTAWA													288 / 463

	REGINA	ST. JOHN, NB.	SAN FRANCISCO, CA.	SASKATOON	SAULT STE. MARIE, ONT.	SHERBROOKE	THUNDER BAY	TORONTO	VANCOUVER	VICTORIA	WINDSOR	WINNIPEG
CALGARY	492 / 792	2890 / 4652	1324 / 2130	294 / 473	1669 / 2685	2383 / 3836	1230 / 1984	2063 / 3321	670 / 1078	738 / 1188	1864 / 2999	795 / 1279
CHICAGO	1147 / 1845	1400 / 2253	2142 / 3448	1304 / 2098	443 / 713	893 / 1437	651 / 1047	492 / 792	2268 / 3651	2336 / 3761	266 / 428	832 / 1339
EDMONTON	481 / 774	2920 / 4700	1661 / 2672	324 / 521	1699 / 2733	2413 / 3884	1260 / 2027	2168 / 3990	848 / 1365	916 / 1474	1967 / 3165	825 / 1328
FREDERICTON	2390 / 3847	62 / 99	3590 / 5776	2534 / 4079	1159 / 1865	2534 / 4079	1548 / 2571	873 / 1405	3498 / 5628	3566 / 5738	1072 / 1725	2033 / 3273
HALIFAX	2682 / 4317	268 / 431	3873 / 6232	2806 / 4549	1451 / 2335	792 / 1275	1890 / 3056	1165 / 1874	3790 / 6098	3858 / 6208	1364 / 2195	2325 / 3743
HAMILTON	1604 / 2581	975 / 1569	2599 / 4184	1851 / 2978	509 / 819	468 / 753	948 / 1525	40 / 64	2848 / 4585	2916 / 4694	191 / 307	1383 / 2225
LONDON	1531 / 2463	1016 / 1635	2526 / 4066	1761 / 2834	386 / 621	509 / 819	825 / 1328	81 / 130	2652 / 4268	2720 / 4379	118 / 190	1260 / 2027
MONCTON	2515 / 4048	101 / 162	3715 / 5978	2659 / 4280	1284 / 2066	625 / 1005	1723 / 2772	998 / 1696	3623 / 5830	3691 / 5939	1197 / 1926	2158 / 3474
MONTREAL	1852 / 2980	600 / 966	2961 / 4765	1996 / 3212	621 / 999	93 / 150	1060 / 1706	336 / 541	2960 / 4765	3028 / 4872	534 / 859	1434 / 2307
NEW YORK, NY.	1949 / 3136	661 / 1064	2934 / 4721	2106 / 3390	900 / 1448	371 / 597	1339 / 2154	469 / 755	3070 / 4939	3138 / 5049	631 / 1015	1634 / 2629
NIAGARA FALLS	1647 / 2650	1055 / 1697	2642 / 4253	1804 / 2903	552 / 888	511 / 822	1151 / 1312	83 / 133	2768 / 4456	2836 / 4565	234 / 377	1360 / 2188
NORTH BAY	1499 / 2412	953 / 1534	2808 / 4520	1643 / 2644	268 / 431	446 / 718	707 / 1138	201 / 323	2607 / 4197	2675 / 4306	400 / 644	1142 / 1837
OTTAWA	1728 / 2781	724 / 1165	2855 / 4596	1872 / 3012	497 / 800	217 / 349	936 / 1506	248 / 399	2836 / 4565	2904 / 4675	447 / 719	1371 / 2206
QUEBEC	2016 / 3246	436 / 702	3122 / 5024	2160 / 3477	785 / 1263	126 / 203	1224 / 1969	497 / 800	3124 / 5026	3192 / 5136	698 / 1123	1579 / 2541
REGINA		2452 / 3947	2113 / 3402	2072 / 3336	1231 / 1981	1945 / 3130	792 / 1275	1654 / 2661	1121 / 1804	1189 / 1913	1413 / 2274	357 / 575
ST. JOHN, NB.			3605 / 5800	2596 / 4179	1221 / 1965	562 / 904	1660 / 2671	935 / 1505	3560 / 5728	3628 / 5838	1134 / 1825	2095 / 3373
SAN FRANCISCO, CA.				1915 / 3081	2585 / 4161	3035 / 4883	2851 / 4589	2625 / 4225	951 / 1530	1019 / 1639	2408 / 3877	1919 / 3088
SASKATOON					1375 / 2212	2089 / 3363	936 / 1506	1798 / 2893	964 / 1551	1032 / 1660	1530 / 2462	501 / 806
SAULT STE. MARIE, ONT.						714 / 1149	438 / 705	423 / 681	2339 / 3765	2407 / 3875	268 / 431	874 / 1406
SHERBROOKE							1153 / 1855	428 / 689	3053 / 4912	3121 / 5022	627 / 1009	1588 / 2555
THUNDER BAY								862 / 1387	1900 / 3057	1968 / 3167	707 / 1138	435 / 700
TORONTO									2733 / 4400	2801 / 4509	199 / 320	1297 / 2087
VANCOUVER										68 / 109	2534 / 4079	1465 / 2357
VICTORIA											2602 / 4189	1533 / 2467
WINDSOR												1126 / 1812

CANADA
Capital: Ottawa
Population: 23,260,600
Area: 3,851,809 sq. mi.

ALBERTA
Capital: Edmonton
Population: 1,838,037
Area: 255,285 sq. mi.

BRITISH COLUMBIA
Capital: Victoria
Population: 2,466,608
Area: 366,255 sq. mi.

MANITOBA
Capital: Winnipeg
Population: 1,021,506
Area: 251,000 sq. mi.

NEW BRUNSWICK
Capital: Fredericton
Population: 677,250
Area: 28,354 sq. mi.

NEWFOUNDLAND
Capital: St. John's
Population: 557,725
Area: 156,185 sq. mi.
112,826 (Labrador)
43,359 (Island of Newfoundland)

NOVA SCOTIA
Capital: Halifax
Population: 828,571
Area: 21,425 sq. mi.

ONTARIO
Capital: Toronto
Population: 8,264,465
Area: 412,582 sq. mi.

PRINCE EDWARD ISLAND
Capital: Charlottetown
Population: 118,229
Area: 2,184 sq. mi.

QUEBEC
Capital: Quebec City
Population: 6,234,445
Area: 594,860 sq. mi.

SASKATCHEWAN
Capital: Regina
Population: 921,323
Area: 251,700 sq. mi.

NORTHWEST TERRITORIES
Capital: Yellowknife
Population: 42,609
Area: 1,304,904 sq. mi.

YUKON TERRITORY
Capital: Whitehorse
Population: 21,836
Area: 207,076 sq. mi.

MAJOR CITIES—POPULATION

Toronto	2,803,101
Montreal	2,802,485
Vancouver	1,116,348
Ottawa-Hull	693,288
Winnipeg	578,217
Edmonton	554,228
Quebec	542,158
Hamilton	529,371
Calgary	469,917
London	270,383

TIME ZONES

Seven of the world's 24 time zones cross Canada. The total difference between the Newfoundland Zone and the Yukon Zone is 5½ hours, because there is only a one-half hour difference between the Newfoundland Zone and the Atlantic Zone. Therefore, when it is noon in Newfoundland, it is 6:30 am in the Yukon.

Newfoundland	Noon
Atlantic	11:30 am
Eastern	10:30 am
Central	9:30 am
Mountain	8:30 am
Pacific	7:30 am
Yukon	6:30 am

PRINCIPAL RIVERS

Mackenzie to the Arctic Ocean	2,635 mi.
Yukon to the Pacific Ocean	1,979 mi.
St. Lawrence to the Atlantic Ocean	1,900 mi.
Nelson to Hudson Bay	1,600 mi.
Saskatchewan to Hudson Bay	1,205 mi.
Peace to the Arctic Ocean	1,195 mi.
Churchill to Hudson Bay	1,000 mi.

PRINCIPAL MOUNTAINS

Mount Logan in The Yukon	19,850 ft.
Mount Fairweather in British Columbia	15,300 ft.
Mount Waddington in British Columbia	13,260 ft.
Mount Robson in British Columbia	12,972 ft.
Mount Columbia in Alberta	12,294 ft.

RECORD TEMPERATURES

Highest recorded temperature in Canada is 115 degrees, officially noted in southern Alberta.

Lowest recorded temperature is 81 degrees below zero, logged at Snag, Yukon Territory, in 1947.

THE FLAG

Canada's flag is an 11-point maple leaf on a white field with two red bands at either end. It was adopted on February 15, 1965. The Union Jack was the Canadian banner from 1763 until 1945, and today it is still flown as a symbol of Canada's membership in the British Commonwealth on Commonwealth occasions or in honor of the Queen.

POSTAL RATES

The postal rate for first-class mail within Canada and to the United States is 14¢ per ounce. This rate applies to postcards as well as letter mail. The rate to all other countries is 25¢ per ounce.

All domestic first-class mail and first-class mail to the United States is carried by air, providing air transmission will expedite delivery and the package does not exceed 66 pounds. All overseas letter mail up to one pound is automatically carried by air.

NEWSPAPERS

Canada's first newspaper was the ***Halifax Gazette,*** first published in 1752. It survives today as the provincial government gazette.

The oldest continuing newspaper in Canada is the ***Quebec Gazette,*** first published in 1764. It is a part of the ***Quebec Chronicle-Telegraph,*** published in Quebec City today.

Canada's largest newspapers are: ***Toronto Star, Toronto Globe and Mail, Vancouver Sun, Montreal La Presse, Calgary Herald, Ottawa Citizen,*** and ***Ottawa Journal.***

METRIC SYSTEM

Canada is on the metric system, and a simple miles/kilometers hint is in order. There are approximately 1.6 kilometers to one mile. This makes it fairly easy to convert in either direction. For instance, if you have 60 kilometers, and want to know miles, multiply 60 times .6, and your answer is 36 miles. If you have 60 miles, and want to know kilometers, multiply 60 times 1.6, and you have 96 kilometers.

Approximate Equivalents

10 mi = 16 km	10 km = 6 mi
20 mi = 32 km	20 km = 12 mi
50 mi = 80 km	50 km = 30 mi
100 mi = 160 km	100 km = 60 mi

CANADIAN FACTS

HIGHEST POINT IN EACH PROVINCE

Alberta	Mount Columbia	12,294 ft.
British Columbia	Mount Fairweather	15,300 ft.
Manitoba	Mount Baldy	2,727 ft.
New Brunswick	Mount Carleton	2,690 ft.
Newfoundland	Lewis Hills	2,672 ft.
Nova Scotia	Cape Breton Uplands	1,747 ft.
Ontario	Mount Ogidaki	2,183 ft.
Prince Edward Island	Queens County	466 ft.
Quebec	Mount Jacques Cartier	4,160 ft.
Saskatchewan	Cypress Hills	4,546 ft.
Northwest Territories	Ellesmere Island	9,600 ft.
The Yukon	Mount Logan	19,850 ft.

NATIONAL HOLIDAYS

New Year's Day
January 1

Good Friday
Friday preceding Easter Sunday

Easter Monday
Monday after Easter Sunday

Victoria Day
Monday preceding May 25

Dominion Day
July 1

Labor Day
First Monday in September

Thanksgiving Day
Second Monday in October

Remembrance Day
November 11

Christmas Day
December 25

Other holidays observed in various provinces:

MANITOBA

Civic Holiday
First Monday in August

NEWFOUNDLAND

St. Patrick's Day
March 17

St. George's Day
April 18

Commonwealth Day
May 24

Orangeman's Day
July 12

ONTARIO

Civic Holiday
First Monday in August

QUEBEC

Saint-Jean Baptiste Day
June 24

NORTHWEST TERRITORIES

Civic Holiday
First Monday in August

YUKON TERRITORY

Discovery Day
Monday preceding August 17

All provinces except Quebec:

Boxing Day
December 26

PACIFIC & ROCKIES

The Fraser River area of British Columbia, Mount Robson in the background

BRITISH COLUMBIA · ALBERTA

THE CANADA THAT TOUCHES THE PACIFIC AND ENCOMPASSES THE ROCKY MOUNTAINS IS A BIG, MUSCULAR PLACE. NOTHING IN BRITISH COLUMBIA OR ALBERTA IS DONE ON A SMALL SCALE. THE MOUNTAINS ARE THE BIGGEST, THE TREES ARE THE TALLEST, THE HARBORS THE GREATEST, THE LAKES THE BLUEST, THE SKI RUNS THE LONGEST—EVERYTHING HAPPENS IN SUPERLATIVES. WHEN GOD DREW HIS PLAN FOR THIS PART OF THE WORLD, HE SKETCHED IN BIG, BOLD STROKES.

Here, perhaps more than in any other part of the country, you feel the pioneering spirit. There is still a strong sense of newness, of the frontier life. Remember, it hasn't been very long since a path was blasted through the mountains to eliminate the isolation of the Pacific coast, tying the nation together with a transcontinental railroad. And the Trans-Canada Highway, that concrete ribbon from St. John's, Newfoundland, to Victoria, British Columbia, is really quite new. Much of the land of these provinces is undeveloped, some even unexplored.

This is country which in many places still belongs to the moose, the elk, the caribou, the salmon, and the big, big trout. Man is almost an intruder; he hasn't quite taken up permanent residence. The prospector still pokes through the remote regions, much as he did a hundred years ago, dreaming of the big strike—and talk of gold and silver spices many a conversation. The lumberjack, though his equipment is now mechanized a bit, still humbles the great craggy Douglas fir pretty much as he has always done. It may not be more than a four-hour drive from the very modern and beautifully gardened streets of Vancouver to a rough-and-tumble backwoods logging camp or a hopeful miner's hillside diggings. That's how close today's living here is to the frontier.

This has been a country of gold and lumber and wheat and fruit, but not long ago a new wealth came gushing up through the narrow-shouldered skeletons you now see in Alberta. Oil and natural gas gave a whole new dimension to the economy.

Other underground treasures still are waiting for discovery. Nearly every known metal is found somewhere in these provinces in abundant supply, and undoubtedly there is more to come, since so much of the country has had little more than a cursory glance.

You'll find as you visit the towns of the area that "old" in these parts isn't really very old. (A home more than a hundred years of age is indeed a rarity.) Old things bespeak a history and a past, but this area is just beginning to write its history, and thus has relatively little past to talk about.

EARLY EXPLORATION

That doughty mariner, Sir Francis Drake, sailed past the coast in 1579, looking for the Northwest Passage, but he paused only long enough to print the name "New Albion" on his charts. During the next 200 years, Russian fur traders came to do business with the Indian tribes along the coast—chiefly because they offered the most luxurious pelts in the world—but they made no effort to settle.

In 1775 the Spanish sent an expedition to claim the area, and left as a heritage such names as the Strait of Juan de Fuca and Quadra Island. Captain James Cook (of Sandwich Island fame), who thought of the Pacific as his private lake, landed at Nootka on Vancouver Island in 1778 and a fur trading post was established, to the alarm of the Spanish. The subsequent dispute was finally settled by the Nootka Convention in 1790, when the coast became British territory.

Captain George Vancouver sailed out of England to take possession of the new land for the Queen in 1792, and that most remarkable and diligent of all trader-explorers, Alexander Mackenzie, then on the last leg of his epoch-making hike across Canada, crossed British Columbia in 1793. To reach the waters of the Pacific he passed through what is now Tweedsmuir Provincial Park, and the trail he cut is still there. He claimed trading rights for the North West Company, and fur commerce with the East was begun. By then, people were calling the land New Caledonia.

The Hudson's Bay Company and the North West Company competed bitterly all across Alberta and British Columbia for the next 30 years. The traders and trappers of these companies explored, mapped, settled, and governed wherever they went. The struggle between the two giants came to an end in 1821, when Hudson's Bay took over North West.

Many of the cities you visit today—Victoria, Nanaimo, and dozens of others—were originally trading forts of the Hudson's Bay Company. In 1849, the company withdrew from the business of government. Fort Victoria was turned over to the Crown, to become the capital city of the new colony of British Columbia.

In 1867 the Dominion of Canada was established when the provinces of Ontario, Quebec, Nova Scotia, and New Brunswick were welded together as the "Canadian Confederation," but British Columbians held out joining for several years—until they were assured that a transcontinental railroad would be built to link them to the East. The promise was made in 1871, and the first train on that railroad chugged into Vancouver on May 23, 1887.

THE MOUNTIES

The first white man to explore Alberta was Anthony Henday, who traveled the area for the Hudson's Bay Company in 1754. It was known as Rupert's Land then, and in the 120 years that followed it was a trading battleground in the struggle between the two competitors—Hudson's Bay and the North West Company. Later it was the stage on which the North West Mounted Police confronted the whiskey traders who had moved up into the country from the Indian Territories below the border.

Canada bought Rupert's Land from the Hudson's Bay Company in 1870 for $1,350,000—one of history's great real estate bargains—and made its new acquisition a part of the Northwest Territories. The Alberta District was separated from the territories in 1882. With the building of the transcontinental railroad in 1885, a steady stream of farmers and homesteaders flowed into Alberta, and it achieved provincial status in 1905.

The great plains of Alberta, Saskatchewan, and Manitoba were the birthplace of one of the world's great police forces: the North West Mounted Police. This unique organization was made official by act of Parliament in 1873, for the specific purpose of bringing law and order to the wild prairie. In those early years, when the scarlet tunics were just beginning to become famous, a force of only 300 men policed an area of more than 300,000 miles—and accomplished what they set out to do.

In 1904, the King honored the Mounties with a new name—the Royal North West Mounted Police—and in 1920, since their work was now on a national scale, they became the Royal Canadian Mounted Police. Today the force totals 8,700 men. They are Canada's federal police force, and they also police all of the provinces except Ontario and Quebec. The familiar scarlet coats are now the force's dress uniform, seen only on state occasions, and their workaday garb is a khaki tunic over blue trousers. But even in such conventional clothes, these men are still the admired Mounties.

The Mounties are a gracious group who welcome visitors to their posts at any time. You'll find displays and museums at those posts where important events in Mountie history took place. Typical is the museum at Fort Macleod, Alberta, where a replica of the first North West Mounted Police fort in western Canada has been built.

British Columbia and Alberta offer you some of Canada's most dazzling sightseeing. Where else could you see Lake Louise, a blue jewel in a rugged mountain setting, the beauty of which cannot be captured in words? Or Banff and Jasper national parks—magnificent panoramas of majestic mountains, ice fields, white-tongued glaciers, pounding rivers and lacy waterfalls, and superb scenic highways.

The drive through Rogers Pass and Glacier National Park is one you won't easily forget. And for variety of landscape, with vistas ranging from tame and orderly farms and orchards to wild white-water cataracts, you shouldn't miss the opportunity to follow the Fraser River, both in its turbulent run south through the awesome Fraser Canyon and in its much gentler flow to the west for a meeting with the Pacific at Vancouver.

Vancouver is the hub of a great wheel of travel pleasure. You can head out in any direction and find delightful spots to visit.

The round trip from Vancouver up the Sunshine Coast, across to Vancouver Island, down the island to Victoria, and back across the Strait of Georgia to Vancouver is a happy combination of good roads, long and colorful ferry rides, picturesque fishing villages, unexcelled scenery, and opportunities to browse and play—all in a surprisingly moderate climate. Though you are in the shadow of the snow-topped giants of the Coast Mountains most of the time, you find yourself reveling in a subtropical climate where snow is a rarity even in midwinter.

For a different kind of trip, drive to the northern end of Vancouver Island, to Kelsey Bay, and there embark on the overnight ferry to Prince Rupert. Spend a bit of time in this port city, then become an explorer and turn your car toward the east. Follow the new Yellowhead Highway, a lovely, though at times lonesome, drive through the midst of some of British Columbia's most ruggedly beautiful country. You might stay on the Yellowhead through to Edmonton, visiting Jasper National Park along the way, or turn south at Prince George to Quesnel, Barkerville, and the Fraser Canyon.

Then, of course, there is the luxurious trip north from Vancouver through the fabled Inside Passage to Skagway, the gateway to the gold rush of 1898. The round trip is six and a half days of cruise fun that are more attractive than an Atlantic crossing because of the constantly changing backdrop of mountains, islands, and fjords.

The big cities in this part of Canada have distinctive personalities and special charms that are all their own.

Victoria, with its quaint Old English atmosphere, its traditional afternoon tea in the lobby of the grand old Empress (which you absolutely should not miss), and its shops, with lovely decorative delicate Irish Balleeks, colorful Scottish woolens, English bone china, and lavender in every imaginable form, will keep you captive for several days. Across the strait, on the mainland, Vancouver, sharp and contemporary, will entertain you with Grouse Mountain, Gastown, the busy harbor, and Skana, the playful killer whale who has captured the heart of the whole city. Skana lives in the aquarium in Stanley Park, where she leaps and frolics and snorts in her own pool, mischievously splashing any visitor who comes too close.

If you can manage to get to Calgary in the early part of July for the Stampede, be there. Don't hesitate. You'll enjoy ten days of whooping Wild West atmosphere and a gala festival that has become world famous, and it all takes place in an atmosphere of the most open and genuine friendliness you've ever encountered. There are dozens of rodeos and stampedes across the region throughout the summer months, and they're all fun. But the Calgary Stampede is still the queen.

There are so many places to interest you that your problem is mostly one of deciding where to go next. You might decide on the prehistoric badlands near Drumheller or the beautiful Waterton-Glacier International Peace Park at Waterton Lakes where the national parks of two nations are joined into a single monument to peace. You might sample the fresh, ripening fruits of the Okanagan Valley, try your luck on the fabulous Kamloops trout, rent a houseboat for a week on Shuswap Lake, or study the petroglyphs in Writing-On-Stone Provincial Park. You could even opt for a trip up the Alaska Highway. It starts at Dawson Creek in British Columbia, and Whitehorse in the Yukon Territory is only 920 miles away.

There are two main streets here in this part of Canada. The Yellowhead Highway begins near Winnipeg and, proceeding in a northwesterly direction, touches the Pacific at Prince Rupert. It is the Main Street of the North. To the south, the Trans-Canada Highway traverses both provinces and manages to come very close to almost everything that would interest a traveler. You'll find Mile 0 of the Trans-Canada marked by a stone in a park in Victoria, a few hundred feet from the southernmost tip of Vancouver Island.

BRITISH COLUMBIA

BARKERVILLE [D-5]* On August 21, 1862, Billy Barker struck pay dirt 40 feet down in his little mine, and before the narrow 600-foot vein petered away he took out $600,000 in gold. That was the beginning of Barkerville, which came to be called the Gold Rush Capital of British Columbia and grew into the largest town north of San Francisco and west of Chicago. The frantic treasure hunt started in 1858, when word leaked out that gold had been found in the sandbars of the Thompson and Fraser rivers, and before long it was every man for himself in the Cariboo Gold Rush. The Cariboo Wagon Road was hewn northward through the awe-inspiring Fraser Canyon, past Yale, Lytton, Clinton, and Quesnel to connect Barkerville and its gold to the rest of the world. Today Highway 97 follows the course of that old wagon road through some of the most spectacular scenery in all Canada. When Barkerville celebrated its centennial a few years ago, only 15 of its original buildings were still standing, but since then constant restoration has been under way. The old buildings have been replaced, and you can see Kelly's saloon, the general store, and other gold rush enterprises. You can pan for gold in the El Dorado Mine and ride a stagecoach. The trip to Quesnel is fun in itself. Then take Highway 26 to Barkerville.

* Letter and number refer to coordinates on map of British Columbia, page 10.

CAMPBELL RIVER [F-4] On Vancouver Island and facing into Discovery Passage, the northern outlet of the Strait of Georgia, the town of Campbell River is a notable vacation area. The salmon are here from July through September, and steelhead, rainbow, and cutthroat bite the year round. Charter a fishing boat, hunt for oysters and clams on remote beaches, cruise to the offshore islands to see Indian villages, or find crabs. This gateway to Campbell Lake and Strathcona Provincial Park is 165 miles north of Victoria on Highway 19. The Tyee Club here has a worldwide membership that includes just about every famous fisherman and a host of celebrities, led by Bing Crosby and Bob Hope. It is named for the fighting Tyee salmon, and a catch of 30 pounds or more entitles you to membership.

CARIBOO COUNTRY The high, rolling plateau that extends west from Wells Gray Provincial Park across British Columbia to Bella Coola on the Pacific coast includes Cariboo and Chilcotin Country—a vast land of gold mines, great cattle ranches, and magnificent hunting and fishing. Gateway to Carboo Country is Cache Creek, and when you drive west from the town of Williams Lake, you enter the Chilcotin. Quesnel and Barkerville are a part of the Cariboo, too.

CHEMAINUS [F-4] South of Nanaimo on Vancouver Island, this is a lumbering center. A boatload of lumber leaves here every day for some place in the world. You can see one of the world's largest sawmills (tours most afternoons) or see pulp

Bronco busting, man and horse in a wild struggle, at Williams Lake Stampede, British Columbia

British Columbia

Population: 2,180,000
(1971 estimate)
Area: 366,255 Sq. Miles
Capital: Victoria

Cities and Towns

Atlin.....A-2
Barriere.....E-5
Beaverdell.....F-6
Beaton.....E-6
Bella Coola.....E-3
Bloedel.....F-4
Blue River.....E-6
Boston Bar.....F-5
Burns Lake.....D-4
Campbell River.....F-4
Canim Lake.....E-5
Castlegar.....F-6
Ceepeecee.....F-3
Chase.....E-5
Chilliwack.....F-5
Clinton.....E-5
Courtenay.....F-4
Cranbrook.....F-7
Creston.....F-6
Dawson Creek.....C-5
Dease Lake.....B-3
Duncan.....F-4
Elko.....F-7
Enderby.....E-6
Fernie.....F-7
Ft. St. James.....D-4
Fort St. John.....C-5
Francois Lake.....D-4
Gerrard.....E-6
Gibsons.....F-4
Hanceville.....E-4
Hedley.....F-5
Hixon.....D-5
Horsefly.....E-5
Hudson Hope.....C-5
Kamloops.....E-5
Kelowna.....F-6
Kelsey Bay.....F-4
Kimberley.....F-7
Kitimat.....D-3
Kitwanga.....C-3
Kleena Kleene.....E-4
Lardeau.....E-6
Lillooet.....E-5
Lumby.....E-6
Lytton.....F-5
McBride.....D-5
Merritt.....F-5
Mission City.....F-5
Nakusp.....E-6
Nanaimo.....F-4
Nelson.....F-6
New Westminster.....F-5
Ocean Falls.....E-3
Oliver.....F-6
100 Mile House.....E-5
150 Mile House.....E-5
Peachland.....F-5
Pemberton.....E-4
Penticton.....F-5
Port Alberni.....F-4
Port Clements.....D-2
Port Hardy.....E-3
Port Moody.....F-5
Powell River.....F-4
Prince George.....D-5
Prince Rupert.....D-2
Princeton.....F-5
Punchaw.....D-4
Quesnel.....D-5
Radium Hot Springs.....E-7
Revelstoke.....E-6
Sicamous.....E-6
Smithers.....C-3
Sooke.....F-4
Sparwood.....F-7
Squamish.....F-4
Summerland.....F-5
Tatlayoka Lake.....E-4
Telegraph Cr.....B-2
Terrace.....C-3
Tete Jaune Cache.....D-5
Tofino.....F-4
Trail.....F-6
Ucluelet.....F-4
Vancouver.....F-4
Vanderhoof.....D-4
Vernon.....E-6
Victoria.....F-4
Wells.....D-5
Westwold.....E-5
Williams Lake.....E-5

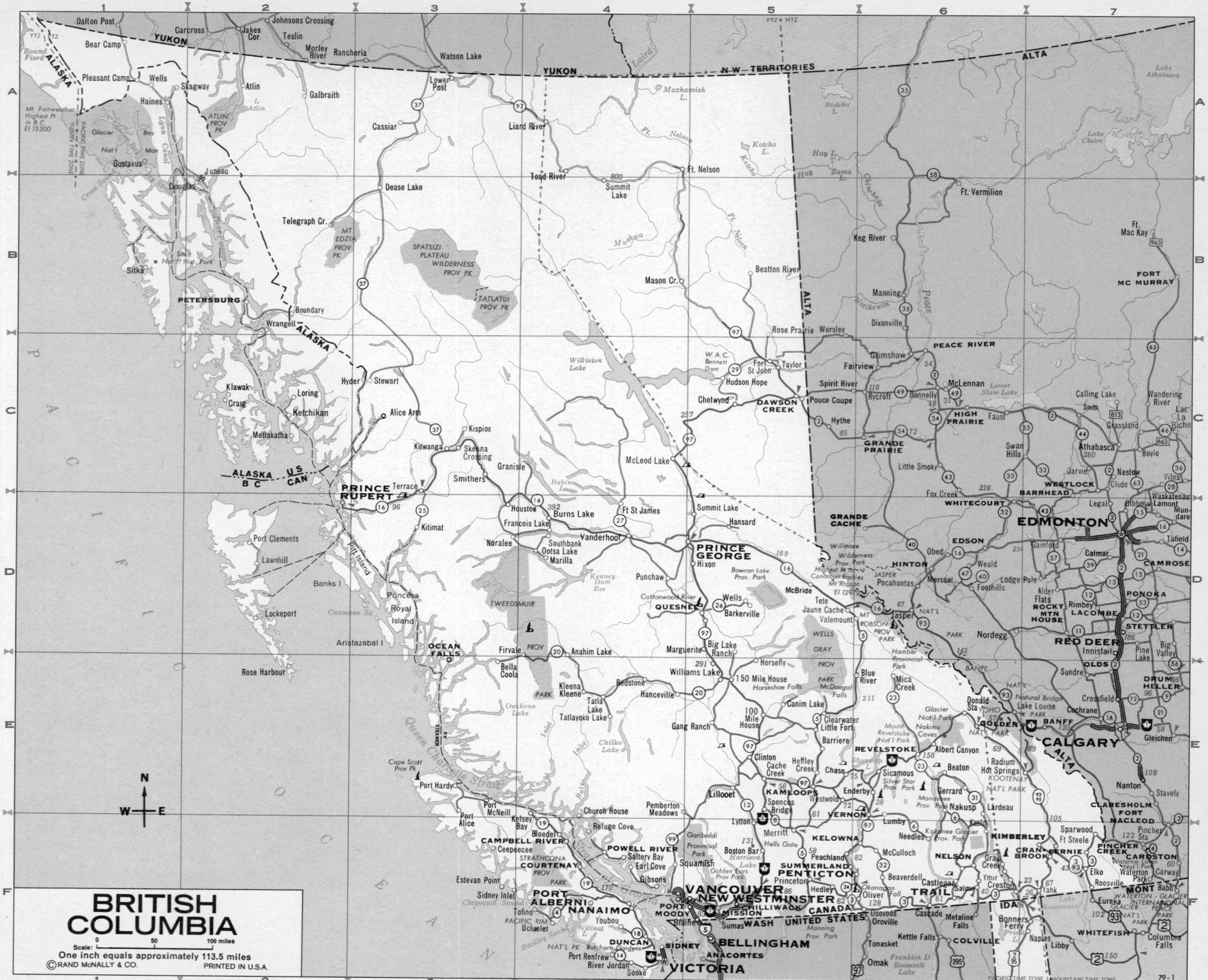

BRITISH COLUMBIA

Scale: 0 — 50 — 100 miles
One inch equals approximately 113.5 miles

PRINTED IN U.S.A.

and paper produced in nearby Crofton (tours on Thursday afternoons). On Bare Point, at the entrance to Chemainus Harbor, visit British Columbia's 100,000-kilowatt gas turbine generating station, one of the largest of its kind in the world.

COURTENAY-COMOX [F-4] They say that in the Comox Valley you can ski in the morning, play golf in the afternoon, and fish in the evening. Courtenay and Comox are twin cities on Vancouver Island facing Comox Harbor. You catch the ferry to the town of Powell River at Little River, just north of Comox. Plenty of sand beaches in the area, with sheltered boating waters and launching ramps, and charter boat fishing is excellent. The Forbidden Plateau rises up to the west of Courtenay in the Beaufort Range, and you can get to picturesque Denman Island by ferry. Visit the museum in Courtenay and the cairn a mile north of town at Sandwick that commemorates the landings of the first settlers in 1862.

DAWSON CREEK [C-5] This is Mile 0 on the Alaska Highway, which strikes north and west through Fort Nelson and Whitehorse to Fairbanks, Alaska, a distance of 1,523 miles. While you are here, drive out to the W. A. C. Bennett Dam, a giant earth-filled dam that harnesses the Peace River and creates 680-square-mile Williston Lake. Have lunch at the damsite and tour the power plant. Near Fort St. John you'll find yourself in the middle of rich gas and oil fields. Whatever time you get here, you'll likely find something going on: the Soap Box Derby championships in mid-June, the Western Canada Midsummer Bonspiel the first week in July, and the regatta staged on nearby Charlie Lake on Dominion Bay. In mid-August, the Fall Fair features a rodeo and horse racing events.

DUNCAN [F-4] Over a million square miles of Canada are covered by usable forests and over 70 percent of the lumber industry's output comes from British Columbia. If you'd like a good look at lumbering equipment—old and new—stop at the British Columbia Forest Museum, a mile north of town. Craggy Douglas firs nearing 300 years old tower over the site, and an old logging locomotive puffs its way around on the Cowichan Valley Railway. If you've a mind for some spectator sports, you'll enjoy the cricket and curling in the Duncan area.

FORBIDDEN PLATEAU The famous Forbidden Plateau, the land of the pink snow, is just west of Courtenay. A legend says that Indian women and children entering the plateau disappeared, and the snow was stained pink by their blood. You can see the pink snow today—made pink by an alpine lichen that flowers on its surface. There is also a legend of hairy giants that are supposed to inhabit the caves of the Forbidden Plateau. Take the Plateau Road from Courtenay to the 2,600-foot level where you'll find the lodge that is headquarters for winter-weekend skiers and summer hikers.

FRASER VALLEY The Fraser River is the great water lifeline of lower British Columbia. The segment from Vancouver east to Hope runs through fertile farmland and lush countryside. At Hope you turn north and the scenery changes as you follow the river into the famous Fraser Canyon—wild, rugged, whitewater country that will provide endless photographic opportunities. Going east from Vancouver, pause to take the boat trip up the Indian Arm for a picnic. Later, as you pass eastward over the Pitt River Bridge, look north to see the Golden Ears Peaks thrusting up from Golden Ears Provincial Park. At

Ducks in Stanley Park, Vancouver. Water-skiing off Vancouver Island. Ski trails at Bugaboo slopes, British Columbia.

Haney, take the ferry across the river to visit old Fort Langley, now a national historic park. Originally built at Derby, the fort burned in 1840 and was rebuilt here. In 1858, it was the seat of government for the Crown Colony of British Columbia, and for many years in the mid-19th century, the Hudson's Bay Company used it as a trading post. The present restoration is based on the fort as it appeared in the 1850s. Nearby, see the Langley Centennial and Agricultural Museums, and stand on the high ground for a fine view of the river. Mission City is a town that grew up around a mission and now has in its midst beautiful Westminster Abbey, a Benedictine monastery that you can visit. There's a fine Logger's Sport Show in town at the end of June. At Harrison Mills, east of Mission City off Highway 7, Acton Kilby's general store is still operating as it did back in 1902. Now it's both a store and a museum, and there's a small charge to enter. Shopping or nosing around the store is an interesting way to spend an hour. All along the Fraser, you'll find good rock hunting on the shore and on the sandbars. One of the best vista points along the river is at Cheam View, after passing lovely Bridal-Veil Falls. You might take a side trip up to lovely Harrison Hot Springs resort and stop at Weaver Creek spawning channel—a spawning ground with 2 miles of artificial zigzag channel, to which thousands of sockeye salmon return in the fall to spawn. At Hope, you turn north, and the country begins to steepen and the roadway gets narrow. The canyon highway to Lytton is 70 miles of engineering marvel, taking you through tunnels, across gaping gorges, and along precipitous canyon walls. Stop at Yale on the way and visit the Church of St. John the Divine, built in 1859 and shaded by a great oak planted when the church was built. At Hell's Gate, ride the air tram down into the Fraser Canyon to see the fish ladders. Near Lytton, at the junction of the Thompson and Fraser rivers, rock hunters find jade and other semi-precious stones along the banks.

GARIBALDI PROVINCIAL PARK [F-5] A 612,615-acre mountain wilderness only 40 air miles or about a two-hour drive from Vancouver. Head north for Horseshoe Bay, then northeast on to Squamish. The Whistler Mountain Ski Area is near the highway on the edge of the park about 35 miles beyond Squamish. Skiing is extremely popular in the winter, and the area provides true high-alpine adventure. The longest vertical drop in North America is served by these lifts, and there are slopes for every class of skier. Mount Garibaldi itself, 8,787 feet tall, stands watch. In the summer there is camping, fishing, and hiking.

GLACIER NATIONAL PARK [E-6] An alpine region with giant mountains, forests, and glaciers between Revelstoke and the Rogers Pass along the Trans-Canada Highway. See National Parks, page 96.

GOLDSTREAM PROVINCIAL PARK [F-4] Bisected by the Trans-Canada Highway, this little park is on Vancouver Island a scant 12 miles northwest of Victoria. Fine campground and picnic areas here, and during the summer, a park naturalist conducts nature walks and talks. Be sure to see the waterfall on Niagara Creek, reached by a fairly easy hike.

GULF ISLANDS [F-4-5] The islands in the Strait of Georgia between the mainland and Vancouver Island are known as the Gulf Islands. You can reach many of them by ferry. Most are quiet, peaceful, little places centered about picturesque villages—good places to step off the world's merry-go-round for a few days of uneventful solitude. There are resorts and motels on most of the islands, and you can swim, sunbathe, picnic, dig for clams and oysters, hunt for rocks and gemstones, and inhale the fresh salt air. Islands you might like include Quadra and Cortes, near the town of Campbell River; Galiano; Saltspring; Mayne; Saturna; San Juan and the other islands between Anacortes (Washington) and Sidney (British Columbia); Denman; and Texada.

HARRISON HOT SPRINGS [F-5] Bathe in 100° mineral water at the Harrison Hotel, a lovely resort amidst 700 acres that include a golf course, quiet gardens, three pools, tennis courts, and an airstrip. The resort is a short jump north of Highway 7 at Agassiz.

HAZELTON [C-3] The Bulkley and Skeena rivers meet here in north central British Columbia, and the Yellowhead Highway passes through on its way from Prince Rupert to Prince George. This area just north of Skeena Crossing has an enviable reputation for large trout. Every year since 1955, the world's largest steelhead have come out of the local rivers. If you are a fisherman, no more need be said. By all means visit the 'Ksan Indian Village here, a living museum where Indians produce, display, and sell their arts and crafts. Visit, also, the Skeena Treasure House Museum in Old Hazelton. In and about the town you'll find the largest gathering of original standing totem poles in the province.

HORSESHOE BAY [F-5] A picturesque village deep in a quiet cove looking out into Howe Sound, a short drive north of Vancouver. If you plan to travel up the Sunshine Coast, the ferry leaves from here to cross Howe Sound and drop you at Langdale. The town is below the main highway, and as you approach, it suddenly comes into view beneath you. The sight will cause you to reach for your camera.

KAMLOOPS [E-5] The North West Company established a post here in 1811. Later the Hudson's Bay Company took it over. Today the area still abounds in brown bear and mountain sheep. There is fine skiing at Lac La Jeune and Tod Mountain. While here, you should visit the historical museum. Kamloops is the home of the world-famous Kamloops trout—a rainbow bigger than any rainbow you ever saw anywhere else. The record catch tops 40 pounds.

KELOWNA [F-5] Ogopogo, a cousin of the Loch Ness monster, is said to romp near here in the waters of Okanagan Lake. There is a statue of the beastie in the city park. Kelowna is one of British Columbia's fruit centers, and while here you can visit fruit-processing plants, as well as three museums, an old mission, and a zoo. Okanagan Lake beaches are sandy and the water is warm, so you'll find many summer resorts in the area, with good swimming, fishing, water-skiing, and skin diving for everyone. The Autumn Grape Festival in September celebrates the harvesting of the grape crop, much of which is used to make British Columbia wines. In mid-November, the Big White Mountain ski area opens. You can skim over runs as long as four miles, and there is good snow until sometime in May.

KELSEY BAY [F-4] If you are driving north on Vancouver Island, this is as far as you can go on the eastern coast. Here you board the British Columbia Ferries' M.V. *Queen of Prince Rupert*, which cruises the Inside Passage between Kelsey Bay and Prince Rupert. The trip time is 20 hours, and the ferry leaves

Kelsey Bay every other day in the summer and twice weekly in winter. Try a round-trip ferry ride with a day's layover in Prince Rupert, or take your car with your on the ferry to Prince Rupert and then drive east along the Yellowhead Highway through some of Canada's most beauitful wilderness. Ferry accommodations are excellent, with cabins and staterooms available.

KEREMEOS [F-6] Originally an Indian settlement on the banks of the Similkameen River, and a Hudson's Bay post until 1872, this tiny town is now one of the province's fruit capitals. If you like your fruit straight from the tree, the cherries are due July 1, the apricots on July 20, peaches on August 10, pears on August 30, the McIntosh apples on September 1, and the Delicious apples on September 10. On the western side of the town you'll see a big rockslide that comes right down to the highway. If you're a rock hunter and are very cautious in probing this dangerous area, you can find rhodonite and hausmannite mixed with a dark red jasper. Located 42 miles southeast of Princeton, Keremeos is one of the delightful towns in the Similkameen Valley.

KOOTENAY NATIONAL PARK [E-7] This park encloses a 65-mile section of the Banff-Windermere Highway in the Rockies. You'll see broad valleys, deep canyons, and hot mineral springs and find good hotel and cabin accommodations in nearby Radium Hot Springs and serviced campgrounds in the park. Park area is 543 square miles. South of Yoho and south and west of Banff National Park. See National Parks, page 96.

THE KOOTENAYS The area south and east of Revelstoke, from the Okanagan east to the Alberta border, is known as the Kootenay Boundary region—10 million acres that include great mountain ranges, deep lakes, and green valleys dotted with orchards and ranches. Kootenay Lake is the home of the Kokanee, a landlocked sockeye salmon, and also boasts of producing the largest rainbow trout in the world. The Arrow Lakes are actually a widening of the Columbia River, and extend for 150 miles south from Revelstoke to Castlegar. Important cities in the area include Nelson and Trail. Kootenay National Park is in the upper eastern corner of the region, adjoining Banff National Park.

LILLOOET [E-5] If you have always wanted to see a gold mine, here is the place for you. There are a number of operating mines in the Bridge River district. Lillooet is on Highway 12, 155 miles north of Hope.

MANNING PROVINCIAL PARK [F-5] As you travel Highway 3 between Hope and Princeton, you pass through the 179,000-acre Manning Provincial Park, a natural museum of mountains and flower-covered alpine slopes, with deer and elk at nearly every turn. The road extends for 27 miles through the park, and there are four campgrounds at convenient points near the road. At Nature House in the park, you can see exhibits of the plants, wildlife, and history of the area. Park headquarters on the highway near the center of the park is the jumping-off point for conducted nature walks through interesting sections.

MOUNT REVELSTOKE NATIONAL PARK [E-6] A rolling mountaintop plateau on the west slope of the Selkirk Range on the Columbia River at Revelstoke is the setting for this magnificent 100-square-mile park. There are no accommodations available in the park, but there are excellent accommodations and campgrounds nearby. Championship ski runs and ski jump. See National Parks, page 97.

Water-skiing on Okanagan Lake, Kelowna

NANAIMO [F-4] The second largest city on Vancouver Island, Nanaimo is set on the island's eastern shore, with a sparkling harbor at its doorstep. The Coast Mountains, 25 miles away, across the bay, fill the horizon with a fascinating silhouette. Two ferry services connect Nanaimo with Vancouver. The Old Bastion, a wooden fortification built in 1853 to protect the Hudson's Bay trading post, still stands in downtown Nanaimo. The city is a sport-fishing center (both freshwater and saltwater) with charter and rental boats available. In the middle of July, the famous and ridiculous Bathtub Race from Nanaimo to Vancouver takes place. Every imaginable type of craft, including real bathtubs, sets out across the strait for Vancouver. Some of them make it. The day before the race, the contestants parade in the harbor. Some of them don't even survive the parade. The stone carvings of an ancient race can be seen in Petroglyph Park south of the city.

NELSON [F-6] The metropolis of the Kootenay Boundary region, Nelson was the first town settled by gold hunters. When visiting the courthouse, look at the Kootenay marble of which it is built. You'll see bits of gold embedded in it. There is good fishing, mountain climbing, and skiing around Nelson, and an excellent museum featuring Indian, pioneer, and Doukhobor artifacts. You can visit a large lumber and plywood mill, and you can get directions locally to numerous ghost towns in the vicinity. To the north of Nelson, Kokanee Glacier Park, as yet undeveloped, is a good place for wilderness hikes, if you're in good shape. Swim from the sandy beach in Lakeside Park and climb to Pulpit Rock for a panoramic view of the whole area. The Midsummer Bonspiel Championships are held in July to produce a curling champion. The festivities last a week and include square dancing and a main-street pancake breakfast. Finally, there's the ferry at Balfour to take you across Kootenay Lake. This cruise is the longest free ride in North America.

NEW WESTMINSTER [F-4] Next door to Vancouver, this is the oldest incorporated city in British Columbia. The Irving House is a fine old Victorian mansion dating back to 1864. A hundred cherry trees comprise the centerpiece of the Japanese Friendship Garden on Royal Avenue. You can visit the Lacrosse Hall of Fame at Sixth Avenue and McBride Boulevard.

THE OKANAGAN When you hear someone say, "In the Okanagan," you know he's referring to the Okanagan River valley, a marvelous summer and winter vacation area and one of Canada's principal fruit-producing sectors. The heart of the valley is an 80-mile stretch along the shores of Okanagan Lake, and activity centers in the towns of Penticton, Summerland, Kelowna, and Vernon. Highway 97 goes north from Osoyoos through Vernon to Kamloops. The Okanagan is about 255 miles by car east of Vancouver.

PACIFIC RIM NATIONAL PARK [F-4] One of Canada's newest national parks is located on the west coast of Vancouver Island, just north of Ucluelet. Beautiful beach area. See National Parks, page 97.

PARKSVILLE [F-4] This village on Vancouver Island north of Victoria has fine sandy beaches for saltwater swimming, and, like the rest of the island, provides great salmon, steelhead, and trout fishing. A good collection of old Edison phonographs is on exhibit in the city's museum. A short jaunt west of the city on Highway 4 brings you to two nice little provincial parks: Englishman River Falls and Little Qualicum Falls, delightful spots with picnicking and camping sites. A bit farther on you find MacMillan Park and the famed Cathedral Grove, where you walk a trail through giant Douglas firs.

PENTICTON [F-5] Known as Peach City, Penticton sits at the southern end of Okanagan Lake in the midst of vast orchards. The first of these were planted in 1874. Because of the clear, warm water of the lake, the area is popular as a summer resort, and with mountains looming on both sides of the valley, it's a major winter sports area, too. Apex-Alpine, where the slopes are open from November to April and the longest run covers a mile and a quarter, is nearby. While here, visit the Okanagan Game Farm, with African and American animals in a natural habitat, and the Dominion Radio Astrophysical Observatory, open to visitors on Sundays during July and August.

PORT ALBERNI [F-4] The isolated villages along the west coast of Vancouver Island get daily mail delivery from the M.V. *Lady Rose*, a small coastal freighter. You can spend an interesting day on the *Lady Rose* as she makes her rounds. The fare is $12; you can make reservations and board her at the dock at the foot of Argyle Street.

POWELL RIVER [F-4] This is the northern end of the Sunshine Coast, where, to the surprise of visitors who haven't been there before, the temperature averages 50° and snow is a very rare occurrence. But you can find all the snow you want a few miles east, among the peaks of the Coast Mountains. The Powell River has been dammed, and now Powell Lake extends back into the mountains east of town. The river, from the mouth of the lake to Malaspina Strait, is called the shortest river in the world. The ferry to and from Courtenay-Comox on Vancouver Island leaves from the town of Powell River. The ferry from Earls Cove lands you at Saltery Bay, 23 miles south of Powell River.

PRINCE RUPERT [D-2] This is Canada's northwestern seaport and the base for some of her largest deep-sea fishing fleets. Prince Rupert is called the Halibut Capital of the World because 18 million pounds of this toothsome fish are landed at its docks each year. One of the good collections of Haida and Tsimshian totem poles is found in the parks here, and the city is noted for its Museum of Northern British Columbia, housing a remarkable collection of ancient Indian relics. The sunken gardens are a delight in the summer, and the fishing fleet, when moored in the harbor, invites creative photography. The harbor, the third largest natural harbor in the world, is ice-free all year. Salmon canneries on the Skeena River operate in July and August and can be toured. This is the western terminus of the Yellowhead Highway and the southern end of the Alaska Marine Highway. The Marine Highway is a tie-up of land and water routes. Ferries provide service through Alaska's southern panhandle, connecting Prince Rupert with Ketchikan, Wrangell, Sitka, Juneau, Skagway, and Haines. From Haines, you drive on to Haines Junction and beyond it to join the Alaska Highway, following the gold rush trail of '98 to such places as Dawson City and Whitehorse.

PRINCETON [F-5] There are more than 60 lakes with great fishing within a radius of 50 miles of town. A lumber center for many years, Princeton is now seeing a revival of mining activities in the area. Major attraction in the summer is Horse Racing Days, a three-day rodeo staged during the second week in July. You'll find a swimming pool, a golf course, and a museum in town. A ghost town is nearby off Highway 64, and you can see ancient Indian rock paintings along Highway 3. Bromley and Stemwinder provincial parks for picnicking and camping are close at hand, and if you are a rock hound, you'll find good pickin's since the area abounds in agate, petrified wood, opal, opalized wood, agatized wood, fossils, and mineral specimens. Ask locally for directions to the best prospecting spots.

QUADRA ISLAND [F-4] The ferry from the town of Campbell River will take you and your car to this island at the head of the Strait of Georgia in an hour. Visit the Indian village here, with its authentic totem poles.

QUALICUM BEACH [F-4] In the original Indian tongue, the name of this seaside resort town means "place where the salmon run"—and they do. A few miles north, on the Big Qualicum River, is one of the few artificial salmon spawning channels in the world. Worth a visit. Qualicum Beach is on Vancouver Island between Parksville and Courtenay.

QUESNEL [D-5] You can pan for your own gold in the Fraser and Quesnel rivers—and probably find some. Or in town you can buy nuggets in almost any kind of setting. This was a major ore-producing area in the Cariboo Gold Rush and there's still a lot of gold here. Barkerville, now restored and once the largest town north of San Francisco, is only a few miles to the east. Hundreds of lakes offer fine fishing, and if you want to hunt moose, mule deer, caribou, black bear, grizzly bear, or mountain goat, you'll find them all here. A good many outfitters and operators of pack trips into wilderness areas center in Quesnel.

REVELSTOKE [E-6] Situated on the banks of the Columbia River, Revelstoke has been famous for furs, lumber, and ore. Rising up behind the town is Mount Revelstoke, the site of a national park. You take a 16-mile winding mountain road to the crest of the mountain, where you'll get one of the most magnificent views in all Canada. Revelstoke is 6,500 feet at the summit, a midget surrounded by the jagged giants of the Selkirk chain. You'll find alpine meadows to explore and hiking paths above the tree line. Silver River Falls is 7½ miles north on Big Bend Highway, the older road from the east which has been replaced by the cut through Rogers Pass. Skiing in the Revelstoke area rivals that of the Swiss Alps. The first European ski-jumping records to be broken in North America fell to jumpers on Nels Nelson Hill here.

ROGERS PASS [E-6] If you travel the Trans-Canada, it will take two hours to drive between Revelstoke and Golden—and these will be two of the most spectacular hours you've ever spent in a car. On this trip, you'll go through Rogers Pass, riding on a road that is a modern engineering miracle and perhaps the most beautiful mountain road in the world. It is four lanes of easy curves and grades, with frequent turn-offs and viewpoints to lure you. The two hours can stretch to four or five if you don't resist—but then, why should you? The road is open all year, with parts of it protected by huge snowsheds. Coming from Golden, you'll be in the Columbia River valley for a bit, then you'll turn west to follow the Beaver River and go through Rogers Pass. Just beyond the pass, you enter Glacier National Park and follow the Illecillewaet River through the park and on to Revelstoke. Ten-thousand-foot peaks will tower on either side of you and provide one huge mountain vista after another —sprawling timberlands, great bluffs and sheer rock faces, towering snowcapped peaks, deep ravines, rushing white-water mountain streams, snowfields, and glaciers. For a flatlander especially, the trip is overwhelming.

ROSSLAND [F-6] A historic gold mining town, it lies 6 miles north of the Canada-U.S. border and 7 miles south of the town of Trail. Here you can take a tour of the famous old Le Roi mine, the only hard-rock workings open to the public in Canada. You'll see mining as it actually was at the turn of the century. The Rossland Historical Museum is near the top of the mine. The mine is open from mid-May through October.

SICAMOUS [E-6] Prospectors on their way to the Columbia goldfields embarked on stern-wheelers at Sicamous to ride north. The Trans-Canada Highway crosses Highway 97 at Sicamous, which is the center of a cluster of towns on Shuswap Lake—a big H-shaped collection of interconnected water bodies that provide fine fishing, boating, and swimming. If you are looking for something different in the way of a vacation, rent a houseboat for a week or two on Shuswap Lake. Plenty of tent and trailer camps in the area, which is west of Revelstoke. Towns on the lake include Chase, Salmon Arm, Enderby, and Celista.

Thousand-year-old fir trees in British Columbia. The Empress Hotel and the harbor at Victoria. Revival of the gold rush days at Barkerville. Indian family history, carefully carved, near Vancouver.

THE SIMILKAMEEN The valley of the Similkameen River begins at Princeton, about 180 miles east of Vancouver, along Highway 3. Here the Similkameen and Tulameen rivers meet. This valley shares the fruit-growing crown with the Okanagan, and the towns of the Similkameen along Highway 3 are all places to see fruit being picked, packed, shipped—and eaten. The blossoms of the Similkameen are breathtaking in the spring, and the fruit is luscious in August and September. Chief towns of the valley are Keremeos and Cawston.

SOOKE [F-4] "All Sooke Day" is celebrated here at this tiny town on Highway 14, 30 minutes west of Victoria. Visitors at the festival can eat the same kind of food the hopeful prospectors did during the Leech River Gold Rush of 1864—barbecued beef cooked underground for 10 hours, salmon grilled over open coals, and a famous clam chowder. Sooke runneth over with people on this day, but reverts to being a picturesque fishing village on the Strait of Juan de Fuca the rest of the year. Vancouver Island's first independent settler took up land here in 1849 but returned to England after four years.

SQUAMISH [F-5] Lumbering village at the head of Howe Sound, 40 miles north of Vancouver, this is the gateway to Garibaldi Provincial Park, which is 21 miles farther on. Look for big log booms being assembled and towed out in the sound. On the first Saturday in August the Logger's Sport Day is the big event, with logrolling, tree-climbing races, and all the contests of the old logging camps. Fun and games for the whole family, beginning with a parade on Saturday morning. To the east of Squamish, the Howe Sound district is noted for fine sport fishing. Cutthroat trout are taken from the tidal estuaries, steelhead and Dolly Varden trout lurk in many of the rivers, and that fisherman's delight, the giant Kamloops trout, can be found in Lake Levette.

STRATHCONA PROVINCIAL PARK [F-4] This area of half a million rugged acres right in the middle of Vancouver Island is the oldest provincial park in British Columbia. You'll find hiking trails of all types, campgrounds, and places to launch your boat. Fishing is excellent, and in the winter there is skiing on slopes up to a mile long on Mount Becher, adjacent to the Forbidden Plateau. The skiing season runs from December to April. You reach the park via Highway 28 from the town of Campbell River. The road goes through the park to the town of Gold River. The Buttle Lake section of the park is 30 miles from Campbell River. You can reach the Forbidden Plateau via 12 miles of gravel road that runs west out of Courtenay. One of the most beautiful drives you can imagine runs south from Highway 28 along the shore of Buttle Lake. You'll be treated to the sight of cataracts and tumbling creeks, placid lake waters, giant firs, and majestic mountain peaks.

SUNSHINE COAST The coastal area on the mainland north of Vancouver, stretching from Gibsons through Powell River to Lund and facing into the Strait of Georgia is happily known as the Sunshine Coast—a name honestly earned. The pretty little villages on the coast here enjoy a remarkably soft and moderate year-round climate that comes close to being tropical. Snow in the villages is almost unheard of, though there is plenty to be seen if you just turn your back to the water and face east, where the great mountains of the coastal range stand in white-topped beauty. Some fingers of the strait run back among these mountains, and you'll get a good look at them—as well as an itchy camera—when you take the ferry rides as you drive up the coast. The first ferry takes you from Horseshoe Bay to Langdale. A bit farther north is the prettiest ride of them all, from Earls Cove to Saltery Bay. The Sunshine Coast is about 90 miles long and includes the towns of Sechelt, Halfmoon Bay, Secret Cove, Pender Harbor, Gibsons, Powell River, and Lund.

TERRACE [C-3] Fishermen prone to exaggerate need particularly vivid imaginations to stay ahead of the truth in this town dedicated to the sport of fishing. Picture yourself standing on a corner in town spinning a yarn about the one that got away —when along trudges this fellow lugging a 92½-pound salmon that he caught on a rod and reel just 2 miles from the center of town. The sight is almost enough to scare you into telling the truth. Terrace is on the slopes of British Columbia's third largest river, the Skeena. Picturesque spots in town include Kay's Tea Barn, where you can stop for a spot of it, and Goat's Foot Gallery. There are unusual lava beds formed about 300 years ago—among the newest in North America—just north of town in the historic Nass Valley. Lakelse Hot Springs, 15 miles away, lets you relax in 100° water. Two provincial parks are nearby. Kleanza Creek is on Highway 16, 12 miles east, where there is a picturesque canyon to explore. Lakelse Lake Park is 12 miles southwest and has picnic grounds and campsites on Furlong Bay.

TRAIL [F-6] South of the southern end of the Arrow Lakes and straddling the Columbia River, Trail is called The Silver City because half of Canada's silver is produced here. Surrounded by great mountains, Trail is a hunting and fishing as well as mining center, and is also the shopping headquarters for a large part of the southern Kootenay Boundary area. You can tour the world's largest zinc plant and one of the largest lead plants while you are here. The drive from Revelstoke south on Highway 23, then through Kaslo, Balfour, and Nelson, to Trail is particularly scenic. Another interesting drive is the Red Mountain Scenic Route on Highway 3B—a 17-mile drive west from Rossland (6 miles south of Trail) to the point where 3B joins Highway 3. Along the way you'll pass through the Nancy Greene Recreational Reserve, and see both Red and Old Glory mountains standing to your south.

TWEEDSMUIR PROVINCIAL PARK Looking at a map of British Columbia, you see a huge area marked Tweedsmuir Provincial Park located east and a bit south of Kitimat. Tweedsmuir is a vast undeveloped wilderness area without roads that is extremely difficult to get to. You can reach the northern edge if you travel by boat and car south on Highway 35 from Burns Lake, which is on Highway 16. There is one small campground on the western edge of the park, and only a dirt road through the southern part of the park east of Bella Coola. There are more than a million completely untouched acres in Tweedsmuir, and the original trail blazed by Sir Alexander Mackenzie on his epic-making journey to the Pacific still exists.

VANCOUVER [F-4] Canada's third largest city, with a metropolitan population of over a million, Vancouver is one of the major ports of the world and the hub of Pacific Canada. For a map of the city and descriptions of its points of interest, see page 23.

VANCOUVER ISLAND A large and long island of great natural beauty across the Strait of Georgia from Canada's mainland, Vancouver Island is connected to the mainland by fine ferry service. You could spend a day or two or several weeks on the island without experiencing a dull moment. A motor trip up island from Victoria to Kelsey Bay, about 180 miles, can be done in a day, or you can stop and poke around and enjoy the sights and take several days or a week. Cities of interest on the island include British Columbia's capital, Victoria; Duncan; Ladysmith, famous for its oysters; Parksville; Qualicum Beach; Courtenay-Comox, where the Powell River ferry lands; Campbell River; Kelsey Bay; Port Alberni; Nanaimo; and Sidney, where the Washington State ferry lands.

VERNON [E-6] Kalamalka Lake changes color right before your eyes. In Polson Park there's a pool where only the kids can fish. Dads can watch but may not drop a line. Vegetable farms and fruit orchards abound, and you'll see the biggest melons you ever laid eyes on. Vernon is at the top of the Okanagan, with the water sports and beaches of both Okanagan Lake and Kalamalka Lake available. There is a fruit cannery to visit in town and a glass factory and the Orchardcroft Arabian Horse Farm. If you bring your boat, there are launching ramps and ample marine facilities. Vernon's Midwinter Carnival brightens the month of February and attracts visitors from all over western Canada. In the middle of July they stage a Tourist Days Festival just to make sure things don't get too quiet—complete with parade, dancing, games, and the like.

VICTORIA [F-4] The capital city of the province of British Columbia, Victoria is on the southern tip of Vancouver Island looking out into the Strait of Juan de Fuca. For a map of the city and descriptions of its points of interest, see page 26.

WELLS GRAY PROVINCIAL PARK [D-5] South and east of Prince George more than 1,300,000 acres of vast, primitive wilderness have been dedicated as Wells Gray Provincial Park. The park is in the Cariboo and Columbia mountains and encompasses the Clearwater River watershed. The Helmcken and Spahats waterfalls are spectacular attractions. Access to the park is from Highway 5 at Clearwater or from Mahood Falls. Park headquarters are just inside the southern boundary north of Clearwater. There are a few developed campgrounds within the park and a lodge near Hemp Creek.

YELLOWHEAD HIGHWAY This is the nation's newest long highway, crossing four provinces and providing a northern scenic route parallel to the Trans-Canada Highway. The road is named after an Iroquois trapper who was called Yellow Head by the voyageurs with whom he dealt. The road begins in the east near Winnipeg, runs north and west to Edmonton, where at Tete Jaune Cache, the Yellowhead divides into two routes, one going to Prince Rupert, and the other southwest to Vancouver. Often lonely, always beautiful, the Yellowhead passes through some of the most scenic and untouched land in Canada—mountains, forests, plateaus. Driving on parts of this road, you will truly sense what a wilderness is—a vast, open, silent, overpowering land, virtually untouched by man.

YOHO NATIONAL PARK [E-6] On the west slope of the Rockies, adjacent to Banff National Park, this park offers serviced campgrounds and the Yoho and Kicking Horse valleys to explore. Hotel and cabin accommodations are available. Park area is 507 square miles. See National Parks, page 97.

Car ferry from Horseshoe Bay on its regular trip to Nanaimo on Vancouver Island

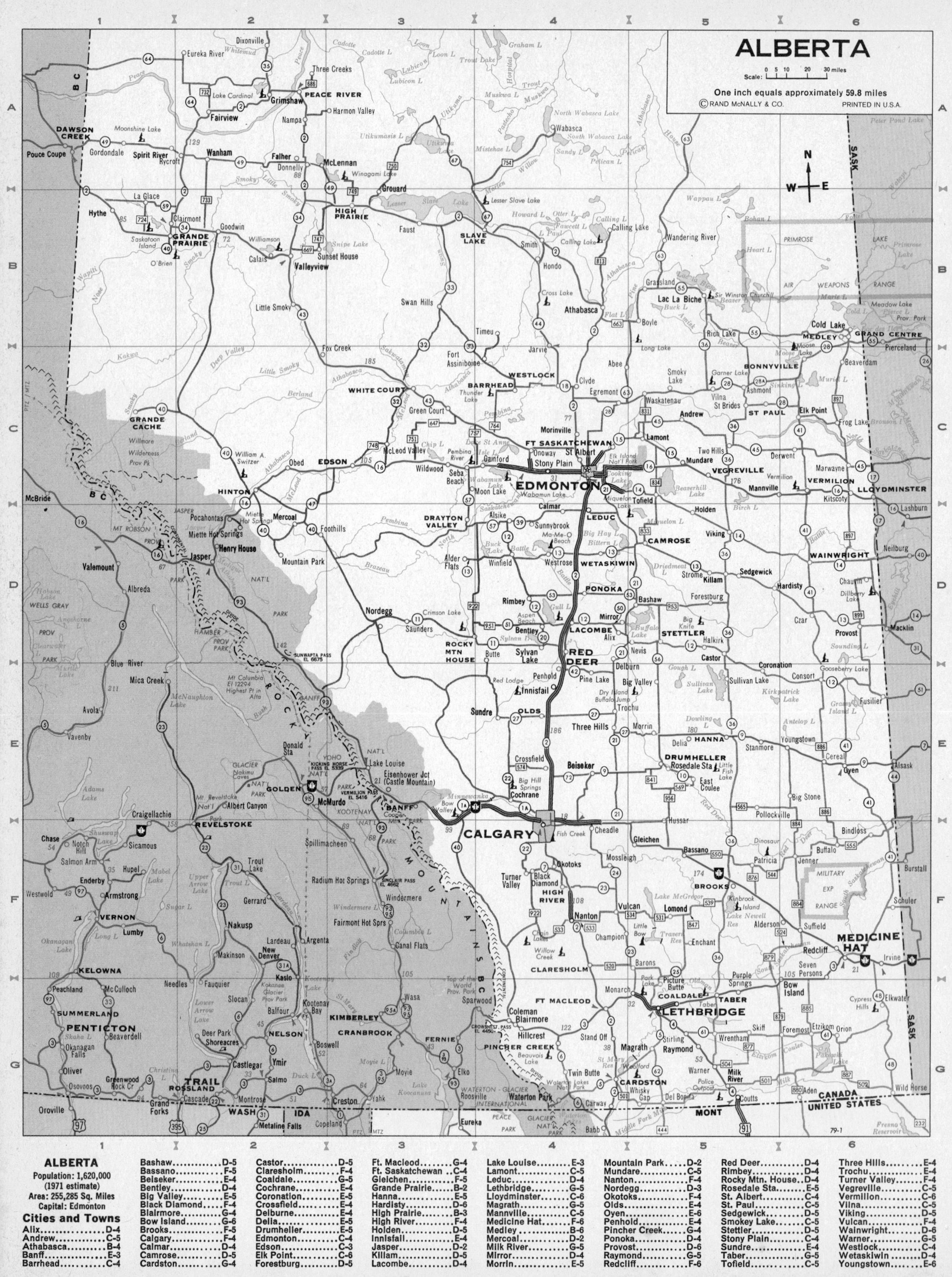
ALBERTA
Scale: 0 5 10 20 30 miles
One inch equals approximately 59.8 miles
©RAND McNALLY & CO.
PRINTED IN U.S.A.
N
W E
EDMONTON
CALGARY
RED DEER
LETHBRIDGE
MEDICINE HAT
GRANDE PRAIRIE
PEACE RIVER
DAWSON CREEK
JASPER
BANFF
ROCKY MOUNTAINS
CANADA
UNITED STATES
SASK
BC
MONT
IDA
WASH
PRIMROSE LAKE AIR WEAPONS RANGE
MILITARY EXP RANGE
79-1
ALBERTA
Population: 1,620,000
(1971 estimate)
Area: 255,285 Sq. Miles
Capital: Edmonton
Cities and Towns
Alix..........D-4
Andrew..........C-5
Athabasca..........B-4
Banff..........E-3
Barrhead..........C-4
Bashaw..........D-5
Bassano..........F-5
Beiseker..........E-4
Bentley..........D-4
Big Valley..........E-5
Black Diamond..........F-4
Blairmore..........G-4
Bow Island..........G-6
Brooks..........F-5
Calgary..........F-4
Calmar..........D-4
Camrose..........D-5
Cardston..........G-4
Castor..........D-5
Claresholm..........F-4
Coaldale..........G-5
Cochrane..........E-4
Coronation..........E-5
Crossfield..........E-4
Delburne..........E-4
Delia..........E-5
Drumheller..........E-5
Edmonton..........C-4
Edson..........C-3
Elk Point..........C-6
Forestburg..........D-5
Ft. Macleod..........G-4
Ft. Saskatchewan..........C-4
Gleichen..........F-5
Grande Prairie..........B-2
Hanna..........E-5
Hardisty..........D-6
High Prairie..........B-3
High River..........F-4
Holden..........D-5
Innisfail..........E-4
Jasper..........D-2
Killam..........D-5
Lacombe..........D-4
Lake Louise..........E-3
Lamont..........C-5
Leduc..........D-4
Lethbridge..........G-5
Lloydminster..........C-6
Magrath..........G-5
Mannville..........C-5
Medicine Hat..........F-6
Medley..........B-6
Mercoal..........D-2
Milk River..........G-5
Mirror..........D-4
Morrin..........E-5
Mountain Park..........D-2
Mundare..........C-5
Nanton..........F-4
Nordegg..........D-3
Okotoks..........F-4
Olds..........E-4
Oyen..........E-6
Penhold..........E-4
Pincher Creek..........G-4
Ponoka..........D-4
Provost..........D-6
Raymond..........G-5
Redcliff..........F-6
Red Deer..........D-4
Rimbey..........D-4
Rocky Mtn. House..........D-4
Rosedale Sta..........E-5
St. Albert..........C-4
St. Paul..........C-5
Sedgewick..........D-5
Smokey Lake..........C-5
Stettler..........D-5
Stony Plain..........C-4
Sundre..........E-4
Taber..........G-5
Tofield..........C-5
Three Hills..........E-4
Trochu..........E-4
Turner Valley..........F-4
Vegreville..........C-5
Vermilion..........C-6
Vilna..........C-5
Viking..........D-5
Vulcan..........F-4
Wainwright..........D-6
Warner..........G-5
Westlock..........C-4
Wetaskiwin..........D-4
Youngstown..........E-6

The fast-moving rodeo event, steer wrestling—always a thrill at the Calgary Stampede

ALBERTA

THE BADLANDS Take the Trans-Canada Highway 6 miles east of Calgary, and turn north on Highway 9, which takes you north and east, where the land begins to change. As you near Drumheller, you can look down on Horseshoe Canyon and drop back a million years in time to the era of the dinosaurs. You are entering Alberta's badlands.

BANFF NATIONAL PARK [E-2-3]* Canada's oldest national park, established in 1885, Banff covers an area of 2,564 square miles in the Canadian Rockies. Lake Louise, one of the world's most beautiful lakes, is the principal attraction in Banff. You'll find 220 miles of scenic roads in the park, which is 81 miles west of Calgary. See National Parks, page 93.

BROOKS [F-5] You'll find the town of Brooks midway between Calgary and Medicine Hat along the Trans-Canada Highway. South of Brooks is Kinbrook Island Provincial Park, on Lake Newell, one of Alberta's largest man-made lakes, where there are pleasant campgrounds, picnic areas, and public shelters. If you've been driving for some time, you might find it worthwhile to spend a relaxing day in these restful surroundings. East of Brooks, the province's Horiticultural Station is a 500-acre experimental farm where new methods of growing field and garden crops, trees, and flowers are tried. Visitors are welcome. You might also look in at the Provincial Pheasant Farm at Brooks.

* Letter and number refer to coordinates on map of Alberta.

CALGARY [F-4] A busy and vigorous metropolis in the foothills of the Rockies surrounded by farms, ranches, and oil wells. If you could bottle the energy displayed by the people here, you could get a good price for it. This energy comes into full play each year during the second week in July when Calgary's citizens stage the internationally known Exhibition and Stampede, ten days of Wild West fun. But Calgary is worth a visit at any time of the year. For a map of the city and descriptions of its points of interest, see page 27 and page 29.

CARDSTON [G-4] A group of Mormons migrated from Utah and platted the township in 1887. Their beautiful temple, built between 1913 and 1921 and surrounded by handsome floral gardens, is a high point of scenic interest. The home of Ora Card, the leader of the original band of settlers, is open to visitors from July 1 to September 1. Waterton-Glacier International Peace Park, which straddles the United States-Canadian border, is less than 30 miles away.

COLUMBIA ICEFIELD [D-2] Midway along the spectacular highway between Banff and Jasper you'll find the greatest known accumulation of ice in the Rockies, covering more than 130 square miles. The ice reaches a depth of 3,000 feet in some places, and runoff from it flows into three river systems. Most accessible glacier in the field is the Athabasca, a tongue of ice 6 miles long and 1,000 feet deep in certain areas. It was receding about 65 feet a year, but is now stabilized. During the summer you can ride a snowmobile for 3 miles over the ice field—a tremendous experience that you'll never forget.

DRUMHELLER [E-5] The center of Alberta's badlands, Drumheller is 86 miles northeast of Calgary. Dinosaurs roamed this area 100 million years ago. Visit the Dinosaur Museum on First Street before taking the Dinosaur Trail, a 30-mile circle tour through Red Deer Valley (400 feet deep in spots), where you'll see plant and animal fossils of great variety, from dinosaurs to oysters. You'll see hoodoos, too—mushroom-shaped mounds formed by the erosion of hills. On the trail you'll also see the Homestead Antique Museum, with a good collection of pioneer and Indian artifacts, and you'll come to a tiny church, big enough for a congregation of six. It is nondenominational, and each year more than 20,000 people pause to push the buttons that bring recorded hymns and sermons. The church was a community project, and all work and materials required to build it were donated.

DUNVEGAN [A-2] A tiny settlement on the Peace River 55 miles north of Grande Prairie on Highway 2, this is the site of Fort Dunvegan, a former trading post, and of the first Roman Catholic mission in the area. Built in 1884 by the Oblate Missionaries, the mission is now maintained as an interesting museum.

EDMONTON [C-4] This is Canada's oil capital and the capital of Alberta, located on the north Saskatchewan River in the center of the province. The tourist can stay busy for a week here. For a map of the city and descriptions of its points of interest, see page 27.

ELK ISLAND NATIONAL PARK [C-5] Elk, moose, and mule deer roam in this 75-square-mile national park 25 miles east of Edmonton. Elk Island is also the home of the plains buffalo. See National Parks, page 94.

FORESTRY TRUNK ROAD If you want an interesting sample of wilderness in western Alberta, you can drive the Forestry Trunk Road. Originally built as a fire road in the foothills on the east side of the Rocky Mountains, the road is 640 miles long. It begins in the north at Highway 34 at Goodwin, 26 miles east of Grande Prairie, and follows a very irregular path south through Hinton, Foothills, Nordegg, and Ghost Lake. South of the Trans-Canada, Highway 1A, it stays in the shadow of the mountains for 140 miles without touching a village or town. There are small campgrounds along the road, most of which have a few tent and trailer spaces, with no luxuries. No oversized trailers are allowed on the road, and if you intend to hunt or camp you must check in at the nearest ranger station on entering and leaving the road. The scenery along the gravel road is spectacular, with snow-crested mountains to the west, clear streams, and flower-dotted alpine meadows.

FORT MACLEOD [G-4] A representation of the first fort built in western Canada by the North West Mounted Police is open daily in the summer. The original fort was built in 1874, when the Mounties came to run the whiskey traders out of Fort Whoop-Up. The museum has a good display of Mountie uniforms and other items and some Indian regalia. Well worth a visit. The Blood Indian Reserve is 18 miles south. Here, every

Snowmobile excursions for a close look at the Athasbasca Glacier in the Columbia Icefield

August, the Bloods stage a two-week-long sun dance. Check with the band council to see this colorful ceremony.

FRANK [G-4] A ledge of limestone 3,000 feet wide and 500 feet thick toppled from the head of Turtle Mountain, and 90 million tons of rock hurtled into the valley, burying a section of this mining town. The slide took place in 1903, and 70 persons died. A winding trail leads to a point where you can look down from 3,000 feet at the amazing sight of a valley 2½ miles wide filled with boulders as big as houses. Frank is on Highway 3, about 60 miles west of Fort Macleod, and east of Blairmore.

GRANDE PRAIRIE [B-2] By 1930, the majestic trumpeter swan was nearly extinct, but a conservation program was undertaken, and today more than 1,000 of the birds nest at Saskatoon Island Provincial Park, 15 miles west of town. You can discover the remains of dinosaurs and other fossils in the Kleskum Hills, a few miles northeast of town, and 7 miles south, at O'Brien Provincial Park beside the Wapiti River, you'll find good camping and picnicking sites. Dawson Creek is only 83 miles up the road toward the northwest.

ICEFIELD HIGHWAY Highway 93 (the Banff–Jasper Icefield Parkway) is a drive no one should miss. It passes 142 miles of glaciers, ice fields, waterfalls, deep canyons, and hot springs, and is the thoroughfare of the Columbia Icefield, 130 square miles of ice up to 3,000 feet deep on the southern boundary of Jasper National Park.

JASPER NATIONAL PARK [D-2] One of the jewels in Canada's star-studded crown of national parks, Jasper extends for 4,200 square miles along the eastern slopes of the Rockies. It is about 100 miles west of Edmonton. See National Parks, page 94.

LESSER SLAVE LAKE PROVINCIAL PARK [B-4] Located 4 miles north of the town of Slave Lake, which is on Highway 2, the park occupies 28 square miles on the shore of Lesser Slave Lake. One of Alberta's largest lakes, Lesser Slave is 55 miles long and covers 17,582 acres. The beaches are wide and white, and the swimming, boating, and fishing are good. You'll find three large campgrounds in the park.

LETHBRIDGE [G-5] On Highway 3 in southern Alberta, southwest of Medicine Hat, Lethbridge is the irrigation capital of Canada—so called because over a million acres of sugar beets and vegetables are under irrigation. The system was devised by Sir Alexander Galt. The city is a sugar beet refining center, and vegetable canning and freezing is also a big industry. To celebrate Canada's 100th anniversary in 1967, the Nikka Yuko Japanese Garden was designed and created by Professor Kobo of Osaka. Features from traditional Japanese gardens are included—bridges, a teahouse, waterfalls, rickshas, and a bell tower. The gardens are located in Henderson Lake Park, adjacent to Henderson Lake, and the lake is annually stocked with 100,000 rainbow trout. (Guess what Lethbridgians do when they want trout for dinner.) Indian Battle Park on the Oldman River is the site of the last Indian battle fought in North America (1870). Inside the park you'll find a reconstructed Fort Whoop-Up, a whiskey fort—so called because it was built and operated by exploiters selling whiskey to the Indians. The North West Mounted Police put the fort out of business and then established Fort Macleod in 1874. Visit also the lovely Galt Gardens and see the historical displays in the Galt Museum. In May there is a band festival with participants from western Canada, while in July you can attend the Whoop-Up Days Rodeo.

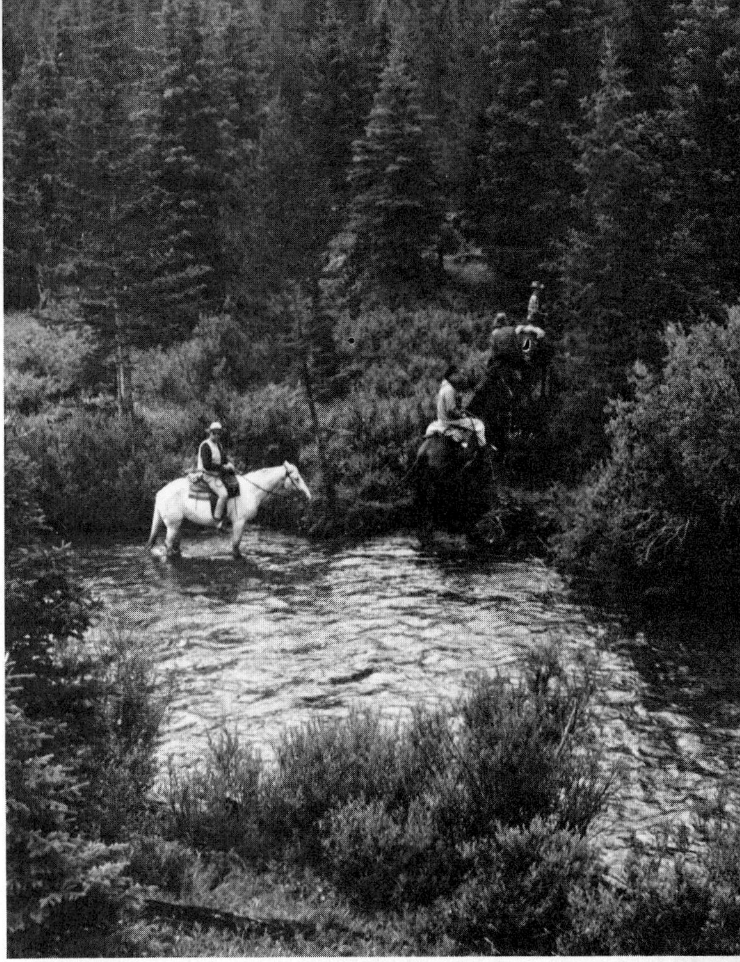

Trail riding in the Canadian Rockies

MEDICINE HAT [F-6] A Cree medicine man, fleeing from a battle between his tribe and the Blackfoot Nation, lost his headdress in the river here—and accidentally named a town. The town sits on top of an enormous deposit of natural gas and is developing strong industry, especially in the manufacture of glass and clay products. Visit the Altaglass plant to see craftsmen deftly blowing exquisite ornaments from glass or tour one of the many giant greenhouses that supply flowers and vegetables to homes all across Canada. The temperate climate of the city will surprise you, but blame it on the warm chinook winds. There's a good display of pioneer utensils and furnishings in the museum near the information booth on the Trans-Canada Highway. Cypress Hills Provincial Park is just a short drive south of the city.

MUNDARE [C-5] You can see an extremely valuable 15th-century handwritten book of the gospels in the museum here that is a part of the Ukrainian Catholic Church complex. Included in the cluster of buildings is a lovely church, a monastery, the museum, and a grotto portraying the life of Christ in pictures and statuary. You can picnic on the grounds if you like. Located on Highway 15, about 50 miles east of Edmonton.

PEACE RIVER [A-2] You are far enough north here in the lovely valley of the Peace River to notice that summer days are very, very long. This is a pleasant area, restful, with good hunting, fishing, and summer living. While here, you'll meet Twelve-Foot Davis—or at least his statue and his life story—

the pioneer from Vermont who "was everyman's friend and never locked his cabin door."

PINCHER CREEK [G-4] The Mounties established a post here back in 1878. Waterton-Glacier International Peace Park is 29 miles to the south. To the southwest is the West Castle Ski Resort, open on weekends and holidays from November 15 to Easter. You'll find slopes for beginners and advanced skiers serviced by four lifts. To the west on Highway 3 is the town of Frank, where the great rockslide of 1903 took place.

RED DEER [D-4] Located midway between Edmonton and Calgary, this thriving city sits at the entrance to the lovely Sylvan Lake Resort area. The Dominion bird sanctuary is nearby and so are the Drumheller Badlands, where dinosaur skeletons and the remains of other prehistoric beasts, including the terrifying 40-foot-long *Tyrannosaurus*, have been discovered.

ROCKY MOUNTAIN HOUSE [D-4] The area between here and Red Deer, 50 miles to the east, is known as the Sylvan Lake Resort region, with lovely lakes and all the summer attractions you'd expect. The town of Rocky Mountain House is in frontier country and is little changed since the days of the fur trade. It serves as the gateway to one of Canada's finest big-game hunting areas, where you can stalk bear, deer, moose, and mountain sheep and goat in season. This is a festive town, with more celebrations than almost any other place in the country. You are likely to find something going on any time you get there. For example: the Kinsman Stampede, the Fish Derby, the Guides and Outfitters Ball, and the Light Horse Association Gymkhana. There's an exciting White Water Canoe Race in mid-August.

WATERTON LAKES NATIONAL PARK [G-4] In 1932, Waterton Lakes National Park was joined to Glacier National Park in Montana to form an international peace park, the first of its kind in the world. See National Parks, page 94.

WETASKIWIN [D-4] A small city 40 miles south of Edmonton where you should stop to visit the Reynolds Pioneer Museum. You'll see a fine collection of early farm machinery, automobiles, and horse-drawn vehicles.

WINAGAMI LAKE PROVINCIAL PARK [A-3] Fifty miles south of Peace River is McLennan, a little town situated between two lakes. The lakes are quite shallow and, for this reason, warm very rapidly in the spring, providing a long season of swimming, boating, and water-skiing. Winagami Lake Provincial Park is a 3,000-acre playground on the eastern lake.

WOOD BUFFALO NATIONAL PARK This untamed park covering 17,300 square miles straddles the line between Alberta and the Northwest Territories. See National Parks, page 95.

WRITING-ON-STONE PROVINCIAL PARK [G-5] In the Milk River valley, southeast of Lethbridge, and not far from the international border, you'll find this small park of sandstone cliffs on which have been inscribed hunting and battle scenes. These ancient petroglyphs are well preserved.

Cowboy skills at Banff Indian Days. Recreation center at Happy Valley, near Calgary. Ceremonial pageantry at Indian Days. Banff Avenue as it crosses the Bow River and stretches back to Cascade Mountain.

VANCOUVER

At noon on any pleasant summer day, if you happen to be in downtown Vancouver, you'll note a sudden tide of traffic—foot, bicycle, and automobile—all headed in the same direction, toward Stanley Park. All cities have parks, and some are very beautiful, but no park is as much a part of the life of its citizenry as is Stanley. On a peninsula, jutting out into Vancouver Harbor, Stanley Park's thousand acres are the city's alfresco lunching spot, its amusement center, and its weekend sports arena.

Vancouver is Canada's third largest city, with a metropolitan population topping a million. It is one of the world's great harbors, and on a tour of the docks you will see the flag of nearly every maritime nation in the world. Blessed (or cursed, depending on whether or not you happen to have an umbrella) with abundant rainfall, the city stays green the year round. One of your first strong impressions will be of the thousands of flower gardens, large and small, everywhere. Vancouverites have green thumbs all the way to the elbows.

It is a modern, young, and vigorous city, with a brief history but a promising future. Vancouverites take their play as seriously as their work—which you discover when you visit the ski run on top of Grouse Mountain, 20 minutes from downtown; or when 30,000 boats, give or take a few, show up on nearby waters on those weekends when the sun sparkles on the water.

There is plenty to do and see here, fine restaurants that offer the cuisines of nearly every nation, and excellent accommodations. The city is interesting itself, or can serve as a base point from which you can make excursions to the Sunshine Coast, Vancouver Island, and the Fraser River valley.

When you travel hereabouts, be prepared to make a good many ferry trips. The boats are commodious and comfortable and very busy in the summer months, making it essential to be at the dock well before sailing time.

Points of Interest

VANCOUVER PUBLIC AQUARIUM. The largest in Canada, this aquarium houses nearly 9,000 specimens of sea life. Up to 700 spectators can enjoy performances by playful dolphins and the killer whales, Skana and Hyak. Here, too, is a pool for beluga whales, as well as galleries devoted to salt and freshwater fish isolated according to species. Best time to see the whales in action is at feeding time. Call 685-3364 for feeding and show times. Admission fee.

BLOEDEL CONSERVATORY. Located in Queen Elizabeth Park at 33rd and Cambie. Beneath the unique 140-foot triadic dome of the conservatory are three separate climate zones—a desert, a rain forest, and the tropics. Fifty kinds of birds and 400 varieties of plants and flowers thrive here. Call 872-5513 for information.

BRITISH PROPERTIES. Exclusive residential area in West Vancouver, with contoured roads, beautiful homes, and lavish gardens, perched on the side of a mountain. Fine view of Vancouver from here. Cross the Lions Gate Bridge from Vancouver. The entrance to the properties is an elaborate mall.

CAPILANO CANYON AND BRIDGE. The Capilano River rushes down from the mountains through a deep canyon, and a park flanks a mile of the canyon. A 450-foot footbridge spans the canyon, swinging giddily 230 feet above the river. This is a spectacular walk, great for photographs. Lighted at night in the summer. Admission fee.

CENTENNIAL MUSEUM. See MacMILLAN PLANETARIUM

CHINATOWN. Vancouver's Chinatown is the second largest in North America. The city's Chinese population is over 25,000, and 4,000 live in Chinatown itself. The area extends along

Theater-goers at the Queen Elizabeth Theatre in Vancouver

East Pender Street, with the heart of the shopping area in the two blocks between Main and Corrall. Visit the Chinese market, a square block on Pender at Main. You'll see jade; ivory and bamboo carvings; gorgeous silk and brocades; and ornate brassware in the shops. You could buy hundred-year-old duck eggs in the market if you wanted. The celebration of the Chinese New Year here is something very special, with dragons parading and fireworks deafening the onlookers.

GASTOWN. The area around Water, Alexander, Columbia, and Cordova streets, just north of Chinatown, is the original heart of Vancouver, where the city began rebuilding after a disastrous fire in 1886. The area deteriorated into a skid road section for years, but is now being restored with shops, boutiques, restaurants, antique specialists, and coffeehouses. Of particular interest is Trounce Alley, a hidden-away little street half a block south of Water Street. Stroll through Gastown, browse in the shops, stop for coffee, or have dinner. You'll learn the history of Gassy Jack Deighton and how it all started. You might discover, too, that a skid road (or skid row) area is so called because it was located on a road down which logs on skids were dragged to the sawmill. It was thirsty work, so a good many saloons sprang up, and itinerants looking for a day's work (but not a regular job) took up residence here since the kind of work they wanted was easy to come by.

GROUSE MOUNTAIN. Looming up 4,200 feet behind North Vancouver, Grouse Mountain boasts an alpine tramway that will take you on a 3,700-foot ride that feels almost vertical. From the top of the mountain the view of the city and surrounding area is unbelievable, especially at night when the city is aglow. There is fine skiing here in the winter, just 20 minutes from the heart of Vancouver. The chalet at the top houses one of the city's fine restaurants, and as you sit at dinner you feel suspended out over the city below. There is also a coffeeshop and bar. There are outdoor grills and places to picnic near the chalet; one of the highlights of a visit to Vancouver. Admission fee for tramway.

HARBOR TOURS. A number of water tours of the harbor and nearby waters are available. Times and destinations change on occasion, so check locally. Boats leave from a pier at the foot of Denman Street near Georgia.

The Capilano Suspension Bridge—450 feet in length and 230 feet above the canyon floor

INFORMATION. Stop first in Vancouver at the Greater Vancouver Visitors Bureau, 650 Burrard St. The pleasant people here have brochures, ferry schedules, maps, and other helpful information. Summer hours: 9 am to 8 pm, Monday through Saturday; 9 am to 5 pm, Sunday and holidays. Winter hours: 9 am to 5 pm. Phone 682-2222.

MacMILLAN PLANETARIUM. Just across the Burrard Bridge and near the foot of Chestnut Street, in one of Vancouver's most beautiful buildings, the planetarium has daily shows of the heavens. No children under 5. Call 736-4431. Here also is the Centennial Museum, housing the Lipsett Collection of British Columbia artifacts.

MARITIME MUSEUM. A block from the MacMillan Planetarium, at the foot of Cypress Street, the museum houses the famous arctic schooner *St. Roch*, first ship to sail the Northwest Passage both ways (1940).

MUSEUM OF ANTHROPOLOGY. A beautiful new building at the University of British Columbia on Northwest Marine Drive, this museum has a famous collection of totem poles which were hidden for years in the basement of the university's library.

OLD HASTINGS MILL STORE MUSEUM. This building housed the first store built on Burrard Inlet, in 1865. It survived the great fire of 1886 and was moved to its present site in 1930. The museum has a collection of memorabilia of old Vancouver. At Point Gray Road and Alma Road.

QUEEN ELIZABETH PARK. A lovely park, the highest point in the city, was built on the site of an old rock quarry. It is now 130 acres of lawns, winding paths, a rose garden, a sunken garden, an arboretum, and the 75th Anniversary Quarry Gardens. Tennis courts, a pitch-and-putt golf course, and a fine restaurant add to its popularity.

ROBSONSTRASSE. Robson Street, in downtown Vancouver, is the center of the city's import shops, and its European atmosphere has earned it the German appellation. Good for browsing and for unique and unusual gifts.

STANLEY PARK. Five minutes from downtown. A thousand acres of pretty and most useful park, dedicated in 1889. Stanley Park is dotted with small lakes, one of which—Beaver Lake—is so unspoiled that a walk around it makes you feel as if you were a million miles from the city. The aquarium is here, and there are three fine beaches, several swimming pools, a cricket field, a pitch-and-putt course, tennis courts, and the zoo. Stroll the 7-mile-long seawall that encircles the park for good sea views, including Siwash Rock. Rent a bicycle to ride the park paths, have lunch or tea at one of several teahouses, hike 50 miles of trails, bowl on the green, see totem poles, see summer theater in the Malkin Bowl and sporting events in the Brockton Oval. There is a miniature train for the children to ride, and a children's zoo, as well as the regular zoo. While you're here, see the famous Nine O'Clock Gun, fired every evening at nine and by which Vancouverites set their watches. Originally it was fired to call fishermen in for the day.

STEAM TRAIN RIDE. The Royal Hudson, last of the great mountain locomotives, takes you on a 6-hour ride through glorious scenery from North Vancouver to Squamish and back, Wednesdays through Sundays, from mid-May to early fall. The fare is $5.50 for adults and $4 for children.

Totem Grove at the University of British Columbia

VanDUSEN BOTANICAL DISPLAY GARDEN. Located at 37th and Oak streets. Enter through the Garden Pavilion, then take an hour to tour the display garden of native and exotic plants. Carvings from the International Stone Carving Symposium, held here in 1975, have been placed throughout the garden. Gardens open at 10 am each day.

VICTORIA

Here is a sedate bit of Old England transplanted. Critics claim the Old English look is fostered for the tourist trade, but these people don't know Victoria very well. A good many Britons have found Victoria to their liking and have settled here, and this, more than anything else, accounts for the Old Empire feeling.

You'll have little trouble in orienting yourself here if you begin by standing in front of the great and imposing Empress Hotel. With your back to the hotel, you face the Inner Harbor. To your left are the buildings of Parliament. To your right is the

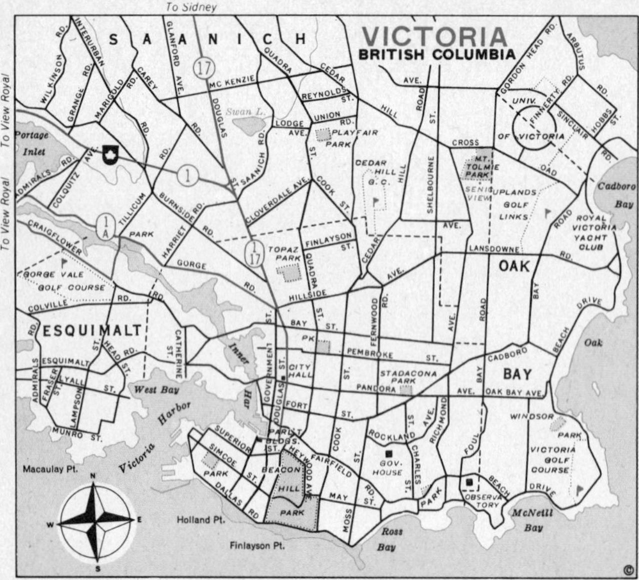

Black Ball ferry dock. The street in front of you is Government Street. Near the ferry dock, in a small building, you'll see the Visitor Information Center.

All of the sightseeing tours leave from this point. You'll be surprised at how many ways you can tour the town. There's the regular sightseeing bus, of course, and there's the old double-decked bus from London. But you also can take a horse-drawn tally-ho. Boat tours of the harbor leave from here, too. If you want to drive your own tour, ask at the Visitor Information Center for a brochure.

One of the first sights to impress you will be the beautiful hanging flower baskets, 650 of which decorate the streetlight poles of the downtown section. They turn the city into a colorful conservatory.

Points of Interest

BASTION SQUARE. You'll find Bastion Square just off Government Street between the 1100 and 1200 blocks. In it there are restored buildings dating back to 1856, including the first jail, the House of Assembly, and the Law Courts. In the buildings now are the Maritime Museum, boutiques, and restaurants. Nice view of Victoria Harbor from the west end of the square.

BUTCHART GARDENS. One of the best known attractions in British Columbia are Butchart Gardens, on an old estate in Brentwood, 12 miles north of Victoria. Over 70 years ago, the Butcharts began to landscape their 125-acre estate, in which there was an old limestone quarry. Now there are 35 acres under cultivation, and in the summer the gardens are absolutely beautiful. You'll see an English rose garden, a sunken garden, a Japanese garden, an Italian garden, and the Ross fountain, all illuminated at night. Ask any Victorian what you should see first in Victoria. The answer, without hesitation, will be Butchart Gardens. Admission fee.

CENTENNIAL SQUARE. On Douglas Street. The square was developed to commemorate the centennial of city government, which began in 1862. Around the square you'll find the City Hall, the McPherson Playhouse and Restaurant, the Senior Citizens Activity Center, the Police Building, the Magistrate's Court, and an arcade of specialty shops. The Centennial Fountain was a gift to the city from neighboring communities.

CLASSIC CAR MUSEUM. Over 40 classic cars, from a 1904 Oldsmobile to a Rolls Royce of the 1930s, are a part of this million-dollar collection at 813 Douglas Street. Admission fee.

CRAIGFLOWER MANOR. Now a national historic site, this old house recaptures the era when the Hudson's Bay Company farmed the fields to provide food for the people of the region. Located at 110 Island Highway, on the beautiful Gorge waterway. Open daily. Admission fee.

EMPRESS HOTEL. The grand old Empress is both a fine hotel and one of the city's attractions—and so must be listed twice. Traditional afternoon tea is served in the lobby every afternoon from 3 to 5, and there is no better way to get a taste of the good old days than to be there.

ENGLISH VILLAGE. At 429 Lampson St. Here you'll find a replica of Anne Hathaway's thatched cottage. Anne was Will Shakespeare's wife, and the 10 rooms of her home are furnished with authentic 16th- and 17th-century items. Also in the village are replicas of Harvard House, Garrick Inn, and Chaucer Lane. Admission fee.

FABLE COTTAGE ESTATE. A fairy-tale cottage with flower-laden gardens and great architectural charm, at 5187 Cordova Bay Rd. Delightful animated creations inhabit the fantasy forest. Open June through October. Admission fee.

FORT VICTORIA. At 340 Island Highway (1A). This is a replica of the fort that stood on Government Street near Broughton in 1843. A plaque marks the original site. The replica has a collection of historical items pertaining to Victoria's early days.

MARINE DRIVE. Follow the seashore beginning at the Parliament Buildings, past Beacon Hill Park, the world's largest totem pole, along Dallas Road and the shore of the Strait of Juan de Fuca. Watch ships come in from around the world, or go beachcombing along the rocky shore.

MARITIME MUSEUM. Fine collection of old maritime items, including ship models, charts, and navy gear and instruments. Located on Bastion Square.

MARKET SQUARE. Restored section of old Victoria, with 30 stores and restaurants that retain the architecture of the turn of the century. In the heart of Old Town.

OLD CRAIGFLOWER SCHOOLHOUSE. Not far from the Fort Victoria replica, this building was constructed in 1855 and is now a museum containing a pioneer schoolroom, a display of old farm implements, and an old stagecoach. Admission fee.

PARLIAMENT BUILDINGS. Open Monday through Friday throughout the year for tours. Tour schedule changes with the season. See the legislative halls, a museum of natural history, excellent mineral exhibits, and libraries and archives where Indian relics and other historic artifacts are displayed.

POINT ELLICE HOUSE. 2616 Pleasant St. The house is occupied by the grandson of the man who built it over 100 years ago. You can see one of the largest and finest collections of furnishings of the Victorian era. Admission fee.

PROVINCIAL MUSEUM. On Belleville St., across from the Empress Hotel, this museum has exhibits relating to the history and industry of the province.

ROYAL LONDON WAX MUSEUM. On the Inner Harbor, across from the Parliament. The collection contains more than 130 life-size figures made by Josephine Tussaud in London. Wax museums aren't unusual anymore, but the good ones are still interesting. You can bring your camera and take pictures here. Admission fee.

SEALAND. This interesting spot is at Oak Bay Marina, Beach Drive and Oak Bay Avenue, on the ocean. See underwater grottos three fathoms beneath the surface of the ocean. Seals, sea lions, and Chimo, the world's only white killer whale, perform. Admission fee.

THUNDERBIRD PARK. At Belleville and Douglas streets, one block up from Government Street and the Parliament Buildings. Neat collection of totem poles. During the summer carvers work on new poles, so you can see just how it's done. Right around the corner is the Helmcken House, the oldest residence in Victoria, built in 1852 when Victoria was still a Hudson's Bay trading fort. Now a museum. Free.

UNDERSEA GARDENS. This attraction is on the Inner Harbor directly in front of the Parliament. You descend below the water's surface to look at marine life through huge windows. You'll see a scuba diving show in the undersea theater.

EDMONTON

In 1891, a spur of the transcontinental railroad was run northward to the little town of Edmonton, population 400, a settlement which had come into existence as a Hudson's Bay Trading Post in 1795. The coming of the railroad, followed by gold rushers pouring through town in '98 on their way to the Klondike, caused the first growth. Then wheat and cattle appeared on the surrounding prairie, and Edmonton boomed.

Today, Edmonton's population approaches 470,000, and the city is a growing industrial center. It is the service and supply center for the oil industry, a major factor since 86 percent of Canada's oil comes from this vicinity.

Edmonton is a modern, vigorous city, clean and open in feeling. It is Alberta's capital and Canada's northernmost major metropolis. It sits in the heart of Alberta's parkland, and good lakes, rivers, and forests are only a short drive in any direction. The Rockies and Jasper National Park are a five-hour drive to the west, and Elk Island National Park is only one hour to the east.

Points of Interest

ALBERTA GAME FARM. Here are 1,400 acres of natural woodland, 1,250 animals, and 1,500 birds representing 132 species, all in enclosures arranged in a series of crescents within easy walking distance of the main gate. Animals include a pair of snow leopards and their twin kits; white rhinos from Africa; and the Przhevalski's horse, once believed to be extinct. The park has a 50-acre picnic area overlooking a lake. Open daily, 9 am to sunset. Admission fee.

EDMONTON VALLEY ZOO. At Buena Vista Road and 134th Street. Two miniature trains tour the grounds of this colorful children's zoo, where the birds and animals live in settings from such fairy tales as "The Three Little Pigs" and "Three Men in a Tub." Open daily, May to October, from noon to 8 pm. Admission fee.

FORT EDMONTON HISTORICAL PARK. This is a theme park, located west of the south end of Quesnell Bridge, in which the history of Edmonton is traced from early Indian villages through today and into the future. The highlight of the park is the reconstruction of the original Fort Edmonton. Guides are on duty from June to September.

LEGISLATIVE BUILDINGS. Erected in 1908 on the site of Fort Edmonton, which had been built in 1795. To commemorate Canada's centennial in 1967, a 305-bell carillon was installed in the dome of this center of provincial government, and concerts are given frequently. The legislative gallery is open when the legislature is in session, usually from mid-February to April 1.

McDOUGALL MEMORIAL SHRINE. At 101st Street and 100th Avenue. This was the first building to be built outside the walls of the old stockade. It was also the first Protestant church in the west. Now a museum with pioneer and early church displays. Open June to September, 2 pm to 5 pm, Tuesday to Saturday, and noon to 1 pm, Sunday.

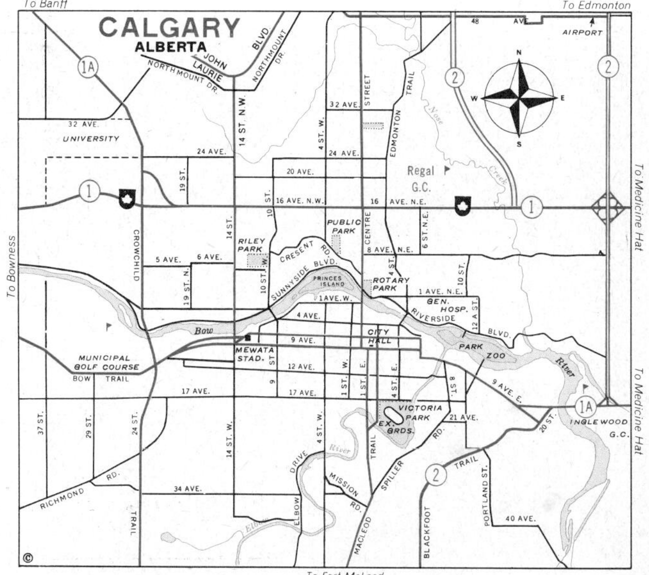

Sightseeing in the fashion of long ago via horse-drawn carriage in Victoria

MUTTART CONSERVATORY AND BOTANICAL GARDENS. Year-round flowers from the world's major climatic zones are here. There is an impressive backdrop of four glass pyramids. Near downtown.

NEW CITADEL THEATER COMPLEX. Features live theater performances by a professional resident company in one of North America's most modern facilities. Check locally for time of performances.

NORTHERN ALBERTA JUBILEE AUDITORIUM. Built in 1955 to commemorate Alberta's Golden Jubilee, this impressive building seats nearly 3,000 people and is used for displays and stage presentations. At 114th Street and 87th Avenue.

QUEEN ELIZABETH PLANETARIUM. In Coronation Park, the planetarium puts on star shows throughout the summer—twice daily on weekdays and three times on Sundays and holidays. Admission fee. No preschool children.

ST. ALBERT MUSEUM. Nine miles north of Edmonton on Highway 2, the museum is a cathedral, built by Father Lacombe in 1861, and has on display weapons from the Riel Rebellion, plow blades, cooking utensils, Father Lacomb's Bible, and an 1870 handpress. Open daily 9 am to 9 pm, Sunday 1 pm to 9 pm.

PROVINCIAL MUSEUM AND ARCHIVES. Located at 12845 102nd Avenue, this museum has exhibits of Alberta wildlife, prehistoric life, early fur trade, Indians, and pioneers. Open 9 am to 9 pm weekdays, 1 pm to 9 pm Sundays, June to September. Closes at 5 pm during the winter. Free.

WATERDALE HISTORIC PARK. At 10627 93rd Avenue. John Walter built this house of hand-hewn logs in 1874. Still on its original site, it is believed to be the first house built outside of Fort Edmonton. It served as the district's first telegraph office. Another house here was built in 1885, and here also is the building which housed Edmonton's first newspaper, *The Bulletin*. Hours are 10 am to 6 pm daily, June to September.

Special Events

KLONDIKE DAYS. In July, Edmonton turns itself inside out and upside down in recalling the days of the gold rush of '98. Big feature of Klondike Days is the Chilkoot Mine built inside a 42-foot mountain. The mine is salted with real gold nuggets, ranging in value from 15¢ to 50¢. Stake your claim in the mine, pan in the stream that runs through it. Take your finds to the assay office, where you can convert them into currency. Or keep them as souvenirs. Along with this annual gold rush, there's a huge livestock show, horse racing, canoe races on the river, flapjack breakfasts, and dozens of other activities. Klondike Kate rides through town, presiding over the whole affair.

CALGARY

The fabulous Calgary Stampede has achieved an international reputation. As a festival it is in the same category as the running of the bulls in Pamplona and the Mardi Gras in New Orleans. *Everyone* knows about it and wants to be there at least once before he dies.

However, if you visit Calgary at any time other than during those 10 rip-snortin' days in July, the truth dawns. Calgary really isn't a Wild West cow town at all. It's an oil town, and has been since 1912 when the first gusher popped in Turner Valley. Mind you, this innocent bit of deception doesn't take one whit from the Stampede. That still rates as one of the truly great shows on earth.

But the first-time visitor who has heard so much about the Stampede has a well-developed image of the place, and in April or October he spends his first day adjusting it. He sees the stockyards and packing plants in town, and he passes the wheat farms and ranches on his way in, but when he gets to town, he realizes this is oil country. He finds there are no less than 400 oil companies in the city—one company for each 800 citizens.

Like a good many other Canadian cities, Calgary began as a North West Mounted Police post, established in 1875 by Col. J. F. MacLeod, first commissioner of the Mounties. The colonel named the new fort after his ancestral estates on the Isle of Mull in Scotland.

The transcontinental railroad went through Calgary in 1885 and gave it a big boost; it became the railhead for a large part of Alberta. Then the discovery of Banff and Lake Louise less than 70 miles away, and their subsequent recognition as outstanding vacation spots, helped. The railroad brought wheat farmers and cattlemen, and at the turn of the century, Calgary *was* a cow town. But everything else was overshadowed when the oil derricks began to appear in the foothills.

There's a good bit to do in Calgary, and many fine restaurants to keep the inner man happy. But one must admit that there is always one great distraction. No matter where you are in the city, you can look to the west and see those giant mountains. And they beckon.

Points of Interest

CALGARY BREWERY GARDENS. The Calgary Brewery established an outstanding aquarium as a public service. The sparkling pools contain a great variety of trout, and the tanks in the aquarium itself have fish from all parts of the world, along with turtles and reptiles. Nearby is the fish hatchery where more than three million fingerling trout are pampered each year. The gardens are open in July and August from 10 am to 9 pm. The brewery grounds are at Ninth Avenue and 15th Street. Small admission fee.

CALGARY ZOO AND DINOSAUR PARK. No, they don't have any live dinosaurs here—just life-size replicas, along with more than 1,200 real live animals of all kinds. "Zooperintendents" supervise the children as they play with the small animals. Located on St. George's Island in the middle of the Bow River, close to the center of town.

GLENBOW FOUNDATION MUSEUM. If you'd like to see what England's Crown Jewels look like, the museum has an excellent set of replicas, along with an extensive gun collection; a coin collection; and displays of artifacts of North and South American Indians, Australian aborigines, and early Canadian pioneers.

HAPPY VALLEY. About 5 miles west of the city, along the Bow River, this is a man-made recreation center. You can camp here, park your trailer, picnic, fish, swim in indoor and outdoor pools, paddle boats, play miniature and regular golf, bounce on a trampoline, visit Frontierland, and more. In the winter there are winter sports here, too. Admission fee.

HERITAGE PARK. This is a re-creation of a 19th-century village on the shore of the Glenmore Reservoir, west and south of town. The park is open weekdays from mid-June through September, and weekends in May and October. Small admission fee.

HORSEMAN'S HALL OF FAME. Also located on the Calgary Brewery grounds, in the aquarium building. The history of famous horsemen of the Old West is re-created.

CALGARY TOWER. A skyscraper that rises 626 feet above the city streets. Up on top there is an observation deck and a revolving restaurant with 210 seats. The view from here is absolutely breathtaking. Lunch in the restaurant is particularly recommended. Between soup and dessert you will have revolved through the entire panorama, and will be left with the impression that you have been able to see virtually all of Canada. Admission fee.

Special Events

THE STAMPEDE. This is the big event, lasting 10 days, beginning the second week in July. The most amazing thing about the Stampede is that it doesn't seem staged. The whole town actually takes on the Stampede spirit and participates "up to here." A gigantic parade gets things whooping and then the festivities become one great kaleidoscope of fun—street dancing, flapjacks and bacon breakfasts served from chuck wagon tailgates, steer wrestling, calf roping, fireworks, fabulous stage shows, Indians, Mounties in scarlet, and much, much more—all topped off by nightly chuck wagon races. These were invented in Calgary and are the most dangerous, thrilling, and hair-raising racing events to come along since Rome's chariot races, which they resemble. To keep you amused and interested, there are a buzzing midway and all kinds of displays on the Exhibition Grounds, including a complete Indian village. If you own boots and a big hat, wear 'em. You'll be right in style.

GREAT PLAINS

Grain elevators and marshland on the plains near Swift Current, Saskatchewan

SASKATCHEWAN MANITOBA

BEFORE THE DAWN OF HISTORY, GIGANTIC TONGUES OF ICE LICKED DOWNWARD FROM THE ARCTIC CIRCLE THROUGH EASTERN AND CENTRAL CANADA. PERFORMING THE GREATEST BULLDOZING FEAT OF ALL TIME, THESE GLACIERS SCRAPED THE AREA DOWN TO ITS VERY ROCK FOUNDATION, AND PUSHED ITS FERTILE SOIL SOUTHWARD TO WHERE YOU'LL FIND IT TODAY—IN THE NORTH CENTRAL AND NORTHERN FARMING AREAS OF THE UNITED STATES AND THE RICH PLAINS OF SASKATCHEWAN AND MANITOBA.

Thus it is probable that Iowa's cornfields, those green dairy pastures in southern Wisconsin, the sturdy vineyards of New York, and the golden grainfields of Manitoba owe their abundant output to rich soil that at one time lay in what is now Hudson Bay.

That great rock plain scraped clean by the icy tongues covers nearly half of Canada's land surface and is known as the Shield. When you travel in Manitoba and Saskatchewan, you can see the southwestern edge of it. You won't find a sharply defined line, of course, but you'll see the three distinct kinds of country it created.

South of the edge, you are in the midst of Canada's great wheat heart, where the soil is rich and deep and returns a hundredfold whatever is planted in it. Along the edge itself there is a wide band of parklands, not rich enough for extensive farming but full of natural advantages that make them the summer playgrounds of the provinces. North of the edge, you will find yourself in a rocky wilderness dotted with more lakes than can be counted. Manitoba alone has more than 100,000 lakes within its borders.

The Shield's edge is an irregular diagonal line running northwest from the Lake of the Woods in Ontario's southwestern corner. It slashes across Manitoba and Saskatchewan, takes in a corner of Alberta, and then heads up into the Northwest Territories, where it crosses through the middle of Great Bear Lake. Some of the world's greatest hunting and fishing is found in the wilderness of the Shield, and large areas of it are practically unexplored. No one yet knows what mineral wealth may be hiding there.

RUPERT'S LAND

Henry Hudson was the first white man to see any of this area. He sailed into the bay now named for him in 1610 and sailed back out without leaving a footprint. Two years later, Sir Thomas Button followed Hudson's watery track into the bay, found the mouth of the Nelson River, and claimed the whole area for the British Crown. For his effort some obscure islands at the entrance of Hudson Strait were named after him. On the early charts, they called this new country Rupert's Land.

In 1670, Rupert's Land was chartered to the enterprising Hudson's Bay Company, which lost no time in opening a trading post at the mouth of the Nelson River. For the next 200 years the ubiquitous Hudson's Bay trading posts were the signs of civilization from Hudson Bay to the Pacific shore.

Until after the first quarter of the 19th century, Rupert's Land, extending from the bay to the mountains, was a trapper's paradise. The world wanted fine furs, especially beaver, and Canada had plenty of them. The North West Company came into the area to compete with Hudson's Bay, and the representatives of both companies tracked and retracked what are now the four western provinces.

In 1731, another complication entered the trapping picture. La Verendrye, a French-Canadian explorer from Quebec, reached the Red River valley—where Winnipeg is now located—and the French Canadians who came with him began to compete with the English for pelts. This French influence is still strong in the great plains today. You'll find St. Boniface, just across the river from Winnipeg, to be the largest French-speaking city in Canada, outside of Quebec.

It was 1817 before the first sod of the great prairie was broken and the first tame seed planted. Then a new kind of struggle began—between the new farmers who planted the wheat and fenced the land and the rough-hewn trappers who had for a hundred years felt free to roam the prairie. Many of these trappers were of French-Indian extraction and were called Metis.

The Canadian government purchased Rupert's Land from the Hudson's Bay Company in 1869, and began the formation of the provinces of Saskatchewan and Manitoba. By now, the Metis were severely restricted by the ever spreading farms. With the purchase of 1869, they felt the new pressure of a much more formal government. Their way of life was threatened, and under Louis Riel they rebelled and formed their own government. This effort was short-lived and things returned to normal until 1884, when the Metis rebelled again. This time they were defeated by Canadian troops in a series of battles, the last of which took place at Batoche Battlefield, 30 miles south and 20 miles west of Prince Albert City.

The transcontinental railroad pushed across the plains in 1885 and determined once and for all the way the life on the great prairie was going to be. The iron horse brought thousands of new farmers from all over the world, and it provided a quick way to ship the produce of the farms to the markets where they were needed.

The plains have served as Canada's melting pot. Their rich land attracted farmers from everywhere—Scandinavia, the United States, Russia, and virtually all the countries of middle Europe. When you travel here now you'll see onion-domed churches straight from the Ukraine, towheaded descendants of the Vikings, and colorful folk costumes from the Balkan countries. You'll find the Julian calendar still used in a few places. If you are at the town of Gimli during the first week of August, you'll participate in the annual Icelandic festival. And when you pass through Steinbach you'll meet the grandchildren of Mennonite settlers who migrated from Russia in 1874 to settle in a number of places in the area.

Perhaps it is the mixture of nationalities here on the plains, or perhaps it is just because the whole area is only a hundred years beyond being a true frontier, but whatever the reason, you soon discover that the people are expansive and friendly. If you are accustomed to the closed society of a big city, the

Bleached animal bones and old wagon wheels at a ranch gate in Saskatchewan

unabashed openness of the prairie people may be disconcerting at first—but you'll soon begin to enjoy it.

The flat provinces of the plains can't offer the traveler the spectacular attractions of their western cousins. They have no towering snowcapped peaks to enthrall you. But they have a beauty and attraction all their own—the beauty of the field, the open land, the quiet lake. To compare the prairie to the mountains is like comparing a pastoral symphony to a great march. One is quiet, restful, soothing. The other is brilliant, stirring, dramatic. Both are beautiful; each has its own appeal.

Where to travel in the plains? Look at the routes of the Trans-Canada and the Yellowhead highways. They pass near dozens of interesting places. Locate the national and provincial parks. And, by all means, draw your route so as to see some of the land both above and below the edge of the Shield.

If you have a yen to experience some of the wilderness without backpacking into a remote region, Manitoba offers a couple of interesting excursions.

One is a five-day boat trip taking you up the full length of Lake Winnipeg. The boat departs from Selkirk on a regular schedule and, on its journey to Norway House, the northernmost port, provides a fascinating view of the lake's unconquered shores.

Another is the 500-mile train ride from The Pas to Churchill, the tiny city on Hudson Bay that serves as Manitoba's only deepwater port. Either of these unusual junkets will provide you with interesting memories, good topics for conversation, and unparalleled photographic opportunities.

Highway 10 is an interesting north-south route to consider. Taking it north from Brandon, you'll pass through Riding Mountain National Park and close to several good provincial parks. You'll get a good look at some wilderness areas and, if you stay on it, will get to visit The Pas and Flin Flon, two "frontier" towns.

The great plains are surprisingly light on precipitation, so you can expect a good many bright, sunny days as you travel in the summer. And if you plan to be anywhere here during the winter, come prepared for deep, deep cold. Winnipeg has been known to go for weeks without seeing the mercury above the zero mark, day or night. It's a dry, brisk, pleasant kind of cold, to be sure—but cold nonetheless.

On clear evenings, beginning sometimes as early as mid-August and extending through the autumn and winter, nature puts on her own fireworks celebration—the brilliant aurora borealis—in the northern sky. If you are traveling anywhere in the west or the northern territories, you may find yourself with a grandstand seat. Pulsing, flaming, flickering, changing color like a psychedelic nightclub scene, the northern lights are caused by electrically charged particles shot from the sun and diverted toward the earth's magnetic poles. En route, they collide with our atmospheric gases and change the polarity of their charge. Displays of the aurora usually begin before midnight and often continue for several hours. At times the waving, shifting, undulating curtains of light cover the whole sky. If you have an opportunity to see this electronic spectacle, don't miss it.

SASKATCHEWAN

BATOCHE BATTLEFIELD NATIONAL HISTORIC SITE [E-3]* At this site the decisive battle between Canadian troops and the Metis ended the Riel Rebellion in 1885. Take Highway 2 south from Prince Albert to Domremy, then go 20 miles west on a gravel road. See National Parks, page 103.

BIG MUDDY BADLANDS [H-3] This valley out of the prehistoric past consists of eroded earth, sandstone hills, and buttes, and creates a desolation that could have been abandoned by the devil himself. Coal seams are visible in the sandstone cliffs. The wildest part is the area around alkaline Big Muddy Lake, about 90 miles south of Regina on Highway 6. The badlands are generally west of the highway. The area is not developed for tourist traffic, and the roads through it are few and poor. There is lodging at Bengough, on Highway 34, and at Minton, on Highway 6. This is a junket for explorers.

CANNINGTON MANOR HISTORIC PARK [G-5] A short drive north of Carlyle you'll find Moose Mountain Provincial Park. Just east of Kenosee Lake in the park, you'll come to this little park, the site of a community established as a colony for English aristocrats in the 1880s. The settlers brought their grand pianos, Wedgwood dinner services, padded commodes, Georgian silver, ancestral portraits, and servants. They built a gristmill, a smithy, a woodworkers' shop, a hotel, and an Anglican church. They imported a pack of foxhounds and established a Hunt Club, which held a grand full-dress ball every year. Cannington Manor lasted only a few years, and now the only surviving building is the little All Saints Anglican Church. Plates have been laid out on the ground describing the former town and the location of its buildings.

CANORA [E-5] This town, with its name made up of the first syllables of Canadian Northern Railroad, is a Ukrainian center north of Yorkton. The homeland traditions have been maintained, and the Julian calendar is still used here. Some of the richest farms in Canada are in the area; they ship a billion and a half bushels of grain a year to the rest of the world.

CYPRESS HILLS PROVINCIAL PARK [G-1] French fur traders who came to this area just south of Maple Creek named these hills for their great stand of lodge pole pines. Later English settlers mistranslated the French, and as a matter of fact there isn't a single cypress tree within miles. The park has delightful hiking and riding trails, and you'll see plenty of antelope, elk, beaver, wild turkey, and other animals. The yucca grass here is subtropical and is believed to have survived high in the hills when the lower areas nearby were under the prehistoric ice cap. Plants like these plus the fossils of crocodiles, turtles, rhinos, and camels found here lead scientists to believe the area was once as tropical as lands near the equator today. Park facilities include modern campgrounds, cabins, a store and snack bar, a playground and a heated swimming pool. Fort Walsh, a restored RCMP fort, is just a short distance away.

* Letter and number refer to coordinates on map of Saskatchewan, page 34.

DUCK MOUNTAIN PROVINCIAL PARK [E-5] On the Saskatchewan-Manitoba border, a few miles east of Kamsack, this small park is one of the most scenic in the province. It is located on a heavily wooded ridge from which you can get a fine view of the surrounding countryside. Pretty blue Madge Lake is in the center of the park, providing swimming, and you'll find many nature trails as well as tent and trailer camping facilities, a store, and a golf course. There also are cabins to rent. Just east of here in Manitoba, is the hundred-times-larger Duck Mountain Provincial Forest ready for exploration.

FORT BATTLEFORD NATIONAL HISTORIC PARK [E-2] A 45-acre park at Battleford with historic buildings of the old North West Mounted Police. See National Parks, page 103.

FORT QU' APPELLE [F-4] First established as a trading post in 1864, this settlement later became a North West Mounted Police post. The name, in French, means "Who calls?" Legend says that a handsome young French trapper, while returning from a long hunt, heard his name echoing across the lake. He cried out, "Qu' appelle?" but heard no reply. Hurrying back to camp, he found that his love, an Indian maiden, had died and with her last breath, had called his name. You'll find four fine lakes for fishing stretched out in a 30-mile chain, with

The village of Lebret in the Qu'Appelle Valley

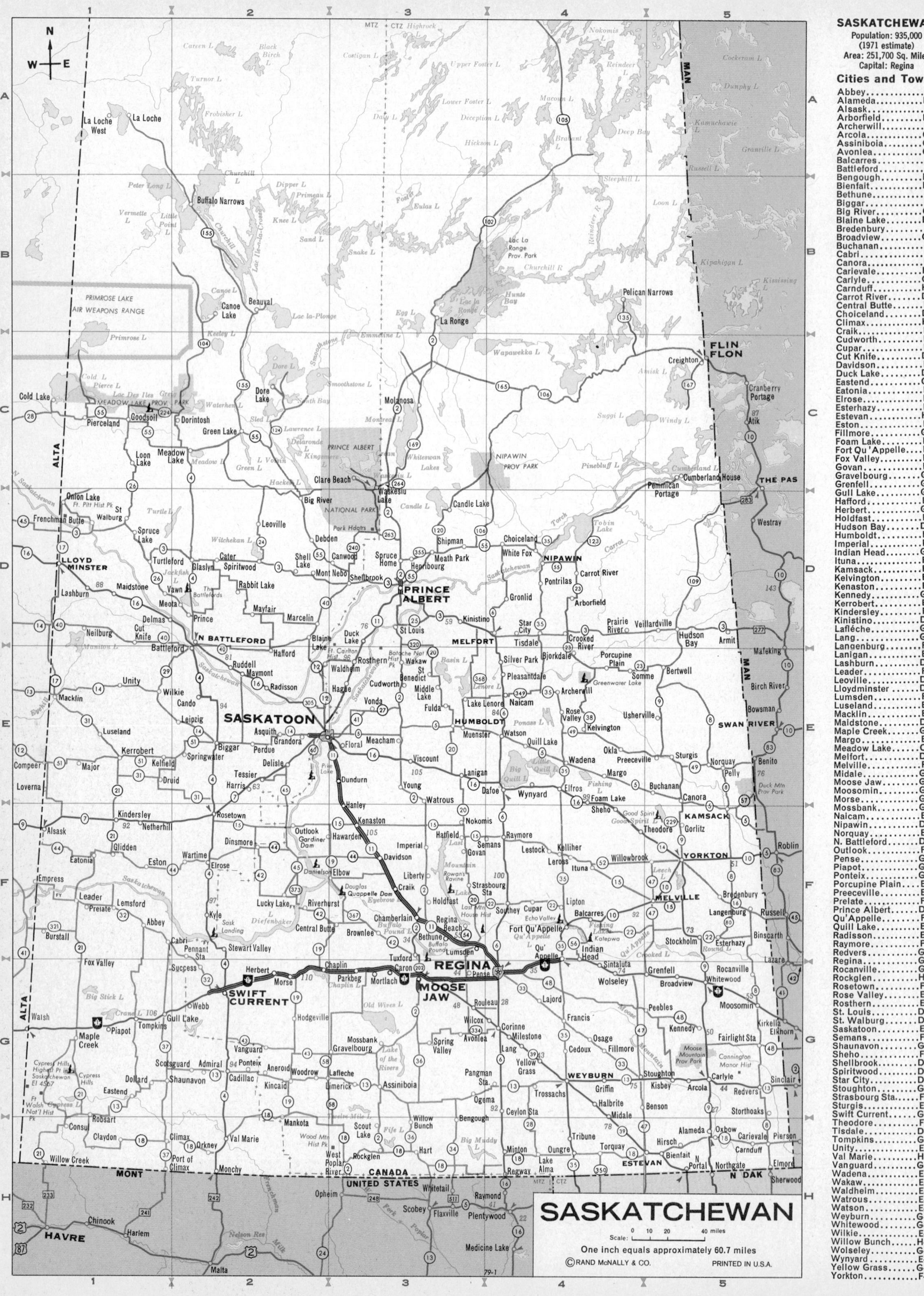

SASKATCHEWAN

Population: 935,000
(1971 estimate)
Area: 251,700 Sq. Miles
Capital: Regina

Cities and Towns

Abbey.....F-1
Alameda.....H-5
Alsask.....F-1
Arborfield.....D-4
Archerwill.....E-4
Arcola.....G-5
Assiniboia.....G-3
Avonlea.....G-3
Balcarres.....F-4
Battleford.....E-2
Bengough.....H-3
Bienfait.....H-5
Bethune.....F-3
Biggar.....E-2
Big River.....C-2
Blaine Lake.....D-2
Bredenbury.....F-5
Broadview.....G-5
Buchanan.....E-4
Cabri.....F-1
Canora.....E-5
Carievale.....H-5
Carlyle.....G-5
Carnduff.....H-5
Carrot River.....D-4
Central Butte.....F-3
Choiceland.....D-4
Climax.....H-1
Craik.....F-3
Cudworth.....E-3
Cupar.....F-4
Cut Knife.....D-1
Davidson.....F-3
Duck Lake.....D-3
Eastend.....G-1
Eatonia.....F-1
Elrose.....F-2
Esterhazy.....F-5
Estevan.....H-4
Eston.....F-1
Fillmore.....G-4
Foam Lake.....E-4
Fort Qu'Appelle.....F-4
Fox Valley.....F-1
Govan.....F-3
Gravelbourg.....G-3
Grenfell.....G-5
Gull Lake.....G-1
Hafford.....E-2
Herbert.....G-2
Holdfast.....F-3
Hudson Bay.....D-5
Humboldt.....E-3
Imperial.....F-3
Indian Head.....G-4
Ituna.....F-4
Kamsack.....F-5
Kelvington.....E-4
Kenaston.....F-3
Kennedy.....G-5
Kerrobert.....E-1
Kindersley.....F-1
Kinistino.....D-3
Lafléche.....G-2
Lang.....G-4
Langenburg.....F-5
Lanigan.....E-3
Lashburn.....D-1
Leader.....F-1
Leoville.....D-2
Lloydminster.....D-1
Lumsden.....F-3
Luseland.....E-1
Macklin.....E-1
Maidstone.....D-1
Maple Creek.....G-1
Margo.....E-4
Meadow Lake.....C-2
Melfort.....D-4
Melville.....F-5
Midale.....G-4
Moose Jaw.....G-3
Moosomin.....G-5
Morse.....G-2
Mossbank.....G-3
Naicam.....E-4
Nipawin.....D-4
Norquay.....E-5
N. Battleford.....D-2
Outlook.....F-2
Pense.....G-3
Piapot.....G-1
Ponteix.....G-2
Porcupine Plain.....E-4
Preeceville.....E-5
Prelate.....F-1
Prince Albert.....D-3
Qu'Appelle.....F-4
Quill Lake.....E-4
Radisson.....E-2
Raymore.....F-4
Redvers.....G-5
Regina.....G-4
Rocanville.....G-5
Rockglen.....H-3
Rosetown.....F-2
Rose Valley.....E-4
Rosthern.....E-3
St. Louis.....D-3
St. Walburg.....D-1
Saskatoon.....E-3
Semans.....F-4
Shaunavon.....G-1
Sheho.....F-4
Shellbrook.....D-2
Spiritwood.....D-2
Star City.....D-4
Stoughton.....G-4
Strasbourg Sta.....F-3
Sturgis.....E-5
Swift Current.....G-2
Theodore.....F-4
Tisdale.....D-4
Tompkins.....G-1
Unity.....E-1
Val Marie.....H-2
Vanguard.....G-2
Wadena.....E-4
Wakaw.....E-3
Waldheim.....E-2
Watrous.....E-3
Watson.....E-4
Weyburn.....G-4
Whitewood.....G-5
Wilkie.....E-1
Willow Bunch.....H-3
Wolseley.....G-4
Wynyard.....E-4
Yellow Grass.....G-4
Yorkton.....F-5

two provincial parks nearby to provide camping facilities. The old fort's museum has some interesting historical displays. Stop at the Hansen-Ross pottery and handicraft center to watch craftsmen shaping native clays. And if you make it in August, you'll be in time for the International Pow Wow held each year on the nearby Sioux Reservation. Fort Qu' Appelle is east and north of Regina, on Highway 35.

FORT WALSH NATIONAL HISTORIC PARK [G-1] After the battle of The Little Big Horn, Chief Sitting Bull led his tribe northward and settled in the area near Cypress Hills Provincial Park. Here 90 Mounties, who had established Fort Walsh the year before, introduced law and order to the tribes. The original fort was restored by the RCMP.

GRAVELBOURG [G-3] The magnificent cathedral in this tiny town south and west of Moose Jaw will remind you of the great churches of Europe. Gravelbourg is a transplanted bit of Quebec, with most of the people speaking French. Gravelbourg College, under the direction of the Oblate Fathers, is affiliated with Ottawa University. Twelve miles south of town, you can swim and fish in Thompson Lake, and picnic on its shores. When you drive hereabouts, keep an eye out for antelope. The region is full of them.

KAMSACK [F-5] Walking down the streets of this little town northeast of Yorkton, you'll see touches of Old Russia, notably in some of the church and building designs and in the richly embroidered shawls worn by the women. Many of the people here are Doukhobors, farmers who came to Canada from Russia. A cyclone very nearly demolished the town in 1944, but there are few traces of the damage remaining.

LAC LA RONGE [B-3] This is a huge lake with more than 1,100 islands dotting its virgin waters. Slightly more than 100 miles north of Prince Albert National Park, it lies in the midst of the wilderness of the Shield. Lac La Ronge Provincial Park extends across the northern end of the lake, with good campsites available, chiefly in the vicinity of the townsite at La Ronge, on the western edge of the lake. Here, too, you'll find a museum and a display of original craft work by the Indians of the region. The lake is noted for its trout, and you can rent boats and fishing equipment at La Ronge to go after them. Take either Highway 2 (paved) or Highway 165 (gravel) north from Prince Albert National Park.

The capitol at Regina

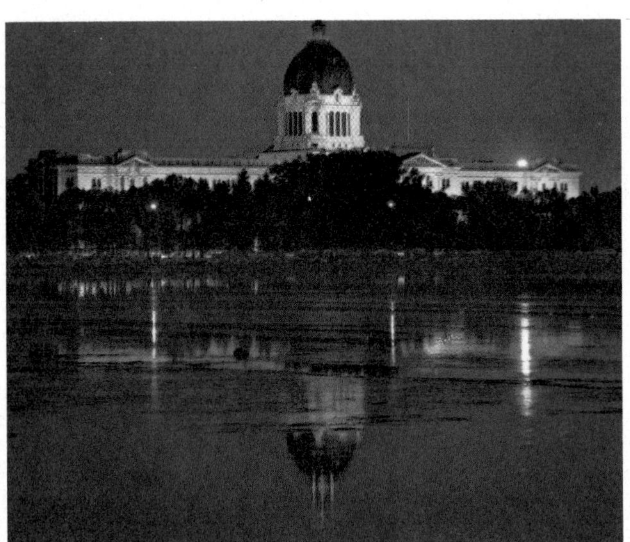

LAST MOUNTAIN LAKE [F-3] If you have a yen to see the whooping crane, the bird that very nearly vanished from this earth a few years ago, this is the place. Wintering at Aransas Pass in Texas, the whooping cranes often travel with sand cranes during the spring and fall migrations—and Last Mountain Lake is an important stopping place on the flyway. This long, narrow body of water situated 25 miles north of Regina is the oldest bird sanctuary in North America. Established in 1887, it covers 2,500 acres.

LLOYDMINSTER [D-1] This little city has the distinction of being in two provinces—Alberta and Saskatchewan—since it sits astride the provincial border. It was first settled by the

Tumbling stream near Lac La Ronge

Barr colonists—2,000 British immigrants led by Isaac Barr who came to the district in 1903—and was named after the group's chaplain, the Reverend G. E. Lloyd. You can camp and picnic in Weaver Park in town, and while there, visit the Barr Colony Museum, which displays items relating to the pioneers. In the museum building you'll also see the Fuchs Wildlife Display of mounted native animals and the 76-picture collection in Imhoff's Art Gallery. The original log church built by the colonists in 1904 is open for visits.

MOOSE JAW [G-3] There must be an unusual story behind a name as odd as Moose Jaw, but no one seems to know it. Legend says that a passing pioneer paused on the bank of a creek to mend his oxcart wheel with the jawbone of a moose he found lying nearby—and named the stream Moose Jaw Creek. More likely, the name came from an Indian word meaning "river that bends like a moose's jaw." The city has a fine 250-acre wild animal park with one of the best collections to be found in Canada—but there isn't a moose to be seen. You'll enjoy the formal gardens and winding streams of Crescent Park, in the center of town, where there are a swimming pool, tennis courts, and a children's zoo. For history buffs and old trail hunters, Highway 2 south of the city, is a remnant of the old Powder River Trail—the main track used by freight wagons and ranchers to travel between Denver and Moose Jaw before the arrival of the railroad. A busy city of 34,000, Moose Jaw's business life revolves around wheat, oil, meat packing, and garment manufacturing. You might enjoy a visit to the stockyards. On the Qu'Appelle River, north of the city, you'll find the headquarters of Saskatchewan's first and most famous yacht club, noted for its class racing activities. In May each year, over 3,000 musicians converge on the city for a musical showdown, the International Band Competition. Another of the city's industries is wine making, and a visit to the wineries during and just after the grape harvest is interesting. Twelve miles north and east of the city is Buffalo Pound Lake, bordered by a provincial park with a large campsite and provisions for swimming, boating, and horseback riding.

MOOSOMIN [G-5] When passing through this town not far from the Manitoba border on the Trans-Canada Highway, you might pause to visit the opera house—an imposing curiosity because it has never had an opera performance. It has served a number of functions, including that of city hall and post office, but has never been used for the purpose for which it was built. One of Saskatchewan's five luxury campsites along the Trans-Canada is located about a mile and a half from town.

NIPAWIN PROVINCIAL PARK [C-4] A wilderness park with campgrounds reached by gravel roads. There is good hunting in the vicinity for moose, deer, bear, and caribou in the nearby Wapaweka Hills. Facilities include accommodations for tents and trailers. You might note that Highway 106 leads north out of the park to Flin Flon. There are good private and government campgrounds as well as service station facilities all along the road, and beaches and boating facilities at many of the lakes you'll pass. Guides for fishing and hunting are also available.

NORQUAY [E-5] A small town on the edge of the wilderness north of Kamsack on Highway 49, Norquay is in the midst of fine hunting and fishing country. Plenty of moose, elk, and deer in season. South of town there are three Indian reservations, and nearby are two historical sites—Fort Livingston and Fort Pelly. Fort Livingston was the original headquarters of the North West Mounted Police.

NORTH BATTLEFORD [D-2] This is the gateway to northern Saskatchewan and was once a trading post and a North West Mounted Police Fort. The city of Battleford, across the river, was the Northwest Territories capital from 1878 to 1882. It was in Battleford that the rebels under Louis Riel surrendered in 1885 and brought an end to the Riel Rebellion. In Battleford, visit the North West Mounted Police Memorial. Fort Battleford National Historic Park is nearby. See National Parks, page 103.

PRINCE ALBERT [D-3] A pretty city high on a bank overlooking the North Saskatchewan River, the city started life as a trading post built by Peter Pond, an ex-soldier from Connecticut, in 1776. Abandoned for a time, it was later settled by Presbyterian minister James Nisbet. His first hand-hewn log church and school building are preserved in Bryant Park. Also in town is the Lund Wildlife Exhibit, containing more than 800 specimens of Canadian wildlife displayed in natural surroundings. Prince Albert is the jumping-off point for hunting and fishing parties heading into northern Saskatchewan and the Northwest Territories, and thus the base of a good many charter flight operations. It is also the headquarters for the smoke jumpers of the Saskatchewan Forest Service—the province's forest fire fighters. Prince Albert National Park is just to the north, while Batoche Rectory National Historic Park is 30 miles south. See National Parks, page 103.

PRINCE ALBERT NATIONAL PARK [C-3] A giant of a park located 50 miles north of Prince Albert. For description, see National Parks, page 103.

REGINA [G-4] This capital city of the province is called the Queen City of the Plains. Its pride is the 1,600-acre Wascana Center built around the shores of manmade Wascana Lake. In this huge parklike development, you'll find government buildings, museums, art galleries, and the Regina Campus of Saskatchewan University. Tour the center on a double-decked bus from London and see the granite fountain which once stood in Trefalgar Square. For a map of the city and descriptions of its points of interest, see pages 43 and 44.

ST. HUBERT [G-5] You won't find this village on many maps because today it is little more than a memory—but it was located south of Whitewood on Highway 9, a few miles north of Moose Mountain Provincial Park. In the early part of the 20th century, a group of French noblemen crossed the Atlantic and set up a unique bit of Old France here. They built palatial homes for themselves and their servants, imported vintage wines and Parisian fashions, drove to local race meets in fancy coach-and-fours—and held court once a year in the Whitewood Hotel. They established commercial enterprises—a chicory farm, a cheese factory, a brush factory, and a sugar beet farm—most of which were not practical for the area—and eventually lost all their money. Then they returned to France, leaving behind memories of gracious hospitality and a string of unpaid bills. The citizens of Whitewood can reduce you to tears with their funny stories about the French counts of St. Hubert.

ST. WALBURG [D-1] Count Berthold von Imhoff, a German artist who traveled and painted in many churches throughout the eastern United States and Canada, settled near this tiny town in 1913. His gallery and studio are located 6 miles southwest of town on Highway 3. In the enormous gallery, you'll see copies of world masterpieces, portraits of British and German royalty, American presidents, saints, popes, and huge biblical scenes. A surprising collection to be found tucked off in a remote corner of the world.

SASKATOON [E-3] The saskatoon is a bush, named by the Indians, which bears a delicious purple berry. Named after it, the city was established in 1882 as a temperance colony by a group migrating from Ontario. Along the way, the city has acquired several descriptive nicknames, including "City of the Bridges" and "Potash Capital of the World." The last name is especially well deserved since one-half of the world's reserve of potash is located in this area. Canada's first potash mine is located 14 miles from the city. The Western Development Museum on Lorne Avenue has a large collection of power tractors, harvesters, and farm implements as well as older horse-drawn implements and pioneer home furnishings. The Mendel Art Gallery, with a fine collection of works by Canadian artists and also a good group of Eskimo carvings, is part of an attractive cultural complex that also includes a theater and a conservatory with magnificent floral displays. A good place to spend an interesting afternoon, especially for the children, is the Golden Gate Wild Animal Park, with a collection of colorful birds and animals from all over the world. Tour the park on a rubber-tired train, let the children take pony rides, and have a picnic. In July you might be here in time to participate in the Saskachimo Exposition, a two-week fair that includes a pageant reenacting Saskatoon's history.

SWIFT CURRENT [G-2] Located on the Trans-Canada Highway 90 miles north of the international border, this was the spot where cowboys from south of the border came north to join the ranch hands on the great Turkey Track and 76 ranches for weekends of ripsnortin' revelry. Oil was discovered in the area in 1952, and the city blossomed from a small town to a population center in a short time. In town, visit the Thorsson Memorial Museum, a good natural history repository, and stop to see Blow Torch, an ingenious mechanical horse which stands guard outside of Bill McIntyre's foundry. Blow Torch has traveled far and wide, performing at Canada's International Trade Fair in Toronto. Frontier Days is a six-day celebration including an excellent rodeo and fair staged during the first week of July.

VAL MARIE [H-2] Did you ever see that lovable little animal, the prairie dog? Their antics can keep you occupied for hours. The only place in Canada when you can watch prairie dogs is Frenchman Creek valley, south of Val Marie, which is 75 miles straight south of Swift Current. In the valley there are six colonies of prairie dogs with a population of over a thousand.

WOOD MOUNTAIN [H-3] This site of a fort established by the Mounties in 1874 is south and west of Moose Jaw—about 140 miles by highway. The post was active until 1918, and today the log barracks have been reconstructed, a museum has been established, and a good model of the original fort has been set up. The Mounties stationed here upheld the law among Indians, whiskey traders, and horse thieves at a time when the area threatened to become a lawless paradise. The park surrounding the fort has picnic grounds, campgrounds, and a swimming pool. Wood Mountain is noted, too, for the oldest continuously operating rodeo in Canada, which puts on its shows at grounds in the park. The park itself is 6 miles south of town.

YORKTON [F-5] A goodly part of Canada's turkeys come from here, so you'll see large flocks on farms as you drive through the area. This is a gateway to the resort area of northeastern Saskatchewan, and one of the points where hunting and fishing expeditions outfit. The Western Development Museum at the airport has a collection of vintage automobiles, carriages, buggies, and early steam, oil, and gas-powered tractors.

"The Star" maneuver performed by the Royal Canadian Mounted Police

MANITOBA

BEAUSEJOUR [G-4]* Forty miles northeast of Winnipeg, this town is where the top racers from Canada and the United States gather in February each year to compete in the Canadian Power Toboggan Races. The races are part of a festival that includes a float parade, pancake breakfast, and the crowning of a queen.

BRANDON [G-2] Aptly called The Wheat City of Canada, Brandon, just south of the Trans-Canada Highway, sits astride the twisting Assiniboine River. Fort Brandon, established in 1791, was the first Hudson's Bay trading post in the area. The original fort has been reconstructed in Churchill Park. The city is a good place from which to sally forth on expeditions to the north (Riding Mountain National Park, Duck Mountain Provincial Park) and to the south (Rock, Pelican, and Killarney lakes and the International Peace Garden). Manitoba's Provincial Exhibition—a fair and industrial and livestock show—is held in mid-June.

CHURCHILL Churchill, on the shores of Hudson Bay, is Canada's northernmost seaport, and makes a deepwater maritime province out of Manitoba. It is an important shipping point for European-bound grain. You can't drive to Churchill, since there are as yet no roads into the area—but you can get there by air or via railroad from The Pas. The 550-mile trip will give you the best look at the wide and empty country of Manitoba's northern wilderness. In the town you'll find an interesting Eskimo museum, and a short boat trip away, you can visit historic Fort Prince of Wales. Fare for the trip to this national historic park is $5.

CLEARWATER PROVINCIAL PARK [B-1] Lake Atikameg and the other lakes in this park just north of The Pas are noted for their remarkable blue-green color. Seen from the air, the lakes are so clear that it is possible to identify objects that lie 120 feet under water from an altitude of 1,500 feet. The park is 20 miles north of The Pas on Highway 10, and has cabins and lodges as well as camping facilities.

* Letter and number refer to coordinates on map of Manitoba.

DAUPHIN [E-2] The chief city in the narrow western part of the province that extends northward in a corridor between Manitoba's giant lakes and the Saskatchewan border. It is important for the vacationer because within easy distance are such attractions as Duck Mountain Provincial Park and Riding Mountain National Park. To the north are the frontier towns of The Pas and Flin Flon. And to the north and east are hundreds of lakes including Dauphin, Manitoba, and Winnipegosis. Dauphin is also the site of the annual National Ukrainian Festival, held during the first week in August, where you can see sturdy Ukrainians in their national costumes doing their colorful dances. These people are Cossacks, and they can really sing and dance. It's a worthwhile festival to see.

DAWSON BAY [C-1] This bay is an arm of Lake Winnipegosis. Highway 10 leads past it going north and takes you through a 10-mile stretch of virgin country that includes the Great Bog, a vast area of floating muskeg, a kind of sphagnum moss, encrusted with reindeer moss and stunted trees. The Pas is just north of the area.

DUCK MOUNTAIN PROVINCIAL PARK [E-1] On the Saskatchewan border, this park encompasses 310,000 acres and has no less than 73 lakes. There are plenty of quiet, well-equipped campsites and good fishing on four of the lakes. Drive to the top of 2,727-foot Baldy Mountain in the southeast corner of the park for a great view of the whole countryside. This is the highest point in Manitoba. The park is located north and a little west of Riding Mountain National Park.

FLIN FLON [A-1] This city has an unusual name and an even more unusual reason for having it. Prospectors who came to the area and discovered rich mineral deposits happened to find a dime novel about a man who found a city of gold in the center of the earth. There were few books available and this one was passed from hand to hand and became an odds-on favorite. The main character in the book was Josiah Flintabbatey Flonatin, shortened in the literary discussions which followed to Flin Flon. A good many decades after the city got its name from this fictional hero, the town fathers instituted a search for the novel. No one could even remember the book's name. Someone finally sniffed it out in a London book-

The history of the Great Plains—his story, too. Manitoba's trails, a rider's delight.

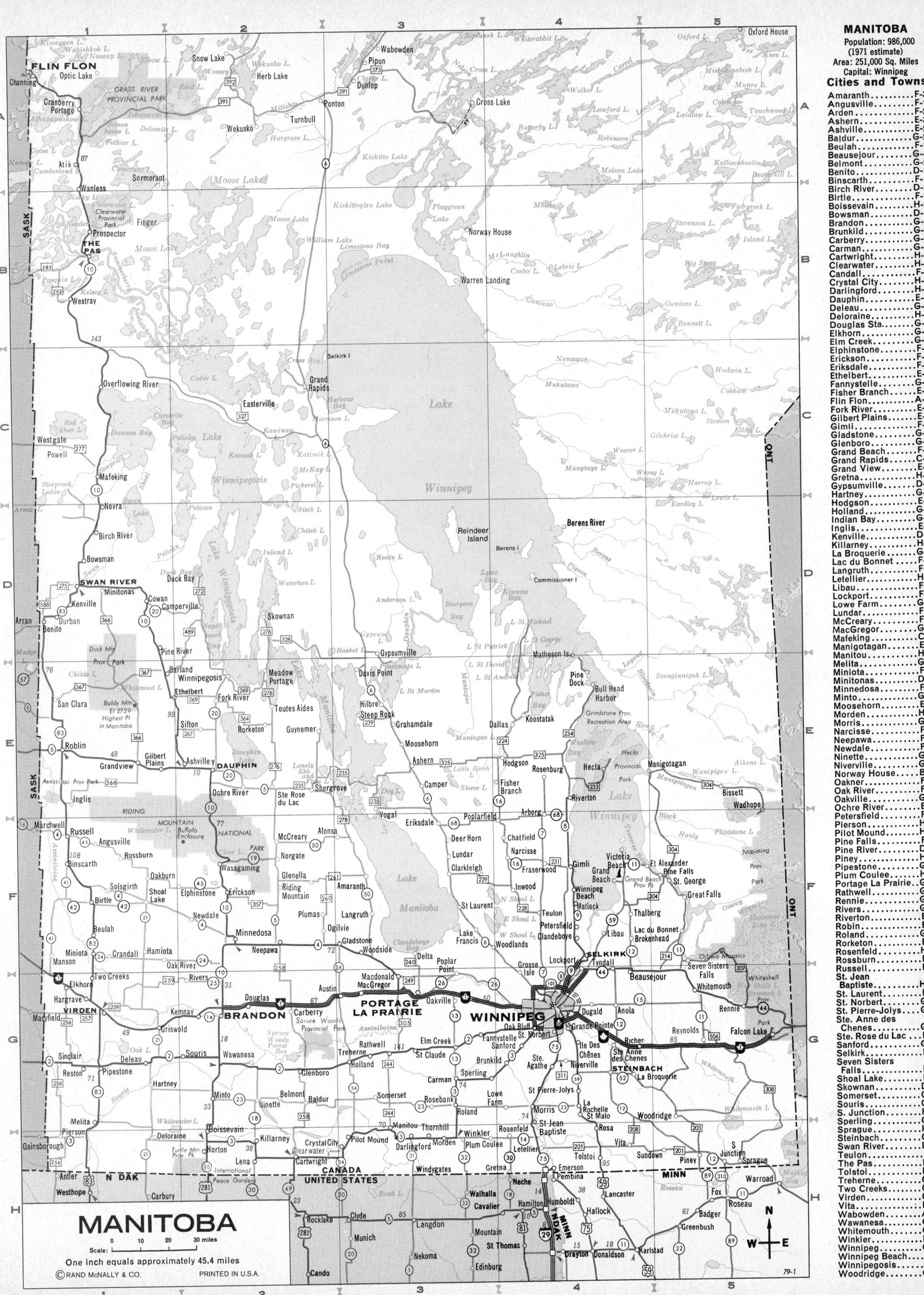
MANITOBA
Population: 986,000
(1971 estimate)
Area: 251,000 Sq. Miles
Capital: Winnipeg
Cities and Towns
Amaranth..........F-3
Angusville..........F-1
Arden..........F-2
Ashern..........E-3
Ashville..........E-2
Baldur..........G-2
Beulah..........F-1
Beausejour..........G-4
Belmont..........G-2
Benito..........D-1
Binscarth..........F-1
Birch River..........D-1
Birtle..........F-1
Boissevain..........H-2
Bowsman..........D-1
Brandon..........G-2
Brunkild..........G-4
Carberry..........G-2
Carman..........G-3
Cartwright..........H-2
Clearwater..........H-2
Candall..........F-1
Crystal City..........H-3
Darlingford..........H-3
Dauphin..........E-2
Deleau..........G-1
Deloraine..........H-1
Douglas Sta..........G-2
Elkhorn..........G-1
Elm Creek..........G-3
Elphinstone..........F-2
Erickson..........F-2
Eriksdale..........F-3
Ethelbert..........E-1
Fannystelle..........G-3
Fisher Branch..........E-4
Flin Flon..........A-1
Fork River..........E-2
Gilbert Plains..........E-1
Gimli..........F-4
Gladstone..........G-3
Glenboro..........G-2
Grand Beach..........F-4
Grand Rapids..........C-2
Grand View..........E-1
Gretna..........H-4
Gypsumville..........D-3
Hartney..........G-1
Hodgson..........E-4
Holland..........G-3
Indian Bay..........G-5
Inglis..........E-1
Kenville..........D-1
Killarney..........H-2
La Broquerie..........G-4
Lac du Bonnet..........F-5
Langruth..........F-3
Letellier..........H-4
Libau..........F-4
Lockport..........G-4
Lowe Farm..........G-4
Lundar..........F-3
McCreary..........F-2
MacGregor..........G-3
Mafeking..........C-1
Manigotagan..........E-4
Manitou..........H-3
Melita..........G-1
Miniota..........F-1
Minitonas..........D-1
Minnedosa..........F-2
Minto..........G-2
Moosehorn..........E-3
Morden..........H-3
Morris..........G-4
Narcisse..........F-4
Neepawa..........F-2
Newdale..........F-2
Ninette..........G-2
Niverville..........G-4
Norway House..........B-3
Oakner..........F-1
Oak River..........F-1
Oakville..........G-3
Ochre River..........E-2
Petersfield..........F-4
Pierson..........H-1
Pilot Mound..........H-3
Pine Falls..........F-5
Pine River..........D-1
Piney..........H-5
Pipestone..........G-1
Plum Coulee..........H-3
Portage La Prairie..G-3
Rathwell..........G-3
Rennie..........G-5
Rivers..........G-2
Riverton..........E-4
Robin..........E-1
Roland..........G-3
Rorketon..........E-2
Rosenfeld..........H-4
Rossburn..........F-1
Russell..........F-1
St. Jean Baptiste..........H-4
St. Laurent..........F-3
St. Norbert..........G-4
St. Pierre-Jolys..........G-4
Ste. Anne des Chenes..........G-4
Ste. Rose du Lac..........E-2
Sanford..........G-4
Selkirk..........F-4
Seven Sisters Falls..........F-5
Shoal Lake..........F-1
Skownan..........D-2
Somerset..........G-3
Souris..........G-2
S. Junction..........H-5
Sperling..........G-3
Sprague..........H-5
Steinbach..........G-4
Swan River..........D-1
Teulon..........F-4
The Pas..........B-1
Tolstoi..........H-4
Treherne..........G-3
Two Creeks..........G-1
Virden..........G-1
Vita..........H-4
Wabowden..........A-3
Wawanesa..........G-2
Whitemouth..........G-5
Winkler..........H-3
Winnipeg..........G-4
Winnipeg Beach..........F-4
Winnipegosis..........E-2
Woodridge..........G-5
MANITOBA
Scale: 0 10 20 30 miles
One inch equals approximately 45.4 miles
©RAND McNALLY & CO.
PRINTED IN U.S.A.
79-1

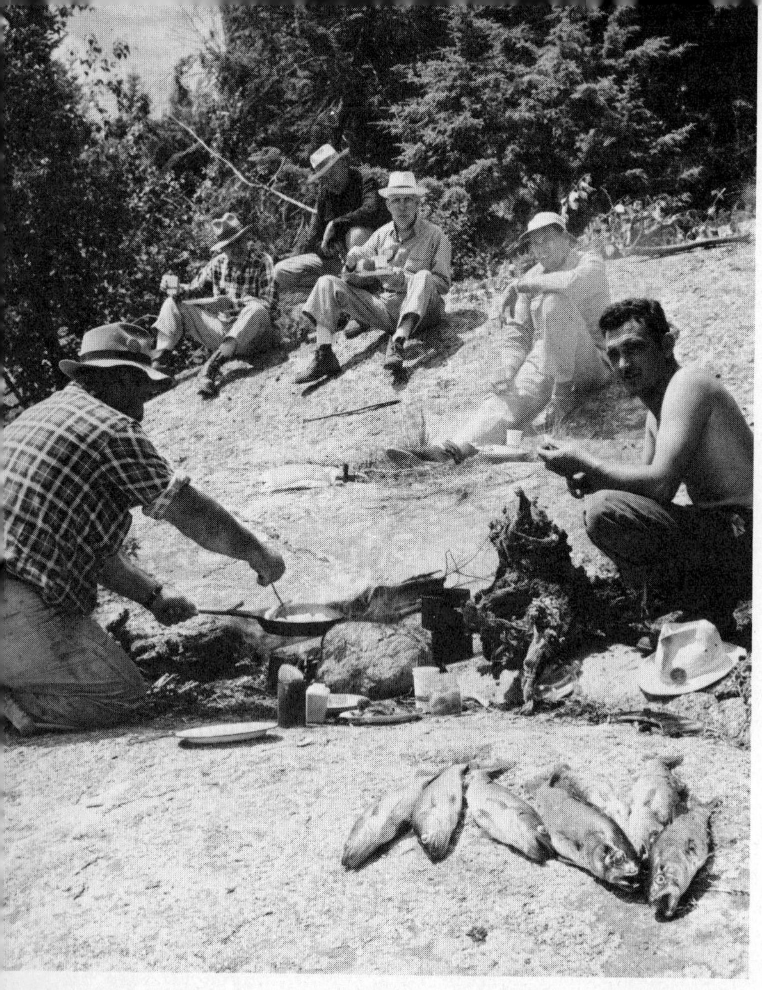

Fresh-caught lunch at a Manitoba lake

stall. The book was *The Sunless City*, and a statue of Flin Flon himself, created by cartoonist Al Capp, stands at the city's edge. One of the world's largest copper mines is near the city, but though mining has been the most important business for years, hunting and fishing in the area are rapidly becoming the city's main enterprises. The Trout Festival, held during the last days in June and the first in July, is becoming world famous as a colorful and fun-filled fiesta. The trout derby is one of the main events, and everyone can enter—but you'd better plan on catching a 40-pounder if you expect to be among the winners. Events of the festival also include the 81-mile Gold Rush Canoe Derby, dancing, fiddling, and a beauty contest.

FORT PRINCE OF WALES Near Churchill on Hudson Bay, this is the northernmost fort in North America. It was built between 1733 and 1771. Can be reached only by boat. See National Parks, page 98.

GIMLI [F-4] This little town on the west shore of Lake Winnipeg, about 60 miles from Winnipeg on Highway 9, is the first of several Icelandic settlements in the region, founded in 1875. Most of the citizens are still of Icelandic origin, and they celebrate their arrival during the first week of August each year with an Icelandic festival. You'll enjoy the singing and dancing.

LOWER FORT GARRY [F-4] At one time this was the Hudson's Bay Company's second most elaborate fur trading post. The governor's residence, built in 1831, is western Canada's oldest building. The fort is a national historic park. See National Parks, page 98.

PORCUPINE PROVINCIAL FORESTS [D-1] North of Duck Mountain along Highway 10 you pass Porcupine Provincial Forests. You can detour for a bit, taking forestry roads to Hart Mountain (2,700 feet) and to campsites on Bell Lake and Steeprock Lakes.

PORTAGE LA PRAIRIE [G-3] In the old fur trading days, the Indians left the Assiniboine River here to begin a portage to Lake Manitoba on their way to York Factory at the mouth of the Nelson River on Hudson Bay. You'll see a cairn a mile southwest of town marking the site of Fort La Reine, established by La Verendrye in 1738. This was headquarters for the explorer and his sons as they probed northward to the Saskatchewan River, southwest in the Mandan Country of North Dakota, and west to the foothills of the Rockies. In the heart of the city, a giant bow of the Assiniboine River forms Crescent Lake. On a beautiful island in the lake is a bird sanctuary and picnic area. You may see the Canada goose here.

RIDING MOUNTAIN NATIONAL PARK [F-2] Covering 1,200 square miles atop a scenic plateau, this park offers a unique combination of tamed and untamed wilderness. Located 70 miles north of Brandon. See National Parks, page 98.

ST. BONIFACE [G-4] Situated on the east bank of the Red River, directly across from Winnipeg, this is the largest French-language speaking city outside of the province of Quebec. You can visit the stockyards here, the largest in the British Commonwealth, and see the monument to the explorer, La Verendrye. Also well worth a visit is the Grey Nun's Home, built in 1845 and now a museum.

SELKIRK [F-4] Located north of Winnipeg on the Red River, this is Lake Winnipeg's busiest port. Fishing vessels and freighters serving the northland via the vast waters of the lake work out of here, and on a bright summer's Sunday afternoon, you'll see hundreds of pleasure craft cruising here on the Red. Just north, on the shore of the lake at Winnipeg Beach, there are dozens of summer resorts taking advantage of the good sandy beaches along the shore. The M.S. *Lord Selkirk II* departs from here for two-to-seven-day cruises up the lake to Grand Rapids—a worthwhile voyage, particularly if you'd like to see what Canada's wilderness looks like. Lower Fort Garry, once a Hudson's Bay Company trading post, is 2 miles south of town. The fort is in "mint" condition. North of town off of Highway 59, you can visit St. Peter's Dynevor Church, from which Anglican missionaries worked among the Saulteaux Indians beginning in 1836.

SOURIS [G-2] There is an agate pit here at this picturesque town 28 miles south and west of Brandon on Highway 2 that will bring a glow to the eye of any rock hound. And if you like exciting bridges, the longest swinging footbridge in Canada—582 feet from end to end—sways across the Souris River. Great for photography and goose pimples.

SPRUCE WOODS PROVINCIAL PARK [G-2] 35 miles west of Austin along the Trans-Canada Highway and then a bit south, you'll come to this new provincial park designed to appeal to those who want a secluded camping vacation. Here are 57,000 unspoiled acres, part of which consists of shifting sand dunes and part of spruce woods, dotted with aspen and wildflowers. Ernest Thompson Seton, naturalist-author who lived for many years in Manitoba, blazed trails that you can follow through the park.

STEINBACH [G-4] The Mennonites came from Russia to Canada in 1874 and settled here and in other places in the wheat provinces. Steinbach is the most ambitious of Canada's Mennonite settlements, boasting a main street that is a mile long. Just north of town you can visit the Mennonite Village Museum, a reconstruction of the pioneer village that was built by the sect in their first year in this country. It was a copy of a village on the steppes of Russia, with farmstead, village streets, and cheese factory. Steinbach is south and east of Winnipeg on Highway 12.

THE PAS [B-1] This is where you discover that the frontier still exists, and also find that hospitality is a true part of frontier life. The name of the town probably comes from the Cree (Indian) word meaning "narrows." You'll be intrigued by the population, a wonderful mixture of miners, prospectors, fishermen, lumbermen, trappers, and Indians. See Christ Church, built in 1840; the Henry Kelsey Cairn, commemorating the first white man to see the region in 1691; and the Sir John Franklin sundial in Devon Park, dating back to 1842. The New Centennial Museum has a fine collection of Indian artifacts and fur trade curios. The big time of the year here comes in February, when the local gentry gather for the Northern Manitoba Trappers Festival. This fabulous bash includes the 150-mile World Championship Dogsled Race, with mushers and their dogs racing for prize purses, canoe packing contests, flour packing contests, in which a winner may carry as much as 700 pounds on his back, squaw wrestling, and—believe it or not—tea boiling contests. It's a great affair. Wear your mukluks and parka. And if you'd like to take the railroad ride of your life, buy a ticket for the 510-mile excursion from The Pas to Churchill, Manitoba's ocean port on Hudson Bay. You live on the train in Churchill while you tour the town and visit Fort Prince of Wales, with its 14-foot-thick walls. You'll see the Arctic poppy growing out of naked rock, perhaps view the white beluga whale playing in the harbor, and be tempted to buy some of the luxurious furs offered for sale.

TURTLE MOUNTAIN PROVINCIAL PARK [H-2] One of the province's smaller parks, covering 47,000 acres of rolling forested hills and fertile valleys. There are 29 lakes in the park, with numerous fishing spots and small campsites. The major attraction in the park is the International Peace Garden, on the Manitoba-North Dakota border. You can reach it via Highway 10. The garden has 1,451 acres in Manitoba and 888 acres in North Dakota, and symbolizes the lasting friendship between the people of Canada and the United States. A series of lakes, drained by ornamental spillways and surrounded by formal gardens, have been jointly developed. A cairn of native stone carries the peace pledge. Each summer, the International Music Camp is held here, along with track and field training camps for boys and girls. The nearest town is Boissevain. The idea for the park was originally conceived by the late Henry J. Moore of Islington, Ontario, in 1928, and was promoted by the National Association of Gardeners of America. The park was dedicated in 1932.

WHITESHELL PROVINCIAL PARK [G-5] The Trans-Canada Highway passes the southern tip of this 675,000-acre park as it crosses the border from Ontario into Manitoba. If you'd like a good close look at the makeup of the Shield, you can have it here, on the Winnipeg River in the northern part of the park, where outcrops of Precambrian rock over 2,600 million years old are visible. The area was originally explored by the French-Canadian explorer La Verendrye in 1733, on his way to the Red River. There are more than 130 lakes and rivers in the park, offering a nearly unlimited opportunity for fishing, boating, swimming, and wilderness canoe trips. Horseback riding and hiking are favorite sports here, too. An extremely interesting drive begins at Seven Sister Falls, just west of the central portion of the park off Highway 11. At Seven Sister Falls, you can see a giant hydroelectric plant. Then, driving east on Highway 307, you'll come to Betula Lake near the winding Whiteshell River, where there are serpentine stone mosaics—including shapes of turtles, snakes, fish, and birds—constructed by the Ojibwa Indians years ago. At Nutimak Lake, visit the interesting little natural history museum, and at White Lake, see lovely Rainbow Falls. Just east of the town of Rennie, you'll find the Alf Hole Sanctuary, where you can see Canada geese at close range. In the spring, the flock totals 600. You'll pass West Hawk Lake—which was formed by a meteor and is 365 feet deep—and visit the nearby fish hatchery. Finally, you'll come to Falcon Lake, with its townsite on the Trans-Canada. The facilities are luxurious and include a shopping center, laundromat, 18-hole golf course, riding stable, ski resort with 14 slopes, and excellent motel accommodations. There are 13 campgrounds scattered through the park, as well as dozens of fine picnic areas.

WINNIPEG [G-4] Accurately described as The Gateway to the West, Winnipeg is the capital of Manitoba and the fourth largest city in Canada. To the east lies that piece of the wilderness which dips down from the north to separate Canada into two distinct parts—The Lake of The Woods Region. To the west, lies the whole western world of the great plains, the Rockies, and the Pacific. For a map of the city and descriptions of its points of interest, see pages 42 and 43.

At the Flin Flon Gold Rush Festival—the Canoe Derby

WINNIPEG

The first citizen of Winnipeg you should meet is the famous Golden Boy, that massive youth carrying a sheaf of wheat atop the Legislative Building. He truly symbolizes the youthful vigor and chief business of the city.

Winnipeg began life as Fort Rouge, established by the French Canadian explorer La Verendrye in 1738. Today, Winnipeg is more than a city. It is a vital hub of Canadian business and cultural life—as an evening at the exquisite Royal Winnipeg Ballet, followed by a visit to the bustling Grain Exchange the next day will prove. Some of the area's unique touches include the onion-domed spires of the Ukrainian church, which punctuate the skyline a bit differently, and Winnipeg's Gallic twin, St. Boniface, just across the Red River, which is the largest French-speaking city in Canada outside of Quebec. The towers of the St. Boniface Basilica here are the "turrets twain" mentioned in Whittier's poem "The Red Voyageur." Like the good metropolis it is, Winnipeg offers a variety of theaters, fine restaurants with cuisines from virtually every nation in the world, a very, very good symphony orchestra, and excellent shopping. For horse enthusiasts, Assiniboia Downs offers racing from mid-May through the end of October—with the first race conveniently scheduled for 6 pm. Your first trip along spacious Portage Avenue, main thoroughfare for shopping, dining, and entertainment, will impress you. If you hail from the east, either in Canada or the United States, you'll immediately become aware of the city's definite western flavor, similar in many ways to that of Denver or Dallas. The hats are a little bigger, the hellos a little louder, the formalities not

Massive bison at the foot of the grand staircase to the legislative building in Winnipeg.
The Royal Winnipeg Ballet Company in a kaleidoscope of color and movement.

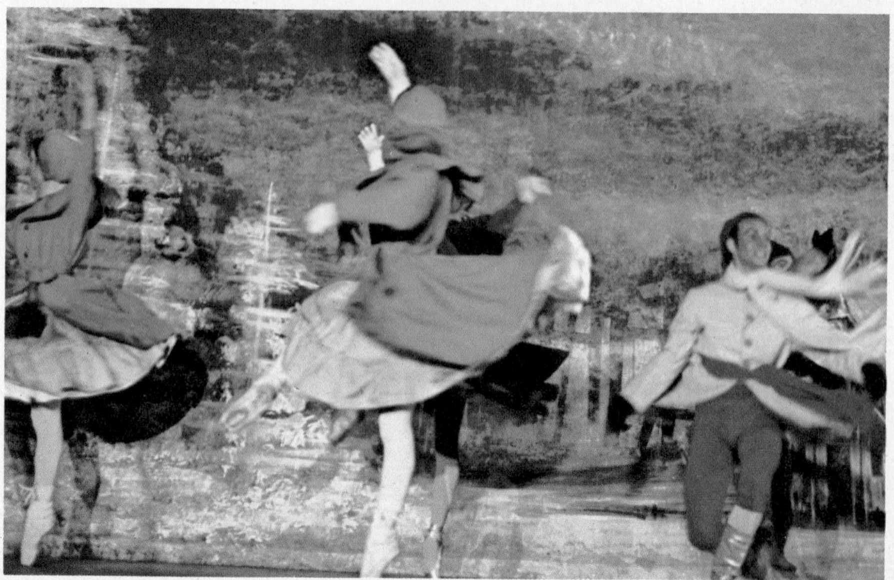

quite so formal, the shirts not quite as stuffed, and everything, including the sky overhead, done on a grander scale. But also, as in Denver or Dallas, this wide open western outlook has a strong overlay of urban sophistication.

Points of Interest

ASSINIBOINE PARK. Located on the west side of the city, on the banks of the Assiniboine River, this park has a conservatory with floral displays changed seasonally, highlighted by a lily display at Easter and a chrysanthemum show in November. Also in the park is a miniature train ride, a delightful formal English garden, and the zoo called Aunt Sally's Farm. Here over 100 animals, from kittens to moose calves, wait to be petted and fed. A bigger zoo is also here and features some exotic species, including the llama and the Mi-lu.

CITY HALL. The two buildings housing the city's administrative offices are joined by an ornamental mall on Main Street. Tours of the buildings can be arranged by phoning the mayor's office.

THE COUNTESS OF DUFFERIN. This fine lady was the first steam locomotive to reach Manitoba, arriving in 1877. She stands just north of the Centennial Centre.

GRAIN EXCHANGE. There is a visitor's gallery here from which you can look into the melee on the trading floor, where every slight hand motion is a signal of some kind in the buying and selling operation. There is a free tour. Hours are 9:30 am to 1:30 pm weekdays. Located at 167 Lombard Avenue.

THE LAST OF THE PRAIRIE. At 2795 Ness Avenue, you'll find a 16-hectare patch of the original prairie that once covered much of North America. Talks and exhibits are free.

THE LEGISLATIVE BUILDING. The province's seat of government is on 30 acres of park between Broadway and the Assiniboine River. You'll see Golden Boy up on top of the dome. The work of French sculptor Charles Gardet, the statue weighs five tons.

MUSEUM OF MAN AND NATURE. The museum, which is devoted to natural history, is located in the Centennial Arts Center, north on Main Street. Located with it is the city's planetarium, where celestial shows are held throughout the year.

OLD ST. ANDREW'S CHURCH. Take Highway 4 north for 12 miles, turn on River Road, to the church. It was erected in 1845.

RAINBOW STAGE. Canada's largest outdoor theater, located in Kildonan Park, is the home of Rainbow Stage Productions, which presents musical comedies alfresco each July and August. It is north of the center of the city off Main Street.

RIVER CRUISES. The M.S. *River Rouge* makes daily 2-hour sightseeing cruises on the Red and Assiniboine rivers, departing from the dock at 312 Nairn Street. Or if you prefer a ride on an old paddle wheeler, go to the wharf on Main Street at the Redwood Avenue Bridge. A longer trip is the 7-hour round-trip criuse to Lower Fort Garry.

ROSS HOUSE. This was the first post office in western Canada; it is located across from the Canadian Pacific depot. Built of logs in 1854, it was the home of William Ross, the first postmaster, and is now a museum.

ROYAL CANADIAN MINT. Located at 520 Lagimodiere Boulevard, the mint, source of all Canadian coins, offers tours at 9 and 11 am and 1 and 3 pm every weekday year round.

SEVEN OAKS HOUSE. Built in 1851, this is one of the oldest buildings in western Canada and was in use until 1954. Now it is a museum displaying articles owned by the original occupants. Located in West Kildonan, just east of Main Street.

TRAIN TRIP TO CHURCHILL. Three times during the months of July and August, a Canadian National Railways train chuffs out of Winnipeg for the ride to Churchill, with stops along the way at Dauphin, The Pas, Thompson, and Flin Flon. There aren't many rides like this remaining, so if you are a history or railroad buff, don't miss it. For details, contact the passenger sales department of the Canadian National at Winnipeg.

WINNIPEG CONVENTION CENTRE. Opened in 1976, this new three-floor center for conventions has meetings rooms, a shopping mall and theater, and a huge room of 78,000 square feet. This area has no pillars to obstruct the view, and 5,000 persons can be accommodated for banquets.

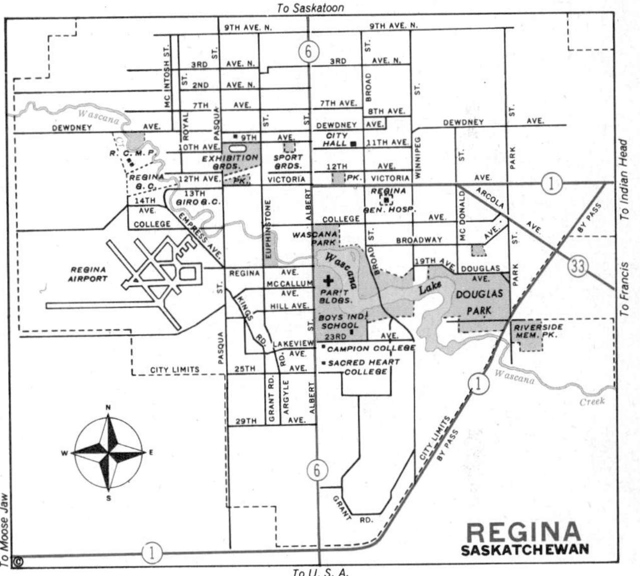

REGINA

Can you imagine a neat, clean, orderly city, capital of the province, named Pile o' Bones, Saskatchewan? It nearly happened. Back in 1882, when the city was no more than a couple of tents on a creek bank, it was called Pile o' Bones because of the enormous pile of buffalo bones left near the spot by Indians after their prairie hunts. Princess Louise, wife of Canada's governor general of the time, saved the day. When the little town was named seat of government for the Northwest Territories in 1883, she suggested it be named Regina, in honor of her mother, Queen Victoria, and the good citizens accepted the idea.

Regina is truly a product of the hand of man, rising out of the prairie without a rock or a river to influence its development. True, it began on the shores of Wascana Creek, but that was damned in 1883 to make Wascana Lake and create a center of interest for the city. You become aware of the geometric precision and the planning behind it almost from

A Canadian giant on display in Regina's museum

your first moment in town. Life revolves around the parklike shores of Wascana Lake, where the Wascana Center is under development. As you tour the center, keep in mind that plans for the area have been projected as far ahead as 100 years. That's planning!

Points of Interest

CURLODROME. Curling is a big sport here, and the Curlodrome on 11th Street is a good place to see some sweeping action. Curling clubs in the city include the Caledonian, the Imperial, the Regina, the Wascana, and the Wheat City.

LAKE SHORE DRIVE. This lovely drive on the south shore of Wascana Lake takes you past the Legislative Building and the Saskatchewan Center of the Arts.

LEGISLATIVE BUILDING. This beautiful building, a part of the Wascana Center, on Legislative Drive, contains 34 different kinds of marble. Guides are available to take you on tours. Way up in the dome, 160 feet above the city, there's an observation spot where you can view the entire city.

Coming down the track in the pacing race—one of the high points of the Regina Buffalo Days

MUSEUM OF NATURAL HISTORY. The museum is in Wascana Park at College Avenue and Albert Street and has a fine specialty collection outlining the natural history of the province. Open daily. Free.

NORMAN MACKENZIE ART GALLERY. The gallery is on the Regina Campus of the University of Saskatchewan, on the north side of Wascana Lake opposite the Legislative Building. You'll see a good collection of Canadian, American, Dutch, and English art, and a display of antiquities from Greece, Egypt, and China. Open every day. Free.

ROYAL CANADIAN MOUNTED POLICE BARRACKS. Located on the city's west side, the barracks are accessible from the 5900 block on Dewdney Avenue. This is the RCMP's western headquarters and the training school for the force. You can visit the museum and the chapel and take a guided tour.

SASKATCHEWAN HOUSE. The original residence of Saskatchewan's first lieutenant governor is located at 4600 Dewdney Ave. Each summer, John Coulter's play "The Trial of Louis Riel" is staged here.

WILD BIRD SANCTUARY. The refuge is on a peninsula jutting out into Wascana Lake. You'll drive past it on Lake Shore Drive. It is particularly interesting in the migrating seasons when birds travel the great central flyway.

Special Events

BUFFALO DAYS. Pemmican Pete rides into town each July astride a snorting buffalo to herald Buffalo Days, Regina's midsummer Old West festival. Rodeo events, singing, dancing, and street parades in costume highlight the affair.

Pedestrian mall in Regina

HEARTLAND

Toronto's city hall—bold, modern expression of a city looking to the future

ONTARIO 

ONTARIO IS MUCH LIKE THAT FAMOUS ELEPHANT ONCE DESCRIBED BY THE THREE BLIND MEN. IT APPEARS DIFFERENT TO ALL WHO LOOK AT IT. TO VANCOUVERITES, IT IS A BIG BUSINESS AND FINANCIAL CENTER BACK EAST. TO NEWFOUNDLANDERS, IT IS THAT PROVINCE TO THE WEST WHERE THE NATIONAL GOVERNMENT HOLDS FORTH. TO AMERICANS FROM THE MIDDLE WEST, IT IS CANADA. (THEY ARE ONLY VAGUELY AWARE OF BRITISH COLUMBIA AND THE ATLANTIC PROVINCES.) TO THE ONTARIANS THEMSELVES—WELL, IT HAS BEEN SAID THAT FEW HAVE EVER REALLY SEEN ALL OF THEIR OWN PROVINCE.

If that last statement is true, it is understandable. Ontario is a lot bigger than most people imagine and has about as much geographical diversity as you can get in one province. It borders on four of the five Great Lakes and also touches Hudson Bay. Its northernmost point, near the spot where the Black Duck River flows into Hudson Bay, is more than 1,100 miles from its southern tip at Point Pelee in Lake Erie. From east to west, Ontario stretches 1,300 miles.

Better than a third of Canada's population lives in Ontario—and most of that population is in the area between Lake Huron and the province's eastern border. In Ontario's north, the moose and the lakes far outnumber the human inhabitants. By contrast, there is the urbanity and sophistication of beautiful Toronto and its 2¼ million citizens.

There are really six Ontarios, and each offers the traveler something different.

NORTHWESTERN WILDERNESS

Beginning at the western border, there is Ontario's northwestern wilderness, a huge block of 200,000 square miles of lake and forest. Some of it is barely explored. In the southern section of this area is the famed Lake of the Woods and its more than 14,000 islands. Here, too, is Rainy Lake, the remnant of a great prehistoric inland sea called Lake Agassiz, which was larger than all the Great Lakes put together.

Kenora is the "fly-in" capital of this country, where you board a float plane to jump to one of the hunting and fishing camps of this wilderness. Northeast of Kenora, in the Red Lake district, you are in rugged gold mine country, where every prospector will tell you that he expects to hit pay dirt tomorrow. North of Red Lake there is raw wilderness.

You *can* sample this wilderness by car if you like. Just drive north on gravel Highway 599, which you join at Ignace on the Trans-Canada. You can do about 200 miles, up to Pickle Crow. The road goes a bit beyond Pickle Crow, but not much. You can fly north of Pickle Crow, to places like Big Beaver House and Weagamow Lake if you hanker to hunt and fish in truly remote places.

If your yen for real adventure is strong, you can make arrangements for a canoe trip across some of this wilderness. With a guide, you leave Osnaburgh House, an old Hudson's Bay trading post a few miles south of Pickle Crow, and travel the length of the rugged Albany River to Fort Albany on James Bay. As the crow flies, it's a 500-mile trip. As the canoe paddles, it's more like a thousand.

The vast Quetico Provincial Park is here in the northwest, too. On the United States-Canadian border, it encompasses 1,750 miles of absolutely unspoiled land. The only road in the park leads to the campground on French Lake. What a place for canoeing! You can lose sight of civilization for a couple of days or a couple of weeks.

Thunder Bay, formerly Port Arthur and Fort William, is the brawny seaport for the northwest. As the western terminus of the St. Lawrence Seaway, it is Canada's third largest port. Vast quantities of wheat and iron ore ship out of Thunder Bay every year.

NORTHEASTERN WILDERNESS

Ontario's second wilderness is its northeast section—the area north and east of Sault Ste. Marie that reaches up to James Bay and extends east to Georgian Bay. This is productive wilderness, pocketed by big mines and wood pulp plants. The paper on which most newspapers in Canada and the United States are printed begins its life in these forests.

Sudbury is the biggest of Ontario's mining centers. More than 39 percent of the world's supply of nickel comes from the mines near here. You'll enjoy a tour of the Numismatic Park in Sudbury, with its collection of gigantic coins up to 30 feet in diameter. Ontario's mining history is still being written, as you can discover at Timmins, where a fabulous zinc and copper lode was discovered as recently as 1963. At Timmins you can see and photograph a rare sight—molten gold being poured into ingots valued at more than $200,000 each.

There's another of those one-of-a-kind train rides here in the northeast. This one is the Polar Bear Express which runs north out of Cochrane to Moosonee near James Bay. There are no roads north of Cochrane, so the Polar Bear becomes the "Deliveryman of the North," bringing all kinds of supplies to the people who live along its 186-mile route. Busiest season for the Polar Bear is in the fall, when hunters jam its cars. They're on their way to meet the millions of Canada geese who pause in the marshes around Moosonee on their migration from the mating grounds on Baffin Bay.

The northeast is not all wilderness. The area adjacent to Georgian Bay, including Lake Nipissing and the French River, is a notable vacationland, rife with beaches and boating opportunities. Not far east of Lake Nipissing is another of those wilderness parks that so delight the Canadian camper. This one is Algonquin, which has 2,910 square miles of lakes and forests for the outdoorsman and his family to enjoy.

As it slices west the Trans-Canada hugs the northern shores of Georgian Bay and Lake Superior. If you want to explore more of the country to the north, take Highway 11. It loops away from the Trans-Canada at Orillia and goes north through North Bay, rejoining it again south of Lake Nipigon.

CENTRAL VACATION AREA

Around the southeastern shore of Georgian Bay you are in Toronto's great holiday land. Just about a hundred miles from the center of the city, it naturally attracts people from there. Look what it has to offer: beautiful Georgian Bay and its islands and beaches; Lake Muskoka, abounding in resorts and surrounded by 600 satellite lakes; and Lake Simcoe, hardly more than 50 miles from the city, with the city of Orillia near its head.

History runs deep in this area. It was originally explored by Samuel de Champlain in 1615. The French Jesuit fathers began their work among the Hurons near Midland in 1639, and during the next ten years, eight of these pioneer black robes were martyred. The Martyrs' Shrine and the restoration of the Jesuit settlement at Ste-Marie-among-the-Hurons memorialize their dedicated efforts.

If you are on the move, you might not want to spend time in resorts, but you could enjoy a cruise up Lake Muskoka on one of the ships which depart daily from Gravenhurst during the summer. Or you might take the "Thirty Thousand Islands" Cruise, a four-hour jaunt through Georgian Bay which begins in Midland.

Northeast of Toronto, but still a part of the central vacation area, you'll find the Kawartha Lakes region, not far from Peterborough. This is another sun-and-water holiday area to which Ontarians stream in the summer months. Champlain intended to use the Kawartha Lakes as a part of an inland waterway connecting Lakes Ontario and Huron. The waterway is there now—the Trent Canal system. This is a 240-mile pleasure route that takes you from Trenton, on Lake Ontario, through the famous lift lock at Peterborough, on through the Kawarthas and Lake Simcoe, to Port Severn on Georgian Bay. On the trip you will pass through 43 locks, be lifted 598 feet and lowered 260 feet.

Incidentally, Lake Simcoe has a remarkable distinction. Though located nearly in the middle of Canada's most heavily populated area, it has the largest number of fish per square mile of any freshwater lake on the North American continent. You would think they would have all been hooked long ago.

THE MUSCULAR SOUTHWEST

Running from Tobermory, on the tip of the Bruce Peninsula, to Windsor, the southwest takes in the shorelines of both Lake Erie and Lake Huron. This is variegated country. Windsor is a muscular industrial giant. Sarnia is a petrochemical king, where the crude oil piped 2,000 miles from the Leduc oil fields of Alberta is processed. Stratford, located (naturally) on the Avon River, is the Shakespearean center of the continent. Her summer festival performances of the bard's works rate with some of the best theater in the world.

Rich little farms are tucked in between these cities of the southwest. From them come ripe red tomatoes, golden corn, and fragrant tobacco. Many of the cities here date back to the 1700s, and most have some historic connection with the War of 1812.

Kitchener is an old German settlement originally established by Amish and Mennonite families migrating from Pennsylvania. The descendants of these original families are still here, maintaining the old customs. Stop at the Farmers' Market on Saturday morning to see the delightful handicraft work and sample the wonderful Dutch food. A couple of days in Kitchener could add ten pounds if you aren't careful.

The historic Bruce Trail, carved through the wilderness by the Huron Indians in their travels between Lake Ontario and Georgian Bay, has its northern terminus at Tobermory. The other end is 433 scenic miles away, near Niagara Falls. This is a fine hiking trail, maintained by conservation authorities and walked by thousands every year. Even if you're not up to 433 miles, you might enjoy hiking parts of the Bruce.

You'll find excellent camping facilities throughout the area, and in particular in the parks on the shores of Lake Erie and Lake Huron. Point Pelee National Park, on Canada's southern tip, provides a unique opportunity: here you can stroll through 3,000 acres of natural freshwater swamp and see the teeming swamp life in close-up vignettes. The trip is made possible by a boardwalk which extends from the shore to an observation tower in the middle of the swamp.

THE GOLDEN HORSESHOE

The area reaching from the Niagara peninsula along Lake Ontario to beyond Oshawa, east of Toronto, is called Canada's Golden Horseshoe. This is Ontario's industrial center, her greatest manufacturing concentration.

If this suggests skies leaden with factory smoke, forget it. Driven by natural gas and the great power from Niagara Falls, the plants in this area are probably the cleanest, most beautiful in the world. Passing through here, you'll be impressed by factories that are architecturally beautiful and landscaped like parks.

Niagara Falls is part of the Golden Horseshoe. This is one of the world's great sights. No matter where in the world you have traveled, you don't qualify as a first-class tourist until you've peered down at the mighty falls or bobbled in the foam at the bottom of the falls on the *Maid of the Mist.*

The Horseshoe and its surrounding countryside has a good many attractions. The Welland Canal, for example, carries the giant ocean freighters through that 326-foot drop between Lakes Erie and Ontario. You can enjoy the exquisite beauty of the Royal Botanical Gardens at Hamilton or see Alexander Graham Bell's childhood home at Brantford.

But the greatest sight of all is Toronto itself, around which the Golden Horseshoe revolves. Toronto is a major metropolis and, like all such giants, is hard to capture in capsule form. Your early impressions will be of wide, bright streets and many parks. Toronto is an open, clean, fresh city. You'll be struck by the number of beautiful new buildings, but remember that much of the city's growth has taken place in very recent years.

Your impression of spacious, open roads will be strengthened if you drive through the city on the broad Macdonald-Cartier Freeway. It is 12 lanes wide, and you won't find a wider road anywhere in the world.

You'll find more things to do in Toronto than you will have time in which to do them. Visit the stock exchange, attend the theater or the symphony, or shop in two of the world's largest department stores, located side by side. Visit the turreted Casa Loma, a 98-room castle, or go to the horse races. See hockey or football games, curling, and sports car racing. Go to the cricket matches, or tour Toronto's busy harbor and its islands by boat.

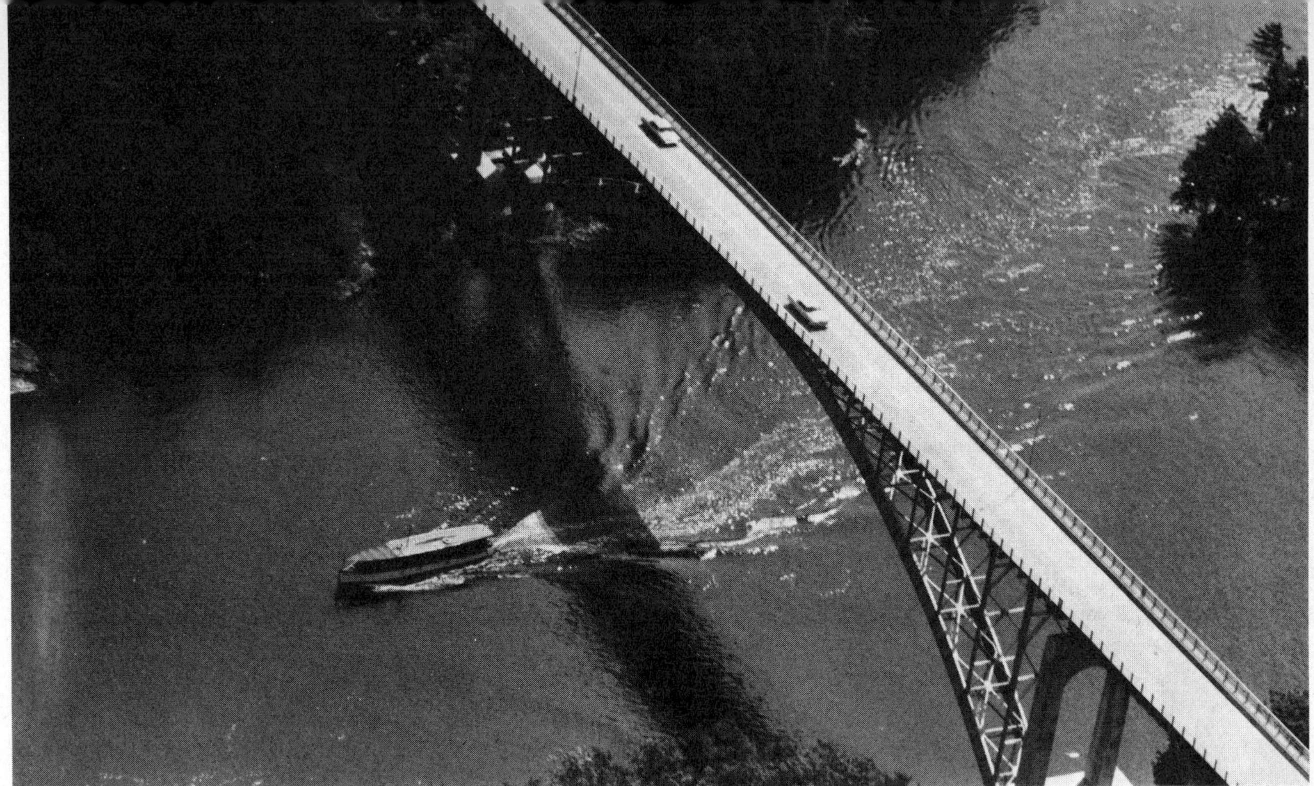

Thousand Islands Bridge—spanning the St. Lawrence, linking the islands

THE SOUTHEAST

Ontario's southeast is a wedge between two great rivers, the St. Lawrence and the Ottawa, and has within its boundaries the nation's capital, the province's oldest fortress, the lovely Thousand Islands, and Upper Canada Village, a page of living history.

As you drive along the St. Lawrence, remember that you are looking at the world's most imaginative inland waterway. Begun in 1954 and completed four years later, the St. Lawrence Seaway gave both Canada and the United States a long-dreamed-of water highway between the Atlantic and the Great Lakes. It travels 2,342 miles through rivers, lakes, canals, and locks, from Montreal to Thunder Bay. It has made busy international seaports out of once-quiet lake harbors.

One by-product of the building of the seaway is Upper Canada Village, on the St. Lawrence east of Morrisburg. To complete the seaway, thousands of acres of land had to be inundated and whole communities moved to higher ground. Buildings of historical value in this area were painstakingly moved, board by board and nail by nail, to the old Crysler Farm—itself a historic spot where in 1813, 800 British and Canadian soldiers defeated a force of 4,000 American troops. More than 40 houses, churches, schools, stores, and other buildings were brought together here.

Under the watchful eye of a committee of historians and antiquarians, Upper Canada Village became a faithful re-enactment of the past, authentic in every dowel and doorknob.

You'll brush against history again at Fort Henry, near Kingston. You'll hear the bugle calls, the fife and drum bands, and the rattle of musketry of 150 years ago in this restored bastion. Inside the walls, 126 rooms have been equipped exactly as they were when the British garrison stood duty here, guarding the western mouth of the St. Lawrence.

Don't miss the opportunity to drive across the Thousand Islands International Bridge a few miles east of Gananoque. From it, you'll have a spectacular view of this beautiful green and blue resort area. The bridge touches Hill Island in its leap across the river, and here you can go up 400 feet in the Thousand Islands Skydeck for an even greater panorama.

Ottawa, fittingly, is a city of pomp and ceremony and deep tradition. Changing the Guard is a ceremony alive with bright color. It is held on the great lawn of the Parliament Buildings. The carillon in the tall, lean central tower—53 bells ranging in weight from 10 pounds to 11 tons—will fill the air around you. If you are there in the spring, two million blooming tulips, a gift from the Dutch royal family, will brighten the city for you.

Once called Bytown, in honor of the man who built the Rideau Canal, Ottawa was selected as Canada's capital in 1857 by Queen Victoria from a number of candidates. Historians say that no one was more surprised at the honor than the citizens of Ottawa themselves.

The Rideau Canal, begun in 1826, was built as a security measure. British gunboats needed a way to get into the Great Lakes without the danger of being fired upon by American batteries along the south side of the international section of the St. Lawrence. By sailing up the Ottawa, passing through the Rideau Canal, and then down the Rideau River, they were able to bypass this danger and make their way into Lake Ontario. Today, the Rideau is a pleasant place for an afternoon cruise while you are visiting Ottawa.

Ottawa is a visit to the Parliament Buildings, the National Gallery of Canada and its fine sculpture and paintings, and the stately old Chateau Laurier—one of Canada's monumental hotels, along with the Empress in Victoria and the Chateau Frontenac in Quebec. Stop in some of the great museums with which the city is blessed, and pause before the National War Memorial in Confederation Square, a truly magnificent sculptured monument to the Canadian soldiers of World War I.

Punctuate your sightseeing in the capital city by crossing the Ottawa River into Quebec and visiting lovely Gatineau Park—a wilderness over 160 miles long that begins only 15 minutes from the center of Ottawa.

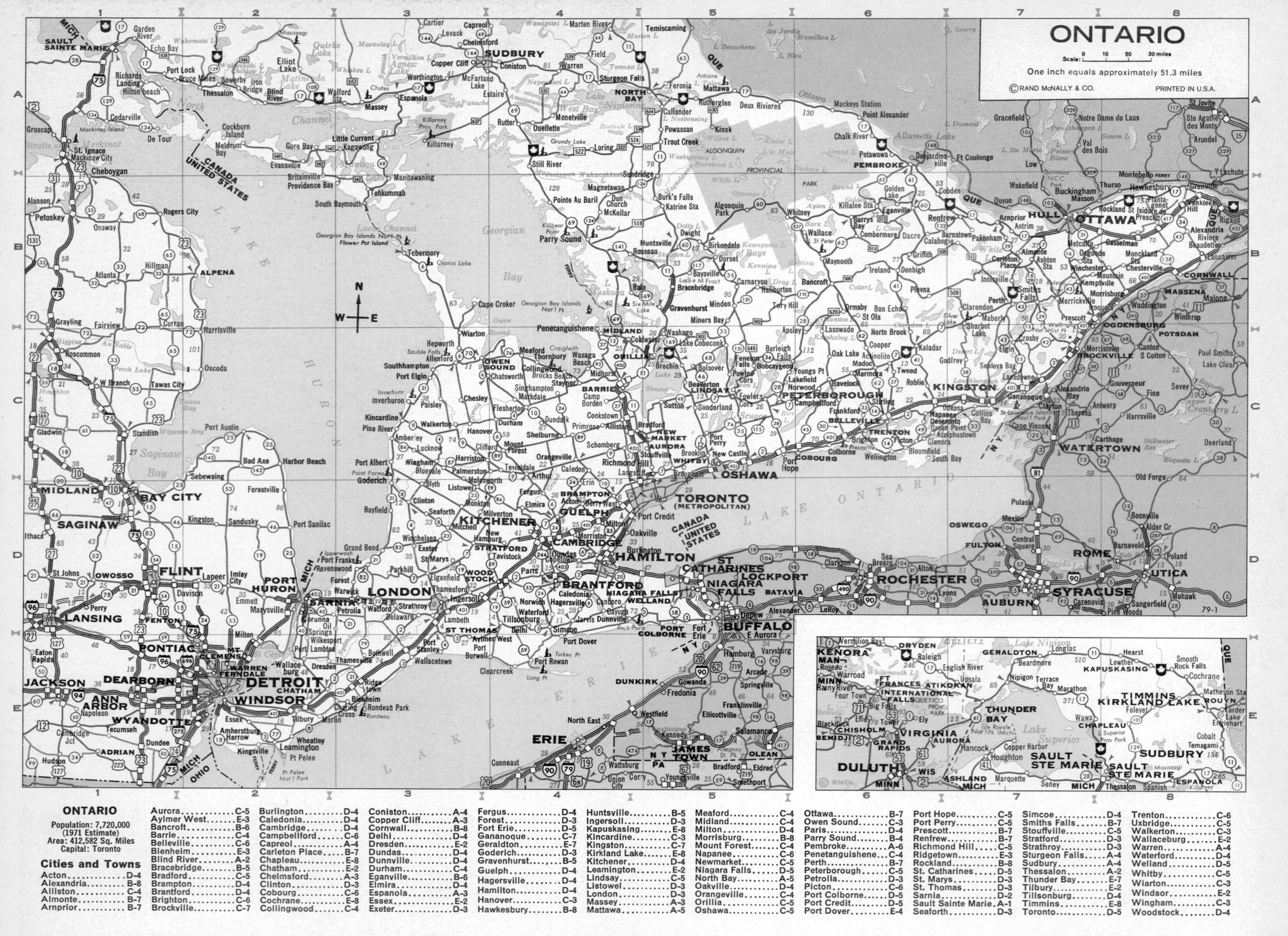

ONTARIO

Population: 7,720,000
(1971 Estimate)
Area: 412,582 Sq. Miles
Capital: Toronto

Cities and Towns

Acton	D-4	Aurora	C-5	Burlington	D-4	Coniston	A-4	Fergus	D-4	Huntsville	B-5	Meaford	C-4	Ottawa	B-7	Port Hope	C-5	Simcoe	D-4	Trenton	C-6
Alexandria	B-8	Aylmer West	E-3	Caledonia	D-4	Copper Cliff	A-3	Forest	D-3	Ingersoll	D-3	Midland	C-4	Owen Sound	C-3	Port Perry	C-5	Smiths Falls	B-7	Uxbridge	C-5
Alliston	C-4	Bancroft	B-6	Cambridge	D-4	Cornwall	B-8	Fort Erie	D-5	Kapuskasing	E-8	Milton	D-4	Paris	D-4	Prescott	B-7	Stouffville	C-5	Walkerton	C-3
Almonte	B-7	Barrie	C-4	Campbellford	C-6	Delhi	D-4	Gananoque	C-7	Kincardine	C-3	Morrisburg	B-8	Parry Sound	B-4	Renfrew	B-7	Stratford	D-3	Wallaceburg	E-2
Arnprior	B-7	Belleville	C-6	Capreol	A-4	Dresden	E-2	Geraldton	E-7	Kingston	C-7	Mount Forest	C-4	Pembroke	A-6	Richmond Hill	C-5	Strathroy	D-3	Warren	A-4
		Blenheim	E-3	Carleton Place	B-7	Dundas	D-4	Goderich	D-3	Kirkland Lake	E-8	Napanee	C-6	Penetanguishene	C-4	Ridgetown	E-3	Sturgeon Falls	A-4	Waterford	D-4
		Blind River	A-2	Chapleau	E-8	Dunnville	D-4	Gravenhurst	B-5	Kitchener	D-4	Newmarket	C-5	Perth	B-7	Rockland	B-8	Sudbury	A-4	Welland	D-5
		Bracebridge	B-5	Chatham	E-2	Durham	C-4	Guelph	D-4	Leamington	E-2	Niagara Falls	D-5	Peterborough	C-5	St. Catharines	D-5	Thessalon	A-2	Whitby	C-5
		Bradford	C-5	Chelmsford	A-3	Eganville	B-6	Hagersville	D-4	Lindsay	C-5	North Bay	A-5	Petrolia	D-3	St. Marys	D-3	Thunder Bay	E-7	Wiarton	C-3
		Brampton	D-4	Clinton	D-3	Elmira	D-4	Hamilton	D-4	Listowel	D-3	Oakville	D-4	Picton	C-6	St. Thomas	D-3	Tilbury	E-2	Windsor	E-2
		Brantford	D-4	Cobourg	C-6	Espanola	A-3	Hanover	C-3	London	D-3	Orangeville	C-4	Port Colborne	D-5	Sarnia	D-2	Tillsonburg	D-4	Wingham	C-3
		Brighton	C-6	Cochrane	E-8	Essex	E-2	Hawkesbury	B-8	Massey	A-3	Orillia	C-5	Port Credit	D-5	Sault Sainte Marie	A-1	Timmins	E-8	Woodstock	D-4
		Brockville	C-7	Collingwood	C-4	Exeter	D-3			Mattawa	A-5	Oshawa	C-5	Port Dover	E-4	Seaforth	D-3	Toronto	D-5		

PROVINCE GUIDE

ONTARIO

AGAWA CANYON [E-8]* The rugged Algoma region is an unspoiled land north of Sault Ste. Marie, a place of lovely, lonesome lakes, pleasant little streams, and big forests. Through this gentle area runs the Agawa River, wild and beautiful and an awesome spectacle. You can get there only by train. From the middle of May to the middle of October, every day in the week, the Agawa Canyon Excursion train of the Algoma Central Railway chugs out of the terminal in Sault Ste. Marie at 8 am and doesn't return until 6 pm. There's a dining car on the train, and you'll make a two-hour stopover at the canyon, where you can walk along the river and see the furious water. A worthwhile trip for train buffs, camera fans, and anyone who enjoys great scenery. Round trip for adults is $14, children through high school age $7. In the autumn, when the leaves turn, the forest becomes a riot of reds, yellows, oranges, and browns, and the train trip becomes almost unbearably beautiful.

ALGONQUIN PROVINCIAL PARK [A-5] The northern route of the Trans-Canada, between Pembroke and North Bay, passes to the north of this giant 2,910-square-mile provincial park. The whole area is a wilderness with few roads. Highway 60 cuts through the southern section, and Highway 630 dips down from the Trans-Canada to touch the northern boundary. Park headquarters are on Highway 60 at the east gate, while the Visitors Center is at Mile 13, on Found Lake. Here you'll find a museum and an audiovisual presentation given hourly on the park's history. There are 11 campgrounds in the park, all along Highway 60, and all have trailer spaces. Chief attractions of the area are fishing—which is sensational—and canoe trips which can be as long and rugged as you want to make them. See also the Pioneer Logging Exhibit at Mile 37.

ATIKOKAN [E-6] Headquarters of the great Quetico Provincial Park are located here. Here, during World War II, a vast iron ore field was discovered, but it was at the bottom of a deep lake. The steel mills of Ontario desperately needed the ore, so engineers drained the lake through tunnels blasted in the rock. They also diverted rivers leading into the lake. The lake bottom became a vast open-pit mine and is still a major supplier of ore. Atikokan is northwest of Thunder Bay.

BANCROFT [B-6] They claim you can find 1,500 different types of gemstones within a 20-mile radius of this town in southeastern Ontario, which lays claim to the title Rockhound

* Letter and number refer to coordinates on map of Ontario.

The world's elite show riders in brilliant array at the annual Royal Winter Fair in Toronto

Capital of the Province. They prove it early in August each year when Bancroft's citizens stage their Gem-Boree, an extensive display of rocks, minerals, and crystal specimens. If you want to swap rocks, this is the place to come.

BRACEBRIDGE [B-5] One of the gateways to the Lake Muskoka vacationland. A three-hour cruise of Lake Muskoka operates from the wharf here from late June to Labor Day. Here, and at other towns in the Lake Muskoka district, Fall Color tours and celebrations take place late in September and early in October.

BRANTFORD [D-4] Chief Joseph Brant and the Six Nation tribes were given land here by the British in 1784 as compensation for their losses in the war, and the river crossing became known as Brant's Ford. The childhood home of Alexander Graham Bell is south of town, and it was here that he conducted his early experiments with the telephone. In 1876, Bell used the wire on farmers' fences to transmit his first message to a friend who lived 3 miles away. The following day, Bell made the first long-distance telephone call, from Brantford to Paris—Paris, Ontario, that is, a town 7 miles away. You can visit the Bell homestead in Tutela Heights and see replicas of the first telephones. The Brant Historical Society Museum has an excellent display of pioneer and Indian relics, including some very old fire-fighting equipment. Two miles southeast of town you'll find St. Paul's Church, Her Majesty's Chapel of the Mohawks. Built in 1785, it is the oldest Protestant church in Ontario and the world's only Royal Indian Chapel. In early August you'll enjoy the Six Nations Pageant, a reenactment of early Indian history presented by an all-Indian cast in colorful tribal regalia.

BROCKVILLE [C-7] This charming little city of tree-lined streets and lovely old homes might be called the eastern gateway to the scenic Thousand Islands. Four-hour boat tours of the islands operate from here from the beginning of June to mid-October. Just southwest of the city, along Highway 401, is the St. Lawrence Islands National Park (see National Parks, page 102) and a number of parks operated by the St. Lawrence Development Commission. The whole area offers a great number of first-class camping facilities, along with ample resort accommodations. The river is lined with good sandy beaches.

BRUCE TRAIL [D-5] The Niagara Escarpment is a cliff formed millions of years ago through the deposit of various kinds of rock, followed by the process of erosion. Niagara Falls tumbles over the escarpment, through the wearing action of the falls has moved its edge back 7 miles from Queenston in the past 12,000 years. With the exception of the falls section, the escarpment runs in a more or less straight line from Queenston north to Tobermory on the tip of the Bruce Peninsula. The Bruce Trail is a hiking path 433 miles long. It follows the escarpment over its entire length. Marked with special trail markers, it begins at Brock's Monument in Queenston, proceeds through Hamilton, and passes Milton, Georgetown, Orangeville, and Collingwood on its way north. It then passes along the south shore of Georgian Bay through Owen Sound and Wiarton to Tobermory. The trail was established in 1965 through the efforts of a number of private citizens and passes for the most part over private lands. If a hike over the trail (all or part of it) appeals to you, first join the Bruce Trail Club, if possible. There are local branches in many cities. Even if you don't join, buy a copy of the *Bruce Trail Guidebook* before starting. Copies are $5 to nonmembers and can be obtained from the Bruce Trail Association, 33 Hardale Crescent, Hamilton, Ontario. The book contains 33 detailed maps and information on campgrounds along the route, general stores, drinking water availability, and other useful bits.

COCHRANE [E-8] This is where a good many big-game hunters outfit for excursions into the wilderness. The Polar Bear Express runs from here to Moosonee on James Bay. Good one-day round trip if you like unusual train rides. The local makes the trip in 2 days and carries some interesting passengers—trappers, Indians, geologists, and adventurers. The train will stop whenever someone wants to get on or off.

DRYDEN [E-6] Driving along Highway 17 a hundred or so miles east of Kenora, you'll encounter a gigantic 18-foot moose. Don't panic. It's just a carving—Dryden's way of telling travelers that the town is the capital of Ontario's northern moose-hunting territory.

ELMIRA [D-4] Early in April in this town a dozen miles north of Kitchener, descendants of early Pennsylvania Dutch settlers don traditional dress and entertain thousands who come to visit the sugar bush. The Maple Syrup Festival has pancakes and syrup, hayrides, auctions, and great fun. Every Saturday morning you can shop in the Farmers' Market, when Mennonite farmers bring their homemade cheese, butter, sausages, and produce to town. There is a great doll collection to be seen at the House of Dolls at 28 South Street.

FERGUS [D-4] In this bit of a town north of Guelph, the pipes skirl, feet fly in the Highland Fling, and the clans gather to compete in the Highland Games each year in mid-August.

FORT FRANCES [E-6] On the international border across the Rainy River from International Falls, Minnesota, Fort Frances is located on the site of old Fort Pierre, a trading station built by Pierre de La Verendrye in 1731 as he pushed his explorations westward. Highway 53 in the United States takes you from Duluth to Fort Frances. The valley of the Rainy River is one of Canada's prime hunting areas. For an interesting auto trip, drive on Highway 11 east of town, where a series of island-hopping bridges provides great scenic views.

FORT HENRY [C-7] Used as a fort in the War of 1812, then redesigned and rebuilt in 1836 to create the mightiest stronghold west of Quebec, Fort Henry stands near Kingston, guarding the junction of the St. Lawrence River with Lake Ontario. Called the Citadel of Upper Canada, the fort was completely restored in 1938, with 126 rooms equipped as they were 150 years ago. See the impressive retreat ceremonies at sunset on Wednesdays and Saturdays during July and August. Museums abound in the area, including the Hockey Hall of Fame.

GANANOQUE [C-7] During the summer months, church services at Half Moon Bay here are conducted from a pulpit located on a rock. The congregation gathers around the rock in small boats. Ushers in canoes pass the hymnals. Gananoque is a center of boat cruises through the Thousand Islands. Most take 3 hours and operate mid-May to mid-October.

GRAVENHURST [B-5] At the southern end of Lake Muskoka, the city is in the midst of a great vacation area only 100 miles north of Toronto. Four-hour lake cruises aboard the 200-passenger *Lady Muskoka* leave here twice daily during the summer months. The two old paddle wheelers that once performed this service are now tied up at Gravenhurst. One is a museum with steam navigation and lumbering displays, and the other is a restaurant. The entire Lake Muskoka area is magnificent when the leaves turn in the fall, and Fall Color tours, parades, and celebrations are staged at towns throughout the area in late September and early October. See Bracebridge and Huntsville.

GEORGIAN BAY ISLANDS NATIONAL PARK [C-4] Located in the southeastern part of Georgian Bay, the park consists of 40 islands. See National Parks, page 101.

GRAND BEND [D-3] During July and August, see comedies and musicals at the Huron County Playhouse in this resort area. The 5 buildings of the Eisenbach Museum, including Ye Olde Country Store, have a display of pioneer items. Nearby provincial parks for camping include Ipperwash and Pinery.

GUELPH [D-4] This town is made particularly picturesque by the fact that all buildings facing its main street are made of native gray limestone—by law. Colonel John McCrae, who wrote the poem "In Flanders Fields," was born here. McCrae Gardens is a memorial to him. The cottage where he was born, displaying his manuscripts and personal effects, is a national historical site adjacent to the gardens. The Gothic church of Our Lady of the Immaculate Conception, whose superb Catherine wheel window is 18 feet in diameter, is a landmark. In Riverside Park a huge 44-foot floral clock made of living flowers actually tells the time. Over 6,000 blooms make up the face. Elora Gorge, 12 miles out of town, is a tiny Grand Canyon carved in limestone and flanked by a beautiful park.

HALIBURTON [B-5] In a land of dense woods dotted with tiny lakes and laced by pretty rivers and streams, Haliburton reaches the apex of its beauty during the latter part of September each year when the leaves turn. Thousands come here from all over eastern Canada to take the Fall Color tours.

HAMILTON [D-4] This is the Steel City of Canada, located on a fine landlocked harbor at the western end of Lake Ontario. For a map of the city and descriptions of its points of interest, see page 59 and page 61.

HEARST [E-8] This is a major moose-hunting center on Highway 11. Civilization is sparse in this area. The next town west of here is Longlac, 151 miles away. You can take a scenic canoe trip of 42 miles through Lakes Ste. Therese, Pivabiska, Hanlan, and Fushimi.

HUNTSVILLE [B-5] This is the northern entrance to the Lake of Bays vacation area, east of Lake Muskoka. The Lake of Bays has 365 miles of shoreline, with numerous resorts and summer homes tucked into little bays and inlets. The aerial chair lift 6 miles east of Huntsville will carry you to the top of Peninsula Peak for skiing in the winter and a panoramic view of Muskoka's lakes in the summer. Town Park has tent and trailer camping facilities along the Muskoka River. The area offers some notable bass and speckled trout fishing, and, in the fall, after the first frost, magnificent color in the trees.

KAKABEKA FALLS [E-7] They say you can see the lithe figure of lovely Greenmantle, daughter of an Ojibwa chief who saved her tribe from massacre, in the mist that hangs above these falls, located 20 miles north of Thunder Bay on Highway 17. Could be—but don't look for Greenmantle on weekdays because the falls flow only on Sundays. The water flow is controlled by a giant hydroelectric plant. The falls, known as the Niagara of the North Country, are 225 feet wide and 128 feet high. The provincial park here has camping facilities, a wading pool, and supervised swimming.

Oxcart ride at Upper Canada Village

KAPUSKASING [E-8] On the northern Trans-Canada route, Highway 11, this is the town where Kleenex is made. They use a pile of logs 4 feet x 4 feet and $1\frac{1}{2}$ miles long each day. That's a lot of tissue.

KENORA [E-6] The Great River Road, which parallels the Mississippi all the way to New Orleans, begins 13 miles east of town. Kenora is the chief city on the Lake of the Woods, a summer resort center, and fly-in headquarters for hunting and fishing camps of the northwest wilderness. Sightseeing cruises of the Lake of the Woods leave three times a day from the foot of Main Street. The Lake of the Woods Museum has a good Indian display, and you can tour the Ontario-Minnesota Pulp and Paper Company's plant. In early August, there is a five-day sailing regatta covering 88 miles in five legs through the 14,632 islands of the lake. The race is followed by a gala celebration.

KINGSTON [C-7] This is the southern end of the Rideau Canal, which starts in Ottawa. The 123-mile trip over this river/canal route is popular with boatmen in the summer. Kingston is a strategic city located at the point where the St. Lawrence joins Lake Ontario. It began life in 1673 as Fort Frontenac and became a military stronghold and guardian of the St. Lawrence. It is still an important military center and the site of the Royal Military College, the Canadian Army Staff College, and the National Defense College. You can visit the museum of the Royal Military College and Fort Frederick to see the excellent Douglas collection of historic weapons and regimental plate. Visit also the Royal Canadian Signals Museum in Vimy Barracks, where a display traces the history of the Royal Canadian Corps of Signals since World War I. Both museums are east of the city on Highway 2. A martello tower, Murney

Redoubt, is located in Macdonald Park. It was built in 1846 as a part of a series of coastal defenses. Tour old Fort Henry, built between 1832 and 1836, now completely restored and operated as a museum of British and Canadian military history. (See page 52.) To the east of here in the St. Lawrence are the beautiful Thousand Islands. Boat cruises covering 80 miles and requiring five hours leave Kingston daily. Check locally for the schedule, which varies according to the time of the year.

KITCHENER [D-4] Back in 1799, when it was founded, this city was named Berlin. The name survived until 1916, when it was renamed for the hero of Khartoum. Most of the early settlers were German Amish and Mennonite farmers relocating from Pennsylvania. Their descendants today hold delightful Saturday morning Farmers' Markets the year round, with additional markets on Wednesdays during the summer. The market is held in the square behind City Hall. You'll find succulent Mennonite specialties to tempt your taste buds, and fascinating local handicrafts. Walper House Hotel features marvelous Dutch cooking, guaranteed to plumpen you up. The home of former Prime Minister Mackenzie King is located in Woodside National Historic Park. Southeast of town, Doon Pioneer Village re-creates the atmosphere of a country village of 100 years ago. South of town on Highway 8 you can visit the unusual African Lion Safari and Game Farm, where you take a bus through 75 acres in which 40 lions roam free. Kitchener's Oktoberfest, held in mid-October, is a nine-day festival of German bands, beer, parades, dancing, sports, tributes to craftsmen, and good fellowship. It culminates in an interfaith Thanksgiving service. Waterloo, Kitchener's twin city, is the home of Seagram's distillery.

KLEINBURG [D-5] Twenty miles north of Toronto off Highway 27, Kleinburg is the home of the McMichael Canadian Collection, the largest permanent display of Canada's Group of Seven—artists who banded together in 1911 and exhibited under that name until 1933. Their common purpose was to represent only Canadian subject matter in their works (which were primarily landscapes), and their style followed that of the impressionists and the school of art nouveau. The collection is housed in the McMichael home, which was presented to the province in 1965. Thirty galleries are filled with over 1,000 paintings, Indian and Eskimo sculpture, and artifacts. The house is open all year, Tuesday through Sunday, from noon to 5:30 pm.

LAKE SUPERIOR PROVINCIAL PARK [E-8] The 526 square miles of this natural park are located on Lake Superior's northeastern shore, 50 miles north of Sault Ste. Marie. The Trans-Canada passes through it. Camping and picnic sites dot the park.

LONDON [D-3] Chief city of southwestern Ontario and bustling with 233,000 people, London takes its name seriously. It is situated in the picturesque valley of the Thames River, and as you tour the city you'll come across names like Pall Mall, Hyde Park, Piccadilly, Trafalgar, and Victoria Park. Storybook Gardens is a seven-acre fairyland for children located in Springbank Park. Museums in the city include Eldon House, the oldest residence in the city, which features 19th-century furnishings, and the Royal Canadian Regiment Museum, with a grand display on Canadian military history. On the campus of the University of Western Ontario, you'll find the interesting Museum of Indian Archaeology and Pioneer Life. Five miles east of the city, you can stop at Fanshawe Pioneer Village, the reconstruction of a typical pioneer village. The log cabins here are originals, moved in toto. Fanshawe Park has facilities for boating, sailing, riding, golfing, swimming, and camping. The village is in the park. The Western Fair is held here in September.

MANITOULIN ISLAND [A-3] This is the world's largest island surrounded by fresh water, and separates Georgian Bay from Lake Huron. There are over 100 lakes on the island to provide top-grade fishing. The hunting is good, too, for deer, wolf, bear, and partridge and duck. You can tour the island by automobile by turning off the Trans-Canada at McKerrow and traveling south on Highway 68. Another way to get here is by automobile ferry from Tobermory on the Bruce Peninsula, a three-hour trip. Scenic cruises around the island leave from the harbor at South Baymouth. While driving around the island, stop at Little Current to see the Howland Centennial Museum, built on the site of a very old civilization. Artifacts found here date back more than 10,000 years. At the town of Gore Bay, you can visit the museum located in the old jail. Another museum at Manitowaning has a pioneer display, including a blacksmith shop and a furnished pioneer home. Not far away, at Wikwemikong, 18 Indian tribes gather each year early in August for a two-day Pow Wow. You're invited to see the tribal dances and traditional ceremonies.

MIDLAND [C-4] On a peninsula jutting out into Georgian Bay, Midland is an optical glass center, a historic site, and a resort capital. Microscopes, optical lenses, color television picture tubes, and Leica cameras are made here. Boat cruises out among the Thirty Thousand Islands of Georgian Bay leave Midland harbor daily during July and August. At the eastern edge of town you'll find the Martyrs' Shrine, dedicated to the eight Jesuit missionaries martyred near here between 1639 and 1649. Just opposite the shrine is a complete reconstruction of the Jesuit mission of 325 years ago, Ste-Marie-Among-the-Hurons. The original of the mission was the most westerly settlement in North America in the mid-17th century. The Jesuits killed by the Iroquois are known as the North American Martyrs and were the first North Americans to be canonized by the Catholic Church. The Huron Indian Village in Little Lake Park is a reconstruction that includes a longhouse, sleeping shelter, and medicine man's lodge. You can watch skilled Indians make pottery, dry fish, and smoke meat. The area around Midland is known as Huronia, and in it are some famous ski slopes—the Blue Mountains of Collingwood, Thornbury, and Owen Sound; Orangeville's Hockley Valley; and Kimberley's Beaver Valley. A number of other facilities are under development.

MOONBEAM [E-8] This town is on the northern Trans-Canada route, Highway 11, west of Cochrane. Remi Lake Provincial Park near here offers excellent camping. If you prefer motel accommodations, you'll find an elegant French chalet here that specializes in gourmet food.

MOOSONEE You can get here via the Polar Bear Express from Cochrane, 186 miles to the south, or you can fly in. A daily train from Toronto makes the connection at Cochrane. Moosonee is a hunting, fishing, and fur trading outpost. It attracts national attention in the fall, when the Canada geese leave their nesting grounds on Baffin Bay and pause in the marshes near here during their migratory flight.

MORRISBURG [B-8] When the St. Lawrence Seaway was under construction during the four years between 1954 and 1958, many acres of land were inundated and many settlements moved to higher ground. Homes, churches, and buildings of historic note in the doomed area were lovingly moved and then reconstructed on the Crysler Farm, 7 miles east of Morrisburg. Crysler Farm was the scene of a decisive battle of the War of 1812, in which 800 British and Canadian soldiers defeated 4,000 American troops. In Upper Canada Village, you can see Cook's Tavern (1835), Providence Church (1845), the general store (1860), a woolen mill, and 35 other old structures placed to form an exciting authentic tableau of pioneer life. Upper Canada Village is one of the finest historic displays in all of Canada. It is open from mid-May to mid-October. Allow yourself at least an afternoon here. It's worth a special trip.

MUSKOKA LAKE REGION [B-5] See GRAVENHURST

NIAGARA FALLS [D-5] One of the world's premier sights and still the honeymoon capital. Three observation towers offer fine views: Oneida Observation Tower, 341 feet above ground, with a Royal Canadian Mounted Police Historical Exhibit at the base; the Skylon Tower in Skylon Park, 520 feet above the ground, with a dining room, lounge, and observation deck in three levels at the top; and Heritage Tower, rising 660 feet above the falls, with a seven-story observation section at the top. One deck is outfitted for photography, with tinted windows and built-in light meters. Having seen the falls from the air, take the elevator down to river level at Table Rock House for a completely different viewpoint. The *Maid of the Mist* cruises to the base of the falls every 20 minutes from

Multilevel observation decks overlooking the thundering waters of Niagara Falls, fringed by Victoria Park

the foot of Centre Street near Rainbow Bridge. Two miles below the falls on River Road, you can board the Whirlpool aerocar, a cable car that carries you across the whirlpool and rapids of the Niagara River. The trip is 1,800 feet each way and takes 10 minutes. For a closer look at the whirlpool and the gorge where the river narrows to 250 feet, take the Great Gorge elevator on River Road 2 miles north of the falls. Here, at the bottom of the descent, a 183-foot tunnel takes you to the brink of the whirlpool. Museums to see in the area include Oak Hall, former home of Sir Harry Oakes; McFarland House at 921 Clifton Hill, where you see a collection of animated hand-carved miniatures carved by violin-maker Moise Potvin; and Canadia, where miniature replicas of historic and cultural landmarks are displayed on 11 acres. Houdini's Magical Hall of Fame is on Centre Street, and Louis Tussaud's English Wax Museum is at the corner of Clifton Hill and Falls Avenue. Finally, the Rainbow Carillon Tower, at Rainbow Bridge, provides daily concerts at 3 and 8 pm during the summer.

NIAGARA-ON-THE-LAKE [D-5] On Lake Ontario, 15 miles north of the falls, this is the home of the Shaw Festival. All summer the works of George Bernard Shaw are presented in the 822-seat Festival Theater. You also can visit the reconstructed Fort George, built originally in 1796, and see 11 buildings furnished as they were in 1812.

OTTAWA An excellent place for a tourist to spend many very interesting days, and also the nation's capital and one of its most beautiful cities. For a map of the city and descriptions of its points of interest, see page 59 and page 60.

OUIMET CANYON [E-7] This 2-mile-long gorge in Ouimet, about 50 miles east of Thunder Bay on Highway 11/17, is a special beauty spot where you look down a drop of 450 feet.

POINT PELEE NATIONAL PARK [E-2] On a point jutting out into Lake Erie, this park is Canada's southernmost tip. See National Parks, page 102.

PUKASKWA NATIONAL PARK [E-7] Created in 1971 and not yet developed for public use, this rugged section of the Precambrian Shield is on the northern shore of Lake Superior. See National Parks, page 102.

QUETICO PROVINCIAL PARK [E-6] Over a million and a quarter acres of completely unspoiled wilderness on the United States-Canadian border, 140 miles west of Thunder Bay, the Quetico offers some of the best canoe/portaging trails in North America. The Canadian entrance to the park is at Dawson Trail Campgrounds, 29 miles east of Atikokan on Highway 11. Park headquarters are located at Atikokan. Entry from the United States is through either Ely or Grand Marais, Minnesota. You won't find any roads in the park, so don't plan to drive through it. Guided canoe trips are available. There are three campgrounds with a total of 100 campsites at Dawson Trail on French Lake, reached via Highway 11.

ST. CATHERINES [D-5] Located on Lake Ontario west of Niagara Falls. The Ontario end of the Welland Canal is here. For a good view of the canal, go to the lookout station at Lock 3. St. Catherines is the scene of the Royal Henley Regatta, one of the continent's oldest and most popular rowing regattas, held each year in early August. The Niagara Grape and Wine Festival takes place here in September.

ST. LAWRENCE ISLANDS NATIONAL PARK [C-7] The park consists of 17 islands and 80 rocky islets of the famous Thousand Islands, in the St. Lawrence River between Kingston and Brockville. See National Parks, page 102.

SARNIA [D-2] The Blue Water Bridge across the St. Clair River connects Sarnia with Port Huron, Michigan. More than a hundred million tons of material is shipped each year through the St. Clair under this bridge—making it the world's busiest waterway. Sarnia is the home of a giant petrochemical complex where more than 200,000 barrels of crude oil are processed daily. Much of the oil comes to Sarnia by pipeline from the Leduc fields of Alberta, 2,200 miles away. Sarnia is blessed with sun-kissed lakeshore beaches, and there are many good beaches along the shores of Lake Huron north of the city.

SAULT STE. MARIE [A-1] Here, in the narrow neck between Lake Superior and Lake Huron, are the world-famous Soo Locks, operated jointly by the United States and Canadian governments. There is something really fascinating about watching the big ore boats go through these 900-foot locks. The Jesuit Father Marquette founded a mission here in 1668, and this was a strategic trading, religious, and military center from that date forward. Longfellow immortalized the region and its Ojibwa Indian tribe in *Hiawatha.* During July, the Ojibwas on the Garden River Reserve celebrate a Hiawatha Pageant. Two-hour boat cruises tour the river and take you through the locks. You are likely to share a lock with a giant oceangoing ore or grain boat—and that's a thrill in itself because the sightseeing boats are so tiny by comparison. Trips are operated from the first of June to the end of September. The "Canoe Canal," built in 1797 to carry the big freight canoes of the voyageurs around the rapids of the St. Mary River, is now reconstructed as a historic site. The Agawa Canyon (see page 51) Excursion train, operated by the Algoma Central Railway, leaves here daily for an all-day tour of the forest wilderness north of here. Just west of the International Bridge, which connects the United States and Canada, is a replica of an early Hudson's Bay Company trading post.

STRATFORD [D-4] The internationally famous Shakespeare Festival in North America makes its home here. It was begun in 1953 under canvas. Today, performances are presented in a concrete and glass Elizabethan-style theater-in-the-round. The stage has seven levels and nine major entrances, while the balcony is encircled by a steep slope seating 2,250 people. No member of the audience is more than 65 feet from the stage. The 22-week Stratford festival extends from mid-May to mid-October, with performances Tuesday through Sunday at 8:30 pm and matinees on Wednesday and Saturday at 2 pm. Play directors and leading actors are always well known in their fields, and critics have acclaimed the quality of these productions. In addition to Shakespearean works, plays by other classic dramatists are performed, and opera, ballet, and contemporary theater are also a part of the season's program.

STURGEON FALLS [A-4] On the northern Trans-Canada route, east of Sudbury, this is the home of a caviar processing plant. Believe it or not, this plant once supplied caviar to Kaiser Wilhelm of Germany and the Czar of Russia—both of whom knew a thing or two about good caviar.

SUDBURY [A-4] You might call Sudbury a money town, because a goodly portion of the world's coinage is made from metals taken from the mines in this area. These mines produce

39 percent of the world's nickel. They are the world's third largest producers of platinum, and the fourth largest of copper. All of this is graphically brought home to the visitor in Sudbury's Numismatic Park—21 acres on a slag hill dominated by a 30-foot replica of the 1951 Canadian commemorative five-cent piece. (Made in stainless steel!) Other giant coins in the park include a 10-foot 1965 Canadian penny; a John F. Kennedy half-dollar, lighted by an eternal flame; a $20 gold piece; and the five-shilling British memorial to Sir Winston Churchill. In the same park, you can don a hard hat and descend into a real mine, or ride a miniature railroad for an excellent view of the mining operations. If you seek a gem of a photograph, be here at night when red-hot rivers of slag are poured. In addition to mining, the country around Sudbury has many resort and vacation attractions. There are no less than 250 lodges and resorts within easy driving distance of the city.

THOUSAND ISLANDS [C-7] There are more than 1,700 islands in this group in the St. Lawrence River between Brockville and Kingston. Some are no more than a bit of rock in the water, but more are big enough to hold one of the area's pretty summer homes. About fifty of the islands and a bit of the mainland make up St. Lawrence Islands National Park. (See National Parks, page 102.) The whole area is a renowned vacation spot with a very pleasant summer climate and every imaginable type of water sport available. Island cruises can be taken from Gananoque, Ivy Lea, Rockport, Brockville, and Kingston. There are good resorts all through the area, should you plan to stay awhile. If you're just passing through, you'd enjoy stopping to swim and sun in the national park, located at Mallorytown. Drive across the Thousand Islands International Bridge, which hops from island to island between Alexandria Bay, New York, and Rockport, Ontario. Part of the way across you land on Hill Island, where you can ride to the top of the 400-foot Skydeck, visit the Arctic Exhibit to see Indian and Eskimo art and craft work, and take the children to Never Never Land to see reproductions of their favorite storybook characters. Skydeck and Never Never Land charge admission.

THUNDER BAY [E-7] This is one of Canada's newest cities, formed on January 1, 1970, through the joining of the twin cities of Fort William and Port Arthur. Thunder Bay is Canada's third largest port, the western terminus of the St. Lawrence Seaway. Golden grain from Canada's plains moves to the world in ships from the elevators here, which store more than 100 million bushels. Iron ore and paper and pulp are major commodities shipped from here also. The voyageurs began the homeward journey to Montreal with canoes loaded with pelts from Fort William, which has been a gateway since its founding. The Sleeping Giant, a rock formation 7 miles long and 1,000 feet high, juts out to form the bay's entrance. You can get a good view of it and the busy waterfront from Hillcrest Park, which also has beautiful sunken gardens. Centennial Park, 3 miles from downtown, is a re-created 1910 lumber camp, complete with bunkhouse, blacksmith shop, stable, cookhouse, and museum. Try a lumberjack-sized meal in the cookhouse. Harbor tours leave from the foot of Arthur Street from May to September. The trip takes one hour.

TIMAGAMI PROVINCIAL FOREST [E-8] The trip on Highway 11 north from North Bay takes you through a number of interesting places. At Marten River, visit the husky dog ranch. At Timagami, you can stop long enough to cruise through some of the 1,600 islands on Lake Timagami, and see the old Hudson's Bay Company trading post on Bear Island, founded in 1821. At Cobalt, the legend says that a blacksmith threw his hammer at a fox and discovered the world's richest vein of silver when he went to retrieve it. The Northern Ontario Mining Museum is interesting. Millionaires Row in Haileybury is where the silver millionaires from Cobalt built their palatial houses. At Englehart, stop in Kap-Kig-Iwan Provincial Park to see the deep gorge with five beautiful cascading waterfalls, some up to 70 feet high. As you pass through Ramore, note that from here all waters flow north, into the Arctic Ocean. At Timmins, you're in gold country, where the second richest gold mine in the world was discovered. Mine tours can be arranged.

TORONTO The capital of the province and Canada's fastest growing city, Toronto is the commercial and financial heart of the nation. For a map of the city and descriptions of its points of interest, see page 58.

UPPER CANADA VILLAGE [B-8] See MORRISBURG

WASAGA BEACH [C-4] A resort on the south shore of Georgian Bay known for its beautiful beach. Nearby are the Blue Mountains of Collingwood and the Blue Mountain ski area. Wasaga Beach Provincial Park, overlooking Nottawasaga Bay, has fine campgrounds. The Museum of the Upper Lakes is on Nancy Island and reached by a footbridge from Mosley Street. H.M.S. *Nancy* was sunk here by an American flotilla during the War of 1812. Currents flowing around the wreck formed the island on which the museum is located. The hull of the *Nancy* was raised and is now a part of the museum's exhibit. You can see a re-creation of the battle in the museum's electronic theater.

WAWA [E-8] The great Canada goose rests on Wawa Lake during the migrating season. Hence the name, which means "wild goose" in the Ojibwa tongue. Wawa is an iron-ore center on the north side of Lake Superior, at the northern tip of Lake Superior Provincial Park. The mines of Algoma Steel are 3 miles from town. Visit Fort Friendship on the banks of the Michipicoten River. This is a reconstructed log redoubt with displays of authentic battlements, blockhouses, and military artifacts. High Falls, on the Magpie River, is a lovely scenic waterfall, 73 feet high and 150 feet wide. You'll find it 2 miles west and a mile south of the junction of Highways 17 and 101.

WINDSOR [E-2] Over 21 million people cross the border between Canada and the United States at this point each year by tunnel and bridge. With a population of 200,000, Windsor is a city of diversified industry. Good industrial tours are available at the Chrysler Canada Corporation automobile plant, the Hiram Walker and Sons distillery, and at the Green Giant plant, largest corn-processing plant in Canada. The Hiram Walker Historical Museum (known originally as the Francois Baby House) is Windsor's oldest brick residence, dating back to 1811. It served as headquarters for U.S. General William Hull during part of the War of 1812. The Dieppe Gardens on the riverfront are beautiful in the summer, especially at night when they are graced by illuminated fountains and ornamental lighting. Also in the summer, you can see hydroplane racing on the Detroit River. Fort Malden National Historic Park is south on Highway 18. See National Parks, page 101.

TORONTO

Toronto's site was first a meeting place of the Huron tribes, then a fort established in 1749 by French fur traders. It was called Fort Rouille until taken over by the British, when it became Fort York. In 1834, with 9,000 citizens, it became Toronto. Today it is not only the capital of the province but one of the fastest growing cities on the continent.

Toronto pleases most visitors immediately. It is a clean, open, contemporary city—chiefly because most of its expansion has taken place in recent years. With the lake as its front porch, the industrial muscle of the Golden Horseshoe to support it, and magnificent vacationlands within a few hours drive to the north, Toronto is an appealing place to live.

Two things can quickly characterize Toronto for the first-time visitor. First, the brochures prepared by the city and distributed at Tourist Information Centers are undoubtedly the warmest, most inviting pieces of literature ever written. Happily, they truly reflect the way Toronto feels about visitors.

The second characterizer is Toronto's City Hall—a strikingly bold and imaginative building whose design could only have been accepted and built by people who are of today yet looking at tomorrow. But for all of its boldness, this complex is tasteful and conservative. It is, in architectural terms, an excellent expression of the city and its people.

Finding your way in Toronto is easy. The city is laid out on a grid, with north-south street numbers beginning at the lake. East-west division is made at Yonge Street.

Points of Interest

CASA LOMA. This 98-room castle, near Davenport Road at Spadina, was begun in 1911; cost $3 million; and is operated by the Kiwanis Club of West Toronto, which uses proceeds for youth programs. See secret passages, magnificent furnishings. Open 10 am to 8 pm (to 4 pm Saturdays) in summer. Other months, 10 am to 4 pm.

CN TOWER. This 1,815-foot tower is the world's tallest free-standing structure. Ride up to a revolving restaurant at the 1,150-foot level, or to observation decks at the 1,136- and 1,465-foot levels. Located at 301 Front Street. Open 9 am to 12 pm daily. Admission: adults, $1 and $2.75; children, $1 and $1.50.

FORT YORK. Built in 1793 to guard Toronto Harbor, the fort fell into ruins after 1841, but was restored beginning in 1936. Eight original structures still stand. The Fort York Guard performs 19th-century drill in the summer. Open daily in summer and daily except Monday in winter. Admission: adults, $1; children, 50¢.

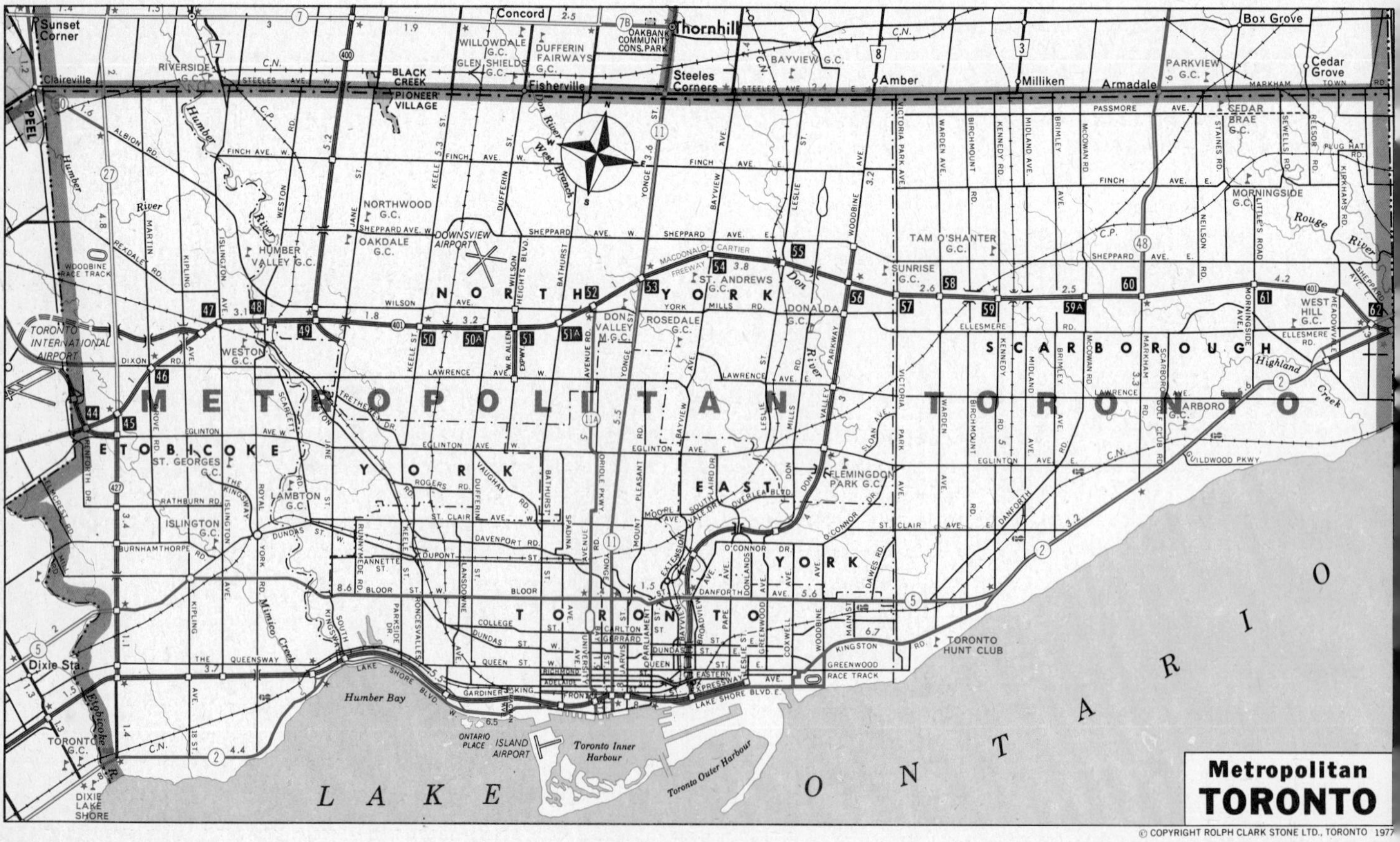

Metropolitan TORONTO

HIGH PARK. At Bloor and Parkside, the park has 353 acres with nature trails, duck ponds, picnic areas, restaurant and refreshment stands, sunken and overhanging gardens, the lovely Hillside Gardens overlooking Grenadier Pond, and a place to rent boats. Bands floating on barges in Grenadier Pond present concerts on summer evenings. Here is a most beautiful and useful park in a city that boasts over 200 park areas.

MacKENZIE HOUSE. Home of William Lyon Mackenzie, Toronto's first mayor in 1837. House has been restored to its original condition. Located at 82 Bond St., two blocks east of Yonge and just south of Dundas. Open daily, 10 am to 5 pm, except Monday, all year.

MARINE MUSEUM. Features marine and shipping displays. It is located in the restored Officers' Quarters of Stanley Barracks, built in 1841. Have lunch in Ship Inn, an 1850-style restaurant. In Exhibition Park. Open daily. Closed Mondays in winter. Admission fee.

ONTARIO PLACE. A thoroughly delightful playground on a lakefront island. See spectacular movies in the Triodetic dome theater called Cinesphere. Concerts and entertainment in The Forum. Take the kids to Children's Village or relax in lovely parks around lakes and reflecting pools. See exhibitions of all kinds. Restaurants for dining. You can drive or get here by public transport.

ONTARIO SCIENCE CENTER. The center is probably the most exciting science museum on the continent. Nearly every exhibit is a working one in which you yourself operate the mechanism. The museum was built with the motto "Please Touch" in mind. You look and feel your way through demonstrations and experiments that go a long way toward explaining what science is up to. It's on Don Mills Road near Eglinton Avenue. Open daily 10 am to 6:30 pm. Admission fee.

ROYAL ONTARIO MUSEUM. Housed in a beautiful building, the museum offers a superb natural history collection. It also has one of the finest collections of Chinese art and archeology in the world. Also in the same complex you'll find the McLaughlin Planetarium, which presents star shows every day except Monday, and the Sigmund Samuel Canadiana Building, with displays of the crafts of early English and French Canada. It is located on Queen's Park Crescent, Queen's Park.

TORONTO CITY HALL. At Queen and Bay Streets, two gracefully curved 27-story office buildings partially surround a three-story domed rotunda. All were designed by Finnish architect Viljo Revell. You can tour the building daily from 10 am to 6:15 pm. View city from the 27th floor deck.

TORONTO STOCK EXCHANGE. Handles a daily volume of stocks second only to New York Stock Exchange. Located at 234 Bay St. Open 10 am to 3:30 pm, Monday through Friday.

OTTAWA

This is more than the capital of Canada. It is also one of the country's most beautiful and interesting places to visit. Its history began in June of 1613, when Champlain passed the site on an exploratory trip. No one settled in the area for the next two hundred years, though during this time the Ottawa River was the fur traders' main highway to the northwestern interior. In 1800 Philemon Wright came from Massachusetts with a group of settlers to build homes where Hull now stands. By 1820 there were villages on both sides of the river. Then, between 1826 and 1832, the British built the Rideau Canal to give their gunboats a route to Lake Ontario that was safe from American guns on the south shore of the St. Lawrence. Colonel John By built the canal, and the town on the south bank honored him by calling itself Bytown. The lumber business boomed and Bytown flourished, acquiring cityship and a new name, Ottawa, in 1854. Three years later, Queen Victoria surprised everyone, especially Ottawa's own citizens, by selecting the new city as capital of the United Provinces of Upper and Lower Canada. The Queen's selection was a masterstroke. Politically, it sidestepped serious tension growing between the four other contenders—Montreal, Toronto, Quebec, and Kingston. Geographically, the city was ideally located between Canada's major population centers.

Today, Ottawa is dominated by the familiar upthrusting green-roofed Peace Tower rising from the Parliament Buildings on Parliament Hill. Visitors to Ottawa start their days in the

city at this point—usually by attending the traditional and colorful ceremony of the changing of the guard, performed each morning at 10 am from mid-June to Labor Day. After this, it's a matter of visiting the interesting places, and enjoying the beauty of Ottawa's beautiful parks, drives, and rivers. If you are here during the last two weeks in May, you'll have a special treat, for that's when the city's two million tulips bloom. These flowers were a gift from the Royal Family of Holland after World War II.

One very good way to orient yourself in the city is to take a sightseeing tour the first day. Sightseeing buses leave hourly for a 27-mile trip from the Chateau Laurier, the Lord Elgin Hotel, and the Colonial Coach Lines headquarters.

Points of Interest—Parliament Hill

PARLIAMENT BUILDINGS. The Center Block was replaced after a fire in 1916. The other two buildings date back to between 1859 and 1865. The Peace Tower, 291 feet high, contains a 53-bell carillon that plays daily concerts at 1 pm, except on Thursdays and Sundays when hour-long recitals are given from 9 to 10 pm. Check locally for the current schedule. The best place to listen to these beautiful bells is on the lawns in front of the House of Parliament. The Memorial Chamber in the Peace Tower contains the Book of Remembrance, in which is inscribed the name of every Canadian who gave his life in World War I. The pages of the book list 66,650 names, and each day a page is turned. Incidentally, a glance at the top of the flagpole on the Peace Tower will tell you whether or not Parliament is in session. The white light at the bottom of the pole is always lighted. The one at the top is lighted only when Parliament sits. In the vicinity of Parliament Hill you can visit:

BYTOWN MUSEUM. On Wellington Street just west of the Chateau Laurier you find the museum's entrance gate. Descend the stairs to Canal Road to find the museum, a small stone building built by Colonel By in 1826, that houses a collection of documents and items relating to Ottawa's history.

BYWARD MARKET. This area, a short distance east of the Chateau Laurier, dates back to the 1830s. It's an open street market where farmers from the surrounding area bring their produce to sell each Tuesday, Thursday, and Saturday morning. The floral displays here are particularly beautiful.

Cinesphere, the triodetic-dome theater at Ontario Place, Toronto

GARDEN OF THE PROVINCES. A few blocks west of the Parliament Buildings, this is a pretty spot in which the flags, coats of arms, and flowers of each province are displayed. It is particularly attractive at night, when it is illuminated.

NATIONAL ARTS CENTRE. This handsome showcase for the performing arts rises from the banks of the Rideau Canal and overlooks Confederation Square. In it are a 2,300-seat opera house, an 800-seat thrust-stage theater, an experimental studio theater, as well as a fine restaurant, a cafe, and a coffee shop and book and record shops. You can tour the building.

NATIONAL LIBRARY AND PUBLIC ARCHIVES. There's an interesting display here in the Historic Museum that includes a model of Quebec in 1860. The building is located across from the Garden of the Provinces.

NATIONAL WAR MEMORIAL. In Centennial Square at Wellington, Rideau, and Elgin streets, this monument commemorates the war dead of World War I.

SPARKS STREET MALL. The three blocks of Sparks Street from Elgin to Banks have been closed to traffic and form an exclusive shopping area and a delightful place for a stroll.

Other Attractions in the City

FESTIVALS. See plenty of theater at the Festival Canada in July and plenty of horses at the Central Canada Exposition late in August. The Ottawa/Outaouais Festival of Spring the last week in May marks the blooming of Ottawa's 4 million tulips.

NATIONAL AERONAUTICAL COLLECTION. At the Canadian Forces Base, Rockcliffe. See a display of more than 50 aircraft dating back to 1908, including Alexander Graham Bell's *Silver Dart*.

NATIONAL GALLERY OF CANADA. The works of famous artists of Canada are displayed here. Elgin Street at Slater.

NATIONAL MUSEUMS OF SCIENCE AND TECHNOLOGY. Fine displays of trains, vintage autos, aircraft, and agricultural implements. On St. Laurent Boulevard at Russel Road.

RIDEAU CANAL AND LOCKS. The Rideau Canal, built in 1826 by Colonel By, is 123 miles long, with 47 locks. The eight locks in the center of Ottawa, known as the Eight Giant Steps, are a historic landmark. Scenic cruises take you through the canal and the Ottawa River.

RIDEAU HALL (Government House). This is the residence of the Governor-General of Canada and is located at the entrance to Rockcliffe Park. The 88 acres of woods, lawns, and formal gardens are open to visitors when His Excellency is not in residence. Just beyond here, on a bluff overlooking the Ottawa River, is the residence of the Prime Minister.

ROYAL CANADIAN MINT. Watch them make money here. Visiting hours are every half hour from 9 to 11:30 am and 1:30 to 3 pm on weekdays by appointment. Call 992-2348.

HAMILTON

At the western tip of Lake Ontario, halfway between Toronto and Niagara Falls, Hamilton is Canada's most important steel-producing center. It is a city of 300,000 with much to offer a visitor—from a genuine castle to a teahouse in a royal garden.

Parliament Buildings at Ottawa's Tulip Festival

Points of Interest

ART GALLERY OF HAMILTON. Formal gardens connect this gallery to the campus of McMaster University. The gallery has a good collection covering several centuries. Open every day except Monday. Free.

BURLINGTON BAY SKYWAY. The Burlington Bay Skyway is a majestic bridge curving high above the entrance to Hamilton's landlocked harbor. The view of the city from the bridge is particularly good.

DUNDURN CASTLE. Built in 1832 by Sir Allan MacNab, it is now furnished as it was when MacNab was Prime Minister of the United Province of Upper and Lower Canada. You tour the mansion, visit the museum, see a sight and sound presentation each Saturday and Sunday evening during the summer months, and see Children's Theater presentations twice weekly. Small admission fee.

GAGE PARK. There are 70 acres of grounds in this park, which is east on Main Street. It offers a fine floral display, and is especially noted for its rose gardens.

HAMILTON BEACH. On the shore of Lake Ontario, this is a 180-acre summer playground for swimming, picnicking, hiking, and games, part of the 2,000-acre Hamilton Park System.

OPEN AIR MARKET. Every Tuesday, Thursday, and Saturday, farmers come to town from all over the Niagara Garden Belt to display their produce. Located at James and York streets, this is Canada's largest open-air market.

ROYAL BOTANICAL GARDENS. Near the western outskirts of the city these 1,900-acre gardens include a famous rock garden clustered about a teahouse; the Spring Garden, where 100,000 flowers riot in May and June; a special Children's Garden; sunken gardens formally trimmed and manicured; and Coote's Paradise, a natural marsh and game preserve.

SAM LAWRENCE PARK. High atop Hamilton Mountain, the park is a good place to get a panoramic view of the city and see an outstanding floral display.

STEEL COMPANY OF CANADA. You can tour the steel plant here Tuesdays through Fridays, by appointment. It's on Wilcox Street, between Sherman and Gage.

LA BELLE PROVINCE

Riding through brilliant autumn maples in the Laurentians at Ste. Adele, Quebec

QUEBEC

IN 1534, JACQUES CARTIER, A SEA CAPTAIN FROM BRITTANY, SAILED WEST FROM THE PORT OF ST. MALO WITH 61 MEN IN TWO SHIPS. HIS OBJECTIVE, LIKE THAT OF MOST EXPLORERS OF THE TIME, WAS TO FIND A NORTHWEST PASSAGE TO THE ORIENT. AFTER 20 DAYS ON THE OPEN SEA, CARTIER SIGHTED NEWFOUNDLAND, SAILED DOWN ITS WESTERN COAST, THEN TURNED WEST, PAST PRINCE EDWARD ISLAND. FOLLOWING THE NEW BRUNSWICK COAST INTO CHALEUR BAY, HE MADE A LANDING ON THE GASPE PENINSULA, WHERE HE PLANTED THE FLAG OF FRANCE.

The next year, Cartier returned with three ships. Passing north of Anticosti Island, he sailed up the broad St. Lawrence to the mouth of the St. Charles, where he found the Indian village of Stadacona. Today, Quebec City is on that site.

The Indians here called the land around them *Kannata*, meaning "place of small villages." Cartier adopted the word and later, in his journals, referred to his explorations of the Isles of Canada. Mapmakers accepted the name and Cartier's spelling of it—and the nation was named.

Leaving two of his ships at Stadacona, Cartier took his smallest vessel up the St. Lawrence to the Lachine Rapids; this was as far as he could go. Here he stopped at the village of Hochelaga, climbed the rocky prominence behind the village, and gave it the name Mount Royal (Mont Real). Returning to Stadacona, he wintered there, then left for France in 1536.

This was the beginning. Cartier returned again in 1541. By 1599, there was a settlement at Tadoussac, at the mouth of the Saguenay. Samuel de Champlain arrived in 1608 and laid the foundations for Quebec City. Paul de Chomedey, sieur de Maisonneuve, established a religious community in the shadow of Mount Royal in 1642. He called his settlement Ville Marie, but the rugged hill behind the village soon asserted its authority, and the place became Montreal.

Thus history has been accumulating along the banks of the St. Lawrence for over 400 years, and when you travel in Quebec an ever present sense of the past is a strong part of the charm and attraction. Even in glass-walled, sky-scraping Montreal, the very old is there beside the very new. You walk from the modern magnificence of the Place Ville Marie to historically steeped Old Montreal in ten minutes—and drop back three centuries.

It is easy to stand on the Governor's Walk, just under the wall of the old Citadel in Quebec City, and visualize the tiny ships of Cartier sailing the river below. You can almost walk the deck with the captain and see the river as he saw it. The wooded heights of Lévis rise from the south bank. Cape Diamond thrusts 360 feet up from the north bank. The river has suddenly narrowed at this point to less than half a mile, and these heights form a natural gateway.

If at that moment one of the glassed-in ferries that ply between Quebec City and Lévis comes into view, it will bring you back to the present. Looking at it, you might suddenly realize that Cartier's ships were probably no more than one-quarter its size. To cross the wild North Atlantic in bobbing corks that small, those Bretons had to be truly intrepid.

This realization gives you an insight into the French Canadian of today. His ancestors were a tough, determined breed who conquered the sea and met and tamed the Quebec wilderness. They fought to force a living from a difficult land. The heritage they forged on this anvil is strong and proud, and you see it today in the survival of the French language and culture of Quebec.

This well-preserved French culture provides a charming appeal for travelers from other parts of Canada and from the United States. It is different—and *vive la différence!* It gives Quebec a touch of Europe close to home. This, coupled with the fact that Quebec is history, a living link with the past, makes it a good place for the tourist to visit.

La Belle Province is Canada's largest province, covering some 600,000 square miles. Like the iceberg, however, most of Quebec is not seen. It is a great trackless wilderness stretching north to Hudson Strait. Much of this northern part of the province hasn't changed from the days of Cartier and Champlain. There are occasional pockets of people, some pulp mills and hydroelectric projects—but mostly it is a vast forest that dwindles into tundra before it reaches the northern coast.

MONTREAL AND QUEBEC CITY

Montreal, over eleven hundred miles from the Atlantic, is a great seaport and Canada's largest city. Better than two-thirds of the people here speak French, making this the second largest French-speaking city in the world—after Paris. Among other things, Montreal has been called the gastronomic capital of North America, a title well deserved, since the city's best restaurants rate among the finest in the world.

In these restaurants, incidentally, you often see "S.A.Q." wines (served in carafes) on the wine lists. This abbreviation of *Societes des Alcools du Quebec* refers to contracts awarded by the province to wine regions in France. These contracts permit vintners to ship wine in large casks to Quebec for bottling here. Some good wines are imported in this manner. So an S.A.Q. carafe (which holds 3 glasses) is a good buy unless you hanker after estate-bottled vintages.

Montreal is a city of special delight for the walking tourist, for there is so much to see and do in the downtown area. There is, first of all, quaint Old Montreal, along the river, reflecting the city's 400-year history. And there is the startling new Montreal, the great underground complex which stretches from towering Place Ville Marie to Place Bonaventure. There is a week of good walking in these places alone.

Quebec City, capital of the province, is the only walled city on the continent, a very quaint and picturesque place. It is graced by the turreted, copper-roofed Chateau Frontenac, which stands high on Cape Diamond's peak. The city is more French than is Montreal, and the past is closer, especially when you ride a horse-drawn *calèche* through the old section.

Highway 138, between Montreal and Quebec City, was Canada's first *Chemin du Roy*, or King's Road. If you choose to drive this old, slower road, you'll see churches, farms, and homes dating back 250 years.

LAURENTIANS AND NORTHWEST

According to geologists, the Laurentians, straight north of Montreal, are the oldest mountains in the world. Peaceful, laced with rivers and streams, speckled with lakes, they are the winter and summer playground of the province. The Laurentians have more resorts and inns than any other place in Quebec, so you can find accommodations at every level—or you can camp. But even if you don't plan to stay, you'll enjoy a tour through this lovely country. During the winter, the Laurentians provide some of the world's best skiing.

Western Quebec begins at Hull, across the river from Ottawa. Here the Gatineau River comes down from the north to join the Ottawa. The Gatineau Valley is a popular resort area, highlighted by Gatineau National Park—88,000 acres of forest and lakes. Skiing is big here in the winter, with hiking, fishing, swimming, and boating serving as summer attractions.

Northwest of Mont Laurier, driving on Highway 117, you pass through La Verendrye Provincial Reserve, then come to the Abitibi region. Settlement here didn't begin until the 1930s. Now it is an area of farming and of mines. It is rich in gold, silver, copper, zinc, and other metals—and in fish and game. If you'd like to take home a picture of a moose, keep your camera ready as you drive through the park and the Abitibi. You are apt to see one crossing the road almost anywhere.

SOUTHERN QUEBEC AND GASPE

Southern Quebec, between the St. Lawrence and the United States border, was originally settled by Frenchmen, who established villages and seigniories along the rivers. Later, Loyalists in the American colonies who opposed the revolution moved north to settle in the area. The result is an interesting mixture of French and English tradition today, though French is still the language you'll hear.

The area directly south of Montreal is the bottom of an ancient sea. Its rich farmlands have gained for it the title Garden of Quebec, and those crisp vegetables on your dinner table in Montreal probably came from here. The flat landscape here is relieved by surprising, isolated mountains which suddenly thrust up from the plain. On a very clear day, you may get a view of these monadnocks from the top of Mount Royal.

Southern Quebec narrows sharply as you travel east of Quebec City. For nearly a hundred miles along the Lower St. Lawrence, it is often no more than 35 miles from the river to the United States border. The farms and little villages along here are old and pretty. You'll pass ancient bogs where peat is being cut and baled for shipment, and in the villages along the river you can stop in the shops of woodcarvers whose work has become world famous.

The Gaspé Peninsula begins at Matane and juts out into the Gulf of St. Lawrence like the thumb of a large glove. For centuries the only way to reach the Gaspé was by boat. Auto roads around the peninsula are relatively recent. As a result the little villages you'll visit here are unspoiled and pretty much as they have been for a couple of centuries. The Gaspé has a wild beauty, highlighted by vistas of capes, sheer cliffs and promontories, narrow valleys, and tablelands so high that even the last glacier didn't cover them. A leisurely trip around the Gaspé is one of the great vacations. Allow yourself a couple of days because you'll drive almost 600 miles and be in and out of the car dozens of times to enjoy the scenery.

Life is peaceful and unhurried in the Laurentians

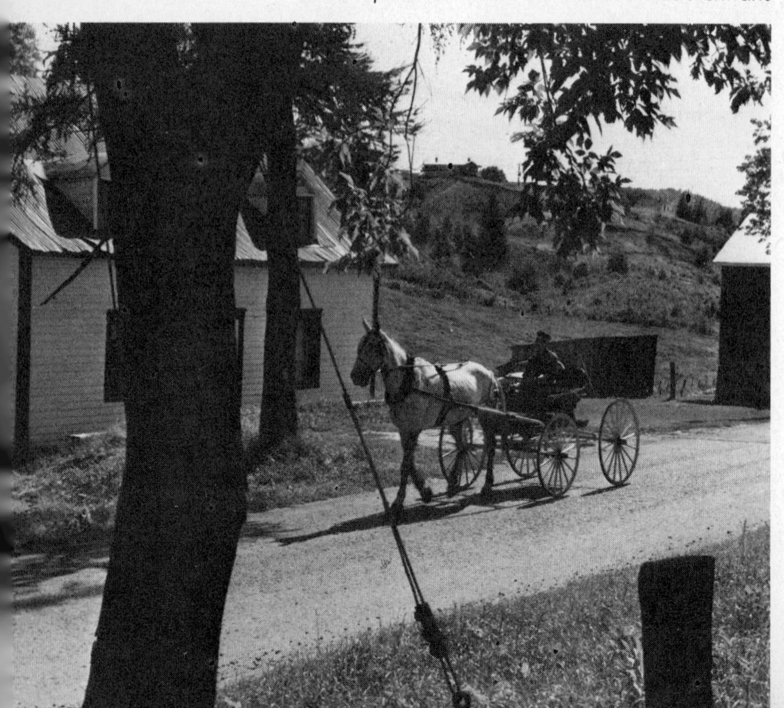

BEAUPRE COAST

The north shore of the St. Lawrence east of Quebec City is a pretty country of hills, woods, and small farms. You'll have an opportunity to see Montmorency Falls, a short distance east of Quebec City, and then to visit the famous shrine of Ste. Anne de Beaupré, which dates back to 1657. The Basilica of Ste. Anne rivals the cathedrals of Europe. On past the Beaupré Coast you can take the ferry across the St. Lawrence from St. Simeon to Riviere du Loup—a pleasant hour-and-three-quarter-ride—or drive on to the site of the first French settlement in Canada, at Tadoussac, on the banks of the Saguenay River.

You might put together an interesting trip by driving up along the Saguenay to Lake St. John (Lac Saint-Jean), then returning to Quebec City through the beautiful Laurentides Provincial Park. Here you'll be driving through the Kingdom of the Saguenay, so-called because Indians told Cartier that the Saguenay River flowed from a kingdom that was rich in precious stones.

LANGUAGE IN QUEBEC

French is spoken throughout Quebec. In the major cities such as Montreal, many people are bilingual, but as you travel into the rural areas and east into the Gaspé, you'll find more and more French and less and less English. However, it isn't a problem, just an interesting complication. Most signs are in both languages, which makes things easier, and the people respond to a smile in any tongue. In a matter of days, you'll find you've picked up a working vocabulary, even though your pronunciation will be less than perfect.

If you have a smattering of French left over from your school days, this is a good time to use it. If you make this much of an effort, you'll get a lot of quick help, along with some broad smiles.

QUEBEC

BAIE ST. PAUL [C-5]* About 57 miles east of Quebec City on the north shore of the St. Lawrence is a popular resort region that begins at Baie St. Paul and extends to La Malbaie. Since the turn of the century people have been coming here in the summer to enjoy the river, the beautiful woodlands, and the resorts. If you are driving east along the river, swing from Highway 138 to Highway 362 to see this area. Resorts and inns have all the amenities, including fine golf courses, in a truly picturesque setting. Pointe au Pic and La Malbaie are particularly notable.

BEAUPRE COAST [D-5] The coast stretches along the north shore of the St. Lawrence, east of Quebec City to Cap Tourmente, for a distance of 25 miles. When Jacques Cartier first saw this area there was a bright meadow along the river's edge, and he is supposed to have exclaimed, "Oh! le beau pré! Quel beau pré!" ("Oh, what a lovely meadow!") The first farms of Quebec were tilled along this coast. The shrine to Ste. Anne de Beaupré is here, as are the beautiful Montmorency Falls.

CHICOUTIMI [B-5] On the Saguenay River, which flows from Lake St. John to the St. Lawrence River between a succession of high cliffs that reminds you of Norway's fjords, is the lovely town of Chicoutimi. The river is extremely deep—as much as 900 feet in some places. Chicoutimi is the northern gateway to the Laurentides Provincial Park. The town was established first in 1676 as a mission, later refounded in 1852. You can see good primitive paintings at the Arthur Villeneuve Museum and the works of local artists at the Maison des Arts. Swimming marathons are held here several times during the summer. The Carnaval-Souvenir is a gay annual historical pageant staged during the week before Ash Wednesday. Everyone dons a costume, the men grow beards, and there are sporting events, street dancing, parades, and auctions. Good fun. Northwest of here is Lake St. John, a big lake surrounded by an agricultural plateau nicknamed the Granary of Quebec. If you like blueberries, visit the towns around the lake. The blueberry crop of this area is worth more than a million dollars each year. The berries are especially delicious with cream for a breakfast treat.

DE LA MAURICIE NATIONAL PARK [D-4] Due north of Trois Rivieres and midway between Montreal and Quebec City, this is a new national park. See National Parks, page 102-3.

FORILLON NATIONAL PARK [F-7] One of the newer national parks, Forillon is located on the tip of the Forillon Peninsula, which thrusts off the end of the Gaspé Peninsula into the Gulf of St. Lawrence. See National Parks, page 103.

FORT CHAMBLY NATIONAL HISTORIC PARK [F-3] On the Richelieu River, about 20 miles east of Montreal, this fort dates back to 1665. See National Parks, page 103.

* Letter and number refer to coordinates on map of Quebec, page 67.

FORT LENNOX NATIONAL HISTORIC PARK [F-3] Fort Lennox is on an island in the Richelieu River, 12 miles south of St. Jean, and was one of the largest forts in Canada. See National Parks, page 103.

GASPE PENINSULA [F-7] For centuries, the Gaspé was locked away from the rest of the world because the only way to reach its settlements was by small boat. Now Highway 132 circumnavigates the peninsula—but the little villages along the shore are still much as they were, and the insular charm remains. The name is a French variation of an old Indian word meaning "land's end"—an apt description. The original settlers were Frenchmen from Brittany, the same area Jacques Cartier came from. They brought with them their language, their love of the sea and fishing, and their distinctive and savory cuisine. A tour of the Gaspé is one of the most beautiful in all Canada. Along the north shore, you'll see a beautifully rough and rugged coast, with tiny fishing villages located in little bays—each separated from its neighbor by gigantic cliffs. The south shore, facing Chaleur Bay, is gentler and less rocky, with many bays and beaches along the way. The eastern end of the peninsula, near Gaspé and Percé, is the high point. If you think of the tour as starting at Ste. Flavie on the lower St. Lawrence coast, where Highway 132 begins, you will drive 560 miles by the time you make a complete circuit of the Gaspé and return to Ste. Flavie. The road is good two-lane asphalt all the way, but not made for high-speed driving, since it follows the contours of the coast and the roll of the land. But then, one doesn't drive the Gaspé at high speeds. This is a place of sightseeing, of stopping to view the magnificent scenery, of pausing to browse in little villages, and of taking pictures of places you'll seldom see anywhere else. Allow at least two or three days for the trip, and spend a night or two at the little inns along the way. You'll find gracious hospitality, eat seafood at its absolute best, and sleep well in the fragrant sea air. If you suffer from hay fever, you'll be glad to know that there is little or no ragweed on the Gaspé. Along the route:

Ste. Flavie [A-7] The Gaspé tour begins and ends here.

Grand Metis [F-6] Visit the Metis Park, a fine collection of flowers and exotic shrubs along a lovely stream spanned by a rustic bridge.

Metis Sur Mer [F-6] A fine 4-mile sandy beach.

Matane [F-6] Good salmon fishing in the river here. A road follows the river for 26 miles, making the salmon pools accessible. Use your waders and stalk these with a fly rod—the only type of fishing permitted. Get a fishing permit from the local office of the Department of Tourism, Fish and Game. Good ski slopes near here, too.

Cap Chat [F-7] Mount Logan rises 3,700 feet behind the town and commands a superb view of the north shore of the St. Lawrence and Egg Island.

Ste. Anne des Monts [F-7] A road from here leads to Gaspesian Provincial Park, which includes 2,498 square miles. At Le Gîte du Mont Albert, you take a guided tour (leaves daily) to the top of Mont Albert. Mount Jacques Cartier, the highest peak in eastern Canada, rises in the distance. Cottages near lakes here can be rented.

Riviere a Claude [F-7] A road from here leads inland to Lac a Claude, where the government owns chalets.

Mont St. Pierre [F-7] You will pass through a number of lovely little fishing villages along this part of the coast. This village is located between two mountains and is an imposing sight. Campground here.

Mont Louis [F-7] Thirteen miles inland is Great Mont Louis Lake, where you can rent cabins from the government and catch speckled trout.

Gros Morne [F-7] The highway runs between the mountains and the sea. The name means "big bluff." Mountains are as high as 2,225 feet.

Riviere Madeleine [F-7] The highway bends away from the sea to the mountains in a sweeping curve and then returns to the sea.

Grand Vallee [F-7] See the *vigneaux,* long tables on which cod are left to dry, and the outdoor bread ovens. The ship aground in the harbor was torpedoed in the St. Lawrence during World War II.

St. Maurice de L'Echouerie [F-7] The cod smacks are blessed each year on the Sunday following the feast of St. Peter.

Riviere au Renard [F-7] The population here is partly Irish because a ship carrying Irish immigrants was wrecked near Cap des Rosiers, and the survivors elected to stay on.

Cap des Rosiers [F-7] The lighthouse here is the highest on the coast. The St. Lawrence is 100 miles wide at this point. West of here, it is the St. Lawrence River. To the east, it is the Gulf of St. Lawrence. From the top of Cap des Rosiers, a French officer sighted General Wolfe's fleet in 1759 and sent a courier with the news to Quebec City. Forillon National Park has been established just beyond here on the Forillon Peninsula, where there are picnic and camping areas.

Grand Greve [F-7] The first mine in Canada was worked in this village in 1665. Three Canadian ships were torpedoed opposite Cap Gaspé during World War II.

Penouille [F-7] Historians suspect that the Vikings established an outpost here in the 11th century. Some also conjecture that the Phoenicians may have been here before the Vikings.

St. Majorique [F-7] The shrine to Our Lady of the Seven Sorrows is here. There are the seven stations of the Way of Sorrows, cast in bronze and a life-size Calvary in the mountains behind the church.

Gaspé [F-7] You can fly to the Magdalen Islands from here. In the gulf, 180 miles east of Gaspé, these islands offer peaceful seashores with warm waters, inviting beaches, curious rock formations, and busy lobster-fishing harbors. Red cliffs and silver dunes give the islands a postcard-picture look. Island fishermen will take you mackerel fishing, and you can dig clams along the dunes. In Gaspé there is an entrance to Gaspesian Provincial Park, leading to Lake Madeleine, and you'll also find a beautiful beach.

Fort-Prevel [F-7] The hotel operated by the provincial government here is luxurious and noted for its cuisine. Tennis courts, golf course, and beach are here for your use.

Percé [F-7] This beautiful village is in the shape of a half-circle formed by two capes. The famous Percé Rock divides the bay the village faces. The rock is a 400-million-ton block of limestone, 1,420 feet long and 288 feet at its highest point. Jacques Cartier anchored his ships behind it in July, 1534. At low tide you can walk to it on a sandbar. Pierced by a central arch 60 feet high, Percé Rock is one of the most noted tourist attractions in Canada. Take the cruiser ride around Bonaventure Island from Percé to see the nesting place of gannets, kittiwakes, herring gulls, razor-billed auks, and even some Arctic puffins. There are two fine lookouts on the mainland, one at Surprise Hill and the other at Pic de l'Aurore.

Grande-Riviere [F-7] The interesting aquarium at the Provincial Fisheries School is stocked with seal, lobster, cod, and other Gaspé marine life.

Port Daniel [F-7] Jacques Cartier stayed in this bay from July 4 to July 12, 1534. Fine beach, hunting, and fishing.

Paspébiac [F-7] Those fishing schooners known as *Gaspésiennes* are built here.

New Richmond [F-7] Indians from the Micmac reservations sell their baskets and other handicrafts near here. The Indian church is built in the form of a tepee.

Carleton [F-7] Founded by fleeing Acadians in 1756. There is a fine beach and campground here, as well as a museum and golf course.

Restigouche [F-6] Visit the Indian mission of Ste. Anne de Restigouche. The church is the twelfth on the site. The little museum of the Capuchin fathers is interesting. Near the monastery is a ship which was stuck in the mud in front of the mission for 178 years before being refloated and brought ashore in 1939.

Matapedia [F-6] You have circled the Gaspé, and now can turn to cross the neck of the peninsula through the Matapedia Valley or turn to the east to tour New Brunswick.

GATINEAU PARK [E-1] Covering an area of 88,000 acres dotted by 44 lakes, this park extends north and west for 35 miles from the city of Hull. There are paved and unpaved roads through the park, a number of lookout points, campgrounds, and picnic sites. Moorside, the summer estate of William Lyon Mackenzie King, the former prime minister, is open to the public. Two rooms are a museum and another is a tearoom. North America's largest ski club, the Ottawa, is located at Camp Fortune in the park. During the summer you can ride the club's chair lift for a fine view of the countryside. Altogether, there are more than 20 ski slopes in the park, served by 14 tows and lifts.

GRANBY [F-3] About 40 miles east of Montreal on Highway 112, Granby has a fine zoological garden housing more than 300 species of animals. There are good restaurants, a place to picnic, and pony and miniature train rides for the children. A favorite excursion spot for Montrealers.

GRAND MERE [D-3] Grandmother Rock, looking like the head and shoulders of a wrinkled old woman, stood in the bed of the St. Maurice River and gave this city of 18,000 its name. When a power dam was built in the river, Grand Mere was moved to the town park. The city is located between Montreal and Quebec City, and the provincial canoe racing championships are held here each year, over a 15-mile course.

QUEBEC
Population: 6,040,000
(1971 estimate)
Area: 594,860 Sq. Miles
Capital: Quebec

Cities and Towns

Acton Vale.........E-4
Alma..............B-4
Amos..............A-2
Asbestos..........E-4
Baie Comeau.......A-7
Baie St. Paul.....C-5
Beauport..........D-5
Bedford...........F-3
Buckingham........E-1
Cap de la Madeleine.........D-3
Cap St. Ignace.........D-5
Causapscal.........F-6
Chambord.........B-4
Charlemagne.........E-3
Châteauguay.........F-3
Chicoutimi.........B-5
Coaticook.........F-4
Cookshire.........F-4
Disraeli.........E-5
Donnacona.........D-4
Dorion-Vaudreuil.........F-2
Drummondville.........E-4
E. Angus.........F-4
Farnham.........F-3
Ferme Neuve.........D-1
Gatineau.........D-1
Granby.........F-3
Grand' Mere.........D-3
Hébertville.........B-5
Hull.........E-1
Huntingdon.........F-2
Iberville.........F-3
Joliette.........E-3
Jonquiere.........B-5
Knowlton.........F-4
La Baie.........B-5
Lac Mégantic.........E-5
La Guadeloupe.........E-5
La Malbaie (Murray Bay).........C-6
Laprairie.........F-3
L'Ascension.........D-2
La Tugue.........C-3
Laurentides.........E-2
Lennoxville.........F-4
Levis.........D-5
Loretteville.........D-5
Magog.........F-4
Maniwaki.........D-1
Marieville.........F-3
Matane.........F-6
Mont Laurier.........D-1
Montreal.........E-3
Montreal Nord.........E-3
Notre Dame du Lac.........C-7
Pierreville.........E-3
Plessisville.........E-4
Pointe Claire.........F-2
Portneuf.........D-4
Princeville.........E-4
Quebec.........D-5
Rimouski.........B-7
Rivière Bleue.........C-7
Rivière du Loup.........C-6
Roberval.........B-4
Ste. Agathe des Monts.........E-2
Ste. Anne de Beaupré.........D-5
Ste. Claire.........D-5
Ste. Marie.........D-5
Ste. Martine.........F-2
St. Felicien.........A-4
St. Ferdinand.........E-4
St. Georges de Champlain.........D-4
St. Hyacinthe.........E-3
St. Jean.........F-3
St. Jean Port Joli.........C-6
St. Jerome.........E-2
St. Lambert.........F-3
St. Michel des Saints.........D-2
St. Pascal.........C-6
St. Raymond.........D-4
St. Tite.........D-4
St. Tite des Capes.........C-5
Scotstown.........F-5
Scott Jct.........D-5
Shawinigan.........D-3
Sherbrooke.........F-4
Sorel.........E-3
Thetford Mines.........E-5
Trois Rivieres.........D-4
Vallée Jonction.........D-5
Valleyfield.........F-2
Victoriaville.........E-4
Waterloo.........F-4
Westmount.........F-3
Windsor.........E-4

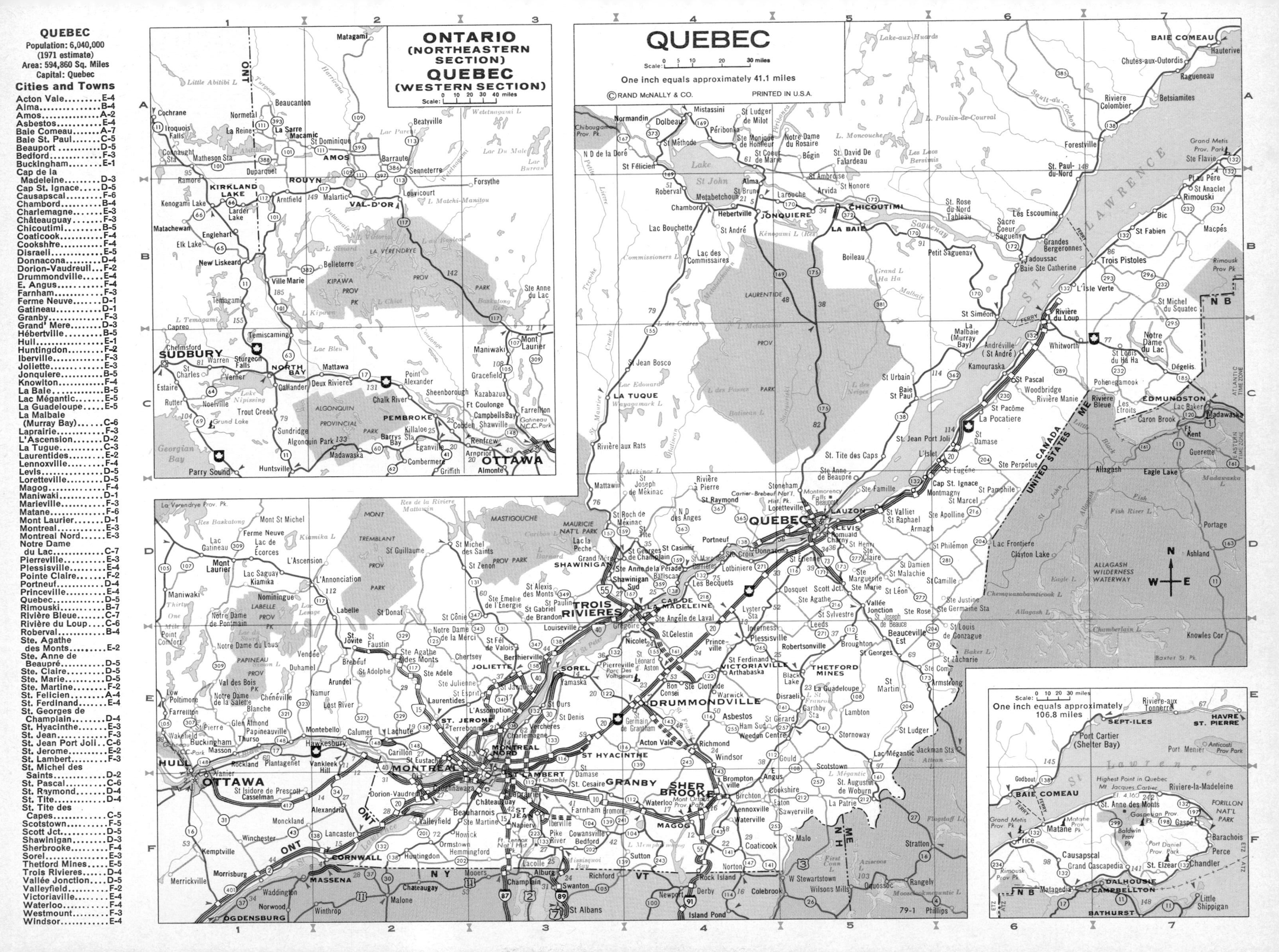

HULL [E-1] The Gatineau River flows down from the north to join the Ottawa at this point. Hull is just across the river from the city of Ottawa. Huge log booms bring raw timber down the Gatineau from the forests in the north, to feed the insatiable appetite of the pulp and paper mills. Hull was established in 1800 by settlers from Massachusetts under the leadership of Philemon Wright. While here, you can follow an old portage path beside the river in the suburb of Val Tetreau. Before the founding of the city this path was used by fur traders and missionaries to bypass the Little Chaudiere Rapids; today these rapids supply electric power for the city. Gatineau Park extends north and west for 35 miles from Hull.

LA BAIE [B-5] A trio of towns, Port Alfred, Bagotville, and Grande Baie, united to form this city on the Baie des Ha! Ha! The strange name has a history: The Indians told Cartier of the legendary Kingdom of the Saguenay, where there was a wealth of precious stones. Later, Champlain heard the same story, but when he investigated, he found no stones or other promised items. In fact, he found no kingdom. Feeling that the joke was on him, he named the bay—and the bitter, ironic name stuck. There are two notable churches to visit: the beautiful St. Alphonse Church, and the Notre Dame de la Baie Shrine.

LA TUQUE [C-3] This is the starting point of the world's toughest, roughest, most exhausting canoe race. Crowds of 150,000 people pace the two-man canoes down the St. Maurice River from here to Trois Rivieres. The race lasts three days, covers 125 miles, and includes three grueling portages. Be there on Labor Day weekend to join the fun. Good campground here.

THE LAURENTIANS The Laurentian Mountains, only 45 minutes by car from Montreal, have become the largest playground in North America. The most popular area is the first 80 miles north of Montreal. It is served by the Laurentian Autoroute, a toll road that shortens the trip to a matter of minutes. In the Laurentians there are 250 resort hotels, 50 ski centers, 120 ski tows serving 300 slopes, 10 golf courses, hundreds of lakes, and more than a hundred campgrounds.

LAURENTIDES PROVINCIAL PARK [B-4-5, C-4-5] A beautiful 4,000-square-mile wilderness bisected by Highways 175 and 169, the park runs from Alma and Chicoutimi to Quebec City, a distance of about 140 miles. At various points you can pitch a tent, park a trailer, rent a cabin or a fishing boat, and buy a snack or a full-course meal. Some of the mountains reach up to 4,000 feet, and the park has more than 1,500 lakes. Parts of the area are still unexplored. If you plan to hike into any of the lesser known areas, hire a guide. Almost anywhere in the park you are apt to see moose, beaver, bear, otter, mink, and marten. In the park, campgrounds have been established at the following sites: Belle Riviere; aux Ecorces; La Loutre; La Mare-du-Sault; des Ilets; Lac Arthabaska; Lac Metabetchouane; and Lac Sainte-Anne. Just outside of the park, Stoneham Park offers 275 sites. The Stoneham gate can be reached by taking Highway 175 north from Quebec City. Another entrance to the park is Highway 381, which leads north from Baie St. Paul and through St. Urbain.

The northern entrance to the park is at Hebertville, just south of Alma. South of Hebertville, at Lake Belle Riviere, 3 miles off the highway, you'll find campgrounds. There also are overnight lodge accommodations about 15 miles south of Hebertville, for which you must have reservations.

LA VERENDRYE PROVINCIAL RESERVE [B-2-3] Studded with lakes, La Verendrye is 5,000 square miles of unspoiled game and fishing reserve. Driving through here, you are likely to see deer or moose crossing the road at any time. Be prepared—both with brakes and camera. Stop to fish and you'll meet king-size northern pike and lake trout. There are wilderness campsites and opportunities for long canoe trips. The park is bisected by a 114-mile paved road, part of Highway 117, and dirt roads lead from it back into the wilderness. Grand Remous is the nearest town, located 12 miles south of the park on Highway 117. There is no hunting in the park, but you can get fishing permits at the reserve's reception office. At Le Domain, a lodge on Lac des Loups, you can have full hotel and restaurant service.

LEVIS [D-5] A city on the heights across the St. Lawrence from Quebec City, General Wolfe's army camped here during the Siege of Quebec in 1759, and bombarded the settlement at the foot of Cape Diamond. You'll find Lévis divided in an interesting way. Schools, colleges, and churches are in one section; wharves, railway yards, and offices are in another. The old houses are of a quaint and unusual style. A ferry connects Quebec City and Lévis, and the views of Quebec City from Lévis and from the ferry are especially interesting. The Trans-Canada is the express road to the east, but Highways 132 and 138 are more scenic.

LONGUEUIL [E-3] Situated on the south side of the St. Lawrence, across from Montreal, you can get a fine view of the big city from here, particularly at night. Longueuil originally was a seigniory granted in 1657 to Charles Le Moyne. One of Le Moyne's sons, Iberville, discovered the mouth of the Mississippi River and founded Louisiana. Another, Bienville, founded New Orleans. Longueuil offers some very old houses to visit.

LOUVICOURT [B-2] Just north of La Verendrye Provincial Reserve on Highway 117, Louvicourt is in the middle of goldfields and log cabins. The hunting and fishing are great. One-third of all the moose killed in Canada are shot near here.

ILE D'ORLEANS [D-5] In the St. Lawrence just to the east of Quebec City, the Ile d'Orleans divides the great river into two parts. You reach the island by a suspension bridge from Highway 138 near Montmorency, 7 miles east of Quebec City. After crossing the bridge to the island, look back toward the north shore of the river for a perfectly beautiful view of Montmorency Falls. Later, from the western tip of the island at Ste. Petronille, you'll have an equally good view of Quebec City. A tour of the island is like touring rural Quebec of a hundred or more years ago. Everything is quaint and old and uncommercial. When Cartier first saw it he called it "Isle of Bacchus" because of the abundance of wild grapes, and today, from its remarkably fertile soil come great quantities of fruits and vegetables. The strawberries, for example, are luscious, and the jam made from them is incomparable. The northern slopes of the island are covered with apple and plum orchards, while great red tomatoes grow everywhere. Near the village of St. Laurent you'll find the ancient Gosselin Mill, which has been converted into a charming restaurant and chamber music center. The village of St. Jean has fine old homes with very photogenic exteriors. You can camp near here, too, at the Park de l'ile d'Orleans. From the eastern tip of the island, you can see the Beaupré Coast and the Basilica of Ste. Anne de Beaupré. Near Ste. Famille, an old farmhouse is now a restaurant that represents French-Canadian life of 200 years ago. You park your car, and are taken to the house in a horse-drawn buggy.

MAGDALEN ISLANDS (See listing under *Gaspé*, page 66). These eight islands are located in the Gulf of St. Lawrence, 155 miles from the tip of the Gaspé Peninsula. Covering 55,000 acres, they can be reached by boat from Montreal and Quebec City, and from Souris, P.E.I. Air service is available from Montreal, Charlottetown, P.E.I., Moncton, N.B., and Gaspé.

MAGOG [F-4] If you have a big taste for landlocked salmon, Magog is the place to go. A popular summer resort southwest of Sherbrooke, it is noted for fishing and most especially for the salmon. South of the town is Lake Memphrémagog, 32 miles long, and 2,600-foot Mount Orford is 5 miles north. There's a provincial park with good camping at the foot of the mountain. In the summer, this is the location of a famous music camp, Le Jeunesses Musicales du Canada, where young people attend performances by internationally known musicians and take courses in music. In the winter months, Mount Orford is the center of a good ski area.

MANIWAKI [D-1] If you are in the market for moosehide moccasins, the Indians on the Algonquin reservation near here will make them to order. Maniwaki was a Hudson's Bay trading post in the 1800s, to which the Indians brought their furs. Today the area is a center for hunting and fishing, and the Algonquins are unexcelled as guides. The big event here is the winter carnival in late January, highlighted by a grueling International Dog Derby. The town is located on Highway 105, 83 miles north of Hull.

MATANE [F-6] The name means "beaver pond" in the Micmac language, but the beavers have gone now, and the silver-sided salmon have taken their place. The Petite Matane River, which comes down to the St. Lawrence from the highlands, is a famous salmon river. The road stays close to the river for 26 miles, making all the salmon pools readily accessible. Most fishing here is done by wading the stream. Matane is connected to the north shore of the St. Lawrence by a ferry that docks at Godbout.

MONT LAURIER [D-1] North of here you are in Quebec's wilderness. To the west, on Highway 117, is La Verendrye Provincial Reserve. To the east is Mont Tremblant Provincial Park. All this should tell you that to travel to Mont Laurier without your fishing gear is a grievous error. Late in August, you can see a 30-mile canoe race in which the contestants must make four portages and shoot several rapids.

MONT SAINTE-ANNE PARK [D-4] A ski paradise 25 miles east of Quebec City with 28 slopes, some steep and some gentle, and 56 miles of cross-country skiing trails, as well as 6 miles of trails for snowshoeing.

MONT TREMBLANT PROVINCIAL PARK [D-2] Just 80 miles north of Montreal, this 990-square-mile wilderness provides two developed campgrounds, rivers and lakes for canoeing and fishing, and woodland trails for hiking. It is a noted ski center and the scene of international competitions. For snowmobilers, there is a wide choice of trails with heated relay stations. Main entry is through St. Jovite, on Highway 117, near the town of Mont Tremblant. Other entrances are through St. Donat on Highway 125, or from St. Faustin, on Highway 117, north through the du Diable River valley.

MONTMORENCY FALLS [D-5] The Montmorency River cascades 274 feet in a gorgeous setting to create this waterfall just 7 miles east of Quebec City on the Beaupré Coast.

MONTREAL [E-3] Canada's largest city and the second largest French-speaking city in the world. For a map of the city and descriptions of its points of interest, see pages 71 and 72.

OKA [F-2] If you know good Canadian cheese, you recognize the name of this town, located on Highway 344 about 30 miles west of Montreal. Here, in one of the largest Trappist monasteries in the world, the famous Oka cheese is made. Other Canadian cheeses high on any gourmet's list are Cheddar, Ermite, and the Raffine from Ile d'Orleans. If you ever are offered the opportunity to enjoy Cheddar and a glass of Caribou, accept with gratitude—and caution. This is an old French-Canadian combination dating back to the days of those hearty voyageurs. The cheese will please your palate, but the Caribou may knock your head off. It is a devilish concoction of sweet red wine and whiskey or white alcohol that could be used as a substitute for nitroglycerine.

PIERREVILLE [E-3] It could be that the fire engine in your home town came from here, where the production of pumpers and ladder trucks is big business. Offering good duck hunting in the fall, Pierreville is on the south side of the St. Lawrence, 70 miles east of Montreal. At the nearby Odanak Indian Reservation you buy baskets and smoked fish from the Indians.

QUEBEC CITY [D-5] Capital of the province and the continent's only walled city. For a map of the city and descriptions of its points of interest, see pages 71 and 72.

RIMOUSKI [B-7] Fire destroyed a quarter of this city in 1950, but all traces of the damage are gone. Established in 1701, Rimouski is on the south shore of the St. Lawrence, 65 miles northeast of Riviere du Loup. The harbor here is open to shipping all year, and ferry service connects it with the north shore. Rimouski Reserve, 300 developed square miles, is about 30 miles south of the city on the Canadian-United States border. You'll find camping facilities, cabins, picnic sites, swimming, and excellent fishing. There are a number of lakes in the park, and you can rent boats in several places. Power boats are permitted only on Lake Kedgwick.

RIVIERE DU LOUP [C-6] A *loup-marin* is a seal, and the city drew its name from seals that once played at the mouth of the river here. Quebec City is 130 miles west via the Trans-Canada. You can take the ferry across the St. Lawrence to St. Simeon, a pleasant hour-and-three-quarters trip. There are eight waterfalls on the river that flows through town, and the highest is in the heart of town. The area has good resorts, sand beaches, and a heated saltwater swimming pool, as well as campgrounds and picnic areas. The Summer Festival, held between mid-July and mid-August, is a series of events that include street dancing, concerts, shows, parades, sporting events, and the crowning of a queen. Incidentally, ferry service stops on January 8, and begins again on April 15.

ST. JEAN PORT JOLI [C-6] Here you'll find the greatest concentration of craftsmen in the entire province. Members of the Bourgault family and other artisans have their shops on either side of the road displaying wood carvings, enamels, copper and wood mosaics, fabrics, paintings—all produced here. Stop in at the church, renowned for its graceful design and beautiful interior, and see the work of famous craftsmen.

STE. ADELE [E-2] This is a resort center and art colony amid the forests of the Laurentians, 40 miles north of Montreal. The annual workshops in writing, ballet, sculpture, painting, and music draw hundreds of students. Near town, visit the Village de Seraphin, a reproduction of a turn-of-the-century village.

STE. AGATHE DES MONTS [E-2] In the lovely Laurentians around the blue waters of Lac des Sables is this water-sport paradise. There are water ski shows every Sunday afternoon, motorboat cruises, regattas, and enough fishing to satisfy St. Peter. There's horseback riding here, too, and a chair lift to take you to scenic heights. In the winter, there's downhill skiing, cross-country skiing, and snowshoeing.

STE. ANNE DE BEAUPRE [D-5] The first chapel was built here in 1658, when the first miraculous cures were reported. Very soon afterward, the Shrine of Ste. Anne became a world-famous pilgrimage goal. A replica of the first chapel is near the great Basilica of Ste. Anne—a magnificent church rivaling the cathedrals of Europe in size and appearance. The faithful pray at the saint's shrine in the basilica, which contains the Miraculous Statue and the major relic, a bone of Ste. Anne. They also climb the Scala Santa, a replica of the 28 stairs Jesus ascended to meet Pilate, on their knees. Life-size bronze stations of the cross are in small grottoes in the hillside across the street from the basilica. Nearby is The Historial, a museum maintained by the priests of the church. It depicts the life of Ste. Anne and the history of the shrine in life-size figures. Also nearby is the Cyclorama, a huge circular painting of the Holy Land which is viewed from a raised platform in the center of the circle.

ST. JEAN [F-3] On July 21, 1836, the first railroad in Canada began operation here, connecting the towns of St. Jean and La Prairie. Originally the site of Fort St. Jean, built in 1666, the city is a few miles southeast of Montreal. The remnants of the old fort can be seen.

ST. JOVITE [E-2] Nestled in the du Diable River valley, close to Mont Tremblant Provincial Park, this is a summer and winter tourist center, one of the oldest in the Laurentians. There is a fine old covered bridge over the du Diable River at Brebeuf, via Highway 323. Winter skiing is at Sugar Peak, where there are 15 slopes.

SEPT ILES [E-7] Don't expect to find seven islands here in the big circular bay, in spite of the name. There are only six. The bay is 7 miles in diameter and the islands are located near its mouth. Sept Iles was an isolated fishing village from 1650 until 1950; then iron mines were opened to the north and it became an important port. You get here by boat from Rimouski or by driving 408 miles from Quebec City through an area yet to be discovered by tourists. At Sept Iles, you'll find inviting beaches, some unforgettable coastal scenery, and wilderness camping.

SHAWNIGAN [D-3] Electric power is generated here, and the city is the cradle of Quebec's chemical industry. Plenty of festivities from the middle of August to Labor Day, when the International Canoe Classics are held on the St. Maurice River. All summer there are open-air concerts on Tuesday evenings at Place Municipale in St.-Marc Park.

SHERBROOKE [F-4] The Queen of the Eastern Townships, Sherbrooke was first settled in 1791 by a Vermonter, Gilbert Hyatt. There are over a hundred industries here, including pulp and paper mills, textile plants, and heavy machinery manufacturers. More than any other city in Quebec, the city is bilingual and bicultural—chiefly the result of the mingling of the original French settlers and the Loyalists who moved into the area from the United States during and after the Revolution. Recently, Sherbrooke has become the center of one of Canada's fastest developing winter sport areas.

SOREL [E-3] A good many of those hard-working Liberty Ships of World War II were born in shipyards here. Midway between Trois Rivieres and Montreal, Sorel is the site of one of the first French forts in Canada. The Chateau des Gouverneurs, built in 1781, was the summer home of the governors of Canada for many years. Christ Church dates back to 1842.

STANBRIDGE [F-3] There are more than two hundred old covered bridges in Quebec—enough to satisfy any photographer. One of them is here at Stanbridge, with a picturesque old mill nearby. You can get here in an hour from Montreal.

THETFORD MINES [E-5] Half of the world's supply of asbestos comes from Quebec's Eastern Townships (the area south of Montreal to the United States border). Thetford Mines, south of Quebec City via Highways 1 and 23, is one of the world's largest asbestos centers. At Black Lake, 7 miles south, you can see open-pit mining operations.

TROIS PISTOLES [B-7] A French sailor paid three pistoles (an old French coin) for a silver goblet, which he lost in the river here. Ile aux Basques, opposite Trois Pistoles, is a bird sanctuary for blue herons, gulls, eider ducks, and other wild birds. If you are a naturalist, a bird watcher, or a photographer, the warden will permit you to visit the island.

TROIS RIVIERES [D-4] The St. Maurice River splits into three channels when emptying into the St. Lawrence, hence the town's name. It is the second oldest French city on the continent, having been founded in 1634. Sieur de La Verendrye, who discovered the Rocky Mountains and established the trading fort that later became Winnipeg, was born here. Buildings in the city go back a long way—the Manor Godefroy de Tonnancour was built in 1690, and the Anglican Church went up in 1699. General Montgomery and Benedict Arnold stayed here during the American army's occupation in 1776. The Ursuline nuns treated wounded American soldiers and later presented a bill of $130 for drugs and bandages. They received a promissory note which has never been honored. Calculated at 6%, that note is now worth $9.5 million. The Ursuline Convent, built in 1697, contains a good museum. Visit the cathedral to see the very beautiful stained glass windows. Across the St. Maurice River at Cap de la Madeleine there is a shrine visited by thousands of pilgrims each year.

WAKEFIELD [E-1] The Lafleche caverns across the Gatineau River from this very picturesque little village are lighted to show off the stalagmites, stalactites, wall encrustations, and other phenomena. To get to the caverns, you cross the river through an old covered bridge. Wakefield is north of Hull.

QUEBEC CITY

Every city has its own character, but this one has more character than most. It is more French than Montreal. It has retained more antiquity and quaintness than almost any city in Canada. The towering Chateau Frontenac, seen from every point in the city and up to twenty miles away from the city, seems to set the pace. There are really two cities here. The Upper City on the head of Cape Diamond, where the Chateau sits and where the old Citadel stands watch. And the Lower Town, the oldest section of Quebec, which sits on the riverbank. The Plains of Abraham, now a part of Battlefield Park, are outside the walls of the city. This is the field on which the British General Wolfe attacked the city defended by the French General Montcalm. The British won the battle, and both generals died in the fray. The city fell in 1759. The great walls surrounding the city, making it the only walled city in North America, were built between 1823 and 1832.

One of the prettiest walks to be found anywhere is that from Battlefield Park along the Governor's Walk, just beneath

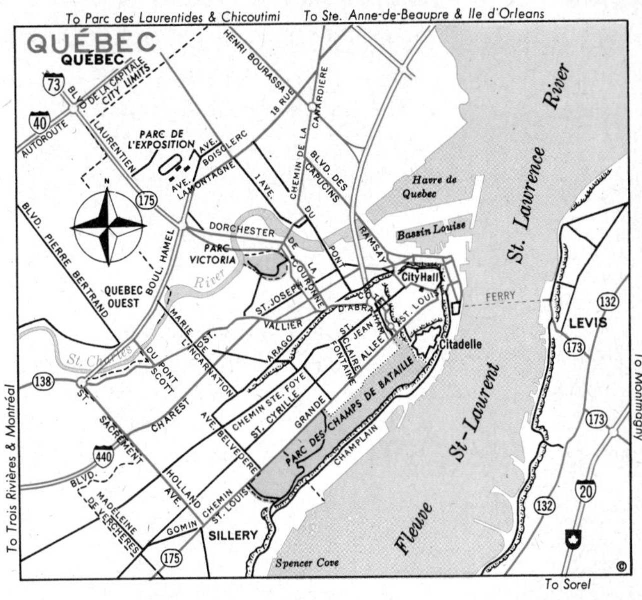

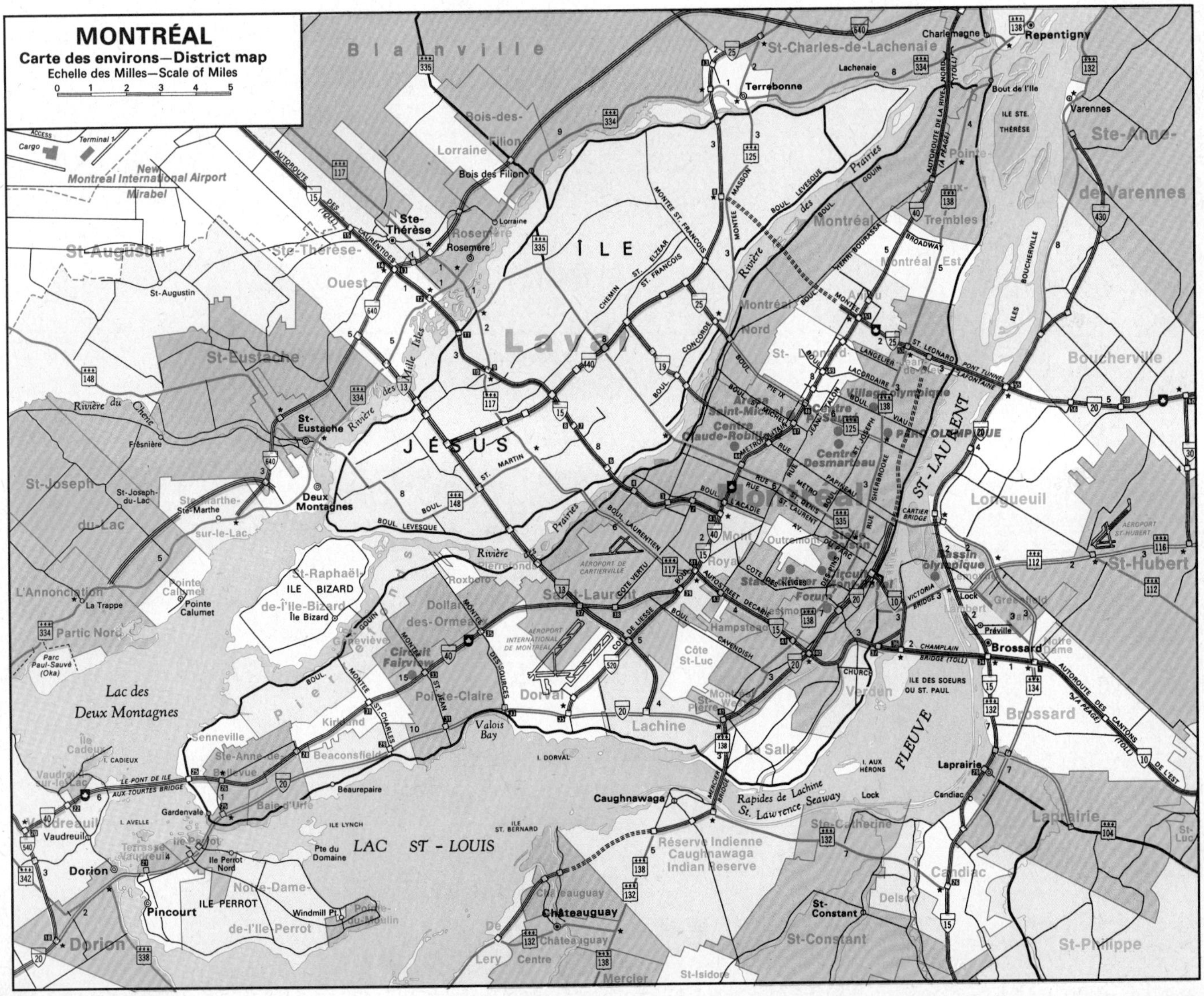

MONTRÉAL
Carte des environs—District map
Echelle des Milles—Scale of Miles
0 1 2 3 4 5

the walls of the Citadel. Following the walk, you descend to Dufferin Terrace, a wide boardwalk promenade adjacent to the Chateau Frontenac. As you follow this walk, you are looking down into the St. Lawrence, at the ships coming in from the Atlantic, and across the river to the city of Lévis.

One of the best ways to see Quebec is by walking—or by combining a long stroll with a ride in a horse-drawn *calèche*. The tourist bureau has a pamphlet outlining an excellent walking tour. The *calèche* can take you out to Battlefield Park and to the Citadel. Incidentally, on a walking tour you can descend to the Lower City via an elevator that drops from the front of the Chateau Frontenac to the old home of Louis Jolliet, discoverer of the Mississippi River, in the Old City below.

Sightseeing bus tours are available, and you also can hire an official guide to ride with you in your own car.

The summer season is the tourist season, but Quebec is very much bright-eyed and alive in the winter.

Points of Interest

ANGLICAN CATHEDRAL. The building dates back to 1804, when the present church was built on the site of the ancient Church of the Recollets.

AQUARIUM. Located in the Parc du Pont at the east end of the Quebec Bridge, the Aquarium has a good collection of freshwater and saltwater fish.

BATTLEFIELD PARK. The Plains of Abraham, where the English under Wolfe attacked the city defended by the French under Montcalm, are a part of the park located just west of the Citadel.

THE CITADEL. This fortress looks down into the St. Lawrence from a height of 360 feet. It was the site of the Quebec Conferences between Winston Churchill and Franklin D. Roosevelt during World War II. The ceremony of the changing of the guard takes place here daily in the summer months at 10 am, weather permitting. Guided tours of the fort are available.

LOWER TOWN. This is Old Quebec, the site of the original city. Notre Dame des Victoires Church here was built in 1688. The altar is shaped like a fortress. Here in the Lower Town you can see the Fargues House, an interesting example of a French-Canadian home of the 18th century.

MUSEE DU FORT. In this small theater you can see a diorama showing the six seiges of Quebec City. It is located opposite the Chateau Frontenac at 10 Rue Ste. Anne. If you stop here before touring the Citadel and the Plains of Abraham, you'll have a better understanding of what actually happened. Fee.

OLD JESUIT HOUSE. Built around 1700, this is one of the oldest homes in Canada, and is now a historical and archeological museum. Located at 2320 Chemin Des Foulons in Sillery.

PARLIAMENT BUILDINGS. You can tour these buildings constructed in ornate 17th-century French Renaissance style and set in beautifully landscaped grounds just outside the St. Louis gate. The interior is decorated with fine sculptures, paintings, murals, and other works of art. Bilingual guides will take you through the buildings.

PROVINCIAL MUSEUM. The museum, located in Battlefield Park, has displays of sculpture, ceramics, paintings, and mosaics.

QUEBEC ZOOLOGICAL GARDENS. Situated 7 miles north of the city on Highway 73, at Orsainville, this zoo has an extensive collection of birds and wild animals, farmhouses and old mills on the river that winds through the park's 30 acres.

STE. ANNE DE BEAUPRE. The world famous shrine is located 21 miles east of Quebec City on the north shore of the St. Lawrence. You can drive, take a regular tour bus, or go by boat from Quebec.

SIGHTSEEING ON THE WATER. Three different cruises on the St. Lawrence are available. A five-hour cruise takes you to Ste. Anne de Beaupré. A two-hour cruise goes past Ile d'Orleans to Montmorency Falls. The third cruise is a three-hour moonlight excursion. Boats leave from Chouinard Wharf, east of the Lévis Ferry Dock.

STREET OF THE ARTISTS. Just off Ste. Anne Street, opposite the Chateau Frontenac, you'll find a tiny street, or alley, just a block long. Here, day and night, artists display their work. You'll see paintings of every description and quality.

URSULINE CONVENT. General Montcalm was buried within the convent walls following the battle on the Plains of Abraham. The convent was founded in Quebec in 1639, but the present convent dates in part back to 1686. The convent was the first girls' school in North America.

Special Events

WINTER CARNIVAL. The famous Quebec Winter Carnival is a gala of long standing, attended by thousands. It opens with a grand parade and continues for two weeks, ending on Shrove Tuesday. Nearly every event you can name is a part of the carnival—from canoe races across the partly frozen river to an international bonspiel, dog derbies, and a peewee hockey championship.

MONTREAL

Canada's largest city, a sophisticated and interesting combination of the Canadian and the European, attracts visitors because of its unique character, its famous restaurants—and because there is so much to see and do.

Two major events, Expo '67 and the 1976 Olympic games, have left impressive landmarks. Man and His World, on the Expo site, is now a permanent exposition on Ile Ste. Helene in the St. Lawrence, and is well worth a visit.

The Olympics centered around Olympic Park, a few miles east of downtown Montreal, across from Maisonneuve Park. The stadium in the complex, protected from the weather by a sliding-membrane roof, will be home to the Expos for baseball and the Alouettes for football. Other Olympic buildings now a permanent part of the city here are the velodrome, the Olympic village (four half-pyramids of bold design built to accommodate 9,019 athletes), and the International Centre.

The entire Olympic complex is connected to the city's famous and quiet Metro by weatherproof walks. And a short underground ride on the Metro brings you to the underground city at Place Ville Marie. One-third of Montreal's city center is connected by underground promenades, so you can live, shop, eat, be entertained, and see sporting events without venturing out into the snow and cold.

Huge Mirabel International Airport was also completed in time for the Olympics. Located 20 miles north of the city via the Laurentian Autoroute toll road, Mirabel has the world's largest airport surface (88,000 acres) and was designed to be the eastern aerial gateway to the continent at some future date.

Points of Interest

LA FONTAINE PARK. A good place to take the children. It has a children's zoo with 250 animals, a lagoon where you can rent a canoe or a paddle-wheeled boat, the Garden of Wonders, with its fairy-tale characters, and snack bars.

MAISONNEUVE PARK. In East Montreal on Sherbrooke, this is the city's largest park. It has a 200-acre botanical garden, rated nearly as good as London's Kew Gardens. You'll see 15,000 species of plants housed in nine large greenhouses.

MAN AND HIS WORLD. Pavilions and exhibits change each year in this outgrowth of Expo '67, now a permanent exposition with 25 pavilions. LaRonde, the amusement park, is a major attraction. On Ile. Ste. Helene, and served by the Metro, Montreal's subway.

THE METRO. The ultimate subway that fulfills the dream of underground riders the world over. Cars are bright, spotless, and rubber-tired (thus quiet). Each subway station is an art gallery in its own right. Don't fail to take at least one ride.

MOUNT ROYAL. There is a park on the summit of Mount Royal (Mont Real) which is an active winter sports center and during the summer, a quiet refuge. Weekly concerts and plays are presented here. Only horse-drawn vehicles are permitted on the top of the mountain. There are miniature train rides, a pretty lake, benches and lookout points, and restaurants. The lighted cross on the mountain fulfills a promise made by Maisonneuve (founder of Montreal) in 1643—to erect a cross for the sparing of the little town from a flood.

OLD MONTREAL. This is the oldest part of the city, located along the river between McGill and Berri streets. You'd enjoy a walking tour through here, to see: Place d'Arms, the original market square of the town; the Sulpician Seminary, with its famous wooden clock; Notre Dame Church, opened in 1829, and possibly the most beautiful church in North America; the Chateau de Ramezay, built in 1705 by Governor Claude de Ramezay; and dozens of other historic sites and buildings. The Chateau de Ramezay is now a museum and worth a visit. In Old Montreal, you'll also find fine little shops where you can buy handwoven linens and woolens, women's clothes, children's clothes, prints of Old Montreal, braided rugs, antiques, and other items. Prices are moderate to expensive.

PLACE DES ARTS. An architectural masterpiece and worth seeing for this reason alone. It was designed as a cultural complex for displays of all of the arts—and a tour through its lobbies and promenades is like a tour through a great art museum. Most of the works you'll see are by local artists, and the quality is superb. The complex has a 1,300-seat theater, an 800-seat recital hall, and a 3,000-seat concert hall, in addition to three-level underground parking, shops, lounges, and landscaped esplanades. Guided tours are available, and you can reach the building by Metro, the subway.

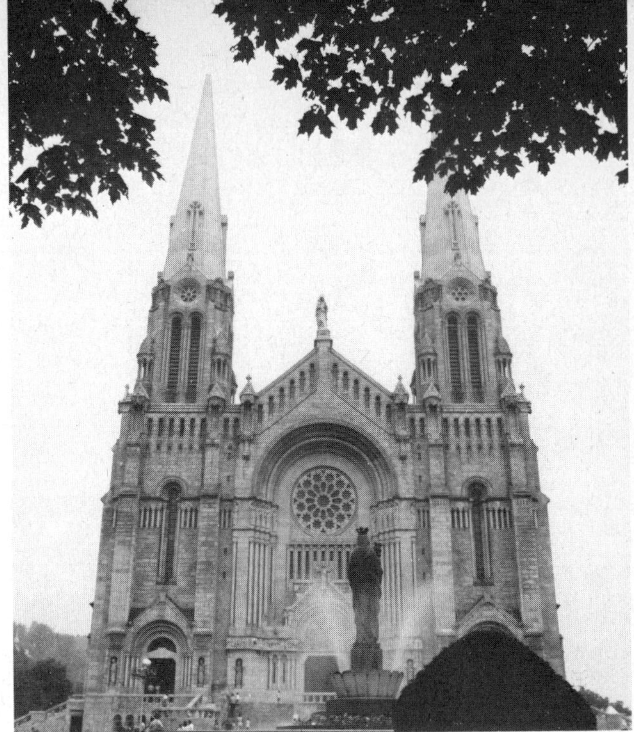

The Basilica in Ste. Anne de Beaupre, east of Quebec City

ST. JOSEPH'S ORATORY. Brother Andre, who is reputed to have brought about many cures through prayer, devoted his life to the building of this great basilica, still not completed. His tomb is in the oratory. The basilica seats 10,000, while the crypt church seats 1,000. A beautiful combination of Renaissance and modern design, the oratory has become famous throughout the world. The view of the city from its steps is excellent.

STOCK EXCHANGE TOWER. You can take a short subway ride from Place du Canada to this financial heart of the city. If you've seen other stock exchanges, this one will be a surprise. It's relatively quiet. The exchange floor is carpeted, and an electronic bidding system has eliminated much of the chaos. Tours are conducted on weekdays between 10 am and 3:30 pm.

THE UNDERGROUND CITY. Montreal has approached city planning in a new way, and the result is the creation of a remarkable city within a city. The heart of this plan is a complex of buildings on either side of Montreal's Central Station. On one side is the towering 45-story Place Ville Marie, an office building in the shape of a cross with a beautiful, terraced plaza, beneath which is a whole city of shops, restaurants, bars, and theaters. The shops are on four vaulted promenades as wide as city streets that are kept at shirt-sleeve temperature all year. From Place Ville Marie, you walk on underground trafficless boulevards through the Central Station—the subway headquarters—to Place Bonaventure, a trade center built over railroad tracks and the subway. This is the second largest commercial building in the world. It, too, has its underground shopping concourse with more than a hundred stores. In its upper reaches, there are five floors of showrooms, an International Trade Center, and the beautiful Hotel Bonaventure, a 400-room luxury hotel that looks out on a great rooftop garden. From Place Bonaventure, continue your underground walk to Place du Canada, containing the 640-room Chateau Champlain, another luxury hotel, 28 floors of offices, more stores, and a theater.

MARITIMES

Lighthouse rising above the rocky, ragged coast at Peggy's Cove, Nova Scotia

ATLANTIC PROVINCES 

THE FOUR PROVINCES THAT MAKE UP ATLANTIC CANADA BELONG TO THE SEA. THE AIR THAT WASHES OVER THEM IS BRISK AND SALTY, AND THE SUN THAT BRIGHTENS THEM IN THE MORNING IS FRESH FROM ITS ATLANTIC CROSSING. THIS IS WHERE NORTH AMERICA BEGAN ITS HISTORY IN 1497, FIVE YEARS AFTER CHRISTOPHER COLUMBUS FOUND THE WEST INDIES. THAT YEAR, JOHN CABOT, WITH 18 MEN IN THE *MATHEW*, SAILED WEST FROM BRISTOL, ENGLAND, AND MADE A LANDING ON THE CONTINENT LATE IN THE AFTERNOON ON JUNE 24, A SATURDAY.

It seems odd that we know the exact hour and day of Cabot's discovery, while the actual site of his landfall is in dispute. It depends on where you hear the story. In Newfoundland, they tell you he first sighted the jutting jaw of Cape Bonavista, on the island's eastern shore north of St. John's. In Nova Scotia, they have erected a bust of this doughty navigator in a little park near the northern end of Cape Breton Island. The place is called Cabot's Landing.

We do know for certain that Cabot gave names to Cape Ray, near Port aux Basques, Newfoundland; to the tiny French islands of St. Pierre and Miquelon; and to the easternmost tip of the continent, now Cape Race, which he called Cape England. We know, too, that when he returned to England in August of 1497, King Henry VII gave him a reward of ten pounds for his discovery.

The easiest way for you to settle this historical mystery is to visit both Cabot's Landing in Nova Scotia and Cape Bonavista in Newfoundland. Then you'll know you've been to the right spot no matter who wins the argument.

VIKING EXPLORATIONS

Of course, Cabot really was a latecomer to these shores. Five hundred years earlier, the Vikings had turned their dragon-prowed boats west. They established settlements in Iceland and then in Greenland. Their sagas tell, too, of another settlement in the west called Vinland, a green and fertile land. Historians and archeologists hunted for years for some signs of this settlement.

Then, in 1963, the Norwegian explorer Helge Ingstad culminated his long search by locating the buried remains of a Viking settlement at L'Anse au Meadow, at the very northern tip of Newfoundland. You can visit Ingstad's excavations there today and see the building foundations and the old iron forge. Whether or not this was the Vinland of the Norse sagas has not been determined. But we do know that this was a Viking settlement, that it was inhabited for a number of years, and that it dates back to somewhere around the year A.D. 1000.

There are more than 17,000 miles of wrinkled coast rimming the Atlantic Provinces, forming uncounted coves and bays and capes and inlets. In some places, sheer cliffs rise out of the sea. In others, long stretches of golden sand fringe the land where it meets the water. No matter where you go there is variety, as one charming vista replaces another.

These provinces wear their 400 years well. Everywhere there is a sense of antiquity, but not the kind that speaks of decay. Instead, it tells you of permanence. This place and these people have been here a long time—and they will be here long into the future. You see this permanence in the rocky cliffs, in the old and pretty villages, and in the faces of the people.

You'll find a wonderful variety of languages in these provinces: Acadian French, Gaelic, the English of Great Britain, and English with the Highland burr and the Irish brogue, along with good, solid Canadian English. You're likely to trip across Portuguese in St. John's and other fishing ports, since the Portuguese fishing fleet spends at least six months a year in the waters just off Canada.

The Atlantic Provinces extend much farther to the east than most people realize. The city of Halifax is at approximately the same longitude as Bermuda—and thus St. John's is more than 500 miles east of Bermuda. New Brunswick, Nova Scotia, and Prince Edward Island are on Atlantic Standard Time, one hour east of Montreal and New York. Newfoundland is in its own time zone, an additional half hour to the east. So when it's 3:30 in Montreal, it's 5:00 in St. John's.

You won't be long in these provinces before you discover that every citizen here is an individualist, and the first place you'll notice it is in the homes you see. Wherever you go there'll be houses, big and small, painted in bright, bright colors—brilliant blues, orchids, greens, chartreuses. You'll also see that each house is a different color than its neighbors. The whole effect is one of cheerfulness, like bright flowers in the spring, and even the drabbest rocky cove is turned into a garden.

And finally, if you enjoy seafood, the Atlantic Provinces will be your downfall. Remember that Prince Edward Island is the home of that gourmet's delight, the Malpeque oyster. And the seas off Nova Scotia provide the succulent Digby scallop. And old redback himself, the lobster, calls these waters home. Then, while you're recovering from these, there are the Atlantic salmon, the cod, the mackerel, and the haddock, not to mention a freshwater entrant such as the trout.

Furthermore, you not only have this huge variety of seafood, you also have people who have been specializing in the tasty preparation of these delights for a long, long time. They know what they're doing.

There are some gustatorial pleasantries here that don't come from the sea, too. The big, juicy blueberries of Newfoundland, the crisp apples of Nova Scotia, and the tasty fiddlehead of New Brunswick—baby ferns cooked tender and touched with butter and salt.

And then there are the chowders—ahhh! They'd fill a book by themselves.

NEW BRUNSWICK

There are three main routes waiting to be explored here. The first is from Quebec to the Bay of Fundy. You pass through Edmundston on the Trans-Canada, and follow the beautiful

Fishing villages dot the rugged coastline of Newfoundland

St. John River through a rolling, forested countryside to Fredericton, the capital of the province, and then on to Saint John, with its harbor on the Bay of Fundy. Highlights of the trip are the world's longest covered bridge, at Hartland, and Kings Landing Historical Settlement, near Fredericton.

The second route is that from the Maine border northeast along the coast to Saint John, and then on to Moncton. On this trip you can see the strange tricks of the tides of the Bay of Fundy—notably the Reversing Falls at Saint John, the high tides at the Fundy National Park, and the Tidal Bore in Moncton's front yard, which is filled twice a day by a swirling flow of water. The tides in some places on the bayshore exceed 50 feet.

The third interesting route is that along the north shore from the Quebec border through the Acadian fishing villages to Moncton and Fort Beauséjour. On this trip you might catch the Salmon Festival at Campbellton on Chaleur Bay, the Acadian Festival at Caraquet (and the nearby Acadian Historical Village), or the Lobster Festival at Shediac. The best way to see this area is to stray off the fast roads, and go to the smaller roads along the coast.

PRINCE EDWARD ISLAND

There are two ferries to take you from the mainland to Prince Edward Island. One plies between Cape Tormentine, not far from Sackville, N.B., and Borden on the island. The other takes you from Caribou, Nova Scotia, to Wood Island, Prince Edward Island.

Prince Edward Island is a quiet place of trim farms and beautiful beaches. Only 140 miles long and 40 miles across at its widest point, it is Canada's smallest province. After you've been there an hour or so, you'll understand why it is sometimes called "The Million Acre Farm."

But the island really isn't all farms, even though you might first be led to believe it. It has 1,100 miles of shore, a good part of it being some of the best sand beach in the hemisphere. By one of those quirks of nature, the north side of the island is blessed with the warmest ocean water north of Florida. Prince Edward Island National Park sits in the midst of this north shore, providing 25 miles of beautiful pink sand for you to play on. Then, when you turn your eyes from the sea, you find rolling sand dunes, terra-cotta cliffs, and green headlands shining in the sun.

There are no less than 28 provincial parks on the island, providing fine camping facilities. And you can fish the streams here for trout, or go for deep-sea adventure, because the giant bluefin tuna are found in abundance here. The world record bluefin was caught off of Cape Breton Island. That giant weighed 1,065 pounds. But a couple of years ago, one weighing a substantial 970 pounds came from Prince Edward Island water.

NOVA SCOTIA

Nova Scotia (New Scotland) is well named. Cape Breton Island looks very much like the highlands of Scotland, and parts of it were settled by clansmen from the land of the heather. On the island and also in the vicinities of Amherst, Pictou, and Antigonish, you'll see the kilt and hear the skirl of the pipe. There are highland games and festivals at Pugwash and at Antigonish and New Glasgow, and on Cape Breton Island, at St. Anns.

The drive around Cape Breton Island on the Cabot Trail is something you shouldn't miss. The mountains, the sea, the forests, and the villages blend into a scene that is positively right out of a picture book. The total distance is about 180 miles and can be done in a day—though it seems a shame to compress so much beauty into such a short time. You'll find the villages along the island's west side mostly French, while those along the east side are Scots. To get to Cabot's Landing, you swing off the Cabot Trail at Cape North and take the road that leads to Bay St. Lawrence. Here, as at other places on Cape Breton, when you hear an unfamiliar language, it is likely to be Gaelic.

One important stop is the Alexander Graham Bell museum at Baddeck. Bell was a man of amazing scientific talents, and the development of the telephone was only one in a series of accomplishments. He was responsible, for example, for the first airplane flight in the British Commonwealth, which took place here at Baddeck in February of 1909.

Another must on your list of places to see has to be the mighty fortress at Louisbourg, south of Sydney. The restoration of this great bastion, which was built between 1717 and 1743, is being done with loving care and in amazing detail. To date, the project has cost the government more than $15 million.

The Citadel at Halifax was built to offset the French power at Louisbourg and today dominates the harbor of this great port. You'll find Nova Scotia's capital city an interesting mixture of today and yesterday.

Another important segment of Canadian history took place at Port Royal. Here you'll see the Habitation of Champlain, where "The Order of Good Cheer" whiled away the winters of the early 1600s with lavish feasting. It was from here, too, that the Acadians were uprooted in 1755.

You'll find Nova Scotia bigger than it looks on the map, with a good many things to see and do. Be sure to allow enough time to enjoy it.

NEWFOUNDLAND

Newfoundland is Canada's youngest province, was once Great Britain's oldest colony, and boasts one of the oldest cities in North America. Labrador, on the mainland, is a part of Newfoundland. You'll discover very quickly after you arrive on the island that the correct pronunciation calls for the accent on the last syllable, so you say Newfoundland to rhyme with the word "understand."

You can fly to Newfoundland or take the ferry from North Sydney, Nova Scotia. The trip across the Cabot Strait takes about seven hours. If you're in the mood for a longer voyage, you can make the overnight jump from North Sydney to Argentia—a pleasant 17-hour cruise along the island's southern coast. Both ferries are run by Canadian National Railways, and you should have reservations, especially during the summer.

The Trans-Canada crosses Newfoundland, from Port aux Basques to St. John's, a distance of over 576 miles. You can create an interesting tour by taking the ferry to Port aux Basques, driving to St. John's, and then returning to the mainland via ferry from Argentia.

Start your tour of St. John's with a visit to Signal Hill, where the Cabot tower sits 600 feet above the narrow gate to the enclosed St. John's Harbor. Drive up here first during the day, and see the city laid out before you. Watch the ships coming and going in the harbor. Then come back at night to see the same places lighted like jewels.

It was from this hill that Marconi received the first transatlantic wireless message in 1901, and from this harbor that the great convoys of World War II set out for the difficult North Atlantic trip to Europe.

If you're a hunter, Newfoundland is one of the great spots for moose, caribou, and black bear. If you're a deep-sea fisherman, it's a fine place to start stalking the bluefin tuna. If you're a photographer, make a leisurely trip to some of the island's fishing villages. Talk to the fishermen and you'll discover that many are pleased to take you out cod-jigging or for a day's trip to inspect the nets. You'll get great pictures.

ST. PIERRE AND MIQUELON

These tiny islands just off the southern coast of Newfoundland are French colonies, the last in North America. St. Pierre, the chief city on the islands, is a typical pretty French village. For an interesting change of pace, you might spend a quiet, pleasant day here. You can fly from Sydney, Nova Scotia, or take the ferry from Fortune, Newfoundland, or North Sydney, Nova Scotia.

In a town that tells time by the ocean clock, fishing nets and a lighthouse

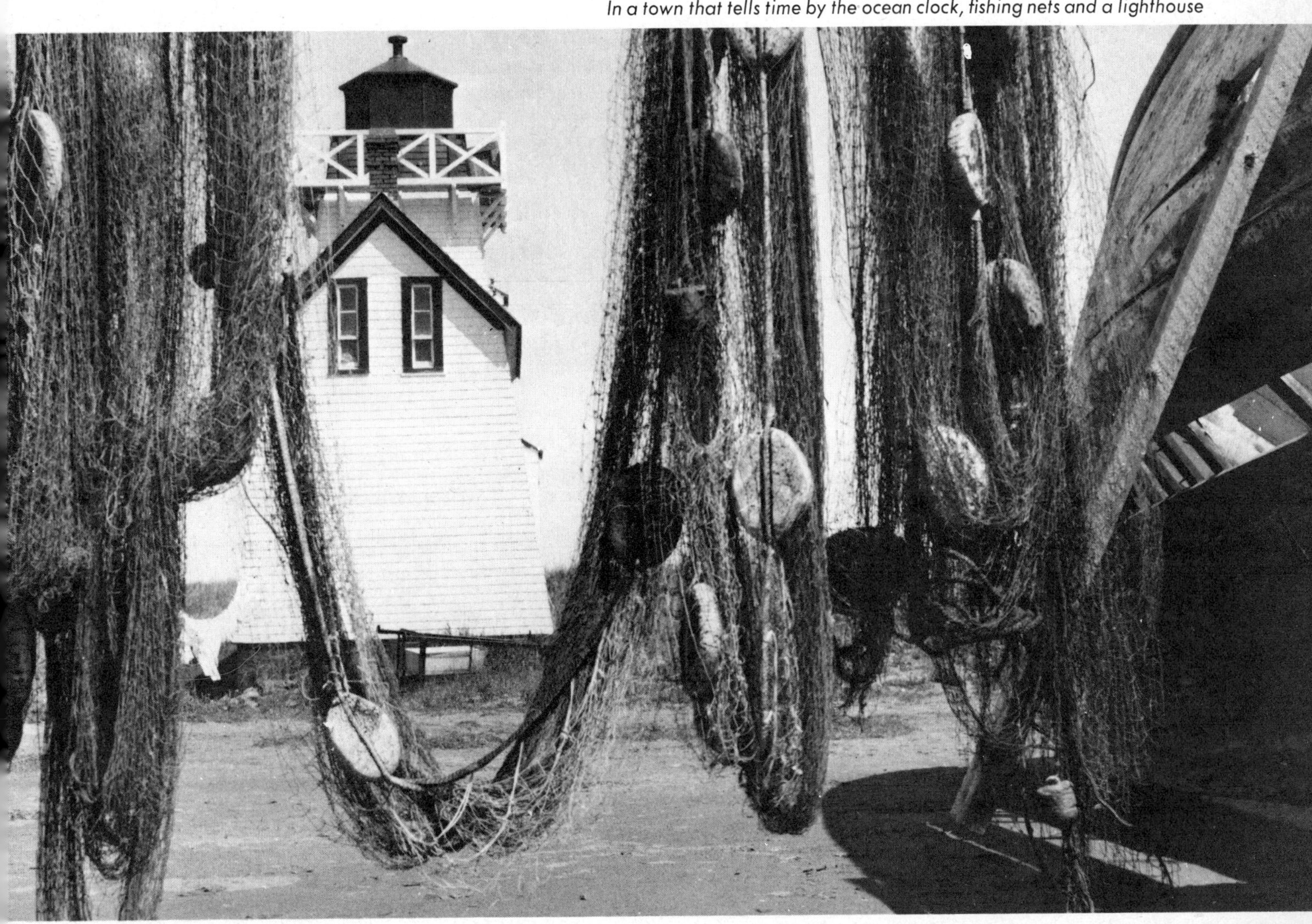

NEW BRUNSWICK

BUCTOUCHE [C-4]* An Acadian fishing town on Highway 11 facing the Northumberland Strait, founded by returning exiles in 1784. Picturesque. The oysters from this bay are exceptional.

CAMPBELLTON [B-3] Salmon fishing on the Restigouche River is world famous. The city is on Highway 11, across the Restigouche estuary from the Gaspé Peninsula. Sugarloaf Provincial Park, south of the city, is an all-season park with camping, picnic areas, and ski-tow rides to the top of Sugarloaf Mountain, 1,000 feet up.

CAMPOBELLO ISLAND [E-2] Once the summer home of President Franklin D. Roosevelt, the island is now an international park. You can camp and picnic here and visit the 34-room Roosevelt "cottage." Campobello Provincial Park looks over the tide-swept shores of Herring Cove, where you also can swim, camp, or play golf on a new, challenging course.

CAPE TORMENTINE [D-5] The car ferry to Prince Edward Island runs from here on a schedule. No reservation needed.

CARAQUET [B-4] Founded in 1757 by Acadians, this is the home of the Atlantic fishing fleets. The Blessing of the Fleet ceremony takes place on a Sunday early in July. Nearby Acadian Historical Village reflects the life style and history of the Acadian people from 1780 to 1880.

DEER ISLAND [E-3] Near Campobello, off the Maine coast, Deer Island is reached by ferry from Letete, New Brunswick, and Eastport, Maine. Good camping weather from June to October. You can hike to see the world's largest whirlpool—the Old Sow—just off the shore. Saltwater fishing is popular.

EDMUNDSTON [B-2] On the Trans-Canada, not far from the Quebec border, Edmundston is important in the pulp and paper industry. Pulp produced here is shipped by pipeline to another plant to be made into paper. The city is also noted for its wood sculptors and hand weavers. West of the city you can visit Jardins Provincial Park and the Cars of Yesteryear Museum. There's good skiing at Mont Farlagne.

FORT BEAUSEJOUR NATIONAL HISTORIC PARK [D-4] The fort, dating back to 1751, is now under restoration. The park is located near Sackville. See National Parks, page 99.

FREDERICTON [D-3] The United Empire Loyalists fled from the United States in 1783 to settle here, and when the colony of New Brunswick was formed, Fredericton became its capital. The Beaverbrook Art Gallery has an impressive collection of 18th- to 20th-century paintings, including some by Winston Churchill. Old Government House, built in 1828 for the colonial governor and recently an RCMP barracks, is now a historical site. Tour Christ Church Cathedral, built in 1853, and see the priceless Audubon bird paintings and a 1783 copy of England's Domesday Book in the Legislative Building. Kings Landing Historical Settlement is 23 miles west of Fredericton on the Trans-Canada, where you get an authentic glimpse of river valley life between 1790 and 1870. Touring the city and nearby areas, you'll find a number of craft studios with weavers, potters, and jewelry makers at work.

FUNDY NATIONAL PARK [D-4] Eight miles of this park front on the Bay of Fundy, where you can watch the highest tides in the world at work. See National Parks, page 99.

HARTLAND [D-2] Driving the Trans-Canada, you cross the St. John River within sight of the world's longest covered bridge—1,282 feet. There are more than 170 covered bridges in the province.

HOPEWELL CAPE [D-4] Near the mouth of the Petitcodiac River, 20 miles south of Moncton on Highway 114, the tides of the Bay of Fundy have carved the Hopewell Rocks—fantastic forms with mysterious caves and caverns carved out of red sandstone. At high tide the rocks look like little islands. At low tide, they are weird top-heavy columns rising from the sea bottom. You can walk out to the rocks at low tide, but be careful. Remember that the Fundy tides come in fast.

KOUCHIBOUGUAC NATIONAL PARK [C-4] A new park on the Northumberland Strait southeast of Chatham with temporary facilities. Access to the grounds is via Highway 117. See National Parks, page 99.

MONCTON [D-4] The tides of the Bay of Fundy, highest in the world, rush up the Petitcodiac River twice a day. Called the Tidal Bore, the water fills the muddy river flats in a few minutes. No longer a spectacular wave because of a causeway above the city, the Bore is still interesting to watch. Five miles north of the city on Highway 126, drive on Magnetic Hill. Put your car in neutral at the bottom of the hill, and in a moment, you coast backward uphill. It's eerie.

ST. ANDREWS [E-2] One of New Brunswick's oldest towns, founded in 1784 with the arrival of the Penobscot Loyalists, it is now a noted summer resort. See historic Greenock Church, the Sunbury Shores Arts and Nature Centre, and the Huntsman Marine Laboratory. Shop for locally crafted woolens of unique design, and attend the summer theater.

SAINT JOHN [E-3] This is New Brunswick's second largest city and dates back to 1631, when it was a French fort and trading post. The world famous Reversing Falls are here at the mouth of the St. John River. The mighty tides of the Bay of Fundy flow in and out of the river through a deep gorge. When the tide rushes in, the water suddenly boils up 11 feet. When the tide goes out, the water reverses and falls 15 feet. Good observation station over the gorge. Plan to see the falls at high and low tides. You can get a good photo of the city from the Carleton Martello Tower, built during the War of 1812. For a city map and a description of its points of interest, see page 83.

SHEDIAC [D-4] The whole east coast is noted for lobsters, and Shediac is the lobster capital. The Lobster Festival, in July, is a good place to gorge yourself. This is a noted resort area with sandy beaches, warm saltwater bathing, and camping.

* Letter and number refer to coordinates on map of Atlantic Provinces.

NEW BRUNSWICK

Population: 623,000
(1971 estimate)
Area: 28,354 Sq. Miles
Capital: Fredericton

Cities and Towns

Bathurst............B-3
Buctouche..........C-4
Campbellton........B-3
Chatham............C-3
Chipman............D-3
Dalhousie...........B-3
Edmundston.........B-2
Fredericton.........D-3
Grand Falls.........C-2
Kedgwick............B-2
Minto...............D-3
Moncton.............D-4
Newcastle...........C-3
Plaster Rock........C-2
Richibucto..........C-4
Saint John..........E-3
St. Léonard.........C-2
St. Quentin.........B-2
St. Stephen.........E-2
Sussex..............D-3

NOVA SCOTIA

Population: 767,000
(1971 estimate)
Area: 21,425 Sq. Miles
Capital: Halifax

Cities and Towns

Advocate Hbr.......E-4
Amherst............D-4
Annapolis Royal....E-3
Antigonish.........D-6
Bass River.........D-5
Bridgetown.........E-3
Bridgewater........E-4
Canso..............D-7
Chester............E-4
Cheticamp..........C-6
Dartmouth..........E-5
Digby..............E-3
Glace Bay..........D-7
Halifax............E-5
Ingonish...........C-7
Kentville..........E-4
Liverpool..........F-4
Lockeport..........F-4
Lunenburg..........E-4
Mahone Bay.........E-4
Middleton..........E-4
New Germany........E-4
New Glasgow........D-5
New Waterford......C-7
North Sydney.......D-7
Parrsboro..........D-4
Pictou.............D-5
Shelburne..........F-3
Springhill.........D-4
Sydney.............D-7
Sydney Mines.......C-7
Tatamagouche.......D-5
Truro..............D-5
Wolfville..........E-4
Yarmouth...........F-3

PRINCE EDWARD ISLAND

Population: 109,000
(1971 estimate)
Area: 2,184 Sq. Miles
Capital: Charlottetown

Cities and Towns

Cardigan...........D-5
Charlottetown......D-5
Georgetown.........D-5
Murray Harbour.....D-5
Port Borden........D-5
St. Peters Bay.....C-5
Summerside.........C-4
Tignish............C-4

NEWFOUNDLAND

Population: 520,000
(1971 estimate)
Area: 156,185 Sq. Miles
Capital: St. John's

Cities and Towns

Bishop's Falls......B-6
Bonavista...........B-7
Corner Brook........B-6
Grand Falls.........B-6
St. John's..........B-7

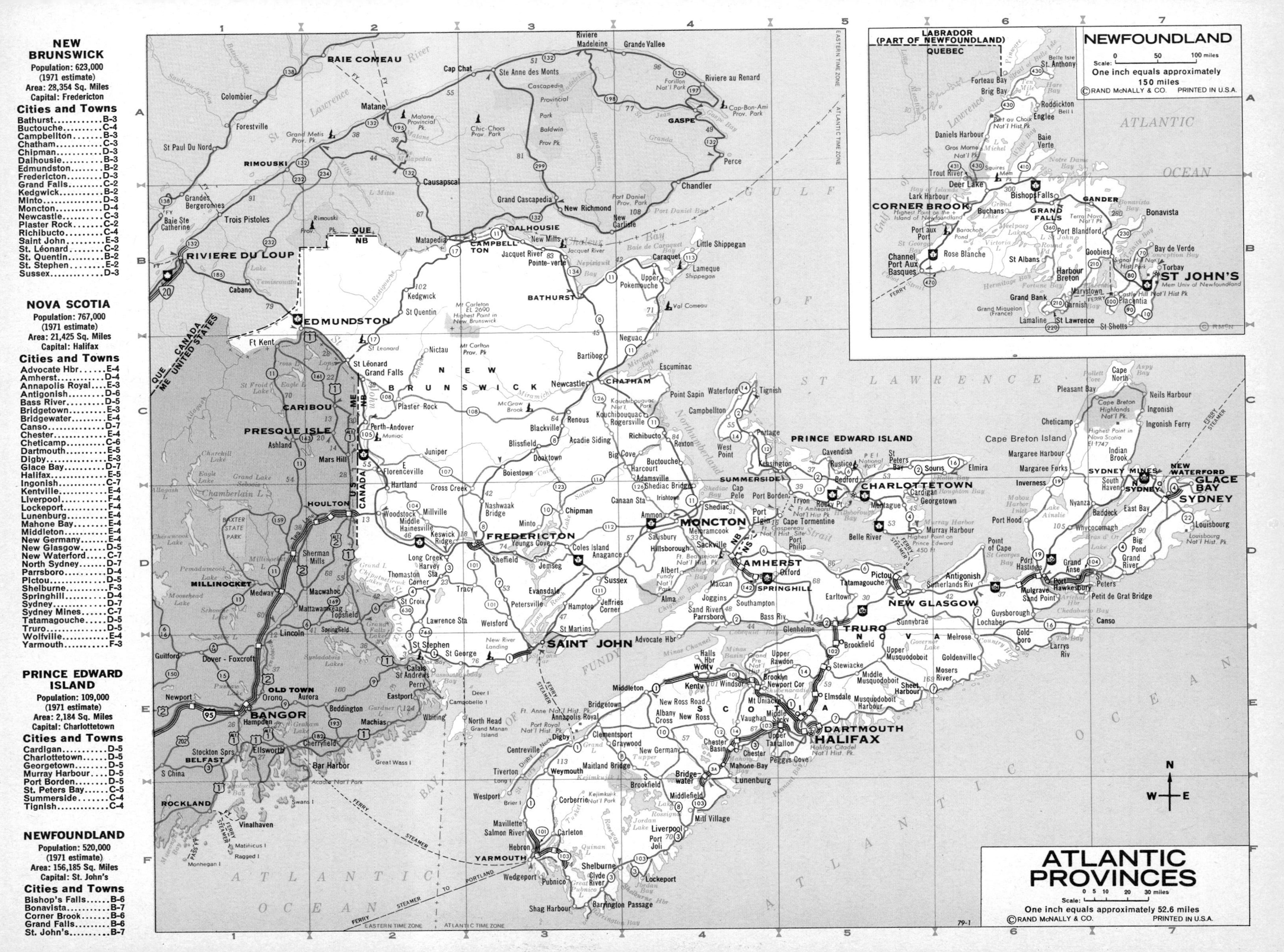

PRINCE EDWARD ISLAND

BURLINGTON [C-5] The Woodleigh Replicas here are an unusual collection of stone and concrete models of famous historical and literary landmarks. You can see such famous places as Glamis Castle, Yorkminster, and Penn Manor House, which was Shakespeare's birthplace.

CAVENDISH [C-5] If you remember reading *Anne of Green Gables*, you'll be pleased to see Green Gables itself here. You can tour the old farmhouse made famous by Lucy Maud Montgomery. Cavendish is located toward the western end of Prince Edward Island National Park.

CHARLOTTETOWN [D-5] Called the birthplace of Canada because the conference that led to the confederation of the colonies was held here in 1864, the city is the capital of Prince Edward Island. It dates back to 1722, when a French post called Port la Joie was located across the harbor. The Charlottetown Festival in July and August features special theater presentations and gallery exhibitions. Old Home Week, in August, is an outstanding fair. The Fathers of Confederation Memorial Center is a complex commemorating the Confederation Conference. It includes a library, art gallery, and 1,000-seat theater. The festival presentations are held here. Visit the beautiful St. Dunstan's Basilica and Province House on Queen Square, a national memorial containing furnishings that were here in 1864 at the Confederation meeting.

FORT AMHERST NATIONAL HISTORIC PARK [D-5] At Rocky Point on Highway 19, this is a park of woods and meadows. It overlooks Charlottetown Harbor and once was the site of an early French settlement, Port la Joie. Good place to picnic.

LADY SLIPPER DRIVE [C-4] A scenic drive around the northwestern end of the island, it begins and ends at Miscouche and takes you along the coast through quaint, out-of-the-way villages. Begin by taking Highway 11 from Miscouche to Union Corner. You'll go through Cape Egmont, Abrams Village, and St. Chrysostom. At Portage, you join Highway 2, the island's main artery, but turn off again at Coleman, to take Highway 14 along the coast to Tignish. Then you can return to Miscouche from Tignish on Highway 2.

MISCOUCHE [C-4] A few miles from Summerside, this is where the island's Acadian Museum is located.

MONTAGUE [D-5] A lovely town, it is located at the point where the Montague River flows into Cardigan Bay. The Garden of the Gulf Museum contains a good collection of relics pertaining to the early history of the island. Moore's Bird Sanctuary, with various species of ducks, Canada geese, and other game birds is worth a visit.

PORT BORDEN [D-5] The big ferry that plies the Northumberland Strait between here and Cape Tormentine, New Brunswick, can carry 190 vehicles and 900 passengers.

PRINCE EDWARD ISLAND NATIONAL PARK [C-5] A beautiful 25-mile stretch of pink-sanded beach on the northern shore of the island. See National Parks, page 102.

SOURIS [C-6] Located near the eastern tip of the island, Souris is a commercial fishing center and a good place to charter a deep-sea fishing boat. The beach here is good for swimming, but then, there is good beach for most of the island's 1,100 miles of coast. Boat trips to the Magdalen Islands, 70 miles north of Prince Edward Island, start here. The beaches on these islands are among the most beautiful in the world. The islands are connected by sand dunes and causeways. Good side trip.

SUMMERSIDE [C-4] Lots of interesting things happen in this well-known summer resort town. For one thing, those fabulous Malpeque oysters come out of nearby Malpeque Bay. For another, this was the headquarters for Canada's silver fox breeding industry. For yet another, the Lobster Carnival held in mid-July keeps things lively for a week.

TIGNISH [C-4] The Tignish Art Foundation offers summer courses to both residents and tourists in Folklore, Conversational French, Art for Children, and other subjects. There also are concerts and motion pictures for children. Tignish is on the northwestern tip of Prince Edward Island.

NOVA SCOTIA

AMHERST [D-4] The gateway to Nova Scotia on the Trans-Canada. The city overlooks the Tantramar Marshes at the extreme end of the Bay of Fundy. You'll see hundreds of dikes used to reclaim land from the sea.

ANNAPOLIS ROYAL [E-3] History runs deep here, back to 1604 when De Monts and Champlain named the place Port Royal. They built the Port Royal Habitation in 1605 and lived in it until July, 1607. Here Champlain organized "The Order of Good Cheer," the first social club in North America, to while away the winter. The Port Royal Habitation was the earliest European settlement of any permanence established in North America north of Florida. It was built two years before Jamestown, three years before Quebec, and 15 years before the Mayflower arrived at Plymouth Rock. The Habitation has been meticulously reconstructed and provides a couple of very interesting hours of sightseeing.

CABOT TRAIL [C-6-7] One of the loveliest tours in all Canada, rivaling that around the Gaspé Peninsula, is the Cabot Trail, which completely circles the northern end of Cape Breton Island. The trail is 184 miles long and can be done in one day—if you insist. But you shouldn't. There is too much beauty to be seen and absorbed. The road passes over timbered mountains and happily settled valleys, and takes you through the magnificent Cape Breton highlands. You'll touch little fishing villages and meet the French on one coast and the Scots on the other. Midway through the trip, you'll go through Cape Breton Highlands National Park. High points on the trail:

Baddeck [D-7] Off the Trans-Canada, on the shores of Bras d'Or Lake, this is where Alexander Graham Bell had his summer home. The Bell museum here is exceptional and worth several hours. The man was one of the geniuses of his century, and the telephone was only a small part of his work. He was also responsible for the first airplane flight in the British Empire. The *Silver Dart*, developed by Bell and his associates, flew here at Baddeck on February 23, 1909.

The Margaree Valley [C-6] Leaving the Trans-Canada, the Cabot Trail cuts across the island through some beautiful scenery in the valley of the Margaree River, a famous salmon stream. Stop to visit the Salmon Museum at Margaree Forks.

The West Coast [C-6] The road follows the coast. You look out into the Gulf of St. Lawrence and pass through a number of pretty Acadian towns—Belle Cote, Terre Noire, Friar's Head, St. Joseph du Moine, and Grand Etang. French is spoken, fish are caught and eaten, and the barns, you will note, are very practically attached to the farmhouses.

Cheticamp [C-6] A snug little fishing harbor renowned for its beautiful hooked rugs and excellent mackerel and cod fishing. The highway passes alongside the tiny harbor, providing a good place to shoot pictures of the colorful fishing boats. Good accommodations and restaurants here.

Cape Breton Highlands National Park [C-7] Three miles north of Cheticamp you enter the park and climb into the highlands. The drive, which has been pretty, now becomes spectacular —mountains, valleys, sweeping views of the sea and waves pounding against rocky promontories. At Pleasant Bay, the road turns inland to cross the island.

Cape North [C-7] There's an interesting side trip to be made from here to Bay St. Lawrence, 10 miles north. You'll see Cabot's Landing and the fishing village at Bay St. Lawrence, where Gaelic is spoken.

South Harbor [C-7] This is a lovely side trip via the dirt road from South Harbor to Neils Harbor past White Point. Slow and narrow, but scenic and very memorable.

East Coast [C-7] Here is Scotland revisited. Just look at the names on the mailboxes or stop to talk to the residents. There are fine accommodations and beaches at Ingonish. A chair lift near Ingonish will take you up for a grand view. Lovely little villages down the coast include Breton Cove and Skir Dhu.

Indian Brook [C-7] Just south of this village, you make a decision. You can proceed on Highway 312 to the ferry and cross St. Anns Bay to Englishtown, on your way to Sydney. Or you can stay on the Cabot Trail and circle the bay, a very beautiful drive. At South Gut St. Anns you visit Gaelic College. The summer school here teaches Gaelic, piping, and Highland folk and clan lore. You might be in time for a pipe concert. This is the home of the colorful Gaelic Mod each August, with piping, dancing, and Scottish games. Passing St. Anns Bay, ponder the unbelievable fact that a bluefin tuna weighing 977 pounds was taken on a rod and line here in 1950.

Iona Village [C-7] The Iona Highland Village here re-creates several historical periods, from the first landing of the Scottish settlers to 1900. Overlooks the Grand Narrows.

CAPE BRETON HIGHLANDS NATIONAL PARK [C-7] A natural wonderland on the northern end of Cape Breton Island. See National Parks, page 100.

CHESTER [E-4] A summer resort area on Mahone Bay originally settled in 1759 by people from Massachusetts. The bay is a famous boating paradise, with yacht races twice a week and tiny sailboats, outboards, and self-paddling sea cycles everywhere. Oak Island, across the bay, is famous as a possible location of Captain Kidd's buried treasure. Men have been looking for it since 1796. You might take the ferry to Tancook Island for a visit to a picturesque, unspoiled area. Some of the local people open their homes and serve meals to visitors.

DIGBY [E-3] Overlooking the Annapolis Basin, Digby is internationally famous for the delicious scallops brought in by its scallop fleet, the world's largest. During the summer months a ferry connects Digby with Saint John, New Brunswick.

GLACE BAY [D-7] Visit the Glace Bay Miner's Museum here, and go underground to the workings.

GRAND PRE [E-4] Ten miles east of Kentville in the Annapolis Valley, this was the major area of expulsion of the Acadians in 1755. Six thousand were deported for refusing to swear allegiance to England. One group settled in Louisiana, west of New Orleans. Longfellow's poem *Evangeline* commemorates the event. Two thousand Acadians eventually made their way back to Nova Scotia. Grand Pre National Historic Park (see National Parks, page 100) has an Acadian museum.

HALIFAX [E-5] The capital of Nova Scotia, with one of the finest harbors in the world, Halifax has been an important naval base since 1749. For a city map, see pages 83 and 84.

KEJIMKUJIK NATIONAL PARK [F-3] Still under development, this is one of Canada's newest national parks. You pronounce it "Kedge-McCoodge-ick." See National Parks, page 101.

LUNENBURG [E-4] You meet a good many Frenchmen and Scotsmen in Nova Scotia, but the Germans settled here, too. Lunenburg was founded by Huguenots and Palatine Germans. This is one of the greatest fishing ports on the continent, and home of the famous racing schooner *Bluenose*, whose picture you find on the Canadian dime. Visit the Lunenburg Sea Products Company to see what happens to fish from the trawler to the can. The Lunenburg Fisheries Museum houses the *Bluenose's* trophies and a good display of items from sailing days.

PARRSBORO [D-4] South of Amherst on the Bay of Fundy, this is a good place for rockhounds. When the sea retreats at low tide, caves and beaches are exposed where you can find amethysts, agates, and other gemstones. The harbor here is completely emptied each day by the tide, leaving giant ocean-going ships high and dry at their docks.

PEGGY'S COVE [E-5] It is difficult to single out one village in Nova Scotia as being the *most* picturesque, but Peggy's Cove possibly should have that honor. It is one of the most painted and photographed seaside villages in North America. It is now being preserved by the Nova Scotia government.

PICTOU [D-5] The ferry service to Prince Edward Island operates from Caribou, about 5 miles from this port town. Pictou is noted as one of the largest live-lobster producing places in the world, and they have a big Lobster Carnival in July. Boat service to the Magdalen Islands also originates here.

PUGWASH [D-4] The Highland clans gather here on the first of July each year. Thousands of people from all over the continent attend this gala, which includes a parade, massed pipe bands, highland dancing, and other attractions.

SYDNEY [D-7] This is the commercial capital of Cape Breton Island and a coal and steel center. The mines in this vicinity extend northward under the Atlantic for up to 4 miles. You'll see the ships of the world in Sydney Harbor. Swim and fish in Bras d'Or Lake, and visit St. George's Church, built in 1786. The church has a chair from Nelson's *Victory*.

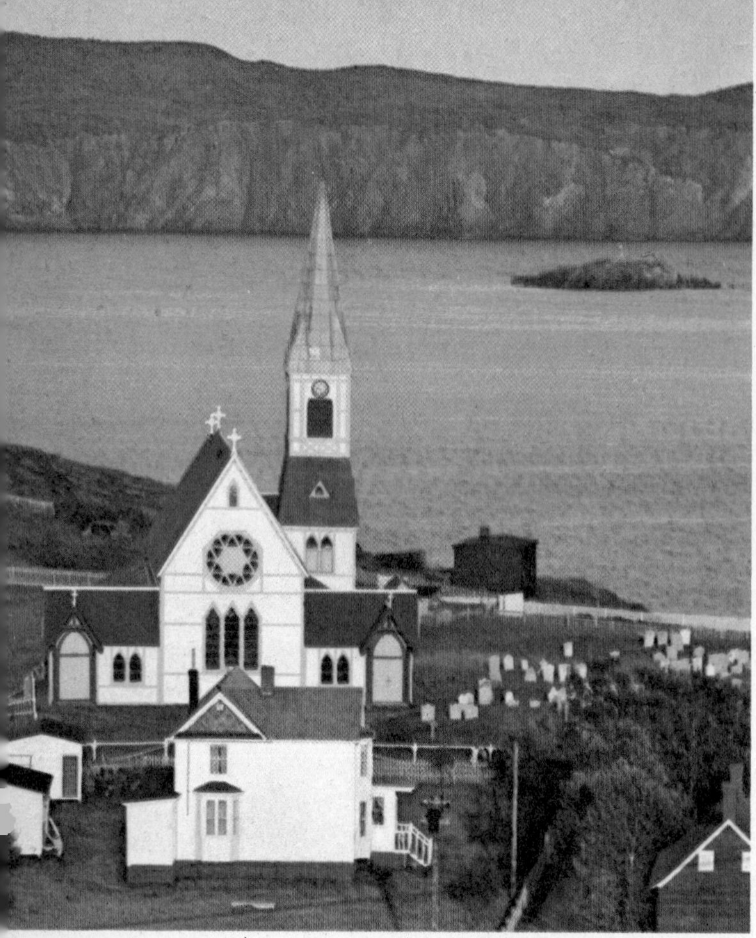

Bonavista Bay, Newfoundland

TRURO [D-5] The town sits in the midst of an important dairy area. See the tidal bore of the Salmon River twice a day, when the rising tides of the Bay of Fundy force a wall of water up the river. Also explore 1,000-acre Victoria Park, graced with two waterfalls and plenty of tent-camping and trailer facilities.

YARMOUTH [F-3] The ferry from Bar Harbor, Maine, docks in this summer resort town on the southwestern tip of Nova Scotia. Visit the Killam Library, where a Norse rune stone is displayed, and the Fireman's Museum with its show of old-time fire equipment. If you are looking for the tartan of your clan or want to buy fine woolen sweaters, while in Yarmouth visit Bonda Textiles, where they weave the tartans, or Gateway Factory Outlet, makers of sweaters. You'll find many quaint villages along the southern shore of the province if you take Highway 3 from here. Shag Harbour offers a magnificent view of famous Cape Sable Island to which you can drive over a 4,000-foot causeway.

NEWFOUNDLAND

BAY DE VERDE [B-7] For an interesting trip through scenic fishing villages and a good look at the Newfoundland coast, follow Highway 70 out of St. John's through Topsail, Holyrood, and other villages. The road circles Conception Bay and brings you to Bay de Verde, a picturesque fishing village on the tip of the Avalon Peninsula. Return from Bay de Verde on Highway 80, along the shore of Trinity Bay.

CORNER BROOK [B-6] Lots of fine salmon fishing and big game hunting near here. Corner Brook is Newfoundland's second largest city and the center of its paper industry.

DEER LAKE [B-6] Surrounded by a magnificent forest, Deer Lake is a hunting headquarters. It's on the Trans-Canada, and if you'd like to visit the Viking village unearthed at L'Anse au Meadow in 1963, turn off that highway here, taking Highway 431 to Highway 430, which goes all the way to the northern tip of the island—a distance of 275 miles over good gravel surface. Along the way, you'll pass through St. Pauls Inlet, where there is fine moose hunting; Portland Creek, noted for excellent sport fishing; and River of Ponds, where there is a provincial campground. River of Ponds is 110 miles from Deer Lake. At Port au Choix, 2 miles off the main road, is an Indian burial ground discovered only a few years ago. Rated as one of the most important archeological finds in North America, this burial ground dates back to 2340 B.C. At L'Anse au Meadow you will find the foundations of 11 buildings dating to around A.D. 1000. Materials found in the area prove that this was a settlement of the Vikings and may possibly have been the long-sought Vinland. Shelters have been erected to protect the excavations. Stand near the greathouse, look out over the bay, and imagine a dragon-prowed boat making for the beach. You'll feel like a Viking yourself.

GANDER [B-7] Before the development of the jet, Gander was the jumping-off point for all Canadian and United States flights bound for Europe. First selected as a transatlantic air base in 1935, the facility was enlarged in World War II and expanded into an International Air Terminal in the 1950s.

GROS MORNE NATIONAL PARK [B-6] Located 50 miles northwest of Cornerbrook, this 750-square-mile area is one of the nation's newest parks. See National Parks, page 99.

HAPPY ADVENTURE [B-7] A town with one of the most inviting names in all Canada. It's a pretty place with a nice beach, a place to change clothes, picnic tables, and fireplaces. The shallow water is safe for children. You'll see a lobster holding pool near here, and during the season you can buy them live or cooked.

LEWISPORTE [B-6] If you want to hunt the bluefin tuna, this is the place to start. An average bluefin will run something over 400 pounds, with line busters hitting the 800 mark. The world's record is 1,065 pounds. This town, on Highway 340 north of the Trans-Canada, faces out into Notre Dame Bay.

PLACENTIA [B-7] The French made a number of efforts to capture St. John's during the 17th century and built a fort here in 1662 to serve as a base for their operations. Remains of the fort can still be seen. Castle Hill, overlooking the town, is a national historic site.

ST. ANTHONY [A-6] At the northern end of the island, this is the headquarters of the Grenfell Mission. Dr. Wilfred Grenfell, a dedicated English doctor, served on the Labrador coast in 1892 and spent the rest of his life raising money for hospitals to provide medical service for the scattered population of northern Newfoundland and Labrador.

ST. JOHN'S [B-7] This oldest of North American cities is Newfoundland's capital and a major port. For a map of the city and descriptions of its points of interest, see pages 83 and 85.

TERRA NOVA NATIONAL PARK [B-7] The Trans-Canada cuts through this national park on the shores of Bonavista Bay. You may be lucky and spot a cruising school of pilot whales while you're here. See National Parks, page 100.

SAINT JOHN

This is a city of firsts. It was Canada's first incorporated city, and Canada's first salaried police force was organized here. Here was the nation's first chartered bank, her first fire insurance company, YWCA, and the first penny newspaper. Though its roots go back to a French fort built here in 1631, the city didn't come into being until 1784, after 4,200 New England Loyalists sought a new land in which to live after the Revolutionary War in the United States. Saint John is on a thumb of land stuck into the mouth of Saint John Harbor, which opens into the Bay of Fundy. The high and fast tides of Fundy rush through the harbor to create that remarkable phenomenon, the Reversing Falls at the mouth of the St. John River. This is a manufacturing center, the commercial and industrial metropolis of New Brunswick. Since the port is open all year, it is a major shipping area.

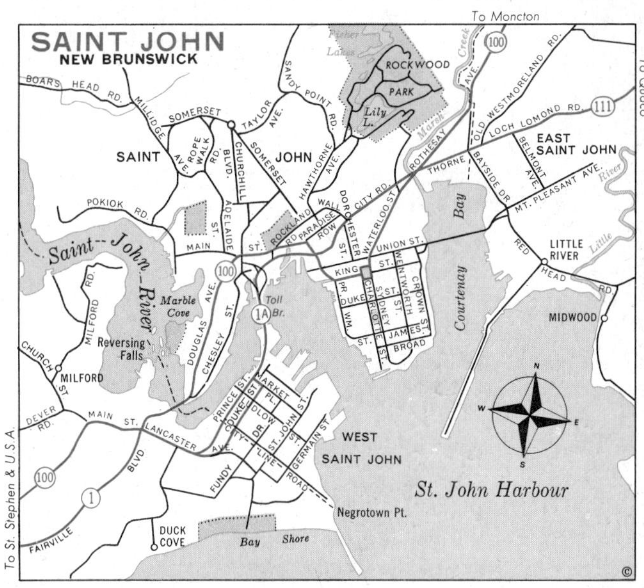

Points of Interest

FERRY SERVICE. Daily service is provided between Saint John and Digby, Nova Scotia, across the Bay of Fundy.

LOYALIST BURIAL GROUND. This old cemetery in the center of the city was in use from 1783 to 1848. Here lie the bones of many of the city's original settlers. The burial ground is at Sydney and King streets.

LOYALIST HOUSE. Now furnished as it was in the 1800s, Loyalist House was built in 1810. It has been completely restored. Located at Germain and Union streets.

MARTELLO TOWER. A national historic site, this round tower followed a design which originated in Europe. It was built to defend the city during the War of 1812, but was never involved in a battle. You can get a fine view of the city and the harbor from its top.

NEW BRUNSWICK MUSEUM. This was Canada's first public museum—another of those Saint John firsts—and features a number of galleries, each with a different kind of display. In the Marine Gallery, for example, are shown supplies and equipment taken from a ship which sank off Deer Island more than 180 years ago. In the Children's Museum, you'll see a fine collection of antique dolls and toys of yesteryear. The Boardman collection of mounted birds and animals is in another gallery, while examples of arts and crafts and fine arts are in the Decorative Arts Gallery. There is more, enough to keep a whole family busy for a full afternoon. Of special interest are the many superb ship models, especially models of old ships that were built in New Brunswick. The museum is on Douglas Avenue. Small admission fee.

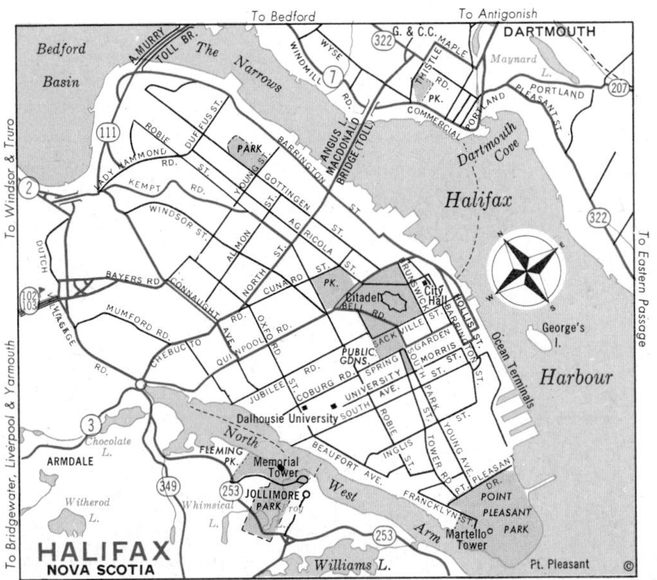

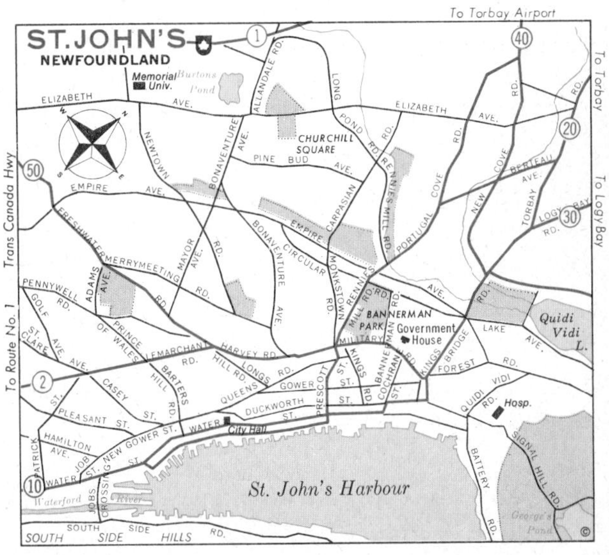

OLD CITY MARKET. The farmers from the area display their produce in open stalls. You'll see flowers, rugs, knitted goods, and other products, including handcrafted baskets brought to the market by Indians. The market is closed on Friday and Sunday, but open all day the rest of the week. It is located between Charlotte and Germain streets in the heart of the city.

REVERSING FALLS RAPIDS. The river recedes into the ocean here at low tide, then rushes upstream with the incoming tide, boiling through the bottom of a 450-foot-deep gorge. There is a viewing deck, with restaurant facilities, that provides the best view of the falls, and you should see them at both high and low tides, and for those few minutes in between, when the water is calm.

ROCKWOOD PARK. A huge natural playground for the city. In these 2,200 acres there are nature trails, swimming, fishing, and boating. Two golf courses are nearby.

SAINT JOHN DRY DOCK. There aren't many places where you can get a good look at a working dry dock. This is one of them. The Saint John Dry Dock is one of the largest in the world. You step to a viewing platform and listen to a recording that tells you about the work in progress at the moment. The description is informative and interesting. Very unusual tourist attraction.

TRINITY CHURCH. This historical church was completed in 1791, destroyed by fire in 1877, and then completely rebuilt in 1880. Among other things, it contains a replica of the Royal Coat of Arms of King George I, who reigned from 1714 to 1727.

HALIFAX

There is no more colorful city in the Atlantic Provinces than Halifax, an absolutely perfect blend of nearly 225 years of life on the seacoast. On the one hand, Halifax is glass and steel and universities and tomorrow. On the other, it is the stone Citadel and Old Dutch Church and old lighthouses and the booming Noon Gun. The contrast is exciting and delightful. Halifax is the capital of Nova Scotia, the largest city in the Atlantic Provinces, and one of the world's great ports. The huge complex of Bedford Basin and the harbor, over 16 miles long, can—and has—housed entire navies. Lord Cornwallis established Halifax in 1749, to defend Britain's North American territory, and it has played a major role in every Canadian war since that time.

In addition to all its other attributes, Halifax is the home of 11 universities and colleges. While the city's business is the sea—shipping, fishing, naval warfare—it is certainly no picturesque fishing village. It is as up to date and modern as tomorrow.

Incidentally, after you arrive here, you might remember that a citizen of Halifax is a Haligonian.

BEDFORD BASIN. This is the spacious inner basin connected to Halifax Harbor. The MacKay Bridge across the mouth of the basin was opened in 1970. The MacDonald Bridge, across the harbor, is the second longest suspension bridge in the British Commonwealth.

HALIFAX CITADEL NATIONAL HISTORIC PARK. There were three other forts on this site before the present star-shaped stone bastion was begun in 1828. A driveway encircles the top of the fort and the view from there is magnificent. For other details, see National Parks, page 100.

MEMORIAL TOWER. This tower, in Fleming Park across the Northwest Arm on the "mainland," commemorates the first parliamentary government in Canada, in Halifax in 1758. You'll get a good picture of the Northwest Arm and the entire peninsula from here.

NOVA SCOTIA MUSEUM. Has good displays related to the natural history and settlement of the province.

OLD DUTCH CHURCH. German settlers of Lutheran persuasion erected this tiny church (only 20 by 20 feet) in 1756—the first Lutheran church in Canada. It is located on Brunswick Street, and you must contact the caretaker if you wish to visit it.

POINT PLEASANT PARK. No cars are permitted to drive in this 186-acre park on the tip of the peninsula. You can follow nature trails, swim at a supervised saltwater beach, or explore the historic sites such as the Prince of Wales Martello Tower, built in 1796.

PROVINCE HOUSE. This is a beautiful example of Georgian architecture, completed in 1818. It is the oldest legislative assembly building in use in Canada. You can see valuable portraits and historic relics on display here. One tablet commemorates the first printing press in British North America, which printed Canada's first newspaper, *The Halifax Gazette*, on March 23, 1752.

PUBLIC GARDENS. There is something pleasant about listening to a summer concert in the park, with the band ensconced in a genuine band shell. It happens frequently in this park. The band shell was built in 1887, to commemorate Queen Victoria's Golden Jubilee. The park has 18 acres of manicured gardens and tree-shaded walks.

ST. PAUL'S CHURCH. This church on Barrington Street is the oldest Protestant church in Canada. The cemetery is three blocks south of the church, and in it are graves of some of the town's founders. The interior of the church has an interesting display. The building is the oldest in Halifax, built with timbers from Boston.

SCOTIA SQUARE. Nineteen acres of rubble and rock in downtown Halifax have been transformed into a shopping, living, and business complex.

THE NORTHWEST ARM. This is the extension of the harbor along the west side of the city. Tour either side; each is lined with summer homes, boating and bathing clubs. The water is usually dotted with pleasure craft.

THE OLD TOWN CLOCK. Located just below the Citadel and not far from the new Scotia Square, this old timepiece was erected in 1803 by Prince Edward, Duke of Kent.

YORK REDOUBT NATIONAL HISTORIC SITE. On Highway 253, 8 miles south of the city, this fort to guard the sea approaches to Halifax Harbor was begun in 1790, but never actually completed until 1945. Drive to the fort, or take a bus from downtown Halifax.

View from The Narrows, looking into St. John's Harbor with the city rising behind it

ST. JOHN'S

The eastern end of the Trans-Canada is here in this oldest of North American cities. Marconi received the first overseas wireless message on Signal Hill in 1901, and Alcock and Brown began the first successful transatlantic flight here in 1919. During World War II the great convoys to Europe formed in this harbor before pushing out into the cold and submarine-infested North Atlantic. The Portuguese fishing fleet, accompanied by its great white mother ship, headquarters in St. John's while fishing on the Grand Banks.

There aren't as many old buildings here as you might expect in a city of these venerable years, because St. John's has been swept by a number of disastrous fires during its history. The outstanding spot for visitors is Signal Hill, a place you should visit both in the daytime and after dark. From here, the city lays out below you like a huge map, and you can watch the ships enter and leave the harbor through The Narrows, the channel connecting the harbor with the Atlantic.

ANGLICAN CATHEDRAL. The present building, an excellent example of ecclesiastical Gothic architecture, dates to 1905. It was designed by Sir Gilbert Scott. The original church was begun in 1816, but was destroyed by fire in 1842. In the Chapter House, there is a gold communion service presented by King William IV. (This William died in 1837 and left no heirs to the throne, so his niece Victoria became Queen, ushering in the Victorian Age and the longest reign in English history.)

BASILICA OF ST. JOHN THE BAPTIST. This great church can accommodate up to 8,000 worshipers. It dates back to 1841. Built in the shape of a cross, the basilica is on Harvey Road.

BOWRING PARK. If you are a stamp collector, this park will have a special meaning for you. Here you'll see the statue of The Fighting Newfoundlander and also that of the Caribou, both of which you'll recognize from the Newfoundland stamps in your collection. Both are World War I memorials. Also in the park is a statue of Peter Pan. You can swim and boat here, and there are picnic facilities and tennis courts. The drive through the park is pretty.

CITY HALL. A new and very modern building in sharp contrast to the Victorian structures in the vicinity. Stroll through it to see the architecture, the displays, and the governmental facilities.

CONFEDERATION BUILDING. This is the capital building of the province. There's a museum of naval and military history here, and on the 11th floor, a public observation room from which you can get a fine view of the city. You can also visit the Colonial Building, which was the seat of government until 1960, and now houses the provincial archives.

NEWFOUNDLAND MUSEUM. The Beothucks were Indians who inhabited the island up to the time of the arrival of the white man. The museum houses a display of relics of this extinct tribe and other historic items, including the original plans for the French fort at Placentia. Highlights of Newfoundland are depicted in a series of paintings and tableaux. Located on Duckworth Street.

OLD GARRISON CHURCH. Built first as a military chapel, this wooden church constructed in 1836 still displays the Hanovarian coat of arms. Located on Cavendish Square.

QUIDI VIDI BATTERY. This battery, built by the British in 1762 to guard the entrance from the sea to Quidi Vidi Lake, has been restored to the way it was in 1812. When the sea is rough, the battery is a good place to see the waves pounding on the rocks beneath the battery wall.

SIGNAL HILL NATIONAL HISTORIC PARK. Cabot tower, built in 1897 to commemorate the 400th anniversary of John Cabot's landfall, is perched on top of this 600-foot hill. On your way up the hill (via Duckworth Street) you'll pass an Interpretation Center. Stop in to see the audiovisual displays. There is also a good display of maritime history in the tower. See National Parks, page 100.

Special Events

ST. JOHN'S REGATTA. Held the first Wednesday in August each year on Quidi Vidi Lake, it is probably the oldest organized sporting event in North America, dating back to 1828.

WILDERNESS

Sturdy cruise boat on the Yukon River—dwarfed by the majesty of the wilderness

YUKON NORTHWEST TERRITORIES

SPREAD OUT ACROSS THE TOP OF CANADA, IN A SWEEP FROM THE ATLANTIC TO THE PACIFIC, IS HER GREAT BARREN WILDERNESS. MUCH OF THE TERRITORY HERE, EXTENDING UP BEYOND THE ARCTIC CIRCLE TO A POINT WITHIN 500 MILES OF THE NORTH POLE, IS UNEXPLORED AND EVEN UNMAPPED. THE NORTHWEST TERRITORIES AND THE YUKON TOGETHER ENCOMPASS MORE THAN 1½ MILLION SQUARE MILES OF LAND, YET THE POPULATION OF BOTH TOTALS LESS THAN 48,000 SOULS. MORE PEOPLE THAN THAT OFTEN CROWD INTO A SINGLE BIG LEAGUE BASEBALL PARK ON A PLEASANT SUNDAY AFTERNOON.

It is only after you have seen all these empty miles on a map that you can begin to believe that Canada is the second largest nation in the world. Like the iceberg, much of Canada is unseen.

This, of course, is a land of the midnight sun, where sunlight lasts 20 hours and longer in the summer, and where they have such extravaganzas as 24-hour golf marathons, simply because there is enough light to play that long.

This, too, is a land where autumn evenings are made brilliant by the aurora borealis. It is divided by the tree line, above which is a treeless windswept tundra, much of it muskeg bog. Most of the eastern portion of the Northwest Territories is north of the tree line, while in the Yukon only the northern tip, on the shore of the Arctic Ocean, is barren.

Here, too, you find the permafrost—the name given to ground that is permanently frozen. Test drillings have shown that the ground is frozen in some spots to a depth of 700 feet. When the permafrost melts during an unseasonably warm spell, it becomes marshy and soft and anything resting on it settles and sinks. Paved roads laid on permafrost tend to heave, crack, and break up, and engineers designing pipelines to carry oil south from the fields on the Arctic Circle are struggling with the problem of what to do about this phenomenon.

Most of the land of the Northwest Territories is a lonely rocky plateau, the scarred track of the glacier, punctuated by unnumbered and unnamed lakes and rivers. The western district is more hospitable.

The Yukon Territory, on the other hand, straddles the northern end of the Rocky Mountain chain, a land of marching mountains interspersed with interesting, pleasant valleys. Within the territory is Canada's highest peak, Mount Logan, a glacier-ribbed giant reaching up 19,850 feet. This is a rich area, with untapped reserves of oil, gold, asbestos, and copper and perhaps more. It has great hydroelectric potential because of its rushing rivers.

The Yukon, on the average, isn't as cold as the northern parts of the Northwest Territories—but it has the distinction, nonetheless, of having the coldest spot in Canada, at Snag, in the central part of the territory, where the all-time record of 81° below zero was established. Even the huskies found that night a bit chilly.

The main water highway of the wilderness is the Mackenzie River, a broad band of water that rises at the western end of Great Slave Lake and runs 1,120 miles northward to empty into the Arctic Ocean. Sir Alexander Mackenzie, when only 25, explored the whole length of this river. The year was 1789, and the immediate result of his trip was a blossoming of the fur trade along the river.

Four years later, Mackenzie became the first man to completely cross the North American continent, when he traveled from a trading post on the Peace River to the Pacific Ocean, passing through what is now Tweedsmuir Provincial Park on the last leg of his journey. Mackenzie's journal, published in 1801, had much to do with the development of northwestern Canada.

WILDERNESS TRAVEL

Travel in the wilderness isn't too easy, chiefly because there just aren't very many roads. You can drive up the Alaska Highway from Dawson Creek, British Columbia—a giant of a trip and one you'll never regret making. Or you can take the luxury route by boarding a sumptuous car ferry at Kelsey Bay on Vancouver Island, disembarking at Haines, and driving north on the Haines Highway. If you wish, you can take the ferry on to Skagway. At Skagway, you and your automobile can board the train to Whitehorse. Once in Whitehorse you can get back on an auto route and take your pick of roads in the wilderness area. You also can take Highway 35, the Mackenzie Route, north from Peace River, Alberta. This will bring you to Great Slave Lake and the gold capital of Canada, Yellowknife. Finally, you can ride the train from The Pas, Manitoba, to Churchill, Manitoba's seaport on the shores of Hudson Bay. Incidentally, twice a year, the Canadian National Railway starts excursion trains at Winnipeg for the run through The Pas to Churchill.

Access to most of the wilderness is via fly-in on small planes. The majority of hunting and fishing parties meet in cities at the northern edge of the provinces to make such flights. Equipped with floats, there is almost no place these little birds can't go. They are flown by those legendary bush pilots, who know every tree and lake of these vast areas by its first name.

The wilderness lands aren't typical vacation spots, and getting to them even over good roads is a bit arduous. But a trip of this kind promises you a holiday that is unique and will provide you with dinnertime conversation material for the rest of your life. A casually dropped line like, "That reminds me of a night in Yellowknife . . ." is guaranteed to immediately put all the other travel talkers out of business for the evening.

A trip to the wilderness is heartily recommended for the jaded traveler who is tired of crowds and touristy spots and commercial attractions. There are interesting things to do and see in wonderful places like Yellowknife, Whitehorse, and Dawson City, and you won't regret the time spent in them—but most of the charm and delight of your trip will come from long and lonesome drives through some of the greatest unspoiled land remaining on the face of the earth.

THE YUKON

DAWSON CITY [D-2]* On August 17, 1896, George Carmack and two Indian companions, "Skookum" Jim and "Tagish" Charlie, made the first gold strike on Bonanza Creek, a tributary of the Klondike River. It took five months for news to reach the outside world and another seven months for the proof to be seen. The world believed the news when miners from Dawson arrived in Portland carrying $2 million in gold. Within a year, 60,000 men had streamed northward to make the gold rush of 1898. The Dawson settlement arose at the confluence of the Yukon and Klondike rivers, and by the end of the summer of '98, its population was more than 25,000. Within five years, the Klondike creeks had given up $104 million in gold. Today you can visit buildings which have survived since the gold rush days—The Red Feather Saloon, Madam Tremblay's, the Flora Dora, and the cabin occupied by poet Robert W. Service. The stern-wheeler, S.S. *Keno*, which transported prospectors upriver to their claims, has been beached and restored, and is now a museum and national historic site, as is the Palace Grand Theater, which opened in 1899 and operated until the town dwindled along with the vanishing gold supply. Today during the summer months you can see "Gaslight Follies" on the Palace's grand old stage. At Service's cabin, you will meet his ghost who gives readings of his poetry. And you can pan for gold yourself along Bonanza and El Dorado creeks. There is a fine view of the city from the top of the Midnight Dome, 3,000 feet above sea level. Discovery Day calls for a celebration each August. Take a two-hour river cruise on the *Yukon Lou* at 10 am or 3 pm any day from June 1 to September 15.

Eskimo carvings relate to life in the Arctic

HAINES JUNCTION [D-3] Located in the Shakwak Valley of the St. Elias Mountains, a range fathering North America's highest peaks. Here the Alaska Highway intersects with the Haines Highway, which leads south to the city of Haines at the head of the Lynn Canal. This is an arm of the sea up which the auto service ferries from Alaska and British Columbia sail. Thus you can drive to Whitehorse and Haines Junction on the Alaska Highway, then return to Haines on the Haines Highway, and sail aboard a ferry back to Vancouver Island. The Alaska Highway was dedicated here in 1942. If you'd like to see where the picture on the Canadian $5 bill originated, take the side trip from Haines to Otter Falls.

KLUANE NATIONAL PARK [D-3] A new national park in the southwest corner of Yukon Territory covering 8,500 square miles. See National Parks, page 103.

WATSON LAKE [F-3] Back in 1942, when they were building the Alaska Highway to connect the U.S. and Alaska, workers put up signs showing the number of miles from their home cities to Watson Lake. Tourists have carried on the tradition, and today the city's milepost collection is an outstanding attraction. Watson Lake is Mile 635 on the Alaska Highway.

WHITEHORSE [E-3] You remember Sam McGee, the prospector who hadn't been warm since he left Tennessee, celebrated in Robert W. Service's poem, *The Cremation of Sam McGee*. McGee's cabin is here for you to visit. And you can see Lake Lebarge, on the marge of which it all took place. Whitehorse is a thriving metropolis, capital of the Yukon Territory and headquarters for the Royal Canadian Mounted Police. Whitehorse is located at Mile 914 on the Alaska Highway. The MacBride Museum has an outstanding gold rush display, including a giant 2,600-pound copper nugget. The Old Log Church, now a museum of Anglican church history, is a pioneer-type skyscraper—being three stories tall. A trip on the Yukon River through the turbulent Miles Canyon on the M.V. *Schwatka* is a good way to spend an afternoon. The canyon, 6 miles south of Whitehorse, was one of the worst hazards on the Trail of '98. Now you can walk a suspension bridge over it to take photographs, and walk a trail following the route of the wooden-railed tramway that was used to haul miner's supplies by horse and wagon around the canyon. Cruises depart at 1:30 each afternoon, take three hours, and are scheduled June through August. Adult fare is $8. Another of those railway trips you shouldn't miss runs between Skagway and Whitehorse. A narrow-gauge line built in 1899, the White Pass and Yukon Railway, follows the original White Pass Trail of '98—the route followed by prospectors who came to Skagway by boat and lit out for the goldfields overland. In addition to its historic value, this rail jaunt is one of the most spectacular from the standpoint of scenery. Trains leave Whitehorse each morning at 8 am and arrive at Skagway at 4:10 pm. Lunch is served at Bennett. A second train departs Skagway each day at 10 am, carrying passengers who have come to the city via ferry up the Inner Passage from Kelsey Bay, and reaches Whitehorse at 3:30 pm. Adult one-way fare is $29, children under 12 half fare. The train can also transport your car, if you choose. The package fare, including the car, two persons and meals, is

* Letter and number refer to coordinates on map of Yukon and Northwest Territories, page 91.

$125. If you are a mountain climber looking for a peak that has yet to be climbed, fly from here to the St. Elias range in the southwestern corner of the territory. It was in this area that the late Senator Robert Kennedy scaled a 13,900-foot peak and named it in honor of his brother, President John F. Kennedy. There are a good many peaks here which have yet to feel the crunch of a climber's boot. Whitehorse sits beside the cold, cold Yukon River—in which you won't swim—and offers almost unending summer days with pleasant temperatures. It is ready to entertain you with no less than 21 hotels, nine smart restaurants, 12 churches, one theater, four cocktail lounges, five cabarets, and five taverns—in addition to two newspapers, two radio stations, and two television stations.

NORTHWEST TERRITORIES

ALEXANDRA AND LOUISE FALLS [H-3] As you travel the Mackenzie Highway north from Alberta you cross into the Northwest Territories at the 60th parallel. At the border you'll find an information center and a campground. Forty-five miles north of the border as you travel close to the Hay River, you come to Alexandra Falls, where the river falls 109 feet. A mile and a half farther downstream, at Louise Falls, the river drops another 46 feet in a series of steps on its way to Great Slave Lake. Below this point, there are 3 miles of magnificent white-water rapids in a gorge 170 feet high that extends downstream for 5 miles. There is a campground adjacent to the river, called Escarpment Creek campground.

BAFFIN ISLAND NATIONAL PARK A new national park located on Baffin Island, it is the first such park to be located above the Arctic Circle. See National Parks, page 100.

FORT NORMAN [F-2] When Alexander Mackenzie discovered the Mackenzie River in 1789, he followed it north to its point of junction with the Great Bear River, which flows out of Great Bear Lake. At this junction, the trading post of Fort Norman was established. You get there by flying in via a scheduled air service. A few miles above the post is a small coal basin containing a low-grade bed of coal. The day Mackenzie first sighted the bed, it was on fire—and it is still burning almost 200 years later. Indian legend tells of giant men and animals who once roamed the area. One of the giants is said to have lighted a campfire on the riverbank and this is what started the fire in the coal beds.

FORT SMITH [H-3] Like so many Canadian cities, this one started out as a Hudson's Bay trading post. It overlooks the Rapids of the Drowned on the Slave River, which flows south out of Great Slave Lake. The city is just north of the Alberta border, and is headquarters for huge Wood Buffalo National Park, sanctuary for thousands of bison. You can drive the loop road around the park beginning at Fort Smith. If you do, watch for animals crossing the road, particularly at dawn and dusk.

FROBISHER BAY Sir Martin Frobisher was one of those hearty British sailors seeking a water route to the riches of the Orient. Coming through the Labrador Sea, he sailed into Frobisher Bay in 1576, and in 1578 attempted to found a settlement for the purpose of hunting for gold. His settlement failed and Sir John Franklin finally discovered the much-coveted Northwest Passage in 1845. Frobisher Bay is a bite in Baffin Island, and Henry Hudson had to sail past it to find his way into the bay which is now named for him. The town of Frobisher Bay was originally a trading post but became an important refuelling point for commercial and military aircraft with the construction of the Distant Early Warning Line of radar stations in 1954. It is the economic and administrative center of the eastern Arctic region. To visit here, you fly in.

HAY RIVER [H-3] Hay River is the transportation hub of all the land north of Great Slave Lake. Located along the Mackenzie Highway on the southern shore of the lake, it is the supply terminal for settlements all the way to the Arctic Circle. Supplies come here via truck and the Great Slave Lake railway, and are trans-shipped to barges which move northward across the lake and up the chain of lakes and rivers that lead to Great Bear Lake and the upper Mackenzie River. You'll find the Vale Island Campsite, operated by the Chamber of Commerce, on the shore of the lake, with a fine sandy beach, picnic tables, toilets, and a log cooking shelter. Local fishing

Canoeists near Dawson City follow the waterways like the voyageurs of old

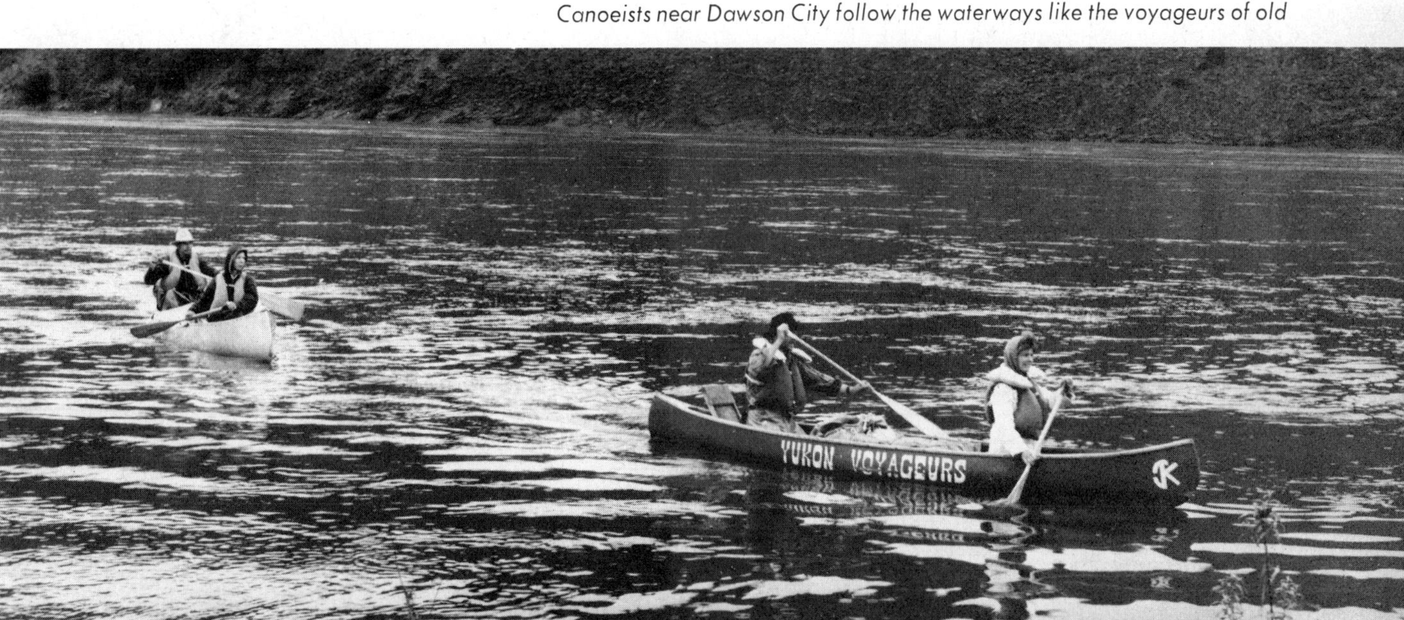

includes lake trout, pike, pickerel, and grayling. The city has stores and services, and ample entertainment facilities.

INUVIK [E-1] A hundred miles above the Arctic Circle on the Mackenzie River, Inuvik is a base for boat and plane trips to the Arctic Ocean and headquarters for hunters and trappers. To reach it, you must fly in. Construction in the city is unusual. The city is built on permafrost—which is permanently frozen earth lying just beneath the ground surface. Permafrost blankets the Arctic region and extends south into many sections of the Yukon and Northwest territories. If the permafrost melts—either from heat from a home built on it or from a spell of mild weather—it becomes marshy. Roadbeds and buildings sink. In Inuvik, the buildings were specially designed for use over the permafrost. Each is built on pilings, suspended over the ground so that no heat from the building can melt the permafrost layer. The pilings are placed by steaming a hole in the permafrost, then driving the pile into place and permitting it to freeze in place before continuing construction.

NAHANNI NATIONAL PARK [F-3] Another of Canada's newly created national parks, Nahanni is located in the southwestern corner of the Northwest Territories. It is a 1,840-square-mile wilderness. See National Parks, page 100.

WOOD BUFFALO NATIONAL PARK [H-3] A giant park of 17,300 square miles in which North America's largest bison herd roams. See National Parks, page 95.

YELLOWKNIFE [H-2] Located on the north shore of the Great Slave Lake, where gold was discovered in 1934, Yellowknife is only 275 miles south of the Arctic Circle. The sun dips below the horizon only for an hour a day in the summer months, and there is daylight for 24 hours. The summer is short here, but pleasant. The air is dry and exceedingly clear. Midday temperatures run into the 70s and sometimes more. Ice on Great Slave Lake does not break up until mid-June—and you know it is autumn by the middle of September. The best time for a visit is from mid-July to the end of August. Yellowknife is the largest settlement in the Northwest Territories and is the capital of the Territories. There are two large gold mines close to town—the Consolidated and the Giant Yellowknife. You can tour the surface facilities of both and see the molten gold being poured into gold bars. No samples are given out.

Cruise boat on the Yukon River. Alexandra Falls, where the Hay River drops 109 feet.

In Yellowknife, you can buy original Eskimo soapstone carvings and collector-quality art prints on paper or sealskin. Also generally available are beautiful handsewn parkas and other handmade garments in leather, fur, and wool, as well as pottery and jewelry set with local gemstones. They have a golf marathon here that lasts 24 hours—thanks to the everlasting summer daylight. Fishing in Great Slave Lake is strictly for big specimens, chiefly lake trout, and you throw back as too small trout that would be bragging size around most southern lakes. Grayling and huge northern pike lurk in the nearby rivers, in case you get bored with the big lakies. During the season, nonresidents can hunt the Dall sheep, mountain goat, caribou, moose, and black and grizzly bear. In spring, great flocks of ducks and geese return from their southland vacations and bagging your limit is easy. While here, remember that Yellowknife is one of Canada's youngest cities, having been born in 1935, yet is already a full-grown city, complete with radio, television, banks, businesses, churches, and entertainment facilities, as well as excellent hotels and motels. If you choose to swim, try McNiven Beach on Frame Lake, a mile south of town. There you'll find a long white sand beach, changing houses, picnic tables, rafts, a diving board, and a fenced wading area for children. Chief sport in Yellowknife seems to be curling, with hockey close behind.

PARKS

The majestic Canadian Rockies tower above the serene waters of Moraine Lake at Banff National Park.

NATIONAL HISTORIC

THE NATIONAL PARKS OF CANADA RANGE FROM THE GREAT FORESTS AND MIGHTY MOUNTAIN STRONGHOLDS OF THE WEST TO THE PRECIPITOUS CLIFFS AND SUN-WARMED BEACHES OF THE ATLANTIC COAST. TOTALING MORE THAN 50,000 SQUARE MILES OF BOTH RUGGED AND DEVELOPED OPEN-AIR MUSEUMS, THE PARKS ARE AS DIFFERENT IN APPEARANCE AND TEMPERAMENT AS THE PEOPLE THEY SERVE. THE LARGEST ENCOMPASSES OVER 17,000 SQUARE MILES—LARGER THAN SOME NATIONS—AND THE SMALLEST SETS APART LESS THAN A SQUARE MILE.

You can see some remarkable sights in these lovely places. In addition to some of the world's greatest scenic views, you can visit the spot where Marconi received the first transatlantic wireless message and the area where Alexander Graham Bell supervised the first airplane flight in the British Commonwealth. Nearly every kind of outdoor activity—with the exception of hunting—is available somewhere in this system, and the facilities are used by 14 million people each year.

In the parks you'll find true wilderness areas, virtually untouched by man's hand and reached only by riding and hiking trails, and somewhat tamer natural areas, developed for vacation pleasure and easily accessible by road. You can simply tour the parks or stay in them for several days and achieve almost any kind of living that suits you, from the very primitive existence of a wilderness camp to the near-luxury living of a fine chalet.

In addition to the 28 national parks, there also are 48 national historic parks and sites across the nation, ranging in size from a tiny fifth of an acre—the boyhood home of Sir Wilfrid Laurier at St. Lin des Laurentides, Quebec, to the 20-square-mile park surrounding the Fortress of Louisbourg in Nova Scotia. Each of these parks preserves a site important in Canada's history.

The parks are open all year, but full facilities generally are operated only from about mid-May to the beginning of October. The exact dates vary from park to park. An annual license, good for unlimited visits during the year, is available for $10. With the exception of Point Pelee, this will admit you to any of the national parks for which a license is required.

Campgrounds cannot be reserved and are allocated on a first-come, first-served basis. At most campgrounds your stay will be limited to two weeks. Daily fees are $3 for an unserviced site, $5 for a site with electricity, and $6 for a site with water, electricity, and sewer connections. If you plan to stay in any of the lodges within the parks, write directly to the facility itself for reservations—and, since more and more people are learning to enjoy the parks, reservations are advisable.

If you have piscatorial leanings, you'll find plenty of places in the parks to fish. You'll need a license, which costs $4. In Ontario, where the national parks border on waters that are not a part of the parks themselves, you must have a provincial license in place of the national parks license. The cost for nonresidents is $6 for three consecutive days, or $10.75 for the entire season.

Your first stop in any national park should be the Information Center, where you'll find leaflets describing the natural beauties and points of interest in the park, and outlining the facilities available. In most parks affable naturalists show films, give entertaining fireside talks, conduct hikes, and answer all of your questions. Activity schedules are posted at the Information Center.

Camping is one of the major activities in the parks, with more than 11,000 tent and trailer sites available within the park limits, and additional thousands ready for you at nearby private, municipal, and provincial facilities.

The national parks give you a wonderful opportunity to get out in the open, breathe deeply, and flex your muscles. There is no better way to get away from it all and to explore nature's wonders firsthand.

In return for all this carefree enjoyment, the nation asks only that you treat each area with respect and loving care—as if it were your very own.

ALBERTA

BANFF NATIONAL PARK [E-3]* Driving west along the Trans-Canada Highway, 81 miles out of Calgary, you'll come to Banff, gateway to Canada's oldest and perhaps most spectacular national park. There you'll turn northwest to pass the beautiful Lake Louise, at which point you can turn west for the Rogers Pass, or continue north to Jasper National Park. Banff is a park of rocky giants, with at least a dozen peaks topping the 9,800-foot mark, and several that are close to 12,000 feet. Park headquarters are in the town of Banff, in the shadow of looming Cascade Mountain. Established in 1885, the park has 220 miles of scenic roads.

In town you'll also find a museum with exhibits of the park's flora, fauna, and geology. It's a good place to visit before you start to explore the park itself. At the edge of town you can stop at the Buffalo Paddocks to see the resident herd of buffalo. And if you'd like to take summer courses in painting, ballet, or any of the handicrafts, what better setting than lovely Banff, where the University of Calgary operates the Banff Centre.

Lake Louise, 35 miles northwest of Banff, is acknowledged by all who have seen it to be one of the most beautiful spots on the continent—if not in the world. A mile and a half long and encircled by towering peaks, the lake is an indescribable blue green jewel—a giant piece of jade in a sculptured setting. The color is not an illusion. Lake Louise is fed by the meltwater from Victoria Glacier, and the color comes from the glacial silt and rock dust in the waters. The lake is too cold for swimming, but you can canoe and row on it. (Motors are not permitted.) Boat rentals are available. You also can rent a saddle horse for trips on some of the mountain trails in the area. Lake Louise was discovered in 1882 by railroad workers and named for Princess Louise, daughter of Queen Victoria.

* Letter and number refer to coordinates on maps included in preceding province guides.

Places you'll want to see within the park, in addition to Lake Louise, include Bow Falls, the Hoodoos, Sundance Canyon, Vermilion Lakes, Mount Norquay Drive, Moraine Lake, and the Valley of the Ten Peaks. There are sky lifts to take you to the summits of several mountains: Mount Norquay, Mount Whitehorn, and Sulphur Mountain.

Winter sports are big in Banff, with major ski areas at Sunshine Village, Mount Norquay, and Lake Louise. Each has a variety of runs for each class of skier.

Accommodations in the park are exceptional, with 46 lodges, hotels, motels, and chalets to take care of more than 5,000 people. In addition, there are 11 campgrounds waiting to receive nearly 2,500 camping parties each night. If you just want to spend a day in the open, there are a dozen developed picnic areas scattered through the park.

Best introduction to Banff are the nature programs conducted by naturalists at both Banff and Lake Louise. Conducted hikes and nature walks also originate in both places.

ELK ISLAND NATIONAL PARK [C-5] This 75-square-mile park 25 miles east of Edmonton is the largest fenced wild-animal preserve in Canada. In it you'll see elk, moose, mule deer, a herd of 600 buffalo, and numerous smaller animals. The Yellowhead Highway passes through the park, and park headquarters are near Astotin Lake. The Sandy Beach Recreational Area, on the lake, has delightful facilities for swimming, boating, golf, camping, and picnicking. Park naturalists at the headquarters conduct many nature hikes and give illustrated fireside talks during the summer months. The park is open all year, but most facilities are serviced only from the middle of May to the middle of September. There is one campground available, located at Sandy Beach.

JASPER NATIONAL PARK [C-1-2] Combined with Banff, its neighbor to the south, Jasper is part of the most popular national park area in all Canada. Jasper itself is 4,200 square miles of mountain playground and wildlife sanctuary on the eastern side of the Continental Divide. It is one vast display of lakes of every size and color, with Maligne Lake the largest and best known. Park headquarters are located at Jasper townsite in the very center of the park at the junction of Highways 16 (the Yellowhead) and 93 (the Icefield).

Activity in the park is almost unlimited. You can fish, boat, or play golf on an 18-hole course, with great mountains peering over your shoulder as you putt. You can take the sky tram to the top of Whistler Mountain and lunch in the teahouse there, 7,350 feet up in the clouds. You can hike, ride, play tennis, and swim in an outdoor heated pool—as a change from swimming in the pretty lakes. You can sit in on illustrated fireside talks and motion pictures and take both self-guided and conducted hikes.

Maligne Lake is 32 miles south of the townsite, and there you'll find sightseeing cruises running on the lake every day; worthwhile trips that provide exceptional views of the mountains. All of Jasper is a photographer's dream, with one gorgeous picture opportunity after another. Those from the sightseeing boats are among the best—and that's saying a good deal.

There are more than 20 lodges and motels within the park, providing accommodations for upwards of 3,500 people, and there are 11 campgrounds for over 1,500 camping parties. Jasper Park Lodge is the center of all activity, and the golf course is adjacent to it.

Winter activities include tobogganing, curling, skiing, playing hockey, and skating. The Marmot Ski Area has one of the finest powder snow slopes in the Rockies, with novice trails up to 3 miles long, exciting advanced runs, and a chair lift and two T-bars to take you to the 7,400-foot level, where the fun begins. The vertical drop of the runs is 2,000 feet. Marmot Basin has all the facilities you need for an outdoor winter vacation.

There's a sky tram 4 miles south of the townsite on Highway 93 at Whistler's Mountain Road. Here enclosed alpine cars start at the 4,200-foot level and zip you to the upper station at 600 feet per minute. At the upper station there are, in addition to the tearoom, picnic sites (and what a place for a picnic!), nature trails, and an observation balcony.

Happily, much of Jasper's great beauty is readily available either by motor road or on improved hiking trails. There are dozens of short and interesting side trips waiting for you. Some of the best are those at Maligne Canyon, Medicine Lake, Lac Beauvert, and Pyramid Lake. Perhaps the most popular trip of all is the one at Mount Edith Cavell. You also should visit Miette Hot Springs, where four hot sulfur springs bubble water at 129°. There's a swimming pool here for mineral baths.

The Icefield highway, connecting Banff and Jasper, is 142 miles of the most scenic driving in Canada. It includes some fine views of the Columbia Icefield—130 square miles of ice that in some places runs 3,000 feet deep. One great side trip is the 3-mile snowmobile trip across the ice field. You'll find the snowmobiles at the point where the Athabasca Glacier licks close to the highway.

ROCKY MOUNTAIN HOUSE NATIONAL HISTORIC PARK [D-3] Located on Highway 11, 60 miles west of Red Deer, this park encloses the remains of the last of a series of fur trading posts built at the junction of the Saskatchewan and Clearwater rivers between 1799 and 1866. Chimneys of the 1866 post are still standing, and an exhibit is located in a trailer.

WATERTON LAKES NATIONAL PARK [G-4] One minute, as you drive toward this area, the land is flat prairie—and the next you find yourself in the midst of mountains. Here is where the Rockies begin. This park is joined to Glacier National Park in the United States to form Waterton-Glacier International Peace Park, the first of its kind in the world. The inspiration for this joint venture came from the Rotary Clubs of Alberta and Montana.

The park is on the international border about 80 miles southwest of Lethbridge. It centers around Waterton Lake, where you'll find the Prince of Wales Hotel, and where the *International* starts its daily trips between the townsite and Goathaunt Landing in Glacier National Park, Montana.

More than 100 miles of trails crisscross the park, bringing you to waterfalls, lovely U-shaped valleys, rock-basin lakes, and vivid alpine meadows. Take your rod and reel along and cast for rainbow, cutthroat, lake, and eastern brook trout. Take the scenic Akamina Highway to the southwestern corner of the park to visit another beautiful spot—Lake Cameron. Or make a photographic expedition to Red Rock Canyon, taking the highway that leads up through Blakiston Brook Canyon. Several of the park's more interesting nature trails start in this canyon.

There are 17 hotels, motels, and lodges in the park, plus a dozen campgrounds, some of which are serviced (electricity, water, etc.) and others which are quite primitive.

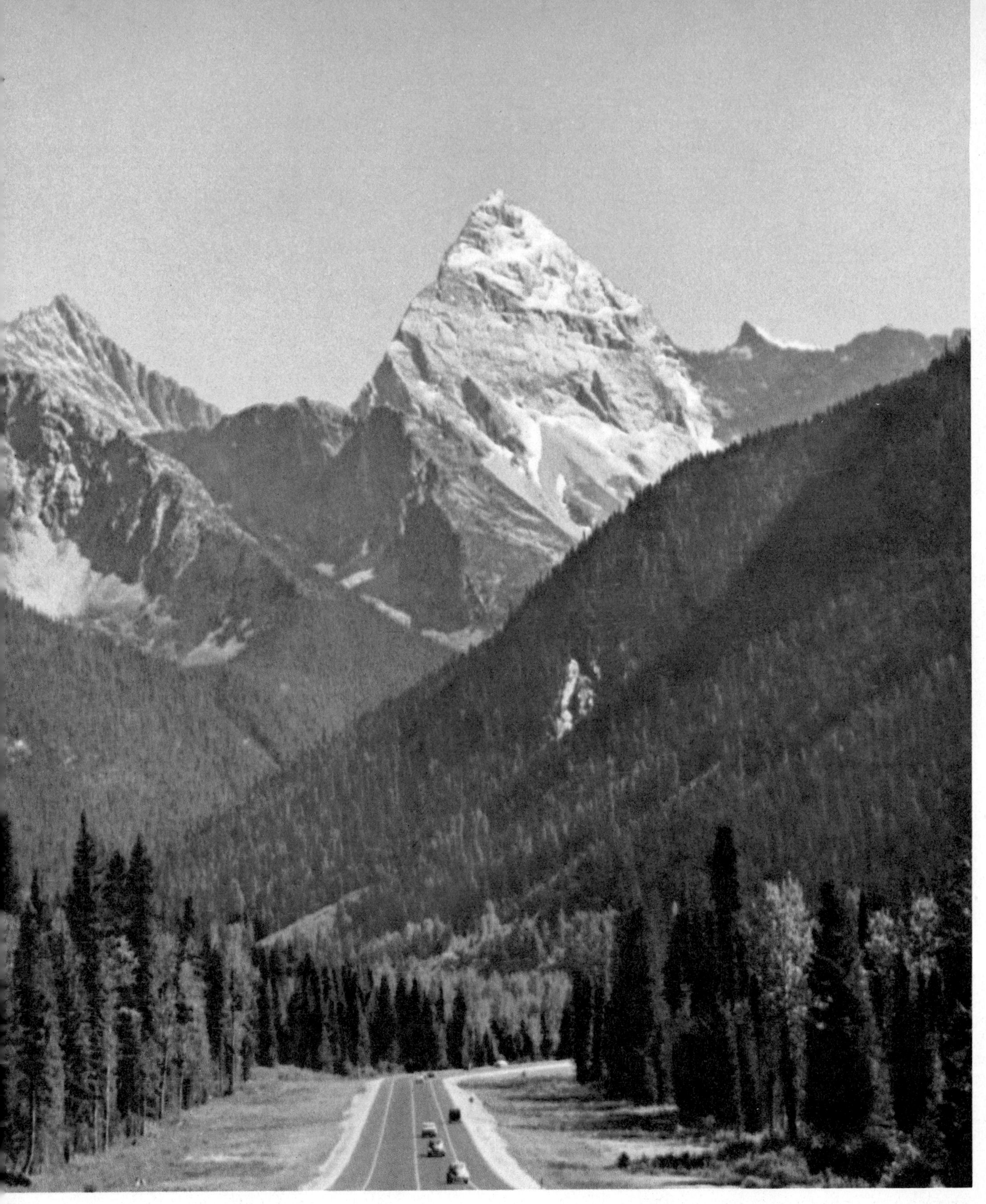

The Trans-Canada cutting through Rogers Pass to Glacier National Park

WOOD BUFFALO NATIONAL PARK A giant untamed region of forests and open plains between Athabasca and Great Slave Lake, Wood Buffalo National Park straddles the line between Alberta and the Northwest Territories. Here are 17,300 square miles that serve as the home of the largest remaining herd of bison on the North American continent. Park headquarters are located at Fort Smith, Northwest Territories. The park currently has only one developed campground. It is located at Pine Lake, about 40 miles southwest of Fort Smith on the shore of Pine Lake, and offers 30 sites.

BRITISH COLUMBIA

FORT LANGLEY NATIONAL HISTORIC PARK [F-5] This is a 9-acre park on the Fraser River, opposite the town of Haney, east of Vancouver on the Trans-Canada Highway. You can visit a reconstruction of the fort, but this shows it as it was in the 1850s when it served as a Hudson's Bay Company post. There aren't any signs of the original fort, built in 1827. You can also tour two museums on the grounds. Take the Albion Ferry across the Fraser from Highway 7 to Fort Langley.

FORT RODD HILL NATIONAL HISTORIC PARK [F-4] You will find a 19th-century British coastal fortification on Highway 1A between Victoria and Sooke. Nearby is the historic Fisgard Lighthouse, the first lighthouse built on the Pacific coast. The fort was in active use until 1956. The lighthouse is an absolute gem of a photographic subject—the kind that makes award-winning pictures.

GLACIER NATIONAL PARK [E-6] This is a grand area of snowcapped mountain peaks flanked by immense ice fields and sparkling glaciers, located 29 miles east of Revelstoke, and entered from the east through the magnificent Rogers Pass section of the Trans-Canada Highway. Rocky giants in the park top 11,000 feet, and, between them, forest-clad slopes lead down to deep canyons cut through the rock by turbulent rivers. Highlighting all of this are waterfalls, alpine meadows, and the glaciers from which the park took its name.

The entire area has been kept in its wilderness condition. Chief activities in Glacier are mountain climbing, skiing, hiking, and camping. There are three campgrounds and at Rogers Pass there is a 60-room motor hotel with an excellent dining room. The campgrounds are open from July through early September, the motor hotel all year.

The park covers 521 square miles and includes such spiky behemoths as Mount Sir Donald (10,818 feet), Mount Eagle, and Mount Uto. They say you haven't tried wilderness skiing until you have been on Asulkan Glacier—but this isn't an activity for beginners. Skiing in the area is top-notch, with 4,000-foot vertical drops and downhill runs as long as 4 miles.

Mountain climbers and overnight campers must register with the park warden. A network of hiking trails will take you to nearly any kind of rugged scenery you want: glaciers, mountain cataracts, great forests, or upland meadows. You can be a long way from civilization on some of these trails.

KOOTENAY NATIONAL PARK [E-6] These precipitous 543 square miles adjacent to the south boundary of Yoho and the west boundary of Banff national parks enclose the Vermilion-Sinclair section of the Banff-Windermere Highway. The park extends for 5 miles on either side of the highway for a distance

Pacific Rim, on the west coast of Vancouver Island, is one of the recently established national parks.

of 65 miles, following the natural avenues formed by the Vermilion and Kootenay rivers. The eastern entrance to the park is through Castle Mountain in Banff National Park on Highway 93. The western entrance is at Radium Hot Springs. Park Information Offices are located near the western entrance and at Aquacourt and Marble Canyon.

The road will take you past awesome Marble Canyon, the odd ocher beds, or "paint pots," the stunning Sinclair Canyon with copper-colored walls that rise 4,875 feet, and the extraordinary hot mineral springs at Radium. You can bathe in either of two outdoor pools where the water is cooled from its natural 114° down to a comfortable 85°.

There are two self-guided walks of special interest. One is the Marble Canyon Nature Trail, and the other is the Paint Pots Nature Trail. Descriptive brochures on both walks can be obtained at the Information Office. If you have time for but one of these walks, lean toward the Marble Canyon hike. The sheer walls here, nearly 130 feet high, are formed of gray limestone and quartzite through which run beautiful veins of white and gray marble.

You must obtain a motor vehicle license at the entrance before driving through the park. Boats, canoes, rafts, and floats are not permitted, and if you plan to take to the mountain trails off the regular park trails, you must register with the district warden.

There are three campgrounds in the park offering nearly 400 sites, and 9 developed picnic areas. Lodge and bungalow accommodations are available in Radium Hot Springs and at Vermilion Crossing in the park, and at Radium Junction, 2 miles from Radium Hot Springs.

MOUNT REVELSTOKE NATIONAL PARK [E-6] Located along the Trans-Canada Highway at Revelstoke, this park is a beautiful rolling mountaintop plateau surrounded by the jagged 10,000-foot giants of the Selkirk Range. A 16-mile winding gravel road, open only in the summer, takes you to the summit of Mount Revelstoke, from which you can look across at platoons of mountains marching in every direction—or look down into the beautiful valley of the Columbia River, where the city of Revelstoke nestles on the bank. The 9-mile trail on the summit, for good mountain hikers, leads through flower-strewn alpine meadows and to one outstanding vista point after another. If you pause for a few moments along the trail to listen, you'll be amazed at the eternal, overwhelming silence around you. Living in a world of noise, you forget that silence of this magnitude can exist.

The park is a noted cross-country ski area, covered by deep snow until mid-June. There are semiserviced campgrounds within the park, which is open all year, and all-year accommodations in nearby Revelstoke.

PACIFIC RIM NATIONAL PARK [F-4] A new park which covers about 45 square miles, is just being developed on the west coast of Vancouver Island between Ucluelet and Tofino. The central part of the park is the beautiful Long Beach. As it is developed, the park will include a Life Saving Trail and a number of islands. This is a good place to observe sea lions and other marine life in a natural habitat. There are campgrounds in the park, and other accommodations nearby. An interpretive program is now under development. Easiest way to drive to Pacific Rim is via Highway 4 west from Parksville or Qualicum Beach to Port Alberni. At Port Alberni, Highway 4 goes north through Stamp River Valley, then west to the park.

Skiing in the Canadian Rockies

VANCOUVER NATIONAL HISTORIC SITE [F-4] The schooner *St. Roch,* the first vessel to navigate the Northwest Passage from west to east, and also the first to completely circumnavigate the North and South American continents, is on display at the Vancouver Maritime Museum.

YOHO NATIONAL PARK [E-6] Freely translated from the original Indian tongue, Yoho means "Wow!"—or more grammatically, "How wonderful!" The name was well chosen for these 507 square miles lying just to the west of the Continental Divide. The Trans-Canada Highway, on its way west, leaves Lake Louise to cross Yoho before cutting through the Rogers Pass.

There are more than 250 miles of improved trails in the park, leading you—hiking or riding—to the curtain of mist hanging over beautiful Laughing Falls, the strangely shaped pillars in Hoodoo Valley, and to the Yoho Glacier. You can drive to the bright green expanse of Emerald Lake, the Natural Bridge on Kicking Horse River, and to the wondrous beauty of Takakkaw Falls—made up of meltwater from the Daly Glacier that plunges 1,248 vertical feet into the Yoho Valley.

Park headquarters are at Field in the center of the park, and four campgrounds can accommodate about 400 camping parties. Six lodges are waiting in the park, and three of these remain open all year.

MANITOBA

LOWER FORT GARRY NATIONAL HISTORIC PARK [F-4] This is one of the forts constructed by the Hudson's Bay Company between 1831 and 1839. Much of it has survived in good condition because it was originally built of stone and because it was in active use as a trading post until 1909. It is located on the west bank of the Red River on a 13-acre site about 20 miles north of Winnipeg.

PRINCE OF WALES NATIONAL HISTORIC PARK The park is located at Churchill on the shores of Hudson Bay, and features a fort originally built in 1733. A partial restoration has been completed. The walls of the fort are an amazing 25 feet thick in places. The park covers 50 acres and can be reached only by water when the weather is good. Churchill, named after a distant relative of the prime minister, is Canada's northernmost deep-sea port. The fare for the trip to the park is $5.

RIDING MOUNTAIN NATIONAL PARK [E-1] This park is on the vast plateau of Riding Mountain which rises up out of the sprawling prairie to a height of 2,480 feet. It's an area of lakes and summer resort activity, a playground of forests and lakes covering 1,148 square miles.

Life in the park centers around the resort town of Wasagaming on the shore of Clear Lake. ("Wasagaming" is the Indian word for "clear lake.") The lake is 9 miles long and 2

A blue ocean backdrop for the Cabot Trail encircling Cape Breton Highlands National Park

miles wide, ringed by sandy beaches, and it attracts regular visitors from the entire central plain. In the park you'll find an 18-hole golf course, tennis courts, lawn bowling, riding, sailing, swimming, fishing, and even a movie house. Clear Lake is stocked with lake trout and pickerel, while native pike, perch, and whitefish strike passing lures when the planted species won't.

Riding Mountain National Park is 160 miles west and north of Winnipeg with plenty of hotel, motel, and cabin accommodations as well as five compgrounds large enough to take 800 camping parties. The Information Center is at Wasagaming, and nature walks and car caravans led by naturalists start from it.

If you are a bird watcher, you'll enjoy a few days here because the park is in the path of migratory flyways, so that more than 200 species can be seen at one time or another.

Sunset at the New Brunswick shoreline

NEW BRUNSWICK

CARLETON MARTELLO TOWER NATIONAL HISTORIC PARK [E-3] Built during the War of 1812, this circular redoubt was one of a number of similar design built in the Atlantic provinces. Located at Saint John.

FORT BEAUSEJOUR NATIONAL HISTORIC PARK [D-4] An 81-acre park surrounds the partially restored fort located on Highway 6, 5 miles east of Sackville. The fort was originally built by order of Canadian Governor Marquis de la Jonquiere in 1750, but was attacked before it was completed and was surrendered to the British, under the command of Lieutenant Colonel Robert Moncton. It was then renamed Fort Cumberland. There is an interesting museum at the fort, which is open from mid-June until mid-September. The restoration is still in progress.

FUNDY NATIONAL PARK [D-4] This picturesque parkland skirts the beautiful Bay of Fundy for 8 miles between Saint John and Moncton, and extends over 9 miles inland. Here the sea has turned sculptor and, using the high and fast tides as a chisel, has carved shapes of ragged grandeur into the sandstone cliffs along the shore. Back from the water's edge, the land is scenic forest and a wildlife sanctuary, with intriguing nature trails and accommodations ranging from alpine chalets to serviced campgrounds.

For recreation, you'll find a nine-hole golf course, tennis courts, a bowling green, open-air theaters, a heated saltwater swimming pool, playgrounds, and a community hall. If the arts attract, bring your sketching pad or camera. You'll find plenty of subjects to challenge your skill. Or sharpen those skills at the New Brunswick School of Arts, which offers art and handicraft courses during July and August.

Park headquarters are on Highway 114, a mile from Alma. There are campgrounds here and at four other locations in the park, or you can stay at motels or chalets in the vicinity of the headquarters. The park is open all year, and most services are available from the end of May to mid-September.

KOUCHIBOUGUAC NATIONAL PARK [C-4] This new park has recently been developed on Kouchibouguac Bay southeast of Chatham on the Northumberland Strait. Quiet lagoons and bays provide excellent protected canoeing. The park's most outstanding feature is a 15½-mile sweep of offshore sandbars. Facilities, including a campground, are open, and swimming is also available. Total area of the park is 87 square miles. Access is via Highway 117 from the town of Kouchibouguac, 27 miles southeast of Chatham.

MOUNT CARLETON PROVINCIAL PARK [B-2] A new wilderness park in the highlands of Restiguoche County, it offers wilderness hiking and primitive camping facilities. Headquarters are at Nictau Lake, reached by taking Highway 385 north from Plaster Rock, then taking a private lumber road.

ST. ANDREWS BLOCKHOUSE NATIONAL HISTORIC PARK [E-2] The only remaining defense work of a series of blockhouses and batteries built by civilians against American privateers, the fortification is located at St. Andrews on Highway 1 near the New Brunswick–Maine border.

NEWFOUNDLAND

CAPE SPEAR NATIONAL HISTORIC SITE [B-7] At this spot near St. John's stands one of the oldest lighthouses on Canada's eastern coast. This is the nearest point in North America to Europe—1,640 miles from Cape Clear, Ireland.

CASTLE HILL NATIONAL HISTORIC PARK [B-7] The French undertook to fortify the harbor at Placentia about 1662. The park takes in the ruins of these fortifications. There is an interpretation center here with displays explaining the ruins. Located at Placentia, not far from Argentia, about 50 miles west and south of St. John's.

GROS MORNE NATIONAL PARK [B-6] A new park now in operation on Newfoundland's western coast, about 50 miles northwest of Corner Brook. It contains the most spectacular section of the Long Range Mountains, which rise majestically and abruptly from the low coastal plain. The name comes from Gros Morne Mountain, 2,651 feet, rising in the midst of the park. The park includes a portion of the seacoast, with its shifting sand dunes, and highlands with fjordlike lakes and dense forests. Total area of the park is 750 square miles. You will find a campground and other temporary facilities ready for use. Take Highway 431 from Deer Lake to Lomond, then Highway 430 north along the coast.

SIGNAL HILL NATIONAL HISTORIC PARK [B-7] Signal Hill, a rocky headland rising 600 feet above the entrance to St. John's Harbor, has been the site of a number of forts because of its strategic location. The major battle fought on the site was the last battle of the Seven Years War. The John Cabot Memorial Tower was erected on the hill in 1897 to commemorate the 400th anniversary of Cabot's landfall. Then, in 1901, the hill continued to live up to its name because it was here that Marconi sat to receive the first transatlantic wireless message.

TERRA NOVA NATIONAL PARK [B-7] If you have a yen to see an iceberg, this may be the place to do it. The cold Labrador Current brushes against these shores, and a shimmering iceberg sailing in the blue waters is a common sight.

The park is located on Newman Sound, an inlet from Bonavista Bay, and owes its beauty to the sea. Glaciers once covered the area to a depth of 750 feet, and deposited boulders, sand, and grooved rock. The rugged coast with its fjords is a result of glacial action. You can take a boat tour of Newman Sound and have a lunch of fish and brewis, a Newfoundland dish of salt cod, while aboard.

Located about 35 miles south of Gander, along the Trans-Canada Highway, the park is home to a good many wild animals, including moose, black bear, red fox, and smaller animals. Headquarters are midway between park boundaries on the Trans-Canada. Near it there are bungalows and a campground, and a nature trail to get you close to the park's beauty. If you crave saltwater fishing, you can charter a boat at any of the towns near here. There is also good freshwater fishing, and you can catch, among other species, the Arctic char. Bird watchers can add new sightings to their collections—many Arctic birds come to the park during the summer.

NORTHWEST TERRITORIES

BAFFIN ISLAND NATIONAL PARK The southern boundary of this isolated new park crosses the Arctic Circle. To get to the area, you fly to Pangnirtung on Baffin Island, 20 miles from the southern boundary. The coastline of the park, facing Davis Strait, consists of great fjords with vertical cliffs rising more than 3,000 feet. Inland is the Penny Ice Cap, covering 2,200 square miles and ranging from 2,000 to 6,000 feet in thickness. The park has no facilities, but there are hotels at Broughton Island and Pangnirtung, on the east and west boundaries.

NAHANNI NATIONAL PARK [F-3] The South Nahanni is one of North America's finest wild rivers and this new park is 870 square miles surrounding most of it. A major sight in the park is Virginia Falls, the most spectacular undeveloped waterfall in America, where the South Nahanni plunges more than 300 feet. The park is 90 miles west of Fort Simpson, and access to it will be by road from Fort Simpson to Fort Liard, near the southern boundary of the park.

NOVA SCOTIA—Cape Breton Island

ALEXANDER GRAHAM BELL NATIONAL HISTORIC PARK [D-7] In the architecturally unusual museum (its plan is based on the tetrahedron) you'll see a fascinating display of relics of experiments in many scientific fields by Alexander Graham Bell and his associates. A good many of these experiments were in aviation. Few people realize that Bell and his fellow workers conducted the first airplane flight in the British Commonwealth here on February 23, 1909. The museum is located at Baddeck, about 20 miles west and north from Sydney, just off the Trans-Canada Highway.

CAPE BRETON HIGHLANDS NATIONAL PARK [C-7] They say you can fairly hear the pipes skirling in this park, so much does it resemble the highlands of Scotland. Spanning the northern end of Cape Breton Island, the park reaches from the Atlantic to the Gulf of St. Lawrence, with an area of 367 square miles. It is encircled by the Cabot Trail, a 184-mile paved highway that climbs four mountains to provide magnificent panoramas of rocks, shores, the sea, and green valleys.

Not only does this area resemble Scotland, but it was settled originally by Scots, and you'll still hear Gaelic spoken in some places nearby.

The park is a typical Acadian forest. Hiking trails have been prepared through the wooded areas, and the most popular path is the one that leads from the Ingonish Information Center up Franey Mountain. There is fine swimming at Ingonish Beach near the eastern entrance to the park, and also freshwater swimming in the park, so you have your choice.

The park has a dozen campgrounds, and a lodge and bungalows are available at Ingonish. Facilities here operate from May 15 to October 15.

FORT ANNE NATIONAL HISTORIC PARK [E-3] The ramparts, bastions, and powder magazine of the original fort can still be seen in this 31-acre park near Annapolis Royal. The museum in the fort has a comprehensive display illustrating the history of the travail at Port Royal, Annapolis Royal, and the forced migration of the Acadian people.

FORTRESS OF LOUISBOURG NATIONAL HISTORIC PARK [D-7] A major restoration of the ruins of a walled city built by the French between 1720 and 1840 is under way here on Cape Breton Island, 3 miles from Louisbourg. Most of the original area of the city, Battery Island in the harbor, and the Royal Battery, 2 miles from the fort, are included in the park area. An easy way to see the fortress and the progress of the restoration is to take a guided bus trip. Buses leave every half hour on summer days from the park entrance.

GRAND PRE NATIONAL HISTORIC PARK [E-4] The Acadians were expelled from Nova Scotia at this point in 1755 and were moved to Massachusetts, Louisiana, and other American colonies. Some eventually found their way back years later. The expulsion is immortalized in the narrative poem *Evangeline* by Henry Wadsworth Longfellow. In all, 6,000 Acadians were expelled because they refused to swear allegiance to England. The Evangeline Chapel in the park is in a beautiful setting, and its museum tells the story of the Acadians. The park is in the Annapolis Valley, 10 miles east of Kentville.

HALIFAX CITADEL NATIONAL HISTORIC PARK [E-5] Work on this fort, located at Halifax, was begun in 1828. Three other forts occupied the site at earlier times in history. The newest structure is one of the largest stone forts in North America. You'll find the view magnificent from the driveway circling the top of the fort. If you are visiting at noon, you'll hear the Noon Gun fired, just as it has been every day for more than 140 years. Three good museums have material and displays about Canada's naval and military history and the history of the province. Free guided tours of the fort are available.

KEJIMKUJIK NATIONAL PARK [E-3] Once the land of the Micmac Indians in west central Nova Scotia, halfway between Digby and Liverpool, this is one of the nation's newer national parks. It covers 150 miles of forests, lakes, and islands. One campground is now ready for campers with tents or trailers, and others are being planned.

At Merrymakedge Beach you can swim in the freshwater lake, boat, fish, hike, and attend a naturalist program. The park has two fine wilderness canoe trails—the Little River Route and the Mersey River Route. On rocks along the lakeshore, you'll find pictographs of battle scenes drawn by the Micmacs.

Winter sports are gaining popularity here, and there are cross-country skiing, snowshoeing, and snowmobiling. Major development of visitor facilities has yet to come, but, even at this point, there is much here to attract. You get to the park via Highway 8.

PORT ROYAL NATIONAL HISTORIC PARK [E-3] This park marks the site of the Port Royal Habitation. Champlain and De Monts arrived in the Annapolis Basin in 1604. The men of the expedition lived in the Port Royal Habitation. The habitation has been reconstructed to the exact dimensions and on the same foundations as the original. You'll find the park 7 miles from Annapolis Royal, on the north shore of the Annapolis River.

PRINCE OF WALES MARTELLO TOWER NATIONAL HISTORIC PARK [E-5] Located at Point Pleasant Park in Halifax, this sturdy circular tower followed a European design proven successful at Cape Mortello in Corsica. This one was built by the British between 1796 and 1798.

YORK REDOUBT NATIONAL HISTORIC PARK [E-5] The park contains the remains of the foundations for a 30-foot stone martello tower and other defense works. The redoubt was first begun by the British in 1793 to defend the port of Halifax. It has a battery of eight 24-pound guns.

ONTARIO

BELLEVUE HOUSE NATIONAL HISTORIC PARK [C-7] The home of Canada's first prime minister, Sir John A. Macdonald, which is located at Kingston, has been declared a national historic park.

FORT GEORGE NATIONAL HISTORIC PARK [D-5] The fort, built between 1796 and 1799, was the principal British post in the Niagara area until its destruction by American forces in 1813. Reconstruction of the fort was completed in 1940. Eleven of the original buildings, including the officers' quarters and soldiers' barracks rooms, the guard room, kitchen, and artificer's shop, have been rebuilt and furnished as they were when in use. The fort is located at the south edge of Niagara-on-the-Lake, and is open from early May to the second week of October each year.

FORT MALDEN NATIONAL HISTORIC PARK [E-2] The British constructed this fort on the banks of the Detroit River in 1797, and it served as their principal frontier post for more than 40 years. British forces rallied here in 1812 for the attack on

Fort Battleford National Historic Park, Saskatchewan

Detroit. The site includes buildings and earthworks of the original fort, and two of the buildings contain museums. The fort is at Amherstburg, 16 miles south of Windsor on Highway 18.

FORT ST. JOSEPH [A-2] Located 40 miles southeast of Sault Ste. Marie, this old fort was built in 1796 as a fur trading post. Destroyed by Americans in 1814.

FORT WELLINGTON NATIONAL HISTORIC PARK [C-7] A massive stone fort, with walls four feet thick, this citadel was built by the British during the War of 1812 and named for the Duke of Wellington. The center of the fort is a great blockhouse, surrounded by pentagonal earthworks, a palisade, and a dry ditch. The ground floor of the blockhouse is now a museum. Stop long enough to see the covered rifleman's post, a sentry station outside of the walls. The fort is open from May 1 to mid-October and is located at Prescott on the St. Lawrence River.

GEORGIAN BAY ISLANDS NATIONAL PARK [B-4] National parks that can be reached only by boat are a rarity, but this is one. The park consists of 50 separate islands in Georgian Bay. Best way to get to the park is to turn off the Trans-Canada Highway at Highway 501 and drive to Honey Harbour on the bayshore. There you'll find boat service to Beausoleil Island, the largest island in the park.

These islands are well known for their unusual geological formations. Ancient glaciers carved rocks on the islands into strange shapes that you can see today. Flower Pot Island, at the northern tip of the Bruce Peninsula, is named for the water-eroded sculptures which do, in fact, resemble flower-pots. You get to Flower Pot Island by boat from the town of Tobermory.

There are no lodge accommodations in the park, but plenty of motels in the nearby towns of Midland, Honey Harbour, and

Penetanguishene. On Beausoleil Island, more than 2,700 acres in size, you'll find nearly one dozen campgrounds, but remember you must take a boat to reach them. The water taxi service will do, or you can rent a boat in any of the bay towns.

The beaches on Beausoleil Island are long and sloping, making for calm, shallow water playgrounds—ideal for children.

POINT PELEE NATIONAL PARK [E-2] Most people don't know that part of Canada is actually south of California's northern border. That southernmost point of Canada is Point Pelee, a thrust of land jutting out into Lake Erie. The point is preserved as a small (9.6 square miles) national park, not because of its location but because it contains the remnants of the original deciduous forest of North America, a unique 2,500-acre freshwater swamp, and some very beautiful sand beaches.

Swimming, water-skiing, and building sand castles are the order of the day here. The park, 30 miles southeast of Windsor, is a favorite picnic spot, and has facilities to accommodate 7,600 people in 11 developed picnic locations.

Nature lovers, who want to study the swamp, can follow a self-guiding woodland nature trail that skirts it, or walk out along a 3,100-foot boardwalk to a 20-foot tower in the center that provides a great view of the marsh's teeming life. Another way to get close to nature here is to rent a canoe in one of the park's four large ponds and paddle out to the wildflowers.

Motel accommodations are available at nearby Leamington. The Nature Center is open from May through August. Start your visit with a tour of the Nature Center, where you can familiarize yourself with the remarkable layout of the park through maps and displays.

PUKASKWA NATIONAL PARK [E-7] On the northern shore of Lake Superior, this new park is 725 square miles of rugged shore line between the Pukaskwa and White rivers. No access roads at present, but one will be developed to lead from the Trans-Canada to a point near the mouth of the White River. The park will be developed as a wilderness recreation area for hiking, canoeing, nature study, and camping. The land of the park is part of the Precambrian Shield, very rugged, with numerous bays, beaches, rocky points and islands along the shore, and wild rivers, creeks, and waterfalls inland.

QUEENSTON HEIGHTS NATIONAL HISTORIC PARK [D-5] Not far from Fort George at Niagara-on-the-Lake, Queenston Heights is the site of a major American invasion, a critical battle, and an American defeat during the War of 1812. There is a monument here to Major General Isaac Brock, killed during the repulse.

ST. LAWRENCE ISLANDS NATIONAL PARK [C-7] Seventeen small islands among the gorgeous Thousand Islands of that portion of the St. Lawrence River between Kingston and Brockville have been set aside to form this pretty and useful recreational park. The actual land coverage of these islands is only 260 acres. They can be reached by water taxi from Gananoque, Mallorytown, and Rockport in Ontario, and from Alexandria Bay and Clayton on the New York side. A portion of the park is on the mainland, and here there is a campground and an excellent beach. All the islands have docks, campsites, and wells for water—and they are a favorite stopping place for the small-boat fraternity who ply the Inland Waterways. Bring your rod and reel because you'll find first-class fishing for bass, pike, and muskellunge near the park islands.

WOODSIDE NATIONAL HISTORIC PARK [D-4] William Lyon Mackenzie King, former prime minister, lived as a boy at 528 Wellington St. in what is present-day Kitchener. This 11½-acre park surrounds his home.

PRINCE EDWARD ISLAND

FORT AMHERST NATIONAL HISTORIC PARK [D-5] Earthworks of the French fort, Port la Joie, are still clearly visible in this park located at Rocky Point across the harbor from Charlottetown. The French built their fort in 1720. It was captured by the British in 1758, renamed Fort Amherst, then abandoned in 1775.

PRINCE EDWARD ISLAND NATIONAL PARK [C-5] The Gulf Stream favors the Gulf of St. Lawrence here, so that the waters rolling on the beaches on the north side of Prince Edward Island are the warmest of any along the Atlantic coast north of Florida. What better place to put a national park, particularly one that is 25 miles of bright sandy beach.

The park is between the harbors of New London and Tracadie and three main areas have been developed for vacationers, with such facilities as cabins, serviced trailer parks and campgrounds, picnic areas, a fine golf course, nature trails —and to top it all off—lakes and streams stocked with fish. Thus, you can have the delights of both fresh- and saltwater fishing on the same day, if you choose.

For a pleasant hike, follow the Bubbling Spring Trail, in the eastern part of the park near Long Pond. One of the earliest roads surveyed, the road leads through the forest and past a number of springs.

To reach the park, take Highway 2 from Charlottetown to Dalvay, 2½ miles from Tracadie. You'll find lodges and hotels at Cavendish, and campsites at Stanhope, Cavendish, and Rustico Island. Park headquarters are at Dalvay. Green Gables, the farmhouse made famous by authoress Lucy Maud Montgomery, in her popular romantic novel, *Anne of Green Gables*, is at Cavendish Beach, and her birthplace is just west of the park.

QUEBEC

CARTIER-BREBEUF NATIONAL HISTORIC PARK [D-4] At the confluence of the St. Charles and Lairet rivers in Quebec City, this park of 14 acres commemorates two important historical events: the first wintering of Europeans in Canada under Jacques Cartier in 1535-36, and the taking possession of the area in September of 1625 by three famous Jesuit fathers—Jean de Brebeuf, Ennemond Masse, and Charles Lalemant, all of whom were later martyred.

COTEAU DU LAC NATIONAL HISTORIC PARK [E-3] This park is the site of the first canal built on the St. Lawrence River, and also marks an 18th-century British military post. Located just off Highway 138, east of Montreal, on the north side of the St. Lawrence.

DE LA MAURICIE NATIONAL PARK [D-4] A new park with an area of 210 square miles has been established in the heart of the lovely Laurentians. Temporary facilities have been prepared for use. The park is heavily wooded and largely untouched, crossed by a number of rivers and dotted with blue lakes. Some small roads are already in the park and will provide access to most areas. The park is about 60 miles north of Trois Rivieres on Highway 157—about halfway between Quebec City and Montreal.

FORILLON NATIONAL PARK [F-7] A brand new national park is located on the scenic tip of the Forillon Peninsula, thrusting out into the Gulf of St. Lawrence from the end of the Gaspé Peninsula. The park is open to the public, but at this time only some temporary facilities are available. Covering an area of 92 square miles, it will be developed to reflect both the unique coastal environment and the rich human history of the famous Gaspé region. An interpretive program has just been started. There is a park campground, with other facilities outside park limits. Park headquarters are in Gaspé.

FORT CHAMBLY NATIONAL HISTORIC PARK [F-3] Captain Jacques de Chambly built the first fort on this site for France in 1665. Located on the Richelieu River at Chambly, about 20 miles east of Montreal, the fort was rebuilt in stone by the British in 1710, then occupied by the French once again during the French and Indian War, by the British in 1760, and by American troops for a time in 1775. The old dungeon and three of the walls have been restored to date, and there is a museum just inside the main entrance.

FORT LENNOX NATIONAL HISTORIC PARK [F-3] First built by the French in 1759, then rebuilt by the British in 1782, Fort Lennox is one of the largest forts built in Canada during the past 200 years. It is well preserved, and notable among the massive stone buildings are the officers' quarters, the guardhouse, the canteen, the barracks, and the commissariat. A moat 10 feet deep and 60 feet across surrounds the fort, which is open from May 1 to October 15. It is located on Ile aux Noix in the Richelieu River near St. Jean.

MAISON LAURIER NATIONAL HISTORIC SITE [E-2] This national historic site, covering one-fifth of an acre at St. Lin des Laurentides, Quebec, is the smallest national historic site. Sir Wilfrid, Canada's prime minister from 1896 to 1911, was born here in 1841, and the home has been restored and is open to the public.

NATIONAL BATTLEFIELDS PARK [D-5] This 235-acre park is the site of the Battle of the Plains of Abraham, fought in 1759 to determine whether Quebec City belonged to the British or French.

QUEBEC CITY WALLS AND GATE [D-5] The old walls and gate, built in the 1700s by the French and reconstructed by the British in 1820, have been dedicated as an historic site.

SASKATCHEWAN

BATOCHE NATIONAL HISTORIC PARK [D-3] The first engagement of the Northwest Rebellion was fought in this vicinity in 1885, and the decisive battle, in which Canadian troops defeated the Metis (fur trappers of French-Indian extraction), was fought at Batoche Battlefield in the park. Near the battlefield are the Metis cemetery and the rectory which houses a historical display telling of the tragedy of Batoche. To reach the park, drive to Domremy, about 30 miles south of Prince Albert National Park on Highway 2, then turn west for an additional 20 miles.

FORT BATTLEFORD NATIONAL HISTORIC PARK [D-2] Fort Battleford was one of the early North West Mounted Police posts, built in 1876 to serve the territory of the Cree Indians. There are five buildings of the original fort to see, housing exhibits of the history of the Mounties and of the Crees. Surrounded by a log stockade, the fort is the center of a 36-acre park located 81 miles northwest of Saskatoon at North Battleford. Take the Yellowhead Highway. Open from May 1 through September 2.

FORT WALSH [G-1] Near Maple Creek, this fort was established by the North West Mounted Police and was the center of law and order for southern Saskatchewan and Alberta until 1833.

PRINCE ALBERT NATIONAL PARK [C-3] North of Saskatchewan's great prairie you'll find a lake- and woodland-studded country that is a legacy of the glacial age. Hundreds of crystal lakes, rimmed by sandy beaches, are connected by a network of rivers that turn the area into an exciting place for canoe safaris. The park's townsite is at Waskesiu, on the eastern edge of the park on Highway 264—about 60 miles north of Prince Albert. Most of the activity in the park is centered at Waskesiu, and the park headquarters are located here, and there are also motel and cottage facilities.

Keep your eyes open as you travel the park roads, especially in the morning and evening, and you'll likely see some of the wildlife that lives in the park—elk, moose, white-tailed deer, mule deer, and black bear. Fishing in the waters here can be particularly satisfying—with northern pike, lake trout, walleye, and whitefish eager to take your lures. You'll need a fishing license, which you can procure at the Information Center.

There are ample lodge facilities at Waskesiu and 18 campgrounds scattered through the park.

THE YUKON

DAWSON CITY [D-2] The Palace Grand Theater, opened in 1899 to bring theatrical entertainment to the brawling gold rushers, has been restored and is now a national historic site. The S.S. *Keno*, a big old stern-wheeler, has been beached and restored and is a national historic site. She carried many a miner upriver and is a colorful remnant of the gold rush.

KLUANE NATIONAL PARK [D-3] A big 8,500-square-mile area in the southwestern corner of the Yukon Territory, this park has as its backbone the great St. Elias mountains. Hoary giant of this chain is the 19,850-foot Mount Logan, Canada's loftiest peak. Peaks in the area have been the North American continent's greatest challenge to mountain climbers. The Alaska Highway runs for 80 miles along the park's northern boundary, and Whitehorse is 100 miles east. No facilities are available; the park will remain a rugged wilderness area.

WHITEHORSE [E-3] The riverboat S. S. *Klondike*, which carried supplies to miners in the area, has also been restored and declared a national historic site.

CAMPING

CANADA IS CAMPING COUNTRY. The land is ideally suited for it. But even more important than the mountains and forests and great undeveloped areas is the fact that planners here have put a priority on camping and outdoor recreation of all kinds. You can see the result of this thinking in big, impressive national and provincial parks all across the country. And when the great Trans-Canada Highway was conceived, an important part of the plan was a series of campgrounds at regular in-intervals along its entire length.

That kind of thinking has made the camper feel welcome and wanted, and has fostered camping.

Whatever kind of camping adventure you want, you can find it here. There is good camping in well-developed areas for the weekend outdoorsman. There are fine facilities for the family on a three-week holiday, with any number of the amenities you desire.

Canada can offer a real test of your skill as a woodsman, too. Here if you want to backpack off into true wilderness, a hundred miles from other humans, you can do it. If you want to portage by canoe along a thousand miles of primeval river, the opportunity is here but don't try it without the services of an experienced guide.

In addition to campgrounds in the national and provincial parks, you'll find hundreds of locally operated grounds, both public and private. Some towns provide camping facilities in parks and on beaches within the city limits. Others have established them nearby. In the more remote areas, nearly every road leads to a lake—and a campground.

Three and a half million people are now camping in Canada, and the number grows every year. Fortunately, the land is vast and the facilities numerous, so serious population pressures have not yet developed. Restrictions on the time you can stay at any campground are reasonable. Expansion of facilities is planned to keep up with the growing interest in outdoor living in the foreseeable future.

The novice camper or the camper new to Canada should be aware of a few things—in addition to the simple but vital fact that he should be a good housekeeper, and leave his campsite in better condition than he found it. People who love the outdoors enough to live in it must lead everyone else toward maintaining its natural order and beauty.

Summer evenings in Canada's mountains and northern areas are sometimes chilly and at other times, very, very cold. Temperatures near freezing are possible even in July and August. When packing for your trip to these places, put plenty of warm clothing and bedding in. Once the sun has come up, the day will warm up pleasantly. You need to be prepared for the nights, and for the evenings and early mornings.

Those who have been there will tell you that Canada's scenic areas are incredibly beautiful—but they breed some pretty voracious insects. These can be a real problem in the late spring and early summer. Don't forget to bring an ample supply of insect repellent with you, and be sure you can effectively screen your tent or trailer.

Another basic rule of camping needs emphasis in Canada. There are many areas here where you may be the only camper in an area of a hundred square miles. Don't go off into remote areas without telling someone where you'll be and how long you expect to be there. In any of the parks, take a moment to check in with the custodian. The rules require that you do it, but it is more than just a matter of rules. It is one of personal safety. If you run into trouble, you'll be missed, and those who can bring you help will know where to look.

It shouldn't be necessary to say so, but in camping as in anything else, you must learn to walk before you start to run. Learn to be a good and self-sufficient camper in a series of easy expeditions, and then take the tougher trips on gradually. Don't attempt to hike in the Rockies of northern British Columbia or the forests of northern Quebec until you've had plenty of practice at less strenuous sites. Know both yourself and your equipment before you tax either too heavily.

Finally, one of the great charms of Canada's mountain and forest lands is the animals who live in them. Treat these animals with a healthy respect. Don't disturb them. Don't feed them. And above all, don't try to pet or play with them. They're wild, they bite, and the larger ones—bears, for example—are capable of killing you with little effort.

To the old hand at camping, much of this advice is unnecessary. But in Canada, campers who have previously ventured only into well-developed campgrounds in protected areas suddenly feel the lure of the more exotic remote sites, where a whole new set of conditions awaits them.

A camper's unexpected treat—discovering an elk at a favorite watering spot

ALBERTA

FOR MAP, SEE PAGE 106

- ●—at the campground
- ○—within one mile of campground
- $—extra charge
- *—see city map
- **—limited facilities during winter months
- 1-5—number of miles in NF within which facility or activity can be found
- A—adults only
- B—10,000 acres or more
- C—contribution
- E—tents rented
- F—entrance fee or permit required—see "Special Information on the Public Areas"
- H—over 9000 feet above sea level
- N—no specific number, limited by size of area only
- P—primitive
- R—reservation required
- S—self-contained units only
- U—unlimited
- V—trailers rented
- Z—reservations accepted
- LD—Labor Day
- MD—Memorial Day
- UC—under construction
- d—boat dock
- g—public golf course within 5 miles
- h—horseback riding
- j—whitewater running craft only
- k—snow skiing within 25 miles
- l—boat launch
- m—area north of map
- n—no drinking water
- p—motor bikes prohibited
- r—boat rental
- s—stream, lake or creek water only
- t—tennis
- u—snowmobile trails
- w—open certain off-season weekends and holidays
- y—drinking water must be boiled
- ⚓ access to ocean
- access to lake
- ≈ access to river
- mountainous terrain
- prairie land
- desert area
- heavily wooded
- urban area
- rural area

CREDIT CARD SYMBOLS:
- A—American Express
- M—Master Charge
- V—Visa/Bank Americard

FEES REFLECT MINIMUM RATE FOR 2 ADULTS AND ARE SUBJECT TO SEASONAL CHANGES

Park number	Map reference	Name of park	Access	Physical environment	Elevation	Acres	Number of tent spaces	Number of trailer spaces	Approximate fee	Credit cards accepted	Season	Time limit	Reservations	Pets permitted	Max. trailer size	Electric hookup	Water hookup	Sewer hookup	Sanitary station	Bottled gas	Air conditioning	Tables	Firewood	Pull-thru spaces	Rec. hall	Flush toilets	Showers	Ice	Auto. laundry	Cafe-snack bar	Store	Swimming pool	Other swimming	Fishing	Boating	Playground	Other	CB channel monitored	Telephone no.	Mail address
		PROVINCIAL PARKS																																						
1	D4	Aspen Beach	Fr Bentley, 5 mi E on Hwy 12		3	386	150	150	1.50		All year	14		•	U				•	o		•	•					o	o	•			•	•	lr	•	gh			Bentley
2	G4	Beauvais Lake	Fr Pincher Creek, 6 mi S on Hwy 6, 8 mi W on country rd		4	1165	22	23	1.50		All year	14		•	U							•	•										•	•	l	•				Pincher Creek
3	E4	Big Hill Springs	Fr Cochrane, 2 mi N, 5 mi E on country rd		4	63	25	25	1.50		All year	14		•	U							•	•													•				Cochrane
4	E3	Bow Valley	Fr Calgary, 45 mi W on TC 1		5	2062	117	118	1.50		All year	14		•	U	•			•			•	•			•	•		•	o				•		•				Seebe
5	B4	Lesser Slave Lk	Fr Slave Lk, 4 mi N on Hwy		2	B	55	50	1.50		All year	14		•	U				•			•	•						o	o			•	•			gp			Slave Lake
6	D3	Crimson Lake	Fr Rocky Mtn House, 4 mi W on Hwy 11, 5 mi N on country rd		3	8507	104	104	1.50		All year	14		•	U	•			•			•	•							•			•	•	dl	•	g			Rocky Mtn House
7	B4	Cross Lake	Fr Jarvie, 6 mi N on Hwy 44, 17 mi NE on country rd		2	4137	40	40	1.50		All year	14		•	U				•			•	•							•			•	•	lr	•				Fawcett
8	G6	Cypress Hills	Fr Medicine Hat, 20 mi E on TC Hwy 1, 21 mi S on Hwy 48		5	B	52	342	1.50		All year	14		•	U	•			•			•	•		•	•	•		•	•	•		•	•	l	•	g			Elkwater
9	G4	Police Outpost	Fr Cardston, 7 mi S, 13 mi SW on country rd		5	362	15	14	1.50		All year	14		•	U							•	•											•	l		p			Cardston
10	D6	Dillberry Lake	Fr Provost, 12 mi E on Hwy 13, 18 mi N on Hwy 17		2	252	30	30	1.50		All year	14		•	U							•	•							•			•	•	l	•				Chauvin
11	D4	Jarvis Bay	Fr Sylvan Lake, 3 mi N on Hwy 20		3	216	70	70	1.50		All year	14		•	U				•	o		•	•			•	•		o	o				•	l		gp			Sylvan Lake
12	C2	William A Switzer	Fr Hinton, 2 mi SW on Hwy 16, 10 mi N on Forestry Trunk Rd		5	6637	40	40	1.50		All year	14		•	U							•	•										•	•	l	•				Hinton
14	F4	Chain Lakes	Fr Nanton, 5 mi W, 21 mi SW on country rd		4	1829	70	70	1.50		All year	14		•	U				•			•								•				•	l		p			Stavely
15	C5	Garner Lake	Fr Spedden, 3 mi N on paved rd		2	182	38	39	1.50		All year	14		•	U	•			•			•	•							•	o		•	•	l	•				Spedden
16	D6	Gooseberry Lake	Fr Consort, 1 mi W on Hwy 12, 7 mi N, 2 mi E		2	128	63	63	1.50		All year	14		•	U	$						•	•							•			•	•	l	•	g			Consort
17	B6	Moose Lake	Fr Bonnyville, 2 mi N, 8 mi W on Country rd		2	1818	29	30	1.50		All year	14		•	U				•			•	•							o			•	•	lr	•	p			Bonneville
18	F5	Kinbrook Island	Fr Brooks, 11 mi S on paved rd		3	95	125	125	1.50		All year	14		•	U							•	•							•			•	•	l	•				Brooks
19	D5	Miquelon Lake	Fr Camrose, 5 mi W on Hwy 13, 22 mi N on Hwy 21 & 10 mi E on paved rd		3	1044	116	116	1.50		All year	14		•	U				•			•	•			•	•			•			•		l	•				Camrose
20	F5	Little Bow	Fr Champion, 10 mi E, 2 mi S on paved rd		3	272	96	97	1.50		All year	14		•	U				•			•	•							•			•	•	l	•				Champion
21	E5	Little Fish Lake	Fr Drumheller, 21 mi E, 8 mi S on country rd		3	151	25	25	1.50		All year	14		•	U							•	•							•			•	•	lr	•				Drumheller
22	B5	Long Lake	Fr Newbrook, 6 mi E, 9 mi N on paved rd		2	1888	163	164	1.50		All year	14		•	U	•			•			•	•						o	•			•	•	lr					Newbrook
23	M	Gregoire Lake	Fr Fort McMurray, 14 mi S on Hwy 63, 4 mi E		3	1676	45	44	1.50		All year	14		•	U							•	•							•	•		•	•	dlr					Ft McMurray
24	D4	Pigeon Lake	Fr Westerose, 3 mi W on Hwy 13, 6 mi N on access rd		3	619	79	79	1.50		All year	14		•	U				•			•	•			•	•			•	o		•	•	dl	•				Westerose
25	A2	Lac Cardinal	Fr Grimshaw, 4 mi W, 2 mi N on country rd		2	300	30	30	1.50		All year	14		•	U							•	•						o	•			•		l	•				Grimshaw
26	A1	Moonshine Lake	Fr Spirit River, 15 mi W on Hwy 49, 7 mi N on paved rd		2	1932	54	54	1.50		All year	14		•	U				•			•	•							•			•	•	l	•				Spirit River
28	G5	Park Lake	Fr Lethbridge, 7 mi N on Hwy 25, 1 mi N, 1 mi W, 1 mi N on paved rd		3	188	26	27	1.50		All year	14		•	U							•	•						o	•			•	•	l	•				Lethbridge
29	C3	Pembina River	Fr Entwistle, 2 mi N on Hwy 11A		3	409	72	72	1.50		All year	14		•	U				•			•	•					o	o	o			•	•		•				Entwistle
30	E4	Red Lodge	Fr Bowden, 9 mi W on paved country rd		3	159	52	52	1.50		All year	14		•	U							•	•							•			•	•	dlr	•				Bowden
31	B5	Sir Winston Churchill	Fr Lac La Biche, 6 mi NE on country rd		2	591	37	38	1.50		All year	14		•	U				o			•	•						o	o			•	•	dlr	•	g			Lac La Biche
32	D5	Rochon Sands	Fr Stettler, 7 mi W on Hwy 12, 9 mi N on paved rd		3	158	17	18	1.50		All year	14		•	U				•			•	•							o			•	•	lr	•				Erskine
33	B1	Saskatoon Island	Fr Grande Prairie, 12 mi W on Hwy 2, 2 mi N on country rd		2	251	21	21	1.50		All year	14		•	U							•	•							•			•		l	•				Wembley
34	F5	Tillebrook	Fr Brooks, 6 mi SE on T-C Hwy 1		3	253	60	15	1.50		All year	14		•	U	•			•			•	•			•	•		•	o							g			Brooks
35	F5	Dinosaur	Fr Patricia, 4 mi NE, 6 mi E on country rd		3	B	20	20	1.50		All year	14		•	U				•			•	•											•		•				Patricia
36	G5	Taber	Fr Taber, 2 mi W on Hwy 3, 2 mi N		3	127	24	24	1.50		All year	14		•	U				•			•	•						o	o			•	•		•				Taber
37	C4	Thunder Lake	Fr Barrhead, 13 mi W on paved rd		2	514	75	75	1.50		All year	14		•	U				•		•	•	•							•			•		l	•				Barrhead
38	D5	Big Knife	Fr Forestburg, 5 mi W on paved rd, 7 mi S on country rd		3	731	26	26	1.50		All year	14		•	U				•			•	•							•				•	l	•				Forestburg
39	C6	The Vermilion	Fr Vermilion, 1 mi N		2	1805	20	21	1.50		All year	14		•	U	•			o			•	•				•	o	o	o			•		l	•	g			Vermilion
40	C4	Wabamun Lake	Fr Edmonton, 38 mi W on Hwy 16, 2 mi S		3	524	182	182	1.50		All year	14		•	U	$			•			•	•			•	•		o	•			•	•	dl	•				Wabamun
41	F4	Willow Creek	Fr Stavely, 5 mi W & 6 mi S on country rd		3	271	25	25	1.50		All year	14		•	U							•	•							•			•	•		•				Staveley
42	A3	Winagami Lake	Fr McLennan, 9 mi S on Hwy 2A, 6 mi E & 2 mi N		2	2992	32	32	1.50		All year	14		•	U				•			•	•				•			•			•	•	l	•				McLennan
43	G5	Woolford	Fr Cardston, 3 mi NE on Hwy 5, 2 mi E, 2 mi S, 2 mi E, 1 mi S, & 1 mi W		4	86	10	10	1.50		All year	14		•	U				•			•	•					o	o				•	•	l	•				Cardston
44	G5	Writing-on-Stone	Fr Milk River, 19 mi E, 3 mi S, 2 mi E, 1 mi S		3	1059	7	8	1.50		All year	14		•	U				•			•	•										•	•		•				Milk River
45	B2	Williamson	Fr Valleyview, 12 mi W on Hwy 34, 1 mi N		2	43	31	31	1.50		All year	14		•	U				•			•	•							•			•	•	lr	•				Calais
		PROVINCIAL PARKS & RESERVES																																						
		Edson Forest																																					403/427-3585	
101	D3	Forks	Fr Edson, 68 mi S		3	250	20				5/1-9/30	14		•								•	•											o			p			Hinton
101	D3	Whitehorse Creek	Fr Edson, 76 mi S		3	30	15				5/1-9/30	14		•								•	•											•			p			Hinton
102	C2	Pierre Grey	Fr Hinton, 58 mi NW on Hwy 40				33	40	None		5/1-9/30	14		•	24							•	•											o	l		p			Hinton
102	C2	Big Berland	Fr Hinton, 43 mi NW on Hwy 40				25				5/1-9/30	14		•								•	•											o	l		p			Hinton
102	C2	Rock Lake	Fr Hinton, 26 mi NW on Hwy 40				14	26	None		5/1-9/30	14		•	24							•	•											o	l		p			Hinton
103	D2	Watson Creek	Fr Hinton, 35 mi S		5		10	15	None		4/1-9/30	14		•	24							•	•	•													p			Hinton
103	D2	Cardinal River	Fr Hinton, 32 mi S, 24 mi E				38	22	None		5/1-9/30	14		•	24							•	•											o			p			Hinton
105	D2	McLeod River	Fr Hinton, 16 mi SE		3	288	9	7	None		5/1-9/30	14		•	24							•	•											•			p			Hinton
106	D2	Fickle Lake	Fr Edson, 24 mi SW		3	250	17				5/1-9/30	14		•								•	•										•	•	l		p			Hinton
		Clearwater/Rocky Forest																																					403/427-3585	
108	E3	Seven Mile	Fr Ricinus, 41 mi NW on Forestry Trunk Rd				20	18	None		5/1-9/30	14		•	24							•	•											o			p			Ricinus
108	E3	Swan Lk	Fr Ricinus, 20 mi NW on Forestry Trunk Rd				16				5/1-9/30	14		•								•	•											o	l		p			Ricinus
108	E3	Ram Falls	Fr Ricinus, 45 mi NW on Forestry Trunk Rd				30	46	None		5/1-9/30	14		•	24							•	•											o			p			Ricinus
109	E3	North Ram River	Fr Nordegg, 18 mi S		5	230	10	10	None		5/1-10/31	14		•	24							•	•	•										•			p			Nordegg
109	E3	Elk Creek	Fr Nordegg, 28 mi S		4	64	9	5	None		5/1-10/31	14		•	30							•	•	•										•			p			Nordegg
110	D3	Elk River	Fr Nordegg, 45 mi N		1	80	5	8	None		5/1-11/30	14		•	24							•	•	•										•			p			Nordegg

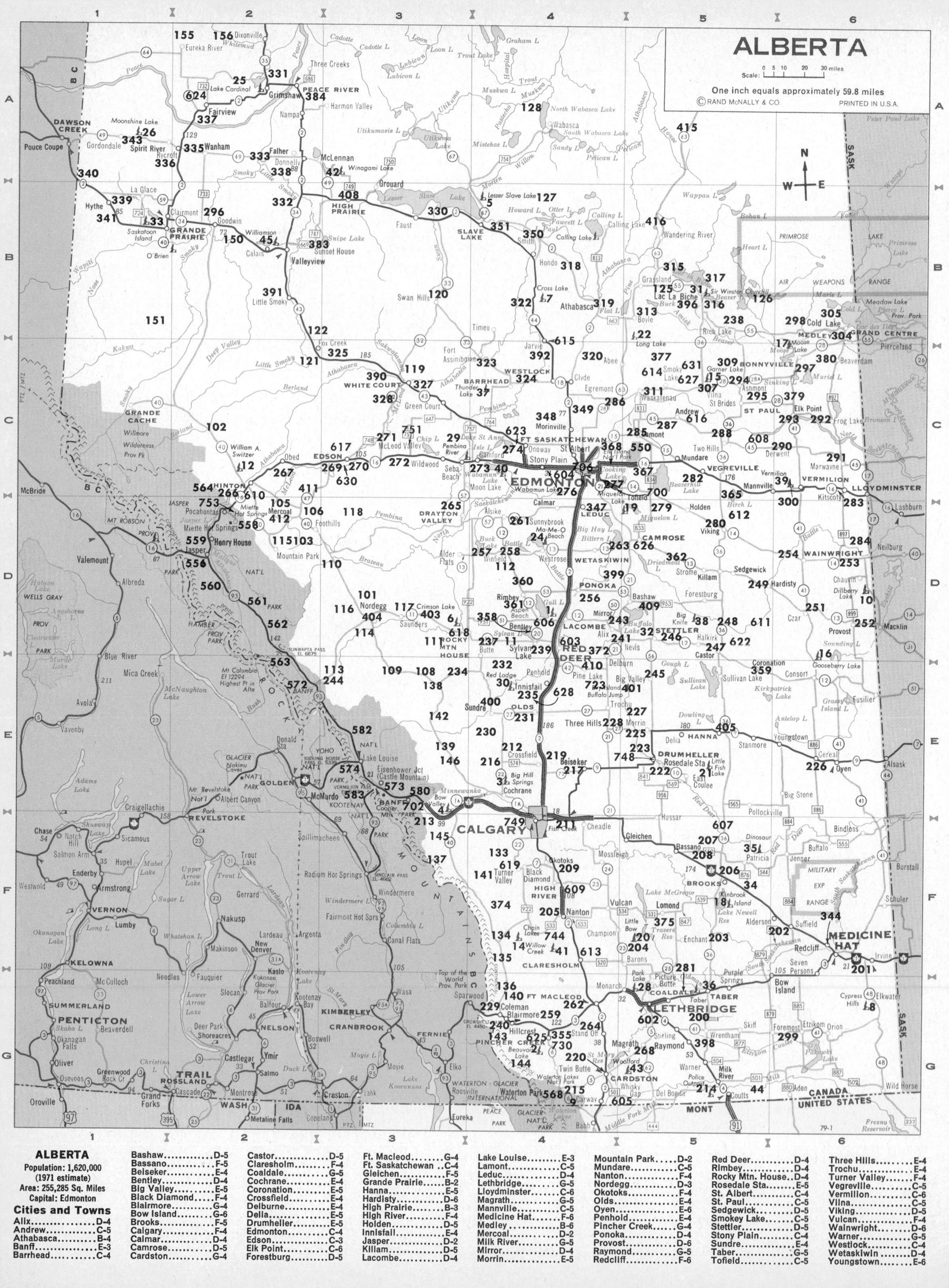

ALBERTA
Population: 1,620,000
(1971 estimate)
Area: 255,285 Sq. Miles
Capital: Edmonton

Cities and Towns

Alix.............D-4
Andrew.............C-5
Athabasca.............B-4
Banff.............E-3
Barrhead.............C-4
Bashaw.............D-5
Bassano.............F-5
Beiseker.............E-4
Bentley.............D-4
Big Valley.............E-5
Black Diamond.............F-4
Blairmore.............G-4
Bow Island.............G-6
Brooks.............F-5
Calgary.............F-4
Calmar.............D-4
Camrose.............D-5
Cardston.............G-4
Castor.............D-5
Claresholm.............F-4
Coaldale.............G-5
Cochrane.............E-4
Coronation.............E-5
Crossfield.............E-4
Delburne.............E-4
Delia.............E-5
Drumheller.............E-5
Edmonton.............C-4
Edson.............C-3
Elk Point.............C-6
Forestburg.............D-5
Ft. Macleod.............G-4
Ft. Saskatchewan.............C-4
Gleichen.............F-5
Grande Prairie.............B-2
Hanna.............E-5
Hardisty.............D-6
High Prairie.............B-3
High River.............F-4
Holden.............D-5
Innisfail.............E-4
Jasper.............D-2
Killam.............D-5
Lacombe.............D-4
Lake Louise.............E-3
Lamont.............C-5
Leduc.............D-4
Lethbridge.............G-5
Lloydminster.............C-6
Magrath.............G-5
Mannville.............C-5
Medicine Hat.............F-6
Medley.............B-6
Mercoal.............D-2
Milk River.............G-5
Mirror.............D-4
Morrin.............E-5
Mountain Park.............D-2
Mundare.............C-5
Nanton.............F-4
Nordegg.............D-3
Okotoks.............F-4
Olds.............E-4
Oyen.............E-6
Penhold.............E-4
Pincher Creek.............G-4
Ponoka.............D-4
Provost.............D-6
Raymond.............G-5
Redcliff.............F-6
Red Deer.............D-4
Rimbey.............D-4
Rocky Mtn. House.............D-4
Rosedale Sta.............E-5
St. Albert.............C-4
St. Paul.............C-5
Sedgewick.............D-5
Smokey Lake.............C-5
Stettler.............D-5
Stony Plain.............C-4
Sundre.............E-4
Taber.............G-5
Tofield.............C-5
Three Hills.............E-4
Trochu.............E-4
Turner Valley.............F-4
Vegreville.............C-5
Vermilion.............C-6
Vilna.............C-5
Viking.............D-5
Vulcan.............F-4
Wainwright.............D-6
Warner.............G-5
Westlock.............C-4
Wetaskiwin.............D-4
Youngstown.............E-6

Park number	Map reference	Name of park	Access	Physical environment	Elevation	Acres	Number of tent spaces	Number of trailer spaces	Approximate fee	Credit cards accepted	Season	Time limit	Reservations	Pets permitted	Max. trailer size	Electric hookup	Water hookup	Sewer hookup	Sanitary station	Bottled gas	Air conditioning	Tables	Firewood	Pull-thru spaces	Rec. hall	Flush toilets	Showers	Ice	Auto. laundry	Cafe-snack bar	Store	Swimming pool	Other swimming	Fishing	Boating	Playground	Other	CB channel monitored	Telephone no.	Mail address
		PROVINCIAL PARKS & RESERVES (CONT'D)																																						
		Clearwater/Rocky Forest (CONT'D)																																						
110	D3	Brazeau Res	Fr Nordegg, 39 mi N		5	13	12	27	None		5/1-10/31	14		•	24							•	•	•										•	I		p			Nordegg
111	D3	Strachan	Fr Rocky Mtn House, 12 mi SW		4	80	12	11	None		5/1-10/31	14		•	24							•	•	•										•			p			Rocky Mtn House
111	D3	Prairie Creek	Fr Rocky Mtn House, 20 mi		4	210	10	25	None		5/1-10/31	14		•	24							•	•	•										•			p			Rocky Mtn House
111	D3	Peppers Lk	Fr Rocky Mtn House, 12 mi S, 28 mi W		5	130	11	9	None		5/1-10/31	14		•	24							•	•	•										•	I		p			Rocky Mtn House
112	D4	Medicine Lk	Fr Rimbey, 23 mi NW		3	90	5	28	None		5/1-10/31	14		•	30							•	•	•										•	I		p			Rimbey
113	E3	Kootnay Plains	Fr Nordegg, 40 mi W		5	260	26	1	None		5/1-10/31	14		•	24							•	•	•										•			p			Nordegg
113	E3	Thompson Cr	Fr Nordegg, 54 mi W		4	20	18	37	None		5/1-10/3	14		•	24							•	•	•										•			p			Nordegg
114	D3	Upper Shunda Cr	Fr Nordegg, 2 mi W		4	110	10	10	None		5/1-10/31	14		•	24							•	•	•						o	o			•			p			Nordegg
115	D2	Brazeau River	Fr Nordegg, 39 mi N		5		6	6	None		4/1-9/30	14		•	24							•	•																	Nordegg
116	D3	Fish Lk	Fr Nordegg, 2 mi W				46	52			5/1-9/30	14		•	24							•	•											o	I		p			Nordegg
116	D3	Goldeye Lk	Fr Nordegg, 2 mi W				11	9	None		5/1-9/30	14		•	24							•	•											o	I		p			Nordegg
117	D3	Chambers Creek	Fr Rocky Mtn House, 25 mi W on Hwy 11		4		14	1	None		4/1-9/30	14		•	24							•	•														p			Rocky Mtn House
		Whitecourt Forest																																					403/427-3585	
118	D3	Wolf Lake	Fr Edson, 15 mi E on Yellowhead Hwy 16, 27 mi S			735	10				5/1-9/30	14		•								•	•											•	I		p			Edson
119	C3	Goose Lake	Fr Whitecourt, 20 mi E, 16 mi N on Hwy 658			110	12				5/1-9/30	14		•								•	•											•	I		p			Lone Pine
119	C3	Carson Lake	Fr Whitecourt, 15 mi N on Hwy 392			577	19	28	None		5/1-9/30	14		•	24							•	•											•	I		p			Whitecourt
120	B3	Swan Hills	Fr Swan Hills, 5 mi W		2	35	7	3	None		5/1-9/30	14		•	24							•	•											•	I		p			Swan Hills
121	C2	Smoke Lake	Fr Fox Creek, 8 mi SW			310	10	12	None		5/1-9/30	14		•	24							•	•											•	I		p			Fox Creek
122	B2	Iosegun Lake	Fr Fox Creek, 7 mi N		2	730	12	18	None		5/1-9/30	14		•	24							•	•											•	I		p			Fox Creek
		Lac La Biche																																					403/427-3585	99 Ave 109 St, Edmonton
125	B5	Touchwood Lk	Fr Lac La Biche, 22 mi E, 7 mi N			60	24	8	None		5/1-11/30	14		•	24							•	•	•									•	•	I		p			Lac La Biche
126	B5	Wolf Lk	Fr Bonnyville, 25 mi N, 10 mi W			430	10	14	None		5/1-10/31	14		•								•	•	•										•	I		p			Bonnyville
126	B5	Seibert Lk	Fr Bonnyville, 28 mi N, 20 mi W			80	17	17	None		5/1-10/30	14		•	24							•	•	•										•	I		p			Bonnyville
		Slave Lk																																					403/427-3585	99 Ave 109 St, Edmonton
127	B4	Fawcett Lake	Fr Slave Lake, 8 mi N, 36 mi E			150	5	10	None		5/1-10/31	14		•	U							•	•	•										•	I		p			Slave Lake
128	A4	North Wabasco Lk	Fr Slave Lk, 88 mi N		2	132	10	8	None		5/1-10/31	14		•	U							•	•	•										•	I		p			Slave Lake
		Footner Lk Forest																																					403/427-3585	
131	M	Hutch Lake	Fr High Level, 14 mi N on Hwy 35, 8 mi W			250		12	None		5/1-9/30	14		•	24							•	•											•	I		p			High Level
		Bow/Crow Forest																																					403/427-3585	
133	F4	Gooseberry Flat	Fr Bragg Creek, 4 mi SW on Co		4	51	10	9	None		5/1-9/30	14		•	24							•	•											o						Bragg Creek
133	F4	Paddy's Flat	Fr Bragg Creek, 9 mi W		5	275	16	21	None		5/1-9/30	14		•	24							•	•	•										o			p			Bragg Creek
133	F4	North Fork	Fr Turner Val, 15 mi NW		5		20	4	None		4/1-9/30	14		•	24							•	•	•																Turner Valley
134	F4	Cat Creek	Fr Longview, 30 mi SW on Co		5	58	10	13	None		5/1-9/30	14		•	24							•	•	•										o						Longview
134	F4	Indian Grove	Fr Coleman, 56 mi N on Forestry Trunk Rd		5		16	12	None		4/1-9/30	14		•	24							•	•	•																Coleman
135	F4	Oldman River	Fr Coleman, 31 mi N on Forestry Trunk Rd				18				5/1-9/30	14		•								•	•											o						Coleman
135	F4	Livingstone Falls	Fr Coleman, 44 mi N on Forestry Trunk Rd				12	4	None		5/1-9/30	14		•	24							•	•											o						Coleman
136	G4	Racehorse	Fr Coleman, 21 mi N on Forestry Trunk Rd				13	6	None		5/1-9/30	14		•	24							•	•											o						Coleman
137	F3	Eau Claire	Fr Seebe, 22 mi S & W on Forestry Trunk Rd		5	213		22	None		5/1-9/30	14		•	U							•	•	•										o			p			Seebe
137	F3	Beaver Flat	Fr Turner Valley, 45 mi WNW via Millarville & Bragg Creek		5	44	10	9	None		5/1-9/30	14		•	24							•	•											•						Turner Valley
137	F3	Spray Lakes	Fr Canmore, 20 mi S		6	2160	26				5/1-9/30	14		•								•	•											•	I		p			Canmore
137	F3	Sibbald Flat	Fr Seebe, 15 mi SE on Forestry Trunk Rd		5	406	32	64	None		5/1-9/30	14		•	24							•	•	•										o			p			Seebe
138	E3	Red Deer River	Fr Cochrane, 68 mi NW on Hwy 1A & Forestry Trunk Rd				18	48	None		5/1-9/30	14		•	24							•	•							o				o						Cochrane
139	E3	Dutch Creek	Fr Coleman, 27 mi N on Forestry Trunk Rd				14	8	None		5/1-9/30	14		•	24							•	•											o						Coleman
139	E3	Waiparous Creek	Fr Cochrane, 37 mi NW on Hwy 1A & Forestry Trunk Rd				18	18	None		5/1-9/30	14		•	24							•	•											o						Cochrane
140	G4	Beaver Mines Lake	Fr Bellevue, 3 mi E, 14 mi N				47	7	None		5/1-9/30	14		•	24							•	•											o	I					Bellevue
140	G4	Chinook	Fr Coleman, 3 mi W on Hwy 3, 3 mi N				20	11	None		5/1-9/30	14		•	24							•	•											o	I					Coleman
140	G4	Allison	Fr Coleman, 2 mi N, 3 mi W				9	8	None		5/1-9/30	14		•	24							•	•											o						Coleman
141	F4	Sandy McNabb	Fr Turner Valley, 15 mi W on Hwy 546		5	330		31	None		5/1-9/30	14		•	24							•	•											o			p			Turner Valley
141	F4	Bluerock	Fr Turner Valley, 4 mi S & 20 mi W on Hwy 546		6	86	13				5/1-9/30	14		•								•	•											•						Turner Valley
142	E3	James-Wilson	Fr Bearberry, 12 mi W on Co, 7 mi SW on Forestry Trunk Rd		4	43	5	10	None		5/1-9/30	14		•	24							•	•	•										o						Bearberry
142	E3	Burnt Timber	Fr Cochrane, 15 mi W on TC 1, 39 mi NW on Forestry Trunk Rd		5	142	10	8	None		5/1-9/30	14		•	24							•	•											•						Cochrane
143	G4	Lynx Creek	Fr Frank, 11 mi SW		5	63	10	6	None		5/1-9/30	14		•	24							•	•											•			p			Frank
143	G4	Castle Falls	Fr Burmis, 10 mi SE on Co		5	76	13	15	None		5/1-9/30	14		•	24							•	•											•						Burmis
144	G4	Castle River Bridge	Fr Hillcrest, 20 mi S on Co		5	90	15	11	None		5/15-9/30	14		•	24							•	•	•										•						Hillcrest
145	F3	Evans-Thomas	Fr Seebe, 17 mi SW		6		34	25	None		4/1-9/30	14		•	24							•	•	•																Turner Valley
146	E3	North Ghost	Fr Cochrene, 40 mi NW on Forestry Trunk Rd		5		11	82	None		4/1-9/30	14		•	24							•	•	•																Sundre
		Grand Prarie Forest																																					403/427-3585	
150	B2	Simonette River	Fr Debolt, 7 mi W on Hwy 34, 5 mi S on Forrestry Trunk Rd		2	70	26				5/1-9/30	14		•								•	•											•			p			Debolt
151	B1	Two Lakes	Fr Grand Prairie, 55 mi S, 25 mi W			3620	26	10	None		5/1-9/30	14		•	24							•	•											•	I		p			Grand Prairie
151	B1	Musreau Lk	Fr Grande Prairie, 50 mi S		3		64	19	None		4/1-9/30	14		•	24							•	•	•																Grande Prairie
		Peace River Forest																																					403/427-3585	
155	A2	Running Lake	Fr Hines Creek, 32 mi N & 18 mi W			330	10				5/1-9/30	14		•								•	•											•	I		p			Hines Creek
156	A2	Sulphur Lake	Fr Dixonville, 35 mi W on Hwy 689			350	10				5/1-9/30	14		•								•	•											•	I		p			Dixonville
		ALBERTA GOVERNMENT HIGHWAY CAMPSITES																																						
200	G5	N of Wrentham	Fr Taber, 14 mi S on Hwy 36			4	N	N	None		5/1-10/1	14		•	U							•	•										o	•	I					161 Transprtn Bldg, Edmonton
201	F6	Pashley	Fr Medicine Hat, 10 mi E on TC 1			15	N	N	None		5/1-10/1	14		•	U							•	•								o									
202	F6	Suffield	Fr Suffield, 1 mi E on TC 1			7	N	N	None		5/1-10/1	14		•	U							•	•								o									
203	F5	Scandia	Fr Vauxhall, 13 mi N on Hwy 36			26	N	N	None		5/1-10/1	14		•	U							•	•											•						
204	F5	Carmangay	Fr Carmangay, 2 mi NW on Hwy 23			12	N	N	None		5/1-10/1	14		•	U							•	•								o			•						
205	F4	Nanton	In Nanton, on Hwy 2			8	N	N	None		5/1-10/1	14		•	U							•	•					o			o									
206	F5	Brooks	Fr Brooks, 2 mi NE on TC 1		3	1	N	N	None		5/1-10/1	14		•	U							•	•								o									
207	F5	Emerson Bridge	Fr Duchess, 14 mi N on Hwy 36		3	10	N	N	None		5/1-10/1	14		•	U							•	•											•						
208	F5	Bassano	Fr Bassano, 2 mi E on TC 1			6	N	N	None		5/1-10/1	14		•	U							•	•								o									
209	F5	Sheep Creek	Fr Okotoks, 5 mi E on Hwy 2			3	N	N	None		5/1-10/1	14		•	U							•	•								o		•	•						
211	F4	Chestermere Lake	Fr Calgary, 6 mi E on Hwy 1A		4	4	N	N	None		5/1-10/1	14		•	U							•	•					o			o		•	•	r					

ALBERTA

FOR FOOTNOTE EXPLANATION SEE FIRST PAGE OF THIS **PROVINCE** FOR MAP, SEE PAGE **106**

Park number	Map reference	Name of park	Access	Physical environment	Elevation	Acres	Number of tent spaces	Number of trailer spaces	Approximate fee	Credit cards accepted	Season	Time limit	Reservations	Pets permitted	Max. trailer size	Electric hookup	Water hookup	Sewer hookup	Sanitary station	Bottled gas	Air conditioning	Tables	Firewood	Pull-thru spaces	Rec. hall	Flush toilets	Showers	Ice	Auto. laundry	Cafe-snack bar	Store	Swimming pool	Other swimming	Fishing	Boating	Playground	Other	CB channel monitored	Telephone no.	Mail address
		ALBERTA GOVERNMENT HIGHWAY CAMPSITES (CONT'D)																																						
212	E4	Cremona	Fr Crossfield, 9 mi NW on Hwy 2A, 11 mi W on Hwy 580			4	N	N	None		5/1-10/1	14		•	U							•	•											•						
213	F3	Lac Des Arcs	Fr Canmore, 12 mi E on TC 1			16	N	N	None		5/1-10/1	14		•	U							•	•										•	•						
213	F3	Deadman's Flat	Fr Canmore, 7 mi E on TC 1			4	N	N	None		5/1-10/1	14		•	U							•	•					○			○			•						
213	F3	Bow River	Fr Canmore, 4 mi E on TC 1			20	N	N	None		5/1-10/1	14		•	U							•	•					○			○			•						
214	G5	Milk River	In Milk Riv vil, on Hwy 4			3	N	N	None		5/1-10/1	14		•	U							•	•					•			○		•	•						
215	G4	Crooked Creek	Fr Waterton Park, 7 mi E on Hwy 5			15	N	N	None		5/1-10/1	14		•	U							•	•											•						
216	E4	Dog Pound Creek	Fr Cochrane, 15 mi N on Hwy 922			3	N	N	None		5/1-10/1	14		•	U							•	•											•						
217	E4	Irricana	In Irricana, on Hwy 9			1	N	N	None		5/1-10/1	14		•	U							•	•								○									
217	E4	Beiseker	In Beiseker, on Hwy 9			3	N	N	None		5/1-10/1	14		•	U							•	•					○			○									
219	E4	N of Crossfield	Fr Crossfield, 2 mi N on Hwy 2			4	N	N	None		5/1-10/1	14		•	U							•	•					○			○									
220	G4	Cardston	In Cardston, on Hwy 2			1	N	N	None		5/1-10/1	14		•	U							•	•			•		•			○		○	•		•				
222	E5	Hoodoos	Fr Drumheller, 9 mi SE on Hwy 10			3	N	N	None		5/1-10/1	14		•	U							•	•					○			○									
223	E5	Munson Ferry (Bleriot)	Fr Drumheller, 7 mi N on Hwy 9, 7 mi W			5	N	N	None		5/1-10/1	14		•	U							•	•																	
225	E5	Morrin Bridge	Fr Morrin, 6 mi W on Hwy 27			2	N	N	None		5/1-10/1	14		•	U							•	•										•	•						
226	E6	Excel	Fr Oyen, 8 mi NW on Hwy 9			4	N	N	None		5/1-10/1	14		•	U							•	•																	
227	E5	Tolman Bridge	Fr Trochu, 11 mi E on Hwy 585			2	N	N	None		5/1-10/1	14		•	U							•	•										•	•						
228	E4	Three Hills	In Three Hills, on Hwy 21			2	N	N	None		5/1-10/1	14		•	U							•	•			•					○		•			•				
228	E4	S of Three Hills	Fr Three Hills, 3 mi S on Hwy 21			1	N	N	None		5/1-10/1	14		•	U							•	•											•						
229	G4	Island Lake	Fr Coleman, 9 mi W on Hwy 3			1	N	N	None		5/1-10/1	14		•	U							•	•											•	l					
230	E4	Fallen Timber Creek	Fr Sundre, 17 mi SW on Hwy 582, 10 Mi W			6	N	N	None		5/1-10/1	14		•	U							•	•											•						
231	E4	Westward Ho	Fr Sundre, 5-1/2 mi E on Hwy 27			30	N	N	None		5/1-10/1	14		•	U							•	•								○		•	•		•				
232	E4	Dickson	Fr Innisfail, 20 mi W on Hwy 54, 5 mi S			3	N	N	None		5/1-10/1	14		•	U							•	•								○			•						
232	E4	Raven	Fr Caroline, 10 mi E on Hwy 54			3	N	N	None		5/1-10/1	14		•	U							•	•								○			•						
234	E3	Tay River	Fr Caroline, 5 mi W on Hwy 54, 12 mi W on Hwy 591			3	N	N	None		5/1-10/1	14		•	U							•	•											•						
235	E4	Bowden	In Bowden, on Hwy 2			3	N	N	None		5/1-10/1	14		•	U							•	•			•					○									
237	D4	Leslieville	Fr Rocky Mtn House, 14 mi E on Hwy 11			2	N	N	None		5/1-10/1	14		•	U							•	•																	
238	B5	Fork Lk	Fr Lac La Biche, 12 mi S on Hwy 36, 24 mi SE		3	3	N	N	None		5/1-10/1	14		•	U							•	•								○		•	•	lr					
238	B5	Pinehurst Lake	Fr Lac La Biche, 12 mi S on Hwy 36, 19 mi NE			48	N	N	None		5/1-10/1	14		•	U							•	•										•	•	l					
238	B5	Ironwood Lake	Fr Lac La Biche, 12 mi S on Hwy 36, 21 mi E			50	N	N	None		5/1-10/1	14		•	U							•	•										•	•	lr					
239	D4	Ft Normandeau	Fr Hwy 2, Red Deer ext, 2 mi W		3	8	N	N	None		5/1-10/1	14		•	U							•	•					○			○		•	•		•				
239	D4	Blindman River	Fr Red Deer, 4 mi N on Hwy 2A			1	N	N	None		5/1-10/1	14		•	U							•	•					○			○		•	•						
240	G4	Frank	Fr Blairmore, 2 mi E on Hwy 3			1	N	N	None		5/1-10/1	14		•	U							•	•								○			•						
240	G4	Lundbreck Falls	Fr Lundbreck, 2 mi W on Hwy 3A			13	N	N	None		5/1-10/1	14		•	U							•	•											•						
241	D4	Tail Creek	Fr Alix, 5-1/2 SE on Hwy 12			1	N	N	None		5/1-10/1	14		•	U							•	•																	
241	D4	Alix	Outskirts of Alix, on Hwy 12			1	N	N	None		5/1-10/1	14		•	U							•	•					○			○				l					
243	D4	The Narrows	Fr Mirror, 3 mi S on Hwy 21, 2 mi E, 2 mi N			3	N	N	None		5/1-10/1	14		•	U							•	•											•						
244	E3	Thomson Creek	Fr Nordegg, 54 mi W on Hwy 11			21	N	N	None		5/1-10/1	14		•	U							•	•																	
244	E3	Kootenay Plains	Fr Nordegg, 40 mi W on Hwy 11			10	N	N	None		5/1-10/1	14		•	U							•	•																	
245	E5	Big Valley	Fr Big Valley, 1 mi E on Hwy 56			2	N	N	None		5/1-10/1	14		•	U							•	•								○									
246	D5	Stettler	In Stettler, on Hwy 12		3	1	N	N	None		5/1-10/1	14		•	U							•	•					○			○					•				
247	D5	Castor	In Castor, on Hwy 12			1	N	N	None		5/1-10/1	14		•	U							•	•								○									
248	D5	Alliance	Fr Alliance, 3 mi S on Hwy 36			5	N	N	None		5/1-10/1	14		•	U							•	•								○									
249	D5	Hardisty	Fr Hardisty, 2 mi SE on Hwy 13			4	N	N	None		5/1-10/1	14		•	U							•	•					○			○									
251	D6	Czar	Fr Czar, 3 mi N on Hwy 41 to jct Hwy 13			10	N	N	None		5/1-10/1	14		•	U							•	•								○									
252	D6	Hayter	Fr Provost, 9 mi E on Hwy 13		3	3	N	N	None		5/1-10/1	14		•	U							•	•								○									
253	D6	N of Chauvin	Fr Chauvin, 13 mi W & N			4	N	N	None		5/1-10/1	14		•	U							•	•																	
254	D6	Fabyan	Fr Wainwright, 7 mi W on Hwy 14			10	N	N	None		5/1-10/1	14		•	U							•	•					○			○									
256	D4	Nelson Lake	Fr Ponoka, 7-1/2 mi E on Hwy 53			4	N	N	None		5/1-10/1	14		•	U							•	•								○		•	•	l					
257	D4	Buck Lake	Fr Winfield, 17 mi W on Hwy 612			2	N	N	None		All year	14		•	U							•	•								○		•	•	lr	•				
258	D4	Modeste Creek	Fr Winfield, 1 mi S on Hwy 12			2	N	N	None		5/1-10/1	14		•	U							•	•								○									
259	G4	Castle River	Fr Pincher Creek, 2 mi N on Hwy 6, 5 mi W			9	N	N	None		5/1-10/1	14		•	U							•	•										○	•						
261	D4	Sunnybrook	Fr Thorsby, 8 mi W on Hwy 39			6	N	N	None		5/1-10/1	14		•	U							•	•																	
261	D4	Mission Beach	Fr Thorsby, 9 mi S on Hwy 778, 3 mi W			5	N	N	None		5/1-10/1	14		•	U							•	•					○			○		•	•	lr					
262	G4	Oldman River	Fr Ft Macleod, 2 mi W on Hwy 3, 1 mi N on Hwy 2			9	N	N	None		5/1-10/1	14		•	U							•	•								○		○	•						
263	D4	Bittern Lake	Fr Camrose, 10 mi W on Hwy 13			5	N	N	None		5/1-10/1	14		•	U							•	•								○									
263	D4	Duhamel	Fr Camrose, 5 mi W on Hwy 13, 4 mi S on Hwy 21			4	N	N	None		5/1-10/1	14		•	U							•	•					○			○									
264	G4	Waterton River	Fr Fort Macleod, 16 mi S on Hwy 2			5	N	N	None		5/1-10/1	14		•	U							•	•										○	•						
265	D3	Drayton Valley	Fr Drayton Valley, 2 mi N on Hwy 57			6	N	N	None		5/1-10/1	14		•	U							•	•					○			○		•	•						
265	D3	Easyford	Fr Drayton Valley, 4 mi N on Hwy 57, 5 mi W on Hwy 621, 2 mi N			14	N	N	None		5/1-10/1	14		•	U							•	•											•		•				
266	C2	Maskuta Creek	Fr Hinton, 11 mi SW on Hwy 16		5	7	N	N	None		5/1-10/1	14		•	U							•	•											•						
267	C2	Roundcroft	Fr Hinton, 12 mi E on Hwy 16			3	N	N	None		5/1-10/1	14		•	U							•	•											•						
267	C2	Obed Lake	Fr Hinton, 24 mi E on Hwy 16			10	N	N	None		5/1-10/1	14		•	U							•	•								○		•	•	l					
268	G5	Magrath	In Magrath, on Hwy 5			5	N	N	None		5/1-10/1	14		•	U							•	•					○			○		○	•						
269	C3	Hornbeck Creek	Fr Edson, 9 mi W on Hwy 16			10	N	N	None		5/1-10/1	14		•	U							•	•											•						
269	C3	Lower Sundance Cr	Fr Edson, 6-1/2 mi W on Hwy 16			3	N	N	None		5/1-10/1	14		•	U							•	•											•						
270	C3	E of Edson	Fr Edson, 5 mi E on Hwy 16			5	N	N	None		5/1-10/1	14		•	U							•	•											•						
271	C3	McLeod Valley	Fr Peers, 3-1/2 mi N on Hwy 32			24	N	N	None		5/1-10/1	14		•	U							•	•								○			•						
272	C3	Mackay	Fr Wildwood, 16 mi W on Hwy 16			8	N	N	None		5/1-10/1	14		•	U							•	•								○			•						
272	C3	Carrot Creek	Fr Edson, 23 mi E on Hwy 16			5	N	N	None		5/1-10/1	14		•	U							•	•								○			•						
273	C4	Gainford	In Gainford, on Hwy 16			2	N	N	None		5/1-10/1	14		•	U							•	•					○			○		•	•	l					
274	C4	Alberta Beach	Fr Alberta Beach, 3-1/2 mi SE on Hwy 33			3	N	N	None		5/1-10/1	14		•	U							•	•					○			○		•	•	lr	•				
274	C4	Gunn	Fr Gunn, 1/2 mi E on Hwy 43			3	N	N	None		5/1-10/1	14		•	U							•	•					○			○		○	○	lr					
276	C4	Spruce Grove	Fr Spruce Grove, 1 mi W on Hwy 16			3	N	N	None		5/1-10/1	14		•	U							•	•					○			○									
277	C4	E of Bretona	Fr Edmonton, 11 mi SE on Hwy 14			6	N	N	None		5/1-10/1	14		•	U							•	•																	
277	C4	Ministik	Fr Tofield, 16 mi W on Hwy 14			8	N	N	None		5/1-10/1	14		•	U							•	•																	
277	C4	Cooking Lake	Fr Edmonton, 18 mi SE on Hwy 14			3	N	N	None		5/1-10/1	14		•	U							•	•							○	○		•		l	•				

 FOR MAP, SEE PAGE 106

Park number	Map reference	Name of park	Access	Physical environment	Elevation	Acres	Number of tent spaces	Number of trailer spaces	Approximate fee	Credit cards accepted	Season	Time limit	Reservations	Pets permitted	Max. trailer size	Electric hookup	Water hookup	Sewer hookup	Sanitary station	Bottled gas	Air conditioning	Tables	Firewood	Pull-thru spaces	Rec. hall	Flush toilets	Showers	Ice	Auto. laundry	Cafe-snack bar	Store	Swimming pool	Other swimming	Fishing	Boating	Playground	Other	CB channel monitored	Telephone no.	Mail address
		ALBERTA GOVERNMENT HIGHWAY CAMPSITES (CONT'D)																																						
279	D5	Amisk Creek	Fr Tofield, 6 mi E on Hwy 14				6	N	N	None	5/1-10/1	14		•	U							•	•					o			o									
280	D5	W of Viking	Fr Viking, 2 mi W on Hwy 14				5	N	N	None	5/1-10/1	U		•	U							•	•					o			o									
280	D5	N of Viking	Fr Viking, 9 mi N on Hwy 36				2	N	N	None	5/1-10/1	14		•	U							•	•								o									
281	F5	Chin Lake	Fr Coaldale, 8 mi E on Hwy 3				4	N	N	None	5/1-10/1	14		•	U							•	•					o												
282	C5	Vegreville	In Vegreville, on Hwy 16				5	N	N	None	5/1-10/1	14		•	U							•	•					o			o			o						Vegreville
283	D6	Kitscoty	Fr Kitscoty, 3 mi W on Hwy 16				3	N	N	None	5/1-10/1	14		•	U							•	•								o									
284	D6	Rivercourse	Fr Lloydminster, 23 mi S on Hwy 17				8	N	N	None	5/1-10/1	14		•	U							•	•																	
285	C5	Bruderheim	Fr Bruderheim, 4 mi W & S				4	N	N	None	5/1-10/1	14		•	U							•	•																	
286	C4	Egremont	Fr Redwater, 7 mi N on Hwy 28				2	N	N	None	5/1-10/1	14		•	U							•	•								o									
287	C5	Andrew	In Andrew on Hwy 45				4	N	N	None	5/1-10/1	14		•	U							•	•								o									
288	C5	Two Hills	Fr Two Hills, 1/2 mi N on Hwy 36				2	N	N	None	5/1-10/1	14		•	U							•	•					o			o									
288	C5	Hairy Hill	Fr Two Hills, 8 mi W on Hwy 45, 7 mi N				3	N	N	None	5/1-10/1	14		•	U							•	•										•	•	l	•				
288	C5	Lac Sante	Fr Two Hills, 8 mi NE on Hwy 36, 7 mi NE on access rd				2	N	N	None	5/1-10/1	14		•	U							•	•										•	•	l					
290	C6	Sunset Lake	Fr Myrnam, 6 mi E on Hwy 45				2	N	N	None	5/1-10/1	14		•	U							•	•								o				l					
291	C6	Hazeldine	Fr Marwayne, 10 mi NW on Hwy 45				5	N	N	None	5/1-10/1	14		•	U							•	•								o									
291	C6	Lea Park	Fr Marwayne, 6 mi N on Hwy 45, 5 mi N on Hwy 897				5	N	N	None	5/1-10/1	14		•	U							•	•											•						
292	C6	Whitney Lake	Fr Elk Point, 15 mi E on Hwy 646				2	N	N	None	5/1-10/1	14		•	U							•	•								o		•	•	l	•				
293	C6	Silver Lake	Fr Elk Point, 8 mi W on Hwy 646, 2 mi S				3	N	N	None	5/1-10/1	14		•	U							•	•										•	•	l					
293	C6	Elk Point Bridge	Fr Elk Point, 2-1/2 mi S on Hwy 41				3	N	N	None	5/1-10/1	14		•	U							•	•					o			o			•						
294	C5	Ashmont	Fr Ashmont, 2 mi S on Hwy 28				3	N	N	None	5/1-10/1	14		•	U							•	•					o			o									
294	C5	Lower Mann Lake	Fr Vilna, 19 mi E on Hwy 28A				17	N	N	None	5/1-10/1	14		•	U							•	•					o			o		•	•	lr					
295	C5	Mallaig Beach	Fr Mallaig, 6 mi S				6	N	N	None	5/1-10/1	14		•	U							•	•										•	•	l					
295	C5	Lower Therien Lake	Fr St Paul, 3-1/2 mi S				14	N	N	None	5/1-10/1	14		•	U							•	•								o		•		l					
295	C5	Vincent Lake	Fr St Paul, 7 mi N on Hwy 881				1	N	N	None	5/1-10/1	14		•	U							•	•								o		•	•						
296	B2	Smokey River	Fr Grande Prairie, 26 mi E				6	N	N	None	5/1-10/1	14		•	U							•	•								o		•	•	l					
297	C6	Bonnyville Beach	Fr Bonnyville, 6 mi SW on Hwy 28, 1 mi W				1	N	N	None	5/1-10/1	14		•	U							•	•										•	•	l					
297	C6	Vezeau Beach	Fr Bonnyville, 3-1/2 mi SW on Hwy 28				3	N	N	None	5/1-10/1	14		•	U							•	•					o		•	o		•	•	lr					
297	C6	Muriel Lake	Fr Bonnyville, 8 mi S				2	N	N	None	5/1-10/1	14		•	U							•	•										•	•	lr					
297	C6	Franchere Bay	Fr Glendon, 8 mi E on Hwy 600				6	N	N	None	5/1-10/1	14		•	U							•	•								o		•	•	lr					
297	C6	Minnie Lake	Fr Glendon, 4 mi E				1	N	N	None	5/1-10/1	14		•	U							•	•					o			o		•	•	l					
297	C6	Eastbourne	Fr Bonnyville, 16 mi SW				6	N	N	None	5/1-10/1	14		•	U							•	•										•	•	l					
298	B6	Manatokan Lake	Fr Iron River, 2 mi N, 1 mi W				3	N	N	None	5/1-10/1	14		•	U							•	•					o			o		•	•	lr					
298	B6	Moore Lake #2	Fr Ardmore, 14 mi N				3	N	N	None	5/1-10/1	14		•	U							•	•										•	•						
298	B6	Moore Lake #1	Fr Ardmore, 12 mi N, 2 mi W				4	N	N	None	5/1-10/1	14		•	U							•	•										•	•						
299	G6	Foremost	In Foremost, on Hwy 61				2	N	N	None	5/1-10/1	14		•	U							•	•								o									
300	D6	Fort Vermilion	Fr Vermilion, 4 mi W				11	N	N	None	5/1-10/1	14		•	U							•	•								o									
304	B6	Frenchman's Bay	Fr Grande Centre, 8 mi N & E				10	N	N	None	5/1-10/1	14		•	U							•	•										•	•	l					
305	B6	Ethel Lake	Fr Cold Lake, 7 mi W on Hwy 662, 7 mi N				1	N	N	None	5/1-10/1	14		•	U							•	•										•	•	l					
305	B6	English Bay	Fr Cold Lake, 10 mi N on access rd				44	N	N	None	5/1-10/1	14		•	U							•	•										•	•	l					
307	C5	Bonnie Lake	Fr Vilna, 4 mi E & N				12	N	N	None	5/1-10/1	14		•	U							•	•					o			o		•	•	l	•				
307	C5	Bellis	Fr Vilna, 10 mi W on Hwy 28				5	N	N	None	5/1-10/1	14		•	U							•	•																	
309	C5	Floating Stone Lake	Fr Vilna, 18 mi NE on Hwy 28 & access rd			3	72	N	N	None	5/1-10/1	14		•	U							•	•										•	•	lr					
311	C5	Warspite	Fr Warspite, 1 mi N on Hwy 28				3	N	N	None	5/1-10/1	14		•	U							•	•								o									
313	B5	North Buck Lake	Fr Caslan, 2 mi N				13	N	N	None	5/1-10/1	14		•	U							•	•										•	•	l					
313	B5	Boyle	Fr Boyle, 4 mi W on Hwy 46				2	N	N	None	5/1-10/1	14		•	U							•	•																	
315	B5	Plamondon Beach	Fr Plamondon, 4-1/2 mi N, 2 mi E				32	N	N	None	5/1-10/1	14		•	U							•	•										•	•	l					
316	B5	Beaver Lake	Fr Lac La Biche, 3-1/2 mi E on access rd				19	N	N	None	5/1-10/1	14		•	U							•	•										•	•	lr					
317	B5	Owl River	Fr Lac La Biche, 20 mi E & N				79	N	N	None	5/1-10/1	14		•	U							•	•										•	•	lr					
318	B4	Lawrence Lake	Fr Athabasca, 30 mi NW on Hwy 2				18	N	N	None	5/1-10/1	U		•	U							•	•										•	•	l					
319	B4	Athabasca	In Athabasca, on Hwy 2				4	N	N	None	5/1-10/1	14		•	U							•	•					o			o			•	l					
320	C4	Rochester	Fr Athabasca, 27 mi S on Hwy 2				5	N	N	None	5/1-10/1	14		•	U							•	•																	
322	B4	Flatbush	Fr Flatbush, 2 mi E				4	N	N	None	5/1-10/1	14		•	U							•	•																	
323	C4	Holmes Crossing	Fr Fort Assinbbine, 2 mi S				5	N	N	None	5/1-10/1	14		•	U							•	•											•						
324	C4	Freedom	Fr Westlock, 16 mi N				2	N	N	None	5/1-10/1	14		•	U							•	•																	
325	C3	Iosegun Creek	Fr Fox Creek, 10 mi SE on Hwy 43, 1 mi S				5	N	N	None	5/1-10/1	14		•	U							•	•																	
325	C3	Two Creek	Fr Whitecourt, 30 mi NW on Hwy 43				3	N	N	None	5/1-10/1	14		•	U							•	•																	
327	C3	Whitecourt	Fr Whitecourt, 1/4 mi E on Hwy 43				3	N	N	None	5/1-10/1	14		•	U							•	•					o			o									
328	C3	Groat Creek	Fr Whitecourt, 13 mi SW on Hwy 947				4	N	N	None	5/1-10/1	14		•	U							•	•																	
329	m	Hotchkiss	Fr Manning, 10 mi N on Hwy 35				5	N	N	None	5/1-10/1	14		•	U							•	•																	
330	B3	Assineau River	Fr Slave Lake, 20 mi W on Hwy 2				6	N	N	None	5/1-10/1	14		•	U							•	•																	
330	B3	Kinuso Beach	Fr Kinuso, 2 mi W on Hwy 2, 5 mi N				7	N	N	None	5/1-10/1	14		•	U							•	•										•	•	l					
331	A2	Grimshaw	Fr Grimshaw, 2 mi N on Hwy 2				6	N	N	None	5/1-10/1	14		•	U							•	•					o												
332	B2	Little Smoky River	Fr Donnelly, 20 mi S on Hwy 2				5	N	N	None	5/1-10/1	14		•	U							•	•																	
333	A2	Watino	Fr Girouxville, 14 mi W				21	N	N	None	5/1-10/1	14		•	U							•	•																	
335	A2	Manir	Fr Wanham, 6 mi W on Hwy 49				6	N	N	None	All year	14		•	U							•	•										o							
336	A1	Woking	Fr Rycroft, 10 mi S on Hwy 2				6	N	N	None	5/1-10/1	14		•	U							•	•																	
337	A2	Dunvegan	Fr Fairview, 16 mi SW on Hwy 2				6	N	N	None	5/1-10/1	14		•	U							•	•										•		l					
338	A2	Peavine Cr	Fr Girouxville, 12 mi S on Hwy 744				14	N	N	None	5/1-10/1	14		•	U							•	•																	
339	B1	Hythe	In Hythe, on Hwy 2				3	N	N	None	5/1-10/1	14		•	U							•	•		•			o			o									
340	A1	Demmitt	Fr Hythe, 20 mi W on Hwy 2				5	N	N	None	5/1-10/1	14		•	U							•	•																	
341	B1	Beaverlodge	In Beaverlodge, on Hwy 2				5	N	N	None	5/1-10/1	14		•	U							•	•								o									
343	A1	Blueberry Mountain	Fr Spirit River, 22 mi W on Hwy 49				5	N	N	None	5/1-10/1	14		•	U							•	•																	
344	F6	Redcliff	In Redcliff, on Hwy 1				3	N	N	None	5/1-10/1	14		•	U							•	•					o			o									
347	D4	Leduc	Fr Leduc, on E edge of town				3	N	N	None	5/1-10/1	14		•	U							•	•								o			•						
348	C4	Sandy Lake	Fr Morinville, 17 mi W on Hwy 642				3	N	N	None	5/1-10/1	14		•	U							•	•										•	•						
349	C4	Vimy	Fr Vimy, 4 mi S				2	N	N	None	5/1-10/1	14		•	U							•	•																	
350	B4	Smith	Fr Smith, 1 mi N on access rd				8	N	N	None	5/1-10/1	14		•	U							•	•																	

ALBERTA

FOR FOOTNOTE EXPLANATION SEE FIRST PAGE OF THIS PROVINCE   FOR MAP, SEE PAGE 106

Park number	Map reference	Name of park	Access	Physical environment	Elevation	Acres	Number of tent spaces	Number of trailer spaces	Approximate fee	Credit cards accepted	Season	Time limit	Reservations	Pets permitted	Max. trailer size	Electric hookup	Water hookup	Sewer hookup	Sanitary station	Bottled gas	Air conditioning	Tables	Firewood	Pull-thru spaces	Rec. hall	Flush toilets	Showers	Ice	Auto. laundry	Cafe-snack bar	Store	Swimming pool	Other swimming	Fishing	Boating	Playground	Other	CB channel monitored	Telephone no.	Mail address
		ALBERTA GOVERNMENT HIGHWAY CAMPSITES (CONT'D)																																						
351	B4	Lesser Slave River	Fr Slave Lk, 11 mi E			5	N	N	None		5/1-10/1	14		•	U							•	•											•	l					
351	B4	Mitsue Lake	Fr Slave Lake vil, 7 mi SE on Hwy 2			3	N	N	None		5/1-10/1	14		•	U							•	•																	
354	m	Twin Lakes	Fr Manning, 37 mi N on Hwy 35			53	N	N	None		5/1-10/1	14		•	U							•	•											•	l					
355	G4	Pincher Creek	In Pincher Creek, on Hwy 6		4	2	N	N	None		5/1-10/1	14		•	U							•	•					o			o		•	•						
358	D4	N Sylvan Lake	Fr Sylvan Lake, 8 mi N on Hwy 20, 6 mi W			1	N	N	None		5/1-10/1	14		•	U							•	•											•	l					
359	E5	Coronation	In Coronation, on Hwy 12			4	N	N	None		5/1-10/1	14		•	U							•	•								o									
360	D4	Rimbey	Fr Rimbey, 4 mi N on Hwy 12			3	N	N	None		5/1-10/1	14		•	U							•	•																	
361	D4	Birch Bay	Fr Bentley, 9 mi N on Hwy 12, 3 mi E			2	N	N	None		5/1-10/1	14		•	U							•	•										•	•	l					
362	D5	Daysland	Fr Daysland, S edge, on Hwy 13			7	N	N	None		5/1-10/1	14		•	U							•	•								o									
365	D5	Birch Lake	Fr Innisfail, 1-1/2 mi S			7	N	N	None		5/1-10/1	14		•	U							•	•										•		l					
365	D5	Ranfurly	Fr Vegreville, 18 mi E on Hwy 16			6	N	N	None		5/1-10/1	14		•	U							•	•																	
367	C5	Elk Island	Fr Edmonton, 23 mi E on Hwy 16			7	N	N	None		5/1-10/1	14		•	U							•	•																	
368	C4	Ardrossan	Fr Edmonton, 11 mi E on Hwy 16		3	8	N	N	None		5/1-10/1	14		•	U							•	•																	
372	D4	Delburne	In Delburne, on Hwy 21			3	N	N	None		5/1-10/1	14		•	U							•	•								o				l					
374	F4	Highwood	Fr Longview, 14 mi SW			4	N	N	None		5/1-10/1	14		•								•	•											•						
375	F5	Travers Reservoir	Fr Carmangay, 22 mi E			8	N	N	None		5/1-10/1	14		•	U							•	•										•	•	l					
377	C5	Hanmore Lake	Fr Smoky Lk, 16 mi N			5	N	N	None		5/1-10/1	14		•	U							•	•											•	l					
379	C6	Kehewin Lake	Fr St Paul, 16 mi E & 4 mi N on Hwy 28			4	N	N	None		5/1-10/1	14		•	U							•	•										•	•	l					
380	C6	Beartrap Lake	Fr Bonneville, 10 mi SW			14	N	N	None		5/1-10/1	14		•	U							•	•										•	•	l					
380	C6	Ernestina Lk	Fr Ardmore, 7 mi SE			16	N	N	None		5/1-10/1	14		•	U							•	•										•	•	l					
380	C6	Angling Lake	Fr Ardmore, 16 mi SE			5	N	N	None		5/1-10/1	14		•	U							•	•										•	•	l					
383	B2	E of Valleyview	Fr Valleyview, 6-1/2 mi E			4	N	N	None		5/1-10/1	14		•	U							•	•										•	•						
384	A2	Peace River	Outskirts of Peace River, Hwy 2			8	N	N	None		5/1-10/1	14		•	U							•	•					o			o									
385	m	Boyer River	Fr High Level, 39 mi S on Hwy 35			6	N	N	None		5/1-10/1	14		•	U							•	•																	
385	m	High Level	In High Level			15	N	N	None		5/1-10/1	14		•	U							•	•					o			o									
387	m	Hay River	Fr High Level, 52 mi N on Hwy 35			2	N	N	None		5/1-10/1	14		•	U							•	•																	
388	m	Steen River	Fr High Level, 86 mi N on Hwy 35			13	N	N	None		5/1-10/1	14		•	U							•	•																	
390	C3	Chickadee Creek	Fr Whitecourt, 12 mi NW on Hwy 43			2	N	N	None		5/1-10/1	14		•	U							•	•																	
391	B2	House River	Fr Little Smoky, 1 mi NW on Hwy 43		3	6	N	N	None		5/1-10/1	14		•	U							•	•										•	•						
392	C4	Jarvie	Fr Jarvie, 2 mi SE on Hwy 44			5	N	N	None		5/1-10/1	14		•	U							•	•																	
396	B5	Missawawi Beach	Fr Lac la Biche, 8 mi S			2	N	N	None		5/1-10/1	14		•	U							•	•										•	•	l					
398	G5	Raymond	In Raymond, on Hwy 52			2	N	N	None		5/1-10/1	14		•	U							•	•					o			o									
399	D4	Red Deer Lake	Fr Bashaw, 12 mi N & W			9	N	N	None		5/1-10/1	14		•	U							•	•										•	•	l					
400	E4	James River Bridge	Fr Sundre, 9 mi N on Hwy 760			2	N	N	None		5/1-10/1	14		•	U							•	•																	
401	E5	Red Deer River	Fr Big Valley, 10 mi W on access rd			8	N	N	None		5/1-10/1	14		•	U							•	•																	
403	D3	Chambers Creek	Fr Rocky Mtn House, 20 mi W on Hwy 11		4	11	N	N	None		5/1-10/1	14		•	U							•	•																	
404	D3	Harlech	Fr Rocky Mtn House, 49 mi W on Hwy 11		4	4	N	N	None		5/1-10/1	14		•	U							•	•																	
404	D3	Shunda Beaverdam	Fr Nordegg, 2 mi E on Hwy 11		4	4	N	N	None		5/1-10/1	14		•	U							•	•																	
404	D3	Haven Creek	Fr Nordegg, 8 mi W on Hwy 11		4	6	N	N	None		5/1-10/1	14		•	U							•	•																	
405	E5	Hanna	Fr Hanna, 5 mi E on Hwy 9			4	N	N	None		All year	14		•	U							•	•																	
408	B3	High Prairie	Fr High Prairie, 1/2 mi E on Hwy 2			5	N	N	None		5/1-10/1	14		•	U							•	•					o			o									
409	D5	Buffalo Lake	Fr Stettler, 16 mi W & N			6	N	N	None		5/1-10/1	14		•	U							•	•												l					
410	E4	Pine Lake	In Pine Lake, on Hwy 42			1	N	N	None		5/1-10/1	14		•	U							•	•								o		•	•	l					
411	C2	Lambert Creek	Fr Robb, 13 mi N			5	N	N	None		5/1-10/1	14		•	U							•	•																	
412	D2	Coalspur	Fr Robb, 4 mi S on Hwy 47			6	N	N	None		5/1-10/1	14		•	U							•	•																	
414	m	Hanging Stone River	Fr Fort McMurray, 22 mi S on Hwy 63			37	N	N	None		5/1-10/1	14		•	U							•	•											•						
415	A5	Mariana Lake	Fr Fort McMurray, 69 mi S				N	N	None		5/1-10/1	14		•	U							•	•											•	l					
416	B5	Wandering River	Fr Wandering River, 7 mi N on Hwy 63			11	N	N	None		5/1-10/1	14		•	U							•	•											•						
		NATIONAL PARKS																																						
		Elk Island NP				B																																	403/998-3781	
550	C5	Sandy Beach	Fr Edmonton, 22 mi E on Hwy 16 to entr gate, 10.5 mi N on pk rd		3	8	115	8	F5.00		5/15-LD	14		•	20	$			•			•	•			•		o		•	•		•	•	dl	•	g			Ft Saskatchewan
		Jasper NP				B																																	403/852-4401	
556	D2	Wabasso	Fr Jasper, 10 mi S on Hwys 93 & 93A		4	10	226		F3.00		5/18-LD	14		•	20							•	•			•								o			k			Jasper
556	D2	Wapiti	Fr Jasper, 2 mi S on Hwy 93		4	93	321		F3.00		5/18-LD	14		•	16				•			•	•			•								o			k			Jasper
556	D2	Whistlers	Fr Jasper, 2 mi S on Hwy 93		4	242	681	77	F6.00		5/4-9/10	14		•	16	•	•	•	•			•	•			•										•				Jasper
558	D2	Miette Hot Springs	Fr Jasper, 27 mi NE on Hwy 16, 11 mi E on Miette Rd		5	7	100		F3.00		5/18-9/10	14		•								•	•			•		•		o	o		o	o		•	h			Jasper
559	D2	Snaring River	Fr Jasper, 7 mi N on Hwy 16, 3.5 mi NW on access rd		4	11	60		F3.00		5/18-LD	14		•								•	•											o						Jasper
560	D2	Mount Kerkeslin	Fr Jasper, 22.4 mi S on Hwy 93		4	4	42		F3.00		6/15-9/30	14		•								•	•											o						Jasper
561	D2	Honeymoon Lake	Fr Jasper, 32.2 mi S on Hwy 93		5	8	30		F3.00		5/18-9/30	14		•	16							•	•											o	l					Jasper
562	D2	Jonas Creek	Fr Jasper, 48 mi S on Hwy 93		6	3	25		F3.00		6/1-9/30	14		•	16							•	•											o						Jasper
563	E2	Columbia Icefield	Fr Jasper, 68 mi S on Hwy 93		7	2	P22		F3.00		6/8-9/30	14		•								•	•							o										Jasper
563	E2	Wilcox Creek	Fr Jasper, 69 mi S on Hwy 93		7	24	46		F3.00		6/15-9/30	14		•	20				•			•	•																	Jasper
564	C2	Celestine Lk	Fr Jasper, 7 mi N on Hwy 16, 22 mi N on Celestine Lk Rd		5	2	P24		None		6/30-10/15	14		•								•	•											o	o					Jasper
		Waterton Lakes NP				B																																	403/859-2262	
568	G4	Waterton Lks Townsite	Fr jct Hwys 5 & 6, 5 mi SW on Hwy 5		5	35	145	96	F6.00		5/17-9/30	14		•	U	•	•	•	•	o	•	•	•	•		•	$	o	o	o	o	$	o	o	dlr		gt			Waterton Park
568	G4	Crandell Mtn.	Fr jct Hwys 5 & 6, 3 mi SW on Hwy 5, 5 mi on Red Rock Pkwy		5	75	129		F3.00		5/18-LD	14		•	20				•			•	•			•							o	o			gt			Waterton Park
568	G4	Belly River	Fr jct Hwys 5 & 6, 17.5 mi S on Hwy 6, 1/4 mi on access rd		5	15	24		F3.00		6/15-9/30	14		•	16							•	•										o	•						Waterton Park
		Banff NP				B																																	403/762-3324	
572	E2	Cirrus Mtn	Mi 65.5 on Banff-Jasper Hwy 93		6	3	16		F3.00		6/29-LD	14		•	16							•	•																	Banff NP
572	E2	Rampart Creek	Mi 54.5 on Banff-Jasper Hwy 93		6	4	50		F3.00		6/14-LD	14		•	16							•	•											o						Banff NP
573	E3	Johnston Canyon	Fr Banff, 16 mi NW on Hwy 1A		5	10	140		F3.00		5/17-9/10	14		•	16				•			•	•			•				o	o			o		•				Banff NP
573	E3	Mosquito Creek	Mi 14.5 on Banff-Jasper Hwy 93		7	3	32		F3.00		6/15-9/17	14		•	16							•	•											o			k			Banff NP
573	E3	Mt. Eisenhower	Fr Banff 15 mi NW on Hwy 1A		5	3	44		F3.00		6/15-8/27	14		•	16							•	•											o						Banff NP
574	E3	Lake Louise	Fr Lk Louise, 7 mi W on TC 1, 5 mi SE on unpaved access rd 1		6	185	221	163	F3.00		5/17-9/17	14		•	U				•	o		•	•			•				o	o			o			k			Banff NP
		Tunnel Mtn	Fr Banff, 1.5 mi E on Hwy 1A		5	235																																		Banff NP
580	E3	Tunnel Mtn #1-Trailers				170		322	F6.00		5/10-9/24	7		•	U	•	•	•	•	o		•	•			•	•	o	•	o	o			o		•	ghtu			

British Columbia

Population: 2,180,000
(1971 estimate)
Area: 366,255 Sq. Miles
Capital: Victoria

Cities and Towns

Atlin....A-2
Barriere....E-5
Beaverdell....F-6
Beaton....E-6
Bella Coola....E-3
Bloedel....F-4
Blue River....E-6
Boston Bar....F-5
Burns Lake....D-4
Campbell River....F-4
Canim Lake....E-5
Castlegar....F-6
Ceepeecee....F-3
Chase....E-5
Chilliwack....F-5
Clinton....E-5
Courtenay....F-4
Cranbrook....F-7
Creston....F-6
Dawson Creek....C-5
Dease Lake....B-3
Duncan....F-4
Elko....F-7
Enderby....E-6
Fernie....F-7
Ft. St. James....D-4
Fort St. John....C-5
Francois Lake....D-4
Gerrard....E-6
Gibsons....F-4
Hanceville....E-4
Hedley....F-5
Hixon....D-5
Horsefly....E-5
Hudson Hope....C-5
Kamloops....E-5
Kelowna....F-6
Kelsey Bay....F-4
Kimberley....F-7
Kitimat....D-3
Kitwanga....C-3
Kleena Kleene....E-4
Lardeau....E-6
Lillooet....E-5
Lumby....E-6
Lytton....F-5
McBride....D-5
Merritt....F-5
Mission City....F-5
Nakusp....E-6
Nanaimo....F-4
Nelson....F-6
New Westminster....F-5
Ocean Falls....E-3
Oliver....F-6
100 Mile House....E-5
150 Mile House....E-5
Peachland....F-5
Pemberton....E-4
Penticton....F-5
Port Alberni....F-4
Port Clements....D-2
Port Hardy....E-3
Port Moody....F-5
Powell River....F-4
Prince George....D-5
Prince Rupert....D-2
Princeton....F-5
Punchaw....D-4
Quesnel....D-5
Radium Hot Springs....E-7
Revelstoke....E-6
Sicamous....E-6
Smithers....C-3
Sooke....F-4
Sparwood....F-7
Squamish....F-4
Summerland....F-5
Tatlayoka Lake....E-4
Telegraph Cr....B-2
Terrace....C-3
Tete Jaune Cache....D-5
Tofino....F-4
Trail....F-6
Ucluelet....F-4
Vancouver....F-4
Vanderhoof....D-4
Vernon....E-6
Victoria....F-4
Wells....D-5
Westwold....E-5
Williams Lake....E-5

BRITISH COLUMBIA

Scale: 0 50 100 miles
One inch equals approximately 113.5 miles

79-1

ALBERTA

FOR FOOTNOTE EXPLANATION SEE FIRST PAGE OF THIS **PROVINCE** FOR MAP, SEE PAGE 106

Park number	Map reference	Name of park	Access	Physical environment	Elevation	Acres	Number of tent spaces	Number of trailer spaces	Approximate fee	Credit cards accepted	Season	Time limit / Reservations / Pets permitted / Max. trailer size	Electric hookup / Water hookup / Sewer hookup	Sanitary station / Bottled gas / Air conditioning	Tables / Firewood / Pull-thru spaces / Rec. hall	Flush toilets / Showers / Ice	Auto. laundry / Cafe-snack bar / Store	Swimming pool / Other swimming / Fishing	Boating / Playground	Other	CB channel monitored	Telephone no.	Mail address
		NATIONAL PARKS (CONT'D)																					
580	E3	Tunnel Mtn #2-Tent Trlrs					246		F3.00		5/15-8/27	7 • U		• o	• •	• • o	• o o	o	•	ghtu			
580	E3	Tunnel Mtn Vil					622		F3.00		5/10-9/24	7 • 16		• o	• •	• • o	o o o	o		ghtu			
580	E3	Two Jack Lk (Main CG)	Fr Banff, 8 mi NE on Hwy 1 at Minnewanka Loop		6	150	381		F3.00		5/17-LD	14 • U		•	• •	•		o	lr •				Banff NP
580	E3	Two Jack Lakeside	Fr Banff, 7-1/2 mi NE on Hwy 1				80		F3.00		6/15-LD	14 • U		o	• • •	•		o	lr	p		403/762-3324	Banff, NP
582	E3	Waterfowl Lake	Mi 35.3 on Banff-Jasper Hwy 93		6	4	145		F3.00		6/21-9/17	14 • 16		•	• •	•		o					Banff NP
583	E3	Protection Mtn	Fr Eisenhower Jct, 7 mi W on Hwy 1A		6	40	89		F3.00		6/28-8/27	14 • U		•	• •	•		o					Banff NP
		CITY, COUNTY & CIVIC																					
602	G5	Henderson Lake CG	SE side of Lethbridge, Hwy 3, 4 & 5	⛵ ♀	3	6	100	36	5.00		5/5-10/10	14 • 24	• • •	• o	• •	• • o	• o o	o	lr •	gh			Lethbridge
603	D4	Red Deer - Lions Cent'l P	In Red Deer, N side of Red Deer Riv, 2 blks E of 49th Ave	≈ ♀	3	4	20	43	5.00		5/19-9/25	7 • U	• • •	• o	• •	• • o	• o o	• •	•	gt			4918-48 Ave, Red Deer
604	C4	Klondike Valley Pk	Fr Hwy 2 in Edmonton, 1 mi S, W on Ellerslie Rd	⊥		60	50	164	6.50		4/30-9/30	14 • U	$ $ $	• o	• • •	• • •	• o •		•				11638 77th Ave, Edmonton
604	C4	Rainbow Valley CG	Fr Hwy 2, 3 mi W at Ave 45	♀ ◢	3	12	120		5.00		15/5-9/15	7 Z •			• •	• • •	• o •		•	h			Edmonton
605	G5	Kimball Park	On Hwy 40, 8 mi SE of Cardston	≈ ѱ	4	10	20	5	None		5/1-10/1	U • 18			• •			• •	•				Cardston
606	D4	Michener Park	Fr Lacombe, 1/2 mi W on Hwy 12	ѱ ◢	3	8	10	16	None		5/18-9/5	7 • U		• o	• •	• o	o o o	o	•	gp			Lacombe
607	F5	Emerson Bridge Pk	On Hwy 36, S end of Emerson Brdg on Red Deer Riv	≈ ♀		90	100				4/1-11/1	U •			• •			o o	•				Brooks
608	C5	Sunset Lake Rec Pk	Fr Myrnam, 6 mi E on Hwy 45, 1 mi N	⛵ ⊥	3	15	20	20	None		5/1-10/1	U • U			• •			•	r •				Two Hills
609	F4	George Lane Mem Pk	Fr High Riv, 1 mi W at jct Hwys 2 & 23	≈ ♀	4	16	20	20	3.00		5/1-9/30	7 • U		o o	• •	• $ o	o o o	o o •	•	gp		403/652-2307	High River
610	C2	Switzer CG	In town of Hinton along Yellowhead Hwy	⋀ ♀	4	20	15	15	2.00		5/15-9/15	7 • 24		• o	• •	• o	o o o			g			Box 818, Hinton
611	D5	Burma Pk	Fr Castor, 30 mi NE	≈ ♀		20	20	20	None		All year	U • U			• •			•	•				Brownfield
612	D5	Birch Lake Pk	1 mi S of Hwy 16, 1 mi S of Innisfree	⛵ ѱ	2	5	5	5	None		5/1-9/30	U • U			• •	o	o o o		l •				Box 69, Innisfree
613	F4	Claresholm Centennial Pk	Fr jct Hwy 2 & 43rd Ave, 3 blks W & 1/2 blk N	ѱ ◢	4	4	8	8	4.00		5/1-10/1	7 • 27	$ $	• o	• •	• • o	o o o	o o	•	t	3/13	403/235-3381	Rec Dept Bx 1000, Claresholm
614	C5	Hanmore Lake	Fr Smoky Lk, 8 mi N, 1 mi W, 3-1/2 mi N	⛵ ♀	3	17	25	20	None		All year	U • U			• •			• •	dl	eu			Smoky Lake
615	B4	Long Island Bch	Fr Westlock, N on Hwy 44	⛵ ♀	3	200	50	25	None		5/15-9/30	U • U		o	• • •			• •	dl •				Jarvie
616	C5	Sandy Lake Rec Park	Fr Willingdon, 10 mi E, 2 mi N	⛵ ѱ	3	10	10	10	None		5/1-10/1	U Z • U			• •			•	r •				Two Hills
617	C3	Edson Lions Campsite	On Hwy 16, E edge of Edson	♀ ◢	4	7	12	18	4.00		5/20-9/5	U • U	$	o o	• • •	• • o	o o o		•	gp			Box 1388, Edson
618	D3	Centennial Park	At Rocky Mtn House on Hwy 11	≈ ⋀	4	5		35	3.00		5/24-10/15	3 • 20		o •	• •	• • o	o o o	o	•	g			Rocky Mtn House
619	F4	Black Diamond	In Black Diamond at jct Hwys 7/22	≈ ⋀	5	15	20	10	1.50		MD-LD	U • U	•	o	• •	o	o o o	o •	•	egu		403/933-4124	Bx 10, Black Diamond
622	D5	Huber Dam Pk	Fr Caster, 7 mi E on Bulwork Rd	ѱ ⊥		22	25				5/30-10/31	U •			• •			•					Castor
623	C4	Summer Vil-Alberta Bch	Fr Edmonton, Hwy 16 to Valleyview Corner, 6 mi N on Hwy 43, 6 mi W on Hwy 33	⛵ ♀	3	12	100	90	3.00		5/15-9/15	U Z • U	$	• o	• • •	• • o	o o o	o o	dlr •	pgh		403/924-3434	Box 278, Alberta Beach
624	A2	Fairview Trlr Ct	Town Center - at 4th Ave & 8th St	ѱ ◢	3	2	5	50	3.00	V	All year	U Z U	$ • •	• o	• •	• • o	• o o	o		g	20	403/835-2032	Fairview
625	G4	Pincher Creek Campsite	Fr Hwy 6, 1 blk W to Scobie, 2 blks N	≈ ♀	4	1	10	10	None		5/1-9/15	3 • 30		• o	• •	• o	o o o	o		ghp			Pincher Creek-Alberta
626	D5	Camrose CG	Fr jct Hwy 13/53rd St, 3/4 mi S	⛵ ѱ	3	15	10	25	2.50		5/15-9/15	14 • 30	$	o o	• • •	• • o	o o o		•	g		403/672-4426	5204-50th Ave, Camrose Canada
627	C5	Mons Lake Camp-site	Fr Smoky Lake, 4 mi E on Hwy 28, 3-1/2 mi N	⛵ ѱ	2	1	10	10	None		All year	U • U			• •			• •		u			Smoky Lake
628	E4	Bowden CG	In Bowden, 25 mi S of Red Deer on Hwy 2	♀ ◢	4	3	35	35	None		All year	U • U		• o	• •	• o	o o o			g			Box 338, Bowden
630	C3	Willmore Rec Pk	Fr Edson, 4 mi S, on McLeod Riv	≈ ♀			40	40	None		All year	•			•			•		k			Box 1388, Edson
631	C5	Bonnie Lake	Fr Vilma, 4 mi E on Hwy 28, 2 mi N	⛵ ⊥	3	2	10	6	None		5/30-10/30	U •			• •			• •	dl				Smokey Lake
		PRIVATE																					
700	C5	Half Moon Lake Resort	Fr Sherwood Pk, 8 mi E on Wye Rd, 4 mi S on oil rd, 2 mi E	⛵ ѱ	3	30	200	200	5.00		5/1-10/31	U Z • U	$ $ $	•	• $ • •	• $ •	• • •	• •	lr •	h		403/922-3045	RR 3, Sherwood Pk
702	E3	Restwell Trlr & Cabins	In Canmore, 1/2 mi W of Hwy 1	≈ ⋀	5	30	90	134	7.00		All year	U Z • U	• • •	• •	• • •	• $ •	• o •	•	•	ghu		403/678-5111	Box 338, Canmore
706	C4	Northgate Motel	On Hwy 2, N city limits of Edmonton	ѱ ◢	4	6	10	S17	4.00	M	5/1-9/15w	U R • 24	$ $ $	• •	• • •	$ o	• o •	o	•	h		403/459-4422	S 8 RR 8 Box 1, Edmonton
723	E4	Leisure CG	Fr Red Deer, 7 mi S on Hwy 2, 16 mi E on Hwy 42	⛵ ♀	3	45	25	163	6.50		4/15-10/15	U Z • 34	• • •	• o	• • •	• $ •	• • •	• •	dlr •	gp		403/886-4705	Pine Lk
730	G4	Cleland's Trailer Park	Fr jct of Hwy 6/Hwy 3, 2 mi S	⋀ ◢	4	3		5	5.00		5/1-10/30	U • 20	• • •	o o	• •	• • o	• o o	o o		g			Pincher Creek
744	F4	Timber Ridge Lodge	Fr SW crnr Nanton, 3 mi W, fol sign S for 11-1/2 mi	⊥	5	1	6	4	3.50		6/1-10/1	U Z •			• •	• •		•	•	hp		403/486-5683	Box 94, Nanton
748	E5	Dinosaur Trail CG	Fr Hwy 9 at Drumheller, 6 mi W on Dinosaur Trail N	≈ ⊥	3	35	122	64	6.00		5/1-9/31	U Z • U	$ $	• •	• • •	• $ •	• •	• • •	r •	gp		403/823-9333	Box 1300, Drumheller
749	F4	Calgary West KOA	Fr Calgary, 1 mi W on TC, S at Esso Station	≈ ⋀	4	33	46	178	6.50		4/15-10/15	U Z • U	$ • $	• o •	• • •	• • •	• o •	• o o	•	gp	10	403/288-0411	Bx 10 Site 12 SS 1, Calgary
751	C3	Arlann CG	Fr Edson 34 mi E on Hwy 16	≈ ⊥	3	12	10	70	4.50		5/15-11/1	U Z $ U	$ •	•	• • •	• • •	o •		•			403/795-2490	Niton Jct
753	D2	Folding Mtn Tourist Ctre	Fr Jasper NP, E gate, 3 mi E on Hwy 16	⋀ ⊥	4	10	100	30	5.50	V	All year	U Z • U	• •	• • •	• • •	• • •	• •		•	ku		403/866-3737	Box 608, Hinton

BRITISH COLUMBIA

FOR MAP, SEE PAGE 111

●—at the campground
○—within one mile of campground
$—extra charge
*—see city map
**—limited facilities during winter months
1-5—number of miles in NF within which facility or activity can be found
A—adults only
B—10,000 acres or more
C—contribution

E—tents rented
F—entrance fee or permit required—see "Special Information on the Public Areas"
H—over 9000 feet above sea level
N—no specific number, limited by size of area only
P—primitive
R—reservation required
S—self-contained units only
U—unlimited

V—trailers rented
Z—reservations accepted
LD—Labor Day
MD—Memorial Day
UC—under construction
d—boat dock
g—public golf course within 5 miles
h—horseback riding
j—whitewater running craft only
k—snow skiing within 25 miles

l—boat launch
m—area north of map
n—no drinking water
p—motor bikes prohibited
r—boat rental
s—stream, lake or creek water only
t—tennis
u—snowmobile trails
w—open certain off-season weekends and holidays

y—drinking water must be boiled
⚓ access to ocean
access to lake
≈ access to river
mountainous terrain
prairie land
desert area
heavily wooded
urban area
rural area

CREDIT CARD SYMBOLS:
A—American Express
M—Master Charge
V—Visa/Bank Americard

FEES REFLECT MINIMUM RATE FOR 2 ADULTS AND ARE SUBJECT TO SEASONAL CHANGES

Park number	Map reference	Name of park	Access	Physical environment	Elevation	Acres	Number of tent spaces	Number of trailer spaces	Approximate fee	Credit cards accepted	Season	Time limit	Reservations	Pets permitted	Max. trailer size	Electric hookup	Water hookup	Sewer hookup	Sanitary station	Bottled gas	Air conditioning	Tables	Firewood	Pull-thru spaces	Rec. hall	Flush toilets	Showers	Ice	Auto. laundry	Cafe-snack bar	Store	Swimming pool	Other swimming	Fishing	Boating	Playground	Other	CB channel monitored	Telephone no.	Mail address
		PROVINCIAL PARKS & CAMPGROUNDS	(For additional CGs, see 'Backpack or Boat Access Areas')																																					
1	F4	Alice Lake	Fr Squamish, 14 mi N on Hwy 99, 1 mi E			979	95	94	4.00		All year	14		●	20				●			●	●			●							●	●						Squamish
2	F4	Roberts Creek	Fr Gibsons, 9 mi W on Hwy 101			100	24	24	2.00		All year	14		●	20				●			●	●										●	●	l					Sechelt
2	F4	Porpoise Bay Prov Pk	Fr Sechelt, 3 mi N, on Sechelt Inlet		0	150	84	84	4.00		All year	14		●	20							●	●										●	●	l		p			Sechelt
3	F5	Golden Ears Park	Fr Vancouver, 30 mi E on Hwy 7 to Haney, 7 mi N			B	351	351	4.00		All year	14		●	20				●			●	●										●	●	l		h			Haney
		Cultus Lake	Fr Chilliwack, 7 mi SW on Hwy 401, SE on access rd			1620																																		Sardis
4	F5	Delta Grove					54	54	4.00		All year	14		●	20							●	●			●							●	●	l					
4	F5	Maple Bay					106	106	4.00		All year	14		●	20				●			●	●			●							●	●	l					
4	F5	Clear Creek					84	84	4.00		All year	14		●	20							●	●			●							●	●	l					
4	F5	Entrance Bay					52	52	4.00		All year	14		●	20							●	●			●							●	●	l					
4	F5	Rolley Lake	Fr Vancouver, 40 mi E on Hwy 7, N on Dewdney Tr Rd, 1 mi W of Stave Falls			285	65	65	4.00		All year	14		●	20							●	●										●	●						Mission
5	C5	Charlie Lk	Fr Ft St John, 5 mi NW on the Alaska Hwy			228	58	58	2.00		All year	14		●	20				●			●	●										●	●	l					Ft St John
6	C5	Moberly Lake	Fr Chetwynd, 15 mi NW on Hwy 29			243	59	59	2.00		All year	14		●	20				●			●	●										●	●	l					Chetwynd
7	E5	Spahats Creek	Fr Clearwater, 10 mi N toward Wells Gray Pk			755	18	18	2.00		All year	14		●	20							●	●											●						Clearwater
7	E5	North Thompson Riv Pk	Fr Clearwater, 1 mi S on Hwy 5		2	317	61	61	2.00		All year	14		●	20				●			●	●										●	●			p			Victoria
8	F5	Nicolum River	Fr Hope, 4-1/2 mi E on Hwy 3			60	8	8	None		All year	14		●	20							●	●											●						Hope
8	F5	Sasquatch Pk	Fr Harrison Hotsprings, 4 mi N, on Deer Lk			3015	100	100	None		All year	14		●	20							●	●										●	●	l					Harrison Hotsprings
		Manning Park				B																																		
9	F5	Cold Spring	Bet Hope & Princeton on Hwy 3; 1 mi W of Manning Pk Lodge				68	68	4.00		All year	14		●	20			●				●	●										●	●			hn			Manning Park
9	F5	Hampton	Bet Hope & Princeton on Hwy 3; 2 mi E of Manning Pk Lodge				80	80	4.00		All year	14		●	20			●				●	●											●						Manning Park
9	F5	Mule Deer	Bet Hope & Princeton on Hwy 3; 6 mi E of Manning Pk Lodge				49	49	4.00		All year	14		●	20			●				●	●			●								●						Manning Park
9	F5	Lightning Lake CG	Fr Manning Pk Lodge, 3-1/2 mi SW on Gibson Pass Rd		5		91	91	4.00		All year	14		●	25							●	●							●	●		●	●	r		hkp			Manning Park
		Strathcona Pk				B																																		
10	F4	Strathcona Buttle Lake	N end of Buttle Lk nr Jct of Gold River				36	36	2.00		All year	14		●	20							●	●											●	l		n			Qjuinsam
11	F4	Ralph River	Fr jct Gold Riv Rd & Battle Lk Rd, 15 mi S				76	76	2.00		All year	14		●	20							●	●											●	l		n			Quinsam
14	F4	Fillongley Prov Pk	On Denman Isl, access by car ferry fr Buckley Bay on Vancouver Isl		1	57	10	10	None		All year	14		●								●															p			Buckley Bay
15	F5	Stemwinder	Fr Princeton, 24 mi E on Hwy 3			9	23	23	2.00		All year	14		●	20							●	●											●						Princeton
15	F5	Bromley Rock	Fr Princeton, 14 mi E on Hwy 3			368	17	17	2.00		All year	14		●	20							●	●										●	●						Princeton
16	F5	Allison Lake	Fr Princeton, 21 mi N on Hwy 5			57	22	22	2.00		All year	14		●	20							●	●										●	●	l					Princeton
17	B4	Prophet River Wayside	At Prophet River Airport, Mi 223 on Alaska Hwy		2		50	50	None		All year	14		●								●	●	●													p			Prophet River
18	F5	Skagit Val RA	Fr Hope, 2 mi W on Hwy 1, 27 mi S on secondary rd			B	45	45	None		All year	14		●	20							●	●											●						Hope
19	E5	Skihist	Fr Lytton, 5 mi E on Hwy 1			82	70	70	2.00		All year	14		●	20				●			●	●			●								●						Lytton
19	E5	Goldpan	Fr Spence's Bridge, 6 mi S on Hwy 1			12	14	14	2.00		All year	14		●	20							●	●											●						Spence's Bridge
20	F6	Okanagan Lake	Fr Penticton, 15 mi N on Hwy 97			198	156	156	4.00		All year	14		●	20				●			●	●			●							●	●	l					Peachland
21	F6	Inkaneep Park	Fr Oliver, 3-3/4 mi N on Hwy 97/3			7	7	7	2.00		All year	14		●	20							●	●											○						Oliver
21	F6	Okanagan Falls	Fr Penticton, 13 mi S on Hwy 97/3			5	20	20	2.00		All year	14		●	20							●	●			●							●	●						Okanagan Falls
21	F6	Vaseux Lk	Fr Oliver, 11 mi N on Hwy 97/3			14	9	9	2.00		All year	14		●	20							●	●										●							Oliver
22	E4	Birkenhead Lake	Fr Pemberton, 23 mi NE on Pemberton-D'Arcy Hwy, 11 mi NW on grvl rd, on Birkenhead Lk		3	9000	88	88	2.00		All year	14		●	20							●	●										●	●	l		p			Pemberton
23	F7	Kikomun Creek	Fr Cranbrook, 40 mi E on Hwy 3/93, 79 mi S; on Lk Koocanusa		3	1384	77	77	2.00		All year	14		●	20							●	●										●	●	l		p			Elko
24	F6	Johnstone Creek	Fr Bridesville, 7 mi E on Hwy 3			93	16	16	2.00		All year	14		●	20							●	●																	Bridesville
24	F6	Boundary Creek	Fr Greenwood, 3 mi SW on Hwy 3			4	17	17	2.00		All year	14		●	20							●	●																	Greenwood
24	F6	Kettle River RA	Fr Rock Creek, 3 mi N on Hwy 33			346	48	48	2.00		All year	14		●	20							●	●										●	●						Rock Creek
25	F6	King George VI	Fr Rossland, 6 mi S on Hwy 22			400	12	12	None		All year	14		●	20							●	●																	Rossland
25	F6	Nancy Greene Prov Pk	Fr Castlegar, 16 mi W on Hwy 3 to jct Hwys 3/3b			451	22	22	None		All year	14		●	20							●	●										●	●						Castlegar
26	F6	Champion Lakes	Fr Fruitval, 4 mi E on Hwy 3A, 6 mi NW to CG			3520	89	89	4.00		All year	14		●	20				●			●	●										●	●	l					Fruitvale
27	E5	Monte Lake	Fr Monte Creek, 13 mi SE on Hwy 97			19	7	7	None		All year	14		●	20							●	●										●	●	l					Monte Creek
28	E6	Blanket Creek	Fr Revelstoke, 14 mi S on Hwy 23		2		64	64	None		All year	14		●	20							●	●										●	●	l		np			Mt Cartier
29	E6	Yard Creek	Fr Revelstoke, 37 mi W on Kamloops-Revelstoke Hwy			150	92	92	2.00		All year	14		●	20				●			●	●			●								●						Malakwa
30	E5	Monck Park	Fr Merritt, 20 mi NE on Hwy 5, W side of Nicola Lk on gravel rd			216	61	61	2.00		All year	14		●	20							●	●										●	●	l					Merritt
31	F6	Kokanee Creek	Fr Nelson, 12 mi NE on Nelson-Balfour Hwy 3A			643	112	112	4.00		All year	14		●	20				●			●	●			●				○			●	●	l					Nelson
32	F6	Lockhart Beach	Fr Creston, 33 mi N on Hwy 3A			7	12	12	None		All year	14		●	20							●	●										●	●						Boswell
33	F7	Yahk	Fr Yahk, 1 mi N on Cranbrook-Creston Hwy 95/3			18	18	18	2.00		All year	14		●	20							●	●											●						Yahk
34	F7	Jimsmith Lake	Fr Cranbrook, 1 mi S on Hwy 3/95, 3 mi W			29	28	28	2.00		All year	14		●	20							●	●										●	●	l					Cranbrook
34	F7	Moyie Lake	Fr Cranbrook, 12 mi S on Hwy 3/95, 1 mi W			153	72	72	2.00		All year	14		●	20				●			●	●										●	●	l					Moyie Lake
35	F7	Wasa Lake	Fr Ft Steele, 13 mi N on Hwy 93			347	105	105	4.00		All year	14		●	20				●			●	●			●							●	●	l					Wasa
36	E7	Thunderhill	Fr Canal Flats, 2 mi N on Hwy 95/93			109	23	23	None		All year	14		●	20							●	●																	Canal Flats
37	E7	Dry Gulch	Fr Athalmar, 7 mi N on Hwy 95/93			72	24	24	2.00		All year	14		●	20							●	●			●								●						Radium Jct
38	E6	Roseberry	Fr New Denver, 3 mi N on Hwy 6			80	22	22	2.00		All year	14		●	20							●	●																	New Denver
39	F7	Mount Fernie	Fr Fernie, 2 mi W on Hwy 3, 1 mi to CG			640	38	38	2.00		All year	14		●	20							●	●			●								●						Fernie

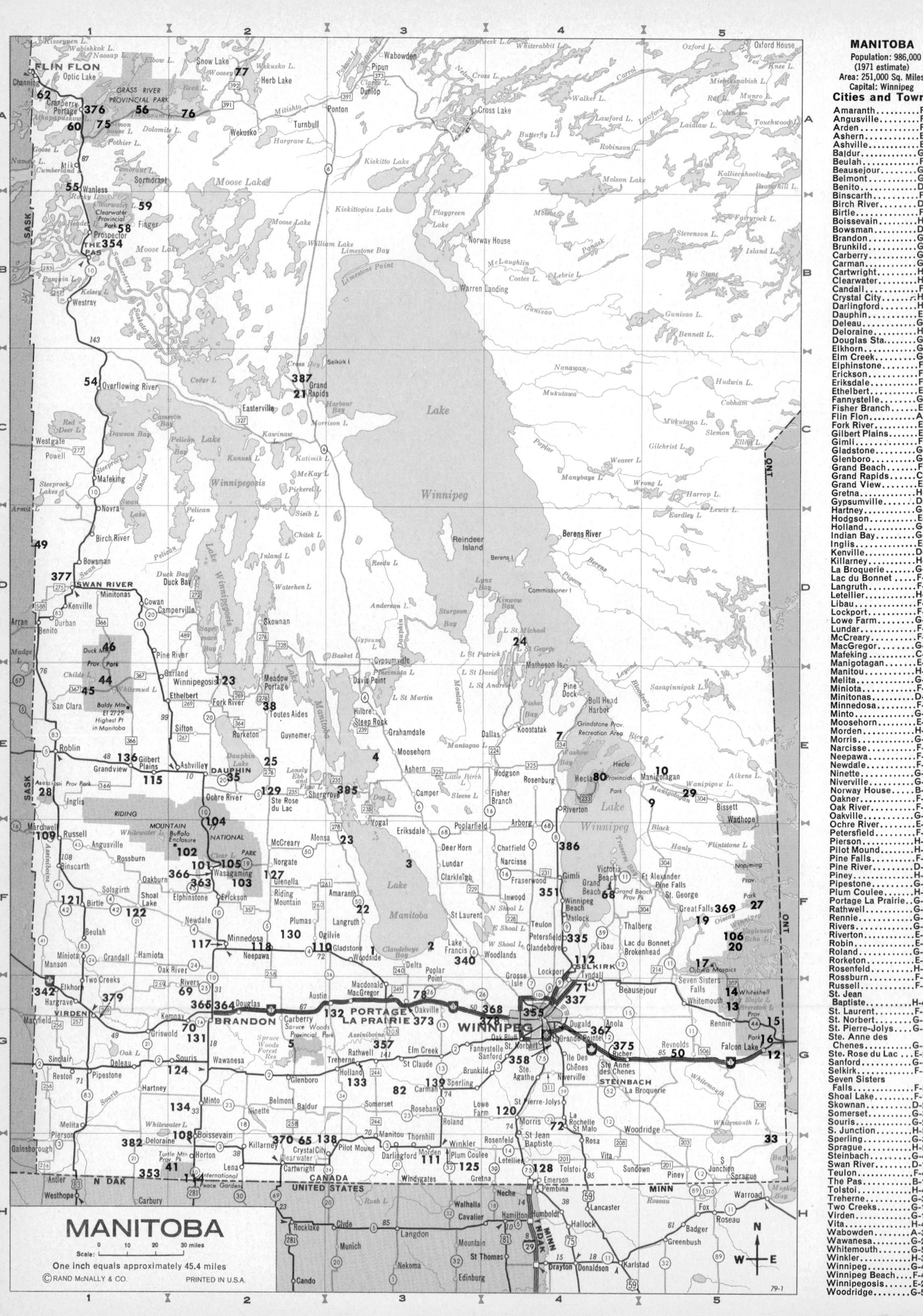

MANITOBA

Population: 986,000
(1971 estimate)
Area: 251,000 Sq. Miles
Capital: Winnipeg

Cities and Towns

Amaranth..........F-3
Angusville..........F-1
Arden..........F-2
Ashern..........E-3
Ashville..........E-2
Baldur..........G-2
Beulah..........F-1
Beausejour..........G-4
Belmont..........G-2
Benito..........D-1
Binscarth..........F-1
Birch River..........D-1
Birtle..........F-1
Boissevain..........H-2
Bowsman..........D-1
Brandon..........G-2
Brunkild..........G-4
Carberry..........G-2
Carman..........G-3
Cartwright..........H-2
Clearwater..........H-2
Candall..........F-1
Crystal City..........H-3
Darlingford..........H-3
Dauphin..........E-2
Deleau..........G-1
Deloraine..........H-1
Douglas Sta..........G-2
Elkhorn..........G-1
Elm Creek..........G-3
Elphinstone..........F-2
Erickson..........F-2
Eriksdale..........F-3
Ethelbert..........E-1
Fannystelle..........G-3
Fisher Branch..........E-4
Flin Flon..........A-1
Fork River..........E-2
Gilbert Plains..........E-1
Gimli..........F-4
Gladstone..........G-3
Glenboro..........G-2
Grand Beach..........F-4
Grand Rapids..........C-2
Grand View..........E-1
Gretna..........H-4
Gypsumville..........D-3
Hartney..........G-1
Hodgson..........E-4
Holland..........G-3
Indian Bay..........G-5
Inglis..........E-1
Kenville..........D-1
Killarney..........H-2
La Broquerie..........G-4
Lac du Bonnet..........F-5
Langruth..........F-3
Letellier..........H-4
Libau..........F-4
Lockport..........F-4
Lowe Farm..........G-4
Lundar..........F-3
McCreary..........F-2
MacGregor..........G-3
Mafeking..........C-1
Manigotagan..........E-4
Manitou..........H-3
Melita..........G-1
Miniota..........F-1
Minitonas..........D-1
Minnedosa..........F-2
Minto..........G-2
Moosehorn..........E-3
Morden..........H-3
Morris..........G-4
Narcisse..........F-4
Neepawa..........F-2
Newdale..........F-2
Ninette..........G-2
Niverville..........G-4
Norway House..........B-3
Oakner..........F-1
Oak River..........F-1
Oakville..........G-3
Ochre River..........E-2
Petersfield..........F-4
Pierson..........H-1
Pilot Mound..........H-3
Pine Falls..........F-5
Pine River..........D-1
Piney..........H-5
Pipestone..........G-1
Plum Coulee..........H-3
Portage La Prairie..........G-3
Rathwell..........G-3
Rennie..........G-5
Rivers..........G-2
Riverton..........E-4
Robin..........E-1
Roland..........G-3
Rorketon..........E-2
Rosenfeld..........H-4
Rossburn..........F-1
Russell..........F-1
St. Jean Baptiste..........H-4
St. Laurent..........F-3
St. Norbert..........G-4
St. Pierre-Jolys..........G-4
Ste. Anne des Chenes..........G-4
Ste. Rose du Lac..........E-2
Sanford..........G-4
Selkirk..........F-4
Seven Sisters Falls..........F-5
Shoal Lake..........F-1
Skownan..........D-2
Somerset..........G-3
Souris..........G-2
S. Junction..........H-5
Sperling..........G-3
Sprague..........H-5
Steinbach..........G-4
Swan River..........D-1
Teulon..........F-4
The Pas..........B-1
Tolstoi..........H-4
Treherne..........G-3
Two Creeks..........G-1
Virden..........G-1
Vita..........H-4
Wabowden..........A-3
Wawanesa..........G-2
Whitemouth..........G-5
Winkler..........H-3
Winnipeg..........G-4
Winnipeg Beach..........F-4
Winnipegosis..........E-2
Woodridge..........G-5

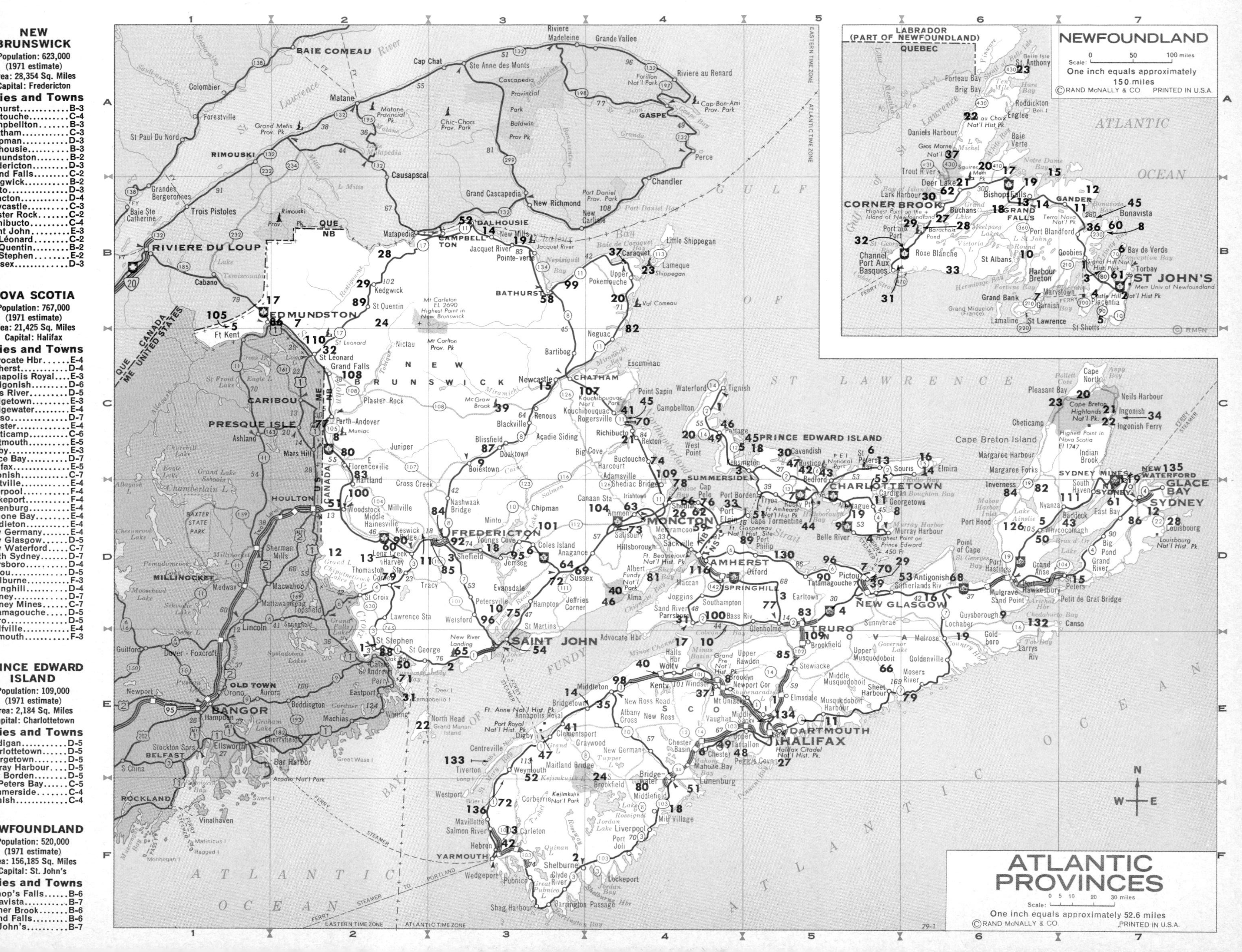

NEW BRUNSWICK

Population: 623,000
(1971 estimate)
Area: 28,354 Sq. Miles
Capital: Fredericton

Cities and Towns

Bathurst..........B-3
Buctouche..........C-4
Campbellton..........B-3
Chatham..........C-3
Chipman..........D-3
Dalhousie..........B-3
Edmundston..........B-2
Fredericton..........D-3
Grand Falls..........C-2
Kedgwick..........B-2
Minto..........D-3
Moncton..........D-4
Newcastle..........C-3
Plaster Rock..........C-2
Richibucto..........C-4
Saint John..........E-3
St. Léonard..........C-2
St. Quentin..........B-2
St. Stephen..........E-2
Sussex..........D-3

NOVA SCOTIA

Population: 767,000
(1971 estimate)
Area: 21,425 Sq. Miles
Capital: Halifax

Cities and Towns

Advocate Hbr..........E-4
Amherst..........D-4
Annapolis Royal..........E-3
Antigonish..........D-6
Bass River..........D-5
Bridgetown..........E-3
Bridgewater..........E-4
Canso..........D-7
Chester..........E-4
Cheticamp..........C-6
Dartmouth..........E-5
Digby..........E-3
Glace Bay..........D-7
Halifax..........E-5
Ingonish..........C-7
Kentville..........E-4
Liverpool..........F-4
Lockeport..........F-4
Lunenburg..........E-4
Mahone Bay..........E-4
Middleton..........E-4
New Germany..........E-4
New Glasgow..........D-5
New Waterford..........C-7
North Sydney..........D-7
Parrsboro..........D-4
Pictou..........D-5
Shelburne..........F-3
Springhill..........D-4
Sydney..........D-7
Sydney Mines..........C-7
Tatamagouche..........D-5
Truro..........D-5
Wolfville..........E-4
Yarmouth..........F-3

PRINCE EDWARD ISLAND

Population: 109,000
(1971 estimate)
Area: 2,184 Sq. Miles
Capital: Charlottetown

Cities and Towns

Cardigan..........D-5
Charlottetown..........D-5
Georgetown..........D-5
Murray Harbour..........D-5
Port Borden..........D-5
St. Peters Bay..........C-5
Summerside..........C-4
Tignish..........C-4

NEWFOUNDLAND

Population: 520,000
(1971 estimate)
Area: 156,185 Sq. Miles
Capital: St. John's

Cities and Towns

Bishop's Falls..........B-6
Bonavista..........B-7
Corner Brook..........B-6
Grand Falls..........B-6
St. John's..........B-7

BRITISH COLUMBIA

FOR FOOTNOTE EXPLANATION SEE FIRST PAGE OF THIS PROVINCE   FOR MAP, SEE PAGE 111

PROVINCIAL PARKS & CAMPGROUNDS (CONT'D)

Park number	Map reference	Name of park	Access	Physical environment	Elevation	Acres	Number of tent spaces	Number of trailer spaces	Approximate fee	Credit cards accepted	Season	Time limit	Reservations	Pets permitted	Max. trailer size	Electric hookup	Water hookup	Sewer hookup	Sanitary station	Bottled gas	Air conditioning	Tables	Firewood	Pull-thru spaces	Rec. hall	Flush toilets	Showers	Ice	Auto. laundry	Cafe-snack bar	Store	Swimming pool	Other swimming	Fishing	Boating	Playground	Other	CB channel monitored	Telephone no.	Mail address
40	E5	Lac Le Jeune	Fr Kamloops, 5 mi W on Hwy 1, 18 mi S on gravel rd			138	144	144	2.00		All year	14		•	20							•	•										•	•	l					Kamloops
41	E6	Shuswap Lake	Fr Hwy 1 at Squalix, 12 mi N			285	294	294	4.00		All year	14		•	20				•			•	•			•							•	•	l					Celista
42	E5	Lac La Hache	Fr Lac La Hache Post Office, 8 mi N on Hwy 97			54	83	83	4.00		All year	14		•	20				•			•	•			•							•		l					Lac La Hache
43	E5	Marble Canyon	Fr Cache Creek, 7 mi N on Hwy 97, 18 mi W on unpaved rd			827	18	18	None		All year	14		•	20							•	•										•	•	l					Pavilion
44	E5	Big Bar Lk	Fr Clinton, 5 mi S on Hwy 97, 22 mi W		4	728	60	60	2.00		All year	14		•	25							•	•										•	•						Clinton
45	D5	Barkerville Historic Pk	At Barkervillestoric Pk			160	200	200	4.00		All year	14		•	20				•			•	•							•										Wells
46	D5	Cottonwood River	Fr Quesnel, 18 mi N on Hwy 97, 6 mi W			164	8	8	None		All year	14		•	20							•	•											•						Quesnel
47	E5	Canim Beach	Fr 100 Mile House, 1/2 mi N on Hwy 97, 21 mi E on gravel rd			13	14	14	2.00		All year	14		•	20							•	•										•	•						Forest Grove
47	E5	Mahood Lk CG	Fr 100 Mile House, 55 mi E on gravel rd				36	36	2.00		All year	14		•	20							•	•										•	•	l					Mahood Lk
48	E5	Bridge Lake	Fr Hwy 97 at 93 Mile House, 33 mi E on Hwy 24			15	32	32	2.00		All year	14		•	20							•	•										•	•						Bridge Lake
49	C4	Topley	Fr Hwy 16 in Topley, 27 mi N on gravel rd			30	5	5	None		All year	14		•	20							•	•											•						Topley
50	C3	Maclure Lake	Fr Telkwa, 1/2 mi W on Hwy 16, fol signs			81	54	54	2.00		All year	14		•	20				•			•	•										•	•						Telkwa
51	C3	Seeley Lake	Fr Hazelton, 4 mi W on Hwy 16			59	8	8	None		All year	14		•	20							•	•											•						Hazelton
52	C3	Kleanza Creek	Fr Terrace, 12 mi E on Hwy 16			143	11	11	None		All year	14		•	20							•	•											•			n			Terrace
53	D3	Prudhomme Lk Pk	Fr Prince Rupert, 10 mi E on Hwy 16			18	17	17	2.00		All year	14		•	20							•	•										•	•						Prince Rupert
54	D3	Exchamsiks River	Fr Terrace, 36 mi W on Hwy 16			38	10	10	None		All year	14		•	20							•	•											•						Terrace
54	D3	Lakelse Lake	Fr Terrace, 16 mi SW on Hwy 25			874	155	155	4.00		All year	14		•	20				•			•	•										•	•	l					Terrace
55	D4	Beaumont Park	Fr Prince George, 80 mi W on Hwy 16			494	49	49	2.00		All year	14		•	20				•			•	•										•	•	l					Fort Fraser
56	F5	Nairn Falls	Fr Pemberton, 2 mi S on Hwy 99			423	86	86	2.00		All year	14		•	20							•	•											•						Pemberton
		Mt Robson Pk				B																																		
57	D6	Robson Meadows	Fr W boundary of pk, 3 mi E on Hwy 16				127	127	2.00		All year	14		•	20				•			•	•											•			n			Red Pass
57	D6	Robson River	Fr W boundary, 2 mi E on Hwy 16				19	19	2.00		All year	14		•	20							•	•											•	l					Red Pass
58	D6	Lucerne	Fr Alberta border, 5 mi W on Hwy 16				32	32	2.00		All year	14		•	20							•	•											•	l		n			Red Pass
59	F4	McDonald	Fr Victoria, 20 mi N on Hwy 17			49	30	30	2.00		All year	14		•	20							•	•																	Sidney
59	F4	Sidney Spit Marine Pk	On N end of Sidney Isle; enter from Haro Strait from Miners Channel			724	6				All year	14		•								•	•																	Sidney Isle
59	F4	Bamberton	Fr Victoria, 20 mi N on TC 1			69	53	53	4.00		All year	14		•	20							•	•			•							•	•						Malahat
59	F4	Pirates Cove Marine Pk	On SE side of De Courey Isle; enter from Pylades Channel			76	9				All year	14		•								•	•																	De Courey Isle
59	F4	Prior Centennial	On North Pender Island, car ferry fr Swartz Bay			39	11	11	None		All year	14		•	20							•	•										•	•						Pender Island
59	F4	Goldstream	Fr Victoria, 12 mi W on Hwy 1			700	160	160	4.00		All year	14		•	20				•			•	•			•								•						Victoria
60	E5	Horsefly Lk Prov Pk	Fr 150 Mi House, 42 mi E on Horsefly-Quesnel secondary rd, on Horsefly Lk			365	22	22	None		All year	14		•	20							•	•										•	•	l					Horsefly
61	E5	Green Lk	Fr 70 Mile House, 12 mi E on secondary rd			280	54	54	4.00		All year	14		•	20							•	•										•	•	l					Mile House
63	F4	Ivy Green	Fr Nanaimo, 12 mi S on Hwy 19			62	51	51	2.00		All year	14		•	20				•			•	•			•							•	•						Ladysmith
65	F4	Englishman River	Fr Parksville, 3-1/2 mi W on Hwy 4			240	105	105	2.00		All year	14		•	20							•	•											•						Parksville
65	F4	Rathtrevor Beach	Fr Parksville, 2 mi S on Hwy 19			859	129	129	4.00		All year	14		•	20				•			•	•										•	•						Parksville
65	F4	Little Qualicum Falls	Fr Parksville, 12 mi W on Hwy 4			365	92	92	2.00		All year	14		•	20							•	•			•							•	•						Parksville
65	F4	Stamp Falls	Fr Alberni, 9 mi N on Stamp River			583	20	20	None		All year	14		•	20							•	•										•	•						Alberni
65	F4	Sproat Lk Pk	Fr Alberni, 8 mi NW on Hwy 4			98	67	67	4.00		All year	14		•	20							•	•										•	•	l					Alberni
66	F4	Miracle Beach	Fr Courtenay, 14 mi N on Hwy 19, 2 mi E			326	185	185	4.00		All year	14		•	20							•	•										•	•	l					Courtenay
67	B4	115 Creek Wayside	Mile 403 Alaska Hwy				8	8	None		All year	14		•	20							•	•																	Summit Lake
68	B4	Bucking Horse Riv Wayside	Mile 175 Alaska Hwyayside				33	33	None		All year	14		•	20							•	•																	Mason Cr
69	F7	Norbury Lk	Fr Ft Steele, 12 mi SE on Ft Steele-Wardner Hwy		3	240	43	43	None		All year	14		•	20							•	•										•	•			p			Ft Steele
69	F7	Premier Lk Pk	Fr Skookumchuck, 13-1/2 mi N on Hwy 93/95, 10 mi E on gravel rd; on S end of Premier Lk			165	40	40	2.00		All year	14		•	20							•	•										•	•	l					Skookumchuck
70	F4	Mouat Park	By ferry to Saltspring Island, 1/4 mi fr Ganges			58	15	15	2.00		All year	14		•	20							•	•																	Ganges
70	F4	Ruckle Pk	At Beaver Pt on Saltspring Island; access by car ferry fr Crofton, Swartz Bay & Tsawwassen			1200	20				All year	14		•								•	•											•						Crofton
71	C5	Sudeten Prov Pk Wayside	Fr Dawson Cr, 20 mi SE on Hwy 2			12	15	15	None		All year	14		•	20							•	•																	Dawson Cr
71	C5	Swan Lk Pk	Fr Dawson Cr, 20 mi S on Hwy 2, 1 mi N, 1 mi E, at Tupper			166	25	25	None		All year	14		•	20							•	•										•	•	l					Tupper
72	F6	Syringa Creek Prov Pk	Fr Castlegar, N to Robson, 10-1/2 mi N of Robson ferry Terminal		2	375	60	60	2.00		All year	14		•	20				•			•	•										•				np			Arrow Lake
73	F4	Montague Harbour Marine	Fr Victoria, 30 mi N; W coast of Galiano Isle			214	31	31	4.00		All year	14		•	20							•	•										•	•	dl					Galiano
75	F4	Elk Falls	Fr Campbell River, 6 mi NW			2686	66	66	123		All year	14		•	20							•	•											•						Campbell River
75	F4	Morton Lake	Fr Campbell Riv, 17 mi NW on Hwy 19 & gravel rd, fol signs			165	24	24	None		All year	14		•	20							•	•										•	•	l		n			Campbell River
		Wells Gray				B																																		
78	E5	Clearwater Lake	Fr Hwy 5, Wells Gray Pk Rd to Pk ent, 20 mi N				35	35	2.00		All year	14		•	20							•	•										•	•	l					Clearwater
79	E5	Dawson Falls	Fr Hwy 5, N on Wells Gray Pk Rd to Pk ent, 5 mi N				11	11	2.00		All year	14		•	20							•	•											•						Clearwater
80	D4	Ethel F Wilson	Fr Hwy 16 in Burns Lk, 11 mi N on Babine Lk Rd			71	10	10	None		All year	14		•	20							•	•											•						Burns Lake
81	F4	Saltery Bay Park	Fr Powell River, 20 mi SE on Hwy 101			25	43	43	2.00		All year	14		•	20				•			•	•										•	•	l					Saltery Bay
82	D5	Ten Mile Lk Pk	Fr Quesnel, 6-1/2 mi N on Hwy 97			596	142	142	4.00		All year	14		•	20				•			•	•	•									•	•	l					Quesnel
83	F4	Gordon Bay	Fr Duncan, 19 mi W on Hwy 18			122	131	131	4.00		All year	14		•	20				•			•	•			•							•	•	l					Lake Cowichan
84	E5	Paul Lk	Fr Kamloops, 3 mi N on Hwy 5, 11 mi E to Pk			993	130	130	2.00		All year	14		•	20				•			•	•										•	•			n			Kamloops
85	D5	Bowron Lk	Fr Quesnel, 70 mi E			B	31	31	2.00		All year	14			20							•	•										•	•	l					Barkerville
86	C5	Kiskatinaw	Fr Dawson Cr, 21 mi N on Alaska Hwy			143	28	28	None		All year	14		•	20							•	•										•							Dawson Creek
87	D5	Purden Lk	Fr Prince George, 40 mi E on Hwy 16			345	78	78	2.00		All year	14		•	20				•			•	•										•	•	l					Prince George
88	A3	Hyland River Wayside RA	Mile 606 Alaska Hwye RA			84	37	37	None		All year	14		•	20							•	•																	Lower Post
90	F5	Ellison Pk	Fr Vernon, 10 mi SW on Okanagan Landing Rd			495	54	54	4.00		All year	14		•	20							•	•			•							•	•						Vernon
91	F6	Haynes Point Pk	Fr Osoyoos, 1 mi S on Hwy 97			13	36	36	4.00		All year	14		•	20							•	•									•	•	•	l					Osoyoos
92	A4	Kledo Creek Park Wayside	Alaska Hwy mi 335Wayside			14	27	27	None		All year	14		•	20							•	•											•						Ft Nelson
93	A4	Liard River Hotsprings	At Mi 493 Alaska Hwygs			1650	21	21	2.00		All year	14		•	20							•	•										•	•						Muncho Lake
94	D5	Crooked River	Fr Prince George, 45 mi N on Hwy 97			2512	93	93	4.00		All year	14		•	20							•	•										•	•						Summit Lake
95	C5	Whiskers Point	Fr Prince George, 79 Mi N on Hwy 97			128	67	67	2.00		All year	14		•	20				•			•	•										•	•	l					McLeod Lake
96	F5	Otter Lk	Fr Princeton, 14 mi W			60	44	44	2.00		All year	14		•	20							•	•										•	•	l		n			Tulameen
96	F5	Emory Creek	Fr Hope, 11 mi N on Hope-Yale Hwy 1			37	32	32	2.00		All year	14		•	20							•	•			•								•						Yale
		Tweedsmuir Prov Pk				B																																		
97	E4	Burnt Bridge	Fr Bella Coola, 30 mi E on Hwy 20		9		6				All year	14		•								•	•											•			hp			Victoria

 FOR MAP, SEE PAGE 111

Park number	Map reference	Name of park	Access	Physical environment	Elevation	Acres	Number of tent spaces	Number of trailer spaces	Approximate fee	Credit cards accepted	Season	Time limit / Reservations / Pets permitted / Max. trailer size	Electric hookup / Water hookup / Sewer hookup	Sanitary station / Bottled gas / Air conditioning	Tables / Firewood / Pull-thru spaces / Rec. hall	Flush toilets / Showers / Ice	Auto. laundry / Cafe-snack bar / Store	Swimming pool / Other swimming / Fishing	Boating / Playground / Other	CB channel monitored	Telephone no.	Mail address
		PROVINCIAL PARKS & CAMPGROUNDS (CONT'D)																				
97	E4	Atnarko River	Fr Bella Coola, 43 mi E on Hwy 20		9		26				All year	14			• •			•	hp			Victoria
		NATIONAL PARKS																				
		Kootenay NP				B															604/347-9615	
100	E7	McLeod Meadows	Fr Radium Hot Springs, 16 mi NE on Hwy 93		4	30	100		F3.00		5/18-LD	14 • U		•	• •	•		o				Radium Hot Springs
101	E7	Redstreak CG	Fr Radium Hot Springs, 3 mi SW on Hwy 95		4	96	153	88	F6.00		5/11-10/15	14 • U	• • •	•	• •	•$ o	o o	o o	•			Radium Hot Springs
105	E6	Marble Canyon	Fr Radium Hot Springs, 53-1/2 mi NE on Hwy 93		5	30	60		F3.00		6/22-LD	14 • U		•	• •	•		o				Radium Hot Springs
		Yoho NP				B															604/343-6324	
106	E6	Chancellor Peak	Fr Field, 14-1/2 mi SW on TC 1		4	16	64		F3.00		5/18-9/30	14 • U			• •			o	•			Field
106	E6	Kicking Horse	Fr Field, 2 mi E on TC 1, 1 mi N on Yoho Valley Rd		9	27			F3.00		6/1-LD	14 • U		• o	• •	•$	o •	o	•			Field
106	E6	Takakkaw Falls	Fr Field, 2 mi E on TC 1, 8-1/2 mi N on Yoho Valley Rd		6	5	35		F3.00		6/15-LD	4 • U			• •			o			604/343-6485	Box 99 Field BC
106	E6	Hoodoo Creek	Fr Field, 14 mi SW on TC 1		1	67			F3.00		6/15-LD	14 • U		•	• •	•		o	•			Field
106	E6	Lake O'Hara	Fr Field, 3 mi E on TC 1, 7 mi S from Lake O'Hara gate				30		3.00		6/25-LD	4 R •			• •		•	•			604/343-6485	Box 99 Field
		Pacific Rim NP				B															604/726-7721	
107	F4	Greenpoint CG	On W shore of Vancouver Island; nr Ucluelet, on Hwy 4		1		92		F3.00		All year	7 • U		•	• •			o •	p			Ucluelet
		Glacier NP				B															604/837-5155	
110	E6	Illecillewaet	Adj to TC Hwy, 1 mi W of Glacier Station		5	8	59		F3.00		6/16-9/15	14 • 12			• •	•			p			Revelstoke
110	E6	Loop Creek	Adj to TC Hwy in Glacier NP, 1 mi E of Glacier Station		4	2	20		F3.00		6/16-LD	14 • 12			• •	•			p			Revelstoke
110	E6	Mountain Creek	Adj to TC Hwy, 2 mi W of E park boundry		3	300	306		F3.00		6/16-LD	14 • U		•	• •	•			p			Revelstoke
		BACKPACK OR BOAT ACCESS AREAS																				
		Provincial Parks																				
112	F4	Newcastle Island Marine	In Nanaimo Harbour, by pedestrian ferry or private boat only			756	18				All year	14 •			• •			•	dl •			Nanaimo
113	E6	Cinnemousun Narrows Pk	Fr Sicamons on TC 1; access by private boat or ferry		2	319	28				All year	14			• •			• •	d			
		CITY, COUNTY & CIVIC																				
118	C3	Riverside Park & Campsite	Fr Smithers, 1/4 mi E on Hwy 16	≈ ᴧ	2	10	30	30	3.00		6/1-10/30	U • U		o	• •	o	o o o	•	• gp		604/847-3251	Box 879, Smithers
119	D2	Roosevelt Trlr Pk	In Prince Rupert	⚓ ᴧ	1	3	10	30	4.00		3/1-10/31	3 Z • U		• o	• • •	• • o	o o o	o o	dlr • gk		604/624-5871	Prince Rupert
120	F5	Coquihalla	In Hope, off Hwy 3, on Coquihalla Riv on Kawkawa Lake Rd	≈ ᴧ	1	30	50	50	3.00		4/15-10/15	U Z • U		o o	• • •	• • o	o o o	$ o •	gp		604/869-5257	Box 609 Hope
121	F6	Grand Forks City Pk	2 blks S of the Southern TC Hwy with directional signs	≈ ᴧ	2	8	15	15	3.00		5/1-9/30	U Z • U	• • •		• •	• • o	o o o	• •	•		604/442-2202	Box 1486, Grand Forks
122	F6	City Tourist Pk	Fr Hwy 3A, 1 blk S in Nelson	♣ ᴧ	2	3	30	10	4.50		5/15-9/30	14 Z • U	• • $	• o	•	• • •	o o o	o o	dlr gt			502 Vernon St, Nelson
122	F6	Nelson Municipal Camp	In Nelson on High Stp	♣ ᴧ	2	5	30	10	4.50		5/15-9/30	U • U	• • •	• o	•	• • o	o o o	o o	dlr g			502 Vernon St, Nelson
124	F7	Cranbrook Mun Tourist Pk	Fr Cranbrook, E on 1st St to 14th Ave	≈ ᴧ	4	10	50	50	5.50		5/13-9/9	14 • 20	• • •	o o	• • •	• • o	o o o	o o	• gpt		604/426-2162	40 10th Ave S, Cranbrook
126	F4	Willingdon Beach Campsite	In Powell Riv, on W side of Hwy 101	⚓ ♀	0	7	38	12	4.50		5/1-10/31	14 Z • U	• • •	• o	• •	• •	o • o	• •	lr • gh			Powell River
127	F6	Peach Orchard	Fr Hwy 97, 1 mi E, at Summerland	♣ ᴧ	2	10	60	60	4.50		5/15-10/1	U Z • 20		o	•	• • o	o o o	o o	• t		604/494-9959	Box 159, Summerland
128	E6	Golden Comm Pk	Fr Hwy 95, 4 blk E, on bank of Kicking Horse Riv	≈ ᴧ	3	341	35	35	4.50		5/15-9/30	14 Z • U	$	• o	• • •	• • o	o o o	$	• h		604/344-2271	Box 350, Golden
129	C5	Mile 'O' Campsite	Fr Dawson Creek, 1-1/4 mi N on Hwy 97 (Alaska Hwy)	♣ ѱ	3	8	10	59	3.00		5/15-9/15	U • U		• o	• •	• • o	• o o		• gp		604/782-3351	Bx 150, Dawson Crk
133	E6	Nakusp Recreation Pk	In Nakusp, 2 blks W off Hwy 23	♣ ᴧ	2	34	25	25	3.00		5/24-9/30	14 • U		o o	• •	• • o	o o o	• o	d • gpt		604/265-3689	Box 280, Nakusp
133	E6	Nakusp Hot Springs CG	Fr Nakusp, 1/2 mi N on Hwy 23, E 7 mi	≈ ᴧ	3	10	8	S30	4.00		All year	U • 28		•	• •	• •		• •	• ghkp			Box 280, Nakusp
		PRIVATE																				
135	F4	Victoria West KOA	Fr Victoria, 16 mi N on TC 1	⚓ ᴧ	1	20	E100	25	5.75		5/1-10/30	U Z • U	$ $ $	• •	• • •	• • •	• o •	• o	lr •		604/478-3332	Malahat
136	D5	Yellowhead Tent & Trlr Pk	Fr Swift Cr Bridge in Valemount, 1/4 mi N on Hwy 5	≈ ᴧ	3	29	20	20	3.75		5/24-8/31	U Z • U	$ $	•	• • •	• • •	o o o	• •			604/566-4227	Valemount
136	D5	Alpine KOA	Hwy 5 at Valemount Crossroads	♣ ᴧ	3	11	E25	60	5.75	AMV	All year	U Z • U	$ $ $	• •	• • • •	• • •	• • •	o o	• kpu		604/566-4312	Bx 217, Valemount
137	F4	4 All Seasons Resort	Fr Nanaima, 2 mi S on TC 1, 4 mi on Cedar-Harmac Rd 6 mi SE on Yellow Pt Rd	⚓ ᴧ	0	15	45	65	6.25	MV	All year	U Z U	$ $ $	•	• • • •	• • •	• •	• • •	dlr • kp		604/245-4243	RR 1 Yellow Pt Rd, Ladysmith
137	F4	The Zuiderzee Campsite	Fr Nanaimo, 9 mi S on Yellow Point Rd (Vancouver Isle)	♣ ♀	1	28	70	16	4.25		All year	U $ U	$ • •	•	• • •	• $ •	•	• •	lr •		604/722-2334	RR 3, Ladysmith
137	F4	Seaside Trlr Pk	Bet Duncan & Nanaimo on Hwy 1A	⚓ ⊥		5		19	4.00		All year	U R 24	• • •		•	• • o	o o o	• $	r gp		604/245-3589	RR 2 Ladysmith
138	E4	F Hansen Family Ranch	Fr Williams Lk, 165 mi W on Hwy 20	♣ ᴧ	4	200	10	8	3.50		5/1-11/1	U R • U			•	• $ •	•	• •	lr h			Kleena-Kleene
139	F4	Ark Resort	Fr Pt Alberni, 5 mi W on Hwy 4, 5 mi N on Grt Central Lk Rd	♣ ᴧ	1	3	8	7	4.50		All year	U • U	$ $ $	•	• •	• •	•	• •	dlr	14	604/723-2657	RR 3, Port Alberni
139	F4	Roger Cr Trlr Pk & Campin	Center of Port Alberni on Hwy 4	≈ ᴧ	1	2	12	8	5.00		All year	U • U	• • •	o o	• •	• • •	• o o	o o	l •		604/723-5090	4837 Roger St, Port Alberni
139	F4	Cameron Lk Resort	Fr Parksville, 14 mi W on Hwy 4	♣ ᴧ	1	7	30	20	4.00		All year	U Z • U	•		• • •	• •	•	• •	dlr g		604/752-6707	RR 2, Qualicum Bch
139	F4	Tall Timbers Resort	Fr Port Alberni, 9 mi W on Hwy 4	♣ ᴧ	1	8	36	90	7.00		4/1-10/31	U Z • U	$ $ $	• •	• • •	• $ •	• o	• o	dl • p		604/724-0014	RR3 Lakeshore Rd,Port Alberni
139	F4	Deep Bay Auto Ct	Fr Qualicum Bch, 17 mi N on Hwy 19, E on Gainsbrg Rd	⚓ ᴧ	0	10		52	5.50		5/1-9/30	U Z • U	• • •		• •	• $ •	• o o	• •	lr •		604/757-8424	RR 3, Qualicum Beach
139	F4	Lakeshore Campgrounds	Fr Port Alberni, 8 mi W on Hwy 4	⚓ ᴧ	1	2	14	8	5.00		6/25-LD	U Z • 24	• • •		• •	• • •	• o o	• $	dl p		604/723-2030	RR 3 Lakeshore Rd, Pt Alberni
139	F4	Little Qualicum Pk	Fr Qualicum Beach, Vancouver Island, 1 mi N on Hwy 19	⚓ ᴧ	0	11	66	34	4.75		4/1-10/31	U Z • 30	$ •	• o $	• • •	• • •	• •	• •	dr • g		604/752-6174	RR 1, Qualicum Beach
141	F4	Big Tent Campsite	Fr Parksville, E on Hwy 19	⚓ ᴧ	1	5	25	10	3.50		5/24-9/30	U Z • 30	• • •	o o	•	• • •	o o o	• •	•			Rt 1, Parksville
141	F4	Park Sands Bch Resort	Fr Nanaimo at Parksville, 20 mi N on Island Hwy E	⚓ ᴧ	0	7	40	40	6.00	V	4/1-11/1w	U Z 20	• • •	• o	• •	• • •	o o o	• o	dlr • ghp		604/248-3171	Box 179 Parksville
141	F4	Paradise Bch Resort	Fr Nanaimo, 22 mi N on Hwy 19, in Parksville	⚓ ⊥	0	5	12	28	6.25		5/1-10/1	U R 30	• • •	o o $	• •	• • •	o o o	• o	• h		604/248-6612	375 Is Hwy 19N, Parksville
141	F4	Parklands Mbl Home Ct	Fr Nanaimo, 9 mi N on Hwy 19	⚓ ⊥	1	4		6	4.00		4/1-10/1	U Z • U	$ $	o	• •	• • o	•	o o	g		604/390-2132	RR 1 Ware Rd, Lantzville
146	C3	Trout Creek	Fr Smithers, 14 mi W on Hwy 16, (Yellow Head)	≈ ᴧ	2	100	5	10	3.00		5/1-11/1	U Z • U			• •		• •	•			604/847-9855	Bx 8, Smithers
148	E6	Willow Shores	Fr Sicamous, 9 mi S on Hwy 97A	♣ ᴧ	2	11	50	75	7.00	M	5/15-9/30	U Z 30	$ $ $	•	• $	• • •	• •	• •	dr • h		604/838-6216	RR 1, Mara
148	E6	Whispering Pines Pk	Fr TC 1, 11 mi S on Hwy 97A	♣ ᴧ	2	11	45	95	6.50		5/24-9/15	U Z • U	• • •	• •	• • •	• • •	• • •	• o o	dlr • gh		604/838-6775	RR 1, Mara
150	D4	Beaver Campsite	Fr Prince George, 40 mi W on Hwy 16 Gateway to Alaska	♣ ♀	3	110	20	20	4.00		5/1-9/30	U Z • U	$	•	• • •	• $ •	• •	o •	•			RR 1, Vanderhoof
151	E4	Dean River Resort	Fr Williams Lk, 190 mi NW on Hwy 20 to Nimpo Lk	♣ ᴧ	4	10	14	14	3.00	MV	All year	U • U	• •	o o	• • •	• o	o o o	• •	dlr • hk	19		P.O., Nimpo Lake
151	E4	Rainbow Lodge	Fr Williams Lk, 180 mi W on Hwy 20, 3 mi S on Nimpo Lk N Rd	♣ ♀	4	16	6	S4	4.00	AM	5/15-10/31	U Z • 24	•		• •	•	o	• •	dr • p			Nimpo Lake
152	F4	Weir's Beach Resort	Fr Victoria, W on Hwy 14, 5 mi S on Metchosin Rd, 2 mi S on William Head Rd	⚓ ᴧ	0	7	30	64	5.25		4/1-11/1	U Z • 30	$ $ $	•	• • •	• $ •	• •	• • •	l • gp		604/478-3323	RR 1, Victoria
152	F4	Sunny Shores Marina	Fr Victoria, 18 mi W on Hwy 14	⚓ ᴧ	0	6	20	20	5.50		All year	U Z • 30	$ $ $	•	• • •	• • •	• o •	• • •	dlr • g		604/642-5731	5621 Sooke Rd RR 1, Sooke
152	F4	Humpback Valley CG	Fr Victoria, 10 mi N on TC 1, 1/2 mi NW on Sooke Lake Rd, 1 mi W on Humpback Rd, 1/2 mi S on Irwin Rd	♣ ᴧ	1	114	124	26	5.00		6/1-9/15	U Z • U	$ $ $	•	• •	• $ •	• o •	•	r • gp		604/478-6960	60 Irwin Rd RR 6, Victoria
152	F4	Ray's Lakeside Trlr Ct	Fr Victoria, 10 mi On Hwy 1A	♣ ᴧ	0	4	30	14	4.50		4/1-10/31	U Z • 31	$ $ $	o o	• •	• • •	o	• •	r • g		604/478-1509	1261 Goldstream Ave, Victoria
152	F4	Thetis Lk CG	Fr Victoria, 5-1/2 mi N on Hwy 1, Vancouver Island	♣ ᴧ	1	13	84	15	5.50		All year	U Z • 30	• • •	• o	• •	• $ •	• •	o o	• gh		604/478-3845	1938 TransCanada Hwy Victoria
152	F4	Ft Victoria Pk	Fr Victoria, 4 mi W on Hwy 1A	⚓ ⊥	1	24	100	50	5.00		All year	U Z • U	$ $ $	• o $	• •	• $ •	• o o	o o	• gp		604/479-8112	340 Island Hwy, Victoria
153	F6	Park Royal	Fr Hwy 97 & Riverside Dr, 1 blk N at N Penticton	♣ ᴧ	1	2	28	27	6.00		5/1-11/1	U Z 22	• •	•	• • •	• • •	• o o	o o	lr • ghpt		604/492-7051	240 Riverside Dr Penticton
153	F6	Golden Sands Trlr Pk	In Penticton on Okanagan Lk	♣ ♀	2	1	24	24	6.50		5/1-10/1	U Z • 22	• • •	• o	•	• • •	• o •	• • •	lr • ght		604/492-4261	1028 Lakeshore, Penticton
153	F6	Golden West Tent & Trlr P	Fr Penticton, 3 mi S on Main St, NE corner of Skaha Lk	♣ ⊥	2	5	72	60	6.00		4/10-10/31	U Z $ U	• • •	o o •	• o •	• • •	• o •	o o	dlr gp	3	604/492-2642	3600 S Main, Penticton
153	F6	Camp-Along Tent & Trlr Pk	Fr Penticton, 2-1/2 mi S on Hwy 97	♣ ᴧ	2	4	54	24	6.25		5/15-9/15	U Z $ 26	$ $ $		•	• • •	• o •	o o	• ghp		604/497-5584	PO Box 544, Penticton
153	F6	Riverside Tent & Trlr Pk	In Penticton, ent on Wylie St off Westminster Ave & Hwy 97	♣ ᴧ	2	2	12	38	6.00		All year	U Z • 18	$ •	o •	•	• • •	• o o	o o	lr • gh		604/492-0594	271 Wylie St, Penticton
153	F6	Wright's Beach Camp	Fr Penticton, 4 mi S on Hwy 97; on Skaha Lk	♣ ᴧ	2	2	30	50	7.00		5/15-9/15	U Z 21	• •	o o	•	• • •	o • •	• •	lr • gh		604/492-7120	Box 4, Rt 2, Penticton

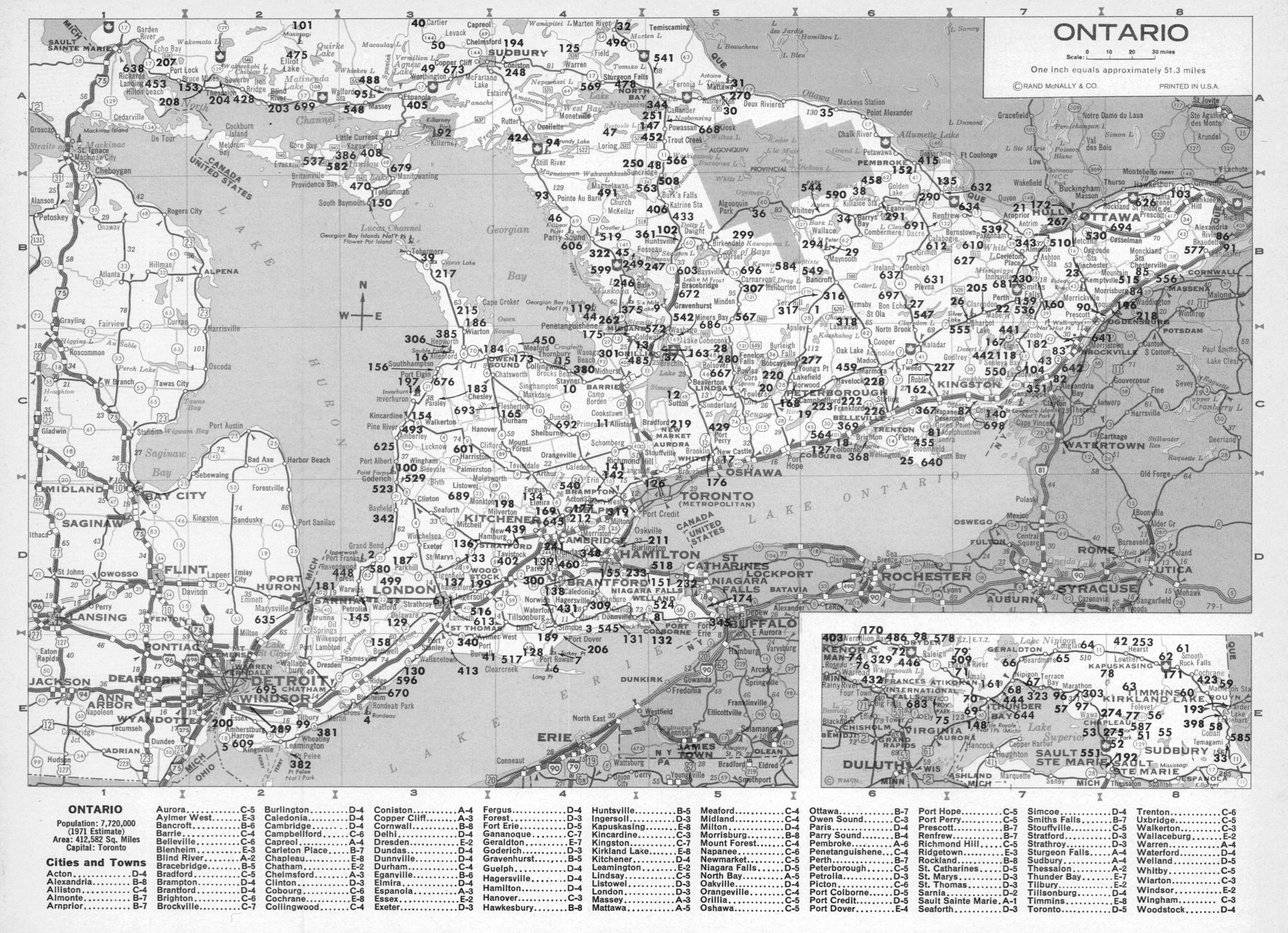

ONTARIO

Population: 7,720,000
(1971 Estimate)
Area: 412,582 Sq. Miles
Capital: Toronto

Cities and Towns

City	Key	City	Key	City	Key
Acton	D-4	Fergus	D-4	Ottawa	B-7
Alexandria	B-8	Forest	D-3	Owen Sound	C-3
Alliston	C-4	Fort Erie	D-5	Paris	D-4
Almonte	B-7	Gananoque	C-7	Parry Sound	B-4
Arnprior	B-7	Geraldton	E-7	Pembroke	A-6
Aurora	C-5	Goderich	D-3	Penetanguishene	C-4
Aylmer West	E-3	Gravenhurst	B-5	Perth	B-7
Bancroft	B-6	Guelph	D-4	Peterborough	C-5
Barrie	C-4	Hagersville	D-4	Petrolia	D-3
Belleville	C-6	Hamilton	D-4	Picton	C-6
Blenheim	E-3	Hanover	C-3	Port Colborne	D-5
Blind River	A-2	Hawkesbury	B-8	Port Credit	D-5
Bracebridge	B-5	Huntsville	B-5	Port Dover	E-4
Bradford	C-5	Ingersoll	D-3	Port Hope	C-5
Brampton	D-4	Kapuskasing	E-8	Port Perry	C-5
Brantford	D-4	Kincardine	C-3	Prescott	B-7
Brighton	C-6	Kingston	C-7	Renfrew	B-7
Brockville	C-7	Kirkland Lake	E-8	Richmond Hill	C-5
Burlington	D-4	Kitchener	D-4	Ridgetown	E-3
Caledonia	D-4	Leamington	E-2	Rockland	B-8
Cambridge	D-4	Lindsay	C-5	St. Catharines	D-5
Campbellford	C-6	Listowel	D-3	St. Marys	D-3
Capreol	A-4	London	D-3	St. Thomas	D-3
Carleton Place	B-7	Massey	A-3	Sarnia	D-2
Chapleau	E-8	Mattawa	A-5	Sault Sainte Marie	A-1
Chatham	E-2	Meaford	C-4	Seaforth	D-3
Chelmsford	A-3	Midland	C-4	Simcoe	D-4
Clinton	D-3	Milton	D-4	Smiths Falls	B-7
Cobourg	C-6	Morrisburg	B-8	Stouffville	C-5
Cochrane	E-8	Mount Forest	C-4	Stratford	D-3
Collingwood	C-4	Napanee	C-6	Strathroy	D-3
Coniston	A-4	Newmarket	C-5	Sturgeon Falls	A-4
Copper Cliff	A-3	Niagara Falls	D-5	Sudbury	A-4
Cornwall	B-8	North Bay	A-5	Thessalon	A-2
Delhi	D-4	Oakville	D-4	Thunder Bay	E-7
Dresden	E-2	Orangeville	C-4	Tilbury	E-2
Dundas	D-4	Orillia	C-5	Tillsonburg	D-4
Dunnville	D-4	Oshawa	C-5	Timmins	E-8
Durham	C-4			Toronto	D-5
Eganville	B-6			Trenton	C-6
Elmira	D-4			Uxbridge	C-5
Espanola	A-3			Walkerton	C-3
Essex	E-2			Wallaceburg	E-2
Exeter	D-3			Warren	A-4
				Waterford	D-4
				Welland	D-5
				Whitby	C-5
				Wiarton	C-3
				Windsor	E-2
				Wingham	C-3
				Woodstock	D-4

QUEBEC

Population: 6,040,000
(1971 estimate)
Area: 594,860 Sq. Miles
Capital: Quebec

Cities and Towns

Acton Vale.........E-4
Alma................B-4
Amos................A-2
Asbestos............E-4
Baie Comeau.......A-7
Baie St. Paul.......C-5
Beauport D-5
Bedford.............F-3
Buckingham.........E-1
Cap de la Madeleine.........D-3
Cap St. Ignace.....D-5
Causapscal.........F-6
Chambord...........B-4
Charlemagne........E-3
Châteauguay........F-3
Chicoutimi..........B-5
Coaticook...........F-4
Cookshire...........F-4
Disraeli.............E-5
Donnacona.........D-4
Dorion-Vaudreuil...F-2
Drummondville.....E-4
E. Angus............F-4
Farnham............F-3
Ferme Neuve.......D-1
Gatineau...........D-1
Granby..............F-3
Grand' Mere........D-3
Hébertville..........B-5
Hull..................E-1
Huntingdon.........F-2
Iberville.............F-3
Joliette..............E-3
Jonquiere...........B-5
Knowlton............F-4
La Baie.............B-5
Lac Mégantic.......E-5
La Guadeloupe.....E-5
La Malbaie (Murray Bay)......C-6
Laprairie............F-3
L'Ascension.......D-2
La Tugue...........C-3
Laurentides.........E-2
Lennoxville.........F-4
Levis................D-5
Loretteville.........D-5
Magog...............F-4
Maniwaki...........D-1
Marieville...........F-3
Matane..............F-6
Mont Laurier.......D-1
Montreal............E-3
Montreal Nord......E-3
Notre Dame du Lac.............C-7
Pierreville..........E-3
Plessisville.........E-4
Pointe Claire.......F-2
Portneuf............D-4
Princeville..........E-4
Quebec.............D-5
Rimouski............B-7
Rivière Bleue.......C-7
Rivière du Loup....C-6
Roberval............B-4
Ste. Agathe des Monts..........E-2
Ste. Anne de Beaupré...........D-5
Ste. Claire.........D-5
Ste. Marie..........D-5
Ste. Martine........F-2
St. Felicien.........A-4
St. Ferdinand.......E-4
St. Georges de Champlain.........D-4
St. Hyacinthe.......E-3
St. Jean............F-3
St. Jean Port Joli..C-6
St. Jerome..........E-2
St. Lambert.........F-3
St. Michel des Saints.............D-2
St. Pascal..........C-6
St. Raymond.......D-4
St. Tite.............D-4
St. Tite des Capes.............C-5
Scotstown..........F-5
Scott Jct...........D-5
Shawinigan.........D-3
Sherbrooke.........F-4
Sorel................E-3
Thetford Mines.....E-5
Trois Rivieres......D-4
Vallée Jonction....D-5
Valleyfield..........F-2
Victoriaville........E-4
Waterloo...........F-4
Westmount.........F-3
Windsor............E-4

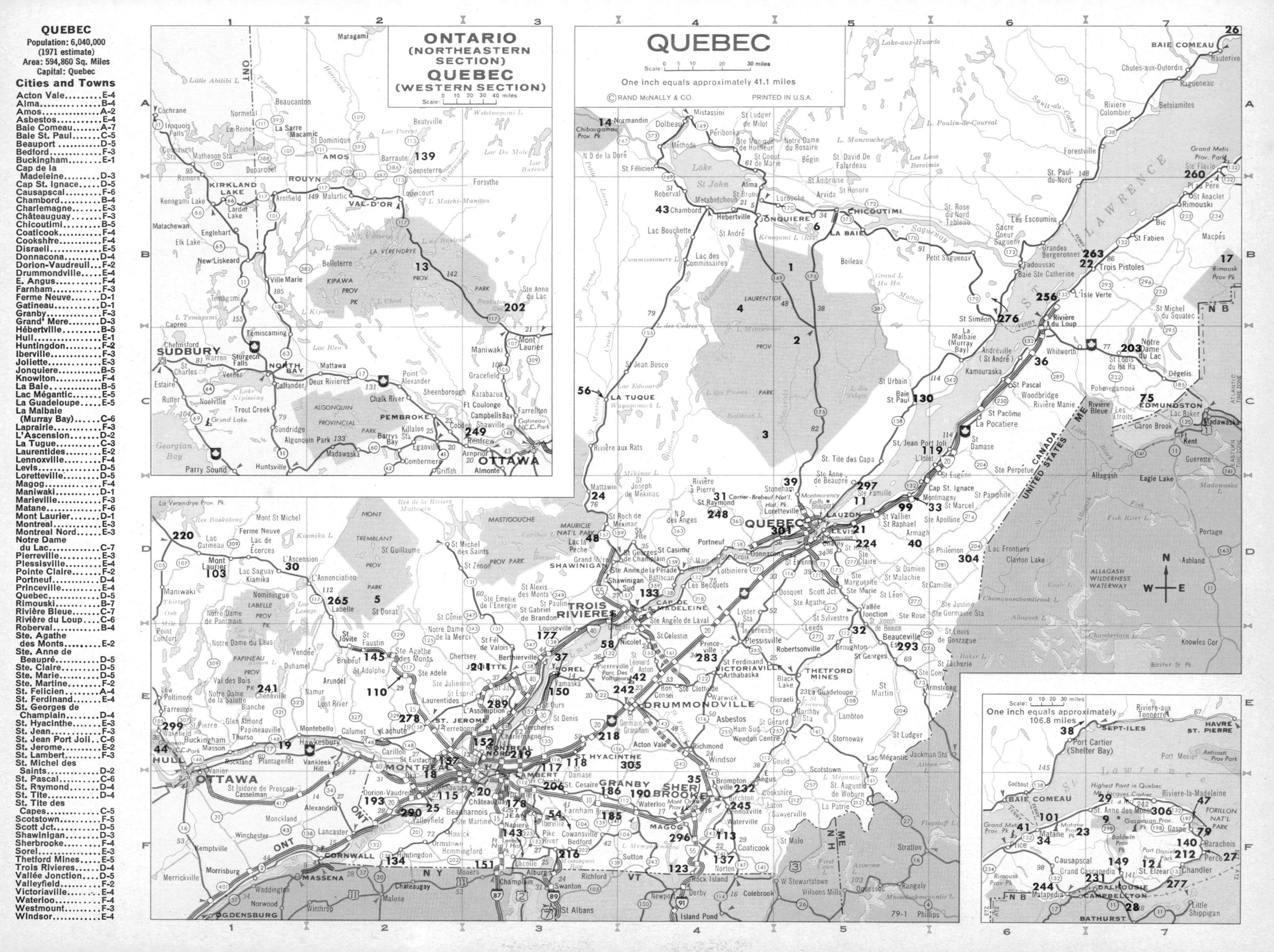

BRITISH COLUMBIA

FOR FOOTNOTE EXPLANATION SEE FIRST PAGE OF THIS PROVINCE   FOR MAP, SEE PAGE 111

Park number	Map reference	Name of park	Access	Physical environment	Elevation	Acres	Number of tent spaces	Number of trailer spaces	Approximate fee	Credit cards accepted	Season	Time limit / Reservations / Pets permitted / Max. trailer size	Electric hookup / Water hookup / Sewer hookup	Sanitary station / Bottled gas / Air conditioning	Tables / Firewood / Pull-thru spaces / Rec. hall	Flush toilets / Showers / Ice	Auto. laundry / Cafe-snack bar / Store	Swimming pool / Other swimming / Fishing	Boating / Playground / Other	CB channel monitored	Telephone no.	Mail address
		PRIVATE (CONT'D)																				
154	F4	Dick & Di's Resort	Fr Courtney, 15 mi N on Island Hwy, 1/2 mi E on Clarkson Rd	⚓		4	20	20	5.50		5/15-9/30	U Z • 28	• $ $	•	• •	• • •	o o	o o	dr •		604/337-5040	Rt 1, Bx 27, Campbell River
154	F4	Owen's Sea-Esta Rsrt	Fr Courtenay, 15 mi N on Hwy 19, 1 mi E to Clarkson Dr, S to Pk	⚓ Λ	0	1		25	5.50		All year	U R • 30	• • •	o •$	• •	• • •	• o •	• •	lr • gkp		604/337-5597	Rt 1, Saratoga Bch Campbell
154	F4	Saratoga Bch Resort	Fr hwy 19, 1/2 mi E on Saratoga Bch	⚓ ⊥	0	2		22	5.50		4/1-10/31	U R • U	• • •	o	• •	• • •	o o o	• •	lr • g		604/337-5511	RR 1, Campbell Riv
157	E5	Walterdale	Fr Kamloops, 24 mi N on Hwy 5	≈ Λ	2	11	100	30	4.50		5/15-10/1	U Z • U	$	•	• • •	• • •		o			604/672-9662	McLure
157	E5	Johnson Lk Fishing Camp	Fr Hwy 5 at Louis Creek, 14 mi E on gravel rd, 9 mi NW on mtn rd	⛵ Λ	5	3	10	10	3.00		5/15-10/31	U Z • 15		•	• • •	• • •	• •	• •	dlr			Rt 1 Box 78, Louis Creek
159	E5	Hilltop Garden's CG	Fr Spences Bridge, 3 mi N on TC 1	≈ Λ	1	5	14	14	3.50		5/1-10/1	U Z • U	$ $	•	• •	• •		o	• p		604/458-2288	Box 119, Spences Bridge
159	E5	Shaw Springs Resort	Fr Spences Bridge, 7 mi W on TC 1	≈ Λ	1	5	30	32	5.50		All year	U Z • U	$ •$	•	• •	•$ •	• •	•	p		604/458-2245	Box 40, Spences Bridge
161	F4	White River Court	Fr Campbell River, 40 mi N on Hwy 19	≈ Λ	0	20	6	14	4.00	M	All year	U Z • U	$ •	• •	• •	• • •	• • •	o o		1	604/282-3265	Sayward
166	F5	Hiawatha Tourist Park	On Hwy 99 nr White Rock, 16565 Beach Rd nr Canadian customs	⚓ ⊥	0	10	60	60	5.25		6/1-9/15	U Z • U	• •	•	•$	•$ •	•	• o	• g		604/536-6184	Box 52, White Rock
166	F5	The Parklander Motor Ct	Fr Blaine, 1 mi N on Hwy 99, 1/2 mi W on Campbell Riv Rd	⚓ ⊥	1	3	20	25	4.50		All year	U Z • U	• •$	• $	•	•$	o	o	gp		604/531-3711	16311 8th Ave, White Rock
166	F5	Sea Crest Mtl & Trlr Pk	At White Rock, corner of Stayte Rd & Campbell Riv Rd	⚓ ▟	0	1	4	17	5.00		All year	U Z • 31	• • •	o o$	•	• •	• o	o o	d • gk		604/531-4720	864 Stayte Rd, White Rock
175	F5	Cedar Brook Mbl Estates	Fr Vancouver, 14 mi E on Hwy 7A to Dewdney Trunk Rd	⚓ ▟	0	4	20	20	4.50		6/1-LD	7 U	$	o	•	• • o	o o •	o o	l		604/461-7698	3315 Dewdney Trunk, Pt Moody
187	F5	Camper's Roost	Fr Hope, 8 mi N on Hwy 1	≈ Λ	1	53	15	36	5.00		3/1-10/25	U Z • U	$ •$	• •	• • •	•$ •	• o •	o o	•	19	604/869-5007	RR3, Hope
187	F5	Green Acres Emory Crk Rsr	Fr Hope, 8 mi, N on TC 1	≈ Λ	1	48	20	100	4.00	M	All year	U Z • U	$ • •	• o	• • •	• • •	• •	• •	• p		604/863-2232	Box 35, Yale
191	E5	Kokanee Beach Rsrt	Fr Merritt, 18 mi N on Hwy 5	⛵ Λ	3	5	24	28	4.00		4/1-10/31	U Z • 28	• •	•	•	• • •	• • •	• •	dlr • g		604/378-4069	Box 101, Merritt
191	E5	Dominic Lk Resort	Fr Kamloops, 12 mi W on TC 1, 16 mi S on gravel rd	⛵ Λ	5	11	10	12	3.50	MV	5/20-12/31w	U Z • 20			• • •	•$ •	• • •	• •	dlr • h		604/376-0881	Box 173, Kamloops
191	E5	Chataway Lks	Fr Hwy 8, 5 mi W of Merritt, N at Lower Nicola, 16 mi on dirt rd	⛵ Λ	5	12	20	12	4.00		5/18-10/30	U Z • 21			• •	• •	•	• •	dlr •			Box 294, Merritt
191	E5	Paradise Lks Rsrt	Fr Quilchene Store, 1/2 mi N on Hwy 5, 27 mi SE	⛵ Λ	6	1	20	20	3.50		5/15-10/15	U R • U	•		• •	•	•	• •	dlr •			Box 204, Merritt
192	E6	Pillar Lake Resort	Fr Falkland, 8 mi NW	⛵ Λ	3	4	15	10	4.50		5/1-10/1	U Z • 16	• •		• •	•$ •	•	• •	dlr • p		604/379-2623	Box 38, Falkland
192	E6	Green Trees Mtl & Trlr Pk	Fr Salmon Arm, 2 mi E on Hwy 1	⛵ Λ	2	5	18	8	5.00		All year	U Z • U	$ •$	o o	• •	• • •	• o o	o o	• gu		604/832-2059	RR 4 1 E, Salmon Arm
192	E6	Ponderosa Resort	Fr TC 1, 2-1/2 mi N at Balmoral, fol signs	⛵ Λ	2	5	4	9	5.50		5/15-9/21	U Z 20	• •	o o	• • •	• • o	o o o	• •	dl • ghp		604/675-2452	Box 21, Blind Bay
192	E6	Lakeview Resorts	Fr Kamloops, 35 mi E on Hwy 1, N at Chase Bus; fol signs	⛵ Λ	2	5	20	65	5.50		4/15-10/15	U Z $ U	• • •	o$	• • •	•$ •	• o •	• o	dlr • gp		604/679-3323	Box 425, Chase
192	E6	Pinaus Lake Resort	Fr Kamloops, 40 mi E on Hwy 97	⛵ Λ	4	10	35	10	4.00		5/1-10/15	U • 20			• •	• • •	•	• •				Falkland
192	E6	Carmel Resort Ltd	Fr TC 1, Balmoral ext, fol signs 4 mi	⛵ Λ		3	5	5	6.00		5/1-10/30	30 Z • U	$ •		• •	• • •		• •	dlr ghp		604/675-2234	PO Box 64, Blind Bay
192	E6	Silvery Beach Resort	Fr Chase, 5 mi E on TC 1	⛵ Λ	2	7	40	40	6.00	V	All year	U Z • U	• • •		• • •	• • •	• •	• •	dlr •	05	604/679-3353	RR1, Chase
192	E6	Old Orchard Trlr Pk	On T C Hwy S to CGk	⛵ Λ	2	5	20	30	4.00		5/15-LD	U Z • 30	$ $ $	• o	• • •	• • •	• • o	o o	dl • g	19		Box 110 Chase
213	E6	Lamplighter Mtl & CG	On Hwy 23 in Revelstoke, 1/4 mi off TC 1 in Big Eddy Dist	≈ Λ	1	3	20	25	4.00	M	5/1-10/31	U U	$ $ $		• • •	• • •	o o o		dl • gh		604/837-3385	Box 150, Revelstoke
213	E6	Revelstoke KOA	Fr Revelstoke, 3 mi E on TC1, 1/2 mi S on gravel rd	≈ Λ	2	15	40	60	6.00	V	4/20-10/15	10 Z • U	$ •$	• •$	•$ • •	• • •	• •	•	• gp		604/837-2085	Box 160, Revelstoke
213	E6	Canyon Hot Springs	In Albert Canyon, on TC 1	≈ Λ	3	240	50	50	4.50		5/24-9/30	U • U		•	• •	• • •	•	$ • •	•		604/837-2526	601 17 Ave SW, Calgary
221	F5	Oliver/Gallagher Lk KOA	Fr Penticton, 20 mi S	⛵ Λ	1	25	67	32	6.00	MV	4/15-10/15	U Z • 30	$ •$	• $	• • • •	• • •	• •	• •	r • gp		604/498-3358	RR 2, Oliver
221	F5	Cherry Grove Mtl & CG	Fr Hwy 97, 1 mi E on Tugulniut Rd in Oliver	⛵ Λ	1	5	40	15	6.00	MV	5/1-10/31	U Z	$ •$	o o$	•$	• • •	o • o	• •	r g		604/498-3613	RR 2, Oliver
221	F5	Peterman's CS	Fr Oliver, 1/4 mi N on Hwy 97	Λ ⊥	1	3	12	12	4.75		6/1-9/30	U Z • 22	$ •		• •	• • •	•	• o	g		604/498-3603	Rt 2, Oliver
224	D4	Kabana Trailer Park	Hwy 97 in Quesnelrk	≈ ▟	2	6	25	28	5.00		All year	U Z • U	• • •	• o	• •	•$ o	o o o	o •	• p	9	604/992-5791	1150 Nelson St, Quesnel
241	E6	Dutch's Tent & Trlr Pk	Fr Vernon, 2 mi S on Kalamalka Lk Rd	⛵ Λ	2	5	45	30	6.25		5/1-9/30	U • U	$ • •	• o	•	• • •	o o	o o	l • gp		604/545-1023	15408 Kal Lk Rd, Vernon
242	F5	Van Acres CS	Fr Osoyoos, 1/4 mi E on Hwy 3	⛵ Λ	1	10	103	35	7.00		5/15-9/15w	U Z 30	• • •	o$	• •	•$ •	• o •	• •	lr • ghp		604/495-6912	RR 1, Osoyoos
244	F6	Tween Lakes Resort	Fr Vernon, 13 mi S on Hwy 97 at S end Kalamalka Lk	⛵ Λ	2	5	48	68	6.50		All year	U Z U	$ $ $	• o	•$ • •	• • •	• • •	• •	dlr •		604/548-3525	Box 67, Oyama
244	F6	Owls Nest Resort	Fr Hwy 97, 200 yds on Evans Rd	⛵ Λ	2	6	40	30	8.00		5/1-10/15	U Z $ 30	$ $ $	o	• • •	• • •	• • •	• •	dlr • p		604/548-3830	Oyama
244	F6	Woodsdale Tent & Trlr Cmp	Fr Hwy 97, 1 mi E at S end of Woods Lk	⛵ Λ		2	32	18	5.50		5/24-10/1	U Z 20	$ $		• •	• • •	•	• •	d p		604/766-3534	RR 2 Site 38, Winfield
261	E5	Evergreen Fishing Rst Ltd	Fr Cache Creek, 13 mi N on Hwy 97, 11 mi E on Loon Lk Rd	⛵ Λ	3	10	24	10	5.00		5/15-10/15	U Z • 28	$ $ $	•	• • •	•$ •	•	• •	dlr		604/459-2372	RR 1, Cache Creek
270	E5	Nelsons' Timothy Lake	Fr Lac La Hache, 10 Mi E on Timothy Lk Rd	⛵ ♀	4	10	8	8	4.50		5/1-11/1	U Z • U	•$		• •	•		• •	lr •		604/396-4427	Box 98, Lac La Hache
270	E5	Crystal Springs CG	Fr Lac La Hache, 8 mi N on Hwy 97	⛵ Λ	3	16	38	22	5.00	V	4/15-9/30	U Z • U	$ $ $	•	• • •	•$ •	• • •	• •	dlr • p		604/396-4497	RR 1, Lac La Hache Vok Ito
270	E5	Big Country KOA	Fr 100 Mile House, 12 mi N on Hwy 97	⊥	3	75	30	32	5.50	M	All year	U Z • U	$ •$	• $	• •	• • •	• •	•	• gp		604/396-7252	Box 37, Lac La Hache
270	E5	Fir Crest Resort	Fr 100 Mile House, 20 mi N on Hwy 97, 1/4 mi W on Emald St o Lac La Hache	⛵ Λ	3	20	30	45	5.00		4/15-10/30*	U Z • U	$ • •	o o •	• • • •	•$ •	• •	• •	dlr •	19	604/396-7337	RR 1, Lac La Hache
278	E6	Fraser Lodge Resort	Fr Lumby, 17 mi E on Hwy 6, 15 mi on Sugar Lk Rd	⛵ Λ	2	3	10	5	3.00		5/15-10/15	U Z 24			• •	• • •	•	• •	lr p		604/JP9-8923	RR 1, Lumby
279	D5	Canyon Creek CS	In Hixon, on Hwy 97	≈ ♀	2	20	26	25	5.00		4/15-10/15	U Z • U	• • •	• o	• • •	• • •	• o o	• •	• p	19	604/998-4307	Bx 390 Hixon
280	D3	Pine Crest Resort	Fr Houston, 10 mi W on Hwy 16 (Yellow Head Hwy)	⛵ Λ	3	120	25	25	3.50		5/1-10/31	U Z • 24	•		• •	• •		o •	dr • p		604/845-2268	Box 245,Houston
288	C5	Paulson's Trlr Pk & CG	In Dawson Creek, on Hwy 97, 1000 ft S of jct John Hart Hwy	⛵ ↓	3	4	30	22	5.00		All year	U Z • U	$ $ $	• •$	• • •	•$ •	• o •	o	kpu	9	604/782-2584	Dawson Creek
293	D4	Beaver Point Resort	Fr Burns Lk, 10 mi S on Hwy 35	⛵ Λ	3	15	52	52	4.00		5/1-10/31	U R • U		•	• •	$ •	• •	• •	dlr •		604/695-6519	Rt 2, Burns Lake
293	D4	Poplar Lodge Trlr Pk	Fr Fraser Lk 3 mi, 7 mi SW at Hwy 16	⛵ Λ	3	6	20	16	5.00		5/15-10/1w	U Z $ 30	• • •		• •	• •	•	• •	dl gp		604/699-6610	Box 9 Endako
293	D4	R & R Lord Fishing Rsrt	Fr Burns Lk, 10 mi S on hwy 35	⛵ Λ	3	15		4	3.00		All year	U Z • U	• • •		•	•		• •	lr k		604/695-6535	Box 273, Burns Lake
297	E5	Lakeview Resort	Fr 100 mile House, E on Hwy 24, NE at Brdg Lk Store, 1/4 mi W on N Shore Rd	⛵ Λ	4	12	5	10	4.00		5/1-10/30	U Z • 30	$ •	• o •	• •	•$ •	• o o	• •	lr • hp		604/593-4434	RR 1 Lone Butte, Cariboo
297	E5	Sandpoint Resort	Fr 100 Mi House, 1/2 mi N, 12 mi E, 14 mi SE fol signs	⛵ Λ	3	12	80	10	5.00		All year	U • U	$ $ $		• •	•$ •	• •	• •	dlr • hku		604/397-2443	Bx 31, Canim Lk
297	E5	Ponderosa Resort	Fr 100 Mile House, 25 mi E to Canim Lake	⛵ Λ	3	5	30	V10	4.50		5/1-10/31	U Z • 30	$ $ $	• •$	• • • •	•$ •	• •	• •	dlr • h		604/397-2243	PO Box 32, Canim Lk
297	E5	Rainbow Resort	Fr 100 mi House, 25 mi E	⛵ ♀	3	60	6	3	4.50		5/1-11/15	U Z • 20	• •$	• •	• • •	• • •	• •	•	dlr •		604/397-2422	Canim Lake
298	E6	Canyon Camp	Fr Radium Hot Springs, 1/4 mi N on Hwy 95	≈ Λ	3	76	150	50	6.50	MV	4/1-11/1W	U Z • U	• • •	• o	• •	•$ •	• o •	o •	• ghpt		604/347-9564	Bx 279 Radium Hot Springs
298	E6	Lake Lillian's Eastlake	Fr Invermere, 4 mi W on Toby Cr & Ski Hill Rds	⛵ Λ	4	8	21	S12	3.50		5/17-LD	U Z • 20			• •	•		• •	dlr		604/342-6108	Box 271, Invermere
298	E6	Radium CG	Fr Hwy 93, 1/4 mi N on Hwy 95	≈ Λ	3	30	100	75	6.50	V	4/1-9/30	U Z • U	• • •	• o •	• • •	• • •	• o o	o	• gh		604/347-9715	Box 28,Radium Hot Springs
301	F4	Bonniebrook Camp & Trlr P	Ferry fr Horseshoe Bay to Langdale; Fr Langdale, 2 mi S to Gower Pt Rd 2 mi	⚓ ⊥	0	125	30	15	4.50		All year	U Z • U	$ •$	•	• •	•$ •	• •	• •	l • gh		604/886-2887	RR 4, Gibsons
301	F4	Duncan Cove Rst	Fr Pender Harbour, 6 mi W on Hwy 101	⚓ Λ	0	5	6	27	6.50		All year	U Z $ 30	• • •	• •	•	•$ •	• o o	•	dlr p		604/883-2424	Box 18 Garden Bay
325	F4	Silver King Trlr Pk	N edge of Campbell Riv on Hwy 19, 1 mi E on Spit Rd	⚓ Λ	1	2		68	6.00		5/20-9/20	U Z • U	• • •	• •	• • •	• • •	• o •	o •	dlr • p		604/286-6142	Box 274, Campbell River
332	D3	Timberland Trlr Pk	Fr Old Skeena Riv brdg, 2-1/2 mi SW on Queensway	≈ Λ	1	11		18	5.50		5/1-10/31**	U Z • U	• • •	•	•	•$	• o		• gp		604/635-5786	4619 Queensway Dr, Terrace
332	D3	Ka-Lum Motel	Fr Terrace, 2 mi W on Hwy 16W	≈ Λ	4	2	10	10	4.50	M	All year	U Z • U	• •	• o	• • •	• • •	• •	•	l • gkpu		604/635-2362	PO Box 593, Terrace
333	E6	Trout Lake Resort	Fr Revelstoke, 30 mi S on Hwy 23, cross free Ferry, 20 mi E on Hwy 31	⛵ Λ	3	5	15	15	4.50		5/1-10/31	U Z • U	• •	• •	• • •	•$ •	o o	o o	dlr • p	19		P O Ferguson, Trout Lake
337	E5	Golden Horn Resort	Fr Kamloops, 14 mi N on Hwy 5, 12 mi E on Tod Mtn Rd	⛵ Λ	4	4	3	12	5.00		5/1-10/31**	U Z • 30	• • •	•	• •	•$ •	• •	• •	dlr		604/578-7113	Box 115, Heffley Creek
337	E5	Heffley Lk Fishing Camp	Fr Kamloops, 14 mi N on Hwy 5, 14 mi E on hard surfaced rd	⛵ Λ	4	6	15	5	4.50		All year	U Z • 30	$ $ $	•	• • •	• • •	•	• •	dlr p	MV	604/578-7251	Box 92, Kamloops
338	E5	Kamloop's View Park	Fr Kamloops, 5 mi E on Hwy 1	⛵ Λ	2	5	10	30	4.00		5/1-10/15	5 Z • 30	$ $ $	• o	• •	•$ • •	•	$ •	• p		604/573-3255	1-4395 E TC Hwy, Kamloops
338	E5	Knutsford Tent & Trlr Pk	Fr Kamloops, 6 mi S on Hwy 5	Λ ⊥	3	20	60	30	4.00		5/1-10/15**	U Z $ 30	$ $ $	• $	• •	•$ •	• o		• p		604/372-5380	Knutsford
347	E6	Holiday Homestead	Fr Sicamous, 3 mi E on TC 1	≈ Λ	2	12	40	40	4.75		4/15-10/15	U Z • U	$ •$	• o •	• • •	•$ •	• o •	•	•		604/836-2583	Box 220, Sicamous
347	E6	Crystal Sands Resort	Fr Sicamous, 9 mi S on Hwy 97A	⛵ Λ	2	30	100	75	7.50		5/15-9/15	U U	$ •	•	• • •	•$ •	• •	• •	lr • h		604/838-6218	RR 1, Mara

 FOR MAP, SEE PAGE 111

Park number	Map reference	Name of park	Access	Physical environment	Elevation	Acres	Number of tent spaces	Number of trailer spaces	Approximate fee	Credit cards accepted	Season	Time limit / Reservations / Pets permitted / Max. trailer size	Electric hookup / Water hookup / Sewer hookup	Sanitary station / Bottled gas / Air conditioning	Tables / Firewood / Pull-thru spaces / Rec. hall	Flush toilets / Showers / Ice	Auto. laundry / Cafe-snack bar / Store	Swimming pool / Other swimming / Fishing	Boating / Playground / Other	CB channel monitored	Telephone no.	Mail address
		PRIVATE (CONT'D)																				
347	E6	Sycamora-Sicamous RKOA	Fr Sicamous, 8 mi E on TC	≈ ⋀	2	95	20	50	6.00	MV	5/15-10/15	U Z • U	$ •$	• •	• • • •	• • •	• ○ •	• •	• h	10	604/836-2507	Bx 310, Sicamous
347	E6	Beachcomber Resort	Fr Sicamous, 2 mi S on hwy 97A	♣ ⋀	2	4	20	35	6.00		6/1-10/1	U Z 30	$ •	• ○	• • •	• • •	•	• •	dlr • hp		604/836-2313	Rt 1 Box 454, Sicamous
347	E6	Hummingbird Resort	Fr Sicamous, 6 mi S on Hwy 97A	♣ ⋀	2	4		60	6.00		5/1-10/1	U Z 31	$ • •	• ○	• • •	• • •	• ○ •	• •	dlr • gh		604/836-2470	RR 1, Mara Lake
352	F6	Hiawatha Trlr Pk	Fr Hwy 97, 3 mi S on Pandosy St, in Kelowna	♣ ⋀	2	4		70	7.00		5/24-9/30	U 26	• • •	○$	• •	• • •	○ ○ ○	○ ○	• g		604/762-3412	3775 Lakeshore Rd, Kelowna
353	F5	Todd's Tent Town	Fr Peachland, 1 mi N on Hwy 97, on lk	♣ ⏊	2	3	35	S5	4.25		6/15-LD	U Z • 15	$ $		• • •	• • •	○ ○ ○	• •	dl •		604/767-2344	Bx 80, Peachland
365	F5	Lombardy Trlr Pk & Cs	Fr TC 1, 2 mi N on Glover Rd, 1 blk W on Mavis	≈ ⋀	1	5	23	12	5.00		5/24-10/1	U Z • 30	$ •$	• •	•	• • ○	• ○ ○	○ ○	l • g		604/534-6266	Box 692, Ft Langley
365	F5	Plaza Mobile & Tourist Ct	In Surrey on Hwy 99A, 10 N of US border	◢	1	9		28	6.00		All year	U Z • 30	• • •	• ○ •	•	• •	• ○ ○	○	gp		604/594-9030	8266 King Geo Hwy 99A,N Surre
365	F5	Mountain Pk	Fr Hwy 11, 3 mi E on Hwy 1, N on Sumas Mtn Rd, fol signs	⋀ ♀	1	40	14	13	3.50		5/15-9/30	U Z • 20	$ •	•	• •	• •	•		• g		604/859-7824	4963 Willet RR 4, Abbotsford
365	F5	Tee Pee Trout Farm	Fr Hwy 401 Sardis Ext, 17 mi S to S end of Cultus Lk	♣ ⋀	2	34	45	205	6.00		3/26-10/10	U Z • 27	• • •	○ •	• • • •	• • •	• •	• ○ •	• ghp		604/858-6193	Box 70, Cultus Lake
367	F4	Talson Tent & Trlr Pk	Fr Comox, 3 mi NE on Lazo Rd	⚓ ⋀	1	7	14	46	5.50		All year	U Z • U	$ •$	• •	• • •	• • •	• •	• •	lr • gkp	11	604/339-3946	RR 1 Lazo Rd, Comox
370	F6	Mountain Shores Rsrt	Fr Creston, 35 mi N on Hwy 3A	♣ ⋀	2	240	15	V42	6.00	M	All year	U Z • U	• • •	• •	• • • •	• • •	• • •	• • •	dlr • kpu		604/223-8258	RR 1, Boswell
370	F6	Kokanee Spgs Pk	Fr Creston, 45 mi N on Hwy 3A	♣ ⋀	2	10		74	5.00		5/1-10/15	U Z • U	• •$	• ○	• •	• • •	• ○ ○	○ ○	l • gt		604/227-9310	Box 62 Crawford Bay
370	F6	Kootenay Kampsites	Fr Creston, 24 mi N on Hwy 3A	♣ ⋀	2	30	3	35	5.50		7/1-8/30	U Z $ U	$ •$	•	•	• • •	• ○	• •	lr • p		604/223-8283	RR 1 Boswell
379	D5	Van Diest's Lake Shore	Fr hwy 97, 150 mi jct turnoff, 58 mi E	♣ ⋀	3	3	10	7	4.00		5/1-11/30	U Z • 20	• •		• •	• ○	○ ○	• •	lr		604/790-2258	Likely BC
385	A4	Klahanie Trlr Pk	Fr Ft Nelson, 5 mi S on Hwy 97; at Mile 295	≈ ♀	2	15	10	25	6.00		5/1-10/1	U Z • U	•	• ○	• •	• • •	• •				604/774-6459	Box 1, Fort Nelson
388	E5	Eleanor Lk Campsite	Fr Yellowhead Hwy 5, 1/2 mi E on Harwood Dr	♣ ⋀	3	12	54	12	4.50		5/15-10/15	U Z • U	$ $	•	• •	• • •	•	•	• p	19	604/673-8316	Bx 13 Blue River
389	F6	Littlejohns Sherwood Frst	Fr Creston, 3-1/2 mi E on Hwy 3	≈ ⋀	2	2	10	17	4.00		5/1-10/1	U Z • 24	$	○	•	• • •	○	○	•	7	604/428-9648	Box 98, Erickson
392	F4	Ruby's Ridge Campsite	Fr Victoria, 29 mi N on Hwy 1	⚓ ⋀	2	3	6	18	4.00		All year	U Z • U	• •	• ○	• • •	• • ○	•		• g	1	604/743-4711	RR 1 Chapman Rd, Cobble Hill
392	F4	Victoria East KOA	Fr Victoria, 11 mi N on Hwy 17 to Mt Newton	⚓ ♀	0	16	102	102	6.50		All year	U Z • U	$ • •	• •	•$ • •	• • •	• •	•	• gp		604/652-3232	RR 1, Mt Newton, Saanichton
395	E5	Star Lake Fishing Camp	Fr Clearwater, 5 mi S	♣ ⋀	4	3		12	3.00		5/25-9/30	U Z • 27			• •	• • •		• •	dlr p			Box 2927, Clearwater
402	F6	Al-Cha-Bel Tent & Trlr Pk	Fr Cascade, 1-1/2 mi N on Hwy 3 to Cross Rd, 1 blk W, 1 blk S	♣ ⋀	2	5	44	16	4.75		5/1-10/30	U Z • U	$ •	• ○	• • •	•$ •	○ ○ •	• ○ ○	dlr • gh			Bx 327, Christina Lk
402	F6	McFarlane CS	Fr Osoyoos, 1 mi E on Hwy 3, 1-1/2 mi S	♣ ⋀	0	3	50	V26	6.00		5/1-10/1	U Z 26	• • •	○	• • • •	•$ •	○ •	• •	l • gh		604/495-7705	RR 1, E Lakeshore Dr, Osoyoos
402	F6	Kingsley's Tent & Trlr Pk	Fr Grand Forks, 14 mi E on Hwy 3	♣ ⋀	2	3	60	20	5.00		5/1-10/1	U Z • 26	• • •	• ○ •	•$	• • •	○ ○	• •	dl gp		604/447-9274	Box 64 Christina Lake
404	E6	Sugar Lake Fishing Camp	Fr Vernon, 33 mi E on Hwy 6, 11 mi N on Sugar Lk Rd	♣ ⋀	2	2	5	5	3.00		5/1-10/30	U Z • U			• •	•	•	• •	dlr • p		604/547-6517	Rt 1, Lumby
405	F5	Pine Crest Lake Resort	Fr Hope, 8 mi N on TC 1, 2-1/2 mi W on gravel rd	♣ ⋀	2	79	15	S10	5.00		6/15-LD	U Z • 12		•	• •	•$	•	• $	dr • p			RR 3, Hope
405	F5	Pine Grove Trailer Pk	Fr jct Hwys 1 & 3, 1/2 mi E on Hwy 3 to 6th Ave, in Hope	♣ ◢	0	30	30	55	5.95		All year	U Z • U	• • •	• ○$	•$ • ○	•$ •	• • •	○ ○ ○	dl gkp		604/869-5024	Box 1118,1350-6thAve, Hope
405	F5	Hope KOA	Fr Hope, 3 mi W on TC 1	≈ ⋀	1	17	35	97	6.00		All year	U Z • U	$ •$	• •	• • •	• • •	• •	•	• gkp		604/869-9857	RR 2, Hope
405	F5	Nendick's Camp	Fr Princeton, 17 Mi E on Hwy 3	≈ ⋀	3	5	18	14	3.50		5/24-10/1	U Z • U	$ •$	• •	• • •	•$ •	○ ○	• •	•			Box 100 Hedley
407	D5	North Country Lodge	Fr Horsefly, 6 mi E	♣ ⋀	3	100	15	S6	5.00		All year	U Z • 30	• •	• •	• • •	• • •	• • •	• •	dlr • hpu		604/620-3434	Bx 100, Horsefly Lake
407	D5	Birch Bay Resort	Fr 150 Mile House, 40 mi E on Horsefly Rd	♣ ⋀	3	450	18	20	5.00		5/1-10/31	U Z • U	• • •	• $	• • •	• • •	•	• •	dlr •	13	604/620-3441	Box 9, Horsefly
412	C5	Alcan Trlr Pk	Fr Dawson Creek, N on Alcan Hwy to milepost 41	Ψ ♀	3	10	15	30	6.00		5/1-10/31	U Z • U	$ $ $	• •	• • •	•$ •	• •		•		604/785-3124	RR 1, Fort St John
416	E7	Kutenai Trlr Pk & CG	Fr Radium Jct, 10 mi S on Hwy 93/95	♣ ⋀	2	25		116	8.00		5/1-9/30	U Z • U	• • •	○	• • •	•$ •	• • •	○	• p		403/342-6663	Box 123, Invermere
416	E7	Fairmont Hot Spgs	Fr Cranbrook, 70 mi N on Hwy 93/95	♣ ⋀	3	1000	150	120	9.00		4/1-11/15	U • U	$ $ $	• ○	• • • •	• • •	○ • ○	$ ○	• ght		604/345-6311	Fairmont Hot Springs
422	D4	Sandy's Camping & Trlr Pk	Fr Burns Lk, 19 mi W at Frangois Lk	♣ ⋀	3	80	20	55	4.50		5/15-10/1	U Z • U	• • •	•	• • •	•$ •		• •	dlr • p		604/695-6321	Box 42 Burns Lake
426	D4	Sawdust Trail CS	Fr Prince George, 22 mi S on Hwy 97, W of Hwy	≈ ♀	2	91	40	20	4.50	MV	5/15-9/30	U Z • U	$ $ $	• •	• •	•$ •	• ○ •	• •	•	6	604/330-4220	RR 7 Stoner Site,PrinceGeorge
430	E5	Overlanders Stopping Plac	Fr Kamloops, 55 mi N on Hwy 5; W side of Hwy	≈ ⋀	2	5		36	3.50	MV	5/1-10/1	U Z • 30	$ •	•	• • •	•$ •	•	•	•		604/677-4289	Box 51, Little Fort
431	D4	Nulki Lk Resort	Fr Vanderhoof, 11 mi S on Kenney Dam Rd	♣ ⋀	3	22	50	40	4.75		5/1-10/1	U Z • U	$ $ $	•	• • •	• • •	• • •	• •	dlr •	11	604/567-9009	Bx 148, Vanderhoof
436	E6	Golden KOA	Fr Golden, 1 mi E on TC	≈ ⋀	3		20	84	6.00		4/1-10/15	U Z • U	$ •$	• •	• • •	• • •	• ○ •	○	•		604/344-6464	P O Box 233, Golden

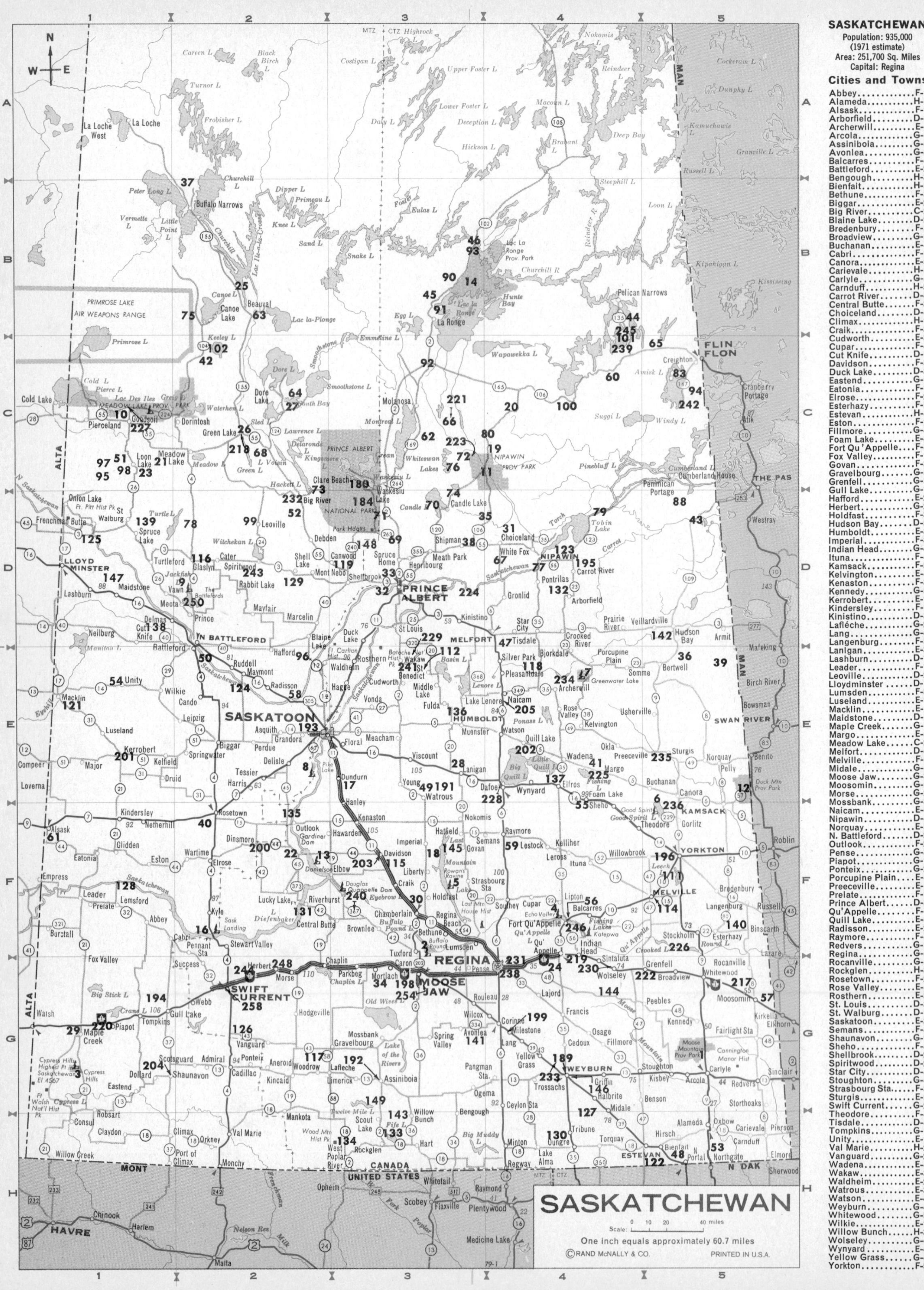
SASKATCHEWAN
Population: 935,000
(1971 estimate)
Area: 251,700 Sq. Miles
Capital: Regina
Cities and Towns
Abbey.............F-1
Alameda...........H-5
Alsask............F-1
Arborfield.........D-4
Archerwill..........E-4
Arcola.............G-5
Assiniboia.........G-3
Avonlea...........G-3
Balcarres..........F-4
Battleford..........E-2
Bengough.........H-3
Bienfait............H-5
Bethune............F-3
Biggar.............E-2
Big River..........C-2
Blaine Lake........D-2
Bredenbury........F-5
Broadview.........G-5
Buchanan..........E-4
Cabri..............F-1
Canora............E-5
Carievale..........H-5
Carlyle............G-5
Carnduff...........H-5
Carrot River.......D-4
Central Butte.......F-3
Choiceland........D-4
Climax.............H-1
Craik..............F-3
Cudworth..........E-3
Cupar.............F-4
Cut Knife..........D-1
Davidson..........F-3
Duck Lake.........D-3
Eastend...........G-1
Eatonia............F-1
Elrose.............F-2
Esterhazy.........F-5
Estevan...........H-4
Eston..............F-1
Fillmore...........G-4
Foam Lake.........E-4
Fort Qu 'Appelle....F-4
Fox Valley.........F-1
Govan.............F-3
Gravelbourg.......G-3
Grenfell...........G-5
Gull Lake..........G-1
Hafford............E-2
Herbert............G-2
Holdfast...........F-3
Hudson Bay.......D-5
Humboldt..........E-3
Imperial...........F-3
Indian Head........G-4
Ituna..............F-4
Kamsack..........F-5
Kelvington.........E-4
Kenaston..........F-3
Kennedy...........G-5
Kerrobert..........E-1
Kindersley.........F-1
Kinistino..........D-3
Lafléche...........G-2
Lang..............G-4
Langenburg........F-5
Lanigan...........E-3
Lashburn..........D-1
Leader............F-1
Leoville...........D-2
Lloydminster D-1
Lumsden...........F-3
Luseland..........E-1
Macklin...........E-1
Maidstone.........D-1
Maple Creek.......G-1
Margo.............E-4
Meadow Lake......C-2
Melfort............D-4
Melville...........F-5
Midale............G-4
Moose Jaw........G-3
Moosomin.........G-5
Morse.............G-2
Mossbank.........G-3
Naicam............E-4
Nipawin...........D-4
Norquay...........E-5
N. Battleford.......D-2
Outlook............F-2
Pense.............G-3
Piapot.............G-1
Ponteix............G-2
Porcupine Plain....E-4
Preeceville.........E-5
Prelate............F-1
Prince Albert......D-3
Qu'Appelle........F-4
Quill Lake.........E-4
Radisson..........E-2
Raymore..........F-4
Redvers...........G-5
Regina............G-4
Rocanville.........G-5
Rockglen..........H-3
Rosetown..........F-2
Rose Valley........E-4
Rosthern..........E-3
St. Louis..........D-3
St. Walburg.......D-1
Saskatoon.........E-3
Semans...........F-4
Shaunavon........G-1
Sheho.............F-4
Shellbrook.........D-2
Spiritwood.........D-2
Star City...........D-4
Stoughton.........G-4
Strasbourg Sta......F-3
Sturgis............E-5
Swift Current......G-2
Theodore..........F-4
Tisdale............D-4
Tompkins..........G-1
Unity..............E-1
Val Marie..........H-2
Vanguard..........G-2
Wadena...........E-4
Wakaw............E-3
Waldheim..........E-2
Watrous...........E-3
Watson............E-4
Weyburn..........G-4
Whitewood........G-5
Wilkie.............E-1
Willow Bunch......H-3
Wolseley..........G-4
Wynyard E-4
Yellow Grass......G-4
Yorkton............F-5
SASKATCHEWAN
Scale: 0 10 20 40 miles
One inch equals approximately 60.7 miles
©RAND McNALLY & CO.
PRINTED IN U.S.A.

●—at the campground
○—within one mile of campground
$—extra charge
*—see city map
**—limited facilities during winter months
1-5—number of miles in NF within which facility or activity can be found
A—adults only
B—10,000 acres or more
C—contribution

E—tents rented
F—entrance fee or permit required—see "Special Information on the Public Areas"
H—over 9000 feet above sea level
N—no specific number, limited by size of area only
P—primitive
R—reservation required
S—self-contained units only
U—unlimited

V—trailers rented
Z—reservations accepted
LD—Labor Day
MD—Memorial Day
UC—under construction
d—boat dock
g—public golf course within 5 miles
h—horseback riding
j—whitewater running craft only
k—snow skiing within 25 miles

l—boat launch
m—area north of map
n—no drinking water
p—motor bikes prohibited
r—boat rental
s—stream, lake or creek water only
t—tennis
u—snowmobile trails
w—open certain off-season weekends and holidays

y—drinking water must be boiled
access to ocean
access to lake
access to river
mountainous terrain
prairie land
desert area
heavily wooded
urban area
rural area

CREDIT CARD SYMBOLS:
A—American Express
M—Master Charge
V—Visa/Bank Americard

FEES REFLECT MINIMUM RATE FOR 2 ADULTS AND ARE SUBJECT TO SEASONAL CHANGES

Park number	Map reference	Name of park	Access	Physical environment	Elevation	Acres	Number of tent spaces	Number of trailer spaces	Approximate fee	Credit cards accepted	Season	Time limit	Reservations	Pets permitted	Max. trailer size	Electric hookup	Water hookup	Sewer hookup	Sanitary station	Bottled gas	Air conditioning	Tables	Firewood	Pull-thru spaces	Rec. hall	Flush toilets	Showers	Ice	Auto. laundry	Cafe-snack bar	Store	Swimming pool	Other swimming	Fishing	Boating	Playground	Other	CB channel monitored	Telephone no.	Mail address
		PROVINCIAL PARKS & RECREATION AREAS	(For additional CGs, see 'Backpack or Boat Access Areas')																																					
1	F3	Lynch's Point	Fr Hwy 4, 6 mi N on Hwy 50, 6 mi E on Hwy 567		1	25	100	100	F4.00		5/15-9/30	21		•	U							•	•										•	•	l	•				Westbourne
2	F3	St Ambroise Beach	Fr Poplar Point, 1 mi W on Hwy 26, 16 mi N on Hwy 430		1	41	99	99	F4.00		5/15-9/30	21		•	U							•	•										•	•	l	•				St Ambroise Beach
3	F3	Lundar Beach	Fr Lundar, 12 mi W on Hwy 419		1	20	50	50	F4.00		5/15-9/30	21		•	U							•	•										•	•	dl	•				Lundar
4	E3	Watchorn Bay	Fr Moosehorn, 7 mi W on Hwy 6		1	10	12	12	F4.00		5/21-9/21	21		•	U							•	•										•	•	l	•				Moosehorn
		Spruce Woods Prov Pk																																						
5	G2	Kiche Manitou	Fr Glenboro, N on Hwy 258			180	76	45	F4.00		5/15-9/30	21		•	U	$			•			•	•			•	•		•				•	•						Brandon
7	E4	Beaver Creek	Fr Riverton, 30 mi N on Hwy 234		1	25	10	10	F4.00		5/15-9/30	21		•	U							•	•										•	•	l	•				Riverton
9	E5	Black River	Fr Pine Falls, 32 mi N on Hwy 304				15	15	F4.00		5/15-9/30	21		•	U							•	•											•			n			
10	E5	Currie Landing	Fr Manigotogan, 5 mi E on Hwy 304				25	25	F4.00		5/15-9/30	21		•	U							•	•											•	l		n			
		Whiteshell Prov Pk																																						
12	G5	Falcon Beach	Fr Winnipeg, 90 mi E on TC 1		2	36	469	255	F4.00		5/15-9/30	21		•	U	$	$	$	•			•	•			•	•	○	○	○	○		•	•	dlr	•	gh			Falcon Lake
12	G5	Toniata Beach	Fr Falcon Beach, 5 mi E on Hwy 301		2	7	26	26	F4.00		5/15-9/30	21		•	U	$				○		•	•			•		○		○	○		•	•	dlr	•	g			Falcon Lake
13	G5	Brereton Lake	Fr Rennie, 2 mi E on Hwy 44, 4 mi N on Hwy 307		2	13	31	31	F4/00		5/15-9/30	21		•	U	$				○		•	•			•		○	•	○	○		•	•	dl	•				Rennie
13	G5	White Lake	Fr Rennie, 2 mi E on Hwy 44, 4 mi N on Hwy 307		2	15	15	15	F4.00		5/15-9/30	21		•	U	$						•	•			•				○	○		•	•	dl	•				Rennie
14	G5	Whiteshell Lake	Fr Hwy 44, 14 mi N on Hwy 307, 10 mi NE on Hwy 309		2	80	57	57	F4.00		5/15-9/30	21		•	U							•	•			•					○		•	•	dl	•				Rennie
14	G5	Lone Island Landing	Fr White Lake, 6 mi N on Hwy 309		1		99	99	F4.00		5/15-9/30	21		•	U							•	•											•	dl					
15	G5	Caddy Lake	Fr Rennie, 15 mi E on Hwy 44		2	20	26	26	F4.00		5/15-9/30	21		•	U	$				○		•	•					○			○		•	•	dlr	•	k			Rennie
16	G5	West Hawk Lake	Fr Rennie, 25 mi E on Hwy 44		2	15	84	73	F4.00		5/15-9/30	21		•	U	$	$	$				•	•			•	•	○		○	○		•	•	dlr	•	k			Rennie
16	G5	Border Reception	On TC Hwy at Manitoba, Ontario Border		1	15	40	40	F4.00		5/15-10/31	7		•	U								•			•							○	○						
17	F5	Opapiskaw	Fr Seven Sisters, 16 mi E on Hwy 307		1	80	83	83	F4.00		5/15-9/30	21		•	U							•	•			•							•	•	dl	•				Seven Sisters Falls
17	F5	Otter Falls	Fr Seven Sisters, 10 mi E on Hwy 307		1	10	75	75	F4.00		5/15-9/30	21		•	U							•	•			•		○		○	○		•	•	dlr	•				Seven Sisters Falls
17	F5	Nutimik Lake	Fr Seven Sisters, 19 mi E on Hwy 307		1	50	146	4	F4.00		5/15-9/30	21		•	U							•	•				•	○		○	○		•	•	dl	•				Seven Sisters Falls
19	F5	Poplar Bay	Fr Hwy 313, 5 mi N on Hwy 315		1	7	45	70	F4.00		5/15-9/30	21		•	U							•	•					○		○	○		•	•	l		n			Lac du Bonnet
20	F5	Sawmill Bay	Fr Lac du Bonnet, 3 mi N on Hwy 502, 22 mi E on Hwy 313		1	2	25	25	F4.00		5/15-9/30	21		•	U							•	•							○	○		•	•	dl		n			Pointe du Bois
20	F5	Eight Foot Falls	Fr Pointe du Bois, 1/2 mi S on access rd		1		20	20	F4.00		5/15-9/30	21		•	U							•	•								○			•	l		n			Pointe du Bois
21	C2	Grand Rapids	Fr Gypsumville, 112 mi N on Hwy 6				15		F4.00		5/21-9/21	21		•								•	•																	Grand Rapids
22	F3	Amaranth Beach	Fr Amaranth, 4 mi E on Hwy 50			5	10		4.00		5/15-9/30	21		•								•	•										•	•			n			Amaranth
23	F3	Margaret Bruce Pk	Fr Alonsa, 1 mi N, 8 mi E on 50			9	15	25	F4.00		5/15-9/30	21		•	U							•	•								•		•			•				Alonsa
24	D4	Lake St George	Fr Dallas, 30 mi N on access rd				10	40	F4.00		5/15-9/30	21		•	U							•	•					•		•	•			•	dl					Hodgson
25	E2	Methley Beach	Fr Ste Rose du Lac, 12 mi N on Hwy 276, 4 mi W			4	50	50	F4.00		5/15-9/30	21		•	U							•	•										•		l					Ste Rose Du Lac
26	m	Burge Lake	Fr Lynn Lake, 3 mi N on Hwy 399			6	25		F4.00		5/15-9/30	21		•								•	•										•	•	dl		n			Lynn Lake
26	m	Zed Lake	Fr Lynn Lake, 12 mi N on Hwy 394			4	35		F4.00		5/15-9/30	21		•								•	•										•	•	dl					Lynn Lake
27	F5	Bird Lake	Fr Hwy 313, 28 mi NE on Hwy 315		1	6	45	45	F4.00		5/15-9/30	21		•	U							•	•								○		•	•	l	•				Lac du Bonnet
27	F5	Black Lake Cg	Fr Lac du Bonnet, N on Hwy 313, 315, 314, to Nopiming Pkwy				72	S72	F4.00		5/12-9/25	21		•	30																		•	•			p			
28	E1	Asessippi Prov Pk	Fr Inglis, approx 5 mi W on Hwy 482			160	88	88	F4.00		5/15-9/30	21		•	U				•			•	•	•		•							•	•	lr	•				Roblin
29	E5	Wanipigow Park	Fr Manigotogan, 15 mi E on Hwy 304		1	6	50	50	F4.00		5/15-9/30	21		•	U							•	•			•							•	•	d					Manigotogan
29	E5	Caribou Landing	Fr Bissett, 3 mi W on Hwy 304, 11 mi SE on access rd		1	2	30	30	F4.00		5/15-9/30	21		•	U							•	•					○			○			•	dlr					Bissett
29	E5	Wallace Lake	Fr Bissett, 17 mi E on Hwy 304				80	80	F4.00		5/15-9/30	21		•	U							•	•					○			○		•	•	dlr	•	p			Bissett
		NW Angle Forest Reserve																																						
33	H5	Moose Lake	Fr Sprague, 23 mi NE on Hwy 308 & access rd		2	25	110	110	F4.00		5/15-9/30	21		•	U							•	•					•		•	•		•	•	dlr	•				Sprague
35	E2	Rainbow Beach	Fr Dauphin, 11 mi E on Hwy 20		1	150	31	31	F4.00		5/15-9/30	21		•	U							•	•			•				•	○		•	•	l	•				Dauphin
38	E2	Manipogo Park	Fr Toutes Aides, 3 mi N on Hwy 276		1	117	134	134	F4.00		5/15-9/30	21		•	U	$						•	•			•		•		•	•		•		dr	•				Toutes Aides
		Turtle Mtn Prov Pk				73																																		
41	H2	William Lake	Fr Horton, 4 mi E on Hwy 341, 5 mi S on Hwy 444		2	293	35	35	F4.00		5/15-9/30	21		•	U							•	•										•	•	dl					Boissevain
41	H2	Max Lake	Fr Boissevain, 4 mi S on Hwy 10, 4 mi W on Hwy 3, 10 mi S on Hwy 446		1	75	35	35	F4.00		5/15-9/30	21		•								•	•										•		dl					Boissevain
41	H2	Adam Lake	Fr Peace Garden, 4 mi N on Hwy 10			180	90	90	F4.00		5/15-9/30	21		•	U				•			•	•			•							•	•	l					Boissevain
		Duck Mtn Prov Pk																																						
44	E1	Blue Lakes	Fr Garland, 20 mi W on Hwy 366		3	100	100	100	F4.00		5/15-9/30	21		•	U							•	•					•		•	•		•	•	dlr					Garland
44	E1	Singush Lake	Fr Garland, 16 mi W on Hwy 367		3	3	15	15	F4.00		5/15-9/30	21		•	U							•	•											•	dl					Garland
45	E1	Childs Lake	Fr Blue Lks, 10 mi W on Hwy 367		3	30	50	50	F4.00		5/15-9/30	21		•	U							•	•					○		○	○		•	•	dl					Garland
46	D1	Wellman Lake	Fr Minitonas, 24 mi S on Hwy 366		3	30	25	25	F4.00		5/15-9/30	21		•	U	$						•	•					•		•	•		•	•	dl	•				Minitonas
		Porcupine Forest Reserve																																						
49	D1	Whitefish Lake	Fr Bowsman, 17 mi NW on Hwy 10		2	25	25	25	F4.00		5/15-9/30	21		•	U							•	•										•	•	dl					Birch River
		Sandilands Prov Forest																																						
50	G5	Pinegrove Halt	Fr Richer, 18 mi E on TC 1				113	113	F4.00		5/15-9/30	7		•	U				•			•	•	•		•	•													Hadashville
54	C1	Overflowing River	Fr Hwy 10 in Overflowing River, 1 mi E		1	10	32	32	F4.00		5/15-9/30	21		•	U							•	•					○		○	○			○	lr	•				Overflowing River
55	A1	Rocky Lake	Fr Wanless, 1 mi W on Hwy 10		1	10	40	40	F4.00		5/15-9/30	21		•	U							•	•					○		○	○			•	dlr					Wanless
56	A1	Iskwasum Landing	Fr Cranberry Portage, 10 mi S on Hwy 10, 26 mi NE on Hwy 391		1	5	20	20	F4.00		5/15-9/30	21		•	U							•	•											•	dl					Cranberry Portage
		Clearwater Provincial Par				230																																		
58	B1	Campers Cove	Fr The Pas, 12 mi N on Hwy 10, 5 mi E on Hwy 287		1	10	40	40	F4.00		5/15-9/30	21		•	U							•	•							○			•	•	l	•				Clearwater Lake

MANITOBA

FOR FOOTNOTE EXPLANATION SEE FIRST PAGE OF THIS **PROVINCE** FOR MAP, SEE PAGE 114

Park number	Map reference	Name of park	Access	Elevation	Acres	Number of tent spaces	Number of trailer spaces	Approximate fee	Credit cards accepted	Season	Time limit / Reservations / Pets / Max. trailer size / Facilities / Activities	Boating / Playground	Other	CB channel monitored	Telephone no.	Mail address
		PROVINCIAL PARKS & RECREATION AREAS (CONT'D)														
58	B1	Pioneer Bay	Fr The Pas, 12 mi N on Hwy 10, 12 mi E on Hwy 287	1	10	62	62	F4.00		5/15-9/30	21 • U •• • • • • • •	dlr •				Clearwater Lake
59	B1	Cormorant Lake	On Cormorant Lk, Rd 287	1		20	20	F4.00		5/15-9/30	21 U •• •	dl				Cormorant
59	B1	Hugo Bay	Fr the Pas, 12 mi N on Hwy 10, 31 mi NE on Hwy 287			150	S150	F4.00		5/15-9/15	21 • 30 • •• • • •	l	p			
60	A1	Cranberry Portage	Fr The Pas, 56 mi N on Hwy 10; on Athapapuskow Lk	1	20	20	20	4.00		5/15-9/30	21 • U •• ○ ○ ○ • •	dl •				Cranberry Portage
62	A1	Bakers Narrows No. 1	Fr Cranberry Portage, 21 mi N on Hwy 10	1	150	57	15	F4.00		5/15-9/30	21 • U $ • •• •• ○ • •	dl •				Flin Flon
64	m	Paint Lake	Fr Thompson, 25 mi S on Hwy 391, E on pk access rd	1	320	135	135	F4.00		5/15-9/30	21 • U • •• •• • • • •	dl •				Thompson
65	H2	Rock Lake	Fr Pilot Mound, 13 mi W on Hwy 3	2	6	35	35	F4.00		5/15-9/30	21 • U •• ○ • •	l •				Glenora
68	F4	Grand Beach	Fr Winnipeg, 57 mi NE on Hwy 59 & 12		60	320	110	F4.00		5/15-9/30	21 • U $ • •• • • ○ ○ ○ • •	l				Grand Beach
69	G2	Rivers	Fr Hwy 25 in Rivers, NE on access rd	2	25	63	63	F4.00		5/15-9/30	21 • U •• • • • •	dlr •				Rivers
70	G2	Grand Valley	Fr Brandon, 6 mi W on TC 1	2	73	42	7	F4.00		5/15-9/30	7 • U $ • •• •• • • ○	•				Brandon
71	G4	Birds Hill	Fr Winnipeg, 14 mi N on Hwy 59		50	335	149	F4.00		5/21-9/30**	10 • U $ $ $ • •• • • • • ○ ○ •		hu			Birds Hill
72	G4	St Malo	Fr St Malo, 1 mi E on access rd	1	20	164	49	F4.00		5/15-10/1	21 • U $ • •• •• • ○ • •	lr •				St Malo
75	A1	Gyles Park	Fr Cranberry Portage, 10 mi S on Hwy 10, 13 mi E on Hwy 391	1	20	20	20	F4.00		5/15-9/30	21 • U •• • •	dl				Cranberry Portage
76	A2	Reed Lake	Fr Hwy 10, 42 mi E on Hwy 391	1	25	46	46	F4.00		5/15-9/30	21 • U •• ○ ○ ○ • •	dl				Cranberry Portage
77	A2	Wekusko Falls	Fr Snow Lk, 11 mi S on Hwy 392	1	10	88	88	F4.00		5/15-9/30	21 • U •• ○ ○ ○	dlr •				Snow Lake
78	G3	Norquay Beach	Fr Portage la Prairie, 6 mi E on TC 1	1	30	100	24	F4.00		5/15-9/30	7 • U $ • •• •• • •	•				Portage la Prairie
		Hecla Island Prov Pk														
80	E4	Gull Harbour CG	Fr North tip of Hecla Island on Hwy 234 & 233			118		F4.00		5/15-9/30	21 • •• • • •	dl •				Gull Harbor
82	G3	Stephenfield Dam RA	Fr Carman, 12 mi W on Rd 245	1		70	70	F4.00		5/15-9/30	21 • U •• • •	l				Carman
		NATIONAL PARKS														
		Riding Mountain NP	(For additional CGs, see 'Backpack or Boat Access Areas')			B									204/848-2811	
101	F2	Wasagaming	Wasagaming Townsite at Clear Lake	3	100	395	379	F3.00		5/15-9/15	14 • 32 $ $ $ ○ ○ • • • • • ○ ○ ○ ○ ○ ○	lr	gh			Wasagaming
102	F2	Lake Audy	Fr Hwy 10 at N side of Clear Lake, 16 mi W on access rd	3	6	50	50	F3.00		5/15-9/15	14 • 32 •• • •	l				Wasagaming
103	F2	Lk Katherine	Fr pk entr, S gate, 7 mi E on Hwys 10 & 19	3	75	110	118	F3.00		6/30-9/15	14 • 17 •• • • •	l				Wasagaming
104	F2	Moon Lk	Fr Clear Lk, 12 mi N on Hwy 10	3	7	50	29	F3.00		5/15-9/15	14 • 17 •• • •	l				Wasagaming
		BACKPACK OR BOAT ACCESS AREAS														
		Riding Mtn NP													204/848-2811	
105	F2	Whirlpool Lk	Fr pk entr, S gate, 15 mi E on Hwys 10 & 19	2	3	15		3.00		5/15-9/15	14 • •• • •	•l				Wasagaming
		Winnipeg Riv Marine CGs														
106	F5	Marine CG #1	Fr Pointe Du Bois 10 water mi; access by boat only			P15		None		5/15-9/30	21 • •• •		n			Pointe Du Bois
106	F5	Marine CG #2	Fr Pointe Du Bois 15 water mi; access by boat only			P12		None		5/15-9/30	21 • •• •		n			Pointe Du Bois
106	F5	Marine CG #3	Fr Pointe Du Bois, 20 water mi; access by boat only			P15		None		5/15-9/30	21 • •• • •		n			Pointe Du Bois
		CITY, COUNTY & CIVIC														
108	G2	Centennial Park	Hwy 10 at Boissevain	2	5	20	S15	1.50		5/14-9/15	U • U $ $ $ • ○ • • • • • ○ ○ ○ ○ $	•	ght			Box 490, Boissevain
109	F1	Russell Tourist Camp	Jct Hwys 4 & 83 at Russell		5	16	16	None		5/1-10/31	U • U • •• • ○ ○ ○ ○	•	g			Russell
110	F2	Williams Park	In NW Gladstone, 1/2 mi off Hwy 4	1	5	8	4	None		5/1-10/1	7 • U • ○ ○ •• • • ○ ○ ○ ○ • •	•	gt		204/385-2332	Box 25, Gladstone
111	H3	Stanley Tourist Park	Fr Moreder, 6 mi S on Hwy 432, 1/2 mi W	2	50	100	100	None		5/1-9/30	U • U • • •	•	gh		204/822-5630	Box 455, Morden
111	H3	Colert Beach	Fr Morden, 1 mi W, 3/4 mi S	2	64	30	60	4.00		5/15-9/15	U Z • U • • ○ ○ • • • • • ○ • • •	dl •	gp		204/822-4991	Box 893, Morden
111	H3	Stanley Centennial Park	Fr Hwy 3 in Morden, 1 mi S, 1 mi W, 2 mi S, 3 mi W	2	56	50		None		1/5-12/10	U • ••	•				Morden
112	F4	Selkirk Park	Fr Selkirk, N on Eve Line St, on Red River, Hwys 4/9	1	240	400	100	2.50		5/1-9/1	U • U • • ○ •• • • • ○ ○ ○ • • •	dlr •	ghp			Selkirk
114	H2	Int'l Peace Garden	Fr Boissevain, 15 mi S on Hwy 10	3	2380	50	50	2.00		5/1-10/31	U • U • •• • • ○ ○				204/534-2510	Box 419, Boissevain
115	E1	Gilbert Plains Cent Pk	In Gilbert Plains, 1 blk N & W of PTH 5	1	180	30	30	3.00		5/15-9/15	U Z • U $ • • • • $ ○ • • •		g		204/548-2118	Gilbert Plains
117	F2	Minnedosa Beach	Fr jct TC1/Hwy 10, 33 mi N, 1.5 mi E on Hwy 262	2	25	30	98	3.75		5/15-9/30	U Z • U $ • ○ •• • • ○ • • • ○	d •	gh		204/867-3450	Box 426, Minnedosa
118	F2	Lake Irwin Pk	Fr Neepawa, 1-1/2 mi S on Hwy 258, 1/2 mi E		20	65	52	3.50		5/15-9/30	U Z • 20 $ • • • • • • ○ •	d •	gp		204/476-2625	Neepawa
120	G4	Big 'M' Centennial Pk	Fr Can-US border, N 28 mi on Hwy 75	1		20	15	2.00		5/20-10/31	U • U • • ○ • $ ○ ○ ○ ○ ○		g		204/746-2552	Box 28, Morris
121	F1	Birtle District Park	Fr Birtle, 1/2 mi W on Hwy 42	2	96	50	15	4.00		4/15-9/30	U R • U • • ○ •• • • ○ ○ ○ • • • •	l •	ghp	8	204/842-3250	Box 57 Birtle
122	F1	Lakeside Pk	Fr Jct Hwys 42 & 21, 1/2 mi SW	2	15	10	4	5.00		5/1-9/30	U Z • 24 • • • ○ •• • • ○ ○ ○ ○ • •	l •	gt			Shoal Lake
123	E2	Winnipegosis Beach	Fr Dauphin, 36 mi N on Hwy 20	1	8	10	10	2.00		5/15-10/15	U Z • U • • ○ •• ○ ○ ○ • •	l •	g		204/656-4791	Bx 370,Winnipegosis
124	G2	Victoria Pk	Fr Hwy 10, 13 mi W on Hwy 2	2	30	20	40	3.75		6/1-10/1	30 Z • 24 $ •• • • • • ○ ○ ○ $ • •	l •	g			Souris
125	H3	Town of Winkler CG	NW edge of Winkler	1	20	20	16	None		6/1-10/15	U • 16 • • • ○ •• • • • ○ ○ ○ $	•	gt		204/325-8211	Box 1055, Winkler
127	F2	Kelwood Centennial Pk	Fr Neepawa, 27 mi N on Hwy 5, 1/2 mi E at Kelwood Corner		3	5	S5	2.00		5/15-9/30	U • U $ • ○ ○ •• ○ ○				204/756-2219	Kelwood
128	H4	Emerson Centennial Pk	In Emerson on Hwy 75k	1	10	20	20	3.00		6/15-9-15	U • U • • ○ ○ •• • • • • ○ • • ○	l •	gp		204/373-2002	Box 340, 104 Church St, Emers
128	H4	Letellier Park	In Letellier on Hwy 201/75	1	7	15	15	3.00		6/1-10/1	U • U • • • • • $ ○ • •		p			Letellier
129	E2	Dollard Pk	Fr Jct Hwy 5 & 276, 1/4 mi N	1	10	10	10	None		5/1-11/1**	U Z • 30 ○ ○ •• ○ ○ ○ •	l	p		204/447-2334	Ste Rose du Lac Rol ISO
130	F2	Lansdowne Centennial Pk	Fr jct Hwy 4 & 352, 3 mi N		40	40	12	2.00		5/1-9/30	U • U • ○ • ○ ○ ○ • •	•				Arden
131	G2	Curran Park	Fr Jct TC 1, & Hwy 10S in Brandon, 2 mi S to Valley Rd, 1-1/2 mi W	2	50	200	80	5.00		5/15-9/15	U • U • • • • • • • • • • • • •	•	g		204/728-7064	Box 960, Brandon
132	G3	Man Agriculture Museum	Fr jct TC 1 & Hwy 34, 1-1/2 mi S	2	36	30	S48	4.00		5/1-10/31	7 • U $ • • • • ○	•	p		204/637-2354	Box 10 Austin
133	G3	Cottonwoods CG	In Treherne on Hwy 2	2	28	25	10	2.00		5/24-10/30	U • U • • ○ • • • • • ○ ○ ○ ○	•	g		204/723-2044	Treherne
134	G2	Whitewater Centennial Pk	On Hwy 23r Centennial Pk	2	13	25	S25	None		5/1-11/30	U • U ○ • • • ○ ○ • •	dl			204/776-2172	Bx 53, Minto
136	E1	Grandview Centennial Pk	In Grandview, fr Hwy 5, ext Main St, L to Rupert Ave to pk		15	15	9	2.00		5/15-9/15	U • U • ○ ○ •• ○ ○ ○ ○ ○				204/546-2792	Box 219, Grandview
138	H3	Mound Park	At jct Hwys 3/253	2	4	4	8	3.00		5/15-9/15	U Z • U • • ○ ○ •• • ○ ○ ○ ○ •		gp		204/825-2130	Pilot Mound
139	G3	Kings Park	In Carman, 4 blks W of jct Hwys 3/13	1	51	30	44	4.00		5/1-9/30	U • 24 • • ○ •• • • • ○ ○ ○ •	•	g		204/745-2684	Bx 127, Carman
140	m	River Rd CS	In Thompson		2	10	24	2.50		5/24-9/15	14 Z • U ○ ○ •• • ○ ○ ○ •	l	tg		204/778-6277	274 Thompson Dr, N Thompson
		PRIVATE														
335	F4	Camp Chesley	Fr Petersfield, 3 mi E on Hwy 9	1	35	100	120	4.00		5/15-10/15	U Z • U $ $ $ • $ • • • • • • • • • • • •	dlr •	p	11	204/738-2250	Petersfield
337	G4	Oasis Beach	Fr Winnipeg, 10 mi N on Hwy 59, 1/2 mi S on Oasis Rd	1	50	100	100	5.00		6/1-LD	U • 26 $ $ • $ • • $ • • •	•	p			Rt 5 Box 117E, Winnipeg
340	F3	Miami Beach	Fr Woodlands, 2 mi W off Hwy 6	1	40	200	50	3.00		MD-LD	U Z • U $ • $ • • $ • $ • • •	•	p		204/383-5664	107 Rex Ave, Winnipeg
342	G1	G & D Service & CG	Jct of Hwy 1 & 41, 3 mi fr Sask. border		8	15	30	3.00	M	4/1-11/1	U Z • U $ • • • • • • • •	•	p	19	204/845-2282	Kirkella
351	F4	Almond's Acres	Fr Winnipeg, 50 mi N on Hwy 8	2	20	30	40	5.00		5/24-9/30	U Z U • •• • • ○ ○	•	gp		204/642-5676	PO Box 1614, Gimli
353	H1	Holiday Hills Resort	Fr Deloraine, 6 mi E on Hwy 3, 13 mi S on Hwy 450	3	153	50	20	6.50		5/1-9/15	U Z • 24 $ ○ •• • • • • • • • •	dlr •	g		204/747-2500	Box 393, Deloraine
354	B1	Atamiskow Lodge	Fr The Pas, 11 mi N on Hwy 10, 12 mi E on Hwy 287	1	1	16	12	4.00		5/15-10/15	U • U • • • • • • • • • • • • • ○ •	dlr •			204/624-5429	Bx 1438,The Pas
355	G4	Summerland Park	In Winnipeg, 1/2 mi W of Metro 90 on Inkster Blvd		80	130	130	6.00		5/15-9/15	15 Z • U •• • • ○ • • • ○ ○ •	•	ghp		204/633-1690	Bx 9 Group 200, RR 2 Winnipeg
357	G3	Bambi Gardens Resort	Fr St Claude, 4 mi W on Hwy 2, 7 mi N on Hwy 305, 1 mi W	1	120	30	20	2.00		5/15-11/15	U Z • U $ $ •• • • • •	•	g		204/749-2083	Box 108, St Claude
358	G4	St Vital Trlr Pk	Fr TC 100 bypass, ext Hwy 150 to St Annes Rd		3	40	41	6.00		All year	U Z • U • • • • • • • • • • • • • ○	•	u		204/257-8269	585 St Annes Rd, St Vital
358	G4	Conestoga Campsites	At Hwy 100 Bypass & St Annes Rd, (Rt 150)	1	13	90	64	6.00		5/1-10/31	U Z • U • • • • • • • • • • • • • ○	•	h		204/257-1754	Lot 143, St Annes Rd,Winnipeg

 FOR MAP, SEE PAGE 114

Park number	Map reference	Name of park	Access	Physical environment	Elevation	Acres	Number of tent spaces	Number of trailer spaces	Approximate fee	Credit cards accepted	Season	Time limit / Reservations / Pets permitted / Max. trailer size	Electric hookup / Water hookup / Sewer hookup	Sanitary station / Bottled gas / Air conditioning	Tables / Firewood / Pull-thru spaces / Rec. hall	Flush toilets / Showers / Ice	Auto. laundry / Cafe-snack bar / Store	Swimming pool / Other swimming / Fishing	Boating / Playground / Other	CB channel monitored	Telephone no.	Mail address
		PRIVATE (CONT'D)																				
358	G4	South Winds Motel & CG	S edge of Winnipeg on Hwy 75 & Metro 42	≈ ⅃	1	1	9		4.50		5/31-10/31	U •			•	• • •	○ ○ ○	○ •	• g			1686 Pembina Hwy, Winnipeg 19
363	F2	Eagle Point	Fr Sandy Lk, 3 mi N off Hwy 45 on Hwy 250, 2 mi W, 1 mi N	▲ Ѱ		20	10	20	3.00		5/1-10/31	U Z • U	$		• •	•		• •	dlr •		204/585-5371	Sandy Lake
364	G2	Kingsway Trlr Pk	Fr Brandon, 1/2 mi S on Hwy 10, 4-1/2 mi S of TC 1	Ѱ ⊥	2	7	10	10	5.00		All year	U Z • U	• • •	• ○	•	• • ○	• ○ ○		• g		204/728-1815	2059 Lyndale Dr, Brandon
365	G2	Meadowlark Campground	At Brandon, fr Hwys 1 & 10, on N Frontage Rd	Ѱ ⅃	2	20	33	45	4.50		5/1-11/1**	U Z • U	$ $ $	• ○ $	• • • •	• $ •	• ○ •		• g	12	204/728-7205	Box 852, Brandon
366	F2	Sportsman's Park	Fr Wasagaming, 1/2 mi S on Hwy 10			30	20	S100	4.00		5/15-9/15	U U	• • •	• •	• •	•	• • •	• ○ ○	dlr ghp			Onanole
367	G4	Yogi Bear Jellystone Pk	Fr Hwy #59, 3 mi E on TC 1, 1/2 mi S on Murdoch Rd	Ѱ ⅃	1	45	50	V232	7.00	MV	5/1-10/31**	U Z • U	• • •	• • •	• $ • •	• • •	• • •	•	• gp		204/256-2186	Bx 1 Group 612 SS6 Winnipeg
368	G4	Whitehorse Plain Park	Fr Winnipeg, 9 mi W on TC 1	≈ Ƥ	1	72	280	280	5.00		5/15-10/15	U Z • U	$ $ $	• ○ •	• • • •	• • •	• • •	•	• gp		204/864-2366	Box 99, Headingley
369	F5	Pioneer Beach	Fr Lac du Bonnet, 24 mi NE on Hwy 315	≈ Ƥ	1	4	40	S60	6.00		5/20-10/13	U • U	$	•	• •	• •	•	• •	dl • p			390 Larsen Ave, Winnipeg
373	G3	Westwinds Camping Rsrt	Fr Portage la Prairie, 6 mi E on TC 1	≈ Ƥ		61	75	75	7.50		5/15-10/1	U Z • U	$ • •	• •	• • •	• $ •	•	•	• pg		204/857-8422	Box 784 Portage la Prairie
375	G4	Lilac Motel & CG	Ft jct TC 1 & Hwy 12, 2 mi E	Ѱ ⊥		12	50	35	4.50		5/1-11/1	U Z • U	$ $ $	•	• • •	• $ •	• •	•	• gp		204/422-5760	Box 96, Ste Anne, Man
375	G4	Ste Anne Tourist Pk	Fr jct Hwy 207/12 in St Anne, or 3-1/2 mi E on Hwy 210 from Hwy 12.	≈ Ѱ		11	20	20	3.00		6/17-9/5	U Z • U	$ •	•	• • •			•	•			50 Galinee Bay, Winnipeg
376	A1	Viking Lodge	At Cranberry Portage	▲ ⅃	1	20	10	50	4.00		5/20-10/14	U • U	• • •	○	•	• • •	• •	•	r •		204/472-9290	Cranberry Portage
377	D1	Green Acres CG	Fr Swan River, 2 blks S on Hwy 83	≈ Ѱ	2	5	20	80	4.00		5/15-10/15	U Z • U	$ $ $	• •	• • •	• • •	• ○ ○		g		204/734-3334	Box 477 Swan River
378	G4	Sunny Harbour Resorts	Fr Winnipeg, 7.6 mi W on TC 1, 1/3 mi S	≈ Ѱ	1	28	100	185	4.50		All year	U Z • U	$ $ $	• ○	• • • •	• $ •	• • •	• •	• gku		204/864-2344	P O Box 279, Headingley
379	G1	Virden Lion's Tourist Pk	Fr Virden, 1 mi W on TC 1 at Virden So access rd	Ѱ Ƥ	2	4	25	25	3.00		5/15-9/15	U Z • U	$ $	• ○	• • •	• $ ○	○ ○ ○		gp			Box 93, Virden
382	H1	Elks CG	In Deloraine on Hwy 21	Ƥ Ѱ		3	15	10	2.00		5/19-10/15	U • U	• •	○ ○	• • •	○	○ ○ ○		• g			Box 48 Deloraine
385	E3	Lake Manitoba Narrows Ldg	Fr Ste Rose du Lac Hwy 235E	▲ Ƥ	1	16	250	100	3.00	M	All year	U Z • U	$ $	•	•	• • •	• •	• •	dlr • u	9	204/768-2749	Oakview PO
386	F4	Spruce Sands Trlr Park	Fr Gimli, 10 mi N on Hwy 8, 1-1/2 mi E	▲ Ƥ	1	45		307	4.00		5/15-10/15	U R • U	$ $ $	• • •	• • •	• $ •	• • •	• •	r • gp	4	204/642-5671	Box 116, Arnes
387	C2	Moak Lodge	Fr Grand Rapids, 6 mi N on Hwy 6, fol signs	▲ Ƥ	2	5	E12	38	3.50		5/15-10/15	U Z • U	$		• • •	•	• •	•	dlr •	11		Grand Rapids

NEW BRUNSWICK

FOR MAP, SEE PAGE 115

●—at the campground
○—within one mile of campground
$—extra charge
*—see city map
**—limited facilities during winter months
1-5—number of miles in NF within which facility or activity can be found
A—adults only
B—10,000 acres or more
C—contribution

E—tents rented
F—entrance fee or permit required—see "Special Information on the Public Areas"
H—over 9000 feet above sea level
N—no specific number, limited by size of area only
P—primitive
R—reservation required
S—self-contained units only
U—unlimited

V—trailers rented
Z—reservations accepted
LD—Labor Day
MD—Memorial Day
UC—under construction
d—boat dock
g—public golf course within 5 miles
h—horseback riding
j—whitewater running craft only
k—snow skiing within 25 miles

l—boat launch
m—area north of map
n—no drinking water
p—motor bikes prohibited
r—boat rental
s—stream, lake or creek water only
t—tennis
u—snowmobile trails
w—open certain off-season weekends and holidays

y—drinking water must be boiled
[ocean]—access to ocean
[lake]—access to lake
[river] ≈—access to river
[mountain]—mountainous terrain
[prairie]—prairie land
[desert]—desert area
[wooded]—heavily wooded
[urban]—urban area
[rural]—rural area

CREDIT CARD SYMBOLS:
A—American Express
M—Master Charge
V—Visa/Bank Americard

FEES REFLECT MINIMUM RATE FOR 2 ADULTS AND ARE SUBJECT TO SEASONAL CHANGES

Park number	Map reference	Name of park	Access	Physical environment	Elevation	Acres	Number of tent spaces	Number of trailer spaces	Approximate fee	Credit cards accepted	Season	Time limit / Reservations / Pets permitted / Max. trailer size	Electric hookup / Water hookup / Sewer hookup	Sanitary station / Bottled gas / Air conditioning	Tables / Firewood / Pull-thru spaces / Rec. hall	Flush toilets / Showers / Ice	Auto. laundry / Cafe-snack bar / Store	Swimming pool / Other swimming / Fishing	Boating / Playground / Other	CB channel monitored	Telephone no.	Mail address
		PROVINCIAL PARKS																				
1	E2	Oak Bay	Fr St Stephen, 5 mi E on Hwy 1			28	113	113	5.50		5/15-10/15	14 • 28	$	•	• •	•	•	•	l •		506/466-2261	St Stephen
2	E3	New River Beach	Fr St John, 24 mi W on Hwy 1			935	111	111	5.50		5/15-10/15	14 • 28	$		• •	•	○ ○	• ○	l		506/755-3804	St George
3	D3	Sunbury-Oromocto	Fr Fredericton, approx 20 mi SE on Hwy 7, 5 mi W to French Lake			200	50	50	5.50		5/15-10/15	14 • 28			• •	•		• •	l •		506/357-3708	Oromocto
5	B1	Lac Baker	Fr Edmundston, 21 mi SW on Hwy 120, 3 mi NW on access rd			12	25	25	5.50		5/15-10/15	14 • 28			• •		○ ○	• ○	l		506/992-2462	Lac-Baker
6	D3	Lakeside	Fr Jemseg, 11 mi E on TC 2			60	135	92	5.50		5/15-10/15	14 • 28	$	•	• •	•		• ○	l •		506/488-2532	Coles Island
7	B2	St Basile	Fr Edmundson, 10 mi SE on TC 2			14	40	40	4.50		5/15-10/15	14 • 28	$	•	• •	•					506/263-5529	Edmundston
8	C2	Muniac	Fr Perth-Andover, 9 mi S on Hwy 105			8	46	46	4.50		5/15-10/15	14 • 28	$		• •			○			506/273-2649	Perth
9	C3	Red Pines Park	Fr Boiestown, 1 mi E on Hwy 8		1	54	88	88	4.50		5/15-10/15	14 • 28	$	•	• •	• •	○ ○	○			506/369-2393	Boiestown
10	D3	Oak Point	Fr Westfield, 16 mi N on Hwy 102			51	25	25	5.50		5/15-10/15	14 • 28			• •		○ ○	•	l •		506/468-2266	St John
11	D2	Mactaquac Rec Pk (3 CGs)	Fr Fredericton, 15 mi W on Hwy 105			1400	297	297	5.50		All year	14 • 28	$	•	• • •	• • •	• • •	• •	dl • gh		506/363-2300	Keswick
12	D2	North Lake	Fr TC 2, 24 mi SW on Hwy 122			115	34		4.00		6/1-10/15	14 •			• •			• •				Canterbury
13	D2	Lake George	Fr Longs Creek, 4 mi W on TC 2, 7 mi S on Hwy 636			29	28	28	5.50		5/15-10/15	14 • 28			• •		○	• ○	l		506/366-2933	Harvey Station
14	B3	Chaleur	Fr Dalhousie, 3 mi S on Hwy 11 to Hwy 280			400	82	82	5.50		5/15-10/15	14 • 28	$	•	• • •	• •		•	p			Charlo
15	C3	The Enclosure	Fr Newcastle, 3 mi SW on Hwy 8			120	101	101	5.50		5/15-10/15	14 • 28	$		• •	•	•	• ○	l •		506/622-3420	Newcastle
17	B1	Les Jardins	Fr Edmundston, 4 mi N on TC 2 to St Jacques			107	60	60	5.50		5/15-10/15	14 • 28		•	• •	• •		• •	• p			St Jacques
18	D3	Grand Lk Rec Pk	Fr Fredericton, 19 mi E on TC 2, 15 mi NE on Hwy 690			212	86	85	5.50		5/15-10/15	14 • 28	$	•	• •	• • •	• ○	•	l •		506/385-2919	Minto
19	B3	Jacquet River	Fr Bathurst, 32 mi NW on Hwy 11			4	57	57	4.50		5/15-10/15	14 • 28	$	•	• •	•	○ ○	• ○			506/237-2826	Jacquet River
20	B4	Val Comeau	Fr Tracadie, 3 mi S on Hwy 11, 5 mi E on access rd			60	55	55	5.50		5/15-10/15	14 • 28	$		• •	•	○ ○	• ○			506/395-4137	Tracadie
21	C4	Jardine Park	Fr Richibucto, 1 mi S on Hwy 11, SE on access rd			12	41	41	5.50		5/15-10/15	14 • 28	$	•	• •	•	• ○	• ○			506/523-4298	Richibucto
22	E2	The Anchorage	Fr Blacks Harbour, ferry to Grand Manan			200	N		5.50		5/15-10/15	14 •			• •	• •		• •	l			Seal Cove, Grand Manan
23	B4	Shippegan	Fr Lamque, 6 mi S on Hwy 113, 2 mi W			74	100	100	5.50		5/15-10/15	14 • 28	$	•	• •		○ ○	• ○	l •		506/336-8673	Shippegan
24	B2	Mt Carleton	Fr Nictau, 20 mi N			B	PN	PN	4.50		5/15-10/15	14 • 28			• •			• •	l			Nictau
26	D4	Parlee Beach Rec Pk	Fr Shediac, 1 mi E on Hwy 15			90	169	169	5.50		5/15-10/15	14 • 28	$	•	• •	• •	• ○	• ○	•		506/532-5885	Moncton
28	B2	Glenwood	Fr Campbellton, 25 mi SW on Hwy 17			68	P19	P19	4.50		5/15-10/15	14 • 28			• •						506/753-4828	Campbellton
29	B2	Kedgwick	Fr Kedgwick, 1 mi E on Hwy 17		1	40	32	32	4.50		5/15-10/15	14 • 28			• •		○ ○				506/284-2295	Kedgwick
31	E2	Campobello Island	Fr Whiting, Me, 11 mi NE on Hwy 189, 8 mi NE on bridge & Hwy 774 to Herring Cove			17	38	38	5.50		5/15-10/15	14 • 28			• •			•	l g		506/752-2396	Wilson's Beach
32	C2	St Leonard	Fr St Leonard, 1 mi E on Hwy 17			88	55	55	4.50		5/15-10/15	14 • 28	$	•	• •		○ ○				506/423-6987	St Leonard
33	D4	Murray Beach	Fr Cape Tormentine, 10 mi NW on Hwy 955			65	110	110	5.50		5/15-10/15	14 • 28	$	•	• •	•	○ ○	• ○	l		506/538-2628	Moncton
37	B4	Caraquet	Fr Caraquet, 2 mi W on Hwy 11			8	25	25	5.50		5/15-10/15	14 • 2$	$		• •		○ ○	• ○			506/727-3474	Ste Anne de Bocaga
		FOREST SERVICE																				
39	C3	McGraw Brook	Fr Renous, 17 mi W on Hwy 108			30	75	S75	2.00		6/1-9/30	U • U			•			•				80 Pleasant, Newcastle
		NATIONAL PARKS																				
		Fundy NP				B															506/887-2000	
40	D4	Headquarters CG	Fr Alma, 1 mi W on Hwy 114 to pk hdqtrs, 1/2 mi N		1	18	121	29	F6.00		5/19-10/9**	14 • U	• • •	• ○	• • •	•$ ○	○ ○ ○	○ ○	gpt			Alma
40	D4	Point Wolfe	Fr pk hdqtrs, 5 mi SW on Pt Wolfe Rd		1	28	212	S212	F3.00		6/12-LD	14 • U			• •	•$	•	○ $	• gtp			Alma
40	D4	Chignecto	Fr pk hdqtrs, 2-1/2 mi W on Hwy 114 (2 CGs)		1	126	468	S55	F5.00		6/30-LD	14 • U		•	• •	•			• gpt			Alma
40	D4	Wolfe Lake	Fr Hwy 2, 15 mi SE on Hwy 114 to info center & CG		1	3	60	S60	F3.00		5/20-10/10	14 • U			• •			• $	gpt			Alma
		Kouchibouguac NP	(For additional CGs, see 'Backpack or Boat Access Areas')			B																
41	C4	South Kouchibouguac CG	Fr St Louis de Kent, 14 mi NW on Hwy 11, 10.6 mi off Hwy 11; 8.5 mi fr main pk entr		1	79	143	S143	F3.00		5/20-10/15	14 • U		•	• •	•		•	lr • p		506/876-2443	Kouchibouguac, Kent Co
		BACKPACK OR BOAT ACCESS AREAS																				
		Kouchibouguac NP																				
45	C4	Petit-Large	Fr St Louis de Kent, 3 mi N on Rt 11, 3 mi E at Pk entrance		1	10	6		F.25		All year	14 R •			• •			• •	dlr kp		506/876-2443	Kouchibouguac Kent Co
		Fundy NP																			506/887-2000	
46	D4	Goose River Pk	Fr Fundy NP interior, 5.5 mi on Marven Lk Trail & Goose River Trail		1						6/30-LD				•			• $	ps			Alma
46	D4	Chambers Lk Pk	Fr Fundy NP interior, 5 mi on Marven Lake Trail		1						6/30-LD				•			$	ps			Alma
46	D4	Marven Lk Pk	Fr Fundy NP interior, 5-1/2 mi on Marven Lk Trail		1						6/30-LD				•			$	ps			Alma
		CITY, COUNTY & CIVIC																				
50	E2	Passamaquoddy Park	Fr Hwy 1, S on Hwy 127, Water St to St Andrews Pt	[ocean] [urban]	0	40	50	75	5.00		5/15-9/30	21 R • U	• • •	•	• • • •	•$ •	○ ○ ○	○ ○	dl • g		506/529-3439	St Andrews
51	D2	Connell Park	Fr downtown Woodstock, 3/4 mi W on Connell St	≈ [prairie]	1	100	90	90	4.00		5/15-10/15	U • U	• •	• ○	• • •	• • •	○ • ○	○	l • gt		506/328-6892	Woodstock
52	B3	Inch Arran Trlr Pk	Fr Hwy 11, in Dalhousie	[ocean] [mountain]		13	10	44	4.50		3/10-9/15	U Z • U	• • $	•	•	• •	• •	• • •	l • gp		506/684-5352	Dalhousie
54	E3	Rockwood Park	In St Johnark	[lake] [mountain]	1	B	100	165	5.00		5/30-9/30	U • U	• •	• ○	• •	• • •	○ • ○	• •	dr • ghp		506/652-4050	Saint John
		PRIVATE																				
58	B3	Youghall Trlr Pk	Fr Hwy 134 in Bathurst, 1-1/2 mi, E at Kent Mtl	[ocean] [urban]	0	20	65	130	5.75		5/1-10/1	U Z • U	$ • $	•	• • • •	• • •	• •	$ ○ •	lr • g			Box 1099 RR 3, Bathurst
59	D4	Border Tent & Trlr Pk	Fr Sackville, 5 mi E on Hwy 2, 1/2 mi NE on Hwy 16	[rural]		1	15	13	5.00		5/15-10/1	U Z • U	• • •	•	• • • •	• • •	○ ○		•		506/536-0564	RR 3, Sackville
60	D2	Katimavik	Fr Fredericton, 20 mi W on TC Hwy	≈ [rural]	1	40	100	45	6.00		6/15-9/15	U Z • U	$ •	• $	•$ •	•$ •	• • ○	• •	•		506/363-9956	Prince William
62	D4	Silver Sands Trlr & Tent	Fr Shediac, 16 mi E on Rt 15	[ocean] [rural]		5	E48	V42	5.00		6/1-LD	U Z • 30	$ $ $	• •	•$ •	• • •	• ○	• ○	dl •		506/577-4623	Cap Pele, Westmoreland Co
63	D4	Green Acres Tent & Trlr P	Fr Ammon, 2 mi S on Hwy 126 to jct with Hwy 2	[mountain] [urban]	0	100	50	V40	6.00	M	5/15-10/15	U Z • U	$ $ $		• •	• • •	•		gp		506/382-0621	RR 8, Moncton
64	D3	Pine Cone Mtl & Pk	Fr Sussex, 4 mi E on TC 2	≈ [wooded]	1	12	25	150	6.00		5/15-10/15	U Z • U	• • $	• ○	• • •	• • •	• • •	• ○ ○	• gp		506/433-3958	RR 1, Penobsquis
64	D3	Millstream Trlr Pk	Fr Sussex, 6 mi W on TC 2	[rural]		13	40	40	6.50	MV	7/1-LD	U R • U	• •	•	• •	•$ •	• • ○	•	• gp	11	506/433-2148	Box 429, Sussex
64	D3	Town & Country Campark	Fr Sussex, E on TC 2	[lake] [wooded]	1	200	100	200	5.50		5/1-11/1	U Z • U	$ $ •	• ○ •	• • •	•$ •	• • •	• • •	l • gku		506/433-3134	P O Box 160, Sussex

 FOR FOOTNOTE EXPLANATION SEE FIRST PAGE OF THIS **PROVINCE** FOR MAP, SEE PAGE 115

Park number	Map reference	Name of park	Access	Physical environment	Elevation	Acres	Number of tent spaces	Number of trailer spaces	Approximate fee	Credit cards accepted	Season	Time limit / Reservations / Pets permitted / Max. trailer size	Electric hookup / Water hookup / Sewer hookup	Sanitary station / Bottled gas / Air conditioning	Tables / Firewood / Pull-thru spaces / Rec. hall	Flush toilets / Showers / Ice	Auto. laundry / Cafe-snack bar / Store	Swimming pool / Other swimming / Fishing	Boating / Playground / Other	CB channel monitored	Telephone no.	Mail address
		PRIVATE (CONT'D)																				
65	E3	Cherry Tree Trlr Park	Fr St John, 20 mi W on Hwy 1				3	10	35	5.50	4/1-10/1	U Z • U	• • •	• ○	•$ •	• • •	• •	• •	l • p		506/659-2860	RR 1, Lepreau
65	E3	Utopia Beach & Campsite	Fr Hwy 1 at Pennfield, 3 mi N on Hwy 785	⛵	ᛘ	1	3	25	10	2.00	6/1-9/30	U Z • U			•	•	○	○ ○	l		506/755-2163	Lk Utopia,St George
66	D4	Gagnon Beach Trailer Pk	Fr Shediac, 9 mi E on Hwy 15	⚓	ᛘ	1	20	30	170	6.00	5/1-10/31	U Z • U	• • •	•	•$ • •	• • •	• • ○	• •	dl • p		506/577-2519	RR 2 Cap Pele, West Co
69	D3	Five Points CG	Fr'Sussex, 12 mi NE on TC 2, in Anagance	≈	♀		3	18	17	4.00	5/18-11/30	U Z • U	$ $	•	•$ •	•$ •	•		• p	11		RR 1, Anagance
69	D3	Lone Pine Pk	Fr Sussex, 12 mi E on TC 2, in Penobsquis	≈	♀	1	12	12	37	4.50	5/24-10/31	14 Z • U	$ $	• ○$	• •	•$ •	•	• • •	• p		506/433-1762	RR 1, Penobsquis
69	D3	Penobsquis KOA	Fr Sussex, 9 mi E on TCH 2, S side of Hwy	≈	♀	1	35	E45	100	5.00 M	All year	U Z • U	$ $ $	• •	•$ • •	• • •	• ○ •	• ○ •	• gkpu		506/433-2870	Penobsquis, King Co
70	C4	Parc Daigles Pk	Fr Kouchibouguac NP, 1-1/2 mi S	ᛘ		1	6	50	40	4.00	5/15-10-25	U • U	$ $ $	•	• •	• • •	• ○	•	•		506/876-2979	RR 1, Bx 95, St Louis de Kent
70	C4	Evergreen Acres	Fr Kouchibouguac NP, 4 mi S on Hwy 11	⚓	⛵		15	40	50	6.00	All year	U Z • U	• •	• •$	•$ •	• • •	○ ○		• gku		506/876-2672	Box 232, St Louis de Kent
71	E2	Deer Island Pt pk	Fr St George, S on Hwy 772 to Letete, Car ferry to Deer Isl	⚓	ᛘ	1	20	70	54	3.50	6/15-9/30	U Z • U	$	• •	•$	• •	•	• •	dl		506/747-2371	Fairhaven, Deer Island
72	D3	Field & Stream CG	Fr Sussex, 2 mi W on Hwy 1	ᛘ			3	14	16	4.50	5/15-10/30	U • U	• • •		• • •	• •		•	g		506/433-3109	RR3, Sussex
72	D3	Tote-M Vacation Park	Fr Sussex, 20 mi W	≈	⋀	0	'17	50	100	4.00	5/24-9/15	U Z • U	• • •	•	•$	•	• •	• •	p		506/485-2345	RR 1, Norton
73	D4	Highland Trlr Pk	Fr Moncton, 12 mi W on Hwy 6, in Salisbury	≈	ᛘ		12	50	26	5.50	5/24-10/15	U Z • U	• • •		•$ •	• • •	• ○ •	$ ○ •	• p		506/372-5968	PO Box 53, Salisbury
74	C4	Allain's Beach Camping	In Bouctouche	⚓	ᛘ	0	2	15	35	5.00	5/24-9/15	U Z • U	$ $ $		• • •	• • •	○	○ •	dl • p			Bouctouche R 1,Bx 84, Kent Co
75	D3	Riverbend Pk	Fr St John, 15 mi NE on Hwy 1, 2 mi E on Stock Farm Rd	≈	⋀	0	10	20	75	4.00	6/1-9/30	U Z • U	• •	•	• •	• •		• •	•		506/832-7419	RR 2, Hampton
75	D3	Chestnut Bch	Fr St John, 11 mi E on Hwy 1, 1/2 mi N on Hammond Riv Rd	≈	⋀	0	4	20	S20	4.50	6/21-9/15	U Z • 30	$ $	• ○	•$	•	○	• •	• p			Rothesay RR1, Kings Co
76	D4	Sandy Beach T&T Pk	Fr jct Hwys 15/950, 1 mi N on Hwy 950, in Cap Pele	⚓	ᛘ	0	30	50	105	5.50	5/24-9/15	U Z • U	$ •$	• •	• •	•$ •	• • •	• •	dl • gp		506/577-2605	RR 2 Site 10 Box 9, Cap Pele
77	C2	Hilltop Camping	Fr Perth-Andover, 2 mi S on TC 2	⋀	ᛘ	1	3	25	20	4.00 MV	6/1-9/30	U Z • U	$ •	•	• •	• • •			• p			RR 4, Perth-Andover
78	D4	Idlewyld Trlr Pk	In Shediac, on Hwy 133	⚓	ᛉ	0	4	E40	V60	6.00 M	5/15-10/15	U Z • U	• • •	• •	• • •	• • •	• •	• ○ •	dlr • ghpt		506/532-3314	PO Box 279, Shediac
78	D4	Bateman Mill Camping Area	Fr jct Hwys 134/11, 2 mi N, 1-1/2 mi W on New Hwy 134	≈	ᛘ	0	200	100	100	4.00	5/1-10/15	U • U	$		• •	• • ○	•	•	•		506/532-3592	Box 32, Shediac
79	D2	Magaquadavic Lake Trlr Pk	Fr Hwy 4, 8 mi NW on Hwy 635	⛵	ᛘ				16	4.50	5/15-10/15	U Z U	• •	○	• •		•	• •	lr		506/366-2979	Harvey Station RR 3,York Cnty
80	C2	Dutch Trlr Pk	Fr Florenceville, 3 mi N on TC 2	≈	⋀	1	6	150	S36	5.00	5/1-9/30	U Z • 32	• •	• ○	•$ •	• • •	•	○ ○	p		506/392-5320	Rt 2, Florenceville
81	D4	Ponderosa Pines Park	Fr Hopewell Cape, 2 mi W on Hwy 114	⛵	⋀	0	150	100	S74	6.00 M	5/1-11/1	U Z • U	$ • •	•	•$ • •	•$ •	• • •	• • •	r • h		506/734-2712	RR 1, Hopewell Cape
82	B4	Wishart Point T & T Pk	Fr Tabusintac, 2 mi N on Hwy 11, 1 mi E on Wishart Point Rd	≈	ᛘ	0		17	22	4.50	6/1-LD	U Z • U	$ $ $	$	•$ •	• • •	• •	• •	dlr •		506/779-9230	RR 2 Box 124, Tabusintac
83	C2	Cloverleaf Trlr Pk	Fr Hartland, 4 mi N on TC 2, ext Lk Mt Pleasant	≈	ᛘ		14	50	20	5.00	5/1-9/15	U Z • U	• •	• $	• • •	• • •	• •		•		506/375-6617	Stickney, Car Co
84	D3	Kelly's Mobile Home Court	In Fredericton, 1/4 mi NW on Rainsford Ln, E on Golf Clb Rd	≈	ᛘ		2	25	25	4.50 V	5/15-10/31	• U	• • •	• ○	• •	•$	• ○		g		506/454-2549	Golf Club Rd, Fredericton
85	D3	Knight Tenting & Trlr Pk	Fr downtown Fredericton, 4 mi W on TC 2	≈	⋀	1	3	38	12	5.00	5/1-10/15	U Z • 28	$ •	•	• •	• • •	○ ○	○	l • g	11	506/455-7640	RR 6, Fredericton
86	B2	Iroquois River CG	Fr Edmundston, 2-1/2 mi E on Hwy 14	≈	⋀	1	8	40	25	3.50	5/15-9/30	U Z • U	$ $ $	•	•$ •	•$ •	○	•	• g		506/735-8782	Edmunston RR2, Iroquois
87	C3	Taylors Tenting & Trlr Pk	Fr Fredericton, 60 mi N on Hwy 8	≈	♀	0	2	25	12	4.50	5/1-10/15	U Z • U	• •$	•	•	• • •	• ○	• ○ •	•		506/365-4617	Doaktown
88	E2	Chamcook's Cozy Cove	Fr St Andrews, 19 mi S on Hwy 127 to Ward St Andrews	⚓	ᛘ	1	14	60	30	3.00	5/15-9/30	U Z • U	$ $ $	•	• • •	•$ •	○	○ ○	•		506/529-8221	Rt 2, St Andrews
89	B2	Castonguay Cmpg	Fr St Leonard, 37 mi NE on Hwy 17	≈	♀		5	22	30	5.50	5/15-11/15	U R • U	• •	•	•$ •	• • •	•	• •	• p	22	506/235-2395	38 Rue Champlain, St-Quentin
90	D2	Great Bear CG	Fr Nackawic, 12 mi E on Hwy 105	≈	♀		25	50	100	5.00 V	6/1-9/30	U Z • U	• •	•	•$ •	• • •	• •	• •	lr • p	11	506/575-8151	Nackawic, Mactguac Co
92	D3	Grant's Tent & Trlr Site	Fr Fredericton, 10 mi E on Hwy 2, on Maugerville Is	≈	ᛘ	0	3	50	50	4.50	6/15-10/31	U • U	•	•	• •	• • •	•		•		506/357-3858	RR 2, Maugerville
92	D3	Over-Niter	In Fredericton, 3 mi fr business district	≈	⋀	1	40	50	S25	5.00	5/1-10/30	U Z • U	$ $	• ○	•$ •	• • •	○ • •	• •	l • gh		506/454-6832	Box 1415, Fredericton
95	D3	Mohawk Campark	Fr Fredericton, 43 mi E on TC 2	⛵	ᛘ	1	12	100	50	4.50	5/15-10/15	U Z • U	$ •$	• $	•$ •	• • •	• • •	• •	l •		506/362-5250	Young's Cove Rd, Waterborough
96	D3	Hardings Point Trlr Pk	Fr St John, 15 mi N on Hwy 7, cross Westfield, Ferry Hwy 845	≈	ᛘ		5	75	80	5.50	4/1-9/30	U Z • 30	• • •	•	• • •	○	○ ○	• •	lr • g		506/763-2517	Westfield
99	B3	Hodnett's Camping	Fr Bathurst, 18 mi E on Hwy 11	⚓	ᛘ	1	6	20	20	4.00	6/15-9/1	U Z • U	$ $	•	• • • •	• • •	•	• •	•	12	506/546-4927	RRH1, Box 10, Site 3,Bathurst
99	B3	Chapman's Tent & Trlr Pk	Fr Bathurst, 9 mi E on Hwy 11	⚓	ᛘ	1	25	50	40	5.00	6/15-9/30	U Z • U	• • •		• • • •	• • •	○ ○ •	• •	• p		506/546-2883	Box 535, Bathurst
100	D2	Kozy Acres CS	Fr TC 2, in Woodstock	ᛘ			8	20	75	5.50	6/15-9/6	U Z • $$	•		•$ • •	• • •	• •	•	• g		506/328-6287	PO Box 198, Woodstock
101	D3	Birches CS	Fr Youngs Cove, 3 mi E on TC 2, in Youngs Cove Rd	♀			5	12	21	5.00	6/15-9/15	U Z • U	• •	•	•$ •	• • •	• •		• p		506/362-5305	Youngs Cove Rd, Queens Cnty
104	D4	Stonehurst Trailer Park	Fr Moncton, 7 mi NW on Hwy 126	♀	ᛘ	1	200	30	100	6.50	6/15-9/15	U Z • U	• • •	•	•$ • •	• • •	•	• •	• g		506/382-1459	585 Mtn Rd, Moncton
105	B1	Camping Chez Ben	Fr Edmundston, 20 mi W on Hwy 120	⛵	≈		2	30	50	5.00	5/15-9/15	U R • U	• • •	• ○ •	•$ •	• •	•	• •	lr •		506/992-2594	Lac Baker
107	C4	Folynwood CG	Fr Chatham, 10 mi S on Hwy 11	≈	ᛘ	1	90	38	10	3.50	5/24-10/31	U Z • U	$ •		• •	• • •	•	○	•		506/773-3984	RR 1 Chatham
108	C2	Mountain View CG	Fr Grand Falls, 8 mi S on TC 2, 4 mi E to Lk Edward	⛵	⋀	1	200	20	32	4.00	5/15-10/8	U Z • U	$ $ $	•	• • •	• • •	•	• •	dl •		506/553-6449	RR 2, New Denmark
109	C4	KOK Caissie Cape	Fr Shediac Bridge, 5 mi NE on Hwy 530	⚓	ᛘ	1	15	50	35	6.00 V	5/20-9/15	U Z • U	• • •	• •	•$ • •	• • •	• ○ •	○ ○	dl • p		506/576-6566	Bx 71A, Caissie Cape
110	C2	Grande Riviere Camp	Fr St Leonard, 2 mi N on Trans-Canada Hwy	≈	⋀	1	10	80	70	6.00	6/1-10/1	U Z • U	• • •	•	•$ •	• • •	○	• • •			506/423-6292	Trans-Canada Hwy, St Leonard
110	C2	Malobiannah Camping	Fr Edmundston, 10 mi SE on TC 2, in Riviere-Verte	≈	♀		3	20	12	6.00	6/15-9/15	U Z • U	• •	• ○	•$ •	• • •	○ ○ ○	• •			506/263-5621	CP 82, Riviere-Verte

NEWFOUNDLAND

FOR MAP, SEE PAGE 115

●—at the campground
○—within one mile of campground
$—extra charge
*—see city map
**—limited facilities during winter months
1-5—number of miles in NF within which facility or activity can be found
A—adults only
B—10,000 acres or more
C—contribution

E—tents rented
F—entrance fee or permit required—see "Special Information on the Public Areas"
H—over 9000 feet above sea level
N—no specific number, limited by size of area only
P—primitive
R—reservation required
S—self-contained units only
U—unlimited

V—trailers rented
Z—reservations accepted
LD—Labor Day
MD—Memorial Day
UC—under construction
d—boat dock
g—public golf course within 5 miles
h—horseback riding
j—whitewater running craft only
k—snow skiing within 25 miles

l—boat launch
m—area north of map
n—no drinking water
p—motor bikes prohibited
r—boat rental
s—stream, lake or creek water only
t—tennis
u—snowmobile trails
w—open certain off-season weekends and holidays

y—drinking water must be boiled
⚓ access to ocean
access to lake
≈ access to river
mountainous terrain
prairie land
desert area
♀ heavily wooded
urban area
rural area

CREDIT CARD SYMBOLS:
A—American Express
M—Master Charge
V—Visa/Bank Americard

FEES REFLECT MINIMUM RATE FOR 2 ADULTS AND ARE SUBJECT TO SEASONAL CHANGES

Park number	Map reference	Name of park	Access	Physical environment	Elevation	Acres	Number of tent spaces	Number of trailer spaces	Approximate fee	Credit cards accepted	Season	FACILITIES: Time limit / Reservations / Pets permitted / Max. trailer size	Electric hookup / Water hookup / Sewer hookup	Sanitary station / Bottled gas / Air conditioning	Tables / Firewood / Pull-thru spaces / Rec. hall	Flush toilets / Showers / Ice	ACTIVITIES: Auto. laundry / Cafe-snack bar / Store	Swimming pool / Other swimming / Fishing / Boating	Playground / Other	CB channel monitored	Telephone no.	Mail address
		PROVINCIAL PARKS																				P O Bx 9340,Stn B, St Johns
		Avalon Region																				
1	B7	Jack's Pond	Fr Whitbourne, 35 mi NW on Hwy 1		1	1200	74	74	F2.50		5/15-9/15	10 • U			• •			• •	l			
2	B7	Gushue's Pond	Fr St John's, 35 mi W on Hwy 1		1	442	121	121	F2.50		5/15-9/15	10 • 30			• •			• •				
2	B7	La Manche	Fr St Johns, 35 mi S on Hwy 10		0	3446	70	70	F2.50		5/15-9/15	10 • 30			• •			• •				
2	B7	Butter Pot	Fr St John's, 22 mi W on Hwy 1		1	4330	122	122	F2.50		5/15-9/15	10 • U		○	• •			• •				
3	B7	Bellevue Beach	Fr St Johns, 70 mi W on Hwy 1		0	194	77	77	F2.50		5/15-9/15	10 • U			• •			• •	l			
3	B7	Backside Pond	Fr Hwy 1, 20 mi N on Hwy 80		1	1390	51	51	F2.50		5/15-9/15	10 • U			• •			• •				
4	B7	Fitzgerald's Pond	Fr Whitbourne, 14 mi SW on Hwy 100		1	2009	23	23	F2.50		5/15-9/15	10 • U			• •			• •	l			
5	B7	Holyrood Pond	Fr jct Hwys 1 & 90, 34 mi S on Hwy 90		1	558	15	15	F2.50		5/15-9/15	10 • U			• •			• •	l			
6	B7	Northern Bay Sands	Fr St John's, 39 mi W on Hwy 1, 49 mi N on Hwy 70		0	34	42	42	F2.50		5/15-9/15	10 • U			• •		○		l			
7	B6	Frenchman's Cove	Fr Marystown, 15 mi W on Hwy 210		0	125	81	81	F2.50		5/15/-9/15	10 • U			• •			• •				
7	B6	Freshwater Pond	Fr Marystown, 8 mi S on Hwy 210, 2 mi W on Hwy 213		1	2204	30	30	F2.50		5/15-9/15	10 • U			• •			• •	l			
8	B7	Lockston Path	Fr Clarenville, 52 mi NE on Hwy 236 to Stock Cove, 7 mi S on Hwy 236		1	498	20	20	F2.50		5/15-9/15	10 • U			• •			• •	l			
10	B6	Jipujijkuei Kuespem	Hwy 360		1	1486	21	21	2.50		5/15-9/15	• U			• •			• •				
		Eastern Region																				P O Box 9340, Stn B, St Johns
11	B7	Square Pond	Fr Gander, 23 mi SE on Hwy 1		1	96	93	93	F2.50		5/15-9/15	10 • U			• •			• •	l			
11	B7	David Smallwood Mem Pk	Fr Gander, 25 mi E on Hwy 1, 7 mi N on Hwy 320		1	130	27	27	F2.50		5/15-9/15	10 • U			• •			• •				
11	B7	Jonathan's Pond	Fr Gander, 12 mi N on Hwy 330		1	1101	96	96	F2.50		5/15-9/15	10 • U			• •			• •	l			
12	B7	Windmill Bight	Fr Gander, 88 mi NE on Hwy 330		0	182	29	29	F2.50		5/15-9/15	10 • U			• •			• •				
13	B6	Beothuck	Fr Grand Falls, 3 mi W on Hwy 1		1	184	64	64	F2.50		5/15-9/15	10 • U			• •			• •	l			
14	B6	Notre Dame	Fr Gander Airport, 30 mi W on Hwy 1		1	278	100	100	F2.50		5/15-9/15	10 • U			• •			• •				Lewisporte
15	A6	Dildo Run	Fr Lewisporte, 43 mi NE on Hwy 340, nr Virgin Arm		0	809	31	31	F2.50		5/15-9/15	10 • U			• •			• •	l			P O Bx 9340, Stn B, St Johns
		Central Region																				
16	m	Pinware River	Fr Deer Lk, 210 mi N on Hwy 430 to St Barbe Bay, ferry to Blanc Sablon, 25 mi NE on Hwy 510		0	168	A25		F2.50		5/15-9/15	10 •			• •			•				
16	m	Duley Lake	In Western Labrador, access only by train fr Sept-Iles, Quebec		2	2180	100	100	F2.50		5/15-9/15	10 •			• •	•		• •	l			
17	A6	Indian River	Fr Windsor, 6 mi NW on Hwy 1		1	79	49	49	F2.50		5/15-9/15	10 • U			• •			• •				
17	A6	Flatwater Pond	Fr Springdale, 7 mi W on Hwy 350 to Hwy 1, 15 mi W to Hwy 410, 30 mi S		1	244	25	25	F2.50		5/15-9/15	10 • U			• •			• •	l			
18	B6	Mary March	Fr Badger, 28 mi SW on Hwy 370		1	79	26	26	F2.50		5/15-9/15	10 • U			• •			• •				
19	B6	Catamaran Brook	Fr Badger, 6 mi NW on Hwy 1		1	111	55	55	F2.50		5/15-9/15	10 • U			• •			• •	l			
20	A6	Sop's Arm River	Fr Deer Lk, 67 mi NE on Hwy 420		0	20	25	25	F2.50		5/15-9/15	10 • U			• •			• •				
21	B6	Squires Mem	Fr Deer lake, 26 mi NE on Hwy 422		1	3890	159	159	F2.50		5/15-9/15	10 • U			• •			• •	r			
22	A6	River of Ponds	Fr Deer Lk, 120 mi N on Hwy 430		0	296	40	40	F2.50		5/15-9/15	10 • U			• •			• •	l			
23	A6	Pistolet Bay	Fr St Anthony, 17 mi NW on Hwy 437		0	2200	27	27	F2.50		5/15-9/15	10 • U			• •			• •				
		Western Region																				P O Bx 9340, Stn B, St Johns
27	B6	Blue Ponds	Fr Corner Brook, 17 mi SW on Hwy 1		1	152	37	37	F2.50		5/15-9/15	10 • U			• •			•				
28	B6	Barachois Pond	Fr Corner Brook, 46 mi Sw on Hwy 1		1	8641	158	158	F2.50		5/15-9/15	10 • U		○	• •			• •	l			
29	B6	Piccadilly Head	Fr Stephenville, 23 mi W on Hwy 463		0	100	50	50	F2.50		5/15-9/15	10 • U			• •			• •				
30	B6	Blow Me Down	Fr Corner Brook, 36 mi W on Hwy 450		0	559	27	27	F2.50		5/15-9/15	10 • U			• •			• •				
31	B5	Grand Codroy	Fr Port aux Basques, 25 mi NE on Hwy 1, 1/2 mi on Hwy 406		0	6	25	25	F2.50		5/15-9/15	10 • U			• •			• •				
31	B5	Mummichog	Fr Port aux Basques, 20 mi N on Hwy 1		0	208	38	38	F2.50		5/15-9/15	10 • U			• •			• •	l			
31	B5	John T Cheeseman	Fr Port aux Basques, 6 mi NW on Hwy 1 & Cape Bay Rd		0	455	103	103	F2.50		5/15-9/15	10 • U			• •			• •				
31	B5	Otter Bay	Fr Port aux Basques, 17 mi E on Hwy 470		0	400	5	5	F2.50		5/15-9/15	10 • U			• •			•				
32	B5	Crabbes River	Fr St George's 28 mi SW on Hwy 1		1	7	32	32	F2.50		5/15-9/15	10 • U			• •			•				
33	B6	Sandbanks Park	Access only by coastal boat fr Port aux Basques		1	569	8		F2.50		5/15-9/15	10			• •			• •				
		NATIONAL PARKS	(For additional CGS, see 'Backpack or Boat Access Areas')																			
		Terra Nova NP																				
36	B7	Newman Sound	Fr Gander, 50 mi SE on TC 1, 1 mi SE on pk rds		1	200	417	406	F3.00		5/21-9/20	14 • 18		•	• •	•$ ○	• ○ ○	•	l •			Terra Nova NP, Glovertown
36	B7	Alexander Bay	On Hwy 39, Midway bet Eastport & TC 1		1	35 B	164	154	F3.00		6/14-9/6	14 • 20			• •	• ○		• •	p			Terra Nova NP, Glovertown
		Gros Morne NP																			709/458-2417	Box 130, Rocky Harbour
37	A6	Berry Hill	Ft TC Hwy 1 at Deer Lk, 45 mi N on Hwy 430		1		160	S2	None		5/15-10/15	14 • U		•	• •	• • ○	○ ○	○ ○	•			Rocky Harbour
		BACKPACK OR BOAT ACCESS AREAS																				
		Terra Nova NP																				Supt, Glovertown
45	B7	South Broad Cove	Fr Gander, 50 mi SE on TC1 to Pk Hdqts, 8 mi E on Newman Sound; access by boat				P6				5/15-10/31	14 •			•			• •	d s			Glovertown
45	B7	Platters Beach	Fr Charlottetown, 2 mi NE on Clode Sound; access by boat only				PN				5/15-10/31	14 •			•			• •	n			Charlottetown
45	B7	Minchin Cove	Fr Gander, 50 mi SE on on TC 1 to Pk Hdqts, 6 mi NE on Newman Sound; access by boat only				PN				5/15-10/31	14 •						• •	d s			Glovertown
		PRIVATE																				
60	B7	Trinity Cabins Trlr Pk	Fr TC Hwy, 40 mi E on Hwys 230 & 239	⚓ ♀	1	1		13	5.00		5/15-9/30	U Z • U	• •	• •	•	• • •	• •	• • •	d • p		709/464-3657	Bx 54 Trinity, TB
61	B7	The Holdin' Ground	Fr St John's City limits, 3 mi W on TC Hwy at Donovan's overpass, jct Hwys 1/60	⚓	1	6	25	75	4.50	MV	5/1-10/30	U • 30	• $ $	• ○	•	• • •	• • ○	○	dl • g		709/368-3191	Bx 8515, St John's

NEWFOUNDLAND

FOR FOOTNOTE EXPLANATION SEE FIRST PAGE OF THIS **PROVINCE** FOR MAP, SEE PAGE **115**

Park number	Map reference	Name of park	Access	Physical environment	Elevation	Acres	Number of tent spaces	Number of trailer spaces	Approximate fee	Credit cards accepted	Season	Time limit	Reservations	Pets permitted	Max. trailer size	Electric hookup	Water hookup	Sewer hookup	Sanitary station	Bottled gas	Air conditioning	Tables	Firewood	Pull-thru spaces	Rec. hall	Flush toilets	Showers	Ice	Auto. laundry	Cafe-snack bar	Store	Swimming pool	Other swimming	Fishing	Boating	Playground	Other	CB channel monitored	Telephone no.	Mail address
		PRIVATE (CONT'D)																																						
62	B6	Bill's Trlr Pk	Fr Corner Brook, 21 mi E on TC 1	⛵ ⋀	1	12	34	68	5.00	M	5/1-10/31		U	•	U	•	•		•			•	•			•	•			•	•	•		•	I	•			709/686-2541	Rt 1, Pasadena

NW TERRITORIES

THESE CAMPGROUNDS NOT MAPPED

●—at the campground
○—within one mile of campground
$—extra charge
*—see city map
**—limited facilities during winter months
1-5—number of miles in NF within which facility or activity can be found
A—adults only
B—10,000 acres or more
C—contribution

E—tents rented
F—entrance fee or permit required—see "Special Information on the Public Areas"
H—over 9000 feet above sea level
N—no specific number, limited by size of area only
P—primitive
R—reservation required
S—self-contained units only
U—unlimited

V—trailers rented
Z—reservations accepted
LD—Labor Day
MD—Memorial Day
UC—under construction
d—boat dock
g—public golf course within 5 miles
h—horseback riding
j—whitewater running craft only
k—snow skiing within 25 miles

l—boat launch
m—area north of map
n—no drinking water
p—motor bikes prohibited
r—boat rental
s—stream, lake or creek water only
t—tennis
u—snowmobile trails
w—open certain off-season weekends and holidays

y—drinking water must be boiled
⚓ access to ocean
⚓ access to lake
≈ access to river
⋀ mountainous terrain
♆ prairie land
♆ desert area
♀ heavily wooded
⊥ urban area
⊥ rural area

CREDIT CARD SYMBOLS:
A—American Express
M—Master Charge
V—Visa/Bank Americard

FEES REFLECT MINIMUM RATE FOR 2 ADULTS AND ARE SUBJECT TO SEASONAL CHANGES

Park number	Map reference	Name of park	Access	Physical environment	Elevation	Acres	Number of tent spaces	Number of trailer spaces	Approximate fee	Credit cards accepted	Season	Telephone no.	Mail address
		DIVISION OF TOURISM											
		NW Territories Campsites										403/873-7200	Travel Arctic, Yellowknife
1	M	NWT-Alberta Border CS	Hwy 1 (Alta Hwy 35) to border info centre, 1500 ft on gravel rd		1	33	6	6	F		5/15-9/30		Enterprise
1	M	Whittaker Falls	Fr Enterprise, 152 mi W on Hwy 1		1	882	5	N	F		5/15-9/30		Ft Simpson
1	M	Fort Providence	Fr Enterprise, 62 mi NW on Hwy 1, 19 mi N on Hwy 3, 1.5 mi NW on Ft Providence access rd		1	24	14	14	F		5/15-9/30		Ft Providence
1	M	Fort Smith	Fr Ft Smith, S on Hwy 5, 1/2 mi on Airport rd to CG		1	86	9	9	F		5/15-9/30		Ft Smith
1	M	Reid Lake	Fr Yellowknife, 40 mi E on Hwy 4		1	2680	20	7	F		5/15-9/30		Yellowknife
1	M	Louise Falls	Fr Enterprise, 5 mi S on Hwy 1 to mi 46.5, 3/10 mi on gravel rd		1	181	9	9	F		5/15-9/30		Enterprise
1	M	Little Buffalo Falls	Fr Hwy River, 133 mi SE on Hwy 5		1	81	5	N	F		5/15-9/30		Fort Smith
1	M	Prelude Lake	Fr Yellowknife, E on Hwy 4 to mi 18.5		1	85	20	3	F		5/15-9/30		Yellowknife
1	M	Sylvia Grinnel	At Frobisher Bay on Baffin Island		1	366	10		F		6/1-9/1		Frobisher Bay
1	M	Hay River (Vale Island)	Fr Enterprise, 27 mi N on Hwy 2, across channel into Old Town		1	35	11	11	F		5/15-9/30		Hay River
1	M	Pitsutinu Tugavik	At Pangnirtung on Baffin Island		1	10	8		F		6/1-9/1		Pangnirtara
1	M	Lady Evelyn Falls	Fr Enterprise, 50 mi NW on Hwy 1 to mi 105.4, 4 mi S		1	12	N	9	F		5/1-9/30		Ft Providence
1	M	Galena	At Pine Point		1	30	6	6	F		5/15-9/30		Pine Pt
1	M	Yellowknife CG	Fr Yellowknife, 3 mi W on Hwy 3 to mi 212.5		1	41	30	13	F		5/15-9/30		Yellowknife
1	M	Fort Simpson CG	Fr Fort Simpson, 1 mi S on Hwy 1; 172 mi NW of jct Hwy 3			42	15	18	F		6/1-9/15		Fort Simpson
1	M	Inuvik Territorial Pk	Fr Inuvik, 3 mi Sl Pk		1	45	5		F		6/1-10/15		Inuvik
1	M	Edzo CG	Fr Yellowknife, 68 mi W on Hwy 3 to Edzo townsite, mi 150		1	3	7	3	F		5/15-9/30		Edzo
1	M	Norman Wells Territorial	Fr Norman Wells, 2 mi Sl Pk		1	10	10		F		5/20-10/15		Norman Wells
		NATIONAL PARKS											
		Wood Buffalo NP				B						403/872-2349	Box 750, Fort Smith
10	m	Pine Lake CG	Fr Ft Smith, 40 mi S on Pk Rd		1		P14	P14	3.00		5/15-10/15		Fort Smith
		Auyuittuq											
11	M	Overlord	Access by plane or boat only			B	12				6/1-8/31	819/437-9962	Pangnirtung
		PRIVATE											
50	m	Paradise Gardens & CG	Fr Enterprise, 8 mi NE on Hwy 2	≈ ♀	1	5	5	15	3.00		5/1-10/30		Box 939, Hay River

Name of park	Time limit	Reservations	Pets permitted	Max. trailer size	Electric hookup	Water hookup	Sewer hookup	Sanitary station	Bottled gas	Air conditioning	Tables	Firewood	Pull-thru spaces	Rec. hall	Flush toilets	Showers	Ice	Auto. laundry	Cafe-snack bar	Store	Swimming pool	Other swimming	Fishing	Boating	Playground	Other	CB channel monitored
NWT-Alberta Border CS	14		●	U							●	●											○	l			
Whittaker Falls	14		●	U							●	●											●			js	
Fort Providence	14		●	U				●			●	●	●				○	○	○	○	○		○	lr			
Fort Smith	14		●	U				●	○		●	●	●			○	○	○	○	○	○		○	l		g	
Reid Lake	14		●	U							●	●										●	●	dl			
Louise Falls	14		●	U							●	●	●										●				
Little Buffalo Falls	14		●	U							●	●														js	
Prelude Lake	14		●	U							●	●					○		○	○		●	●	dlr	●		
Sylvia Grinnel	14		●								●	●							○	○			●				
Hay River (Vale Island)	14		●	U					○		●	●	●				○	○	○	○		●	○	l			
Pitsutinu Tugavik	14		●								●								○	○			○			k	
Lady Evelyn Falls	14		●	U							●	●										●	●			s	
Galena	14		●	U							●	●					○	○	○	○						g	
Yellowknife CG	14		●	U				●	○		●	●	●		●		○	○	○	○		●	○	l		g	
Fort Simpson CG	14		●	U				●	○		●	●	●				○	○	○	○		●	●	l			
Inuvik Territorial Pk	14		●								●	●														k	
Edzo CG	14		●	U							●	●															
Norman Wells Territorial	14		●								●	●											○				
Pine Lake CG	15		●	U							●	●										●	●	l		ps	
Overlord			●								●	●															
Paradise Gardens & CG	U	Z	●	U	$			●			●	●				●	●					●	●	l		p	

NOVA SCOTIA

FOR MAP, SEE PAGE 115

●—at the campground
○—within one mile of campground
$—extra charge
*—see city map
**—limited facilities during winter months
1-5—number of miles in NF within which facility or activity can be found
A—adults only
B—10,000 acres or more
C—contribution

E—tents rented
F—entrance fee or permit required—see "Special Information on the Public Areas"
H—over 9000 feet above sea level
N—no specific number, limited by size of area only
P—primitive
R—reservation required
S—self-contained units only
U—unlimited

V—trailers rented
Z—reservations accepted
LD—Labor Day
MD—Memorial Day
UC—under construction
d—boat dock
g—public golf course within 5 miles
h—horseback riding
j—whitewater running craft only
k—snow skiing within 25 miles

l—boat launch
m—area north of map
n—no drinking water
p—motor bikes prohibited
r—boat rental
s—stream, lake or creek water only
t—tennis
u—snowmobile trails
w—open certain off-season weekends and holidays

y—drinking water must be boiled
⚓ access to ocean
⛵ access to lake
≈ access to river
ʌ mountainous terrain
ѱ prairie land
℘ desert area
♀ heavily wooded
▙ urban area
⅄ rural area

CREDIT CARD SYMBOLS:
A—American Express
M—Master Charge
V—Visa/Bank Americard

FEES REFLECT MINIMUM RATE FOR 2 ADULTS AND ARE SUBJECT TO SEASONAL CHANGES

Park number	Map reference	Name of park	Access	Physical environment	Elevation	Acres	Number of tent spaces	Number of trailer spaces	Approximate fee	Credit cards accepted	Season	Time limit / Reservations / Pets permitted / Max. trailer size	Electric hookup / Water hookup / Sewer hookup	Sanitary station / Bottled gas / Air conditioning	Tables / Firewood / Pull-thru spaces / Rec. hall	Flush toilets / Showers / Ice	Auto. laundry / Cafe-snack bar / Store	Swimming pool / Other swimming / Fishing	Boating / Playground / Other	CB channel monitored	Telephone no.	Mail address
		PROVINCIAL PARKS																				
1	E5	Laurie	Fr Waverly, N on Hwy 2 to Grand Lake			71	71	71	4.00		5/18-9/4	14 • 25		•	• •		o				902/861-2560	Waverly
2	F3	The Islands	Fr Shelburne, 1/4 mi W on Hwy 3, 1/2 mi S		0	62	70	70	4.00		5/18-9/4	14 • 25		•	• •		o				902/742-4196	Shelburne
3	D5	Wentworth	Fr Amherst, 50 mi E on TC 104 to Wentworth			243	51	51	4.00		5/18-9/4	14 • 25		•	• •		o				902/895-1591	Oxford
4	D5	Salt Springs	Fr Truro, 24 mi E on TC 104		1	76	50	50	4.00		5/18-9/4	14 • 25		•	• •		o o				902/863-4513	New Glasgow
5	D6	Whycocomagh	Fr Whycocomagh, 2 mi E on TC 5/105			503	160	160	4.00		5/18-9/4	14 • 25		•	• •		o o				902/295-2554	Baddeck
6	E4	Graves Island	Fr Chester, 2 mi E off Hwy 3, 1/4 mi S		0	123	64	64	4.00		5/18-9/4	14 • 25		•	• •						902/543-8167	Bridgewater
7	D5	Caribou	Fr Pictou, 5 mi N on Hwy 106, E on access			78	78	77	4.00		5/18-9/4	14 • 25		•	• •			•			902/863-4513	New Glasgow
8	E4	Smiley's	Fr Windsor, 13 mi E on Hwy 14, 1/2 mi S			100	84	103	4.00		5/18-9/4	14 • 25		•	• •		o				902/861-2560	Windsor
9	D6	Boylston	Fr Guysborough, 3 mi N on Hwy 16			225	35	35	4.00		5/18-9/4	14 • 25			• •						902/863-4513	Guysborough
10	E4	Five Islands	Fr Parksboro, 15 mi E on Hwy 2		0	1020	90	90	4.00		5/18-9/4	14 • 25		•	• •		o				902/895-1591	Truro
11	E5	Porter's Lake	Fr Dartmouth, 15 mi E on Hwy 7, 3 mi S		0	216	165	165	4.00		5/18-9/4	14 • 25		•	• •						902/861-2560	Waverley
12	D7	Mira River	Fr Sydney, 13 mi SE on Hwy 22 & rd to Mira		0	216	141	141	4.00		5/18-9/4	14 • 25		•	• •						902/564-6389	Sydney
13	F3	Ellenwood Lake	Fr Yarmouth, 10 mi NE on Hwys 1 & 340			281	98	55	4.00		5/18-9/4	14 • 25		•	• •		o	•			902/742-4196	Yarmouth
14	E3	Valley View	Fr Bridgetown, 3 mi N			134	30	30	4.00		5/18-9/4	14 • 25		•	• •						902/584-3383	Lawrencetown
15	D7	Battery	Nr St Peters, off Hwy 4			114	55	45	4.00		5/18-9/4	14 • 25		•	• •						902/564-6389	St Peters
16	D6	Beaver Mountain Pk	Off TC 104, at Beaver Meadow, bet New Glasgow & Antigonish			329	45	45	4.00		5/18-9/4	14 • 25			• •						902/863-4513	Antigonish
17	E4	Blomidon Pk	Fr Blomidon, 5 mi N off Hwy 358		1	1718	70	70	4.00		5/18-9/4	14 • 25		•	• •						902/584-3833	Lawrencetown
18	F4	Risser's Beach Pk	Fr Bridgewater, 16 mi S on Hwy 331			181	90	54	4.00		5/18-9/4	14 • 25			• • •	• •	•	•			902/543-8167	Bridgewater
19	E6	Salsman Pk	Fr Goshen, 8 mi S on Hwy 316		1	26	15	15	4.00		5/18-9/4	14 • 25			•						902/533-3503	Box 50, Guysborough
		NATIONAL PARKS																				
		Cape Breton Highlands NP				B															902/285-2270	
20	C7	Big Intervale	Fr Cape North Vil, 7 mi W on Cabot Trail		1	1	10	10	F3.00		5/15-10/15	14 •			• •			o o	•			Ingonish Beach
20	C7	Macintosh Brook	Fr Pleasant Bay Vil, 2 mi E on Cabot Trail		1	4	20	20	F3.00		All year	14 •			• •	•		o o	•			Ingonish Beach
21	C7	Black Brook	Fr Ingonish Bch Pk entr, 12.6 mi N on Cabot Trail		1	100	187	187	F3.00		6/15-9/15	14 •		•	• •	•		o o	l			Ingonish Beach
21	C7	Broad Cove	Fr Ingonish Bch Pk Entr, 7 mi N on Cabot Trail		1	65	198	83	F6.00		5/15-10/15	14 •	• • •		• •	•$ o	• o o	o o	l • g			Ingonish Beach
22	C7	Ingonish Beach	Fr Ingonish Bch pk entr, 1 mi N on Cabot Trail		1	8	99	99	F3.00		6/15-9/15	14 •			• •	•$ o	• o o	o o	l • g			Ingonish Beach
23	C6	Cheticamp	At Cheticamp Pk entr on Cabot Trail		0	75	220	124	F6.00		5/15-10/15	14 • U	• • •	•	• •	•$	o o	o o	•			Ingonish Beach
23	C6	Corney Brook	Fr Cheticamp entr, 6 mi N on Cabot Trail		0	4	20	20	F3.00		5/15-10/15	14 •			• •	•		o o	•			Ingonish Beach
		Kejimkujik NP	(For additional CG's see 'Backpack or Boat Access Areas')			B																
24	E4	Jeremy Bay CG	Fr Maitland Bridge, 6 mi SW on access rd off Hwy 8		1	500	329	329	F3.00		5/19-10/9**	14 • 30		• o	• • •	•$ o	o o	• $	dlr • p		902/242-2770	PO Bx 36, Maitland Bridge
		BACKPACK OR BOAT ACCESS AREAS																				
24	E4	Kejimkujik NP Wildrnss CS	Fr Maitland Bridge, 1 mi SW on access rd off Hwy 8		1	B	101		None		All year	U •			• •			• $	psu		902/242-2770	PO Box 36,Maitland Bridge
		CITY, COUNTY & CIVIC																				
27	E5	Shubie Park	Fr Dartmouth, 1.7 mi N on Rt 18	⛵ ▙	1	30	28	S34	6.00		5/15-9/15	7 Z • U	•	•	• •	• • o	• o	• •	dl • tp		902/435-3346	PO Box 817, Dartmouth
28	D7	Stone Wall	Fr Louisburg, 5 mi N on Hwy 22	⛵ ⅄		50	40	30	5.50		5/15-10/15	U Z • U	• $ $	• •	• • •	• • •	• •	• •	dr		902/733-2058	RR 1, Louisburg
29	D6	Steeltown Centennial Pk	In Trenton	⛵ ♀		600	56	56	5.00		6/20-9/6	U • U			• •	• •	o • o		• g			Main St, Trenton
31	D4	Glooscap Municipal	3 mi fr Center of Parrsboro	⚓ ▙	1	40	35	34	3.50		6/15-9/15	U Z • U	$ $ $	•	• • • •	• •	•	• •	r • gp		902/254-2529	Parrsboro
		PRIVATE																				
34	C7	Smokey Ridge Pk	At Ingonish Harbor, off Cabot Trail	≈ ʌ	1	90	100	100	7.00		6/10-9/15	U Z • U	• • •	• o •	• $ • •	• • •	• o •	• •	• ghp		902/285-2327	Ingonish Beach
35	E4	Holiday Haven Cmpg Pk	Fr Hwy 101, 1 mi S	ʌ ⅄		75	40	200	6.00		5/24-9/1	U • U	• • $	• o $	• $ • •	• $ •	• •	•	• ghpt			Box 91, Kingston Kings Co
37	E4	Bar-S CS	Fr Halifax, 40 mi NW on Hwy 101	≈ ♀		28	40	40	6.00		5/1-10/15	U Z • U	$ •	• o	• • •	• • •	• •	• •	• p		902/757-3372	Scotch Village, Hants Co
39	D5	Birchwood	Fr Pictou Rotary, 3 mi on Hwy 376	⛵ ⅄		10	10	12	4.00		6/1-9/30	U Z • U	• •	o	• • •	• $ o	o o	o			902/485-4660	RR 2, Pictou
39	D5	D & B Trlr Pk & CS	In New Glasgow& CS	⚓ ʌ	0	30	10	65	6.00		6/15-9/15	U Z • U	• • $	• $	• $ •	• • •	• o •	•	l • gp		902/752-3621	Box 622, New Glasgow
39	D5	Forbes' CG	Fr New Glasgow, 8 mi E on Hwy 289 to Little Harbor	⚓ ⅄		30	28	56	6.00		6/15-9/11	U Z • 28	$ $ $	• •	• $ • •	• $ •	• • •	• •	• p		902/752-3631	New Glasgow
40	E4	Pine Grove Cabins & CG	Fr jct Hwys 1/101, 1/10 mi W	≈ ▙	1	4	60	52	6.50		5/1-11/30	U Z • U	• • $	•	• • •	• • •	• o •	• o	•		902/678-3868	Box 455, Kentville
40	E4	Palmeter's Tent & Trlr Pk	Fr Kentville, 2 mi W on RR 1	≈ ⅄	0	40		60	6.50		5/15-10/15	U Z • U	• • •	• $	• $	• $	•	•	• g			655 Park St, Kentville
40	E4	Camelot Camping Pk	Fr Hwy 1, 3/4 mi S on Canaan Ave in Kentville	≈ ▙	1	150	70	50	6.50		5/15-10/15	U Z • U	• •	• o $	• $ • •	• • •	• • o	• • •	• gp		902/678-3343	Box 343, Kentville
40	F4	The Plantation	Fr Hwy 101, ext 15, 2 mi N	⅄	1	31	30	200	4.50		5/12-10/15	U Z • 28	$ • $	• •	• $ • •	• $ •	• • •	•	r •		902/538-3634	Box 453, Berwick
41	E3	Dunromin CS	Fr Annapolis, 1 1/2 mi E on Hwy 1, E of Causeway	≈ ʌ	1	30	103	32	5.50		4/1-10/15	U Z • U	• • •	• •	• $ • •	• • •	• o •	• •	dlr •		902/532-2808	Granville Ferry
42	F3	Shatfords Trlr & Camping	Fr Yarmouth, 2 mi N on Hwy 1	⚓ ⅄	0	4	20	12	4.50	AMV	5/1-10/1	U • U	$ • $	•	• • •	• $	o • o	•			902/742-7157	Box 1020 RR 1 N, Yarmouth
42	F3	Doctor Lk Camping Pk	Fr Yarmouth, 2-1/2 mi N on Hwy 1	⛵ ⅄	1	22	32	58	4.50		5/1-10/30	U Z • U	$ $ $	•	• $ • •	• $ •	o o	• •	dlr • gp		902/742-8442	Bx 1040 RR 1, Yarmouth
42	F3	Loomer's Camper's Haven	Fr Yarmouth, 3 mi E on Hwy 3 in Arcadia	⛵ ♀	1	60	85	165	7.00		5/15-10/15	U Z • U	• • •	• •	• $ • •	• • •	• • •	• •	dlr •	5	902/742-4848	Rt 4, Yarmouth
43	D7	Inlet CGs	Fr Baddeck, 5 mi W on TC 105, ent to Cabot Trail	⛵ ʌ		40	47	47	4.50		6/1-10/30	U Z • U	$ $	• •	•	• $ •	• •	• o o	• gt	11	902/295-2417	Bx 292, Baddeck
47	E3	Fundy Spray Trlr Pk & CG	Fr Digby, 2 mi E on Hwy 217, 1-3/4 mi E on Hwy 101, 1/4 mi on Hwy 1-Smith's Cove	⚓ ⅄	1	10	32	53	5.50		4/15-9/30	U Z • U	$ • $	• • $	• $ • •	• • •	• o •	• o	• g	11	902/245-4884	Box 74, Digby
48	E4	Red Arrow-Wayside Camping	Fr Upper Tantallon, Hwy 333 to Glen Margaret, on Peggy's Cove Rd	⚓ ♀	1	200	70	80	6.00	V	All year	U Z • U	$ $ $	• •	• • •	• • •	• o •	• •	lr •	4	902/823-2271	Glen Margaret
49	E4	Hubbard's Bch	Fr Halifax, 28 mi W on Hwy 103, ext 6, 1.5 mi fr jct Hwy 103/3	⚓ ⅄	1	10	60	40	4.50		5/15-10/15	U • 30	$ • $	•	• $	• $ •	• • o	• •	dlr •			Hubbards Beach
50	D6	Glenview Trlr Pk	Fr TC 105, 1/5 mi N on Hwy 252	≈ ʌ	1	10	30	64	5.00		5/15-10/15	U Z • 32	$ $ $	• o $	• $ •	• $ •	• o •	• • •	l • p	1	902/756-2867	Box 70, Whycocomagh
51	F4	Zinck's Trlr Pk	Fr Bridgewater, 10 mi E on Hwy 332, at E La Have	⚓ ⅄	1	2	15	14	5.00		6/1-9/30	28 R • 14	• $ •	• •	• •	• •	•	• •	lr • p		902/766-4862	Rt 3, Bridgewater
52	E3	Marshalltown CG	Fr Hwy 101, Digby ext W 1/2 mi, 1 mi S at rr underpass	ʌ ⅄	1	100	20	30	5.50		5/15-9/15	U Z • U	• •	• o •	• $ •	• • •		$	g	11	902/245-2050	RR 2, Digby

NOVA SCOTIA

FOR FOOTNOTE EXPLANATION SEE FIRST PAGE OF THIS **PROVINCE** FOR MAP, SEE PAGE **115**

Park number	Map reference	Name of park	Access	Physical environment	Elevation	Acres	Number of tent spaces	Number of trailer spaces	Approximate fee	Credit cards accepted	Season	Time limit / Reservations / Pets permitted / Max. trailer size	Electric hookup / Water hookup / Sewer hookup	Sanitary station / Bottled gas / Air conditioning	Tables / Firewood / Pull-thru spaces / Rec. hall	Flush toilets / Showers / Ice	Auto. laundry / Cafe-snack bar / Store	Swimming pool / Other swimming / Fishing	Boating / Playground	Other	CB channel monitored	Telephone no.	Mail address
		PRIVATE (CONT'D)																					
53	D6	Mason's Heath-Ty CG	Fr New Glasgow, 7 mi E on TC 104, 6-1/2 mi N on Hwy 245	⚓	⋀		28	100	68	4.50		5/15-10/1	U Z • U	$ $ $	ᴗ	• • • •	•$ •	•	• •	lr •			902/926-2488	Box 9, Merigomish
53	D6	Merry-Go-Park CG	Fr New Glasgow, 7 mi E on TC 104, 4 mi NE on Hwy 245	⚓	⊥	1	40	35	25	5.00		6/24-10/1	U Z • U	$ •	•	• • •	•$ •	• •	• o		p		902/926-2059	Merigomish
61	D7	Driftwood Tent & Trlr Pk	Fr Bras d'Or (Hwy 105), 1-1/2 mi W on George Riv Hwy	⛵	⊥	0	4	30	20	6.00		6/20-9/30	U Z • 31	$ $ $	•	• • •	•$ •	o	• •	dl •				Box 222, N Sidney
66	E5	Sunset Camps	Fr Sheet Harbour, 7 mi N on East River	⛵	⊥	1	12	20	25	3.50		5/1-9/30	U Z • U	$ $ $	•	•$ •	•$ •	• •	• •	lr •	p		902/885-2534	Sheet Harbour
68	D6	A E Whidden Trlr Ct	In Antigonish, W end of Main St (Hwys 4, 7 & 245)	≈	◢	1	15	100	100	6.50		All year	U • U	• • •	• •	• • •	• • •	• o o		•	gp		902/863-3736	Box 1744, Antigonish
68	D6	Farm View Camp & Trlr Pk	Fr Antigonish, 2 mi W off Hwy 104	≈	⋀	1	30	20	20	6.00		6/1-9/15	U Z • U	• • •	• o $	• • •	• • •	•	o o	•	g	7	902/863-6747	RR 2, Antigonish
70	D5	Harbour Light Trlr Ct	Fr Traffic Circle, Pictou ext, 2 mi E	⚓	⊥	1	20	75	75	6.50		6/1-10/15	U • U	$ $ $	• •	• •	•$ •	o o	•	•			902/485-5733	Braeshore, RR 1, Pictou
72	F3	La foret du Voyageur CG	Fr Digby, 28 mi S on Hwy 1, 8 mi E on Patria Comeau Rd	⛵	⚲	1	70	E50	V65	6.50	V	All year	U Z • 30	• •	• •	•$ •	•$ •	• • •	• • •	dlr •	ghkp	13	902/769-3477	Box 36, Saulnierville DigbyCo
72	F3	Belle Baie Pk Ltd	Fr Digby, 26 mi S on Rt 1	⚓		1	35	10	35	6.00		5/20-9/15	U Z • U	• •	•	• • •	• • •	• • o	• • •	•	g		902/769-3160	Church Pt RR 1, Digby Co
77	D5	Campers Villa	Fr Glenholme, 3 mi N on TC 104	⊥		1	45	24	122	6.00		5/1-10/15	U Z • U	• •	• •	•$ • •	• • •	• • •	•	•	t		902/662-3086	RR 1, Dabert
79	E6	Dolphin Tent & Trlr Pk	Fr Sheet Harbour, 8 mi E on Hwy 7	⚓	⊥		3	17	10	3.50		6/15-10/5	U Z • 30	$ $ $		•$	•$ •	• o	• •	•			902/654-2479	Port Dufferin
79	E6	Ocean View Tent & Trlr Pk	Fr Sheet Harbour, 7 mi E on Hwy 7	⚓	⊥	0	8	19	16	3.50		6/15-9/30	U Z • U	• •	•	• • •	•$ •	• o	• •	l •			902/654-2910	Beaver Harbor
80	F4	Lakeland Retreats KOA	Fr Hwy 103 at Bridgeport, ext 13, 4 mi NW on Hwy 325, W on Hwy 210 to Labelle Rd	⛵	⚲	1	70	60	V73	6.25	V	All year	U Z • U	$ •$	• •	•$ • •	• • •	• • •	• •	dl •	hp	12	902/685-2222	Site 1, Bx 1, RR 1,Greenfield
80	F4	Ponhook Lodge Trlr Pk	Fr Bridgewater, 20 mi W on Hwy 210	⛵	⚲	1	50	45	75	7.00		5/1-9/15	U Z • U	• • •	•	•$ •	• • •	• •	• •	dlr •	p		902/685-2346	Greenfield
82	D6	MacLean's Riverside Camp	Hwy 19, Strathlorne Camp	≈	⊥		6	20	22	6.00		6/1-10/1	U Z • U	• • •	•	•$	•$ •	•	•	•	p		902/258-2448	Church St, Box 338, Inverness
82	D6	Trout Riv Trlr Pk&Cottage	Fr Whycocomagh, 12 mi N on Rt 395	⛵	⋀	1	2	5	20	4.50		5/1-10/30	U Z • U	• • •	o	• •		o o	• •	dlr •	hp	4	902/258-2391	RR 1, Whycocomagh
83	D5	Nuttby Mountain CG	Fr Truro, 12 mi NE on Hwy 311	≈	⋀	2	75	25	30	4.50		6/1-9/15	U Z • U	$ •	• o	• • • •	• •	•	• •	•	p		902/893-3540	RR 6 Col Co, Nuttby
83	D5	Elm River Pk	Fr Truro, 10 mi W on TC 104	≈	⊥	0	10	50	150	5.50	A	5/15-10/30	U Z • U	• •$	• •	•$ • •	•$ •	• o •	• •	•			902/662-3162	RR 1 Debert Col Co
84	D6	MacLeod's Beach CS	Fr Inverness, 7 mi N on Hwy 19	⚓	⊥	0	100	120	100	5.00		6/15-10/20	U Z • U	$ • •	• •	•$ • •	•$ •	• •	• •	•	p		902/258-2433	RR 1, Inverness
84	D6	Cameron's CG	Fr Hwy 19, 1/2 mi on Sight Pt Rd, in Inverness	⚓	◢	1	50	50	40	4.50		6/15-9/30	U Z • U	$ •$	• o	•$ • •	•$ •	o o	• o	dl •	p		902/258-2886	Banks Rd, Inverness
85	E5	Green Acres	Fr Hwy 215 N, ext 10, 1/2 mi of Hwy 102	≈	⊥	1	53	50	95	6.00		5/1-10/1	U Z • U	$ •$	• •	•$ • •	•$ •	• • •	• •	•	p	11	902/758-2177	RR 4, Shubenacadie
86	D7	Spruce Point Pk	Fr Hwy 125, Marion Brdg ext, S on Hwy 327 to Hillside Rd, 3 mi E	≈	⚲	1	150	60	60	6.00		6/1-9/10	U Z • U	$ $ $	•	•$ • •	•$ •	• o •	• •	dlr •	p		902/727-2981	Box 16, Marion Bridge
89	D5	Searidge Camp	Fr Amherst, 16 mi E to Shinimicas Brdg, 5 mi N, 1 mi E	⚓	⋎	1	25	45	50	6.00		6/1-9/1	U Z • U	$ $ $	•	•$ • •	•$ •	• o •	• •	l •	gp			Northport
90	D5	Brule Bch Rsrt	Fr Tatamagouche, 7 mi E on Hwy 6	⚓	⊥	0	50	75	V52	6.50		6/8-9/9	U Z • U	• •	• • $	•$ • •	•$ •	o •	•	r •	gp		902/657-2450	Bx 261, Tatamagouche
96	D5	Harbour View Tent & Trlr	Fr Amherst, 50 mi E on Hwy 6, at Wallace	⚓	⊥	1	15	25	10	5.00		6/1-10/31	U Z • 30	• •	• •	•$ •	• •	•	•	dl •	p			Box 176, Wallace
98	E4	Sherwood Forest Cmpg Pk	Fr Kentville, 4 mi W on Hwy 1	⚓	⊥		200	50	210	5.50		5/15-10/15	U Z • U	• • •	• •	• • • •	• • •	• • •	• • •	•	g		902/678-7477	RR 1 Kentville,Colbrk Kngs Co
98	E4	O Q Mtl & CG	Hwy 1 in Middleton	≈	◢	1	5	30	17	5.50	M	5/1-9/31	U Z • 31	• • •	• o	• • •	• • •	• o o	• o	•	ghp		902/825-4801	Main St Box 249, Middleton
98	E4	White's Tent & Trlr Park	Fr Middleton, 1 mi E on Hwy 1	≈	⋀	0	20	E20	20	5.00		4/1-10/30	U Z • U	$ • •	• o	• • •	•$ •	o o •	• •	l •			902/825-4380	Wilmot
100	D4	Sand Point Pk	Fr Parrsboro, 15 mi E on Hwy 2 to Five Islands	⚓	⊥	0	20	40	72	5.50		5/1-9/30	U Z • U	$ $	• •	•$ • •	•$ •	• • o	• •	dl •	p	23	902/254-2755	Five Islands Col Co NS
100	D4	Shea's Trlr Ct & CGs	Fr Parrsboro, 12 mi E on Hwy 2 to Five Islands	⚓	⊥		3	E7	16	5.50		5/15-10/15	U Z • U	• • •	• o	• •	• • o	o o	• •	l •			902/254-2839	Lower Five Islands, Col Co
109	E5	Playland Camping Pk	Fr Hwy 102, ext 12 or 13	⚲	⊥	1	160	45	75	5.50		6/1-9/30	14 Z • U	$ $	•	•$ •	•$ •	• •	•	•	p		902/893-3666	RR 1 Brookfield
111	D7	Fraser's Trlr Pk & CS	Fr Baddeck, 4 mi W on T/C 105	⛵	⊥	0	22	33	56	3.50		5/15-11/30	U Z • U	$ $ $	• •	•$ •	• • •	• • •	• • •	dlr •		11	902/295-2329	PO Box 4, Baddeck
111	D7	Baddeck-Cabot Trail KOA	Fr Baddeck, 5 mi W on TC 105	⛵	⋀		140	60	90	6.50		5/15-10/15	U Z • U	$ $ $	• •	•$ • •	• • •	• • •	• • •	lr •			902/295-2288	Box 417 Baddeck
116	D4	Gateway Parklands	Fr Hwy 104, E on Ft Lawrence Rd 500 yds	⊥		1	57	50	50	5.50		6/20-9/10	U Z • U	• •$	•	• • •	• • •	• o •	•	•	g		902/667-8436	Bx 521 Amherst
116	D4	Riverside Trlr Ct	Fr Amherst, 3 mi N on Hwy 6, 13 mi on Hwy 366	≈	⚲		50	100	200	5.50		6/1-11/1	U Z • U	• •$	•	• • •	•$ •	• •	• •	dlr •		11	902/538-2839	RR 2 Rt 366, Amherst
116	D4	The Barrel Trlr Pk	Fr TC 104, S Albion St ext, 1/2 mi on Hwy 2; in Amherst	⚓	◢	1	2	15	25	5.50		5/1-10/15	U Z • U	• • •	• •	• •	• • •	• o o	o	•			902/667-2040	Box 452, Amherst
116	D4	Loch Lomond T & T Pk	Fr Amherst, 1 mi S on Hwy 2	⚓	⋀		20	50	50	5.50		5/15-10/15	U Z • U	• •$	• o	•$ •	•$	• o o	• •	dl •	gp		902/667-9036	Amherst
119	D7	Seal Island Tent&Trlr Pk	Fr Baddeck, 22 mi toward N Sidney, on TC 105 & New Harris Rd at Seal Is Bridge	⚓	⋀	0	100	50	100	5.50		5/15-10/15	U Z • U	$ $	• • $	•$ • •	•$ •	• o •	• • •	dlr •	p	18	902/674-2145	New Harris Rd RR 1 Bras D'Or
119	D7	Mtn View by the Sea	Fr Sydney, 20 mi NW on T.C. 105, NE 4 mi on Hwy 5	⚓	⋀	1	16	E10	V10	4.50		All year	U Z • U	$ $ $	•	•$ •	• • •	• •	• •	dl •	kp		902/674-2384	RR 1, Big Bras d'Or
126	D6	MacQueen's Trlr Ct	In Whycocomagh, on Hwy 105	⛵	⋀		5	10	32	5.50		5/24-11/15	U Z • U	• • •	•	• •	• •		• •	dl •	p		902/756-2443	Box 125, Whycocomagh
130	D5	Gulf Shore Camping Pk	Fr Amherst, 30 mi E on Hwy 6 to Pugwash, 7 mi NE on Gulf Shore Rd	⚓	⊥	0	225	40	50	4.25		6/15-9/7	U Z • U	$ •	•	• • •	• •	•	•	l •	gp	19	902/243-2489	RR 4, Pugwash
130	D5	Hillcrest CG	Fr Amherst, 30 mi E on Hwy 6 (S of Pugwash)	⊥		1	6	20	15	3.50	V	6/15-9/30	U Z • U	• •	o o	•$ •	• • •	•			p	1	902/243-2727	Box 264, Pugwash
132	D6	Sea Breeze Camp & Trlr Pk	Fr Canso, 7 mi W on Hwy 16	⚓	⊥	1	30	25	40	6.00		All year	U Z • U	$ $ $	• $	•$ •	•$ •	• •	• •	lr •			902/366-2352	Bx 142, Canso
133	E3	Champlain Tent & Trlr Pk	Fr Digby, 20 mi SW on Hwy 217	⚓	⊥	1	70	30	72	6.50		5/15-10/15	U Z • U	• •	•	•$ •	• • •	• • •	• o •	dl •	gt		902/834-2594	Digby County, Sandy Cove
134	E5	Woodhaven Pk	Fr Halifax, 7 mi N on TC 102, ext 3, 4 mi W on Hwy 213	⊥		1	25	25	75	5.50		6/1-9/30	U Z • U	$ $ $	•	•$ • •	•$ •	• •		•	gp		902/835-2271	70 Lorne Ave, Dartmouth
134	E5	Haverstock's CG	Fr Halifax, 6 mi N on Hwy 102, 3 mi W on Hwy 213, ext 3	⛵	⊥	1	4	24	28	5.50		5/15-10/15	U Z • U	$ •$	•	•$ •	• • •	•		•	gp		902/835-2562	Bedford, RR 1, RSB 60
134	E5	Smith Campground	Fr Halifax, 7 mi N on Hwy 1 to Bedford	⚓	⊥	0	2	50	30	5.00		5/1-11/30	14 • U	•		• •	• •	o •	•	•	gp		902/835-9027	RR 2, Bedford
135	C7	Arm of Gold CG & Trlr Pk	In Cape Breton & Trlr Pk	≈	⊥	1	35	47	56	5.00		5/15-10/15	U Z • U	• •$	• o	•$ • •	•	• •	•	•	gp		902/736-6516	Bras d'Or, Cape Breton
136	F3	Kiwanis Kampers Kourt	In St Bernard, 1 mi off Hwy 1	⛵	⚲	1	8	8	22	5.00		5/20-10/15	U Z • U	• •		•$ •	• • •	•	• •	l •			902/837-4331	Box 24, Weymouth

ONTARIO

FOR MAP, SEE PAGE 118

- ●—at the campground
- ○—within one mile of campground
- $—extra charge
- *—see city map
- **—limited facilities during winter months
- 1-5—number of miles in NF within which facility or activity can be found
- A—adults only
- B—10,000 acres or more
- C—contribution
- E—tents rented
- F—entrance fee or permit required—see "Special Information on the Public Areas"
- H—over 9000 feet above sea level
- N—no specific number, limited by size of area only
- P—primitive
- R—reservation required
- S—self-contained units only
- U—unlimited
- V—trailers rented
- Z—reservations accepted
- LD—Labor Day
- MD—Memorial Day
- UC—under construction
- d—boat dock
- g—public golf course within 5 miles
- h—horseback riding
- j—whitewater running craft only
- k—snow skiing within 25 miles
- l—boat launch
- m—area north of map
- n—no drinking water
- p—motor bikes prohibited
- r—boat rental
- s—stream, lake or creek water only
- t—tennis
- u—snowmobile trails
- w—open certain off-season weekends and holidays
- y—drinking water must be boiled
- ⚓ access to ocean
- ⛵ access to lake
- ≈ access to river
- ⋀ mountainous terrain
- ¥ prairie land
- ⅌ desert area
- ♀ heavily wooded
- ▟ urban area
- ⫛ rural area

CREDIT CARD SYMBOLS:
- A—American Express
- M—Master Charge
- V—Visa/Bank Americard

FEES REFLECT MINIMUM RATE FOR 2 ADULTS AND ARE SUBJECT TO SEASONAL CHANGES

Park number	Map reference	Name of park	Access	Physical environment	Elevation	Acres	Number of tent spaces	Number of trailer spaces	Approximate fee	Credit cards accepted	Season	Time limit	Reservations	Pets permitted	Max. trailer size	Electric hookup	Water hookup	Sewer hookup	Sanitary station	Bottled gas	Air conditioning	Tables	Firewood	Pull-thru spaces	Rec. hall	Flush toilets	Showers	Ice	Auto. laundry	Cafe-snack bar	Store	Swimming pool	Other swimming	Fishing	Boating	Playground	Other	CB channel monitored	Telephone no.	Mail address
		PROVINCIAL PARKS																																						
1	B6	Silent Lk	Fr Peterborough, 50 mi N on Hwy 28		2	2000	145	S20	5.50		5/16-9/17	28		●	16				●			●	●			●	●	○	●	○	○		●	●	dr		p		613/339-2807	Bancroft
2	D3	Pinery	Fr Grand Bend, 5 mi S on Hwy 21		1	5500	913	337	7.50		All year	23		●	24	$			●			●	$			●		●	●	●	●	●	●	●	l		ghkp			Grand Bend
2	D3	Ipperwash	2 mi off Hwy 21, bet Ravenswood & Pt. Franks		1	201	200	66	7.50		5/9-9/30	23		●	24	$	●		●			●	$			●		●	●	●	●		●	●	l		g			Forest
3	D4	Selkirk	Fr Selkirk, 2 mi SW		1	160	160		5.00		5/15-9/30	28		●	U	$			●			●	●	●				○	○	○	○		●	●	l				416/776-2600	Selkirk
4	E3	Rondeau	Fr jct Hwys 3 & 21 at Morpeth, 3 mi S		1	B	261	12	7.50		All year	23		●	28	$			●			●	$			●		●	●	●	●		●	●	dl	●	ght			Morpeth
5	E2	Holiday Beach	Fr jct Hwys 18 & 18A, 2 mi S; 7 mi W of Harrow		1	201	23	23	7.50		5/9-9/30	23		●	24				●			●	●			●		●	●	●			●	●	l	●				Amherstburg
6	E4	Long Point	Fr Courtland, 23 mi S on Hwy 59		1	848	129	141	5.00		5/15-9/30	28		●	U	$			●			●	●	●		●		○	○	○	○		●	●	lr		g		519/586-2133	Port Rowan
7	E4	Turkey Point	Fr Delhi, 4 mi E on Hwy 3, 9 mi S		1	778	200		5.00		5/15-9/30	28		●	U				●			●	●			●		○	○	○	○		●	○	lr	●	g		519/426-3239	Turkey Point
8	D5	Rock Point	Fr Dunnville, 8 mi S on Haldimand Co Rd	⛵ ⫛	1	279	130		5.50		5/12-9/4	28		●	U				●	○		●	$			●	●		●				●	●					416/774-6642	Box 158, Dunnville
9	B5	Six Mile Lake	Fr Pt Severn, 8 mi N on Hwy 69	⛵ ♀	1	177	145	45	5.00		5/9-9/21	23		●	U				●			●	●					○		○	○		●	●	dl				705/686-3342	Coldwater
10	C4	Devils' Glen	Fr Collingwood, 8 mi S on Hwy 24, in Blue Mtns	⫛	2	150	20	20	5.00		5/9-9/21	23		●	U							●	●					○			○			●					705/455-3088	Collingwood
11	C4	Earl Rowe	Fr Alliston, 2 mi W on Hwy 89	⫛	2	773	241	350	5.50		5/9-9/21	28	Z	●	U	$			●			●	●	●		●		●	○	●	●		●	●		●	g		705/435-4331	Box 1063, Alliston
12	C5	Sibbald Point	Fr Sutton, 2 mi E on Hwy 48, 1/2 mi N	⛵ ♀	1	500	200	456	7.00		All year	23	Z	●	U	$			●			●	●	●		●		●		●	●		●	●	dlr	●	gku		416/722-3268	RR 2, Sutton West
13	C5	Bass Lake	Fr Orillia, 2 mi W on Hwy 12, 1/2 mi SE	⛵ ⫛	1	170	80	13	5.50		5/9-9/21	23		●	U				●	○		●	●	●		●		○	○	○	○		●	●	l	●	g		705/326-7054	Box 2178,Orillia
14	C3	MacGregor Point	Fr Port Elgin, 3 mi S on Hwy 21, 1-1/2 mi W	⛵ ♀	1	1900		142	5.50		5/8-10/20	23		●	U	$	$		●			●	●	●		●	●						●	●			g		519/832-9055	Box 539, Pt Elgin
15	C4	Craigleith	Fr Collingwood, 8 mi W on Hwy 26 nr Craigleith	⛵ ⫛	1	27	68	102	5.50		5/8-9/20	23		●	U	$			●	○		●	$	●		●				●	●		●	●	l	●	gh		705/445-4467	Collingwood
16	C3	Sauble Falls	Fr Hwy 6 in Hepworth, 9 mi W to Sauble Bch, 1 mi N	≈ ⫛	1	43	58	88	5.50		5/8-9/20	23		●	U				●			●				●								●		●			419/422-1952	Wiarton
17	C5	Darlington	Fr Oshawa, 4 mi E on Hwy 401	⛵ ⫛	1	380	258	102	5.50		5/7-10/11	23		●		$			●			●	$	●		●	$		●				●	●	dl				416/723-4341	RR 2, Bowmanville
18	C6	Presqu'ile	Fr Brighton, 3 mi S on Ontario St & access rd	⛵ ♀	1	2170	500	500	5.50		5/15-9/30	23		●					●			●	●			●		●	●		○		●	●	dl				613/475-2204	RR No 4, Brighton
19	C6	Serpent Mounds	Fr Peterborough, 7 mi E on Hwy 7, 8 mi S on Rd 10 thru Keene		1	70	113	113	3.50		5/14-10/11	28		●					●			●	$			●		○	●	○	○		●	●	dl	●			705/295-6879	RR 3, Keene
20	C5	Emily	Fr Omemee, 2 mi E on Hwy 7, 3 mi N on Co 16		1	167	193	106	5.50		5/14-10/11	23		●	U	$	●		●	○		●	$	●		●		●	○	○	●		●	●	dl				705/799-5170	RR 4, Omemee
21	B7	Fitzroy	Fr Hwy 17, NW thru Galetta to Fitzroy Harbor, 2 mi N		1	486	251	150	5.00		5/12-9/16w	28		●	26				●			●	●			●		○			○		●	●	dl	●			613/623-5159	Fitzroy Harbour
22	B7	Silver Lake	Fr Perth, 18 mi W on Hwy 7, just W of Maberly		1	76	150	24	5.50		5/14-10/31	23		●	U				●			●	●	●		●		○	○	○	○		●	●	dlr	●	p		613/268-2489	Maberly
22	B7	Murphy's Point Prov Pk	Fr Perth, S on Co 1 to Co 21, Co 21 to CG		1	2650	N	SN	5.50		5/14-9/30	23	Z	●	U				●				$	●		●	$		●				●	●	dlr		p		613/267-5060	RR 5, Perth
23	B7	Rideau River	Fr Kemptville, 3 mi N on Co 13		1	208	185	185	5.00		5/12-9/16w	28		●	26				●			●	●	●		●		○		○	○		●	●	dlr	●	g		613/258-2740	Box 908, Kemptville
25	C6	Outlet Beach	Fr Picton, 10 mi SW on Co 10 & 11	⛵ ♀	1	305	480	480	5.50		All year	23			30				●			●	●			●		●		●	●		●	●	dl	●	h		613/393-3314	RR 1, Picton
25	C6	Sandbanks	Fr Picton, 12 mi SW on Co 10 & 11	⛵ ♀	1	1210	50	50	5.50		5/8-9/19	23		●	22							●	●			●		○			○		●	●					613/393-3314	RR 1, Picton
26	B7	Sharbot Lk (Black Lk)	Fr Sharbot Lk townsite, 4 mi NW		1	99	200	200	5.50		All year	23		●	30				●			●	$			●		○		○	○		●	●	dl				613/335-2814	RR 2, Sharbot Lk
27	B6	Bon Echo	Fr Kaladar, 20 mi N on Hwy 41		1	B	525	260	5.50		5/12-9/14**	23		●	30				●			●	$	●		●		○					●	●	dl	●			613/336-2228	RR 1, Cloyne
28	C5	Balsam Lk	Fr Coboconk, 4 mi W on Hwy 48		1	1040	475	33	5.50		5/14-10/11	23				$			●			●	$	●		●	●	○	●		○		●	●	dl	●			705/454-3324	RR 1, Kirkfield
29	B6	Lake St Peter	Fr Maynooth, 7 mi N on Hwy 127, 1 mi E	⛵ ♀	2	61	60	60	5.50		5/13-9/6**	28		●	30				●			●	●			●				○			●	●	dlr				613/338-5312	Lake St. Peter
30	A5	Samuel de Champlain	Fr Mattawa, 8 mi W on Hwy 17		1	5800	190	26	5.50		5/11-9/09	23		●	U				●			●	●	●		●							●	●	dl	●			705/744-2276	PO Box 147, Mattawa
31	A5	Antoine	Fr Mattawa, 5 km N on Hwy 533, 5 km N on Hwy 656		1	30	24	6	5.00		6/1-9/3	23		●	U				●			●	●	●										●	l				705/744-2251	PO Box 147, Mattawa
32	A4	Marten River	Fr North Bay, 58 km N on Hwy 11		1	1075	193	23	5.50		5/18-9/9	23		●	U				●	○		●	●	●		●		○		○	○		●	●	dlr					Marten River
33	E8	Finlayson Point	Fr Temagami, 1/2 mi S on Hwy 11, 1/2 mi W	⛵ ♀	1	74	114	114	5.50		6/4-LD	21		●	24				●	○		●	●	●	●	●		○	○	○	○		●	●	dlr		p		705/569-3622	Box 38, Temagami
34	B6	Carson Lake	Fr Barry's Bay, 4 mi W on Hwy 60	⛵ ♀	1	15	30	14	5.00		12/5-3/9	28		●	U							●	●					○		○	○		●	●	l				613/756-5123	Barry's Bay
35	A6	Driftwood	Fr Pembroke, 45 mi NW on Hwy 17	≈ ⫛	1	640	72	8	5.00		5/19-9/11	28		●	U				●			●	●								○		●	●	l				613/586-2553	Stonecliffe
		Algonquin	(Tents can be rented at service center)			B													●																				705/637-2780	Box 219, Whitney
36	B5	South Tea Lake	Fr W Gate, 7-1/2 mi E on Hwy 60	⛵ ♀	1		50	24	5.00		6/23-9/4	28		●	U							●	$										●	●	l					Algonquin PP
36	B5	Canisbay Lake	Fr W entr, 15 mi E on Hwy 60, 1 mi N	⛵ ♀	1		100	152	5.50		6/23-9/4	28		●	U							●	$			●			●				●	●						Algonquin PP
36	B5	Mew Lake	Fr W entr, 20 mi E on Hwy 60	⛵ ♀	1		105	50	5.50		6/23-9/4	28		●	U							●	$			●	●	○	●	○	○		●	●						Algonquin PP
36	B5	Lake of Two Rivers	Fr W entr, 21 mi E on Hwy 60	⛵ ♀	1		150	93	5.50		5/19-10/9	28		●	U							●	$			●	●	○	●	●	●		●	●	l					Algonquin PP
36	B5	Pog Lake	Fr W entr, 24 mi E on Hwy 60	⛵ ♀	1		200	107	5.50		6/23-9/4	28		●	U							●	$			●	●		●				●	●						Algonquin PP
36	B5	Kearney Lake	Fr W entr, 24 mi E on Hwy 60	⛵ ♀	1		55	50	5.50		6/23-9/4	28		●	U							●	$				○		○				●	●						Algonquin PP
36	B5	Rock Lake (Coon Lk)	Fr W entr, 26-1/2 mi E on Hwy 60, 5 mi S	⛵ ♀	1		100	76	5.00		5/19-9/4	28		●	U							●	$										●	●	l					Algonquin PP
36	B5	Opeongo Lake	Fr W entr, 30-1/2 mi E on Hwy 60, N to CG	⛵ ♀	1		23		5.00		5/18-10/9	28		●								●	$					●		●	●			●	l					Whitney
37	C5	McRae Point	Fr Orillia, 7 mi E on Hwy 12, 3 mi SW	⛵ ⫛	1	170	70	130	5.50		5/9-9/21	23		●	U	$			●	○		●	●	●		●		○		○	○		●	●	l				705/325-7290	Box 607, Orillia
37	C5	Mara	Fr Orillia, 3 mi E on Hwy 12, 2 mi S at Atherley	⛵ ⫛	1	99	75	25	5.50		5/9-9/21	23	Z	●	U				●			●	●	●		●		○		○	○		●	●			g		705/326-4451	Box 607, Orillia
38	B6	Bonnechere	Fr Pembroke, 25 mi SW on Hwy 62	⛵	1	250	70	44	5.00		11/5-3/9	28		●	U				●			●	●					○		○	○		●	●	l				613/757-2103	Bonnechere
39	B3	Cyprus Lake	Fr Tobermory, 6 mi S on Hwy 6, 3-1/2 mi E	⛵ ⫛	1	1149	140	100	5.00		5/8-9/20	23		●	U				●			●	$	●									●	●	dl				2263	Tobermory
40	A3	Halfway Lk	Fr Sudbury, 60 mi N on Hwy 144			B	215	215	5.50		5/15-9/10	23		●	U				●			●	●			●	●		●				●	●	dl				705/965-2702	Levack
41	E4	Iroquois Beach	Fr Tillsonburg, 18 mi SW to Port Burwell via Hwy 19	⛵ ▟	1	560	232	232	5.50		5/15-LD**	23		●	U				●	○		●	$			●		○		○	○		●	○	dl	●			519/874-4691	Port Burwell
42	E8	Fushimi Lake Prov Pk	Fr Hearst, 16 mi W on Hwy 11, 8 mi N on Fushimi Rd	⛵	1	9000	40	40	5.00		6/2-LD	23		●	25				●			●	●	●									●	●	dl				705/362-4346	Box 670, Hearst
43	C7	Charleston Lake	Fr Gananoque, 9 mi E on Hwy 401, 10 mi N on Reynolds Rd		1	6000	227	227	5.50		5/14-9/19	23		●	24				●			●	$			●							●	●	dl				613/659-2065	RR 4, Lansdowne
44	B4	Awenda	Fr Penetanguishene, 10 mi N on Co 26			5000	125	25	5.50		5/10-9/21	23		●	U				●			●	●			●	●		●				○	○			gp		705/549-2231	Box 973, Penetang
45	B4	Oastler Lake	Fr Parry Sound, 6 mi S on Hwy 69	⛵ ♀	1	50	115	37	5.50		5/11-8/10	23		●	U				●	○		●	●	●		●		○		○	○		●	●	dlr	●	g		705/378-2401	Parry Sound
46	B4	Killbear Pt	Fr Parry Sound, 8 mi NW on Hwy 69	⛵ ♀	1	2345	443	450	5.50		5/11-8/10	23		●	18				●	○		●	●			●		○		○	○		●	●	l	●			705/342-5492	Parry Sound
47	A4	Restoule	Fr Nipissing, 23 km W on Hwy 534, 10 km NW		1	2400	246	32	5.50		5/11-9/16	23		●	U	$			●			●	●	●		●							●	●	dl				705/729-2010	Restoule
48	A5	Mikisew	Fr Hwy 11 in South River, 12 mi W	⛵ ♀	2	300	265	265	5.50		5/15-9/19	21		●	U				●			●	●	●		●							●	●	dl	●			705/386-7762	Box 400, South River
49	A3	Fairbank	Fr Worthington, 13 mi N on Hwy 658			216	160	160	5.50		5/19-9/10	23		●	U				●			●	●			●	●		●				●	●	dl				705/965-2703	Worthington
50	A3	Windy Lake	Fr Sudbury, 30 mi NW on Hwys 144 & 544			293	65	11	5.50		5/15-9/10	23		●	U				●			●	●			●				○	○		●	●	dl		g		705/966-2315	Levack
51	E8	Five Mile Lk	Fr Chapleau, 23 mi S on Hwy 129	⛵ ⫛	2	1009	87	20	5.00		6/7-9/28	28		●	25				●			●	●										●	●	dl					Chapleau
52	E8	Pancake Bay	Fr Sault Ste Marie, 50 mi N on Hwy 17		1	1151	144	90	5.50		6/1-9/15	23		●	21	$			●			●	$	●		●		○	○	○	○		●	●	l					Sault Ste Marie
53	E7	Lake Superior	Fr Sault Ste Marie, 80 mi N on Hwy 17	⛵ ⋀		B																																	705/856-2396	Box 1160, Wawa

ONTARIO

FOR FOOTNOTE EXPLANATION SEE FIRST PAGE OF THIS **PROVINCE** FOR MAP, SEE PAGE **118**

Park number	Map reference	Name of park	Access	Physical environment	Elevation	Acres	Number of tent spaces	Number of trailer spaces	Approximate fee	Credit cards accepted	Season
		PROVINCIAL PARKS (CONT'D)									
53	E7	Crescent Lake	1 mi off Hwy 17, 1 mi N of S boundary of pk, at mi 81	⛵ 🌳	2	100	102	16	5.00		6/1-9/10
53	E7	Agawa Bay	At Mi 87 on Hwy 17, 5-1/3 mi N of S boundary of pk	⛵ 🌳	1	96	140	32	5.00		6/1-9/10
53	E7	Rabbit Blanket Lake	At Mi 120 on Hwy 17, 15 mi S of N boundary of pk		2	50	42	22	5.00		6/1-9/10
55	E8	Wakami Lk	Fr Chapleau, 18 mi S on Hwy 129, 15 mi E on rd to Sultan, S to pk	⛵ 🌲	2	B	48	40	5.00		6/7-9/28
56	E8	Ivanhoe Lk	Fr Foleyet, 7 mi E on Hwy 101, 2 mi S	⛵ 🌲	2	3000	129	16	5.50		5/15-9/15
57	E7	White Lake	Fr White River, 22 mi W on Hwy 17		2	3980	187	100	5.50		6/1-9/10
58	E8	Kap-Kig-Iwan Prov Pk	Fr Hwy 11 in Englehart, 1-1/2 mi S on secondary rd		1	784	32	32	7.00		6/1-9/3
59	E8	Esker Lks Prov Pk	Fr Kirkland Lk, 10 mi E on Hwy 66, 12 mi N on gravel rd		2	8000	130	6	5.50		6/1-9/3
60	E8	Kettle Lakes	Fr Porquis Jct, 12 mi W on Hwy 67		1	2304	75	75	F5.50		5/20-9/30
61	E8	Greenwater	Fr Cochrane, 11 mi NW on Hwy 11, 9 mi N		1	B	70	40	5.00		6/1-9/3
62	E8	Remi Lk Prov Pk	Fr Kapuskasing, 13 mi E on Hwy 11, 6 mi N on Hwy 581		1	7540	70	30	5.00		5/30-LD
63	E8	Missinaibi Lk	Fr Chapleau, 55 mi N on gravel rd	⛵ 🌳	2	B	20	30	5.00		6/7-9/28
64	E7	Klotz Lake	Fr Longlac, 30 mi E on Hwy 11		2	210	15	15	5.00		2/6-LD
65	E7	MacLeod	Fr Longlac, 19 mi W on Hwy 11	⛵ 🌲	2	200	57	28	7.00		2/6-LD
66	E7	Lake Nipigon	Fr Nipigon, 40 mi N on Hwy 11, 3 mi W	⛵ ⋀	1	3353	60	20	5.00		6/2-9/9**
67	E7	Rainbow Falls	Fr Terrace Bay, 16 mi W on Hwy 17	⛵ 🌳	1	1422	212	18	5.50		6/4-9/12
68	E7	Sibley	Fr Thunder Bay, 20 mi E on Hwy 17, 23 mi S on Hwy 587		2	B	205	20	5.00		5/21-9/12
69	E7	Middle Falls	Fr Ont-Minnesota border, 2 mi N on Hwy 61, 1 mi W on Hwy 593		1	2000	20	10	5.00		7/1-9/5
70	E7	Kakabeka Falls	Fr Thunder Bay, approx 20 mi NW on Hwy 17		1	1010	151	20	5.00		5/24-9/15
71	E7	Inwood	Fr English River, 32 mi SE on Hwy 17		2	81	40	40	5.00		6/1-9/15
72	E6	Aaron	Fr Dryden, 10 mi E on Hwy 17		2	238	75	23	5.50		5/23-9/11
72	E6	Blue Lake Provincial Pk	Fr Vermilion Bay, 5 mi NW on Hwy 647		2	873	146	42	5.50		5/23-9/11
74	E6	Rushing River	Fr Kenora, 11 mi E on Hwy 17, 3 mi S on Hwy 71		2	395	158	35	5.50		5/19-3/8
		Quetico Dawson Trl CGs	Quetico		2	B	67	68	5.00		5/16-9/15
75	E6	Dawson Trail	Fr Atikokan, 27 mi E on Hwy 11 to French Lk	⛵ 🌳	2	200	135	135	5.00		5/3-10/1
76	E6	Sioux Narrows	Fr Sioux Narrows, 3 mi N on Hwy 71		2	284	62	10	5.50		5/19-3/8
76	E6	Lake of the Woods	Fr Sleeman, 19 mi N on Hwy 621	⛵ 🌳	2	2673	70	30	5.00		5/15-9/15
76	E6	Caliper Lake	Fr Nestor Falls, 3 mi S on Hwy 71, 1 mi W	⛵ 🌳	2	246	60	32	5.50		5/15-9/15
77	E8	Shoals	Fr Chapleau, 32 mi W on Hwy 101	⛵ 🌲	2	B	24	56	5.00		6/4-9/12
78	E8	Nagagamisis	Fr Hwy 11, 26 mi S on Hwy 631	⛵ 🌳	2	B	165	100	5.50		5/26-LD
79	E7	Sandbar Lake	Fr Ignace, 7 mi N on Hwy 599		2	7787	57	18	5.50		5/15-9/15
80	m	Pakwash	Fr Red Lk, 30 mi S on Hwy 105	⛵ 🌳	2	1507	57	57	3.50		6/1-9/5
		St Lawrence Parks Commis									
81	C6	Adolphustown	Fr Kingston, 30 mi W on Hwy 33		1	70	82	53	7.00		5/15-10/15
82	C7	Ivy Lea	W of Ivy Lea Bridge, 1000 Island Parkway		1	48	109	34	7.00		5/15-10/15
83	C7	Brown's Bay Camp	Fr Brockville, 11 mi W on 1000 Island Parkway		1	165	61	51	7.00		5/15-10/15
84	B8	Riverside	Fr Morrisburg, 3 mi E on Hwy 2		1	84	163	61	7.00		5/15-10/15
84	B8	Cedar Camp	Fr Morrisburg, 4 mi E on Hwy 2		1	87	189	52	7.00		5/15-10/15
85	B8	McLaren Camp	Fr Ingleside, 1 mi E on Long Sault Pkway		1	90	161	50	7.00		5/15-10/15
85	B8	Woodlands Camp	Fr Ingleside, 2-1/2 mi E on Long Sault Pkway		1	65	186	48	7.00		5/15-10/15
85	B8	Morrison & Nairne Isl	Fr Ingleside, 2-1/2 mi W on Hwy 2		1	29	104	20	7.00		5/15-10/15
85	B8	Dickinson Camp	Fr Ingleside, 3 mi E on Long Sault Pkway		1	32	232		5.00		5/15-10/15
85	B8	Farran Park	Fr Morrisburg, 12 mi E on Hwy 2, adj to Ingleside		1	88	62	53	7.00		5/15-10/15
85	B8	Mille Roches	Fr Cornwall, 10 mi SW on Long Sault Parkway		1	52	217	17	7.00		5/15-10/15
86	B8	Raisin River	Fr Cornwall, 14 mi E on Summerstown Rd		1	84	52	51	7.00		5/15-10/15
87	C7	Fairfield Park	Fr Kingston, 12 mi W on Hwy 33		1	7	P20		5.00		5/15-10/15
90	B8	Grenville Park	Fr Prescott, 3 mi E on Hwy 2, on St Lawrence River		1	115	71	44	7.00		5/15-10/15
91	B8	Glengary	Fr Lancaster, 1 mi E on Service Rd, on Lake St Francis		1	62	190	54	7.00		5/15-10/15
91	B8	Charlottenburgh	Fr Cornwall, 12 mi E on Hwy 2, on Lk St Francis		1	50	113	46	7.00		5/15-10/15
92	A3	Killarney	Fr Sudbury, 25 mi S on Hwy 69, 40 mi SW on Hwy 637			B	100	36	5.00		5/15-9/10
93	B4	Sturgeon Bay	Fr Parry Sound, 25 mi N on Hwy 69 to Pte au Baril, 3 mi N on Hwy 529	⛵ 🌳	1	35	75	7	5.00		5/11-8/10
94	A4	Grundy Lk	Fr Parry Sound, 50 mi N on Hwy 69, E one mile on Highway 522 Channal Rd		1	6100	479	41	5.50		5/11-9/17
95	A3	Chutes	Fr Massey, 1/2 N on Hwy 553	≈ 🌲	1	270	91	91	7.00		5/15-10/15
96	E7	Neys Provincial Park	Fr Marathon, 16 mi W on Hwy 17	≈ ⋀	1	8150	120	30	7.00		6/1-9/9
97	E7	Obatanga	Fr White River, 22 mi E on Hwy 17		2	B	77	40	5.50		6/1-9/10
98	E6	Ojibway	Fr Dinorwic, 30 mi N on Hwy 72		2	6130	27	23	5.00		5/17-9/14
99	E2	Wheatley	Fr Wheatley, 1 mi E on Hwy 3		1	596	167	100	7.50		5/9-9/30
100	C3	Point Farms	Fr Goderich, 2 mi N on Hwy 21		1	600	126	74	F7.00		5/24-LD
101	A2	Mississagi	Fr Elliot Lk, 20 mi N on Hwys 108 & 639		2	7124	51	50	5.00		5/15-9/15
102	B5	Arrowhead Pk	Fr Huntsville, 5 mi N on Hwy 11		2	2000	289	115	7.00		5/15-9/10
103	B8	Carillon	Fr Montreal, 45 mi W on Hwy 417	≈ 🌲	1	B	50	366	7.00		5/1-10/31
		NATIONAL PARKS									
		St Lawrence Islands NP	(For additional CGs, see 'Backpack or Boat Access Areas)								
104	C7	Mallorytown Landing	Fr Brockville, 7 mi S on Hwy 2, 8 mi SW on 1000 Islands Pkwy			97	64		2.00		5/15-9/31
		Georgian Bay Islands NP	(For CG information, see 'Backpack of Boat Access Areas')								
		BACKPACK OR BOAT ACCESS AREAS									
		Grenadier Island	(Additional primitive camping areas on 16 islands)								
118	C7	Grenadier Landing	On Grenadier Island, access by boat or water taxi			213	P30		F2.00		5/15-10/15
119	B4	Georgian Bay Islands NP	Fr Honey Harbor, 3 mi W by boat or water taxi to Beausoleil Island (16 CGs)		1	3460	265		3.00		All year
		CITY, COUNTY & CIVIC									
125	A4	Parc River Valley Camping	Fr Warren, 16 mi N on Hwy 539	≈ ⋀	1	350	50	50	3.00		5/15-10/15

Park number	Name of park	Time limit	Reservations	Pets permitted	Max. trailer size	Electric hookup	Water hookup	Sewer hookup	Sanitary station	Bottled gas	Air conditioning	Tables	Firewood	Pull-thru spaces	Rec. hall	Flush toilets	Showers	Ice	Auto. laundry	Cafe-snack bar	Store	Swimming pool	Other swimming	Fishing	Boating	Playground	Other	CB channel monitored	Telephone no.	Mail address
53	Crescent Lake	21		•	21					○		•	•	•				○		○	○		•	•	dl				705/856-2396	Box 1160, Wawa
53	Agawa Bay	21		•	21				•	○		•	•	•				○		○	○		•	•					705/856-2396	Box 1160, Wawa
53	Rabbit Blanket Lake	21		•	21							•	•										•	•	dl				705/856-2396	Box 1160, Wawa
55	Wakami Lk	28		•	U				•			•	•										•	•	dl					Chapleau
56	Ivanhoe Lk	28		•	U	$			•			•	•			•							•	•	l					Foleyet
57	White Lake	23		•	U				•			•	•	•		•	•		•				•	•	dl	•			807/822-2250	White River
58	Kap-Kig-Iwan Prov Pk	23		•	U	•			•	○		•	•	•		•	•	○	○	○	○	○		•	l	•			705/544-2050	Englehart
59	Esker Lks Prov Pk	23		•	U				•	•		•	•	•		•		•	•	•	•		•	•	dlr	•			705/642-3222	Box 129, Swastika
60	Kettle Lakes	23	Z	•	30	$			•			•	$			•	$	•	•	•	•		•	•	l	•	p		705/264-1262	Connaught
61	Greenwater	23		•	30				•			•	•	•			$		○				•	•	d	•			705/272-4365	Box 730, Cochrane
62	Remi Lk Prov Pk	28		•	U	$			•			•	•	•		•	•		•					•	dl		p			Kapuskasing
63	Missinaibi Lk	28		•	25				•			•	•										•	•	dl					Chapleau
64	Klotz Lake	23		•	30		•		•			•	•										•	•	dl		p			Bx 640 Geraldton
65	MacLeod	23		•	30	$			•			•	•	•		•			•				•	•	l		gp			Geraldton Bx 640
66	Lake Nipigon	23		•	30				•			•	•	•									•	•	dl				807/887-2120	Box 970, Nipigon
67	Rainbow Falls	28		•	30				•			•	•	•		•	•	○	•	○	○		•	•	l					Box 280, Terrace Bay
68	Sibley	U		•	U				•			•	•										•	•	dl	•				Pass Lake
69	Middle Falls	28		•	30							•	•			•				○	○			•						RR 3, Pigeon River
70	Kakabeka Falls	28		•	U	$			•			•	•			•	•	○		○	○		•							Kakabeka Falls
71	Inwood	28		•	30				•			•	•							○	○		•	•	dl					Upsala
72	Aaron	23		•	U	$			•			•	•	•				○		○	○		•	•	dl	•	p			Box 3000, Dryden
72	Blue Lake Provincial Pk	23		•	U	$			•			•	•	•		•	$	○		○	○		•	•	dl	•	p			Box 3000, Dryden
74	Rushing River	23		•	U	$			○	○		•	•	•		•	$	○		○	○		•	•	dlr	•			807/848-4351	808 Robertson St, Kenora
	Quetico Dawson Trl CGs				30				•			•	•	•									•	•					807/597-6971	Ministry of Ntl Rs, Atikokan
75	Dawson Trail	28		•	U				•			•	•	•		•					•		•	•	dl				807/597-6971	Atikokan
76	Sioux Narrows	23		•	U				•			•	•	•		•							•	•	dl	•				Box 5080, Kenora
76	Lake of the Woods	28		•	U				•			•	•	•									•	•	dl	•			807/488-5531	RR 1, Sleeman
76	Caliper Lake	28		•	U	$			•			•	•	•		•	$						•	•	dl	•			807/484-2181	Nestor Falls
77	Shoals	28		•	30				•			•	•	•									•	•	dl					Chapleau
78	Nagagamisis	23		•	25				•	○		•	•	•		•		○	○	○	○		•	•	dl				705/362-4346	Box 670, Hearst
79	Sandbar Lake	28		•	U	•			•			•	•	•		•	•						•	•	dl	•			807/934-2995	Ignace
80	Pakwash	28		•	U				•			•	•	•									•	•	dl	•				Box 323, Red Lake
	St Lawrence Parks Commis																												613/543-2951	Box 740, Morrisburg
81	Adolphustown	23		•	25	•			•	○		•	$			•		○			○		•	•	l	•			613/543-2951	Morrisburg
82	Ivy Lea	23		•	25	•			•	○		•	$			•		○	○	○	○		•	•	l	•			613/543-2951	Morrisburg
83	Brown's Bay Camp	23		•	25	•			•	○		•	$			•		○		○			•	•	l	•	g		613/543-2951	Morrisburg
84	Riverside	23		•	25	•			•	○		•	$			•		•	○	○	○		•	•		•	gh		613/543-2951	Morrisburg
84	Cedar Camp	23		•	25	•			•	○		•	$			•		•	○	○	○		•	•	l	•	gh		613/543-2951	Morrisburg
85	McLaren Camp	23		•	25	•			○	○		•	$			•		•		○	○		•	•		•	gh		613/543-2951	Morrisburg
85	Woodlands Camp	23		•	25	•			○	○		•	$			•		•		•	○		•	•	l	•	gh		613/543-2951	Morrisburg
85	Morrison & Nairne Isl	23		•	25	•			○	○		•	$			•		•		○	○		•	•		•	gh		613/543-2951	Morrisburg
85	Dickinson Camp	23		•					○	○		•	$					•		○	○		•	•		•	gh		613/543-2951	Morrisburg
85	Farran Park	23		•	25	•			•	○		•	$	•		•		•		○	○		•	•	l	•	gh		613/543-2951	Morrisburg
85	Mille Roches	23		•	25	•			•	○		•	$			•		•		•	○		•	•	l	•	gh		613/543-2951	Morrisburg
86	Raisin River	23		•	25	•			•	○		•	$			•	•	•	•		○	•		•	dl		p		613/543-2951	Morrisburg
87	Fairfield Park	23		•								•	$						○					•	l	•			613/543-2951	Morris
90	Grenville Park	23		•	25	•			•	○		•	$			•		○		•	○		•	•		•	g		613/543-2951	Morrisburg
91	Glengary	23		•	25	•			•	○		•	$			•		•	○	•	○		•	•	dl	•			613/543-2951	Morrisburg
91	Charlottenburgh	23		•	25	•			•	○		•	$			•		•		•	○		•	•	l	•			613/543-2951	Morrisburg
92	Killarney	23		•								•	•										•	•	dl				705/287-2368	Killarney
93	Sturgeon Bay	23		•	U				•	○		•	•					○		○	○		•	•	l	•			705/366-2521	Parry Sound
94	Grundy Lk	23		•	18				•	○		•	•	•		•		•		○	○		•	•	l	•			705/383-2369	Britt
95	Chutes	28		•	U	$			•	○		•	$			•	•	○	○	○	○		•	○	l		g			Massey
96	Neys Provincial Park	28		•	30	•			•			•	•	•		•	•	○	•		○		•	•	l					Box 280, Terrace Bay
97	Obatanga	23		•	U				•			•	•	•		•	•		•				•	•	dl				807/822-2250	White River
98	Ojibway	28		•	U				•			•	•	•									•	•	dl	•			807/737-1140	Box 309, Sioux Lookout
99	Wheatley	23		•	28				•			•	$			•		○	○	○	○		•	•	l	•	g			Wheatley
100	Point Farms	23		•	U	$			•	○		•	○	•	•	•				○	○		•		l		g		519/524-7124	RR 3, Goderich
101	Mississagi	23		•	21				•			•	•	•									•	•	dl				705/848-2806	Box 190, Blind River
102	Arrowhead Pk	21		•	U	•			•			•	•	•		•			○	○	○		•	•	l	•	ku		705/789-5105	RR 3, Huntsville
103	Carillon	23		•	30	$			•			•	$	•		•	•	○	•		○		•	•	dl	•	g		613/674-2825	Chute A Blondeau
	St Lawrence Islands NP																												613/923-5241	Box 469 RR 3, Mallorytown
104	Mallorytown Landing	14		•								•	•			•		○		○			•	•	dl	•				Mallorytown
	Grenadier Island											•	•			•							•	•	d				613/923-5241	Box 469 RR 3, Mallorytown
118	Grenadier Landing	14		•								•											•	•						
119	Georgian Bay Islands NP	14		•								•	•			•	•						•	•	d	•	ekpu		705/756-2415	Box 28, Honey Harbor
125	Parc River Valley Camping	U		•	U				○	•		•	•	•				○		○	○		•	•		•	p		705/758-6576	River Valley

ONTARIO

FOR FOOTNOTE EXPLANATION SEE FIRST PAGE OF THIS **PROVINCE** FOR MAP, SEE PAGE 118

Park number	Map reference	Name of park	Access	Physical environment	Elevation	Acres	Number of tent spaces	Number of trailer spaces	Approximate fee	Credit cards accepted	Season	Max. trailer size / Pets permitted / Reservations / Time limit	Electric hookup / Water hookup / Sewer hookup	Sanitary station / Bottled gas / Air conditioning	Tables / Firewood / Pull-thru spaces / Rec. hall	Flush toilets / Showers / Ice	Auto. laundry / Cafe-snack bar / Store	Swimming pool / Other swimming / Fishing	Boating / Playground / Other	CB channel monitored	Telephone no.	Mail address
		CITY, COUNTY & CIVIC (CONT'D)																				
126	D5	Indian Line Tourist CG	Fr Hwy 401, 1 mi N on Airport Expwy, Indian Line ext, 1/2 mi N to CG		1	50	125	124	5.00		5/1-9/30	7 Z • U	$	•	• •	• $ •		• •	lr gp		416/661-6600	5 Shoreham Dr, Downsview
127	C6	Victoria Pk Tourist Camp	Fr Hwy 401, Division St ext (Hwy 45), S to Harbour			17	20	77	5.00		5/24-10/1	U R • U	• • •	• ○	• $ •	• • •	○ • ○	• • ○	d • gp		416/372-8641	19 Charles St, Coburg
128	E4	Backus Conservation Area	Fr Port Rowan, 2 mi Nrea		1	200	60	16	6.00		5/15-10/15	U • U	• •	• ○	• • •	○	○ ○ ○	• •	l		519/426-4623	Box 525, Simcoe
128	E4	Deer Creek Con Area	Fr Hwy 3, 12 mi S on Hwy 59		1	250	30	20	5.00		5/15-9/15	U • 20		•	• $			• •	l p		519/426-4623	Box 525, Simcoe
129	D3	Melwood CA	Fr Kerwood, 4-1/2 mi S on Middlesex Co 6		1	225	28	37	7.00		MD-LD	28 • 24	• •	•	• •	• •	•	• •	•		519/245-3710	205 Mill Pond Cresc,Strathroy
130	E3	Pt Glasgow Trlr Pk	Fr Hwy 401, ext 15, 6 mi S to New Glasgow		1	20	75	125	4.00		5/15-10/15	U Z • U	• • $	• ○ •	• • •	• • •	• •	• •	dl •			Rodney
131	E4	Byng Island Cons. Area	Fr Dunnville, Hwy 3 to Co across Grand River, 2 mi S		1	469	130	100	5.00		5/1-10/15	14 • 24		•	• •	• $ ○	○ ○ ○	$ • •	dlr		416/774-5755	11 Haldimand Trail, Dunnville
132	E5	Long Beach Cons. Area	Fr Port Colborne, 10 mi W on Hwy 3 & Lakeshore Rd		1	140	300	300	5.00		5/15-9/1	14 • U	$ $	•	• $	• $ •	○ ○	• •	• •		416/899-3462	Wainfleet
133	D3	Wildwood Park	Fr Stratford, 7 mi W on Hwy 7		2	200	186	190	5.00		5/1-10/15	14 • U	$ •	• •	• $	• $ •	○ •	• •	l g		519/284-1381	RR 2, St Mary's
134	D4	Elora Gorge Cons Area	Fr Guelph, 2 mi N on Hwy 6, 10 mi N on Elora Rd		2	326	460	88	5.00		5/15-10/15	14 • U	$ •	•	• •	• $ •	○ • ○	• •	•		519/846-9742	PO Box 356, Elora
135	B6	Overnite Tent & Trlr Pk	Hwy 17 in Cobden, 90 mi NW of Ottawa			3	25	19	3.50		5/24-9/3	U • 20	$		•	• ○	○ ○ ○	○ ○	dl			Box 40, Cobden
136	D3	Stratford Trlr Camp	In Stratford, 4 blks N of Hwy 8, on Fairgrounds		2	20	150	150	4.00		5/1-10/31	U • U	$ $ $	○	• •	• • •	○ ○ ○	○	r • gh		519/271-5130	Stratford
137	D3	Fanshawe Cons Area	Fr London, 6 mi E to Clarke Side Rd, 2 mi N to sign		1	1000	278	315	5.00		5/1-10/15	U • U	$ •	•	• $	• $ •	○ ○ •	• • •	r • gp		519/451-1760	RR 6 Bx 6278 Stn "D", London
138	D4	Brant Cons Area	Fr Brantford, W on Hwy 53 to Oakhill Dr to Jennings Side Rd			446	100	100	5.00		5/1-10/15	14 • U	$	•	• $	• •	○ •	$ •	r • gp		519/752-2040	Box 691, Brantford
139	D4	Pinehurst Lake Cons Area	Fr Paris, 4 Mi N on Hwy 24 A		1	257	100	80	5.00		5/1-10/15	14 • U	$	•	• $	• $	○ ○	• •	r •		519/442-4721	RR 3, Ayr
140	C7	Lake Ontario Park	Fr Hwy 401, ext 101 S to Hwy 2, E on Hwy 2, 2 mi S on Portsmouth Ave, W on King St			25	100	100	5.50		5/1-10/1	14 • 24	• • $	•	•	• • •	○ ○ ○	• •	l • g		613/542-6574	City Hall, Kingston
141	C4	Albion Hills Cons Area	Fr Hwy 7, 14 mi N on Hwy 50 (4 mi N of Bolton)		1	927	60	60	4.00		5/1-9/30	U Z U			• •	• • •		• •				5 Shoreham Dr, Downsview
142	D4	Terra Cotta Cons. Area	Fr Hwy 10 at Victoria,5 mi W on Co to Terra Cotta, 1 mi N on Town Line Rd		2	350	200	25	3.00		5/24-9/5	7 Z • 24		•	• • •	• • •	• ○	• •	•		416/451-1615	Meadowvale
145	D3	Warwick CA	Fr Hwy 7 in Warwick, 1/2 mi S		1	215	48	26	5.00		MD-LD	28 • 24	• •	•	• •	• •	○ ○	• •	• p		519/245-3710	205 Mill Pond Cresc,Strathroy
147	A5	Muni. Camping Park	Fr Lk Shore Drive in North Bay, SW on Judge Ave, NW on Queen Street		1	2	45	45	5.50		5/15-10/15	U • 30	$ $ $	• ○	• •	• • ○	○ ○ ○	• •	dlr • gh			North Bay
148	E7	Chippewa Park	Fr Thunder Bay City Hall, 7 mi S on City Rd		1	350	80	60	5.50		5/15-9/15	15 Z • 30	$ •	•	• • • •	• • •	• • •	• ○	r •		807/623-3912	Thunder Bay "F"
150	B3	John Budd Memorial Pk	Fr Espanola, 72 mi S on Hwy 68		1	5	10	5	3.00		5/15-10/20	U Z • 16	$		• $		○ ○	○ ○	dl p			RR 1, Tehkummah
151	D5	Balls Falls Conserv Area	Fr QEW at Prudhommes, 3-1/2 mi S on Hwy 24		1	179	75	75	5.00		5/15-10/15	14 • U		•	• $	○	○ ○		• g		416/562-5235	Jordan
151	D5	Charles Daley Pk	Fr St Catharine's, 6 mi W on Queen Elizabeth Way, 7th St ext, fol signs		1	28	37		5.50		5/15-9/15	U Z •	$	•	•	• •	•	• •	dl •			Box 150, Niagara Falls
152	A6	Riverside Pk	Hwy 17 bet Ottawa & North Bay at Pembroke			42	57	100	7.00		5/17-10/1	U Z • U	• • •	• ○	• $	• • •	• • ○	• •	• g		613/735-1007	Pembroke
153	A2	Thessalon Lakeside Park	Fr Thessalon, W on Hwy 17 to 17B, 1/2 mi to Pk		1	23	40	40	6.00		5/14-LD	U Z • U	• •	• ○	• • •	• • ○	○ ○ ○	• ○	dl • pt		705/842-2523	Box 220, Thessalon
154	C3	Blue Water Trlr Pk	Kincardine, Hwys 21 & 9		1	3		35	5.50		5/19-10/9	U Z • 30	• •	• ○	•	• • ○	○ ○ ○	• ○	• gh		519/396-2082	Kincardine
155	D4	Hamilton Confederation Pk	Fr Queen Elizabeth Way, Fruitland Rd ext, N to service rd to 601 Grays Rd			37	10	42	6.00		5/15-10/15	U Z U	• •	•	• $ •	• $ •	• •	•	•		416/561-2206	Hamilton
156	C3	Southampton Mun Camp	In Southampton, Hwy 21		1	8	100	150	4.50		5/1-9/30	U Z • U	• •	•	•	• •		• •	• gh		519/797-3648	Southampton
158	E3	Shetland CA	Fr Lambton Co 2 in Shetland, 1 mi N		1	17	8	4	7.00		MD-LD	28 • 24	• •	○	• •		○	• •	dl • p		519/245-3710	205 Mill Pond Cresc,Strathroy
159	B7	Last Duel Trlr Pk	Fr Perth, 1 mi fr #7 on 43			30	50	40	4.00		5/24-9/15	14 Z • U	$ $	• ○	• $ •	• • ○	○ ○ ○	• •	dlr g		613/267-4975	25C Robinson St, Perth
160	B7	Victoria Pk CG	In Smith Falls, jct Hwys 15 & 29 off Lombard St		1	8	40	60	4.50		5/15-10/15	U Z • U	$ •	• • •	• ○	• • •	○ ○ ○	• • •	dl • gp		613/283-1334	Town Hall, Smith Falls
161	E7	Trowbridge Falls	Fr Hwy 11/17 in Thunder Bay, Hodder Ave Ext, 300 yds N on Copenhagen Rd		1	B	100	60	5.50		5/15-9/15	U Z • 30	$ •	•	• • •	• $ •	• ○ •	○	• g		807/683-6661	Thunder Bay
162	C6	Vanderwater Cons. Area	Fr Belleville, 18 mi N on Hwy 37		1	600	40	10	5.00		5/15-10/15	28 • 18			• •			• •	l •		613/968-3434	308 N Front St Belleville
163	C5	James B. Tudhope Mem Pk	In Orillia, jct Hwys 12 & 12-B By-pass		1	56	150	150	7.00		MD-LD	28 • 30	• •		•	• • •	○ • •	• •	r • gp		705/325-2831	Bx 966 Orillia
165	C4	Durham Conservation Area	Fr Hwy 6 in Durham, 1 mi E on Durham Rd		2	146	350	350	6.00	V	5/24-10/30	14 • U	$	•	• •	• • ○	○ ○ ○	• •	• p		519/364-1255	RR 1, Hanover
167	C7	Westport Municipal Trlr P	Fr Crosby, 9 mi W on Hwy 42		1	8	25	15	3.00		5/15-9/15	U Z • U	$	•	• • •	○	○ ○ ○	○ ○	lr gp		613/273-2191	Westport
168	C5	Beavermead Park	Fr TC 7, 1/2 mi N on Ashburnham Dr		1	53	285	96	7.00		5/12-10/15	28 • 25	$ •	• ○	• • • •	• • •	• • •	• •	dlr • ghp		705/745-0518	610 Parkhill Rd W,Peterboroug
168	C5	Hope Mill Cons Area	Fr Peterborough, 6 mi E on Hwy 7, 2.5 mi S on Cty 34, fol signs		1	122	65P		4.00		5/24-10/10	14 •			• $			• •	r gp			727 Landsdowne, Peterborough
168	C5	Warsaw Caves Cons Area	Fr Peterborough, 14 mi N & E on Co 4, E at sign		1	554	50P	7	4.00		5/24-10/12	14 •			• $		○	• •	lr gp			727 Landsdowne, Peterborough
169	D4	Guelph Twp Rec Pk	Fr Hwy 6 in Guelph, 2 mi E on Co 30			64	30	20	4.00		5/15-10/15	U Z • 28	$ $		• •		•	•	p		519/822-1759	Guelph
170	E6	Anicinabe Park	Fr TC 17, S on Golf Course Bay at Kenora		2	5	25	32	5.00		5/15-9/15	5 • U	• •	• ○	• •	• • ○	○ ○ ○	• •	dl gh		807/468-6878	Box 1110, Kenora
171	E8	Drury Park	Fr Kirkland Lk, 80 mi NW on TC 11			75	65	75	3.50		6/1-9/15	U • 30	$	○ ○	• •	• • ○	○ ○ ○	○ •	•		705/272-4361	Box 490, Cochrane
172	B7	Ottawa-Nepean Tnt & Trlr	Fr Ottawa, 9 mi W on TC 17 to Moodie ext, 1/4 mi N, 1-1/2 mi W on Corkstown Rd		1	200	150	150	4.00		5/15-9/30	4 Z • U	• •	•	• $	• • •	• •	○	• h		613/828-6632	3825 Richmond, Ottawa
173	C4	Meaford Memorial Pk	Fr Hwy 26, SE Meaford limits, N on St Vincent, 1/4 mi E over tracks, 500 yds S		1	25	50	160	4.50		5/15-10/31	21 • U	$ •	• ○	• • • •	• • •	○ • •	• •	dlr • gt			Box 758, Meaford
174	D5	Miller's Creek Park	Fr Niagara Falls, 14 mi S on Niagara Pkwy			15	38	16	5.50		5/15-9/7	U Z • 19	$ •	•	•	• • •	• •	○ ○	l •			PO Box 150, Niagara Falls
175	C4	Little Lake Park	At Midland via Hwys 11, 27, 400 & 12		1	500		49	5.00		5/24-9/5	U Z U	• • •	• ○	•	• • •	○ • •	• • •	• ght		705/526-9395	Box 12, Midland
176	D5	Heber Down Conserv Area	Fr Hwy 401 at Whitby, N on Thickson Rd, 3 mi W on Hwy 7 1 mi S on Coronation Rd		1	590	50	50	6.00		5/1-10/31	14 • 24	• •	•	• •	• $	•	• •	gp		416/579-0411	1650 Dundas St E, Whitby
177	D4	Rockwood Cons Area	Fr Guelph, 7 mi E on Hwy 7		2	200	40	20	5.00		5/1-10/15	14 • U			• $	• •	•	• ○	dlr		519/856-9543	Box 60, Rockwood
181	D2	Huron View Park	Fr Sarnia, N on Christina St, 5 mi E on Lkshore Rd		1	94	86	64	5.50		5/24-9/10	28 • U	$ •	•	• $	• • •	○ ○ •	• •	• g			City Hall, Sarnia
182	C7	Lower Beverley Lk Tnshp P	In Delta, 1/2 mi off Hwy 42		1	106	100	150	5.50		5/15-10/15	U • U	$ •	•	• $ • •	• $ •	• • ○	• •	dlr • hp		613/928-2881	Delta
183	C3	Saugeen Bluffs Cons Area	Fr Paisley, 2-1/2 mi N on Bruce Co 3, 1 mi W on Twp Rd 8		1	507	75	S75	6.00	V	5/24-10/11	14 • U			• • •	• •		•	p		519/364-1255	RR 1, Hanover
184	C4	Harrison Pk Tst Camp	Owen Sound, Hwys 6/10/21/26		1	96	50	75	5.00		5/1-9/1	14 • U	$ •	○ ○	• •	• • ○	○ • •	$ • •	r • g		519/376-0265	Owen Sound
186	B3	Blue Water Beach Pk	Fr Hwy 6 in Wiarton, 2 blks E on Williams St		1	12	50	72	6.00		5/15-10/15	28 Z • U	• •	• ○	• $ •	• • •	○ ○ ○	• •	d • gpt		519/534-2592	Wiarton
187	D3	Parkhill Cons Area	Fr Parkhill, 1-1/4 mi E on Hwy 7, 1 mi N on Centre Rd		1	1885	60	100	5.00		5/15-10/15	U Z • 30	$ •	•	• $	• • ○	○ ○ ○	• •	dr •		519/294-0114	Box 459, Exeter
189	E4	Norfolk Cons Area	Fr Simcoe, 7 mi S on Hwy 24, Twp Roads to Lkshore		1	46	120	66	6.00		5/15-9/15	U • 20	$ •	• ○	• • • •	• • •	•	• ○	l •		519/426-4623	Box 525, Simcoe
189	E4	Hay Creek Cons Area	Fr Simcoe, 5 mi S on Hwy 24, 1 mi E on Radical Rd		1	98	25	S25	5.00		5/15-9/15	U • U		• ○	• $ •	○	○	• •	dl • gp		519/426-4623	Box 525, Simcoe
192	E8	Pointe des Chenes Pk	Fr Sault Ste Marie, 14 mi W on Hwys 550 & 565		1	75	81	81	5.50		6/1-LD	14 • 31	$	•	• •	• $	•	• •	•		705/256-2232	Box 580, Sault Ste Marie
193	E8	Raven Beach Park	Fr Larder Lk, 1/2 mi on Hwy 66 & 624		1	10	40	40	3.00		6/15-9/30	U Z • U	• •	•	• •	• • •	○ •	• •	lr •			Larder Lk
193	E8	Culver Pk Trlr Camp	Fr Kirkland Lk, 4 mi W on Hwy 66			40	122	50	3.50		5/1-11/30	U • 30	• •	• •	• • •	• •	• • ○	• •	r •		705/567-4340	Box 1051, Kirkland Lk
194	A4	Moonlight Beach Trlr Pk	Fr Sudbury, 5 mi E on T/C 17, fol signs		1	20	35	35	5.00		6/1-9/7	U Z • U	• •	•	•	• • ○	• • ○	• •	• g		705/566-9201	Box 1000, Sudbury
196	B8	Iroquois Mun Pk	Fr Border, E on Hwy 401 to Ext 118, S on Carman Rd		1	20	15	17	4.00		6/15-9/30	28 Z • U	$	•	• •	• • ○	○ ○ ○	• •	dl • g		613/652-2121	Iroquois
197	C3	Brucedale Cons Area	Fr Port Elgin, 7 mi S on Hwy 21, 4 mi W on CR 10 & 11		1	10	40	40	6.00	V	5/24-10/30	14 • U			• •			• •	• p		519/364-1255	RR 1, Hanover
198	D4	Laurel Creek Cons Area	Fr Kitchener, N on Hwy 85 to Northfield Dr, 2 mi E		2	750	50	50	5.00		5/1-10/15	14 • U	$ •		• $	• $ •	○ • ○	• •	dr p		519/884-6620	RR 3, Waterloo
198	D4	Conestogo Lk Cons Area	Fr Elmira, on Hwy 86 to Dorking, N 3 mi		2	400	200	50	5.00		5/1-10/15	14 Z U	$	•	• $ •	• $ •	•	• •	d •		519/638-2873	RR 2, Wallenstein
199	D3	Pittock Camp	Fr Hwy 2, 1 mi N on Hwy 59			2150	56	94	5.00		5/1-10/15	14 • U	$ •	•	• $	• $ •	•	• •	lr •		519/539-6013	RR 6 Bx 6278 Stn D, London

ONTARIO

FOR FOOTNOTE EXPLANATION SEE FIRST PAGE OF THIS **PROVINCE** FOR MAP, SEE PAGE 118

Park number	Map reference	Name of park	Access	Physical environment	Elevation	Acres	Number of tent spaces	Number of trailer spaces	Approximate fee	Credit cards accepted	Season	Time limit / Reservations / Pets permitted / Max. trailer size	Facilities	Activities	Playground / Boating	Other	CB channel monitored	Telephone no.	Mail address
		CITY, COUNTY & CIVIC (CONT'D)																	
		PRIVATE																	
200	E2	Yogi Bear's Jellystone Pk	Fr Amherstburg, 2-1/2 mi E on Pike Rd		1	22	75	175	7.00	MV	All year	U Z • U	• • • • •$ • • • •	• • • •	•	gp	12/13	519/736-3201	RR 1, Amherstburg
200	E2	Windsor South KOA	Fr Hwy 3, S on Howard Ave to Texas Rd, 1/4 mi W		1	25	105	65	5.50	MV	4/1-10/31	U Z • U	• • • • • • •$ • • • • •	• • • •	•	ghp	12	519/726-5200	Box 59, McGregor
203	A2	Sunset Pt CG	Fr Hwy 17 in Blind River, 1 mi N on Hwy 557	≈	2	4	25	25	5.00		5/1-11/1	14 Z • U	$ •$ • ○ •$ • •$ •	• ○ ○ • •	dlr	t		705/356-7580	Bx 668 R, Blind River
204	A2	Brownlee Lk Tent & Trlr P	Fr Thessalon, 6 mi E on Hwy 17, 1 mi N on Brownlee Rd		1	63	35	30	4.00		All year	U Z • U	$ •$ • ○ • • • • • •	• ○ • •	dlr •	p	19	705/842-5346	Rt 2, Thessalon
205	B7	McGowan Lk Family CG	Fr Perth, 12 mi W on Hwy 7		1	100	55	105	5.50		5/20-9/15	U Z • U	• • • • • • • • • • • ○ •	• •	r •	hp		613/268-2234	Hwy 7, Maberly
206	E4	Bonnie View Lodge Trlr Pk	Fr Hwy 6 in Port Dover, 1 mi W on Nelson St			2		S10	4.50		All year	U Z 32	• • • $ • • • •	• • • •	l •	gp		519/583-1480	Box 583, Port Dover
206	E4	County Mtl & Trlr Pk	Fr Hwy 24 in Simcoe, 1 mi W on Hwy 3		1	3	10	20	5.50	M	All year	U Z U	• • • • ○$ • • • •	○ ○ •		gp		519/426-2954	486 Queensway West, Simcoe
206	E4	Shore Acres Park	Fr Hwy 6 in Port Dover, 1 mi W on Nelson St		1	15	28	166	5.00		4/1-11/30**	U 30	• • • • ○ • • • ○	○ ○ ○ • •	•	gp		519/583-2222	Port Dover
207	A1	Trudeau's Tent & Trlr Pk	Fr Sault Ste Marie, 18 mi E on T/C 17	^	2	5	52	30	6.50		5/1-10/1	U Z • U	$ • • $ • • • • •$ •	• ○	•			705/248-2880	RR 4, Echo Bay
208	A1	Pine Crest Tent & Trlr Pk	Fr Thessalon, 1 mi W on T/C 17		1	22	26	24	5.25		5/15-10/9**	U Z • U	$ $ • • • • • • • ○ ○ ○	• •	• •	p		705/842-2635	PO Box 517, Thessalon
211	D5	Lawson Pk	Fr 401, 2 mi E on Conc X1, in E Flamborough		2	50	125	175	6.00		5/15-9/15	U Z • U	$ $ • $ •$ • • • •	• • •	•	gpt		416/659-3395	RR 1, Freelton
211	D5	Courtcliffe Pk	Fr Hwy 6, 1 mi N on Carlisle Rd (12 mi N of Hamilton)	≈	2	100	200	500	7.50		All year	U Z • U	$ $ • •$ •$ • • • • •	• • • •	•	hkp		416/689-4421	Carlisle
212	D4	Nor-Halton Pk	Fr Milton, 10 mi NW on Hwy 25, 1-1/4 mi SW on Halton Rd 12		2	63	20	80	6.00		5/1-10/15	U Z • U	• • • • • • • • • • •	• • •	•			519/853-2959	RR 1, Acton
215	B3	Roth Park	Fr Wiarton, 1 mi N on Hwy 6, E on Bruce Rd 9, N to Lk		1	47	100	100	5.50	V	All year	U Z • U	$ • •$ • • • • •	• • •	dlr	u		519/534-0145	Rt 4, Wiarton
215	B3	LarBerMoe Pk	Fr Wiarton, 1 mi N on Hwy 6, 1000 ft E on Bruce Co 9, 2 mi N on Berford Lk Rd		2	5	12	26	6.50		5/1-10/31	U Z • U	$ $ • •$ • •$ • ○ • •	• ○ $	l •	ghp		519/534-0809	RR 4, Wiarton
217	B3	Summer House Camping Pk	Fr Wiarton, 32 mi N on Hwy 6, 2 mi E on Miller Lk Rd		1	85	150	A77	7.00		All year	U Z • 26	$ $ • • •$ • • • • • •	• •	dlr •	p		705/519-7712	Miller Lake
218	B8	Cardinal KOA	Fr Hwy 401, ext 117, N 3.8 mi, 1/4 mi S			20	25	60	5.00		5/1-9/30	U Z • U	$ • • $ •$ • • • • •	• •	•	p		613/657-4536	RR 1, Cardinal
219	C5	Ponderosa CG & Ski Resort	Fr Hwy 401 in Toronto, 25 mi N on Hwy 48		1	94	100	150	7.50		All year	U Z • U	$ •$ • • •$ • • • • •	• • ○	•			416/473-2607	Box 53, Mt Albert
219	C5	Cedar Beach Pk	Fr Hwy 48 in Ballantrae, E to Mussleman's Lk, fol signs		2	48	67	338	7.50		5/1-10/15	U Z • U	• • • • • • •$ • • • • •	• •	r •	ghp		416/640-1525	RR 2, Stouffville
219	C5	Grangeways Trlr Pk	Fr Hwy 401, 23 mi N on Hwy 48, 5 mi E on Herald Rd	≈		50	8	150	6.00	M	5/1-10/31	U Z • U	• • • • • • • • • • • •	• • • • •	•	ghp		416/852-3260	Sandford
220	C5	Deer Bay Park	Fr Hwy 28, 9 mi NW on Hwy 507, 2 mi E at 16th Line		1	30	10	55	4.00		5/24-10/15	U Z • 24	$ • • • • • •	○ ○ • •	dlr •	p	10	705/742-0262	288 Lake St, Peterborough
220	C5	Birch Pt Cmp & Marina	Fr Fowlers Corners, 9 mi N of Hwy 7			4	10	10	5.50		5/1-11/15	U Z • U	$ $ • • • • • •	$ • •	dlr •	gp		705/292-9461	RR 2, Ennismore
220	C5	Pratt's Marina	Fr Peterborough, N on Hwy 28 to Hwy 507, N to Selwyen, 1-1/2 mi W to Lk Chemong																
220	C5	Green Acres Camp	Fr Bobcaygeon, 1-1/2 mi S on Hwy 36, 2 mi SE on Victoria Rd 17 to Pigeon Lk		1	7	16	22	6.50		5/1-11/1	U Z • U	$ •$ • •$ • • • •	• • • •	dlr •	gpu		705/652-8058	RR 3, Lakefield
220	C5	Cadigan's Camp	Fr Enismore, 5 mi N to Pigeon Lk, fol signs			10	5	30	6.00		5/15-10/15	U Z • 28	$ •$ • •$ • •	• •	dlr	p		705/738-3112	RR 2, Bobcaygeon
220	C5	Elliot's Lodge	Fr Peterborough, N on Hwy 28 to Hwy 507, W on 12th Concession		2	20	30	30	6.00		All year	U Z U	• • • • • • • • • • ○	• •	dlr •			705/292-9403	RR 1, Peterboro
220	C5	Buckhorn Narrows	Fr Hwy 507, 3 mi W on Lakehurst Rd, in Buckhorn		1	63	8	S17	6.50		5/15-10/15	U Z • U	• • • • • • • • • • • •	• • •	dlr •	gp		705/652-8058	RR 3, Lakefield
220	C5	Six Foot Bay Resort	Fr Peterborough, Hwy 28 N to Hwy 507 to Buckhorn, fol signs 6 mi		1	120		65	7.50		5/1-10/30	U R • U	• • • ○ • • • • • • • •	• •	dlr •	p		705/657-8802	Buckhorn
220	C5	Skyline Tourist Park	Fr Fowlers Crnrs, 4-1/2 mi E on Hwy 78, NW on Chemung Rd, Cross Bridgenorth Causeway, fol signs E		1	30	110	150	6.50		5/14-10/15	U Z • U	• $ • • •$ • • • • • • ○ •	• •	dlr •	p		705/657-8788	Rt 1, Lakefield
220	C5	Wood Wharf Pt	Fr Peterborough, N on Hwy 28 to Hwy 507, N to Deer Bay Rd, fol signs W	^	2	165	100	200	7.50	M	5/1-10/15	U Z • U	• • • • • • •$ • • • • • • • •	• • •	dlr •	ghp		705/292-9811	RR 1, Ennismore
222	C6	Austin Tent & Trlr	On Rice Lk at Keene		1	4	5	20	6.00		5/1-11/30	U R • 24	• • • • •$ • • • •	• • •	dlr •	p		705/657-8843	RR 1 Lakefield
222	C6	Fisherman's Paradise	Fr Campbelleford, 7 mi N on Co 37, on E side of Trent Waterway			2	6	25	5.50		5/1-11/1	U Z • U	• • • • • • ○	• •	lr •			705/295-6940	Rt 3, Keene
222	C6	Lang's Marina Resort	Fr Roseneath, 1 mi N on Merrill Rd off Hwy 45, fol signs		1	5	20	30	6.50	V	5/15-10/15	U R • 30	• • • • • • • • • • •	• • • •	lr •	gh		705/653-1537	Bx 190, Campbellford
223	C6	Sandercock's Camp	Fr Toronto, E on Hwy 401, N on Hwy 45, W on Rice Lk Rd			5	10	31	5.00		5/15-10/15	U Z • 18	$ • • •$ • •$ • •	• •	lr •	hgp		416/352-2308	Rt 3, Roseneath
223	C6				0	7	22	40	4.50	M	5/1-11/30	U Z • 25	• •$ • • • • • • • • • ○ • •	• •	dlr •	hp	4	416/352-2469	RR 2, Roseneath KOK 2XO
226	C6	Carleton's Cove	Fr Belleville, 2-1/2 mi N on Hwy 14/62, 1/4 mi E	≈	L	10	20	30	6.00		5/1-10/31	U Z • U	• • • • • • ○ ○	• •	•	gp		613/962-6344	Rt 1, Foxboro
227	C6	Greenwood Pk	Fr Tweed, 3-1/2 mi E on Co 9			50	30	80	5.00		All year	U Z • U	$ • • • • • • • • • •	• •	dlr •	gpu		613/478-3620	Box 188, Tweed
228	C6	Lakeview Farms-Pitts Lndg	Fr Madoc, 2 mi SE, 1 mi S of Hwy 7		1	80	32	25	3.75		5/1-11/1	U • 30	$ • • • • • •	• •	lr •	p		613/473-2032	RR 2, Madoc
228	C6	Crystal Bch Madoc Pk	Fr Madoc, 2 mi E on Hwy 7, 1 mi S on Crystal Bch Rd		1	160	150	150	4.00		5/15-10/15	U Z$ 24	$ $ $ • ○ •$ • •$ • • •	• •	lr •	h		613/473-2098	Madoc
230	B7	McCrearys Beach Rsrt	Fr Perth, 8 mi NE on Hwy 7, 1 mi E on Mississippi Lk Rd		1	25		175	7.00		5/1-9/30	U Z • U	$ $ $ • •$ •$ • • •$ • • •	• •	dlr •	gpt		613/267-4450	RR 6, Perth
230	B7	Mississippi Wonderland	Fr Ottawa, 20 mi W on Hwy 7	≈		100	50	S54	6.50		5/1-10/15	U Z • U	• • • • • •	• •	dr •	gp		613/257-4757	Box 76, Carleton Place
232	D5	Niagra Mdows Hol Trvl Pk	Fr Buffalo, 15 mi N on Queen Elizabeth Hwy, ext Lyon Creek Rd W	≈	1	23	100	180	8.50		All year	U Z • U	$ $ $ • • • •$ • • • • • • • • •	• ○	l •	ghkp	14	416/354-1432	8676 Montrose Niagara Falls
232	D5	Niagara Glen-View T & T	Fr Niagara Falls, 1-1/2 mi N on Niagara Pkwy	≈	1	20	150	100	7.75		5/1-11/15	U Z • U	$ $ $ • • •$ • • • • • •	• ○	•	g		416/358-8689	3950 Victoria, Bx2087, Nia Fls
232	D5	Log Cabin Trlr Pk	Fr Queen Elizabeth Hwy, ext Mountain Rd E, left on Regional Rd # 100			18	50	100	5.00		5/1-10/31	U • U	• • • • • • • • • ○ ○ •	○ ○	•	g		416/262-4562	Box 85, St Davids
232	D5	The Big Valley CS Resorts	Fr Queen Elizabeth Way, 7th St ext, 4 mi S, 1 mi W on Co 81		1	24	40	100	5.50		4/1-10/31**	U Z • U	$ $ $ • •$ •$ • • • • • ○ ○	• ○	•	gt		416/562-5616	RR 1 St Catharines
232	D5	Niagara Mdws/Edgewater	Fr Queen Elizabeth Way, 1/4 mi W on McLeod	≈		95	200	300	6.00		All year	U Z • U	$ $ $ • • •$ • • • • • • ○	• ○	•	gh		416/354-1432	8676 Montrose, Niagara Falls
232	D5	Orchard Grove Tent Trlr P	Fr Queen Elizabeth Way, 1/2 mi W on Hwy 20		1	40	100	300	6.50		4/1-10/31	U Z • U	$ •$ • $ •$ • • • • • •		•	gp			8123 Lundy's Ln, Niagara Fls
232	D5	Paradise Acres	Fr QEW, 1-1/2 mi E on Lyons Creek Rd	≈	1	50	100	100	3.00		6/15-9/15	U Z • U	$ $ •$ • • • •	○ •	l •	gh		416/295-3122	Box 568, Niagara Falls
232	D5	Niagara Falls KOA	Fr Queen Elizabeth Hwy, 1 mi W on Hwy 20		1	21	65	300	6.00	MV	4/1-11/1	U Z • U	$ $ $ • • •$ • • • • • ○ •	•	•	g		416/354-6472	8625 Lundy's Ln Niagara Falls
232	D5	Riverside Pk CG	Niagara River Pkwy bet Fort Erie & Niagara Falls, 1 mi E of Queen Elizabeth Way on Black Creek Rd	≈	1	17	100	100	5.00		5/15-10/15	U Z • U	$ •$ • • •$ • • • • •	•	l •	h		416/382-2204	13541 Niagara Pkwy, NiagaraFal
233	D5	Jorden Valley Cmpg	Fr St Catherine, 6 mi W on QE Way, 2 mi S on Jordan Rd, 1 mi W fol signs		1	40	30	40	5.50		5/1-10/31	U Z • U	$ •$ • ○$ •$ • • • • ○ ○ ○	• •	dlr •	gp		416/562-7245	RR 1, Jordan
241	D4	Barber's Beach	Fr Hwy 401, S on Hwy 24 to Galt, E at first turnoff			75	50	60	5.50		5/1-9/15	U Z • 27	• • • • • • • • •$ • ○ • •		lr •	gp		519/658-9644	Co Rd 32, Cambridge
241	D4	Hillside Lake Park	Fr Galt, 5 mi SW on Hwy 24A			43	100	85	6.50		All year	U Z • U	$ $ • • •$ • •$ • • •	• ○	•	gpu		519/632-7572	R R 3, Ayr
246	B4	Bala Woodlands	Fr Bala, 2 mi N on Hwy 169 on Medora Lk Rd			162	20	50	5.00		5/24-10/15	U Z • U	$ $ • •$ •$ • • •	• •	dlr •	p		705/762-3332	Box 227, Bala
247	B5	Inverness Trlr Pk	Fr Hwy 141, S on Musk Rd 24, 2 mi E on N Shore Rd		1	35	10	30	5.25		5/15-10/15	U Z • 25	$ $ • •$ • • •$ • • •	• •	dlr •	gp		705/769-3721	Windermere
247	B5	Glenwood Park	Fr Bracebridge, 15 mi W on Hwy 118 at Port Carling		1	60	30	30	5.00		5/15-10/15	U Z • U	$ $ $ • • •$ • • • • ○ ○ ○	• •	dlr •	ghpt		705/765-3067	RR1, Port Carling
248	A4	Carol CS	Fr Sudbury, 8 mi S on Hwy 69	^	1	10	40	100	7.00		5/15-10/15	U Z • U	$ •$ • •$ •$ • •$ •	•	•			705/522-5570	RR 3, Site 14, Box 8, Sudbury
249	B4	Butterfly Lk Campgrounds	Fr Gravenhurst, 22 mi N on Hwy 169, .1 mi E on Hwy 118 to White's Rd, fol signs		1	16	26	70	5.00		5/15-10/15	U Z • 28	$ •$ • • • •	• •	lr •			705/765-3927	RR 3, Port Carling
250	A4	Dur-Bay Campsite	Fr Sundridge, 7-1/2 mi W on Hwy 124, 7 mi N on Pearcley Rd		2	200	70	30	3.50		6/1-10/1	U Z • 26	• • • •	• •	rl				Rt 2, Sundridge
251	A5	Camp Ohio	Fr North Bay, S on Hwy 11, SW on Hwy 654, W on South River Rd	≈		5	10	6	6.00		5/15-10/15	U Z • U	• • ○ • • • • •	○ • ○ • •	dlr •	p		705/724-5253	Nipissing
251	A5	Link's CG	Fr Callander, 1 mi S on Hwy 11, 9 mi W on 654, 1-1/2 mi on Sunset Cove Rd		1	190	35	20	5.00		All year	U Z • U	• • • • • ○ •	• •	lr	ku		705/752-1266	RR 1, Callander

ONTARIO

FOR FOOTNOTE EXPLANATION SEE FIRST PAGE OF THIS **PROVINCE** FOR MAP, SEE PAGE **118**

Park number	Map reference	Name of park	Access	Physical environment	Acres	Number of tent spaces	Number of trailer spaces	Approximate fee	Credit cards accepted	Season	Time limit / Reservations / Pets permitted / Max. trailer size	Electric / Water / Sewer hookup	Sanitary station / Bottled gas / Air conditioning	Tables / Firewood / Pull-thru spaces / Rec. hall	Flush toilets / Showers / Ice	Auto. laundry / Cafe-snack bar / Store	Swimming pool / Other swimming / Fishing	Boating	Playground	Other	CB channel monitored	Telephone no.	Mail address
		PRIVATE (CONT'D)																					
251	A5	Green Rd Cottage Trlr Ct	Fr Hwy 11, E at S edge of Callander			5	E6	V8	7.00		5/15-10/31	U Z • 30	• •	•	• ○	• • •	○ ○ •	• •	dlr	•	gp		705/752-2910	80 Green Rd, Callander
251	A5	Birchwood Cottages	Fr Powassan 8 mi W on Hwy 534, N 1 mi on Hwy 654, 2 mi to Wades Landing, 1 mi W on gravel rd		1	4	9	7	6.00		5/15-10/15	U Z • U	• • •	•	• •	• • •		•	dr	•			705/724-5250	RR 1, Nipissing
253	E8	Breezy Acres Camping Area	Fr Kapuskasing, 16 mi W on Hwy 11			12	30	18	5.00		5/24-10/10	U Z • 20	•	• •	• •	• •	•		r	•	p		05/335-4969	Harty
253	E8	Shallow Lk Trlr Pk	1/4 mi W of Mattice, 1-1/2 mi N of Hwy 11		1	196	60	45	5.00		5/15-10/1	U Z • U	• • •	•	• •	• • •	•	• •	dlr	•	p		705/364-4411	Box 12, Mattice
262	B4	Bayfort Camp	Fr Midland Bay, 3/4 mi E on Hwy 12 at Ogden Bch Rd		1	25	120	120	4.50		5/24-10/12	U • U	$	○	•$ •	• •	• •	• •	lr	•	gh		705/526-8704	Box 44, Midland
262	B4	O'Hara Pk	Fr Gloucester Pool at Pt Severn, 7 mi by boat; on Severn Riv Waterway (water access only)	≈	1	96	30		2.00		5/24-10/15	U Z •	•		• • •	• •	• •	• •	dr	•	p	13	705/756-2284	605 Bayview Drive, Midland
262	B4	Mariner's Paradise Trlr P	Fr Barrie, 30 mi NE on Hwy 400, 4 mi N on Hwy 69		1	30	42	58	5.00		5/15-10/15	U Z • U	$ $ $	• •	•$ • •	• • •	• ○ •	• •	dlr	•			705/538-2590	Waubaushene
262	B4	Picnic Island Resort	Muskoka Rd 5 to Honey Harbour			9	40	60	5.00		5/15-10/15	U • U	•	• •	• •	•	○ •	• •	dlr		g		705/756-2421	Honey Harbour
262	B4	Sunnylea Trlr Pk	Fr Port Severn, 1 mi W on Hwy 5			5	12	28	5.50		5/15-10/15	U • U	• •	•	• ○	• • ○	• ○	• •	dl		ghp		705/538-2812	Box 83, Port Severn
262	B4	Hidden Glen Camp	Fr Pt Severn, 7 mi N on Hwy 69, W on Hidden Glen Rd			200	25	75	7.00	V	5/24-10/15	U Z • U	$ •$	• ○	• • •	• • •	• •	• •	dlr	•	g	12	705/756-2675	PO Box 141, Pt Severn
267	B7	Rideau Heights Campsite	Fr Ottawa, 1/2 mi S on Hwy 16	≈	1	5	30	65	6.50		5/15-10/15	U Z • 30	• • •	•	•$ •	• • •	• ○	•	lr	•	p		613/825-1217	38 Rideau Hgts Ottawa
270	A5	Sid Turcotte Park	In Mattawa, on S shore of Mattawa Riv	≈	1	25	150	160	5.50		1/15-9/30	U Z • U	$ •$	• • •	• • • •	• • •	• • •	• •	dlr	•	gp		705/744-5375	Box 549, Mattawa
274	E8	Big Sky Trlr & Tent Pk	Fr Wawa, 1 mi S at Jct K Hwy 17/101	≈	2	24	30	50	4.50		5/15-10/1	U Z • U	$ $ $	• ○	• • •	• • •	○ • •	○ ○	d	•	g		705/856-7040	Box 581, Wawa
274	E8	Twin Lakes Camps	Fr Wawa, 8 mi E on Hwy 101		1	11	10	25	4.25	V	5/15-10/7	U Z • 30	$ $ $		• •	•$ •	•	• •	lr	•			705/856-2793	Box 642, Wawa
275	E8	Oski-Wawa	Fr Wawa, 3-1/2 mi S, corner of Hwy 17 & Mission Rd	≈	1	15	20	60	4.00		5/1-10/15	U Z • 31	$ •	•	•$ •	• • ○	• ○	• •	lr	•	gp		705/856-2413	Box 1192, Wawa
277	C6	Julian Lake Camp	Fr Peterborough, 25 mi N on Hwy 28		2	15	32	8	4.00		5/20-9/2	U Z • U	$ •	•	• •	○	○	• •	dlr				705/654-3835	Woodview
277	C6	Lovesick Lake Campsites	Fr Peterborough, 20 mi N on Hwy 28			22	60	40	5.00		5/15-10/15	U Z • U	$ •	• •	•$	• • •	•	• •	dlr				705/654-3587	Burleigh Falls
280	C5	Fenelon Falls Trlr Camp	In Fenelon Falls, off Hwy 121, W on Louisa St		1	4	10	43	5.50		5/10-10/15	U Z • 30	• • •	○$	•	• • ○	○ ○ ○	• •	dr	•	g		705/887-2310	Box 412, Fenelon Falls
280	C5	Gypsy Point	Fr Bobcaygeon, 3 mi N on Hwy 36, on Pigeon Lk, fol signs		1	9	4	14	5.50		5/1-11/30	U Z • U	• •	○	•$	• •	○ • •	• •	dlr	•	gp		705/738-2731	RR 3, Bobcaygeon
289	E2	Maple Leaf Beach Pk	Fr Hwy 401, ext 4, N to Lk St Clair, 1 mi W on Tecumseh Rd		1	10	20	65	6.00		5/15-9/30	U Z • U	$ •	•	•$	• • •	• •	• •	l	•	g		519/735-4428	Bx 9,556 Tecumseh, Emeryville
289	E2	Windsor KOA/401	Fr Hwy 401E,ext Co 46 (interchange 2) follow E		1	50	50	150	6.50	MV	5/15-10/10	U Z • U	• •	• •$	•$ • •	• • •	• •	• •	r	•	gp		519/735-3660	RR 3, Maidstone
290	B6	Smith's Bay	Fr Eganville, 4 mi N on Hwy 41, 1/2 mi to S shore of Lk Dore			25	75	25	3.50		5/15-10/15	U Z • U	•		• •	•	•	• •	r	•			613/628-5264	RR 1, Eganville
291	B6	L'Escale Camping	Fr Killaloe, 3 mi E on Hwy 60			54	20	280	7.25		5/15-10/15	U Z • U	$ •$	• •	•$ • •	• • •	• • •	• • •	dlr	•	hpt		613/757-2391	Rt 2, Golden Lake
291	B6	Golden Lk Tent & Trlr Pk	Fr Pembroke, 20 mi S on Hwy 41, 13 mi W on Hwy 60			4	20	20	3.50		5/15-10/15	U Z • 30	$ •	•	• •								613/625-2842	Rt 2, Golden Lake
291	B6	Nien-Mar Campsite	Fr Jct Hwy 60/62/512, at Killaloe, 6 mi E on Hwy 512			10	5	25	3.75		6/1-9/30	U Z • 24	$	•	• •	•	•	• •	lr	•			613/625-2431	Rt 4, Killaloe
294	B6	Serene-Vu Camping Pk	Fr Lake St Peter, 1 mi E on Lake St Peter North Rd		2	5	25	25	6.50		All year	U Z • 30	• • •	• •	• • •	•$ •	•	• •	dlr	•	pu		613/338-5636	Lake St. Peter
299	B5	Livingstone Lodge	Fr Dorset, 15 mi NE on Fletcher Lk Rd		2	10	10	5	5.50		5/1-11/15	U Z U			• •	• •		• •	lr	•				Bx 53, Dorset
300	D4	Crestwood Lake	Fr Woodstock, 7 mi E on Hwy 53, 1 mi N on Crestwood Lk Rd			25	25	200	5.00		5/1-10/1	U • U	• •$	•	• • •	• • •	• •	• •	l	•			519/458-4229	RR 1, Burford
300	D4	Little Austria Trlr Pk	Fr Brantford, 10 mi W on Hwy 53, 1/2 mi N	≈	1	50	45	200	5.50		5/1-10/30	U Z • U	• •$	• ○$	• • • •	• • •	• •	• • •		•	g		519/449-5612	RR 3, Burford
301	C4	Maple Park	Fr Wasaga Beach, 1-1/2 mi E on Hwy 92, fol signs			10	40	20	5.00		5/15-9/15	U Z • U	$ $	•	•$	• • •	•	○		•	ghp			RR 2, Elmvale
301	C4	Wasaga Cmpg	Fr Wasago Beach, 2 mi E on Hwy 92			57	20	40	7.00		5/24-9/30	U Z • U	• •	•	•$ •	• • •	•	• ○ ○		•	gh			Bx 180, Wasaga Bch
301	C4	Wasaga Beach KOA	Fr Hwy 27 in Elmvale, 2-1/2 mi W on Hwy 92		1	56	30	92	6.50		5/15-9/7w	U Z • U	• •$	• •	•$ • •	• • •	• ○ •	•		•	gp		705/322-2727	Box 193, Elmvale
302	D4	Knights Dunmark Pk	Fr Hamilton, 15 mi W on Hwy 2			200	200	400	6.00		5/24-10/1	U • U	$ $ $	•	•$ •	• • •	• • •	• •	r	•	gpt		416/648-3355	229 King St E, Hamilton
303	E7	White River	Fr Elgin St in White River, 1/2 blk E on Hwy 17		2	15	13	30	5.00		5/15-10/1	U Z • U	$ $ $	• ○ •	• •	•$ ○	• ○ ○	○ ○	r	•			807/822-2598	Box 158 White River
306	C3	Sauble Beach KOA	Fr Sauble Bch, 1 mi E on Co 8		1	23	50	150	8.00	MV	5/1-10/15	U Z • U	• • •	• • •	•$ • •	• • •	• ○ •	• ○ ○		•	ghst		519/422-1101	Rt 2, Sauble Bch
306	C3	Sauble Falls Family Camp	Fr Southampton, 14 mi N on Hwy 21		1	27	50	90	7.00		5/1-10/31	U Z • U	• • •	• ○$	• • •	•$ •	○ ○ •	○ ○		•	ghpt		519/422-1322	Rt 3, Wiarton
306	C3	Carson's Family Camp	In Sauble Beach Camp		1	69	26	481	6.75		5/1-9/15	U Z • U	$ •$	• •$	•$	•$ •	• ○ •	○ ○		•	h	12	519/422-1143	Sauble Beach
306	C3	Woodland Park	In Sauble Beach		1	85	100	200	6.75		5/1-9/15	U Z • U	$ •$	• •$	•$	•$ •	• ○ •	○ ○		•	hp	23	519/422-1161	Sauble Beach
307	B5	Northern Eagle Tent & Trl	Fr Minden, 8 mi E on Hwy 121N, S on Caribou Lodge Rd		2	37	30	80	6.00		5/15-10/15	U Z • U	$ $ $	• $	•$ • •	• • •	• • •	• •	dlr	•	ghp		705/286-2837	RR 1, Minden
307	B5	Edgewater Beach CG	Fr Minden, 5 mi E on Hwy 121, 5 mi on S Kashagawigamog Rd		2	20	160	160	5.50		5/15-10/15	U Z • 26	$ $	•	•$	• • •	•	• •	lr	•	gp		705/457-2277	Rt 2, Haliburton
307	B5	Paradise Cove Trlr Pk	Fr Haliburton, 4-1/2 mi E on Hwy 121, E end Paradise Lk		2	8	25	19	6.00		All year	U Z • 27	• •	•	•$	• • •	•	• •	r	•	gp		705/457-1953	RR 2, Haliburton
309	D4	Grand Oaks Park	Fr Hwy 3 in Cayuga, 1 mi N on Hwy 54	≈	1	40	40	140	5.50		5/15-10/15	U • 30	$ •	•	•$ •	•$ •	○ • •	• • •	lr	•			416/772-3713	Rt 5, Cayuga
309	D4	Sunnibank Park	Fr Dunnville, 4-1/2 mi W on Haldimand Rd 17	≈		10	30	30	5.00		5/1-10/1w	U • U	$	•	• • •	• • •	•	• •	lr	•	gp	8	416/774-7052	RR 5, Dunnville
316	B6	The Homestead	Fr Bancroft, 16 mi S on Hwy 28, fol Dyno Rd 2 mi		2	200	10	90	7.50		All year	U Z • U	• •$	• •	• • • •	• • •	•	• •	lr	•	u		613/339-2500	RR 3, Bancroft
316	B6	Lavallee Tent & Trlr Pk	Fr Bancroft, 4 mi SW on Hwy 28, 7 mi S on Lower Farraday Rd		2	B	419	125	7.00		5/15-10/15	U Z • 30	• •	•	•$ •	• • •	•	• •	dlr	•	gp		613/332-2015	RR 3, Coe Hill
317	B6	Parkwood Beach	Fr Bancroft, 8 mi S on Hwy 28, 2-1/2 mi W on Hwy 121, 1 mi E on Bicroft Mine Rd		2	15	25	40	5.00		All year	U Z • U	• • •	•	•$ •	•$ •	•	• •	dl	•	kp	10/11	613/339-2718	61 Spruce Ave, Cardiff
318	B6	Red Eagle T&T Pk	At Coe Hill on Hwy 620, bet Hwys 28 & 62, 1 mi S to lake		2	40	75	178	5.50		5/15-10/9**	U Z • U	$ •	•	• • •	• • •	• • •	• •	dlr	•	p		613/337-5587	Box 119, Coe Hill
322	B4	Roll-in-G Campsite	Fr Parry Sound, 14 mi S on Hwy 69 to Clear Lake Rd		1	40	12	38	4.50		6/15-10/15	U Z • U	$	○	• • • •	•$ •	○ ○	• •	r	•	p		705/375-5304	Rt 2, Parry Sound
323	E7	Travel Rest	On Hwy 17, NW edge of Schreiber		2	40	12	33	7.00		5/1-12/1	U Z • U	$ •$	• ○$	• • •	• • •	○ ○ •	○ ○	dlr				807/824-2617	Box 373, Schreiber
329	E6	Tomahawk Trlr Pk Resort	Fr Sioux Narrows, 1 mi S on Hwy 71, 1/2 mi E on Tomahawk Rd		2	15	10	60	6.50	M	5/1-10/15	U Z • U	• • •	• ○ •	• •	• • •	• ○ ○	• •	dlr	•	p	12	807/226-5622	Box 27R, Sioux Narrows
340	E3	Red Oak Travel Pk	Fr Alymer, 8 mi E on Hwy 3		1	35	20	80	None		4/1-11/1	U Z • U	$ •	•	•$ • •	• • •	• ○ •	•		•	p		519/866-3504	RR 1, Eden
340	E3	Bee-Lin Trailer Park	Fr Aylmer, 10 mi S on Hwy 73, 1/4 mi E at Brdg, fol signs		1	4	15	63	4.50		5/1-10/15	U Z • U	$ $ $	• •	•$ •	• • ○	○ •	• ○	dlr	•	p		519/773-8999	1832 Royal Cres London
342	D3	Paul Bunyan Camp	Fr Bayfield, 1-1/4 mi S on Hwy 21, fol signs		3	50	300	V300	7.00		5/24-10/31	U Z • U	• • •	• •	•$ • •	•$ •	• • •	• •		•	gh		416/565-5355	Box 46, Bayfield
342	D3	Blue Anchor	Fr Bayfield, 1/4 mi N on Hwy 21 to Jowett Rd			20	25	100	4.50		5/1-10/31	U Z • U	$ $ $	•	•$ •	•$ •	• •	• •	dl	•	g		519/565-2661	Box 38, Bayfield
343	B7	Mississippi Lk Camping	Fr Carleton Place, 1 mi W on Hwy 7, at jct Hwy 7/7B		1	36	175	100	5.00		5/1-10/1	U • U	$ •$	• •$	•$ •	•$ •	• • •	• •	lr	•	gp	12	613/257-3216	Box 337, Carleton Place
343	B7	Riverbend Pk	Fr Pakenham, 1 mi S on Hwy 29	≈		12	15	75	3.50		5/15-10/15	U Z • U	$ •	•	•$	• •	○ •	• •	dlr	•			613/624-5426	Pakenham
344	A5	Champlain T & T Park	Fr North Bay, 6 mi S on Hwy 11B, SW on Premier Rd to end			4	20	35	6.00		5/1-10/1	U Z • 28	• • •	• ○ •	•$ •	• • •	• • •	• •	lr	•	ghpt	12	705/474-4779	1202 Premier Rd, North Bay
345	D5	Knight's Hide-Away Pk	Fr Buffalo, NY, 8 mi N on Hwy 3 to Stevensville Rd jct; fol signs		1	28	30	120	6.50		5/1-10/31	U Z • 30	$ •	• $	•$ • •	• • •	• •	• ○		•	gh		416/894-1911	RR 2, Ridgeway
348	D4	Copetown Holiday Park	Copetown, 500 yds S of Jct Hwys 99 & 52 on Hwy 52		1	50	50	50	4.50		5/24-9/15	U • U	$ $ $	•	•$	• • •	• ○	• •	d	•	g		416/648-3108	Box 94, Copetown
348	D4	Olympia Village	Fr jct Hwys 5/6, 1 mi N on Hwy 6, 6 mi W on concession 4		1	48	200	300	5.50		5/1-10/9	U Z • U	$ $ $	•	•$	• • •	• •	•		•	gp		416/627-3212	RR 1, Waterdown
350	m	Goose Bay Camp	Fr Ear Falls, 4 mi S on Hwy 105			4	E6	6	4.00		All year	U Z • U	• • •	• •	• •	• •	• • •	• •	dlr	•			807/222-3313	Ear Falls
350	M	Hoover's Tall Pines Pk	Fr Vermilion Bay, 45 mi N on Hwy 105		1	6		12	4.00		5/15-10/30	U Z • U	• • •	•	• •	• • •		•	dr				807/529-6443	Rt 105, Perrault Falls
350	m	Timberlane Lodge	Fr Vermilion Bay, 63 mi N on Hwy 105, 2-1/2 mi E on Hwy 657		2	2	4	6	5.00		5/15-10/15	U Z • U	• • •	• ○	• •	•	• •	• •	dlr	•			807/222-3131	Ear Falls
350	M	Flying Bait Service & Pk	Fr Vermilion Bay, 25 mi N on Hwy 105 to Camp Robinson Rd		2	8	50	33	7.00		5/1-10/15	U Z • U	• • •	• $	• •	• • •	• •	• •	dlr	•			807/529-6561	Camp Robinson
351	C7	Landon Bay	Fr 1000 Islands Bridge, 5 mi W on 1000 Islands Pkwy	≈	1	175	70	80	5.00		5/15-10/15	21 Z • U	$ $	•	•$ •	•$ •	•	• ○ ○		•	gp		613/382-2719	Box 668, Gananoque
351	C7	Ivy Lea KOA	Fr Hwy 401, ext 108 S to 1000 Isl Pkwy, 2 mi W	≈	1	100	E25	V95	6.50		5/16-10/15	U Z • U	• •	• •$	•$ • •	• • $	• •	• ○	dlr	•	gp		613/659-2817	Box 30, Lansdowne
351	C7	1000 Islands CG	Fr 1000 Islds Brdg, 1/4 mi W on 1000 Islds Pkwy	≈	1	30	15	10	6.00		5/15-9/15	U • U	• •	•	• •	• • •	•	• •	d					RR 1, Landsdowne
351	C7	Crazy Horse CG	Fr Hwy 401, ext 109, 4 mi W of 1000 Island Brdg	≈	1	108	40	100	6.50		All year	U Z • U	• •	• •$	•$ • •	• • •	• •	• ○ ○	lr	•	ghpt		613/659-3058	RR 1, Lansdowne
351	C7	St Lawrence Beach	Fr Gananoque, 1 mi W on Hwy 2, 1 mi S on Howe Islnd Frry Rd	≈	1	10	15	10	4.00		5/1-10/31	U U	$		• •	• • •	○ • •	• •	dr		gp		613/382-3552	Bx 636 RR 3, Gananoque

ONTARIO

FOR FOOTNOTE EXPLANATION SEE FIRST PAGE OF THIS PROVINCE FOR MAP, SEE PAGE 118

Park number	Map reference	Name of park	Access	Elevation	Acres	Number of tent spaces	Number of trailer spaces	Approximate fee	Credit cards accepted	Season	Time limit / Reservations / Pets permitted / Max. trailer size	Electric hookup / Water hookup / Sewer hookup	Sanitary station / Bottled gas / Air conditioning	Tables / Firewood / Pull-thru spaces / Rec. hall	Flush toilets / Showers / Ice	Auto. laundry / Cafe-snack bar / Store	Swimming pool / Other swimming / Fishing	Boating	Playground	Other	CB channel monitored	Telephone no.	Mail address
		PRIVATE (CONT'D)																					
361	B5	Casablanca CG	Fr Huntsville, 1-1/2 mi W on Muskoka Rd #3W		8	26	44	5.50		5/15-10/15	U Z • 30	$ $		•$	• • •	• •	• •	dlr	•	g		705/789-4764	Rt1 Muskoka Rd#3W, Huntsville
361	B5	Lagoon Trlr Pk	Fr Huntsville, 4 mi N on Muskoka Rd #3	2	49	24	51	5.50		5/15-10/15	U Z • 32	$ $ $	• •$	•$ •	•$ •	○ • •	• •	r	•	g		705/789-5011	Huntsville
361	B5	Silver Sands Park	Fr Huntsville, 4 mi N on Hwy 11 (Huntsville By-Pass), W on Old N Rd	1	86	50	100	7.00		5/1-10/30	U Z • U	• • •	• ○ •	•$ •	• • •	• ○ •	• •	dlr	•	ghp		705/789-5383	Box 219, Huntsville
367	C6	Mohawk Bay Trlr Pk	Fr Hwy 401, ext 95 to Deseronto, fol signs	1	10	45	145	7.00	V	5/1-10/15	U Z • U	• • •	• •$	•$ • •	• • •	○ ○ •	• • •	r	•	gt		613/396-3730	Box 441, Deseronto
368	C6	Camp Barcovan	Fr Brighton, 7 mi E on Hwy 2, S on Stoney Pt Rd, fol signs	1	120	50	30	7.00		4/1-10/1	U • U	$ •$	• •	• •	• • •	• ○	○ •	lr	•	p			Rt 2, Carrying Place
368	C6	Sunset Tent & Trlr Pk	Fr 401, Wooler Rd, S to Co 29, 1/2 mi W on Co 29	2	22	20	80	7.00		5/15-10/15	U Z • U	• • •	•	•$ •	• • •	• • •	• •	dlr	•	g		613/392-1968	Box 107, Consecon
368	C6	Lk Consecon Rsrt	Fr Jct Hwys 401/33, 11 mi S on Hwy 33, 2 mi E on Co 1	1	13	5	70	6.00		5/1-10/15	U Z • U	• • •	•	•$ • •	• • •	• ○ •	• •	dlr	•	gp		613/399-5518	RR 2, Consecon
368	C6	Cedardale Beach Park	Fr Brighton, E 3-1/2 mi on hwy 2, S at Stoney Pt Rd, cross Murray Canal, fol signs	1	25	25	75	7.00		5/15-10/15	U Z • U	• •$	• $	•$ • •	• • •	○ •	• ○		•	gp		613/475-0212	R R 2, Carrying Place
368	C6	Willow Grove	Fr Trenton, 11 mi S on Hwy 33, ext to Co 29, 1-1/4 mi on Stinson Blk Rd		8	42	42	6.00		5/1-10/31	U Z • U	• • •		•$	•		• •	dlr	•	gp		613/392-4272	Rt 3, Consecon
369	C6	Cedar Creek Trlr Pk	Fr Hwy 401, 2-1/4 mi N on Hwy 30		15	20	45	6.00		5/15-10/15	U Z • U	• • •	•	• • •	•$ •	○ ○	• •			gp		613/475-0640	RR 7 Brighton
369	C6	KOA-Brighton-401	Fr Hwy 401, ext 86, 1000' n, 1/2 mi W on Telephone Rd	1	53	35	102	5.50	V	5/15-10/15	U Z • U	$ •$	• $	•$ •	• • •	• ○ •	•		•	g	10	613/475-2186	Box 176, Brighton
375	B4	Tamarack Park	Fr Hwy 12 in Coldwater, N on Co 17 to Severn Falls	1	10	20	10	4.00		5/1-11/1	U Z • 20	$		•$	• •	○ •	• •	dlr			13	705/686-7935	RR 1, Coldwater
375	B4	The Lantern Marina	Fr Orillia, N on Hwy 11, 9 mi W on Kilworthy Rd	0	130	30	20	5.00	M	4/1-11/1	U Z • U	• • •	• •	• • •	• • •	• •	• •	dlr	•	g	13	705/687-4184	Rt 1, Kilworthy
380	C4	Jell-E-Bean Pk	Fr Collingwood, 7 mi E on Hwy 26	1	10		140	6.50		All year	U Z • U	$ $ $	• •$	•$	•$ •	• ○ •	○ ○		•	u		705/429-5418	RR 4, Stayner
380	C4	Cedar Grove Pk	Fr Stayner, 3 mi N on Hwy 26		20	150	150	6.00		5/15-10/15	U Z • U	• $ $	• ○$	•$ •	•$ •	• ○ •	• •	dl	•			705/429-2134	Box 4,Stayner
381	E2	Camper's Cove	Fr Wheatley, 2 mi E on Hwy 3, 1/4 mi S on Campers' Cove Rd	1	61	40	270	7.00		5/15-9/30	U Z • U	• •	• •	•$ •	• • •	• •	• •		•	gp		519/825-4732	Wheatley
382	E2	Sturgeon Woods Camp	Fr Leamington, 3 mi S on Pt Pelee Rd, E on Rd C	1	57	275	275	6.00		4/15-10/15	U Z • U	• •$	• •$	•$ • •	• • •	○ •	○ •	d	•	gh		519/326-1156	RR 1, Leamington
385	C3	Spry Lake Camp	Fr Sauble Bch, 7 mi N on Sauble Bch Rd, E 1/4 mi	1	5	3	72	7.00		5/24-10/15	U Z • 31	$ • •	• •	•$	•$ ○	○ ○	• •	dlr	•	p		519/534-0192	RR 3, Wiarton
385	C3	Cam-Rene	Fr Hwy 6 in Wiarton, 8 mi W	1	30	20	10	6.00		5/1-11/1	U • U	$ $	○	• •	• ○	○ ○	○ ○	lr	•	g		519/534-0405	Oliphant
386	A3	Norm's Resort Pk	Fr Kagawong, 1 mi S on N end of Kagawong Lk; fol signs	1	97	40	60	7.00	M	5/1-10/1	U Z • U	• •	• ○	• • •	• • •	• ○ •	• •	dlr	•			705/282-2827	Kagawong
386	A3	Lacodia Resort	Fr Manitoulin Isl Bridge, W on Hwy 540, S to Manitou Lk, 6 mi on Bidwell Rd		5	10	5	4.50		5/15-10/15	U Z • U	$		• •	• •	•	• •	r				705/377-4965	RR 1 Box 133 Mindemoya
386	A3	Mike's Pk	Fr Little Current, 29 mi W on Hwy 540, Manitoulin Island		200	30	30	6.00		6/1-9/15	U Z • U	$ $	•	•$	• • •	○ ○	• •	dlr	•			705/282-2745	Kagawong
398	E8	Rose Point Lodge	Hwy 560 in Charlton, 6 mi off Hwy 11	2	14	12	7	4.00		5/1-11/1	U Z • 20	•		• •	• •	○ ○	• •	dlr	•	p		705/544-7665	Box 29, Charlton
402	D4	Willow Lake Park	Fr Woodstock, 2-1/2 mi N on Hwy 59	2	13	20	80	5.50		5/15-10/15	U Z • 32	$ $	•	•$ •	• • •	• • ○	•		•	g		519/537-7301	RR 6, Woodstock
402	D4	Park Haven Lake	Fr Toronto, SW on Hwy 401, 4 mi W on Ext 32, fol signs	1	75	50	150	5.00		5/1-10/15	U Z • U	$ •	• •	•$ •	• • •	• •	• •	dlr	•			519/469-3501	Rt 2, Innerkip
403	E6	Sauve's Arrowhead Camp	Fr Kenora, 10 mi E on Hwy 17, 1-1/2 mi W on Longbow Lk Rd	3	5	7	7	4.00		5/18-10/7	U R • U	$ •	○ ○$	• • •	• • •	• ○ •	•$	dr	•	g		807/548-4666	Box 68, Kenora
403	E6	Pleasant Point Lodge	Fr Kenora, 28 mi E off Hwy 17, on Willard Lk Rd	2	4	10	12	3.00		5/15-9/30	U Z • 30	$		• •	• •	○ •	• •	dlr	•				PO Box 324, Kenora
403	E6	Hampton's Tent & Trlr Pk	Fr Kenora, 9 mi E on Hwy 17; Fr Jct Hwy 17/71, 3 mi W	2	7	20	33	7.00	MV	5/15-9/15	U Z • U	$ $ $	• •	• •	•$ •	• ○ ○	• •	dr	•	gp		807/548-5444	Longbow Lake, Kenora
403	E6	Primmer's Court	Fr Kenora, 10 mi E on Hwy 17 (Longbow Lk Rd)	2	5	20	30	6.00		5/15-9/30	U R • U	• •	•	• •	• •		• ○	dlr	•			807/548-4844	P O Box 615, Kenora
403	E6	Pye's Landing T & T Pk	Fr Kenora, 16 mi W on Hwy 17	1	10	30	48	5.50		5/15-11/1	U Z • U	$ $ $	• ○$	• • •	• • ○	○ ○	• •	dlr	•	p	2	807/733-2098	PO Box 626, Kenora
403	E6	Redden's Trlr Pk	Fr Kenora, 9 mi E on Hwy 17	2	2		20	6.00		5/1-11/1	U Z • 30	• • •	○ •	•	• • •	• ○ •	• •	dlr	•			807/548-4066	Longbow Lake PO, Kenora
403	E6	Hillylake Camp	Fr Kenora, 5 mi E on Hwy 17	2	24	31	31	5.00		5/1-10/1	U Z • 28	$ $ $		• •	• • •	•	• •	dlr	•			807/548-5015	RR 2, Kenora
403	E6	Bigstone Lodge & Trlr Pk	Fr Kenora, 7 mi E on Hwy 17, 1-1/2 mi N on Bigstone Bay Rd	1	10	24	24	5.00		5/1-10/31	U Z • 20	• •		• • •	• • •	•	• •	dlr	•	g		807/548-5077	Box 459, Kenora
403	E6	Birch Dale Camp	Fr Kenora, E on Hwy 17 to Waldhof Rd, S to Eagle Lake	2			12	5.50		5/15-10/15	U Z • 20	$ •	• •	• • •	• • •	• •	•	dlr	•			807/227-5225	Waldhof
405	A3	Caruso Resort	Fr Espanola, 2 mi S on Hwy 68, 1/4 mi E on Anderson Lk Rd	1	7	24	18	4.50	M	5/1-10/31	U Z • U	$ •	• ○	•$ •	•	○	• •	dlr	•	gh		705/869-4895	Box 1968, Espanola
405	A3	Queensway Trlr Pk	Fr Hwy 17, 3 mi S on Hwy 68	1	4	6	22	5.00		5/15-10/15	U Z • U	$ $	• ○ •	•$ •	• • •	• ○ ○	○ ○		•	g	9	705/869-1065	Box 1213, Espanola
406	B5	Lillie Kup Kamp	Fr Hwy 11 in Katrine, 1/4 mi W on Doe Lk Rd		10	40	50	6.00		All year	U Z • U	$ $	• •$	• • •	• • •	• • •	• •	dlr	•	gkpu		705/382-3410	Box 33, Katrine
406	B5	Almaguin Parklands CG	Fr Hwy 11 in Katrine, E on Three Mi Lk Rd 1-1/4 mi	1	100	100	120	7.00		All year	U Z • U	$ $ $	• ○$	•$ • •	• • •	• • •	• • •	dlr	•	ghpu	11	705/382-3802	Box 40, Katrine
406	B5	Katrine Golf & Trlr Pk	Fr Burk's Falls, 4 mi S on Hwy 11	1	100	20	20	5.50		5/1-10/1	U Z • U	$ $ •		•$ •	• • ○	○ ○ ○	○ •	l	•	gp		705/382-5012	Box 84, Katrine
408	A3	Green Acres Tent & Trlr	Fr Espanola, 35 mi S on Hwy 68, Manitoulin Island	1	20	50	70	5.00	MV	All year	U Z • U	$ •	•	•$ •	• • •	• •	• •	dlr	•	pu	7/22	705/368-2428	Sheguiandah
408	A3	Batman's Tent & Trlr Pk	On Manitoulin Is; Fr Little Current, 8 mi S on Hwy 68	2	80	50	100	6.00	M	5/15-10/1	U Z • U	$ •$	• •	•$ •	• • •	• •	• •	dlr	•		55	705/368-2180	Sheguiandah, Manitoulin Isle
413	E3	Pt Stanley Marina Trlr Pk	Fr Hwys 3 & 401, S on Elgin Rd 20	1	14	100	36	5.00	V	All year	U Z • U	• •	• •	• • • •	• • •	○ • ○	• •	dl	•	ghu		519/782-3481	Bx 1, 301 Carlow, Pt Stanley
415	A6	White Sands Trlr Pk	Fr Pembroke, 5 mi NE off Hwy 17 on Co 21	6	6	20	45	4.75		6/1-9/15	U Z • U	$	•	• • •	•$ •	○ ○	○ •	lr	•			613/582-9202	RR 1, Pembroke
415	A6	Pine Ridge Pk & Resort	Fr Pembroke, 4 mi W on Hwy 17, 1 mi N on Radke Rd	1	15	10	40	6.00	M	5/1-11/15	U Z • U	$ •$	•	•$ •	•$ •	• • •	• •	dlr	•	gp		613/732-9891	RR 6, Pembroke
423	E8	Cameron's Beach	E of jct of Hwys 578 & 11, follow signs	1	4	100	25	5.00		6/1-9/1	U Z • U	• •		• •	○	○ ○ ○	• •	dl				705/258-3546	Box 268, Iroquois Falls
424	A4	Hass' Camp & Pk	Fr Sudbury, 40 mi S on Hwy 69, E on Hwy 607 to 607 A, S to Hass Rd		25	50	50	4.50	AV	5/1-10/15	U Z • U	• •$	• ○ •	• • •	• • •	○ • •	• •	dlr		g	14	705/857-2175	Rt 2, French River, Alban
428	A2	Timberwolf Park	Fr Iron Bridge Village, 1/2 mi E on Hwy 17E, 1/4 mi S, fol signs		80	45	14	5.00		5/1-10/31	U Z • U	• • •	• ○	• • •	• • •	○ ○ •	• •	lr	•			705/843-2223	Box 283, Iron Bridge
428	A2	Viking Tent & Trlr Pk	Fr Iron Bridge, 1 mi W on Hwy 17	1	18	E50	50	3.00		5/18-10/14	U Z • U	$ •$	• ○ •	• • •	•$ •	• ○ •	○ ○	lr	•			705/949-0124	Box 19, Iron Bridge
429	C5	Goreski Summer Resort	Fr Port Perry, 1/2 mi E on Hwy 7A, 4 mi N on Co 7		43	100	100	7.00	M	5/1-10/15	U R • U	• • •	• ○ •	•$ • •	•$ •	• • •	• •	lr	•		13	416/985-3068	Rt 3, Port Perry
429	C5	Poplar Pk	Fr Hwy 7, 2 blks S on Arrow St	1	30	10	6	3.50		5/24-9/1	28 Z • 30	$ •		• •	○	○ • ○	• ○ ○	l	•	g		416/985-2809	Box 433, Port Perry
431	D4	Willow Lake Park	Fr Brantford, W 4 mi on Hwy 53, S 7 mi on Hwy 24, E on Brant Co 4		50	80	155	6.00		5/15-9/15	U Z • 27	$ $	•	• •	•$ •	• •	• •		•	gh		519/446-2513	RR 1, Scotland
432	E6	Swenson's Resort & Trlr C	Hwy 71 W to Hwy 11, N on Hwy 621 to Morson		210	10	10	6.50		5/1-11/1	U Z • U	• • •	○ ○	• •	• •	○ •	• •	dlr	•			807/488-5641	Morrson
432	E6	Camp of the Woods	Fr Intnatl Brdg at Rainy River, 3 mi N on Hwy 600, 3.3 mi W on River Rd	2	97	30	20	5.50		5/1-10/15	U Z • U	$ •	• •	• • •	• •	•	• •	dlr	•	g		807/852-3739	RR #1, Rainy River
432	E6	Crawford's Res & Trlr Pk	Fr Nestor Falls, 7 mi N on Hwy 71	2	6	10	24	6.00		5/1-10/15	U • U	• • •	•	•	• • •	• •	• •	dlr	•			807/484-2183	Nestor Falls
432	E6	Parkview Trlr Pk	Fr Nestor Falls, 4 mi S on Hwy 71	2	5	10	25	5.50		5/1-10/31	U Z • U	• • •	• •	• • •	• • •	• ○ •	• •	dlr	•			807/484-5337	Nestor Falls
432	E6	Walleye Trailer Park	Fr Ft Francis, 1 mi W on Hwy 11/71		10	10	25	4.00		All year	U Z • U	• • •	• ○	• •	• • ○	• ○ ○	○ ○	lr	•	g		807/274-6456	1231 K Hwy, Ft Frances
433	B5	Whip-Poor-Will	Fr Huntsville, 18 mi N on Hwy 11, 3.8 mi E on Deer Lk Rd	2	38	50	50	4.00		5/1-10/1	U Z • 30	$ •		• • •	• • •	•	• •	dlr	•	gh		705/382-5410	PO Box 40, Emsdale
433	B5	Sandhurst Vacationland	Fr Huntsville, 20 mi N on Hwy 11 to Hwy 518, 12 mi E	1	135	30	80	7.50		5/24-10/20*	U Z • U	• •$	• •	•$ • •	• • •	• • •	• •	dlr	•	p		705/636-7705	RR #1, Kearney
439	D4	Country Gardens Pk	Fr Hwy 401, Interchange 34 W to New Dundee, N 3 mi, fol signs	1	30	50	150	6.00		6/1-9/1	U Z • U	$ • •	•	•$ • •	• • •	•	• •		•	p		519/696-3230	Rt 2, Petersburg
439	D4	Holiday Beach	Fr New Hamburg, Hwys 7 & 8, 4 mi S, Twp Rd 12 to Haysville, through to Twp Rd 14	2	120	100	100	6.00		5/24-10/15	U Z • U	$ • •	•	•$	• • •	• ○	• •	r	•	g		519/662-1475	RR 2, New Hamburg
441	C7	Rideau Lakes Park	Fr Crosby on Hwy 15, NW 12 mi on Narrows Lock Rd		2000	80	S20	6.00	V	5/15-10/15	U Z • 22	$	•	•$	•	• •	• •	dlr				613/267-1700	PO 307, Perth
441	C7	Hudson Bay Tent & Trlr Pk	Fr jct Hwys 15 & 42, 1-1/2 mi N on Narrows Locks Rd, 1 mi W	1	99	38	V40	5.00		5/1-10/15	U Z • U	• •	•	• • •	• • •	○ •	• •	d	•	ghp		613/272-2927	Box 37, Portland
441	C7	Sunnyside CG	Fr Westport, 2 mi SE on Hwy 42 to Golf Course Rd	1	170	30	86	4.75		5/15-10/15	U Z • U	$ $	•	•$	• • •	•	• •	dlr	•	gp		613/273-5434	RR 2, Westport
441	C7	Rideau Lks KOA	Fr Crosby, 4 mi N on Narrows Lock Rd	1	80		50	6.50		5/22-10/11	U Z • U	• • •	•	•$ •	• • •	• •	• •	dlr	•	p		613/272-2907	Box 4 RR 1, Portland
441	C7	Skycroft Family Camps	Fr Elgin N on Hwy 15, 9 mi W on Chaffey's Lock Rd	1	2000	30	30	7.00		6/15-10/15	U Z • 20	•		• • •	• •		• •	lr		p		613/359-5491	Rt 1 Chaffey's Lock, Elgin
442	C7	Canoe Lake Tent & Trlr Pk	Fr Godfrey, 11-1/2 mi E on Westport Rd, 1-1/2 mi S on dirt rd	1	600	10	60	5.50		5/1-10/31	U Z • U	• • •	•	•$	• • •		• •	lr	•		13	613/273-5232	Rt 2, Godfrey

Park number	Map reference	Name of park	Access	Physical environment	Elevation	Acres	Number of tent spaces	Number of trailer spaces	Approximate fee	Credit cards accepted	Season	Time limit	Reservations	Pets permitted	Max. trailer size	Electric / Water / Sewer hookup	Sanitary station / Bottled gas / Air conditioning	Tables / Firewood / Pull-thru spaces / Rec. hall	Flush toilets / Showers / Ice	Auto. laundry / Cafe-snack bar / Store	Swimming pool / Other swimming / Fishing	Boating	Playground	Other	CB channel monitored	Telephone no.	Mail address
		PRIVATE (CONT'D)																									
442	C7	Desert Lk-Verona KOA	On Hwy 38 N to Verona, 6 mi E on Desert Lk Rd		1	50	50	75	5.50	V	All year	U	Z	•	U	• •	• $	•$ • •	• • •	• •	• ○	dlr	•	pu		613/374-2196	RR 1, Hartington
444	E7	Bellevue Tent & Trlr Pk	Fr Nipigon, 8 mi W on Hwy 17		1	16	25	14	5.00		6/1-9/30	U	Z	•	U	• • •	•	• • •	•$ •	• •	○ ○		•			807/886-2440	RR 1, Nipigon
444	E7	Hillside Acres Trlr Pk	1/4 mi off Hwys 17 & 11, W side of Nipigon Riv Bridge		1	116	28	52	4.00		5/1-10/31	U	Z	•	U	$ $	• ○	•$ •	•$ •	○ ○ ○	• •	dlr	•			807/887-3232	Box 540, Nipigon
444	E7	Stillwater Trlr Pk	Fr Nipigon River Bridge, 3 mi W on Hwy 11/17		2	57	40	100	4.99	MV	5/15-10/15	U	Z	•	U	• •$	• •	•$ •	• • •	•	• •	r	•	g		807/887-3701	Rt 1, Nipigon
444	E7	Wolfe River Campground	Fr Nipigon, 22 mi W on Hwy 17			18	30	50	4.00		5/1-10/3	U		•	U		○	• •	○	○ ○ ○	• •		•	h		807/857-2307	Dorion
446	E6	Cobble Stone Resort	Fr Ignace, 15 mi W on Hwy 17, at Raleigh Falls		2	5	6	12	6.50		5/1-10/15	U	Z	•	U	• • •	•	• •	•$ •	• •	• •	dlr	•			807/934-2345	Bx 375, Ignace
446	E6	Tee Pee Trlr Pk & CG	Fr Dryden, 13 mi E on Hwy 17, at Wabigoon		2	3	12	23	5.00		All year	U	Z	•	U	• •$	•	• •	• • •	• ○ ○	○ ○		•				Box 46, Wabigoon
448	D3	Our Ponderosa	Fr Grand Bend, 16 mi S on Hwy 21, W on Ipperwash Rd			130	100	220	6.00	M	5/15-10/15	U	Z	•	U	• •	• •$	•$ • •	• • •	○ • •	• ○ ○		•	ghp		519/873-2031	RR 2, Forest
448	D3	Woodhaven Trlr Pk	Fr Ravenswood, N on Centre Ipperwash Rd			50	30	60	6.50		5/15-9/15	U	Z	•	U	$ $ •	• ○	• • • •	• • ○	○ ○ ○	• ○ ○	dl	•	g		519/243-2183	RR 2, Forest
450	C4	Fairview Trlr Camp	Fr Meaford, 1 mi W on Hwy 26, 2 mi N on Grey Rd #22		1	5	40	48	6.00		5/1-10/30	U	Z	•	30	$ •$	• ○ •	•$	•$ •	• •	• • •	dlr	•	gp		519/538-2631	Box 428, Meaford
452	A5	Harrison's Holiday Haven	Hwy 11 N to Powassan, W on 534 12 mi, 1/2 mi to Lk		2	10	15	5	5.00		5/15-11/15	U	Z	•	24	$ $		• •	•		• •	dr				705/729-5518	Rt 1, Nipissing
452	A5	Munro Pk	Fr Hwy 11 at Powassan, 3-1/2 mi W on Hwy 534, 1-1/4 mi S on Co			50	20	30	5.00		5/15-9/15	U	Z	•	U	$ •	•	•$ •	•$ •	•	• •	r	•	p		705/724-2539	RR 2, Powassan
453	A1	Hilton Bch Tourist Pk	Fr Hwy 17, 1-1/2 mi S on Hwy 548 to St Joseph Is; fol signs			10	10	60	6.00		5/1-9/30	U	Z	•	U	• •	• •	•$	• • •	• ○ ○	• •	dlr		p		705/246-2389	Box 9, Hilton Bch
453	A1	Twin Lakes Campsite	Fr Sault Ste Marie, 29 mi E on Hwy 17, 6 mi E on Hwy 548, 2-1/2 mi W on Hilton Rd			4	15	35	6.00		5/1-11/1	U	Z	$	U	• • •	•	• • •	• • •	• •	• •	dlr	•	h		705/246-2636	RR 1, Hilton
455	C6	Adolphous Reach Fun Farm	Fr Picton, E on Hwy 33 to Lk of Mountain Rd, 5 mi to CG		1	94	15	S15	3.00		6/15-9/9w**	U	Z	•	U			• • • •	• •	• •	• •	dlr	•	p		613/476-4203	RR 4, Picton
455	C6	Battle Hill Pk	Fr Picton, 7 mi E on Hwy 33, 1 mi N on Co 8		1	225	200	96	6.00		5/1-10/8	U	Z	•	U	• •	• $	•$ • •	• • •	• •	• • •	r	•	hkp		613/373-2651	RR 2, Napanee
458	B6	Bonnechere Bay CS	Fr Killaloe, 6 mi N on Hwy 62		1	4	40	40	3.50		5/24-9/15	U	Z	•	U	$ •		• •	•		• •	dlr	•			613/757-2731	RR 5, Killaloe
459	C6	Bayview Pk	Fr Marmora, 3 mi W on Hwy 7, 1 mi N on Bayview Pk Rd		1	125	40	50	6.00		5/15-10/30	U	Z	•	28	$ $ $	•	•$ •	•	○ ○ ○	• •	lr	•			613/472-2283	Rt 3, Marmora
459	C6	Happy Lands KOA	Fr Marmora, 2-1/2 mi E on TC 7, 1/2 mi S on 7th Concession Rd		1	200	40	64	5.50		5/1-9//30	U	Z	•	U	• •	•	• • • •	• • •	• •	• ○		•			613/472-2233	RR 2, Marmora
459	C6	Crowe Valley Camp	On Hwy 7, in Marmora, on Norwood Rd		1	130	30	10	4.00		5/1-11/30w	U	Z	•	25	•		• •		○ ○ ○	• •	dlr	•	p		613/472-3241	Norwood Rd, Marmora
459	C6	Blairton Trlr Pk	Fr Havelock, 5 mi E on Hwy 7, 1/4 mi N on Blairton Rd		1	10	10	130	7.00		5/1-10/30	U	Z	•	U	• •	• •	•$ •	•$ •	• •	• •	lr	•	gp		705/778-2557	Rt 3, Havelock
459	C6	Glen Allan Pk	Fr jct Hwys 7 & 14, in Marmora, 3 mi N, fol signs			100	125	80	7.00		All year	U	Z	•	U	• •	• •$	•$ • •	•$ •	○ • •	• •	dlr	•	kptu	10	613/472-2415	Box 219, Crowe Lk, Marmora
460	D4	Shamaranne Pk	Fr Brantford, N on Hwy 24, 2-1/2 mi W on Hwy 5 at Kitchen Rd		1	17	40	40	5.00		5/1-10/1	U	Z	•	31	• • •	• $	•$ •	• •	• •	• •		•	g		519/442-6102	Rt 1, Paris
460	D4	Everglades Park	Fr Galt, 4 mi S on Hwy 24, on Glenmorris Rd		1	13	10	5	5.00		5/24-10/31	5	Z	•	20	• • •	•	• •	•	○	• •			h		519/621-0159	Rt 5, Galt
460	D4	Ontario Park	Fr Brantford, 5 mi N on Hwy 24		1	32	100	80	4.00		5/1-10/31	U	Z	•	U	$ •$	• •$	•$ • •	• • •	• • •	•		•	gh		519/448-1801	Rt 1, St George
470	B3	Providence Bay Pk	Fr Mindemoya, W on 542 to 551, fol signs		1	300	65	85	7.00		5/1-10/31	U	Z	•	U	$ •$	• $	•$ • •	•$ •	• • •	• •	l	•			705/377-4550	Providence Bay
470	B3	L & J Trlr Pk	Fr Manitowaning, 10 mi S on Hwy 68, 4 mi W on Eagle's Nest Rd			26	40	25	6.00		5/1-11/1	U			U	$	•	• •	• • •	•	• •	dlr	•	p		705/859-3154	RR 2, Manitowaning
475	A2	South Bay Pk	Fr Elliot Lk, 6 mi N on Hwy 108, 1 mi W on S Bay Rd		2	4	15	10	4.00		5/24-9/15w	U		•	24	$ •		• • •	•	• •	• •	dlr	•	p		705/848-2804	Box 153, Elliot Lake
478	A4	Laronde Creek Pk	Fr North Bay, 12 mi W on Hwy 17		2	6	25	30	5.00	M	5/15-9/30	U		•	U	• • •		• • •	• • •	• •	• •	lr	•			705/753-1338	RR 4, North Bay
478	A4	Meadowside Lodge	Fr North Bay, 12 mi W on Hwy 17		1	600	25	20	5.00		5/14-10/31	U	Z	•	U	$	•	• • •	• • •	• ○ •	• •	dlr	•			705/753-0190	RR 4 Bx 4,North bay
485	C4	The Hammock	Fr Orillia, Hwy 12 E at Atherley, 1/2 mi N on Rama Rd, fol signs		1	50	20	160	7.00		5/1-10/9	U	Z	•	30	• •	• •	•$ •	• • •	• ○ •	• • •	dlr	•	gp	20	705/326-7885	Box 921, Orillia
485	C4	To Jo	Fr Hwy 93, 1-1/2 mi W			49	40	60	5.50		5/24-10/10	U	Z	•	30	$ •	•	•	• •	• •	• •	r		gp			RR 3, Elmvale
485	C4	The Grove	Fr Orillia, 3-1/2 mi N on Hwy 11, E on Big Chief Rd			4	12	20	5.00		5/1-10/12	U	Z	•	U	• • •	○	• •	○	○ ○	• •	lr				705/325-7103	Rt 3 Big Chief Rd, Orillia
485	C4	Oro Camping	Fr Barrie, 10 mi N on Hwy 11		1	31	60	60	5.50		5/1-11/30	U	Z	•	U	$ $	•	•$ • •	• • •	• • •	•		•	g		705/487-2610	RR 2, Oro Station
485	C4	Cedarwood KOA	Fr Barrie, 3 mi E on Hwy 400, 1 mi E on Hwy 11, 7 mi N on Hwy 93		2	60	35	65	7.00		5/1-11/1	U	Z	•	31	$ •	• •$	• • • •	• • •	• •	• •		•	g		705/726-6128	RR 1, Barrie
486	E6	Carl's Pine Hill Trlr Pk	Fr Dryden, 2 mi W on Hwy 17			6	15	30	6.00		4/1-10/1	U	Z	•	25	•$ $	•	• • •	• • •	•	$		•	h		807/937-5542	Box 481, Dryden
486	E6	Crystal Lk Trlr Pk	Fr Vermilion Bay, 3 mi W on Hwy 17, 1/2 mi S on Hanslip Rd		1	150	40	20	3.00		5/1-10/1	U	Z	•	U	• • •	•	• • •	• • •	• •	• • •	dlr	•	h		807/227-2112	Box 7, Vermilion Bay
486	E6	Brownie's Fairview Camp	Fr Jct 17/72, 9 mi N on Hwy 72			9	15	23	4.00		5/1-11/1	U	Z	•	31	• • •	•	• •	• •		• •	dlr	•			807/938-6638	Dinorwic
486	E6	Deer Trail Lodge	Fr Vermilion Bay, 4 mi E on Hwy 17, 2 mi S on Waldhof Rd		2	68	20	10	4.00		5/15-10/1	U	Z	•	30	• •	•	• • • •	• •	• • •	• •	dlr	•			807/227-5205	Waldhof, Ont
486	E6	Nugget Camp & Trlr Pk	Fr Dryden, 13 mi E on Hwy 17, at Wabigoon		2	3	12	6	5.00		5/1-9/30	U	Z	•	U	• • •	•	• • •	• • •	○ ○ •	• •	dlr		p		807-938-6304	Box 70 Wabigoon, Ont
486	E6	Polar Star Lodge	Fr Dryden, 13 mi E on Hwy 17, 1/2 mi on Polar Star Rd		2	10	25	12	5.00		5/15-10/31	U	Z	•	U	•		• •	• • •	○ •	• •	dlr				807/938-6336	Wabigoon
486	E6	Blue Bird Trlr & Campsite	Fr Vermilion Bay, 1 mi E on Hwy 17, S on Meyers Rd to Eagle Lk		2	267	40	70	6.50		5/1-10/15	U	Z	•	U	$ • •	• •	• • •	• • •	• ○ ○	• •	dlr	•			807/227-2042	Waldhof
488	A3	Mitch's Motel & Trlr Pk	Fr Sudbury, 50 mi W on Hwy 17 to Webbwood		1	7	50	30	5.00		5/1-10/1	U	Z	•	U	$ •$	• •	• • •	• • •	• • ○	•		•			705/869-1771	Webbwood
491	B4	Lost Forest Pk	Fr Parry Sound, Hwy 124 to Ahmic Harbour, 6 mi S		1	50	100	100	5.75	MV	5/15-10/15	U	Z	•	30	$ •	• •	•$ •	•$ •	• •	• •	dlr	•	p		705/387-3346	RR 1, Magnetawan
491	B4	Allendale Tourist Camp	Fr Burks Falls, 12 mi NW on Hwy 520			20	15	26	4.50		5/10-10/15	U	Z	•	U	$ •	$	• • •	•		• •	dlr	•	gp		705/387-3791	RR 3, Burks Falls
491	B4	Spring Hill Park	Fr Magnetawan on Hwy 520, 3 mi S on Old Nippising Rd			10	15	10	4.75		5/1-11/1	U	Z	•	28	$		• •	•		• •	dlr	•	g		705/387-3353	RR 1, Magnetawan
491	B4	Ahmic Lk Tent & Trlr Camp	Fr Burks Falls, 18 mi W on Hwy 520 to Hwy 124		1	150	70	70	5.00		5/1-10/15	U	Z	•	U	$ $ $	• • •	• • •	• • •	○ •	• •	dlr	•	g		705/387-3853	PO Box 18, Ahmic Harbour
493	C3	Aintree Trlr Pk	Fr Kincardine, 2 mi S on Hwy 21, 3/4 mi W on Aintree Rd		1	14		160	6.60		4/15-10/11	U	Z	•	33	• • •	• •	• • • •	• • ○	• ○ ○	○ ○	l	•	gp		519/396-3605	Box 790, Kincardine
496	A4	Land O'Lakes Lodge	Fr North Bay, 35 mi N on Hwy 11 N		1	10	E7	16	6.00	M	5/1-10/30	U	Z	•	U	• • •	• •	• •	• • •	• •	• • •	dlr	•				Marten River
499	D3	Rock Glen Fam CG	Fr Hwy 7 in Arkone, 1 mi SE, 1 mi N on Co 12			33	30	150	7.00		5/15-10/15	U	Z	•	U	• • •	• •$	•$ •	• • •	• • •	• ○		•	h	12	519/828-3456	RR1, Arkona
499	D3	Shady Pines KOA	Fr Alisa Craig, 2 mi S fr Hwy 7		2	110	100	250	5.00		All year	U	Z	•	U	$ $		• • •	• • •	• •	• •		•	h		519/232-4210	RR 1, Alisa Craig
508	B5	Lake Bernard Park	Fr Sundridge, 5 mi S on Hwy 11, 3 mi E on S Lk Bernard Rd		2	95	60	105	6.50		5/15-9/30	U	Z	•	30	$ •	•	•$ • •	•$ •	• • •	• •	dlr	•			705/384-5455	Box 99, Sundridge
509	E7	Thunderbird Resort	Fr Thunder Bay, 90 mi NW on Hwy 17, 6 mi S on lac Des Mille Lac Rd		2	6	20	20	5.00		5/13-10/22	U	Z	•	U	• •	•	• •	• • •	•	• •	dlr				807/986-2332	Upsala
510	B7	Canadian Outdoors T& T Pk	Fr Ottawa, 16 mi W on Hwys 7 & 15, at Dwyer Hill Rd		1	30	25	89	4.00		All year	U	Z	•	U	$ $ $	• •	•$ • •	• • •	• • •	•		•	gp		613/257-3958	RR 4, Ashton, Ont
515	B8	Upper Canada CG	Fr Morrisburg, 5 mi E on Hwy 401, Exit 120		1	65	60	60	5.00		5/15-10/15	U	Z	•	U	$ $	• $	•$ •	• • •	○ •	• ○ ○	l	•	gh	19/10	613/543-2201	Bx 127, Morrisburg Ontario
516	D3	Anthony's MHP	Fr London, 7 Mi E on Hwy 401, Dorchester ext 23, 1 blk N on Dorchester Rd		1	50	25	25	5.00		LD-MD	U	Z	•	U	$ •$	• $	• • •	• • ○	• ○ ○			•	g		519/268-3131	RR 2, Dorchester
516	D3	Golden Arrow Park	Fr London, 15 mi E on MC Fwy, 1/4 mi S at ext 25 on Putnam Rd, E on first rd		1	48	30	60	5.00		All year	U	Z	•	U	$ •	○	•$ •	• • •	• ○ •	• •$		•	g		519/485-0679	Rt 2, Mossley
517	E4	Sand Hill Pk Family Farm	Fr Hwy 19, 8 mi E, nr Clearcreek		1	30	100	50	4.00		4/1-11/30	U		•	U	•	• •	• •	• • •	• • ○	• ○		•	p		519/875-2329	RR 2, Port Burwell
518	D5	Holiday Harbour	Fr Q.E.W in Grimsby, ext N on Bartlett Ave to N Service Rd, 1/2 E to Book Rd, fol signs		1	6	40	20	5.00		5/1-10/30	U	Z	•	U	$		•$	• • •	•	• •		•			416/945-4779	375 Book Rd N, Grimsby
519	B4	Hutch's Haven	Fr Parry Sound, 5 mi E off Hwy 69 on McDougall Rd		1	210	75	75	4.75		All year	U	Z	•	U	$ •		•$ • •	•$ •	• ○ •	• •	r	•	hkpu		705/746-5762	Rt 1, Parry Sound
519	B4	Richmond Lake Trlr Pk	Fr Parry Sound, 1-1/2 mi S on Hwy 69			90	50	50	6.00		5/1-12/1	U		•	U	$ $ $	• ○	•$	• • •	○ ○ •	• •	dlr	•	ghp			Rt 2, Parry Sound
523	D3	Bluewater Golf Course CGs	Fr Bayfield, 1 mi N on Hwy 21			100	49	49	5.00		5/1-10/30	U	Z	•	30	• • •	• ○	•$ •	• • •	○ • •	• ○ ○	dlr	•	g		519/482-7473	RR 1, Bayfield
524	D5	Bissell's Hideaway Resort	Fr Niagara Falls, 15 mi W on Hwy 20, 1/2 mi N on Effingham Rd		1	100	100	250	7.00		5/1-10/1	U	Z	•	U	$ •	• ○	•$ • •	• • •	• • •	•		•	gp		416/892-5706	Rt 1, Ridgeville
524	D5	Scotts Trlr Pk	Fr Queen Elizabeth Way, 1 mi W on Hwy 20			16	150	127	5.50	13	4/1-11/1	U	Z	•	U	$ $ $	• • •	•$ • •	• • •	• •	•		•	ghpt		416/356-6988	8845 Lundy Ln, Niagara Falls

ONTARIO

FOR FOOTNOTE EXPLANATION SEE FIRST PAGE OF THIS **PROVINCE** FOR MAP, SEE PAGE 118

Park number	Map reference	Name of park	Access	Elevation	Acres	Number of tent spaces	Number of trailer spaces	Approximate fee	Credit cards accepted	Season	Time limit / Reservations / Pets / Max. trailer size / Electric hookup	Boating / Playground	Other	CB channel monitored	Telephone no.	Mail address
		PRIVATE (CONT'D)														
524	D5	Guenther's Grove	Fr Port Colborne, 1 mi W on Lakeshore Rd		14	30	50	4.00		5/1-10/1	U • U	dlr	gp		416/835-5606	Rt 2, Port Colborne
529	D3	Huron Haven	Fr Goderich, 2-1/2 mi N on Hwy 21	1	164	85	40	6.00	V	5/1-11/1	U Z • U		gp		519/524-6384	RR 6 Bx 128 Goderich
530	B7	Hither Hills	Fr Ottawa city limits, 6 mi S on Hwy 31 at S Glousester	1	75	100	50	4.00		4/1-10/31	U Z • U		gh		613/822-0509	Rt 6, Box 130, Ottawa
530	B7	Poplar Grove Camp	Fr Ottawa, 8 mi S on Hwy 31, at Greely	1	60	80	120	5.00		5/1-10/31	U Z • U		gpt	13	613/821-2973	Rt 2 Greely
536	B7	Sandy Beach Tourist Resor	Fr Smith Falls, 10 mi S on Hwy 15	1	8	2	36	4.50		6/1-10/1	U Z • U	dlr	gp		613/283-2080	RR 1, Lombardy
537	A2	Indian Point Tent & Trlr	In Evansville, Hwy 540 (Manitoulin Island)	1	10	40	30	6.00	M	6/1-9/30	U Z • 30	lr		9	705/282-2698	Evansville
539	B7	Mississippi Villa	Fr Arnprior, 5 mi E on Hwy 17 & Proven Line Rd at Brdg		2	10	12	4.50		5/1-10/1	U Z • U	dl			613/623-3501	RR 1, Arnprior
539	B7	T-Bell Resort	Fr Arnprior, 10 mi SW on White Lk Rd	1	17	140	140	6.50	V	5/15-10/15	U Z • U	dlr			613/623-3897	White Lake
539	B7	Grainger's Tent & Trlr Pk	Fr Arnprior, 10 mi E on Hwy 17, at Grainger Camp Rd		100	75	65	5.00		5/15-11/1	U • U				613/839-5297	RR 1, Kinburn
540	D4	Havsumfun Pk	Fr Fergus, 6 mi E on Co 18	2	170	100	300	6.50		5/15-10/15	U • U	dlr	gp		519/843-2220	Rt 4, Fergus
540	D4	The Breezes	Fr Acton, 1 mi NW on Hwy 7, 1 mi S on 1st Line	2	17	100	75	6.00		4/1-10/1	U • U	dlr	g			Rt 1, Acton
540	D4	Highland Pines CG	Fr Fergus, 6 mi E on Co 19 (Garafraxa St)	2	44	10	260	6.50		5/15-10/15	U Z • U	d	gp		519/843-2537	Rt 1, Belwood
541	A5	Pine Lane Pk	Fr North Bay, 1/4 mi N on Hwy 11 to Airport Rd, E on Carmichael Dr, N to Chadbourn Dr, 1/2 mi to CG	2	120	35	50	5.50		5/15-9/30	U Z • U	l	gp		705/472-1479	RR # 1 North Bay
542	B5	Hillbilly Estates	Fr Gravenhurst, 7 mi S on Hwy 11	1	125	25	100	6.50		5/15-10/15	U Z • U		ghp		705/689-2366	R R 2, Kilworthy
544	B6	Riverland Camp	Fr Barry's Bay, 18 mi W on Hwy 60/523	2	28	P70	90	6.50	12	All year	U Z • U	dlr	hku		705/637-5338	PO Box 98, Madawaska
545	D4	Murphy's Harbour & Cmpg	Fr Jarvis, 16 mi E on Hwy 3, 6-1/2 mi S on Cheapside Rd to Lk	0	10	25	84	6.25		5/1-10/31	U Z • 30	dl	ghp		416/776-2355	Rt 2, Nanticoke
545	D4	Knights Beach	Fr Dunnville, 8 mi W on Co 11 (Dover Rd)		200	100	130	6.00		5/1-10/15	U Z • U	lr	hp	11	416/774-4566	Rt 9, Dunnville
547	B6	Holiday Haven Pk	Fr Kaladar, 15 mi N on Hwy 41		20	50	50	5.00		5/24-10/12	U Z • 30	dr	gp		613/336-8849	RR 1, Cloyne
547	B6	Sherwood Park	Fr jct Hwys 7/41, N on Hwy 41, 1/4 mi E on Hwy 506	1	58	50	50	5.00		5/1-11/1	U Z • U	dr	gp		613/336-8844	Cloyne
548	A3	Mitchells' Camp	Fr TC 17 in Spanish, 1/2 mi S, fol signs	1	4	10	10	4.00		6/1-9/31	U Z • U	dlr				Spanish
549	B6	Forest View Lodge	Fr Bancroft, 4 mi N on Hwy 62, 14 mi W on Lk Baptiste Rd	2	15	50	20	6.75		5/1-10/31	U Z • U	dlr	p		613/332-3173	PO Box 1171, Bancroft
549	B6	Bancroft (Rockhound) KOA	Fr Bancroft, 4 mi N on Hwy 62, 1/4 mi W on S Baptiste Rd	2	186	25	100	5.50	MV	5/15-10/15	U Z • U	dr	gp	11	613/332-3673	Box 669, Bancroft
550	C7	Log Cabin Villa	Fr Kingston, 22 mi N on Co 10		4	10	10	3.00		5/1-10/15	U 22	lr			613/273-5510	Rt 1, Perth Rd
550	C7	Rideau Acres CG	Fr Kingston, 6 mi N on Hwy 15, 1/4 mi W on Cunningham Rd	1	116	20	100	5.00		5/15-10/1	U Z • U	dlr	gp		613/546-2711	RR 6, Kingston
550	C7	Burega's Loughboro Lk	Fr Hwy 401, ext 101, 7 mi N on Co 9 (Sydenham Rd)		10	25	50	5.50		5/1-11/1	U Z • U	dlr	p		613/376-6655	RR 1, Elginburg
550	C7	Ray's Place	Fr Hwy 401, Ext 101, 10 mi N on Sydenham Rd, 2 mi E & 1 mi S		5	40	20	4.00	MV	5/1-10/15	U Z • 30	dlr	p		613/376-3020	Box 22 Sydenham
550	C7	Hogan's Haven	Fr Hwy 401 10 mi W on Hwy 32, 2 mi S on Hwy 15, 3 mi W to Burnt Hills area		30	35	30	4.50		5/15-10/15	U Z • U	lr			613/387-3432	Rt 3, Seeley's Bay
551	E7	Sault Ste Marie KOA	Fr Hwy 17 N, 1/4 mi on 5th Line	1	77	35	65	6.00		5/1-10/31	U Z • U		g		705/256-2806	RR3, Sault Ste Marie
551	E7	Rock Shop Trlr Pk	Fr Sault Ste Marie, 8 mi N on Hwy 17	1	2	10	12	4.50	MV	5/1-10/31	Z Z • U				705/777-2177	Box 1079, Sault Ste Marie
551	E7	Pioneer Trlr Pk	Fr Sault Ste Marie, 8 mi N on Hwy 17	1	28	30	40	3.50		6/1-9/30	U Z • U		g		705/777-3186	RR 2, Sault Ste Marie
555	C7	O'Reilly Lk Cmpg Resort	Fr Kaladar, 18 mi E on Hwy 7, S on Frontenac Rd	1	100	50	110	6.75	V	5/1-9/10	U Z • U	lr	g	10	613/335-5643	RR 1, Mountain Grove
556	B8	Harold's Camping Grounds	Fr Ingleside, 1/2 mi E on Hwy 3	1	15	20	46	4.50		5/15-10/1	U Z • U	dlr	ghp		613/537-2318	Rt 1, Ingleside
556	B8	Vin Vista CG	Fr Ingleside, 2 mi E on Hwy 2	1	40	210	210	7.00		5/15-10/15	U Z • U	dlr	p		613/537-2300	PO Box 47, Ingleside
563	B5	Ye Olde Cutter Camp	Fr Hwy 11, ext Ontario St at Burk Falls	1	6	13	17	5.00		All year	U Z • 30	dlr	gkpu		705/382-3811	Box 12, Burks Falls
564	C6	Cobourg East KOA	Fr Hwy 401, ext 84, 1 mi E on Hwy 2, at Benlock Rd	1	42	14	97	5.25	M	5/1-10/31	U Z • U				416/349-2594	RR 1, Grafton
564	C6	Kenwin Pk	Fr Cobourg, 10 mi E on Hwy 2, S on Kenwin Pk Rd	1	79	100	100	5.00		All year	U Z • U				416/349-2154	RR 3, Colborne
566	A5	Algonquin Motel & Trlr Pk	Fr Sundridge, 4 mi N on Hwy 11		17	20	14	5.00	M	5/1-10/30	U • U		g		705/386-2641	Box 115, South River
566	A5	Camp Pocono	Fr South River, 12 mi W on Deer Lk Rd	2	10	10	5	4.00		6/1-10/15	U Z • 16	dlr	p		705/386-2834	South River
567	B5	Miners Bay Lodge-Trlr Pk	Fr Minden, 9 mi S on Hwy 35	2	200		70	4.50		5/15-10/15	U Z 30	dlr	p		705/286-2978	RR 1, Norland
569	A4	Riverside Lodge	Fr Sturgeon Falls on Hwy 17, S on Nipissing St	1	2	15	8	4.00		5/15-10/15	U Z • U	dlr			705/753-2120	RR 1, Sturgeon Falls
569	A4	Big Oak Tent & Trlr Pk	Fr Hwy 17 in Sturgeon Falls, 2-1/2 mi N on Nipissing St		80	18	12	6.00		5/24-9/15	U Z • U	dlr	gp		705/753-0679	RR 1, Sturgeon Falls
569	A4	Nipressing Lodge	In Sturgeon Falls, 4 mi S of TC 17	1	5	10	12	4.00		5/15-10/14	U Z • U	dlr	gp	5	705/753-2870	River Rd, Sturgeon Falls
569	A4	Musky Bay Camp	Fr Hagar, 12 mi S on Hwy 535	1	12	15	15	4.00		5/1-10/31	U Z • 24	dlr	p	11	705/867-5630	Rt 3, St Charles
572	C5	The Baer's Den	Fr Jct K Hwy 12/103, 2-1/2 mi W on K Hwy 12, 1/8 mi S on Concession 8	2	19	60	40	6.00		5/1-11/1	U Z • 28	d	gp		705/538-2898	RR 1, Waubaushene
577	B8	Lancaster Pk	Fr Hwy 401, ext 127, E on So Service Rd, on Lk St Francis	1	45	100	200	5.00		5/15-10/1	U Z • U	dlr	p		613/347-3452	Bx 115, Lancaster
577	B8	Curry Hill Pk KOA	Fr Hwy 401, ext 128, 2 mi N		28	35	54	6.25	M	5/20-10/30	U Z • U		gp		613/347-2130	RR 1, Bainsville
578	E6	Abram Lake Pk	Fr Dinorwic, Jct Hwy 17/72, 40 mi NE on Hwy 72 to Sioux Lookout	2	48	65	50	5.50		5/15-10/15	U Z • U	dlr			807/737-1247	RR 1, Sioux Lookout
578	E6	Lincoln Pk	TC Hwy 17 to Hwy 72, N toward Sioux Lookout, 1-1/2 mi E on Drayton Rd	2	25	20	10	6.00		5/15-10/20	U Z • U	dlr			807/737-3299	Box 444, Sioux Lookout
580	D3	Klondyke Goldrush CG	Fr Grand Bend, 3-1/2 mi S on Hwy 21	1	25	100	185	6.00		4/1-11/1	U Z • U		ghp		519/238-8348	RR 2, Grand Bend
580	D3	Sunny Side Trailer Park	Bet Port Franks & Ravenswood, 2 mi N on Hwy 21 on E Ipperwash Rd		25	35	60	6.50		5/15-10/1	U • U		gp	10	807/243-2952	RR 1, Forest
580	D3	Parkside	Fr Hwy 21, Ipperwash Bch, 2 mi N on Army Camp Rd, on Lk Huron	1	3	20	15	7.00		6/25-LD	U • U	l	gp		519/243-2657	Rt 2, Forest
580	D3	Happy Days CG	Fr Grand Bend, 4 mi S on Hwy 21		25	E50	V250	6.00		5/24-10/31	U Z • U		gp		519/243-2538	Phillips St RR 1, Thedford
582	A2	Stanley Pk CG	Fr jct Hwys 540/551, S to Monument Corners, fol signs N		105	70	150	6.50		5/10-9/15	U Z • U	dlr	g		705/337-4661	Spring Bay
582	A2	Idyll Glen Resort	Fr Mindemoya, 1 mi N on Hwy 551	1	8	25	100	5.50		5/1-9/30	U Z • U	dlr	gp		705/377-4095	Box 74, Mindemoya
584	B5	Rip's Sleepy Hollow Resor	Fr Haliburton, Hwy 35 N to Hwy 530, E to W Guilford, on N side of Pine Lk		90	80	80	5.50		All year	U Z U	lr	gkp		705/754-2057	Rt 1, Haliburton
584	B5	The Glens	Fr Bancroft, 7 mi SW on Hwy 28, W on Hwy 121, N on Hwy 648 to Wilberforce	2	300	75	S75	5.50		5/15-LD	U Z • U	dlr	p		705/448-2756	Wilberforce
585	E8	Old Mission Resort	Fr Cobalt, 16 mi SW off Hwy 11B	1	3	A30	A25	3.00			U R U	dlr	gp		705/647-5421	Box 636, New Liskeard
585	E8	Loon Lk Tent & Trlr Pk	Fr Cobalt, 4 mi on TC 11, 1 mi on Cobalt By-Pass, 1/8 mi W on Portage-Bay Rd	2	30	50	50	5.00		5/1-11/1	U Z • U	dr	p		705/679-8992	Box 1592, New Liskeard
585	E8	Marsh Bay Tourist Rsrt	Fr Cobalt, 1-1/2 mi E of Hwy 11		9	23	12	4.00		All year	U Z • U	dlr	ghu		705/679-8810	RR 1, Cobalt Marsh Bay Rd
585	E8	'Ravenscroft'	Fr Hwy 11, 1/8 mi on Jumping Caribou Lk Rd	2	5	2	7	7.50		5/1-10/30	U Z • 20	dlr			705/569-3865	Rt 1, Temagami
587	E8	Five Mile Lake Lodge	Fr Wawa, 89 mi E on Hwy 101, 17 mi S on Hwy 129	2	3	12	12	5.00		5/15-10/30	U Z • 25	dlr	p		705/864-0201	Box 516, Chapleau
590	B6	North Shore Camp	Fr Barrys Bay, 4 mi W on Hwy 60, 2 mi N on Arbor Vitae Rd	2	5	25	12	5.00		7/1-LD	U Z • U	lr	p			Box 122, Barrys Bay
596	E3	Duttona Tent & Trlr Pk	Fr Hwy 401, ext 17, 5 mi S to Hwy 3, 2 mi S on Coyne Rd		140	50	250	5.50		4/15-10/15	U Z • U	l	p		519/762-9922	RR 1, Wallacetown
596	E3	Lakewood Trlr Estates	Fr Rodney, 6 mi S on Hwy 401, ext 15, 1 mi S on Hwy 3	1	33	10	225	6.00		5/15-10/15	U Z • 31	l	p		519/785-0590	RR 3, Rodney
597	m	Steven's Gullrock Bay	Fr Vermilion Bay, 100 mi N on Hwy 105 to Red Lake Rd	2	1	10	10	5.00		5/15-10/1	U Z • 20	dlr			807/727-2708	Box 417, Red Lake

ONTARIO

FOR FOOTNOTE EXPLANATION SEE FIRST PAGE OF THIS **PROVINCE** FOR MAP, SEE PAGE 118

Park number	Map reference	Name of park	Access	Physical environment	Elevation	Acres	Number of tent spaces	Number of trailer spaces	Approximate fee	Credit cards accepted	Season	Time limit / Reservations / Pets permitted / Max. trailer size	Electric hookup / Water hookup / Sewer hookup	Sanitary station / Bottled gas / Air conditioning	Tables / Firewood / Pull-thru spaces / Rec. hall	Flush toilets / Showers / Ice	Auto. laundry / Cafe-snack bar / Store	Swimming pool / Other swimming / Fishing	Boating / Playground / Other	CB channel monitored	Telephone no.	Mail address
		PRIVATE (CONT'D)																				
599	B4	Brandywine Campsites	Off Hwy 69 on Queen's Walk Rd in Torrance	⛵	♀	1	2	18	6	6.00		5/24-10/15	U Z • 30	$		• •	•	○	• •	dl •		705/762-5497	Torrance
601	C3	Driftwood Beach Pk	Fr Hwy 9 in Clifford, 4-1/2 mi W on Huron Co 30	⛵	┴	2	60	100	100	5.00		5/15-10/15	U Z • U	$ $ $	•	• • •	• • •	• •	• •	dlr • p		519/327-8535	R R 1, Clifford
603	B5	Earth Park	Fr Bracebridge, 2 mi N on Hwy 11, 10 mi E on Hwy 117	⛵	⋀	2	50	40	30	5.50		All year	U Z • 28	• •	•	• • • •	• • •	○ ○ ○	• • ○	r • gkp		705/767-3781	Gen Del, Baysville
606	B4	Point Pleasant Marina	Fr Parry Sound, S at Sequin Riv Brdg on Great North Rd to Emily St, W on Pt Pleasant Rd	⛵	┴	1	7	4	12	7.00		5/15-10/15	U R • 33	$ $ $	• ○	• • •	• • •	•	• •	dlr • ghp		705/746-9671	Box 85, Parry Sound
606	B4	Parry Sound KOA	Fr Parry Sound, 5 mi S on Hwy 69, 2 mi W on Rankin Lk Rd	⛵	┴		70	30	50	6.00		5/1-10/31	U Z • U	$ •	• • $	• $ •	• • •	• •	• • ○	l • pu		705/378-2721	Rankin Lk Rd,RR 2,Parry Sound
609	E2	Twin Gables	Fr Colchester, 6 mi E on Hwy 18A	⛵	┴		10	30	24	3.50		6/1-9/30	U R U	$ $		•			•	p			RR 1, Harrow
609	E2	Ravine Cottages, Trlrs &	On K Hwy 18A, at Oxley & CS	⛵	♀	1	22	5	131	6.00		5/24-9/15	U Z • U	• • •	• •	• $ •	• • •	○	• • •	• ghp		519/738-2620	RR 1, Harrow
610	B7	Pickeral Bay	Fr Pakenham, on Hwy 29, 17 mi W on Bellamy Rd	⛵	♀	1	10	5	5	4.00		5/1-10/15	U R • 21	• $	• •	• $	• $ •	• • •	• •	dlr		613/623-3344	Rt 2 White Lake
611	D3	Argyle Acres	Fr London, 4 mi E on Hwy 2	ѱ	┴	1	13	10	10	3.50		5/1-10/31	U Z • 24	•	•	•	• • •	• ○		• gp		519/268-7271	RR 2, Thorndale
612	B6	Snider's Tent & Trlr Pk	Fr Hwy 41 in Griffith, 11 mi, fol signs	⛵	⋀	2	400	75	75	3.50		5/1-11/30	28 • U		•	• •	•	•	• •	lr •		613/333-5551	R 3, Dacre
613	D3	London KOA	Fr Hwy 401, ext 22 on Hwy 74 to 2nd Concession, 1/8 mi E	┴			25	50	102	5.50		5/1-10/31	U Z • U	$ •	• • $	• $ • •	• • •	• ○ •	•	• gp		519/644-0222	RR 7, London
625	C3	MacKenzie Trlr Ct	Fr Goderich, 17 mi N on Hwy 21, 1 mi W on Rd 22	⛵	┴	1	16	75	80	7.00		5/15-10/15	U Z • U	• • •	•	• $ •	• • ○	• ○	•	l • p		519/529-7536	Rt 3, Goderich
626	B8	L'Orignal Pk	Fr Hawksbury, 5 mi W on Hwy 17, 1 mi S	≈	♀	1	18	10	24	3.50		6/1-9/15	U Z •	$		• •	○	○ ○	• •	dlr • p		613/675-2294	Box 271, L'Orignal
626	B8	Evergreen Pk	Fr Alfred, 1 mi W on Hwy 17	⛵	♀	1	48	24	S16	4.00		All year	U Z • U	$ •	• ○	• • •	•	○ ○	○ ○	dlr • kp		613/679-2943	RR 1, Evergreen Park
627	B7	Sugar Bush Hill	Fr Hwy 7 in Perth, 20 mi N on Lanark Rd	⛵	┴	1	10	10	30	5.00		5/24-10/1	U Z • 22	•		• $	○	○ ○	• •	dlr • p		613/278-2774	Box 367 Perth, Ont
631	B6	Lk Palmerston Resort	Fr Plevna, 6 mi NE on Hwy 509 off Hwy 506	⛵	♀	1	15	100	100	3.50		4/25-11/1	U • U	$ $	○ ○	• ○ •	•	• •	• •	dlr •	10		Ompah
632	B7	Cedar Haven Pk	Fr Cobden, 1/2 mi E on TC 17, 3 mi NE on Cedar Haven Pk Rd	⛵	♀	1	24	100	140	4.25		5/15-10/15	U Z • U	$ $ $	• •	• $ • •	• • •	• • •	• •	dlr • p		613/646-7989	RR 1, Cobden
632	B7	Yonder Hill Cmpg	Fr Renfrew, 11 mi W on Hwy 17	⛵	♀	1	75	128	128	5.50		5/1-9/15	U Z • U	• •	•	• • • •	• • •	○ •	• •	dlr • gp		613/432-6584	Haleys Station
634	B7	Renfrew KOA	Fr Renfrew, 5 mi W on Hwy 17 1/2 mi on Storyland Rd	⛵	♀		200	15	85	6.00		5/1-10/15	U Z • U	$ •	• • •	• $ • •	• • •	• •	• •	r • gp	19	613/432-6280	RR 5, Renfrew
635	D2	Bluewater Country KOA	Fr Blue Water Brdg, 5 mi E on Hwy 7, 1/4 mi S on Blackwell Rd	ѱ	◢	1	50	150	150	6.00		5/1-10/31	28 Z • 31	$ $	• • $	• $ • •	• • •	• ○ •	•	• g		519/542-7800	1144 Blackwell S Rd, Sarnia
637	B6	Sun 'N' Sand	Fr Cloyne, 15 mi N on Hwy 41	⛵	⋀	1	5	15	25	4.50		All year	U Z • 30	$	○ ○	• $ •	•	○ • •	• •	dlr • hku	10	613/336-2294	RR 1, Cloyne
638	A1	Fred's Tent & Trlr Pk	Fr Sault Ste Marie, E on Hwy 17, S on Hwy 548	⛵	⋀		5	15	20	5.50		5/1-11/1	U Z • U	• • •	• ○	• • • •	• •	• ○ ○	• •	dlr • p			St Joseph Island
640	C6	Smugglers Cove CG	Fr Milford, 7 mi SE on Co 9	⛵	┴	1	20	50	72	5.00		6/1-9/30	U Z • U	$ $ $	•	• • •	• • •	• • •	• •	dlr • p		613/476-3522	Box 1357, Picton
641	C7	Cedar Forest Pk	Fr Hwy 401, Brockville ext (ext 112) 7 mi N on Hwy 29, fol signs	⛵	♀	1	9	35	25	5.00		5/15-9/15	U Z • U	$ $	•	• • •	•	•	• •	dl • ghpt		613/923-5726	Graham Lk, RR4 Mallorytown
642	C7	1000 Islands KOA	Fr Hwy 401, ext 110, Mallorytown Rd to Hwy 2 W	≈	┴		60	55	110	6.00		5/15-10/15	U Z • U	• • $	• •	• $ • •	• • •	• •	• ○ ○	• g		613/923-5339	Box 29, Mallorytown
642	C7	Rockport Tent & Trlr Camp	Fr Brockville, 21 mi W on 1000 Isl Pkwy	≈	♀	1	26	100	60	4.50		5/1-10/15	U • U	• •	• ○ •	• •	• • •	• •	• •	dlr hp		613/659-3402	Rockport
644	E7	Happyland Pk	Fr Thunder Bay, 11 mi W on Hwy 11/17	≈	┴	2	24	30	70	5.00		All year	U Z • U	$ $ $	• ○ •	• • • •	• $ •	○ ○ •	○	•		807/939-0531	RR5, Thunder Bay
644	E7	Maple Leaf CG	Fr Nipigon, 20 mi W on Hwys 11/17	≈	♀	1	8	10	S30	5.00		5/1-10/1	U Z • U	$ •		• $ •	• • •	•		•		807/857-2386	RR 1, Hurkett
644	E7	Thunder Bay KOA	Fr Thunder Bay, 4 mi E on Hwy 11/17; S on Spruce Riv rd	⛵	⋀	1	90	E35	115	6.00		5/1-10/15	U Z • U	• • •	• •	• $ • •	• • •	• •	•	• g	2	807/683-6221	RR 13, Thunder Bay,Sta P
645	D4	Bingeman Park	Fr Kitchener, Victoria St N, Hwy 7 on Bingeman Pk Rd	≈	◢	1	130	100	170	7.50		All year	U • U	$ $ $	• ○ $	• $ • •	• • •	• • ○	•	• gk		519/744-1555	1208 Victoria St N, Kitchener
667	C5	Wanna Sta CS & Marina	Fr Lindsay, NE 5 mi on Hwy 36 to Snug Harbour Rd, N to Sturgeon Lk	⛵	ѱ	1	20	50	150	5.50		5/1-10/15	U Z • 30	$ • $	• •	• $ •	• • •	• • •	• • •	dlr • gp		705/324-4735	RR 6, Lindsay
668	A5	Nosbonsing Marina & Pk	Fr Hwy 11 in Callander, 7 mi N on Hwy 654	⛵	⋀	1	25	20	S10	6.00	M	5/15-11/15	U • 28	• •	•	• •	• •	• •	• •	dlr		705/752-2690	RR 1, Astorville
670	E3	Rondeau Shores Trlr Park	Fr Hwy 3 in Morpeth, 2 mi S on Co, fol signs	⛵	ѱ		10	7	120	6.50		5/15-10/15	U Z • U	• •	• •	• $ •	• • •	• •	• • •	l • ghp		519/674-3330	RR1, Morpeth
670	E3	Jellystone Pk	Fr Morpeth, 2 mi S on Co 17	⛵	┴	1	130	E50	V50	5.50		5/1-11/1	7 Z • U	• • $	• •	• • • •	• • •	• •	• • •	• p		519/674-5516	RR 1, Morpeth
672	B5	Reay Park KOA	Fr Gravenhurst, 4 mi N on Hwy 11, 1/4 mi E on Reay Rd	⛵	♀	1	200	14	120	6.00		All year	U Z • 31	• •	• • $	• $ • •	• • •	• •	• • •	r • egku		705/687-2333	RR #3, Gravenhurst
672	B5	Inn on the Lake	Fr Gravenhurst, 2 mi to Muldrew Lk Rd, W to camp	⛵	⋀	1	69	20	40	5.50	MV	All year	U Z • U	• •	• •	• • • •	• • •	• • •	• •	dlr • gpu		705/687-3679	Box 130, Gravenhurst
672	B5	Whispering Pines Trlr Pk	Fr Bracebridge, 3 mi W on Hwy 118 - Golden Beach Rd	⛵	♀	1	10	20	100	6.25		5/15-10/15	U Z • 28	$ • $	• •	• $ •	• • •	•	○ •	dl • gh		705/645-5682	RR 1, Bracebridge
673	A3	Holiday Bch CG	Fr Sudbury, 12 mi W on TCH 17	⛵	♀	2	26	35	35	5.00		5/15-10/30	U Z • U	$ $	•	• $ • •	• • •	• •	• •	• g		705/866-2976	Bx 142, Whitefish
676	C3	Port Elgin KOA	Fr Port Elgin, 1 mi N on Hwy 21	⛵	┴		15	40	160	6.50		5/1-11/15	U Z • U	$ $ $	• • $	• $ • •	• • •	• • •	• •	dlr • gp		519/832-5183	RR 2, Port Elgin
679	A3	Holiday Haven Resort	Fr Manitowaning, 3 mi N on Hwy 68, 1 mi W at Bidwell Rd	⛵	┴	1	30	75	75	7.00		4/15-10/15	U Z • U	$ •	•	• • • •	• • •	• •	• •	dlr •	7	705/859-3550	RR1, Manitowaning, Manitoulin
681	B7	McCullough's Landing	Fr Perth, 8 mi NE on Hwy 7, 1 mi E on West Shore Rd	⛵	ѱ	1	35	25	125	6.00		5/15-10/1	U Z • U	• •	• • $	• $ • •	• • •	• •	• •	lr • gp	10/19	613/267-4310	RR 6, Perth
683	E6	Bear Pass Trading Post	Fr Ft Frances, 20 mi E, S on Crawford's Rd	⛵	♀	2	3	30	S10	5.00	V	5/14-9/30	U Z • 25	$ $	•	• • •	• • •	•	• •	dlr			Box 57, Fort Francis
686	C5	Black River Pk	Fr Toronto, E on Hwy 401, N on Hwy 12, 12 mi N on Hwy 169	≈	♀	1	179	35	18	5.00		5/24-LD	U Z • 24	$		• •			• •			705/689-5947	Rama Rd Post Office, Rama
689	D3	Family Paradise	Fr Seaforth, 6 mi N on Co 12, 3 mi E	⛵	┴		118	45	80	5.00		5/1-10/30	U • 24	• •	•	• • •	• • •	•	• •	• g		519/527-0629	RR 4, Walton
691	B6	White Cedars	Fr Eganville, 10 mi S on Hwy 41	⛵	⋀	1	360	40	40	5.50		5/1-10/30	U R • U	• • •	• $	• $	• • •	•	• •	dlr • p		613/649-2255	RR 4, Eganville
692	C4	Primrose Park	Fr Shelburne, 3 mi E at jct Hwy 10/24/89 at Primrose	≈	♀	2	60	100	133	5.50	V	5/1-10/15	U Z • U	$ $ $	• •	• $ • •	• • •	• • •	•	• g		519/925-2848	RR 4, Shelburne
693	C3	River Bend Camp	Fr Durham, 7 mi N on Hwy 6	≈	♀		127	30	32	5.00	MV	All year	U Z • U	$ •	•	• $ •	•	• •	• •	• kpu	10	519/369-5642	RR 1, Durham
694	B8	Camp Kittawa	Fr Ottawa, 20 mi E on Hwy 417, Limoges ext, 1/2 mi N	ѱ	┴	1	135	30	150	6.00		5/15-10/15w	U Z • U	$ • $	• ○	• $ •	• • •	• ○ •	•	• p		613/443-3040	Box 59, Limoges
695	E2	Tilbury Trlr Camp	Fr Tilbury, W on Hwy 2, E of W Inter 8 on Hwy 401	⛵	┴		25	50	50	5.00		5/1-10/31	U • 34	$ $ $	• •	• • •	• • •	○ ○ •	• •	• g		519/682-1350	RR 5, Tilbury
696	B5	Sandy Lane Resort	Fr Minden, 16 mi N on Hwy 35	⛵	⋀		4	15	15	7.00		All year	U R U	$ •		• $	•	○ ○	• •	dlr • ghpu	9	705/489-2020	Halls Lk Rt 2, Minden
697	B6	Brown's Cg	Fr Hwy 401 (Napane ext), 54 mi N on Hwy 41	⛵	ѱ	1	100	75	S75	5.00		5/1-10/1	U Z • U	$		• •	• • •	○ ○ ○	• •	dlr		613/336-2504	RR 1, Cloyne
698	C7	Cedar Rails KOA	Fr Hwy 401, ext 100, N on Hwy 38 to Cordukes Rd	ѱ	┴		33	34	72	5.50	MV	5/15-10/15	U Z • U	$ $	• ○ $	• $ • •	• • •	•	•	• gh		613/546-6140	Cordukes Rd,RR 8, Kingston
699	A2	North Channel KOA	Fr jct Hwys 108 & 17, 1 1/2 mi W on TC 17	⛵	┴	1	500	E18	76	5.50		MD-LD	U Z • U	$ $ S	• • $	• $ • •	• • •	• ○ •	• • •	l •		705/849-2210	Box 27, Spragge

PRINCE EDWARD ISLAND

FOR MAP, SEE PAGE 115

●—at the campground
○—within one mile of campground
$—extra charge
*—see city map
**—limited facilities during winter months
1-5—number of miles in NF within which facility or activity can be found
A—adults only
B—10,000 acres or more
C—contribution

E—tents rented
F—entrance fee or permit required—see "Special Information on the Public Areas"
H—over 9000 feet above sea level
N—no specific number, limited by size of area only
P—primitive
R—reservation required
S—self-contained units only
U—unlimited

V—trailers rented
Z—reservations accepted
LD—Labor Day
MD—Memorial Day
UC—under construction
d—boat dock
g—public golf course within 5 miles
h—horseback riding
j—whitewater running craft only
k—snow skiing within 25 miles

l—boat launch
m—area north of map
n—no drinking water
p—motor bikes prohibited
r—boat rental
s—stream, lake or creek water only
t—tennis
u—snowmobile trails
w—open certain off-season weekends and holidays

y—drinking water must be boiled
⚓ access to ocean
⫯ access to lake
≈ access to river
∧ mountainous terrain
ѱ prairie land
⅌ desert area
♀ heavily wooded
⊥ urban area
⫛ rural area

CREDIT CARD SYMBOLS:
A—American Express
M—Master Charge
V—Visa/Bank Americard

FEES REFLECT MINIMUM RATE FOR 2 ADULTS AND ARE SUBJECT TO SEASONAL CHANGES

Park number	Map reference	Name of park	Access	Physical environment	Elevation	Acres	Number of tent spaces	Number of trailer spaces	Approximate fee	Credit cards accepted	Season	Time limit	Reservations	Pets permitted	Max. trailer size	Electric hookup	Water hookup	Sewer hookup	Sanitary station	Bottled gas	Air conditioning	Tables	Firewood	Pull-thru spaces	Rec. hall	Flush toilets	Showers	Ice	Auto. laundry	Cafe-snack bar	Store	Swimming pool	Other swimming	Fishing	Boating	Playground	Other	CB channel monitored	Telephone no.	Mail address
		PROVINCIAL PARKS																																						
1	C4	Jacques Cartier	Fr jct Hwys 2 & 151, E on Hwy 151 to Alberton, 4 mi N on Hwy 162		0	22	60	12	5.00		6/10-9/5	14		●	U	$	$		●			●	●			●	$		●		○		●	○	l	●	h			Alberton
3	C4	Linkletter	Fr jct Hwys Summerside & 11, 4 mi W on Hwy 11, S on access rd		0	15	52	32	5.00		6/10-9/5	14		●	U	$	$		●			●	●			●	$		●	○	○		●	○		●	g			Summerside
4	D5	Northumberland Park	Fr Wood Island Ferry Terminal, 2 mi E on Hwy 4		0	75	57	45	5.00		6/10-9/5	14		●	U	$	$					●	●		●	●	$	○	●	○	○		●	●	l	●				Wood Island
5	C4	Green	Fr Richmond, E & N on Hwy 167 to Port Hill		0	110	72	24	5.00		5/15-10/10	14		●	U	$	$	$	●			●	●			●	$		●	○	○		●	●	l	●	h			Summerside
6	C5	Crowbush Cove	Fr Charlottetown, 22 mi E on Hwy 350, in W St Peters		1	90	20	40	5.00		6/10-9/5	14		●	U	●	●					●	●			●	●		●				●			●				Charlottetown
7	D5	Strathgartney	Fr Charlottetown, 13 mi SW on TC 1		0	40	48	12	5.00		5/15-10/10	14		●	U	$	$					●	●			●	$		●	○	○			●		●	gh			Strathgartney
8	D5	Panmure Island	Hwy 17 to Gaspereaux, then N			19	50	10	5.00		6/10-9/5	14		●	U	$	$		●			●	●			●	$		●	●			●		l	●				Murray Harbour
9	D5	Lord Selkirk	Fr Wood Islands, 15 mi NW on TC 1		0	114	52	20	5.00		6/10-9/5	14		●	U	$	$		●	○		●	●			●	$		●		○		●	●	l	●	h			Eldon
11	D5	Brudenell River	On Hwy 3, bet Poole's Corner & Georgetown		0	1285	108	12	5.00		5/15-10/10	14		●	U	$	$		●			●	●			●	$		●	○	○		●	○	l	●	gh			Georgetown
13	C5	St. Peters	Fr Charlottetown, 30 mi NE on Hwy 2		0	17	18	12	5.00		6/10-9/5	14		●	U	$	$			○		●	●			●	$			○	○		●	●	l	●				St Peters
14	C6	Red Point	Fr Souris, 8 mi NE on Hwy 16		0	5	24	12	3.75		6/10-9/5	14		●								●	●			●	$						●		l	●				Souris
16	C6	Campbell's Cove	Fr Elmira, 3 mi NW on Hwy 16		0	7	30		3.75		6/10-9/5	14		●								●	●			●	$	○					●	●	l	●				Souris
18	C5	Cabot Park	Fr Kensington, 10 mi NW on Hwy 20, at Malpeque		0	261	114	30	5.00		5/15-9/5	14		●	U	$	$			○		●	●			●	$	○	●	○	○		●	●	l	●				Kensington
19	D5	Sir Andrew MacPhail Mem	At Orwell, off TC 1 Mem		0	143	P24		3.75		6/10-9/5	14		●								●	●							○	○		○	●		●				Orwell
20	C4	Cedar Dunes	At West Pt, off Hwy 14		0	100	36	10	5.00		6/10-9/5	14		●	U	$	$		●			●	●			●	$	○	●		○		●	●	l	●				O'Leary
		NATIONAL PARKS																																						
		Prince Edward Island NP																																						PO Box 487, Charlottetown
30	C5	Stanhope	Fr Charlottetown, N on Hwys 2 & 6		0	5	103	14	F6.00		5/18-10/14	14		●	U	●	●	●	●			●	●			●	●	○	●	○	○		●	○	l	●	g			
30	C5	Rustico Island	Fr Charlottetown, 19 mi on Hwy 15 & Gulf Shore Rd		0	113	148		F3.00		6/15-9/7	14		●								●	●			●				○			●		l	●	g			
30	C5	Cavendish	Fr Charlottetown, 27-1/2 mi on Hwy 7 & 6 or Hwy 2 & 13		0	62	226	78	F6.00		5/18-10/14	14		●	U	●	●	●	●			●	●			●	●	○	●	○	○		●	○	l	●	g			
		PRIVATE																																						
42	C5	Dunwurkin By The Sea	Fr Charlottetown, 13 mi N on Hwya 15/6 to 6W	⚓ ⫛	0	50	75	25	6.00		6/1-9/30	U	Z	●	U	●	●	●	●			●	$	●	●	●	●	●	●	○	●		●	○		●			902/672-2243	Brackley Beach
43	C5	Ideal CG	Fr Dalvey Bch, 1-1/2 mi on Hwy 6	⚓ ⫛		12	98	36	5.50		6/24-9/15	U	Z	●	U	●	●	●	●	●		●			●		●	●	●	●	●	●			l	●			902/672-2273	Grand-Tracadie
43	C5	Bagnalls Trlr Pk	Fr Charlottetown, 4 mi E on Hwy 2E, 10 mi N on Hwy 25 to Bayshore Rd	⚓ ⫛	0	1		40	5.50		6/15-LD	U	R	●	U	●	●	●				●	●			●	●	○			○		○	○		●	gh		902/672-2239	Stanhope
44	D5	Holiday Haven	Fr Charlottetown, 8 mi W on Hwy 1, on Hwy 248 at Cornwall	≈ ⫛	1	50	75	250	7.00	MV	5/15-10/30	U	Z	●	U	●	●	●	●	●		●		●	●	●	●	●	●	●	●	$	●		l	●			902/675-2421	Box 129 Cornwall
45	C5	Twin Shores Camping Area	Fr Kensington, 10 mi N on Hwy 20, W at Darnley School	⚓ ⫛	0	100	218	218	5.00		6/15-9/4	U	Z	●	U	$	$	$	●			●	$	●	●	●	$	●	●	●	●		●	●		●	p		902/836-5152	Darnley Point
46	C4	Foxley River Haven CG	Fr Hwy 2, 2-1/2 mi N on Lady Slipper Dr/Hwy 12	⚓ ⫛	1	10	25	38	5.00		6/1-10/31	U	Z	●	U	●	●	$				●	●			●	●	●	●			●	●	●		●	p		902/831-2382	Portage RR 1
47	C5	Harbourvue	Fr Charlottetown, 20 mi N on Hwy 6	⚓ ⫛		20	200	100	5.50		6/20-LD	U	Z	●	U	●	●	●	●			●	●	●	●	●	●	●	●		●		●	○	l	●	ghpt		902/963-2511	PO Bx 54, North Rustic
47	C5	Forest Hills Pk	On Rt 6, in Cavendish	⚓ ⫛		200	270	480	6.25		6/25-8/31	U	Z	●	U	●	●	●	●	○		●	$	●	●	●	●	●	●	●	●	●	○	○	r	●	gh		902/964-2432	Hunter River
47	C5	Cavendish Sunset CGs	Fr Jct Hwys 6/13, 1-1/2 mi W	⚓ ♀	1	300	225	115	7.00		6/22-9/3	U	Z	●	U	$	$	$	●			●	$	●	●	●	●	●	●	●	●	●	○	○		●	pt	14	902/436-6641	Box 1506, Summerside
49	C4	Pate Orchard View Cabins	Fr Summerside, 36 mi W off Hwy 2	⫛		23	A20	A10	7.00		5/31-9/30	U	R	●	U	$	$	$					●			●	●		○	○	○						g			O'Leary Village
51	D5	Surfside Trlr & CG	Fr TC 1, 6 mi S on Hwy 10	⚓ ⫛	1	15	35	40	5.00		5/15-9/15	U	Z	●	30	●	●	$	●	●		●	$	●		●	●	●	●		●		●	○		●	p			RR 1, Borden
54	C5	Stanhope Bay	Fr NE Charlottetown, 13 mi N on Hwys 2/25 (St Ptrs & York rds)	⚓ ♀	1	9	70	V30	5.25		6/15-9/10	U	Z	●	25	$	$	$				●	●	●	●	●	●	●	●	○	●		○	○		●	ghp		902/672-2826	Bx 1172, Charlottetown

QUEBEC

FOR MAP, SEE PAGE 119

●—at the campground
○—within one mile of campground
$—extra charge
*—see city map
**—limited facilities during winter months
1-5—number of miles in NF within which facility or activity can be found
A—adults only
B—10,000 acres or more
C—contribution

E—tents rented
F—entrance fee or permit required—see "Special Information on the Public Areas"
H—over 9000 feet above sea level
N—no specific number, limited by size of area only
P—primitive
R—reservation required
S—self-contained units only
U—unlimited

V—trailers rented
Z—reservations accepted
LD—Labor Day
MD—Memorial Day
UC—under construction
d—boat dock
g—public golf course within 5 miles
h—horseback riding
j—whitewater running craft only
k—snow skiing within 25 miles

l—boat launch
m—area north of map
n—no drinking water
p—motor bikes prohibited
r—boat rental
s—stream, lake or creek water only
t—tennis
u—snowmobile trails
w—open certain off-season weekends and holidays

y—drinking water must be boiled
access to ocean
access to lake
≈ access to river
mountainous terrain
prairie land
desert area
heavily wooded
urban area
rural area

CREDIT CARD SYMBOLS:
A—American Express
M—Master Charge
V—Visa/Bank Americard

FEES REFLECT MINIMUM RATE FOR 2 ADULTS AND ARE SUBJECT TO SEASONAL CHANGES

Park number	Map reference	Name of park	Access	Physical environment	Elevation	Acres	Number of tent spaces	Number of trailer spaces	Approximate fee	Credit cards accepted	Season
		PROVINCIAL PARKS & RESERVES	For additional CGs, see 'Backpack or Boat Access Areas'								
		Laurentides Pk									
1	B5	Belle Riviere	Fr Alma, 20 mi S on Hwy 169		3		40	40	3.00		5/26-LD
1	B5	Lac Arthabaska	Fr Quebec, 100 mi NW on Hwy 175		2	3	25	25	3.00		5/25-LD
1	B5	Des Islets	Fr Quebec, 120 mi N on Hwy 175		2		25	25	2.00		5/25-LD
2	C5	La Mare du Sault	Fr Quebec, 50 mi N on Hwy 175		3		112	10	3.00		5/25-LD
2	C5	La Loutre	Fr Quebec, 75 mi N on Hwy 175		3		110	36	4.00		5/25-LD
3	C4	Lac Ste Anne	Fr Quebec, 65 mi NW on Hwys 40 and 365		2		20	20	2.00		5/25-LD
4	B4	Aux Ecorces	Fr Quebec, 120 mi N on Hwys 175 & 169		2		25	25	3.00		5/26-LD
4	B4	Lac Metabetchouane	Fr Chambord, 40 mi S on Hwy 175		2		15	15	2.00		5/26-LD
		Mt Tremblant									
5	D2	La Menagerie	Fr Montreal, 60 mi N on Rt 117		1		204	39	4.00		5/26-10/9
5	D2	La Volieri	Fr St Donat, on Hwy 125, 10 mi NW on access rd		1		150		3.00		5/26-9/9
		Parc Kenogami									
6	B5	Lac Kenogami	Fr Jonquiere, 15 mi S on access rd		2		85	60	4.00		5/25-LD
		Parc de la Gaspesie				B					
9	F7	Mont Albert	Fr Ste Anne-des-Monts, 26 mi SE on Hwy 299		4		43	16	3.00		6/15-9/3
9	F7	Lac Madeleine	Fr Ste Anne Des Monts, 30 mi SE on Hwy 299		3		10	10	3.00		6/7-9/3
11	D5	St-Jean-Ile-D'Orleans	Fr Quebec, NE on Hwy 368 ovr Ile d'Orleans brdg to rd to St Jean		1	33	268	268	4.00		5/26-9/5
12	F7	Parc Port Daniel	Fr Port Daniel, 4 mi N on access rd		1	B	24	9	4.00		5/25-LD
		Parc de La Verendyre			2	B					
13	B2	Lac la Vieille	Fr Mont-Laurier, 42 mi N on Hwy 117		2		138	50	4.00		5/17-9/20
13	B2	Lac Savary	Fr Mont-Laurier, 60 mi N on Hwy 117		2		44	10	4.00		5/16-9/15
13	B2	Lac Dozois	Fr Mont-Laurier 132 mi N on Hwy 117, 6 mi S on paved rd		2		50	50	3.00		5/17-9/20
		Parc du Chibougamau				B					
14	A3	Lac du Milieu	Fr St Felicien, 25 mi NW on Hwy 167				10	10	3.00		5/26-9/4
14	A3	Lac d'Argenson	Fr St Felicien, 66 mi NW on Hwy 167		2		25	25	3.00		5/26-9/4
		Parc Mistassini				B					
16	M	Riviere Chalifour	Fr Chibougamau, 48 mi N on Hwy 167		2		15	15	3.00		6/1-9/15
16	M	Baie Penicouane	Fr Chibougaman, 20 mi N on access rd		2		30	30	3.00		6/1-9/25
16	M	Lac Albanel	Fr Chibougamau, 95 mi N on Hwy 167		2		50	50	3.00		6/1-9/15
17	B7	Parc Rimouski	Fr Rimouski, 60 mi SE on Ste 232 & secondary rd			B	14	6	4.00		5/25-9/2
18	F2	Paul-Sauve	Fr Oka, 1 mi E on Hwy 344		1	600	774	301	4.00		5/17-9/29
19	E1	Plaisance	Fr Hull, 30 mi E on Hwy 148			40	86	29	3.00		5/12-9/5
20	F3	Cote Sainte-Catherine	At Ste Catherine d'Alexandrie on Hwy 131			128	300	75	3.00		5/31-9/8
21	D5	Parc de Vincennes	Hwy 132 E of Quebec at Beaumont, S of St Laurent		1	40	43	35	5.00		5/31-9/3
22	B6	Parc Trois-Pistoles	Fr Riviere-du-Loup, 28 mi NE on Hwy 132		0		100	35	4.00		6/21-9/3
		Parc Matane				B					
23	F6	Etang de la Truite	Fr Matane, 30 mi SE on Hwy 195				16	58	3.00		5/25-LD
23	F6	La Barriere John	Fr Matane, 20 mi SE on Hwy 195				12	12	4.00		5/25-10/13
		Parc St Maurice				B					
24	D3	Lac Inman	Fr Shawnigan, 40 mi N on Hwy 155 to Mattawin, access by ferry		1		10	10	3.00		5/26-9/4
24	D3	Lac Dunbar	Fr Shawnigan, 40 mi N on Hwy 155 to Mattawin, access by ferry		1		12	12	3.00		5/24-9/8
24	D3	Lac Normand	Fr Shawnigan, 40 mi N on Hwy 155 to Mattawin; access by ferry		1		40	15	4.00		5/24-9/8
24	D3	Lac Tousignant	Fr Shawnigan, 40 mi N on Hwy 155 to Mattawin, access by ferry		1		10	10	3.00		5/24-9/8
25	F2	Pointe des Cascades	Fr Montreal, 30 mi W on Hwys 340/540			45	144	144	4.00		6/7-9/3
25	F2	Coteau Landing	Fr Montreal, 25 mi SW on Hwy 20		1		144	144	4.00		6/7-9/3
26	A7	Parc Moisie	Fr Sept Iles, NE on Hwy 138				40	7	4.00		5/31-9/3
27	F7	Parc de Perce	Fr Perce, W on Hwy 132		1	40	120		3.00		6/21-9/3
27	F7	Perce Trlr Pk	Fr Perce, 4 mi on Hwy 132		1	63		98	4.00		6/21-9/3
28	F7	Parc Carleton	Fr Carleton, on Hwy 132		1		150	24	4.00		6/21-9/3
29	F7	Mont St-Pierre	Fr Mont St-Pierre, W on Hwy 132		1		79	44	5.00		6/21-9/3
30	D1	Parc Ste-Veronique	Fr Ste Veronique, E on Hwy 117		1		91	53	4.00		6/7-9/3
31	D4	Lac Bellevue	Fr St Raymond, N on Hwy 367				30	30	3.00		5/24-9/8
32	E5	St Joseph-de-Beauce	Fr St Georges, 20 mi N on Hwy 173		1		13	13	5.00		6/2-9/5
33	D6	Parc de la Pte-aux-Oies	At Montmagny on Hwy 20s				100	100	5.00		6/21-9/3
34	F6	Riviere Matane	Fr Matane, S on Hwy 195		1		89	33	4.00		5/25-LD
35	F4	Parc du Mont Orford	Fr Sherbrooke, 17 mi SW on Hwys 112 & 10		2	9600	280	54	4.00		5/12-9/24
36	C6	Parc St-Alexandre	Fr Riviere du Loup, SW on Hwy 20, S on Hwy 51				59	59	3.00		6/21-9/3

Park number	Name of park	Time limit	Reservations	Pets permitted	Max. trailer size	Electric hookup	Water hookup	Sewer hookup	Sanitary station	Bottled gas	Air conditioning	Tables	Firewood	Pull-thru spaces	Rec. hall	Flush toilets	Showers	Ice	Auto. laundry	Cafe-snack bar	Store	Swimming pool	Other swimming	Fishing	Boating	Playground	Other	CB channel monitored	Telephone no.	Mail address
1	Belle Riviere	14			U				•			•	•		•	•	•						•	$	r		p			Laurentides Park
1	Lac Arthabaska	14			U							•	•			•		•					•	$	r		p			Laurentides Park
1	Des Islets	14			U																			$						Laurentides Park
2	La Mare du Sault	14			U				•			•	•		•	•	•	•	•	•				$	lr		p			Laurentides Park
2	La Loutre	14			U	•	•	•	•			•	•			•	•	•	•	•			•	$	r		p			Laurentides Park
3	Lac Ste Anne	14			U																			$			p			Laurentides Park
4	Aux Ecorces	14			U							•	•											$			p		418/846-2811	Laurentides Park
4	Lac Metabetchouane	14			U								•											$			p			Laurentides Pk
5	La Menagerie	14			U	•	•	•	•			•				•	•	•			•		•		r				819/688-2281	Mont Tremblant
5	La Volieri	14										•				•	•						•	$	r				819/688-2281	Mont Tremblant
6	Lac Kenogami	14			U	•	•	•	•			•	•			•	•		•		•		•	•	l		p		418/344-1142	Jonquiere
9	Mont Albert	14			U		•	•	•			•	•			•	•						•	$			p		418/763-3301	Ste Anne des Monts
9	Lac Madeleine	14			U							•												$			p		418/763-3331	Ste Anne Des Monts
11	St-Jean-Ile-D'Orleans	14			U	•	•		•			•	•		•	•	•	•	•	•	•						p		418/663-7897	Montmorency House
12	Parc Port Daniel	14			U		•	•				•	•		•	•	•	•					•	$	r		p		418/752-2211	New Carlisle
13	Lac la Vieille	14			U	•	•	•	•			•				•	•	•					•	$	r					Le Domaine Inn
13	Lac Savary	14			U		•					•	•			•							•	$	lr					Le Domaine Inn
13	Lac Dozois	14			U	•			•			•				•	•	•					•	$	r					Le Domaine Inn
	Parc du Chibougamau																												418/275-1702	
14	Lac du Milieu	14			U							•	•											$	r				418/275-1702	Roberval
14	Lac d'Argenson	14			U							•	•			•	•	•			•		•	$	lr				418/275-1702	Roberval
16	Riviere Chalifour	14			U													•					•	$	lr				819/276-6144	Chibougamau
16	Baie Penicouane	14			U							•	•					•						$					819/276-6144	Chibougaman
16	Lac Albanel	14			U							•	•					•					•	$					819/276-6144	748 Blvd Marcotte, Roberval
17	Parc Rimouski	14			U		•	•				•	•		•	•	•	•					•	$			p		418/724-7032	Rimouski
18	Paul-Sauve	14			U	•	•	•	•			•	•		•	•	•	•	•	•			•	•	lr		gh		514/473-1460	Oka
19	Plaisance	14			U				•			•	•		•	•	•	•		•				•					819/771-6629	Hull
20	Cote Sainte-Catherine	14			U				•			•	•			•	•	•		•			•				g		514/632-1510	Ste Catherine d'Alexdrie
21	Parc de Vincennes	14			U	•	•	•	•			•	•			•	•	•	•			$				•	gp		418/833-2245	Beaumont
22	Parc Trois-Pistoles	14			U	•	•	•	•			•	•			•	•	○		○	○			○					418/851-2867	Trois Pistoles
	Parc Matane																												418/562-3700	
23	Etang de la Truite	14			U		•	•				•	•			•	•	•						$	r		p			
23	La Barriere John	14			U	•	•	•				•	•			•	•	•							r		p			
24	Lac Inman	14			U											•	•	•	•				•	$			p		819/537-6674	Shawnigan
24	Lac Dunbar	14			U																		•	$			p		819/537-6674	Shawnigan
24	Lac Normand	14			U		•	•				•	•			•		•					•	$	lr		p		819/537-6674	Shawnigan
24	Lac Tousignant	14			U																		•	$	r		p		819/537-6674	Shawnigan
25	Pointe des Cascades	14			U	•	•	•				•	•			•	•						•			•	p		514/455-2501	Pointe des Cascades
25	Coteau Landing	14			U	•	•	•				•	•			•	•	•					•				gp		514/267-9242	Coteau Landing
26	Parc Moisie	14			U	•	•	•				•	•			•	•	•						•	r				418/962-9876	Sept Isles
27	Parc de Perce	14										•	•			•	•	○	○	○	○	○		○			p		418/782-2846	Perce
27	Perce Trlr Pk	14			U	•	•	•	•	○		•	$	•	•	•	•	○	•	○	○	○	○	○	r		p		418/723-9215	Perce
28	Parc Carleton	14			U	•	•	•	•	○			$			•	•			○	○		•	○	r		p		418/752-2211	New Carlisle
29	Mont St-Pierre	14			U	•	•	•	•			•	•			•	•	○		○	○	•		○		•	p		418/797-2250	Mont St-Pierre
30	Parc Ste-Veronique	14			U	•	•	•	•						•	•	•	•	•	•			•	○		•	h		819/275-2155	St Veronique
31	Lac Bellevue	14			U											•	•						•	$			p		418/323-2021	Riv-a-Pierre
32	St Joseph-de-Beauce	14			U	•	•					•	•	•		•	•	•	•	○	○	•					p		418/397-5953	St Joseph de Beauce
33	Parc de la Pte-aux-Oies	14			U	•	•	•	•			•				•	•	○		○	○	•					gp		418/248-3522	Montmagny
34	Riviere Matane	14				•	•	•								•	•							$					418/562-3700	Matane
35	Parc du Mont Orford	14			U	•	•	•	•			•	•		•	•	•	•	•	•		•	•	•	r	•	ghp		514/297-2222	Mont Orford Pk
36	Parc St-Alexandre	14			U							•				•													418/495-2502	St Alexandre (Kamouraska)

QUEBEC

FOR FOOTNOTE EXPLANATION SEE FIRST PAGE OF THIS **PROVINCE** FOR MAP, SEE PAGE 119

Park number	Map reference	Name of park	Access	Physical environment	Elevation	Acres	Number of tent spaces	Number of trailer spaces	Approximate fee	Credit cards accepted	Season	Time limit / Reservations / Pets permitted / Max. trailer size	Facilities	Activities	Other	CB channel monitored	Telephone no.	Mail address
		PROVINCIAL PARKS & RESERVES (CONT'D)																
37	E3	Ste Anne de Sorel	Fr Sorel, 3 mi E on Hwy 132			2		150	50	4.00		5/25-LD	14 U	• • • • • • • • ○	○ r	p		819/873-2763 Montreal
38	E6	Lac Walker	Fr Sept Iles, 25 mi NW on Hwy 138 and access rd			2		60	60	3.00		5/25-LD	14 U	• • • •	• $ r	p		418/962-9876 Sept Iles
39	D5	Stoneham	Fr Quebec, 15 mi N on Hwys 173 & 175			1		189	61	5.00		6/21-9/3	14 U	• • • • • • • • •	○ ○ ○ •	p		418/848-2235 Stoneham
40	D5	St Camille	Fr Quebec 60 mi S on Hwys 20 and 281			1		25	25	3.00		6/21-9/3	14 U	•		p		418/663-7897 Montmorency House
41	F6	Parc Amqui	Fr Ste Flavie, 40 mi SE on Hwy 132			1	66	89	30	4.00		6/15-LD	14 U	• • • • • • • • •	• • • dlr	p		418/629-3433 Amqui
42	E4	Voltigeurs Park	Fr Drummondville, 1 mi E on Hwy 20			1	300	281	282	5.00		5/17-9/15	14 U	• • • • • • • • • •	• • • •	gp		819/477-1360 Drummondville
43	B4	Val Jalbert	Fr Roberval, 6 mi S on Hwy 169			1	480	129	42	4.00		7/31-9/3	14 U	• • • • • • • • •	• • $	p		418/275-3132 Val Jalbert
		FEDERAL PARKS																
		National Capital Comm																48 Rideau St, Ottawa
44	E1	Gatineau (Lac Philippe)	Fr Hull, 25 mi N on Hwy A5, Hwy 105 to 366 W			1	B	184	122	3.00		5/19-10/15	7 18	• • • • • •	• • • • r	p		705/827-2711
		NATIONAL PARKS																
		Forillon NP					B											418/368-5505
47	F7	Cap-Bon-Ami	Fr Gaspe, 24 mi E on Hwy 132			1	40	85	85	3.00		6/9-LD	14 U	• • • •	• ○ dl •			CP 1220, Gaspe
47	F7	Petit Gaspe	Fr Gaspe, 20 mi NE on Hwy 132			1	40	136	136	3.00		6/23-LD	14 U	• • • • • •	• ○ •			CP 1220, Gaspe
		La Mauricie NP					B											
48	D3	Camping Mistagance	Fr Shawinigan, 15 mi N on Hwy 351 S			1	29	91	91	3.00		6/1-LD	14 U	• • • • • ○	○ ○ ○ lr			819/536-2638 465 5th St, Shawinigan
48	D3	Canoe-Camping	Fr Shawinigan, 15 mi N on Hwy 351S					39				5/1-11/1	14	• •	• r			
48	D3	Riviere a la Peche	Fr Grandmere, 15 mi N of St Jean des Pilers			1	300	128	138	3.00		6/1-LD	14 U	• • • •	•	p		
48	D3	La Clairiere Group CG	Fr Shawinigan, 15 mi N on Hwy 351S					100		F		All year	14 R	• •	•			
		BACKPACK OR BOAT ACCESS AREAS																
		Provincial Parks																
50	M	Grand Entree	Fr Prince Edward Is, NE to Isle-de la-Madeleine; access by ferry		0			38	38	3.00		6/21-9/3	14 U	• • • • • ○ ○	○	p		418/985-2848 Isle de la Madeleine
50	M	Gros Cap	Fr Prince Edward Is, NE to Isle-de-la-Madeleine; access by ferry					33	5	4.00		6/21-9/3	14 24	• • • • • • • • ○ ○	○ •	p		415/986-3066 Isle de la Madeleine
		CITY, COUNTY & CIVIC																
54	F3•	Camping Caravelle	Fr St Jean, E on Hwy 35, Iberville/Cowansville ext, at Hwy 104E	♀			82	100	200	6.00		5/15-9/15	U Z • U	• • • • • $ • $ • • • $ • • • •	• ○ •	ghp		514/293-3987 770 Lkshore Dr PH4, Dorval
56	C3	Camping Mun La Tuque	In La Tuque on Hwy 155N	≈ Λ		1	50	200	200	6.00		6/1-LD	U Z • 30	• • • • ○ • $ • • • • • •	• • • dlr •	gpt		819/523-5533 Box 580, La Tuque
58	E3	St Quentin Island Mun Pk	In E part of Trois-Rivieres, on Hwy 138	≈ ♀		1	50	69	56	4.00		6/18-9/11	U Z • U	• • • ○ • $ • • • • ○ ○ ○	• • • dl •	gp		819/374-9675 1450 Des Chenaux, Trois Rivie
		PRIVATE																
75	C7	Nadeau's Sporting CG	Fr New Brunswick-Que boundary, 2 mi NW on Hwy 289, 4 mi E															
79	F7	Paradise Point	Fr Gaspe, 28 mi S on Hwy 132	⛵ Λ		1	4	10	5	3.00		6/1-10/1	U Z • U	$ $ $ • • $ • • $ • •	• • dl •			418/853-5528 Gerry Lake
79	F7	Camping Baie de Gaspe	Fr Gaspe, 20 mi N on Hwy 132	⚓ Λ		0	25	30	24	3.50		6/15-9/15	U • U	• • • $ • • ○ •	• • d •			418/645-2883 St Geo de Malbaie, Gaspe Co
99	D5	Aux Islets de Berthier	Fr Montmagny, 10 mi SW on Hwy 2	⚓ ψ		1	25	30	100	5.00		6/1-10/15	U Z • U	• • • • • • • • • • ○ ○	○ l •			418/892-5777 C P 79, Forillon
				≈ ψ		1	8	45	75	5.00		5/15-9/15	U Z • U	• • $ • ○ • • • • • • • •	•			418/259-7655 Berthier Sur Mer
101	F6	Parc Azur	On Hwy 132 bet Ste Flavic & Matane, in Metis Beach	≈ ⚘		1		20	80	5.00		6/1-9/30	U Z • 30	• • • • • $ • • • ○ ○	• • •	gp		418/936-3524 Box 63, Metis Bch
101	F6	Au Coin De La Baie	Fr Ste Flavie, 14 mi NE on Hwy 132	⚓ ⚘		1	4		33	5.75		5/1-10/31	U U	• • • • • • • •	• •	g		418/936-3855 Metis Sur Mer Metis Beach
101	F6	Camping Daniel	Fr St Ulric, 4 mi NE on Hwy 6	≈ ψ			5	20	20	4.00		5/15-10/1	U Z 30	• • • • ○ • • • • • • •	• $ ○ $ •	gh		418/737-4541 RR 1 St Ulric
103	D1	A La Clairiere	Fr Monte-laurier, 4 mi S on Hwy 309, 2 1/2 mi on Monte-Des-Iles	⛵ Λ			20	45		3.00		6/1-9/15	U Z 30	$ $ $ • • • •	•			RR 3 Mont-Laurier
110	E2	Laurentian Camping	Fr Ste Adele, 7 mi N on Hwy 117	⛵ Λ		2	10	30	12	6.50		All year	U Z • 32	$ • • • ○ • $ • • • • ○ ○	• ○ •	gkp		514/632-2856 Box 399, Val David
113	F4	Chez Ben Camping	Fr Hwy 55 ext 18E, 1/2 mi E on Katevale Rd	⛵ ψ			65	64	20	5.00		5/1-10/1	U Z • U	• • • • • • • • • •	• •	p		819/843-5337 Katevale
115	F2	Sugar Bay Trailer Park	Off Hwy 2/20, ext Blvd Perrot, Ile Perrot S, 3 mi E	⛵ ♀		1	15	7	13	4.50		5/1-10/30	U Z • U	• • • • • • • • • •	dl •			514/453-2725 1288 Perrot Blvd, Perrot N
115	F2	Parc ABC Camping	Fr jct Hwys 132/138, 2 mi S on Hwy 138	aa ⛵		1	2	15	23	5.50		5/15-9/30	U Z • 33	• • • • ○ • $ • • • • ○ ○ • ○	•	g		514/691-0306 285 St-Jean Baptiste, Mercier
117	E3	Camp Laurier	Fr Montreal, 20 mi NE on Hwy 116	≈ ψ			25	211	140	6.00		5/1-10/1w	U Z • U	• • • • ○ • $ • • • • • ○ ○	•			514/467-2518 745 Laurier, St Hilaire
117	E3	Camping-Ste-Madeleine	Rte 20 E, at ext 73; 20 mi fr Montreal	ψ ♀			30	120	90	4.00		5/1-10/1	U Z • U	$ $ $ • • • $ • • • • • •	•	g		514/795-3888 St Madeleine Vercheres
118	E3	Domaine de Rouville	Fr Hwy 20, ext 69, 2 mi S on Hwy 21 to Hwy 229, 4 mi N	⛵ Λ		1	500	559	989	6.00		5/15-9/15	U Z • U	• • • • • • • $ • • • • •	r •	g		514/467-6867 St Jean Baptiste de Rouville
119	C6	Demi-Lieue Camping	Fr Quebec, 60 mi E on Hwy 20, ext 256	≈ ψ		1	90	102	175	6.00		5/15-10/15	U Z • 27	$ • • • • • • • • • • •	•	p		418/598-6108 St Jean Port Joli
123	F4	Bernie's Camping	Fr jct Hwys 143 & 55 in Stanstead, 1/2 mi N on Hwy 143	⛵ Λ		2	6	36	V22	3.50		5/15-10/15	U Z • U	$ • • • • • • • • • • • ○ ○ ○	r •	g	13	819/876-2105 RR 2, Stanstead
123	F4	Rock Island-Stanstead KOA	Fr US 91, 1 mi N at jct Hwys 143 & I-55	⛵ Λ			24	40	64	6.00	AMV	5/1-10/15	U Z • U	• • $ • ○ $ • $ • • • • • • ○ ○	lr •	gp		819/876-5676 Box 329, Stanstead
130	C5	Camping Le Genevrier	In Baie St-Paul, fr TC 138, on La Marre St	⛵ Λ		0	30	500	200	6.00		5/15-9/15	U Z • U	• • • • ○ • • • • • • ○ • ○ • •	r •	gpt		418/435-6520 80 La Marre Baie St Paul
133	D4	Camp Royal	Fr Trois Rivieres, 10 mi E on Hwy 138	≈ ψ		1	3	7	6	4.00		5/15-10/15	U Z • U	• • • • • • • • ○				819/295-3441 590 Hwy 138, Champlain
134	F2	Moonlight Lake	Fr Huntington, 6 mi S on Hwy 52, 2 mi W, fol signs	⛵ ψ		1	40	74	38	5.50		5/15-9/15	U • U	$ • • • • • • • • •	•			514/264-5548 Athelstan
137	F4	Piskiart Tent & Trlr Pk	Fr Coaticook, 5 mi N on Hwy 141 to Barnston, 7 mi S to Lk Lyster	⛵ Λ		2	150	48	12	6.00		5/20-9/15	U Z • 25	• • • • $ • $ • • ○ ○	• • lr	hts		819/849-3929 RR 5,Coaticook
140	F7	The Evergreens	Fr Perce, 12 mi N on Hwy 132	≈ Λ		1	3	20	6	5.00		5/15-10/1	U Z • U	• • • ○ • $ • ○ ○ •	• • •			418/645-2654 Rt 1, Barchois W
143	F3	Remember Point	Fr Hwy 202, 1 1/2 mi N, E end of Richelieu Riv Brdg, on N Shore Rd															
145	E2	Domaine Des Jardins	Fr Hwy 117 in St Faustin, 1/2 mi S	≈ ♀		1	10	30	25	4.50		5/15-9/30	U Z • 25	• • • $ • • • ○ • • •	• • lr •	gp		514/294-5648 RR 2 Clarenceville, Noyan
149	F7	MacKenzie's Camp	Fr Now Richmond, 2 mi E on Hwy 132	⛵ Λ		2	100	66	32	6.00		5/15-LD	U Z • U	• • • • • • $ • $ • • ○ •	• • •	ghpt		819/688-2179 St Faustin
149	F7	Spruce Grove	Fr Maria, 2 mi E on Hwy 6	⚓ ♀		1	5	20	10	4.00		6/1-10/15	U • U	• • ○ • $ • $ ○ ○ ○	○ • d •			418/392-5566 PO Box 25, Black Cape
149	F7	Village Guite Cmpg	Fr Perce, 110 mi SW on Hwy 132	⚓ ⚘				42	26	4.50		6/1-10/15	U Z • U	• • • • $ • • $ • • ○	• •	gp		RR 1, Box 866, Maria, Bon Co
150	E3	Camping Bellerive	Fr Sorel, 6 mi S on Hwy 133 N, at St Ours	⚓ ψ		0	6	25	8	4.00		6/1-10/1	U Z • U	$ • $ • • • • • • •				418/759-3536 Box 802, Maria
151	F3	Motel Guay's Trlr Pk	Fr US border, 500 ft N on Hwy 9 & Hwy 15, Montee Guay ext 1	≈ ♀			40	220	100	7.00		5/1-10/1	U Z • U	• • • • • • • • • •	• • lr •	ghp		514/785-2272 St Ours Sur Richelieu
				⛵ ♀		1	110	90	50	5.50	AMV	5/1-12/1	U Z • U	$ • $ • • • • • • • • • • • •	• •	gp		514/246-3861 St Bernard de Lacolle
152	E3	Parc Bel-Air	Fr Montreal, Hwy 40E, ext 55, 2-1/2 mi on Hwy 138	♀ ⛵			15	65	65	8.00		5/20-9/30	U Z • 30	$ $ $ • • • • $ • • • • • • • •	•	gp		514/642-3680 Pointe-Aux-Trembles
152	E3	Henry's Camps	Fr Montreal, E on Hwy 40, ext 55, fol signs	≈ ψ		1	14	60	40	5.00		5/15-10/15	U Z • U	$ $ $ • ○ • • • • • • • •	•			514/642-5477 14678 Notre Dame, E, Montreal
157	E2	El Paraiso	On Hwy 344 bet St Eustache & Oka	⛵ ψ			7	6		6.00		4/1-9/30	U Z • U	• • • • • • $ • • • •	• • dlr	p		1181 Blvd Prouly Pt Calumet
177	E3	Camping DuVieux Moulin	Fr St Barthelemy, 3 mi NW on St Laurent	⛵ ♀		1	30	108	85	6.50		5/15-10/1	U Z • U	• • • • ○ • $ • • • • • • •	r •	p		514/885-3591 St Barthelemy
178	F3	Relais des Pins	Fr St Jean, 4 mi N on Hwy 35, ext St Luc	ψ ♀		1	10	78	22	6.00		5/15-10/1	U Z • U	• • • ○ • $ • • • • • • • ○	l •			514/348-5818 233 Avenue du Parc, St Luc
178	F3	KOA Montreal South	Fr Montreal, Hwy 15S to ext 24, 1 mi E	⚘		1	23	28	152	6.75		5/1-10/27	U Z • U	• • $ • • $ • $ • • • • • • • ○ •	•	g		514/659-8626 St Philippe de Laprairie
178	F3	St-Claude Camping	Fr Montreal, 15 mi S on Hwy 15, E thru St Philippe	♀ ⚘		1	60	60	40	6.50		5/1-10/1	U Z • U	• $ $ $ • • • • • • • • $	•	p		514/659-8258 St-Philippe, Cte LaPrairie
178	F3	Cmpg Joie de Vivre	Fr Montreal, 12 mi S on Hwy 104	≈ ♀		1	40	200	100	5.00		5/15-9/15	U Z • U	• • • • • • • • • • •	•			514/348-0715 975 Boul, St Luc, St Jean Co
185	F3	Plage Carrousel Camping	Fr Montreal, E on Hwy 10, ext 74, 3 mi S on Hwy 241	⛵ Λ		1	36	150	68	4.50		5/1-10/1	U • U	• • • • • $ • $ • • • • •	•	gh		514/534-2404 Bromont
185	F3	Parc Bromont	Fr Granby, 7 mi SE on Hwy 10, ext 78	⛵ Λ		1	30	35	112	7.00		All year	U Z • U	• • • • • • $ • $ • • • • • • ○	r •	hkpt		514/534-2669 Box 26, Bromont
186	F3	Camping Bon-Jour	Fr Granby, 3 mi W on Hwy 112	⛵ ♀		1	20	120	80	5.00		5/15-10/15	U Z • U	• • • • $ • • • • • • •	•	gp		514/378-9479 Rt 112, Granby
186	F3	Tropicana Plage Camping	Fr Granby, 3 mi W off Hwy 112	⛵ ψ		1	200	200	535	6.50		All year	U Z • U	• • • • $ • • $ • • • • • •	•	gkp		514/378-9410 1680 Main St, Granby
190	F4	Camping Lemay	Fr Waterloo, NE on Hwy 243	⛵ ψ		2	150	50	50	3.75		5/1-10/1	U Z • U	$ $ • • • • $ • • • • • • • •				514/539-2707 Rt 1 Ste-Anne De La Rochelle

Park number	Map reference	Name of park	Access	Physical environment	Elevation		Acres	Number of tent spaces	Number of trailer spaces	Approximate fee	Credit cards accepted	Season	Time limit / Reservations / Pets permitted / Max. trailer size	FACILITIES: Electric hookup / Water hookup / Sewer hookup	Sanitary station / Bottled gas / Air conditioning	Tables / Firewood / Pull-thru spaces / Rec. hall	Flush toilets / Showers / Ice	Auto. laundry / Cafe-snack bar / Store	ACTIVITIES: Swimming pool / Other swimming / Fishing	Boating / Playground / Other	CB channel monitored	Telephone no.	Mail address
		PRIVATE (CONT'D)																					
190	F4	Brodeur Camping	Fr Waterloo, 1 mi E on Hwy 112	⛵	⋀		30	150	90	5.25		5/1-9/30	U Z • U	• • •	• •	• • • •	• • •	• • •	• • •	• ghp		514/539-1470	Rt 112 CP 1171, Waterloo
193	F2	Daoust Camping	Fr Hwy 40, ext 17, 1-1/2 mi W on Hwy 342	⛵	Ϙ		20	90	50	6.00		5/1-10/31	U Z • 30	$ $ $	• ○	• • • •	• • •	• • •	• ○ ○	dr • gh		514/458-7301	Hwy 342,3844 Hardwood, Hudson
193	F2	Tepee CG	Fr Ontario Line, 10 mi NE on Hwy 338	⛵	Ψ	1	10	32	64	6.00		5/15-10/20	U Z • U	• • •	• •	•$ • •	• • •	• • •	• • •	dlr • gp			254 Principale, St Zotique
193	F2	KOA Montreal West	Fr Montreal, 30 mi W on Hwy 20, ext 10 to Hwy 338, 3/4 mi W	≈	Ϙ	1	21	14	65	6.75		5/1-10/12	U Z • U	• •$	• •$	•$ • •	• • •	• ○ •	• ○	• g		514/763-5625	Coteau du Lac
202	B3	RV Camping	Fr Maniwaki, 28 mi NW; off Hwy 117, on Barrage Mercier Rd	⛵	⋀		8	E37	35	4.00	V	5/15-10/3	U Z • U	$ •$	• •	•$ • •	• • •	• • •	• •	lr •		613/722-4217	Box 6163 STN J, Ottawa
203	C7	Camping Mun Cabano	Fr Cabono, E on Hwy 185	⛵	⋀	1	2	58	29	5.50		6/1-9/30	U Z • U	• • •	• ○	•$ •	• • •	• ○ •	○ ○	dr •		418/854-2116	79 Commerciale St, Cabano
206	F3	Camping Pinvert	Fr St Jean, N on Hwy 223N to St Therese Island, fol signs	≈	Ϙ	1	37	75	210	6.00		5/15-9/15	U Z • 26	• • •	• •	•$ • •	• • •	• • •	• • •	l • gh		514/348-8082	600Baillargeon,Ile St Therese
211	E3	Park Kelly Cmpg	Fr Ste Julienne, 1 mi N on Hwy 18	⛵	⋀	1	60	125	70	6.00		5/15-10/1	U Z • U	• • •	• •	• • •	• • •	• • •	• •	•		514/831-2422	Ste Julienne
212	F7	Camping 'Gazon Vert'	Fr Chandler, 2 mi E on Hwy 132	⚓	⊥	0		14	11	4.00		6/1-9/30	U Z • U	• • •	•	•	• • •	○ ○		d h		418/689-3022	Box 59, Pabos Gaspe South
216	F3	Missisquoi	Fr border, 14 mi on Hwys 133 & 227	⛵	Ψ	0	20	20	80	6.00		5/15-10/8	U Z 30	• • •	• •	•$ •	•$ •	• ○ ○	• •	lr • ghp		819/244-5323	109 E Rt 227,Venise-en-Quebec
218	E3	Camping Plage La Liberte	Fr Hwy 20, ext 90 to Upton	⛵	Ψ	1	24	300	300	6.50		6/1-9/6	U Z • 30	$ •$	•	•$ •	• • •	• • •	•	• p			St Hyacinthe
219	E3	Camp Alouette	Fr Montreal, 8 mi E on Hwy 20, ext 64	⋀	Ϙ	1	60	80	120	5.50		5/20-10/1	U Z • U	$ $ $	• •	• • •	• • •	• • •	•	•		514/464-1661	Box 155, Sta A, Longueil
220	D1	Grand Camping	Fr Maniwaki, 18 mi N on Hwy 105 to Jct Hwy 117	≈	⋀	1	50	15	50	4.50		5/15-9/15	U Z • U	$ •$	• •$	•$ •	• • •	• • •	• ○ •	r • p		819/438-2974	PO Box 48 Grand Remous
224	D5	Imperial Camping & Trlr P	At TC 20, Westbound, ext 192	≈	Ϙ			15	30	5.00		5/1-11/1	U Z • U	• • •	• •	• •	• • •	• • •	• •			514/831-2969	152 Blvd DuPont, St Nicholas
224	D5	KOA Quebec City	Fr Quebec City, 3 mi W on Hwy 20, bet exts 188 & 192	⊥		1	21	32	97	7.00		5/1-10/12	U Z • U	• •$	• •$	•$ • •	• • •	• •	•	• p		418/831-1813	684 Chemin Olivier, Bernieres
224	D5	Auberge de La Colline Pk	Fr Quebec City, 1 mi W on Hwy 20 to ext 192, 1/5 mi N	≈	⋀	1	10	40	60	5.50		5/1-11/1	U Z • U	• • •	• •	•$ •	• • •	• • •	• • •	• ghp		418/831-0848	385 Blvd du Pont, St Nicolas
231	F7	Camping Belle Vue	Fr New Richmond, W on Hwy 6 to Nouvelle	⚓	Ψ		1	24	6	4.00		5/15-9/30	U • U	• • •	•	• •	• • •	• • ○	○				RR 1 St Omer BP 70, Nouvelle
232	F4	Camping Park Ascot	Fr Sherbrooke, 7 mi E on Hwy 112	⛵	⋀	3	90	70	15	5.00		5/1-10/31	U Z • U	• •		•$ •	• • •	• • •	•	• ghp		819/832-2043	C P 78 Ascot-Corner
241	E1	Camping Paradise	Fr Papineauville, NW on Hwy 321 to Cheneville, W to Lk Simon	⛵	⋀	4	339	30	46	6.00		5/15-10/15	U Z • U	• • •	• ○ •	• • •	• • •	• • •	• •	dlr • gh	7	514/428-3131	Cheneville
241	E1	Canard Blanc Camping	Fr Hwy 321, Cheneville-Lac Simon ext, 3 mi W	⛵	⋀	1	220	A100	A25	4.50		6/12-9/12	U Z 24	$ • •		• • •	• • •	• • •	• •	dl gp		819/428-3346	Lac Simon
242	E4	Camping L'Escargot	Fr Drummondville, 3-1/2 mi N on Hemmings Falls Rd	≈	⊥	1	6	78	48	5.50	AM	5/1-9/30w	U Z • U	• • •	•	• • •	• • •	• • •	• • •	dr • ght		819/478-5701	Drummondville
244	F6	Matapedia Valley Camping	Fr Matapedia, 4-1/2 mi W on Hwy 132	≈	⋀	1	5	50	26	5.00		5/1-10/31	U Z • U	$ $ $		•$ •	•$ •	•	○ ○	•		418/865-2206	Rt 1, Matapedia
245	F4	Homestead Tent & Trlr Pk	Fr Sherbrooke, 5 mi S on Hwy 143, 1/4 mi on Hwy 147	≈	⋀	1	75	80	14	5.00		All year	U Z • U	• • •	•	• • • •	•$ •	• • •	• ○ ○	• ghu		819/569-2671	Rt 2, Lennoxville
245	F4	Jardin Prevert Camping	Fr Sherbrooke, 13 mi E on Hwy 108 to jct 210	⛵		2	80	10	242	5.75		5/15-9/15	14 Z • 28	$ •$	• •	•$ • •	• • •	• • •	• • •	• p		819/875-3327	RR 3 Cookshire, Birchton
248	D4	Camping Claire Fontaine	Fr Quebec City, 35 mi SW on Hwy 2 (Lk Rd 365N)	≈	⋀	1	19	80	80	6.50		6/1-9/15	U • 26	• • •	• ○	• • •	• • •	• •	• ○	• gp		418/337-2744	Grand Rang St Raymond
249	C3	Pine Lodge	Fr Hull, N on Hwy 148, S on Mi 44	≈	Ϙ		300	32	32	4.00		4/1-10/30	U Z • 18	• •	•	• • •	• •	• •	• •	• gp		819/647-2805	Bristol
256	B6	Camping Dunnigan	Fr Riv-du-Loup, 6 mi NE on Hwy 132	≈	Ψ	1	2	15	4	4.00		5/1-10/31	U Z • 24	•		•	• •		• •	l • g		418/862-6940	Cacouna
260	A7	La Luciole	Fr Rimouski, 7 mi E on Hwy 132	≈	Ϙ	1	2	26	22	5.50		6/1-9/1	U Z • U	$ • •	•	• •	• • •	○ •	○ ○	dl •		418/739-3258	RR 1, Ste Luce
263	B7	Camping Plage 3 Pistoles	Fr Trois-pistoles, 3 mi E	⚓	⋀	1	30	105	90	5.00		5/15-9/30	U Z • U	• • •	• • •	• • • •	• • •	• • ○	• •	d • gp		418/851-2403	Rt 132, Trois Pistoles
265	D2	Camping Hautes Rives	Fr Labelle, 2-1/2 mi N on Macaza Rd	≈	⋀		85	40	8	5.00		6/15-9/15	U Z • 24	• • •		• •	• • •		• •	• gp		819/686-5577	RR 2 Labelle, Co Labelle
276	B6	Camping Maurice	Fr Village St Simeon 3 mi E	⛵	Ψ	1	6	40	12	4.50		5/15-9/15	U Z U	$ $	$	• • •	• •	•	•	l • p		418/638-2753	Rt 138,St SimeonCo Charlevoix
277	F7	Bay View	Fr Chandler, 22 mi S on Hwy 132	⋀	⚓	1	5	E100	V10	5.00	V	6/1-10/22	U Z • U	• • •	• ○	• • •	• • •	• • •	○ ○	dlr • p			Port Daniel
277	F7	Au Ruisselet	Fr St Chas de Caplan, 2 mi on Hwy 132	⚓	Ϙ		11	30	100	5.50		4/1-10/31	U • U	• • •	•	• •	• • •	• • •	• • •	lr •		418/388-2138	Ruisseau Leblanc
277	F7	Au P'tit Ruisseau	Fr Bonaventure, on Hwy 6	⚓	⊥	1	3	30	20	4.50		5/1-10/1	U Z • U	$ $ •	•	• •	• • •	• ○ ○	$ • ○	r • h		418/534-2150	RR 1 Bx 896, Bonaventure
278	E2	Lac Claude Camping	Fr Montreal, 29 mi N on Hwy 15 ext 45 St Jerome, 2 mi N	⛵	⋀	1	5	50	50	3.50		5/1-10/31	U Z • U	$ •$	• ○	• • • •	• •	○ • •	• •	r • g		514/438-7532	RR 3, St Jerome
283	E4	Plage des Sables	Fr Princeville, 4 mi W on Hwy 116	⛵	Ψ			50	100	6.00		5/1-9/30	U Z • 32	• • •	• ○	•$ • •	•$ •	• • •	•	• gp			425 Rt 116, Princeville
289	E3	Camping LD	On Hwy 40, ext 122N	⛵	⊥	0	10	50	75	6.00		5/1-10/10	U Z • U	$ •$	• $	•$ • •	• • •	• ○ •	•	• gp		514/586-9914	81 Point du Jour Sud,Lavaltri
290	F2	Riverview Trlr Pk	Fr Dorion, 2-1/2 mi W towards Pointe Cascades	⛵	Ψ	1	3	10	30	4.00		5/1-9/30	U Z • 24	• • •	• ○	• •	• • ○	○ ○	• •	r		514/455-4932	RR 2, Vaudreuil
293	E5	Relais Des Pins	Fr St Gearges, 2 mi N on Hwy 173	≈	⊥	1	3	25	22	6.00		6/1-10/1	U • 30	• • •	•	• •	• • •	○ ○ ○	• • •	•		418/774-9460	C P 13, Notre Dame Pins
296	F4	Bacon's Bay Pk	Fr Hwy 55, 2 mi E on Hwy 141, fol signs	⛵	⋀		50	86	24	4.00		5/15-9/15	U Z • 30	• • •	• ○	•$ • •	• •	• • •	• •	dlr • p		819/838-4940	Box 187, Ayer's Cliff
297	D5	Ste Anne Camping Enr	Fr Quebec, NE on Hwy 138 to SE Anne de Beaupre	⋀	⊥		2	90	20	4.50		5/1-10/1	U Z • U	• • •	• ○	•	• • ○	○ ○ ○	○			418/827-4206	Ste Anne de Beaupre
297	D5	Camping Plage Fortier	Fr Quebec City, 3 mi N on Hwy 138 or 360, 3 mi past Montmorency Falls	⛵	⋀	1	75	250	50	7.25		5/15-9/15	U Z U	$ •$	• • •	• • • •	• • •	• • •	• •	•		418/822-1935	Ange-Gardien
299	E1	Hide-A-Way Camping Pk	Fr Hull, 21 mi N on Hwys 5 & 105, 4 mi W on Rupert Rd or Maple Dr	⛵	⋀	1	15	50	10	4.50		5/24-9/15	U Z • U	$		•$	• • •	• ○	• •	r •			Alcove RR 1
300	E4	Camping Baieville	Fr Nicolet, 10 mi W on Hwy 132	Ψ	⊥	1	20	70	30	5.50		5/1-10/31w	U Z • U	• • •	•	•$ • •	• • •	• •	•	• p		514/783-6238	134 Marie Victorin, Baieville
301	D5	Mtl Canadien Trlr Cmpg Pk	Fr Quebec City, 1/4 mi E on Hwy 138, 1 mi fr jct 540	Ψ	◣	1	3	55	25	5.00	MV	4/1-11/1	U Z • U	$ $ $	• •	•	• • •	• •	•	• gh		418-872-7801	4030 Hamel Blvd, Anc-Lorette
301	D5	Camping Nadeau	In Quebec, Notre Dame du Portage, Co Riviere-Du-Loup	⚓	⋀		6	24	14	4.00	AMV	5/15-10/15	U Z • U	• • •	• •	•	•		○	g	10	418/862-0683	412 Rt deLaMontagne,NotreDame
304	D6	Domaine d'Evangeline	Fr Montmagny, 36 mi SE on Hwy 283 to St-Fabien-de-Panet	Ψ	⊥			24	6	2.50		6/1-9/1	U Z • 30	$ $ $	•	• • • •	• •	• ○ ○	• •	r • p		418/249-4281	St Fabien de Panet, Montmagny
305	E4	Camping de L'ile	Fr Hwy 20, ext 90, Hwy 116 W to Hwy 139 S	≈	Ψ	0	45	150	50	5.00		4/1-11/1**	U Z • U	$ •$	•	•$ • •	• • •	• • •	• • •	• ghp		514/548-2495	290 Richelieu, Beloeil
306	F7	Camping Mont-Marthe	Fr Gaspe, W on Hwy 132	≈		1	3	52	52	4.50		3/1-12/1	U Z • U	• • •	• ○	•$ • •	• • •	• •	• •	• p		418/288-5544	Hwy 132, St Marthe, Gaspe NW

SASKATCHEWAN

FOR MAP, SEE PAGE 122

•—at the campground
○—within one mile of campground
$—extra charge
*—see city map
**—limited facilities during winter months
1-5—number of miles in NF within which facility or activity can be found
A—adults only
B—10,000 acres or more
C—contribution

E—tents rented
F—entrance fee or permit required—see "Special Information on the Public Areas"
H—over 9000 feet above sea level
N—no specific number, limited by size of area only
P—primitive
R—reservation required
S—self-contained units only
U—unlimited

V—trailers rented
Z—reservations accepted
LD—Labor Day
MD—Memorial Day
UC—under construction
d—boat dock
g—public golf course within 5 miles
h—horseback riding
j—whitewater running craft only
k—snow skiing within 25 miles

l—boat launch
m—area north of map
n—no drinking water
p—motor bikes prohibited
r—boat rental
s—stream, lake or creek water only
t—tennis
u—snowmobile trails
w—open certain off-season weekends and holidays

y—drinking water must be boiled
⚓ access to ocean
access to lake
≈ access to river
mountainous terrain
prairie land
desert area
heavily wooded
urban area
rural area

CREDIT CARD SYMBOLS:
A—American Express
M—Master Charge
V—Visa/Bank Americard

FEES REFLECT MINIMUM RATE FOR 2 ADULTS AND ARE SUBJECT TO SEASONAL CHANGES

Park number	Map reference	Name of park	Access	Physical environment	Elevation	Acres	Number of tent spaces	Number of trailer spaces	Approximate fee	Credit cards accepted	Season	Telephone no.	Mail address
		PROVINCIAL PARKS											
1	G5	Moose Mtn Prov Pk	Fr Carlyle, 14 mi N on Hwy 9		3	B	243	243	F2.00		5/1-9/30		Carlyle
2	F3	Buffalo Pound Prov Pk	Fr Tuxford, 8 mi E on Hwy 202		2	2368	98	98	F2.00		5/1-9/30		Moose Jaw
3	G1	Cypress Hills Prov Pk	Fr Maple Creek, 18 mi S on Hwy 21, 3 mi W		5	B	207	207	F2.00		5/1-9/30		Maple Creek
4	F4	Echo Valley Prov Pk	Fr Fort Qu Appelle, 5 mi NW on Hwy 210		2	1318	238	238	F2.00		5/1-9/30		Ft Qu'Appelle
5	F3	Rowan's Ravine Prov Pk	Fr Southey, 14 mi W on Hwy 22, 3 mi N on Hwy 20, 14 mi W on Hwy 220		2	659	60	60	F2.00		5/1-9/30		Bulvea
6	E5	Good Spirit Lk Prov Pk	Fr Yorkton, 20 mi N on Hwy 9, 11 mi W on Hwy 229		2	3232	61	61	F2.00		5/1-9/30		Yorkton
7	E4	Greenwater Lake Prov Pk	Fr Kelvington, 26 mi N on Hwy 38		2	B	67	67	F2.00		5/1-9/30		Greenwater Lake
8	E2	Pike Lk Prov Pk	Fr Saskatoon, 4 mi SW on Hwy 7, 15 mi S on Hwy 60		2	1235	70	70	F2.00		5/1-9/30		Pike Lake
9	D2	The Battlefords Prov Pk	Fr North Battleford, 26 mi N on Hwy 4, 3 mi NW on access rd		2	1472	170	170	F2.00		5/1-9/30		Cochin
10	C1	Meadow Lk Prov Pk	Fr Goodsoil, 3 mi W on Hwy 224		2	B	300	300	F2.00		5/1-9/30		Dorintosh
11	C4	Nipawin Prov Pk	Fr Candle Lake, 36 mi NE on Hwy 120		2	B	35	35	F2.00		5/1-9/30		Smeaton
12	E5	Duck Mtn Prov Pk	Fr Kamsack, 15 mi NE on Hwy 57		3	B	290	290	F2.00		5/1-9/30		Kamsack
13	F2	Danielson Prov Pk	Fr Elbow, 10 mi N on Hwy 19, 14 mi W on Hwy 345		2	7200	49	49	F2.00		5/1-9/30		Cutbank
13	F2	Douglas Prov Pk	Fr Elbow, 8 mi N on Hwy 19, 10 mi W		2	B	49	49	F2.00		5/1-9/30		Cutbank
14	B3	Lac La Ronge Prov Pk	Fr La Ronge, 35 mi N on Hwy 2		2	B	PN	PN	F2.00		5/1-9/30		La Ronge
16	F2	Saskatchewan Landing	Fr Swift Current, 30 mi N on Hwy 4		3	B	35	35	F2.00		5/1-9/30		Swift Current
		PROVINCIAL HIGHWAY CAMPSITES											
17	E3	Blackstrap Lk RA	Fr Dundurn, 4 mi E		2	960	25	25	F2.00		5/1-9/30		Dundurn
18	F3	Etters Beach RA	Fr Imperial, 8 mi S on Hwy 2, 6 mi E		2	364	20	20	F2.00		5/1-9/30		Stalwart
19	C4	McDougal Cr	Fr Smeaton, 53 mi N on Hwy 106		2	2	PN	PN	F2.00		5/1-9/30		Smeaton
20	C4	Jay Jay Lake	Fr Hwy 120, 45 mi N on Hwy 106, 5 mi E X				PN	PN	F2.00		5/1-9/30		Candle Lake
21	C1	Little Birch Lk	Fr Meadow Lake townsite, 12 mi SW on Hwy 304		2	8	N	N	F2.00		5/1-9/30		Meadow Lake
22	F2	Coldwell Park	Fr Delisle, 42 mi S on Hwy 45		2	156	N	N	F2.00		5/1-9/30		Cutbank
23	C1	Loon Lake RA	In Loon Lake Vil at Hwy 26		2	2	20	20	F2.00		5/1-9/30		Loon Lake
23	C1	Pine Cove	Fr Loon Lake, 6 mi NW on Hwy 26 & access rd to Makwa Lk		2	3	8	8	F2.00		5/1-9/30		Loon Lake
24	G4	McLean TC Hwy	Fr McLean, 2 mi W on TC 1, 1/2 mi S		3	80	154	154	F3.00		5/1-10/31		McLean
25	B2	Little Amyot Lake	Fr Beauval, 12 mi NW via Hwy 155		2	5	8	8	F2.00		5/1-9/30		Ile a la Crosse
26	C2	Green Lake	At Greenlake, on Hwy 55		2	2	7	7	F2.00		5/1-9/30		Green Lake
26	C2	Cowan River	Fr Green Lake, 11 mi N on Hwy 155			5	N	N	F2.00		5/1-9/30		Green Lake
27	C2	Michel Point	Fr Green Lake, 50 mi NE via Hwys 55 & 124			3	15	15	F2.00		5/1-9/30		Green Lake
28	E3	Lanigan	Fr Lanigan, 3 mi W on Hwy 20			12	12	12	F2.00		5/1-9/30		Lanigan
29	G1	Maple Creek TC Hwy	Fr jct Hwy 21, 3 mi W on TC 1		3	80	116	116	F3.00		5/1-10/31		Maple Creek
30	F3	Arm River	Fr Findlater, 2 mi NW on Hwy 11, 2 mi N on Hwy 2		2	24	18	18	F2.00		5/1-9/30		Regina
31	D4	Torch River	Fr Nipawin, 12 mi N on Hwy 35, 8 mi N to Torch Riv Vil, 5 mi W			2	PN	PN	F2.00		5/1-9/30		Nipawin
32	D3	Shell River	Fr Prince Albert, 5 mi W on Hwy 3		2	10	80	80	F2.00		5/1-9/30		Prince Albert
33	D3	Nisbet	Fr Prince Albert, 2 mi N on Hwy 2		2	20	97	97	F3.00		5/1-9/30		Prince Albert
34	G3	Besant Park TC Hwy	Fr Mortlach, 4 mi E on Hwy 1, 1/2 mi S		3	150	79	79	F3.00		5/1-10/31		Mortlach
35	D4	Torch Riv CG	Fr Smeaton, 17 mi N on Hwy 106 (Hanson Lk Rd)		2		5	5	F2.00		5/1-9/30		Smeaton
36	E5	Dagg Creek	Fr Hudson Bay, 16 mi S on Hwy 9		2	3	N	N	F2.00		5/1-9/30		Hudson Bay
37	B2	Taylor Lake	Fr Buffalo Narrows, 20 mi N on Hwy 155			5	10	10	F2.00		5/1-9/30		Buffalo Narrows
38	D3	Smeaton	Fr Smeaton, 6 mi E on Hwy 55			5	8	8	F2.00		5/1-9/30		Smeaton
39	E5	Small Fish Lk	Fr Armit, 24 mi S on access rd				N	N	F2.00		5/1-9/30		Hudson Bay
40	F2	Rosetown	Fr Rosetown, 1 mi W on Hwy 7			5	6	6	F2.00		5/1-9/30		Rosetown
41	E4	Margo Hwy Site	Fr Margo, 5 mi W on Hwy 5		2	1	7	7	F2.00		5/1-9/30		Wadena
42	C2	Low Creek	Fr Dorintosh, 34 mi N on Hwy 104			2	N	N	F2.00		5/1-9/30		Dorintosh
42	C2	Perch Lake	Fr Dorintosh, 48 mi N on Hwy 104			1	N	N	F2.00		5/1-9/30		Dorintosh
43	D5	Mountain Cabin	Fr Hudson Bay, 92 mi N on Hwy 109			1	N	N	F2.00		5/1-9/30		Hudson Bay
44	B5	Mirond Lk	Fr Pelican Narrows, 12 mi S on Hwy 135				N	N	F2.00		5/1-9/30		Creighton
45	B3	Waden Bay	Fr La Ronge, 18 mi N on Hwy 102		2	4	25	25	F2.00		6/1-9/30		La Ronge
45	B3	McLeans Beach	Fr La Ronge, 16 mi N on Hwy 102		2		N	N	F2.00		5/1-9/30		La Ronge
45	B3	Little Deer Lk	Fr La Ronge, 33 mi N on Hwy 102		2	1	P5	P5	F2.00		5/1-9/30		La Ronge
46	B3	Otter Rapids	Fr La Ronge, 52 mi NE on Hwy 102		2	3	9	9	F2.00		6/1-9/30		La Ronge
47	D4	Melfort	Fr Melfort, 1 mi S on Hwy 6		2	27	41	41	F2.00		5/1-9/30		Melfort
48	H5	Roche Percee	Fr Estevan, 13 mi SE on Hwy 39		2	160	35	35	F2.00		5/1-10/31		Esteven
49	E3	Watrous	Fr Watrous, 2 mi N on Hwy 365			18	35	35	F2.00		5/20-9/6		Watrous
50	E2	David Laird	Fr North Battleford, 2 mi E on Hwy 5		2	94	54	54	F2.00		5/1-10/1		N Battleford
51	C1	Mewasin Beach	Fr Loon Lake, 4 mi W on access rd		3	6	14	14	F2.00		5/1-9/30		Loon Lake
52	D2	Big Riv Hwy Site	Fr Big River, 10 mi S on Hwy 55		2	2	10	10	F2.00		All year		Big River
53	H5	Souris Prov Hwy Site	Fr Northgate, at US border, 7 mi N on Hwy 9		3	28	10	10	F2.00		5/15-9/15		Estevan
54	E1	Unity Hwy 14 CG	Fr Unity, 1.5 mi W on Hwy 14			18	19	19	F2.00		5/20-9/6		Unity
55	F4	Foam Lake	Fr Foam Lake town site, 1/2 mi S			26	14	14	F2.00		5/20-9/6		Foam Lake
56	F4	Valley Center Beach	Fr Fort Qu'Appelle, 1 mi N on Hwy 35		2	3	N	N	F2.00		5/1-9/30		Ft Qu'Appelle

Park number	Name of park	Time limit	Reservations	Pets permitted	Max. trailer size	Electric hookup	Water hookup	Sewer hookup	Sanitary station	Bottled gas	Air conditioning	Tables	Firewood	Pull-thru spaces	Rec. hall	Flush toilets	Showers	Ice	Auto. laundry	Cafe-snack bar	Store	Swimming pool	Other swimming	Fishing	Boating	Playground	Other	CB channel monitored
1	Moose Mtn Prov Pk	21		•	32	$			•	○		•	•		•	•	•	•	○	•	•		•	•	dl	•	gh	
2	Buffalo Pound Prov Pk	21		•	32	$			•			•	•			•	•			•	•		•	•	dl	•	h	
3	Cypress Hills Prov Pk	21		•	32	$			•			•	•		•	•	•	•	○	•	•	•	•	•	dlr	•	gh	
4	Echo Valley Prov Pk	21		•	32	$			•			•	•			•	•		•	•	•		•	•	dl	•	gh	
5	Rowan's Ravine Prov Pk	21		•	32	$			•			•	•			•	•			•	•		•	•	dl	•		
6	Good Spirit Lk Prov Pk	21		•	32	$						•	•				•			•	•		•	•	dlr	•		
7	Greenwater Lake Prov Pk	21		•	32	$			•			•	•			•	•	•	•	•	•		•	•	dlr	•	gh	
8	Pike Lk Prov Pk	21		•	32	$			•			•	•				•			•	•		•	•	dl	•	g	
9	The Battlefords Prov Pk	21		•	32	$			•			•	•			•	•	•	•	•	•		•	•	dlr	•		
10	Meadow Lk Prov Pk	21		•	32	$			•			•	•			•	•	•	•	•	•		•	•	dl	•		
11	Nipawin Prov Pk	21		•	32							•	•							○	○		•	•	l			
12	Duck Mtn Prov Pk	21		•	32	$			•			•	•			•	•	•	•	•	•		•	•	dl	•	g	
13	Danielson Prov Pk	21		•	32	$						•	•										•	•	l			
13	Douglas Prov Pk	21		•	32							•	•										•	•	l			
14	Lac La Ronge Prov Pk	21		•	32							•	•										•	•	l	•	n	
16	Saskatchewan Landing	21		•	32	$						•	•	•									•	•	dl			
17	Blackstrap Lk RA	21		•	32							•	•	•									•	•	dl	•		
18	Etters Beach RA	21		•	32							•	•							○			•	•	l	•		
19	McDougal Cr	21		•	32							•	•											•			s	
20	Jay Jay Lake	21		•	32							•	•										•	•			s	
21	Little Birch Lk	21		•	32																		•	•				
22	Coldwell Park	21			32							•	•															
23	Loon Lake RA	21			32							•	•							○	○		•	•	l	•	g	
23	Pine Cove	21			32							•	•											•		•	g	
24	McLean TC Hwy	21		•	32	$			•			•	•			•	•	•	•									
25	Little Amyot Lake	21		•	32							•	•										•	•	l			
26	Green Lake	21			32							•	•							○	○		○	•	r			
26	Cowan River	21		•	32							•	•															
27	Michel Point	21		•	32							•	•															
28	Lanigan	21		•	32							•	•															
29	Maple Creek TC Hwy	21		•	32	$			•			•	•			•	•		•	○	○					•		
30	Arm River	21		•	32							•																
31	Torch River	21		•	32																							
32	Shell River	21		•	32	$						•	•															
33	Nisbet	21		•	32				•			•	•			•												
34	Besant Park TC Hwy	21		•	32	$			•			•	•			•	•	•	•	•	•		•	•		•		
35	Torch Riv CG	21			32								•											•				
36	Dagg Creek	21		•	32							•	•															
37	Taylor Lake	21		•	32							•	•										•	•				
38	Smeaton	21		•	32							•	•															
39	Small Fish Lk	21		•	32																		•	•				
40	Rosetown	21		•	32							•	•															
41	Margo Hwy Site	21		•	32							•	•															
42	Low Creek	21		•	32																							
42	Perch Lake	21		•	32																		•	•				
43	Mountain Cabin	21		•	32																							
44	Mirond Lk	21		•	32								•										•	•				
45	Waden Bay	21			32				•			•											•	•	l	•		
45	McLeans Beach	21		•	32																		•	•				
45	Little Deer Lk	21		•	32							•	•										•	•			s	
46	Otter Rapids	21			32							•												•				
47	Melfort	21		•	32	$						•	•			•												
48	Roche Percee	21		•	32	$						•	•															
49	Watrous	21		•	32							•		•						○	○		○				gp	
50	David Laird	21		•	32				•			•	•			•		○	○	○	○							
51	Mewasin Beach	21		•	32							•	•										•	•				
52	Big Riv Hwy Site	21		•	32							•	•															
53	Souris Prov Hwy Site	21		•	32							•	•															
54	Unity Hwy 14 CG	21		•	32					○		•						○	○	○	○						gp	
55	Foam Lake	21		•	32					○		•							○	○	○						p	
56	Valley Center Beach	21		•	32					○		•	•					○	○	○	○		•	•	l	•	gh	

SASKATCHEWAN

FOR FOOTNOTE EXPLANATION SEE FIRST PAGE OF THIS **PROVINCE** FOR MAP, SEE PAGE 122

Park number	Map reference	Name of park	Access	Physical environment	Elevation	Acres	Number of tent spaces	Number of trailer spaces	Approximate fee	Credit cards accepted	Season	Time limit	Reservations	Pets permitted	Max. trailer size	Electric hookup	Water hookup	Sewer hookup	Sanitary station	Bottled gas	Air conditioning	Tables	Firewood	Pull-thru spaces	Rec. hall	Flush toilets	Showers	Ice	Auto. laundry	Cafe-snack bar	Store	Swimming pool	Other swimming	Fishing	Boating	Playground	Other	CB channel monitored	Telephone no.	Mail address
		PROVINCIAL HIGHWAY CAMPSITES (CONT'D)																																						
57	G5	Moosomin TC Hwy	Fr Moosomin, 1 mi N on Hwy 1		2	80	90	90	F3.00		5/1-10/31	21		•	32	$			•	○		•	•			•	•	•	•	○	○					•				Moosomin
58	E2	Borden Bridge	Fr Saskatoon, 28 mi NW on Hwy 5		2	6	29	29	F2.00		5/1-9/30	21		•	32	$						•	•											•						Borden
59	F4	Raymore	Fr Raymore, 4 mi S on Hwy 6		3	26	12	12	F2.00		5/1-9/30	21		•	32							•	•																	Raymore
60	C4	Limestone Lk	Fr Creighton, 66 mi W on Hwy 106			1	P6	P6	F2.00		5/1-9/30	21		•	32							•	•										•	•			s			Creighton
61	F1	Alsask	Fr Alsask, 1 mi E on Hwy 7			11	6	6	F2.00		5/1-9/30	21		•	32							•	•																	Alsask
62	C3	Birch Creek	Fr jct Hwy 2, 38 mi NE on Hwy 169			1	P10	P10	F2.00		5/1-9/30	21		•	32							•	•														n			Montreal Lake
		PROVINCIAL FORESTS																																						
63	B2	La Plonge Lake	Fr Beauval, 5 mi E on access rd		2	3	7	7	F2.00		5/1-10/31	21		•	32				•			•	•								○		•	•	l					Beauval
64	C2	Smoothstone Lk	Fr Big River, 33 mi N on Hwy 55, 41 mi NE on Hwy 124 & branch road				N	N	F2.00		5/1-9/30	21		•	32																		•	•						Green Lake
65	C5	Leaf Rapids	Fr Creighton, 34 mi W on Hwy 106			3	13	13	F2.00		5/1-9/30	21		•	32							•	•																	Creighton
66	C3	East Trout Lake	Fr Candle Lake, approx 10 mi NE on Hwy 120, 45 mi N on access rd via Piprell Lk		2	16	19	19	F2.00		5/1-9/30	21		•	32							•	•										•	•						Candle Lake
67	D4	Gronlid Ferry	Fr Choiceland, 17 mi S on Hwy 6		2		14	14	F2.00		5/1-9/30	21		•	32							•	•																	Choiceland
68	C2	Cowan Dam	Fr Green Lake, 22 mi SE on Hwy 55			1	5	5	F2.00		5/1-9/30	21		•	32							•	•										•	•						Green Lake
69	D3	Murray Point	Fr Prince Albert, 33 mi NW on Hwy 2 & Emma Lk Rd		2	10	71	71	F2.00		5/1-9/30	21			32							•	•							○	○		•	•	l					Emma Lake
70	D3	Sandy Bay	Fr Meath Pk, 20 mi N on Hwy 120, approx 10 mi Nw to lk		2	25	56	56	F2.00		5/1-9/30	21		•	32	$						•	•							○	○		•	•	l	•				Candle Lake
71	D3	Anglin Lake	Fr Prince Albert, 37 mi N on Hwy 2 & Anglin Lk Rd		2	2	29	29	F2.00		5/1-9/30	21			32							•	•								○			•	l					Anglin Lake
72	C3	Piprell Lake	Fr Candle Lake townsite, 45 mi N on Hwy 120 & Piprell Lk Rd		2	2	10	10	F2.00		5/1-9/30	21			32							•	•							○	•		•	•	l					Candle Lake
73	C2	Nesslin Lake	Fr Big River, 12 mi NE on access rd		2		PN	PN	F2.00		5/1-9/30	21		•	32							•	•										•	•	l					Big River
74	D3	Minowukaw Beach	Fr town of Candle Lake, 5 mi N on Hwy 120		2	3	86	86	F2.00		5/1-9/30	21		•	32							•	•										•	•	l					Candle Lake
75	B2	Canoe Lake	Fr Hwy 104, E on access rd		2	3	6	6	F2.00		4/1-9/30	21		•	32							•	•			•							•	•	r					Dorintosh
76	C3	Whelan Bay	Fr Candle Lk townsite, 29 mi N on Piprell Lk Rd, 3 mi W		3	6	17	17	F2.00		5/1-9/30	21		•	32							•	•										•	•	l					Candle Lake
77	D4	Tobin Lake	At Nipawin, on Hwy 35		2		30	30	F2.00		5/1-9/30	21		•	32	$						•	•			•							•	•						Nipawin
78	D2	Turtle Lake	Fr Glaslyn, approx 20 mi N on Hwy 4, 10 mi W			5	10	10	F2.00		5/1-9/30	21		•	32							•	•										•	•						Glaslyn
79	D4	Squaw Rapids	Fr Carrot River, 6 mi N on Hwy 23, 23 mi NE on Hwy 123		2	10	55	55	F2.00		5/1-9/30	21		•	32	$						•	•			•					•			•	l					Carrot River
80	C4	Little Bear Lake	Fr Smeaton, 63 mi N on Hwy 106, 2.5 mi W		3	10	30	30	F2.00		5/1-9/30	21		•	32							•	•							•	•		•	•	l					Smeaton
83	C5	Denare Beach	Fr Creighton, 13 mi SW on Hwy 167		2	4	63	63	F2.00		5/1-9/30	21		•	32	$			•			•				•				•	•			•	dl					Creighton
88	D5	Dragline Channel	Fr Carrot River, 6 mi N on Hwy 23, 46 mi NE on Hwy 123				P10	P10	F2.00		5/1-9/30	21		•	32							•	•												l		s			Cumberland House
90	B3	Mackay Lake	Fr La Ronge, 35 mi N on Hwy 102		2	2	6	6	F2.00		6/1-9/30	21			32							•												•	l					La Ronge
91	B3	English Bay	Fr La Ronge, 12 mi N on Hwy 102		2		PN	PN	F2.00		6/1-9/30	21			32							•												•	l		s			La Ronge
91	B3	Nemeiben Lake	Fr La Ronge, 18 mi NE on Hwy 102		2	2	P22	P22	F2.00		6/1-9/30	21			32							•												•	l		s			La Ronge
92	C3	Montreal River	Fr La Ronge, 40 mi SW on Hwy 2		2		PN	PN	F2.00		5/1-9/30	21		•	32							•	•											•			s			La Ronge
93	B3	Missinipe	Fr La Ronge, 48 mi NE on Hwy 102		2		N	N	F2.00		6/1-9/30	21			32							•											•	•	l					La Ronge
94	C5	Tyrrell Lake	Fr Creighton, 14 mi W on Hwy 106		2	5	10	10	F1.00		5/1-9/30	21		•	32							•	•										•	•	l					Creighton
95	C1	Little Fishing Lk	Fr Loon Lake townsite, 38 mi SW on access rds		3		34	34	F2.00		5/1-9/30	21		•	32							•	•								•		•	•	l					St Walburg
95	C1	Peck Lk	Fr St Walburg, 26 mi NW on access rds		3	5	12	12	F2.00		5/1-9/30	21		•	32							•	•										•	•	l					St Walburg
96	E2	Petrofka Bridge	Fr Saskatoon, 35 mi NW on Hwy 12			62	10	10	F2.00		5/1-9/30	21		•	32							•	•											•						Waldheim
97	C1	Ministikwan Lake	Fr Loon Lake townsite, 18 mi W on access rd		2	4	20	20	F2.00		5/1-9/30	21			32							•											•	•	l					Loon Lake
98	C1	Jumbo Beach	Fr Loon Lake townsite, 3 mi W		3	6	26	26	F2.00		5/1-9/30	21		•	32							•	•		○		•			•	•		•		l					Loon Lake
99	D2	Chitek Lake	Fr Leoville, approx 8 mi N on Hwy 24, 8 mi W on access rd		2	40	20	20	F2.00		5/1-9/30	21		•	32							•	•							•	•		•	•	l					Chitek Lake
99	D2	Pelican Beach	Fr Leoville, 8 mi N on Hwy 24, 8 mi W to Chitek Lake, 3 mi N		2	5	N	N	F2.00		5/1-9/30	21		•	32																		•	•						Chitek Lake
100	C4	Puskwakau River	Fr Creighton, 90 mi W on Hwy 106; 10 mi SW of Ballantyne Bay		2	4	15	15	F2.00		5/1-10/31	21		•	32							•	•											•	l					Creighton
101	C4	Jan Lake	Fr Creighton, 44 mi W on Hwy 106, 5 mi N on Hwy 135		2	30	20	20	F2.00		5/1-10/31	21		•	32							•	•					•		•	•		•	•	dl					Creighton
102	C2	Keeley Lake	Fr Dorintosh, 49 mi N on Hwys 4 & 104, 5 mi NE		2	5	8	8	F2.00		4/1-9/30	21		•	32							•	•					○			○		•	•	r					Dorintosh
		REGIONAL PARKS																																						
111	F5	York Lake	Fr Yorkton, 3 mi SW on Hwy 10				N	N	F2.00		5/15-9/15	21		•	32	•			•			•	•			•				•			•	•		•	g		306/783-3614	Box 400, Yorkton
112	E3	Wakaw Lake	Fr Wakaw, 1 mi N on Hwy 2, 6 mi E				N	N	F2.00		5/15-9/15	21		•	32	•						•	•							•			•	•	l	•	g		306/233-4424	Wakaw
114	F5	McLeod	In Melville, at NE city limits on Hwy 10				N	N	F2.00		5/15-9/15	21		•	32	•						•	•			•					○	•				•	g		306/728-5426	Box 1358, Melville
115	F3	Craik	Fr Hwy 11 in Craik, 1 mi E, 1 mi N				N	N	F2.00		5/17-9/2	21		•	32	•						•	•			•	•					•				•	g		306/734-2610	Craik
116	D2	Little Loon	Fr Glaslyn, 3 mi E on Hwy 3		3	90	10	10	F2.00		5/15-9/15	21		•	32							•	•							•			•	•	l	•	g		306/342-2015	Glaslyn
117	G2	Thomson Lake	Fr Lafleche, 4 mi N on Hwy 58		3	109	N	N	F2.00		5/15-9/15	21		•	32	•						•	•			•	•			•		•		•		•	g		306/648-2412	Gravelbourg
118	E4	Kipabiskau Lake	Fr Tisdale, 20 mi S on Hwy 35, 6 mi W		2	584	50	50	F2.00		5/15-9/15	21		•	32	•						•				•				•			•	•	l	•			306/873-2335	Box 1175, Tisdale
119	D3	Canwood	Fr Canwood, 3-1/2 mi E on Hwy 55		2	320	40	25	F2.00		5/17-9/2	21		•	32	•						•	•													•	g			Box 159, Canwood
121	E1	Macklin Lake	Fr Macklin, 3/4 mi S on Hwy 31, 1/4 mi W		3	180	N	N	F2.00		5/15-9/15	21		•	32	•				○		•	•							•			•			•	g		306/753-2128	Box 103, Macklin
122	H5	Woodlawn	Fr Estevan, 1 mi E		3	200	40	40	F2.00		5/15-9/15	21		•	32							•	•			•	•			○		•		•		•	g		306/634-2222	Estevan
123	D4	Nipawin	In Nipawin, on Hwy 35		2	422	5	8	F2.00		5/15-9/15	21		•	32	•			•	○		•	•			•	•	○	○	•	•			•	l	•	g		306/862-5318	Box 1330, Nipawin
124	E2	Glenburn	Fr Maymont, 5 mi S on Hwy 15		3	240	6	6	F2.00		5/15-9/15	21		•	32	•						•	•							•		•				•	g			Ruddell
125	D1	Sandy Beach	Fr Lloydminster, 11 mi N on Hwy 17, E to pk				N	N	F2.00		5/15-9/15	21		•	32	•						•	•			•				•			•	•	l	•			306/825-4160	4909 - 50th Av. Lloydminster
126	G2	Lac Pelletier	Fr Swift Current, approx 20 mi S on Hwy 4, W on Hwy 343		4	500	25	10	F2.00		5/15-9/15	21		•	32	•						•								•			•	•		•	g			Box 1210, Swift Current
127	H4	Dr Mainprize	Fr Midale, 5 mi W, 3 mi S		3	220	10	10	F2.00		5/15-9/15	21		•	32							•	•			•				•		•		•		•	g		306/458-2244	Midale
128	F1	Lemsford Ferry	Fr Lemsford, 9 mi N on Mun Rd		3	171	10	10	F2.00		5/15-9/15	21		•	32	•						•	•			•	•			•		•		•		•	g		306/463-3338	Glidden
129	D2	Memorial Lake	In Shell Lake		3	220	5	12	F2.00		5/15-9/15	21		•	32	•						•	•							•			•	•	dl	•	g		306/427-2272	Shell Lake
130	H4	Oungre Memorial	Fr Hwy 35 in Oungre, 3 mi N		3	165	25	6	F2.00		5/15-9/15	21		•	32	•						•	•			•	•			•		•		•		•	g		306/456-2749	Oungre
131	F2	Palliser	Fr Riverhurst, 5 mi SW		3	320	50	26	F2.00		5/15-9/15	21		•	32	•						•				•				•			•	•	l	•	g		306/796-4441	Riverhurst
132	D4	Pasquia	Fr Carrot River, 7 mi S on Hwy 23		2	211	2	6	F2.00		5/15-9/15	21		•	32							•	•			•	•			•		•				•	g		306/862-5847	Aylsham
133	H3	Rockin Beach	Fr Rockglen, 4 mi E on Hwy 2		3	230	10	10	F2.00		5/15-9/15	21		•	32	•						•	•			•				•			•			•	g		306/476-2640	Rockglen
134	H3	Wood Mountain	Fr Wood Mountain, 4 mi S on Hwy 358			75	10	10	F2.00		5/15-9/15	21		•	32	•						•	•			•				•		•				•	g		306/266-4742	Wood Mountain
135	F2	Outlook	Fr Outlook, 1/2 mi W on Hwy 15		3	80	12	12	F2.00		5/15-9/15	21		•	32	•						•				•	•			•		•		•		•	g		306/867-8214	Outlook
136	E3	Waldsea Lake	Fr Humboldt, 2 mi W on Hwy 5, 5 mi N		3	50	N	N	F2.00		5/24-LD	21		•	32	•						•	•							•			•			•				Humboldt
137	E4	Fishing Lake	Fr Foam Lake, 14 mi N on Hwy 310 & local rd			118	13	17	F2.00		5/15-9/15	21		•	32	•			•			•	•							•	•		•	•	l	•	g		306/338-2231	Wadena
138	D1	Atton's Lake	Fr Cutknife, 7 mi E on Hwy 40, 6 mi N				N	N	F2.00		5/17-9/2	21		•	32	•						•	•			•				•			•	•		•	g		306/398-2383	Cutknife
139	D1	Brightsand	Fr St Walburg, 13 mi E				N	N	F2.00		5/17-9/2	21		•	32							•	•							•			•	•		•	g			St Walburg
140	F5	Carleton Trail	Fr Spy Hill, 4 mi N on Hwy 8				N		F2.00		5/17-9/2	21										•	•							•			•	•		•	g		306/534-2022	Spy Hill
141	G3	Donnett	Fr Avonlea, 2 mi SE on Hwy 334				N	N	F2.00		5/17-9/2	21		•	32							•				•				•		•				•			306/868-2221	Avonlea
142	D5	Hudson Bay	Fr Hudson Bay, 1-1/2 mi S				N	N	F2.00		5/15-9/15	21		•	32	•						•	•													•	g		306/865-2274	Box 552, Hudson Bay

SASKATCHEWAN

FOR FOOTNOTE EXPLANATION SEE FIRST PAGE OF THIS **PROVINCE** FOR MAP, SEE PAGE 122

Park number	Map reference	Name of park	Access	Physical environment / Elevation	Acres	Number of tent spaces	Number of trailer spaces	Approximate fee	Credit cards accepted	Season	Time limit / Reservations / Pets permitted / Max. trailer size	Facilities & Activities	Playground / Boating	Other	CB channel monitored	Telephone no.	Mail address
		REGIONAL PARKS (CONT'D)															
143	H3	Jean Louis Legare	Fr Willow Bunch, 1-1/2 mi SE			N	N	F2.00		5/15-9/15	21 • 32	• • • •	•	g		306/473-2421	Willow Bunch
144	G4	Kemoca	In Monmartre			N	N	F2.00		5/15-9/15	21 • 32	• • • • • •	•	h		306/424-2242	Monmartre
145	F3	Last Mountain	Fr Govan, 10 mi W, 2 mi N			N	N	F2.00		5/15-9/15	21 • 32	• • • • • •	•			306/487-2177	c/o Credit Union, Govan
146	G4	Nickle Lake	Fr Weyburn, 3 mi SE on Hwy 39			N	N	F2.00		5/15-9/15	21 • 32	• • • • • •	dl •				Weyburn
147	D1	Silver Lake	Fr Maidstone, 12 mi N & E on Hwy 21 & access rd			N	N	F2.00		5/15-9/15	21 • 32	• • • • • • •	•	g		306/893-2547	Box 307, Maidstone
148	D3	Sturgeon Lake	Fr Holbein, 12 mi N			N	N	F2.00		5/15-9/15	21 • 32	• • • • • •	•			306/747-2926	Site 4-447 RR 1, Shellbrook
149	G3	Sylvan Valley	Fr Assiniboia, 17 mi SE on Hwy 2 & access rd			N	N	F2.00		5/15-9/15	21 • 32	• • • • ○ •	•				St Victor
		NATIONAL PARKS															
		Prince Albert			B											306/663-3511	
180	C3	Beaver Glen	Fr Prince Albert, 65 mi N, 1/2 mi E of Waskesiu	2	74	213		F3.00		5/15-10/15	14 •	• ○ • • •$ ○ ○ ○ ○ ○ ○	dl				Waskesiu
180	C3	The Narrows CG	Fr Waskesiu Lake, 12 mi W	2	2	61		F3.00		6/1-10/15	14 •	• • • • • ○ ○ ○ • •	dlr •				Waskesiu Lake
180	C3	Waskesiu Trlr Pk	Fr Prince Albert, 65 mi N; in Waskesiu townsite	2	8		160	F6.00		5/15-10/15	14 • U	• • • ○ • • • • • ○ ○ ○ ○ ○ ○ •	dl •	gh			Waskesiu Lake
184	D3	Namekus Lake	Fr Waskesiu, 6 mi SW on Hwy 263	2		21		F3.00		All year	14 •	• • • •	dl				Waskesiu Lake
184	D3	Halkett (Sandy) Lake	Fr Prince Albert, 24 mi N on Hwy 2, 15 mi NW on Hwy 263	2	2	P20		F3.00		All year	14 •	• • • •	dl	s			Waskesiu Lake
		CITY, COUNTY & CIVIC															
189	G4	River Pk	In Weyburn, 3 blks SE of jct Hwys 35 & 39	≈ 2	6	30	20	3.50		5/15-9/31	5 • 20	$ $ • ○ • • • • ○ ○ ○ ○ ○ •	•	g		306/842-4911	Bx 370, Weyburn
191	E3	Manitou Beach	In Manitou Beach, 3 mi N of Watrous, Hwy 365	2	40	30	8	2.00		5/24-9/30	U Z • U	• • • • • • ○ ○ ○ ○		gh		306/946-2102	RR 1, Watrous
192	G3	Assiniboia Trailer Camp	Hwys 2 & 13 at Assiniboia	3	4	20	8	3.50		All year	U • U	• • • ○ ○ • • • • ○ • ○ ○ ○	•	g		306/642-4424	Assiniboia
193	E2	Gordon Howe Pk CS	In Saskatoon, on Ave P, S of 11th st	≈ 2	6	100	138	4.50		5/1-10/15	U • U	• • • • • • • • ○ ○ ○ ○	•	gh		306/653-5387	City Hall, Saskatoon
194	G1	Gull Lake Camp Site	Fr jct Hwy 37 & TC 1, 2 blks S, 4 blks E	3	2	35	20	3.50		5/20-9/30	U Z • U	• • • ○ • • • •$ ○ ○ ○ ○	•	gp			Box 128, Gull Lake
195	D4	Carrot Riv Overnite Pk	Fr Hwy 23, 1 blk E Birch Rd		1	3	5	None		6/1-9/30	14 • U	• ○ ○ • • ○ ○ ○ ○				306/768-2515	Box 147
196	F5	Yorkton Camping Grounds	In Yorkton, 1 mi N of Hwys 14/10, 1-1/4 mi W	2	8	10	20	4.00		5/24-9/30	U • 16	• • • • ○ ○ ○ ○ ○	•	gp			Box 400, Yorkton
198	G3	River Park CG	SE corner of Moose Jaw, in city limits	≈ 2	12	60	46	5.50		5/1-10/31	U Z • U	• •$ • • • • • • ○ ○ ○ ○ ○	r •	ghp		306/692-5474	Moose Jaw
199	G4	Town of Milestone CG	In Milestone, on Railway Ave E		4	10	6	3.00		5/24-9/1	U • U	• • • •$ ○ ○ ○ $	•				Box 247, Milestone
200	F2	Dinsmore Centennial Pk	In Dinsmore on Hwy 44k	3	10	5	5	None		4/1-10/31	U Z • U	• • • ○ • • • ○ ○ ○	•			302/842-2220	Dinsmore
201	E1	Wild Horse Motel	In Kerrobert	3	5		5	1.75		6/1-9/1	U Z • U	• • • • ○ ○ ○ ○		gp			Kerrobert
202	E4	Quill Lk CS	In Quill Lk on Hwy 5		1	10	10	None		All year	U • U	• • ○ ○					Quill Lake
203	F3	Davidson CG	In Davidson	2	3	10	15	3.00		5/20-9/30	U Z • U	$ • ○ • • • • ○ ○ ○ ○ $	•	gp			Box 2, Davidson
204	G1	Shawnee CG	In Shaunavon		4	10	10	2.00		5/1-10/31	U • U	• • • ○ ○	•	gp			Box 820, Shaunavon
205	E4	Spalding CG	Fr Naicam 6 mi S on Hwy 6, in Spalding	2	2	6	6	None		5/15-9/15	U Z • U	• ○ • • •		p		306/872-2276	Spalding
		PRIVATE															
217	G5	Bri-Ma-Del CG	Fr Moosomin, 7 mi W on T/C 1	2	30	30	68	6.00		6/1-9/30	U Z • U	• • • • • • •$ • • • •	•	p		306/435-8922	Box 1138 Moosamin Sask
218	C2	O'Briens Lodge	Fr Meadow Lk, 30 mi E on Hwy 55	2		20	20	5.00		5/1-10/10	U Z • U	• • • $ • • • • •	dlr •	p		306/832-2070	Green Lk, SASK
219	G4	Sunny Vw-Superior Wstrn	Fr TC 1, on town limits of Indian Head		18	55	112	3.50		5/10-9/10	U • U	$ • • ○$ • • • • • • • •	•	g		306/695-3635	Gen Del, Indian Head
220	G1	Wheel Inn CG	At jct TC1 & Piapot, in Piapot		4	40	30	3.00	MV	6/1-9/30	U Z • U	$ • • • • • • • •$ • •	•	p		306/262-2066	Box 99, Piapot SASK
221	C3	Pine Grove Rsrt	Fr Candle Lk, N on Hwy 120 to mi mrkr 33, N on Whelan Bay Rd fol signs (60 mi N of Candle Lk)	2	5	15	11	3.50		5/15-9/5	U R • U	• ○ ○ • • ○	dlr •			306/374-7721	714 East Dr, Saskatoon
222	G5	Mitchell's Trailer Park	Fr TC 1 in Grenfell, 2 blks N, 1 blk W	2	12	50	30	3.00		All year	U Z • U	$ $ $ • ○ • • • • • • ○ ○	•	gkp		306/697-2718	Box 415, Grenfell
223	C3	Rainbow Lodge	Fr Candle Lk, N on Hwy 120 to mi mrkr 33, NE on Whiteswan Rd to mi mrkr 28	1	1		S7	2.00	M	5/1-10/1	U Z • U	• • • • • • •	dlr •	p			Box 40, Meath Pk SASK
224	D3	Horseshoe Bend Trlr Pk	Fr Hwy 3 in Kinistino, 20 mi N on Grid Rd, 1 mi E	≈ 2		25	20	5.00		7/1-8/31	U Z • U	• • • • • • • • • • •	dl •		9	306/864-3431	Box 321, Kinistino
225	E4	Leslie Bch Rec Co-op	Fr Foam Lk, 12 mi N on Hwy 310		170	10	44	5.00		5/15-9/15	U Z • U	• • ○ • • • •	lr •	gp			Box 1224, Wynyard SASK
226	F5	Maple Grove Rsrt	Fr Whitewood, 14 mi N on Hwy 9, 8 mi W on Hwy 247		10	10	25	3.50		5/1-9/30	U Z • U	• • • • • • • •	dlr •		19	306/696-2862	Box 147, Dubuc SASK
226	F5	Sunset Beach Rsrt	Fr Broadview, 10 N on Hwy 201, 7 mi W on Hwy 247		10	20	20	3.00		5/15-9/30	U • U	○ • • • • • • •	dlr •	g		306/696-2948	Gen Del, Marieval SASK
226	F5	Moose Bay Rsrt	Fr Hwy 9, 20 mi W on Hwy 247 to Crooked Lk		14	10	S10	3.50		5/21-9/6	U Z • U	• • ○ • • • • • • •	dlr	gp		306/696-2876	Box 271, Grayson SASK
226	F5	Bird's Point	Fr TC 1, N on Hwy 9, W on Hwy 247			P20	S11	3.50		5/1-10/10	U Z • U	$ $ ○ • • • • •	dl •			306/696-3586	Box 324, Stockholm
227	C1	Silver Bay Cbns & Trlr Pk	Fr Goodsoil, 1 mi N on Hwy 26, 3 mi W on Hwy 224, 2 mi N	2	6	4	18	5.00		5/1-10/15	21 • 30	• ○ ○ • • • • • •	lr •	p	11	306/238-4607	Box 28, Goodsoil SASK
228	E4	Werner's	Fr jct Hwy 6/16, 1 mi N of Dafoe on Hwy 16		5	10	15	3.00		5/24-9/30	U • U	$ • ○ • •	•				Dafoe, SASK
229	D3	Lakeside Cabins Row	Fr Wakaw, 3 mi N on Hwy 2, 9 mi E on Grind Rd		2	7	8	2.50		5/1-9/15	U Z • 22	$ • • • • • •	lr •	gp		306/233-4986	Domreny Bch, Box 133, Wakaw
230	G4	Sleepy Hollow	Fr TC1, W ent of Wolseley		12	40	30	4.50		5/15-10/15	U Z • U	• • • • • • •$ ○ ○ ○	•	gp		306/698-2408	Box 603, Wolseley SASK
231	G4	Holiday Wheels CG	Fr Regina, 1 mi E on TC1		10	100	100	5.00		All year	U Z • U	$ $ $ • ○ • • • •$ • ○ ○ ○ • •	•	g		306/525-3712	Box 815 TC 1 E, Regina
232	D2	Goulds Cabins & CG	Hwy 55, at town of Big River	2	11	16	14	3.00	M	5/1-11/30	U Z • U	$ $ $ • • • • • • ○ ○ ○ • ○ ○	•	g	19	306/469-2169	Box 414, Big River
233	G4	La Clare CG & Trlr Pk	W edge of Weyburn, Hwy 39 N of Hwy 13 jct	≈ 0	6	20	20	3.00		All year	ZA • U	$ $ $ • • • • ○ ○ ○	•	g		306/842-4522	General Delivery, Weyburn
234	E4	Barrier Beach	Fr Archerwill, 7-1/2 mi NE on Hwy 35	1	120	15	S10	3.00		5/1-9/30	U Z • U	$ • • • • • •	dr •			306/323-4713	Archerwill
235	E5	Black's Resort	Fr Canora, 17 mi N on Hwy 9	2	15	6	S4	3.00		6/1-10/30	U Z U	• ○ •$ • • • • • •	d •	gp		306/548-4607	Box 275, Sturgis
236	F5	Crystal Lk Rsrt, Wm's Bch	Fr Yorktown, N on Hwy 9	2	3	8	S8	4.50		4/15-11/15	U R • U	• ○ • • • • • • • •	dlr •	ghpt		306/563-5968	Box 463, Canora
238	G4	Buffalo Lookout	Fr Regina bypass, 3 mi E on Hwy 1, 50 yds S, 1/4 mi E	2	13	77	40	6.00		6/1-8/31	U Z • U	$ • • • • • • • • • •	•	h	19	306/527-5095	23 Marquis Cr, Regina
239	C4	Jan Lk Ldge	Fr jct Hwys 106/135, 4 mi N on Hwy 135		3	15	15	4.00		5/20-9/20	U • U	• • • • • • • x ○ •	dlr			306/632-4416	2418 Broadway Ave, Saskatoon
239	C4	Great North Lodge	Fr jct Hwys 106/135, 5 mi N on Hwy 135	2	2	4	10	6.00		5/15-9/15	U Z • U	• • $ • • • ○ •	dlr	p		306/632-4516	Box 237, Flin Flon
240	F3	Tugaske Trlr Ct	Fr Moose Jaw, 50 mi W on Hwys 42/367, in Tugaske	3	3	5	23	3.50		6/1-9/1	U Z • U	• • • • • • ○ ○ ○ ○		g		306/759-2243	Ogemia St, Bx 219, Tugaske
241	E3	Wakaw Lk Lodge	Fr Wakaw, 1/2 mi S on Hwy 2, 3 mi E	2	80	40	40	4.00		5/1-9/15	U Z • U	$ • • • • • • • • • • • •	dlr •	g		306/233-4980	Wakaw
242	C5	T & D Amisk Cabins	Fr Creighton, 27 mi S on Hwy 167		2		S10	2.00		5/20-10/1	U Z • 28	• • • • •	dr		12		Box 161, Creighton SASK
243	D2	Shady Bay Beach	Fr N Battleford, 54 mi NE on Hwy 378	3	29	12	S24	4.00		5/15-9/15	U Z • U	• • • • • • •	dlr •			306/824-4538	2105 Herman Ave, Saskatoon
244	G2	Ponderosa CG & Trlr Ct	Fr Swift Current, 1 mi E on TC 1	≈	10	100	56	3.75		All year	U Z • U	$ $ $ • • • • • • • • • • •	•	gp		306/773-5000	49 Ponderosa, Swift Current
245	B4	Bayview Lodge	Fr Creighton, 43 mi W on Hwy 106, 14.2 mi N on Hwy 135	2	4	24	S24	4.00		5/25-9/20	U Z • U	$ • • • • • •	dlr	p		204/687-4582	Box 325, Flin Flon
246	F4	Triple C Trailer Ct	3 blks E on Main St in Ft QuAppelle		10	6	6	4.00		All year	U Z • 30	• • • • • • ○ ○		gku		306/332-5773	Bx 1194 Ft Qu Appelle
248	G2	Lone Eagle Tent & Trlr Pk	In Herbert Tent & Trlr Pk		2	30	50	2.50	MV	5/1-10/15	U Z • U	$ $ $ • • • • • ○ ○	•	g			Box 177, Herbert
250	D2	Pirot's Trlr Pk	Fr N Battleford, 20 mi N on Hwy 4	2	2	10	20	2.50		5/15-9/15	U • 30	$ $ ○ • • • ○ • • • • •	dlr •	gh		306/386-2207	Cochin
254	G3	Prairie Oasis	Fr Moose Jaw, 1 mi E on TC 1	2	82	50	87	6.00	M	All year	U Z • U	• $ $ • • • • • • • • • • • • •	•	g		306/692-2323	Box 250, Moose Jaw
258	G2	Trail CG	Fr Hwy 1, 800 ft N on 11th Ave NW, Exit in Swift Current	3	20	10	150	4.50		5/15-11/1	U Z • U	$ $ $ • ○ •$ • • • • • • •	•	gp	19	306/773-8088	160-6th Ave NE, Swift Current

YUKON TERRITORY

THESE CAMPGROUNDS NOT MAPPED

●—at the campground
○—within one mile of campground
$—extra charge
*—see city map
**—limited facilities during winter months
1-5—number of miles in NF within which facility or activity can be found
A—adults only
B—10,000 acres or more
C—contribution

E—tents rented
F—entrance fee or permit required—see "Special Information on the Public Areas"
H—over 9000 feet above sea level
N—no specific number, limited by size of area only
P—primitive
R—reservation required
S—self-contained units only
U—unlimited

V—trailers rented
Z—reservations accepted
LD—Labor Day
MD—Memorial Day
UC—under construction
d—boat dock
g—public golf course within 5 miles
h—horseback riding
j—whitewater running craft only
k—snow skiing within 25 miles

l—boat launch
m—area north of map
n—no drinking water
p—motor bikes prohibited
r—boat rental
s—stream, lake or creek water only
t—tennis
u—snowmobile trails
w—open certain off-season weekends and holidays

y—drinking water must be boiled
⚓ access to ocean
⛵ access to lake
≈ access to river
⋀ mountainous terrain
ψ prairie land
℘ desert area
⚲ heavily wooded
▟ urban area
⊥ rural area

CREDIT CARD SYMBOLS:
A—American Express
M—Master Charge
V—Visa/Bank Americard

FEES REFLECT MINIMUM RATE FOR 2 ADULTS AND ARE SUBJECT TO SEASONAL CHANGES

Park number	Map reference	Name of park	Access	Physical environment	Elevation	Acres	Number of tent spaces	Number of trailer spaces	Approximate fee	Credit cards accepted	Season	Telephone no.	Mail address
		TERRITORIAL CAMPGROUNDS & REST STOPS											
1	C5	Watson Lake CG	Mile 632, Alaska Hwy		3	8	34	34	F		5/1-10/15		Watson Lake
2	C5	Big Creek CG	Mile 674, Alaska Hwy		3	5	18	18	F		5/1-10/15		Watson Lake
3	C5	Rancheria CG	Mile 710, Alaska Hwy		3	9	15	15	F		5/1-10/15		Watson Lake
4	C5	Morley River CG	Mile 777, Alaska Hwy		3	4	17	17	F		5/1-10/15		Teslin
4	C5	Swift River Rest Stop	Mi 733, Alaska Hwytop		4	1	11	11	F		5/1-10/15		Teslin
5	C5	Teslin Lake CG	Mile 813, Alaska Hwy		3	4	21	21	F		5/1-10/15		Teslin
6	C5	Squanga Lake CG	Mile 850.5, Alaska Hwy		3	12	15	15	F		5/1-10/15		Teslin
7	C5	Judas Creek CG	Mile 872, Alaska Hwy		3	6	6	6	F		5/1-10/15		Whitehorse
7	C5	Tagish Bridge	Mile 21, Tagish Rd		3	10	38	38	F		5/1-10/15		Carcross
7	C5	Marsh Lake CG	Mile 890, Alaska Hwy		3	4	12	12	F		5/1-10/15		Whitehorse
7	C5	Wolf Creek CG	Mile 906, Alaska Hwy		3	15	58	58	F		5/1-10/15		Whitehorse
8	C5	Francis Lake Rest Stop	Mile 90, Watson Lk-Ross Riv Rd, N of Watson Lk		3	10	11	11	F		5/1-10/15		Watson Lk
9	C5	Jackson Lk Rest Stop	Mile 15, Fish Lk Rd (W of Whitehorse)		4	3	20	20	F		5/1-10/15		Whitehorse
10	C4	Mendenhall CG	Mile 960, Alaska Hwy		3	6	10	10	F		5/1-10/15		Whitehorse
11	C4	Pine Creek CG	Mile 1013, Alaska Hwy		3	6	16	16	F		5/1-10/15		Haines Jct
11	C4	Otter Falls CG	Mile 18, Aishihik Hwy		4	10	19	19	F		5/1-10/15		Whitehorse
12	C4	Horseshoe Bay CG	Mile 1064, Alaska Hwy		3	15	28	28	F		5/1-10/15		Destruction Bay
12	C4	Sulphur Lake	Mile 1038, Alaska Hwy		3	2	9	9	F		5/1-10/15		Haines Jct
13	C4	Burwash Flats CG	Mile 1105, Alaska Hwy		3	5	10	10	F		5/1-10/15		Destruction Bay
13	C4	Lake Creek CG	Mile 1152, Alaska Hwy		3	6	17	17	F		5/1-10/15		Destruction Bay
15	C4	Lake LaBerge CG	Mile 21, Mayo Hwy		4	8	8	8	F		5/1-10/15		Whitehorse
15	C4	Fox Lake CG	Mile 35, Mayo Hwy		3	8	13	13	F		5/1-10/15		Whitehorse
16	C4	Twin Lakes Rest Stop	Mile 70, Mayo Hwytop		3	2	7	7	F		5/1-10/15		Carmacks
17	C4	Tatchun Creek CG	Mile 118, Mayo Hwy		3	5	14	14	F		5/1-10/15		Carmacks
17	C4	Frenchmans Lk CG	Fr mi 118, Mayo Rd, 15 mi on Frenchmans Lk Rd		3	1	16	16	F		5/1-10/15		Carmacks
18	B4	Mayo River CG	Mile 245, Mayo Hwy		2	4	4	4	F		5/1-10/15		Mayo
18	B4	Ethel Lk CG	Fr Mi 206.5, Mayo Hwy, 15 mi on Ethel Lk Rd		3	5	13	13	F		5/1-10/15		Mayo
20	B4	Klondike CG	Mile 102, Dawson Road		2	10	32	32	F		5/1-10/15		Dawson
20	B4	Yukon River (Dawson)	Mile 112, Stewart-Dawson Hwy 3			29	70	70	F		5/15-9/15		Box 2703, Whitehorse
20	B4	West Dawson	Fr Hwy 3 in Dawson City, W across Yukon Riv; Free 24 hr ferry		2	10	30	30	F		5/15-9/15		Dawson
22	C5	Quiet Lake CG	Mile 59.5, Canol Road		3	2	8	8	F		5/1-10/15		Whitehorse
22	C5	Fisheye Lake	Mile 258, Robt Cambell Hwy		2	3	3	3	F		5/15-10/15		Faro
23	C5	Simpson Lake CG	Mile 60-Watson Lk-Ross River Rd, N of Watson		3	10	16	16	F		5/1-10/15		Watson Lake
24	C4	Snag Junction	Mile 1188, Alaska Hwy		3	5	20	20	F		5/1-10/15		Beaver Creek
24	C4	Kusawa CG	Fr mi 959, Alaska Hwy, 20 mi S on Kusawa Lk Rd		3	2	10	10	F		5/1-10/15		Whitehorse
26	B4	Tombstone	Mile 45, Dempster Hwy 11			320	5	5	F		5/15-9/15		Box 2703, Whitehorse
26	B4	Ogilvie River	Mile 123, Dempster Hwy 11			6	4	4	F		5/15-9/15		Box 2703, Whitehorse
		NATIONAL PARKS											
		Kluane NP				B							
35	C4	Kathleen Lk	Fr Haines, AK, NW on Haines Hwy to Km 229		3	20	30	30	3.00		6/15-9/15		Haines Jct
		PRIVATE											
57	C5	The Halsteads Fox Point	Fr Teslin, 2-1/2 mi Nnt	⛵ ⋀	3	20	30	24	6.00	V	6/1-10/1		Teslin
58	C4	Mackintosh Lodge	On Alaska Hwy 1, 6 mi W of Haines Jct	≈ ⋀	2	160	N	10	8.00	MV	All year	403/634-2301	Mile 1022, Alaska Hwy, Yukon
59	C5	Paddle Wheel Village	On Alaska Hwy Mile 913	≈ ⋀		10	40	20	5.00		6/1-9/30	604/668-2896	Box 4336, Whitehorse, Yukon
60	C5	The Teri-Tori Trlr Pk	Mile 797, Alaska Hwyk	⛵ ⋀	3	5	10	30	3.50	MV	5/1-10/1	403/390-3507	Teslin

Park number	Name of park	Time limit	Reservations	Pets permitted	Max. trailer size	Electric hookup	Water hookup	Sewer hookup	Sanitary station	Bottled gas	Air conditioning	Tables	Firewood	Pull-thru spaces	Rec. hall	Flush toilets	Showers	Ice	Auto. laundry	Cafe-snack bar	Store	Swimming pool	Other swimming	Fishing	Boating	Playground	Other	CB channel monitored
1	Watson Lake CG	14		●	U				●			●	●	●				○	○	○	○		●	●				
2	Big Creek CG	14		●	U				●			●	●											●				
3	Rancheria CG	14		●	U				●			●	●							○	○			●				
4	Morley River CG	14		●	U				●			●	●							○	○			●				
4	Swift River Rest Stop	14		●	U							●	●															
5	Teslin Lake CG	14		●	U				●			●	●										●	●	r			
6	Squanga Lake CG	14		●	U							●	●							○				●	l			
7	Judas Creek CG	14		●	U							●	●															
7	Tagish Bridge	14		●	U				●			●	●								○		●	●	l			
7	Marsh Lake CG	14		●	U				●			●	●										●	●				
7	Wolf Creek CG	14		●	U				●			●	●											●				
8	Francis Lake Rest Stop	14		●	U							●	●											●	l		s	
9	Jackson Lk Rest Stop	A			U							●	●											●				
10	Mendenhall CG	14		●	U							●	●															
11	Pine Creek CG	14		●	U				●			●	●							○	○		●	●				
11	Otter Falls CG	14		●	U							●	●										●	●	l			
12	Horseshoe Bay CG	14		●	U				●			●	●							○			●	●	lr			
12	Sulphur Lake	14		●	U							●	●										●	●	l			
13	Burwash Flats CG	14		●								●	●															
13	Lake Creek CG	14		●	U							●	●											●				
15	Lake LaBerge CG	14		●	U							●	●										●	●	l			
15	Fox Lake CG	14		●	U				●			●	●										●	●	lr			
16	Twin Lakes Rest Stop	14		●	U							●	●										●	●	l			
17	Tatchun Creek CG	14		●	U				●			●	●											●				
17	Frenchmans Lk CG	14		●								●	●										●	●	l		s	
18	Mayo River CG	14		●	U							●	●							○	○			●				
18	Ethel Lk CG	14		●	12							●	●										●	●			s	
20	Klondike CG	14		●								●	●											○				
20	Yukon River (Dawson)	14		●								●	●					○	○	○	○			○	dl			
20	West Dawson	14		●						○		●	●					○	○	○	○						p	
22	Quiet Lake CG	14		●	U							●	●										●	●	l			
22	Fisheye Lake	14		●	U							●	●	●									●	●			ku	
23	Simpson Lake CG	14		●	U							●	●										●	●	l			
24	Snag Junction	14		●	U				●			●	●										●	●				
24	Kusawa CG	14		●	10							●	●										●	●	l		s	
26	Tombstone	14		●	U							●	●											●			p	
26	Ogilvie River	14		●	U							●	●														p	
	Kluane NP																											
35	Kathleen Lk	14		●								●	●							○	○		●	●				
57	The Halsteads Fox Point	U	Z	●	U	●	●		●			●	●	●		●	●	●		●	●		●	●	r	●		
58	Mackintosh Lodge	U		●	U	$	$		●			●	●	●		●	$	●	●	●	●			●		●		
59	Paddle Wheel Village	U	Z	●	U	$	$	$	●			●	●	●		●	●			●							g	
60	The Teri-Tori Trlr Pk	U	Z	●	U				●			●	●	●		●	●	●		●			●	●				

HUNTING ✦ FISHING

CANADA OFFERS HUNTERS AND FISHERMEN a huge wilderness paradise that is equaled nowhere else in the world. This vast preserve—more abundant than any royal shooting preserve of bygone days—covers nearly 3 million square miles and includes every kind of topography, from great thrusting mountain ranges to endless undulating tundra. Laced and spotted through Canada are sparkling lakes and rivers that contain no less than one-quarter of the entire world's supply of fresh water.

Much of this paradise is so remote it can be reached only by air. Some of it, in fact, remains unexplored and only sketchily mapped. But millions of acres are close enough to Canada's great cities so that fine hunting and fishing are readily available to every citizen and visitor. Unless you study a map, it is difficult to believe that there is rugged wilderness, big-game hunting, and true lunker fishing within 100 miles of every major Canadian city except Toronto. Those who live in southern Ontario have to travel 200 miles or so to enjoy a wilderness experience.

No other developed nation on earth can offer the outdoorsman this combination of opportunity and accessibility. But the outstanding fact about hunting and fishing in Canada is not the vastness of the lands, the abundance of the wildlife, nor the accessibility. It is that Canada's vast open land and water areas stand as the most intelligently regulated in the world.

Many who have watched it happen in other countries fear that man will overrun Canadian wildlife and trample these wilderness areas into submission. They grant that, because of Canada's great size, this will take time. But they feel that inevitably there will come an end to wildlife as we know it now because of man's avaricious slaughtering habits. They point to the decimation of the great buffalo herds of the United States as an example of what will happen here.

White-tailed deer spotted in Quebec's Patapédia Valley

Fortunately, it isn't happening and probably won't. Canada protects and manages its wilderness lands and their inhabitants. Because of this management, wildlife is actually increasing—not diminishing—in those areas where the land can support more life. In those places where the wildlife population has reached the balance point between sufficient food and overpopulation, the game is carefully controlled.

Hunting and fishing in Canada today are sports, but they also are an integral part of wildlife management—more so than in perhaps any other country. Hunting and fishing bag limits and the annual duration of each season are set with the balance of nature in mind. Continuing wildlife census studies indicate when a species has multiplied beyond the ability of the land to support it—and also when human or natural pressures have reduced a population below the level of optimum balance.

The story of the moose in Newfoundland provides an excellent example of wildlife management in Canada. Prior to 1905, there were no moose in the province. In that year, four animals were introduced. This small herd grew during the ensuing years, with its growth accelerating in the 1930s, when heavy cutting of pulpwood in the Newfoundland forests resulted in an improved range for the animals.

Eventually, the moose herd grew to the point where there were as many as 12 animals per square mile. This was severe overpopulation, since the forests couldn't provide food for so large a group. The moose herds faced a lean existence, and perhaps starvation.

Hunting limits were raised to three animals per hunter to control the herd, and in time, this hunting pressure reduced the herd to a size the forest could sustain. Today, the moose population of Newfoundland has stabilized, and the natural balance is maintained when 5,000 to 10,000 animals are harvested each year. Without such a harvest, the herd would expand once more to numbers that would bring about starvation.

In another example of wildlife management, white-tailed deer were introduced into Nova Scotia in 1896. They were completely protected for 20 years, during which time the herd expanded into its surroundings. Only then was hunting permitted. Today, herd maintenance requires a harvest that sometimes runs as high as 23,000 animals per year to maintain balance.

Wildlife managers say that the moose population of the western provinces has stabilized and is now showing signs of increasing. In the same area, the woodland caribou, which at one time was decreasing in number, is also increasing. In both eastern and western provinces, the black bear population has increased dramatically—so much so that some provinces have opened special spring hunting seasons to prevent overpopulation.

Population control is successfully sustaining the wildlife of Canada, but it is only one of the tools used in wildlife management. Another is the maintenance and improvement of the lands in which game breeds and lives. For example, 70 percent of the continent's most hunted migratory birds use prairie potholes to nest and raise their young. These nesting holes have been threatened by cyclical drought and competing land users. The Canadian Wildlife Service, to counteract this threat, has implemented a preservation program in which landowners agree not to drain, burn, or fill their wetlands. Such agreements now cover thousands of acres.

Perhaps at some time in the distant future, the land and hunting demands of our expanding human population may change all of this, and Canada's wilderness and wildlife may be threatened. But the present regulatory effort appears to reach into the future, and appears to have been begun in time to offset this threat.

Hunting and fishing in Canada is a working part of this regulatory program. Outdoorsmen who recognize this, adhere to the rules, and are actively concerned with the preservation of the areas which they enjoy, are welcomed to the Canadian wilderness. Others are not.

HUNTING

Each province sets its own regulations in regard to open seasons for game, bag limits, and licenses for hunting game and nonmigratory birds. The Canadian Wildlife Service, working within the Migratory Bird Treaty with the United States, sets the regulations for hunting migratory birds.

The dates for open hunting seasons vary from year to year, as do the bag limits on different species. The dates, limits, and latest regulations are published each year shortly before the hunting season opens. In some provinces, certain animals may not be hunted when wildlife census figures indicate that these species need to be protected. By the same token, for species that have multiplied too rapidly, there may be both a spring and fall hunting season.

When planning a hunting trip, write to the province you intend to visit to obtain the latest information. The address of the provincial authority is given in the provincial listings which follow. For the most recent information on hunting migratory birds throughout Canada, write: Director General, Canadian Wildlife Service, Department of the Environment, Ottawa, Ontario.

If you come to Canada from the United States, you don't need a passport or visa, but should carry some identification papers. A birth or baptismal certificate or a voter's registration card will do. If you drive across the border, get from your insurance agent before you start a Canadian Non-Resident Interprovince Motor Vehicle Liability Insurance card. This simply shows that your insurance company agrees to accept the minimum limits of financial responsibility prevailing in Canada.

If you come from another country, you must carry a passport, and in some instances, a visa from the Canadian representative in your country. You must also have proof of vaccination against smallpox.

You will find no problems in bringing hunting, fishing, and camping equipment into Canada. You don't need a permit for rifles, shotguns, or fishing tackle and can bring 200 rounds of ammunition with you duty free. However, fully automatic firearms are not admissable. It is also against the law to bring revolvers or pistols, unless you can prove that you are attending a marksmanship contest.

It is a good idea to make a list of such portable items as radios, television sets, electrical appliances, outboard motors, guns, and the like, showing the serial number of each. Carry three copies of this list with you, and file one with the customs agents when you enter Canada. Later, when you leave Canada, this will serve to verify that you didn't purchase the equipment in Canada.

If you drive, your U.S. driver's license is valid anywhere in Canada. Your car and trailer are admitted free to Canada, but you must have your motor vehicle registration with you.

Hunting dogs from the United States are welcome if they have a certificate of vaccination against rabies issued within the previous year.

There are many fly-in fishing resorts in Manitoba

Facilities and Seasons

In most of the popular hunting areas in Canada, you'll find a wide range of comfortable lodges with good facilities and services. There are luxury lodges, and there are cabins where you must provide your own sleeping bags and food. Many can be reached by automobile, or by automobile plus a horseback or canoe trip. But some can be reached only by air. The expense of your trip can vary widely, depending on how far into the wilderness you want to go and how luxurious you like your accommodations. Wherever you go, you'll find facilities for handling and shipping trophy heads, hides, and meat.

The skill of Canadian guides is legendary, and there is no better insurance for a successful trip than a good guide. In some provinces and for certain big game, you are required by law to hire a guide. Lists of registered guides and outfitting services are available from each province and territory.

Most Canadian hunting is done in the autumn—but remember that autumn in the Far North begins in August. You'll find spring hunting for bear, wolf, and mountain lion is allowed in some years. Not all guides work in the spring, so make your arrangements early to be sure your man is waiting.

Giant elk grazing in Banff National Park

The sport of hunting with a bow and arrow has grown popular in recent years, and just about every species of large and small game has been taken with archery equipment. Most provinces offer special hunting opportunities to archers—including advance seasons.

Another blossoming sport is the photographic safari—hunting with a camera. There was a time when a guide would have curled his lip at a hunter armed with a telephoto lens, but that day is past. Now he'll happily lead the two- or three-day trek needed to find a majestic Dall sheep poised on a pinnacle of rock. Canada's national and provincial parks, where no hunting is permitted, usually have abundant game and provide a good many special photographic opportunities.

Keep in mind that you must have a license from the province in which you hunt. The cost of this license will range from a few dollars for a small-game permit to as much as $125 for a big-game license. Some provinces issue less expensive big-game permits, then require a trophy fee for each trophy taken. And to export game in some provinces you need a license, which may be free or cost a few dollars.

If you intend to hunt migratory birds, you need both the provincial hunting license and the Canada Migratory Bird Hunting Permit. The latter costs $3.

In many areas, you cannot hunt on Sunday. Some provinces have specific requirements for the outer clothes big-game hunters must wear—chiefly as a matter of safety for the hunter himself. The object of these clothes is to make the hunter visible to other hunters.

As you read the following province-by-province rundown on hunting, keep in mind that any regulations which are mentioned are subject to change, and may in fact have changed by the time you read this. The final word on regulations is to be found in the latest publications of the province in which you will hunt.

ALBERTA. The top trophy in Alberta is the Rocky Mountain bighorn sheep, an animal ranging up to 300 pounds, with massive curling horns. A ram with prize horns (more than 40 inches around the outside curl) is at least 12 or 13 years of age, just past his prime. His life expectancy at this time is a year or two, and for this reason, wildlife managers permit him to be taken—if you can get to him. His eyesight is the equivalent of perfect human eyes looking through eight-power binoculars, so there is a good chance he'll see you before you even know he's there.

Alberta has an interesting variety of hunting lands—the mountains, plus rolling ranchland foothills to the east of them, plus heavy forests and muskegs to the north. The variety of terrain gives variety to the hunting, and it is possible to hunt big game, upland birds, and waterfowl in the same area.

The province is noted for fine goose shooting. Canada, snow, and white-fronted geese pass through east-central Alberta on their way south from the northern breeding areas.

There is a special spring hunting season for both grizzly and black bear in Alberta, and a special archery season for moose, deer, and bear. In some areas of the province, you must employ a registered guide when hunting big game. In other areas, you need only be accompanied by a resident hunter. Hunting is not permitted on Sunday except in the northern parts of the province. You need an export license, which is free.

For the latest hunting information, write: Fish and Wildlife, Department of Recreation, Parks and Wildlife, 9833 109 Street, Edmonton, Alberta, T5K 2E1.

For migratory bird hunting, write: Director General, Canadian Wildlife Service, Department of the Environment, Ottawa, Ontario.

BRITISH COLUMBIA. British Columbia's 366,000 square miles include some of the roughest topography on the continent, a goodly amount of which is raw wilderness. This wilderness has produced some of the world's great hunting trophies—along with some of the world's weariest hunters. One very successful trophy hunter claims he trains for three months before a trip into British Columbia's mountains because "sore muscles and blistered feet have ruined more good hunting trips than bad weather or a lack of game ever will."

The big trophy game—the Rocky Mountain bighorn sheep—in British Columbia is the same as in Alberta, for the provinces share the rugged Rockies. In the mountains, you may also meet the grizzly bear—500 pounds or more of angry trouble looking for a fight. The mature grizzly has tremendous power, and can kill an 1,800-pound bull moose with one swipe of his paw. You don't stalk such an animal without care and preparation.

Other big game in British Columbia include Stone sheep, the beautiful Dall sheep, elk, moose, two species of caribou, mountain goat, grizzly and black bear, wolf, cougar, and three kinds of deer: white-tailed, black-tailed, and mule.

Waterfowl are plentiful on the province's many small lakes and in swamps drained by the Columbia, Kootenay, and Chilcotin rivers. Seven species of native grouse, including three kinds of ptarmigan, provide the food for many a hunter's table.

In British Columbia, you buy a hunting license plus a tag license for each species of big game. When you take a big-game animal, you cancel the appropriate tag license and pay a trophy fee to the nearest government agent or conservation officer. This fee includes an export permit.

For the latest hunting information, write: Fish and Wildlife Branch, Department of Recreation and Travel Industry, Parliament Buildings, Victoria, British Columbia.

For migratory bird hunting, write: Director General, Canadian Wildlife Service, Department of the Environment, Ottawa, Ontario.

MANITOBA. The sport in Manitoba is very much like that in Saskatchewan. The wildfowl population during the migration season is enormous, and many lodges throughout the area cater to bird-hunting sportsmen. Many sportsmen employ guides who know the flyways, to assure themselves of a successful trip—though guides aren't required by law.

Manitoba requires big-game hunters to wear a complete outer suit of white, with either a white or "blaze orange" cap, for reasons of safety.

Population control has required a close watch on certain species of birds and game, most especially Barren-Ground and woodland caribou, pheasant, pinnated grouse, and wild turkey. Whether or not these species can be hunted is determined each year by wildlife census figures. Black bear and moose have proliferated, so that two seasons each year are likely. The moose seasons usually are set for early and late fall, while the bear seasons run in May and June, and earlier in the spring.

For the latest hunting information, write: Renewable Resources and Transportation Services, 1495 St. James Street, Winnipeg, Manitoba.

For migratory bird hunting, write: Director General, Canadian Wildlife Service, Department of the Environment, Ottawa, Ontario.

NEW BRUNSWICK. Over 80 percent of New Brunswick is forestland, providing an ideal habitat for white-tailed deer, black bear, and ruffed grouse. In addition, most hunting areas of the province are readily accessible.

The province has long been known as Canada's Woodcock Capital, but in 1970, the woodcock season had to be canceled, due to the high residue of DDT found in these birds. The Canadian Wildlife Service has a continuing study of these birds under way, and as the use of toxic chemicals in the forests of the province decreases, hunting for this little game bird may return to normal.

New Brunswick has more inland waters for its size than any other area on the continent, and one of the results is excellent duck and goose shooting. Black duck and scaup are plentiful; there is fine shooting for Canada geese and brant along the coast. Wilson's snipe is found in all the marshes.

Nonresident hunters must be accompanied by a licensed guide when after big game. A guide must accompany every two hunters when hunting game birds.

For the latest hunting information, write: Fish and Wildlife Branch, Department of Natural Resources, Fredericton, New Brunswick.

For migratory bird hunting, write: Director General, Canadian Wildlife Service, Department of the Environment, Ottawa, Ontario.

NEWFOUNDLAND. Newfoundland includes two parts: the island of Newfoundland and the area of Labrador on the mainland east of Quebec. Travel to the hunting areas on

A resident of Terra Nova National Park, Newfoundland

the island is excellent, even though many are in a near-wilderness state. Labrador is remote, and much of the travel there is by float-equipped plane.

There are three big-game animals in Newfoundland—the moose, the caribou, and the black bear. Hunters may take as many as 10,000 moose in a year because of the size of the island's herd. Caribou hunting may be more limited, since the herd is still growing toward its ideal size.

The Newfoundland moose differs from those found elsewhere in Canada. It tends to be smaller, but with antlers which rise high rather than spread wide. This characteristic has developed since the island was first stocked with four animals in 1905.

Nonresident big-game hunters must be accompanied by a registered guide, with at least one guide employed for each two hunters.

For the latest hunting information, write: Director of Wildlife, Department of Mines, Agriculture, and Resources, St. John's, Newfoundland.

For migratory bird hunting, write: Director General, Canadian Wildlife Service, Department of the Environment, Ottawa, Ontario.

NORTHWEST TERRITORIES. If there is a complete wilderness anywhere, this is it. The Northwest Territories cover 1,300,000 square miles—with a population of less than 40,000 people. There are great reaches which seldom if ever feel the imprint of a human foot.

Hunting has been a major activity in the Northwest Territories for generations, and it continues to attract a great many visitors—but the winds of change are blowing. Some aspects of it, notably hunting for buffalo and polar bear, are now limited, and more limitations are in sight. This is due in part to dwindling numbers of certain types of game and in part to the fact that there are fewer outfitters.

At the same time, there has been a strong rise in the number of people interested in nonshooting activities in the wilderness, including the long canoe portage trip, nature study, and photography. Only recently, several lodges which cater to the advocates of these activities almost exclusively have been opened.

Visiting hunters are required to employ native outfitters for polar bear, seal, and whale hunting, and in some areas, Eskimo or Indian outfitters are required for all hunting. You won't have to have one for hunting game birds, but if you intend to strike out into a remote area, an outfitter is highly recommended. This is a big empty country up here, like nothing you've ever experienced before. Don't take chances.

The major centers for wilderness activity are Yellowknife, Rankin Inlet, and Frobisher Bay. You can drive to Yellowknife, reach Rankin Inlet by taking a train from The Pas to Churchill, then fly to the inlet, and get to Frobisher Bay by air from Montreal. If you drive to Yellowknife, plan carefully, because settlements are far apart. The Mackenzie Highway is good gravel road, as are most other roads in the Northwest Territories, but repair and fuel facilities can be scarce.

Most game and sea mammal hunting begins in late July or the first of August and extends to the end of November. But this country is at or near the Arctic Circle, and even in early September, you can expect freezing temperatures. Winterize your firearms and photographic equipment, and equip yourself with Eskimo parkas and footwear.

For the latest information on hunting sea mammals, big game, and upland game birds, write: Superintendent of Fish and Wildlife, Yellowknife, Northwest Territories.

For maps, an accommodation guide, and general travel information, write: TravelArctic, Yellowknife, Northwest Territories.

For migratory bird hunting information, write: Director, General Canadian Wildlife Service, Department of Environment, Ottawa, Ontario.

NOVA SCOTIA. The principal game animal is the handsome white-tailed deer, descended from nine deer introduced into the province in 1896. The next is the black bear. Nova Scotia waters provide major resting places for migrating ducks and Canada geese traveling along the Atlantic flyway. Thousands of geese winter along the southeastern coast, providing fine shooting on inland lakes and in the tidal mud flats.

The best hunting of the season, veteran hunters say, is a little later in Nova Scotia than elsewhere in Canada. They like early November for all game which doesn't leave for the south until the first winter snows arrive.

There is no open season for moose for nonresidents of Nova Scotia. All visiting hunters are required to employ guides or to hunt with a resident who has written permission from the Minister of Lands and Forests. A guide may be employed by up to three hunters at one time.

At the conclusion of your hunting trip, you are asked to fill out the report cards attached to your license and turn them in. This is one method of checking the hunting pressure.

For the latest hunting information, write: Director of Wildlife Conservation, Department of Lands and Forests, Halifax, Nova Scotia.

For migratory bird hunting, write: Director General, Canadian Wildlife Service, Department of the Environment, Ottawa, Ontario.

Fox exploring his snowy home in northern Canada

ONTARIO. Most of Ontario's 400,000 square miles are wooded and support good game populations. The best moose and bear hunting is in the northern half of the province, and there is deer and bear hunting in the south. Ruffed grouse are found everywhere, and you'll see Hungarian partridge and woodcock in the farmlands of the south and east. You also can hunt pheasant, rabbit, hare, quail, and the sharp-tailed grouse.

The southern end of James Bay—the northern terminus of the Polar Bear Express on its run from Cochrane—is renowned for its goose and duck hunting. Here Indian guides build willow blinds on the tidal mud flats and make decoys by turning blocks of mud with a shovel and decorating them with a few white goose feathers. The method looks funny and unworkable until the guides begin to call the high-flying honkers. Doubting Thomases stop laughing as the big flying birds wheel and settle in around the decoys.

Ontario requires that nonresident hunters show proof that they are at least 16 years old. A birth certificate or a hunting license from another province or a previous year will do. When hunting big game in the Rainy River district, nonresidents must be accompanied by one licensed guide for each two hunters.

Hunting licenses are not valid for most fur-bearing animals, such as beaver, marten, and otter, but there are no restrictions on hunting wolf, raccoon, and fox.

For the latest hunting information, write: Fish and Wildlife Branch, Ministry of Natural Resources, Queens Park, Toronto, Ontario.

For migratory bird hunting, write: Director General, Canadian Wildlife Service, Department of the Environment, Ottawa, Ontario.

PRINCE EDWARD ISLAND. Nine miles from the Canadian mainland, this beautiful island is known as the Garden of the Gulf. More than half of it is under cultivation, and there is very little forest. No big game has ever settled in its green fields. You can, however, find good goose and black duck shooting, along with ruffed grouse and Hungarian partridge. Game populations have been increasing in recent years, partly as a result of wildlife management work to increase cover for upland game birds.

Canada goose enjoying the Gorge, Victoria, British Columbia

For the latest hunting information, write: Fish and Wildlife Division, Department of Fisheries, PO Box 2000, Charlottetown, Prince Edward Island.

For migratory bird hunting, write: Director General, Canadian Wildlife Service, Department of the Environment, Ottawa, Ontario.

QUEBEC. Hunting in Quebec is a little different. A large amount of hunting territory is leased to private clubs or professional outfitters who completely control the hunting on the leased land. To hunt in a leased area, you must use the facilities of the outfitter. The system works well. The outfitters specialize in accommodating hunting parties, providing skilled guides, and in protecting wildlife. The number of hunters in each party is kept low, so that everyone has a piece of the country to himself.

Quebec has more than 300,000,000 acres of virgin forest, highlands, rivers, and lakes, and there is plenty of land which hasn't been leased. Thus the hunter who prefers to organize his own trip has an opportunity to do so.

The moose is the favorite big game of Quebec, and it is hunted by stalking or by calling. The calling technique is the most exciting. The hunting season coincides with the moose mating season, and during this time, the female moose advertises her amorous desires vocally, morning and evening. A good Canadian moose guide can duplicate her call, and sweet-talk the wariest old bull right down to the wooded edge of a lake or stream.

It sounds easy, but there's a catch. The bull is extremely cautious and unwilling to take the last few steps into the open until he is absolutely certain that a lady awaits. The hunt becomes a suspenseful contest between the bull and the caller. Will he or won't he? When he does, the hunter may collect a trophy with antlers having a spread of six feet or more. When he doesn't, the contest begins all over again the next morning.

One of the best hunting opportunities in Quebec is for caribou in the northeastern part of the province, where a herd of more than 60,000 animals produces an unusually high number of trophies with "double shovels," the most highly prized of all caribou racks.

There is fine migratory bird hunting along the St. Lawrence, especially for black duck, scaup, and greater snow geese. The goose flights peak about the third week in October. Quebec also has white-tailed deer and upland game hunting, chiefly for grouse and snowshoe hare. The whole province is noted for partridge.

Big-game hunters must have a Forest Travel Permit. Licenses are issued for certain groups of animals rather than for each species.

For the latest hunting information, write: Department of Tourism, Fish and Game, 150 East Blvd. Saint-Cyrille, Quebec, Province of Quebec, G1R 4Y3.

For migratory bird hunting, write: Director General, Canadian Wildlife Service, Department of the Environment, Ottawa, Ontario.

SASKATCHEWAN. Saskatchewan has been called North America's duck factory, because two of the continent's main migration channels converge over it. The potholes and ponds of the province offer resting spots for one of the largest concentrations of migratory birds in the world—and great flocks fatten on grain left in the fields after the autumn harvest.

The geese—Canada, blue, white-fronted, and snow—begin to arrive in mid-September from the north. They settle in

Hunters canoeing the saltwater flats at James Bay

to feed until the latter part of October, when they begin the next leg of their journey south. Through these weeks, sportsmen have a field day, not only with geese but also with grouse, pheasant, duck, snipe, ptarmigan, and Hungarian partridge.

White-tailed and mule deer are found throughout Saskatchewan, while moose, caribou, and black bear are in the northern half of the province. Saskatchewan and Manitoba offer perfect browsing conditions for deer, and the result is larger-than-average specimens. Nearly half of the entries for large white-tailed deer in the Boone and Crockett Record Book come from the plains provinces.

When you hunt big game in Saskatchewan, you must wear an outer suit of white or scarlet or bright yellow and a scarlet or yellow cap. Wildlife managers ask you to report your hunting luck at checking stations located throughout the province, to aid them in planning conservation programs.

There have been closed seasons on pheasant, elk, antelope, and caribou in the past, and game management officers are carefully watching these species. At the same time, the season for bear and moose has at times been expanded.

For the latest hunting information, write: Saskatchewan Travel and Extension Services, Department of Tourism and Renewable Resources, 1825 Lorne Street, Regina, Saskatchewan S4P 3N1.

For migratory bird hunting, write: Director General, Canadian Wildlife Service, Department of the Environment, Ottawa, Ontario.

YUKON TERRITORY. If you are looking for the largest Dall sheep and moose, you'll find them in the high mountains of the Yukon. These animals, along with grizzly bear and caribou, are the most sought-after big game in the area. Hunters also go after black bear and the mountain goat.

In the Yukon, government-registered outfitters are allotted specific territories for their hunting parties, and nonresident hunters must use the services of an outfitter. The hunting season generally extends from the beginning of August to the end of November, but the best months are August and September. After that, the weather can get rough, with severe cold and snow at the higher elevations.

You can fly to the Yukon, take a bus, or drive your own car up the Alaska Highway to Whitehorse. Or, if you want to combine a restful vacation with your hunting, you can cruise by boat from Vancouver to Skagway, Alaska, and take the train to Whitehorse. The Yukon, because of its rugged beauty, the abundance of game, and its gold rush history, is particularly popular with photographers venturing out on camera hunts.

For the latest hunting information, write: Director of Game, PO Box 2703, Whitehorse, Yukon Territory.

For migratory bird hunting, write: Director General, Canadian Wildlife Service, Department of the Environment, Ottawa, Ontario.

FISHING

No one has ever published an official count of the number of freshwater lakes in Canada, but we know there are several hundred thousand of them, ranging in size from overgrown puddles to the big waters of the Great Lakes. Add to this the fact that thousands of rivers and streams flow through the land of the maple leaf, and you begin to get some kind of picture of the fishing opportunities that await you.

And this is only the freshwater angling. Canada's thousands of miles of coastline—east, west, and north—add a magnificent saltwater dimension to the picture.

Whether you are a purist addicted to waders and a fly rod or prefer to harness yourself into the swivel chair of a tuna cruiser, Canadian waters have something for you. There are dozens of ways to enjoy fishing here and more than 40 varieties of game fish to go after.

The most exotic method is to go with a fishing party to a remote camp that can be reached only by air. A number of outfitters specialize in organizing trips of this kind, with camp accommodations ranging from minimal to luxurious.

Other camps, only a little less remote, are located in the northern sectors of many provinces and tied to the rest of the world by gravel roads. You can get to them by car or bus, and the fishing is reported to be spectacular there, too. Closer in, you'll find resorts with full facilities that can offer fine fishing along with other amenities. These are excellent places to take the family because there is something for everyone to do.

The easiest method of all is to simply select a town in an area that has the kind of fish you want to catch, and make a reservation at a local hotel or motel. Then tell the desk clerk or any local resident that you'd like to catch some fish. In fifteen minutes you'll know every hot fishing spot within ten miles.

Fishing for steelhead trout on the coast of British Columbia

It's a beauty! caught in Miramichi River, New Brunswick

Waiting for salmon at New Brunswick's popular Miramichi River

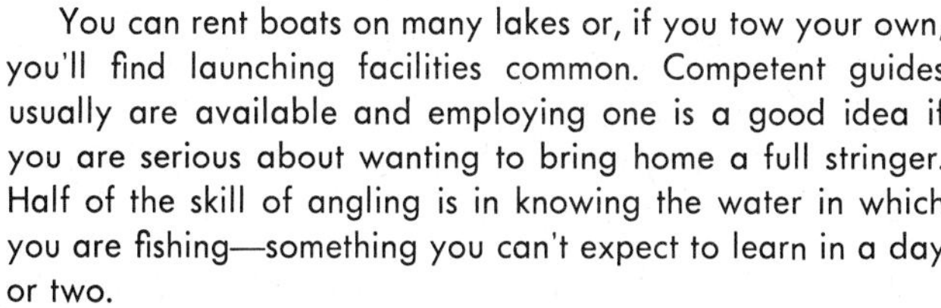

"The jumpingest thing on fins": Quebec's ouananiche

You can rent boats on many lakes or, if you tow your own, you'll find launching facilities common. Competent guides usually are available and employing one is a good idea if you are serious about wanting to bring home a full stringer. Half of the skill of angling is in knowing the water in which you are fishing—something you can't expect to learn in a day or two.

If you want to try deep-sea fishing, you can charter a boat or join a party on a daily fishing cruise. The charter boats usually go after the big ones, like the bluefin tuna. The world record bluefin tuna, weighing in at over 900 pounds, was caught in the waters off Cape Breton. But stripers, mackerel, haddock, and other saltwater varieties, even though less spectacular, can provide a day's fun. The deep-sea boats usually have tackle on board.

As far as freshwater tackle is concerned, be guided by your own experience—plus the advice of people who have fished the area. If you are trying to outwit a brook or other small trout, the 9-foot, 5-ounce fly rod is fine, and so is spinning gear. However, heavier fly rods are recommended for steelhead and Kamloops trout. You *can* land these tigers on standard gear, but the risk is high.

If you are after lake trout, be prepared to troll deep with a wire line during the summer months, when these fellows hug the bottom. You can troll for muskies, too, though most of them are taken on standard bass bait casting tackle. A big one may be too much for a 14-pound test line, so a good many experts use a 20-pound line—just in case. Remember that an average muskie runs around 30 fighting pounds—and 60-pound lunkers are not uncommon.

Kinds of Fish and Where to Find Them

The following list identifies the most popular sport fish to be found in Canada, and names the provinces in which they are most abundant. Some species are found in virtually every province, but only those provinces are listed in which they are high in supply or popularity. Also, some species have local names not shown here. You may hear the northern pike called a jackfish, for example.

ARCTIC CHAR: British Columbia, Labrador, Manitoba, Northwest Territories, Yukon

ARCTIC GRAYLING: Alberta, British Columbia, Manitoba, Northwest Territories, Saskatchewan, Yukon

BASS, LARGEMOUTH: British Columbia, Ontario, Quebec

BASS, SMALLMOUTH (BLACK): Manitoba, New Brunswick, Nova Scotia, Ontario, Quebec

BASS, STRIPED: New Brunswick, Nova Scotia, Quebec

GOLDEYE: Alberta, Saskatchewan

KOKANEE (LANDLOCKED SOCKEYE SALMON): British Columbia, Yukon

LANDLOCKED SALMON: New Brunswick, Nova Scotia

OUANANICHE (LANDLOCKED NATIVE SALMON): Newfoundland, Labrador, Ontario, Quebec

PIKE AND NORTHERN PIKE: Alberta, Labrador, Manitoba, Northwest Territories, Ontario, Quebec, Saskatchewan, Yukon

PERCH: Alberta, British Columbia, Ontario, Saskatchewan

POLLOCK: New Brunswick, Nova Scotia

MUSKELLUNGE (MASKINONGE): Ontario, Quebec

SALMON, CHINOOK AND COHO: British Columbia

SALMON, ATLANTIC: Labrador, New Brunswick, Newfoundland, Nova Scotia, Prince Edward Island, Quebec

SPLAKE: Ontario

STEELHEAD: British Columbia, Yukon

STURGEON: Quebec

SWORDFISH: Nova Scotia, Newfoundland

TOMMY COD: Quebec

TROUT, BROOK: Alberta, British Columbia, Manitoba, New Brunswick, Quebec, Saskatchewan

Cameron Lake, in Waterton Lakes National Park

TROUT, BROWN: Alberta, British Columbia, Nova Scotia, Newfoundland, Ontario, Quebec, Saskatchewan

TROUT, CUTTHROAT: Alberta, British Columbia

TROUT, DOLLY VARDEN: Alberta, British Columbia, Yukon

TROUT, KAMLOOPS: British Columbia

TROUT, LAKE: Alberta, British Columbia, Labrador, Manitoba, Northwest Territories, Nova Scotia, Ontario, Quebec, Saskatchewan

TROUT, RAINBOW: Alberta, British Columbia, Manitoba, Nova Scotia, Newfoundland, Ontario, Quebec, Prince Edward Island, Saskatchewan, Yukon

TROUT, SEA: New Brunswick, Nova Scotia, Quebec

TROUT, SPECKLED: Labrador, New Brunswick, Newfoundland, Ontario, Quebec

TUNA: Newfoundland, Nova Scotia

WALLEYE AND PICKEREL: Alberta, Manitoba, Northwest Territories, Ontario, Quebec, Saskatchewan

WHITEFISH: Ontario, Quebec, Saskatchewan

WHITEFISH, ROCKY MOUNTAIN: Alberta, British Columbia

Fishing in Each Province

ALBERTA. Alberta is true trout country, and six varieties can be taken in the mountain streams of the western section. Rainbow trout are also found in many lakes as well as in the rivers. Lake trout, for the most part, inhabit the remote lakes of the north reached chiefly by air.

The northern pike is very common, found in most of the lakes and rivers. You won't find as many walleye, but they live in the same waters as the pike. Arctic grayling are native to the Athabasca and Peace river systems and the Martin River, north of Lesser Slave Lake.

During August and September, the Rocky Mountain whitefish bites in nearly all of the Alberta rivers.

For the most recent regulations, write: Fish and Wildlife, Department of Recreation, Parks and Wildlife, 9833 109 Street, Edmonton, Alberta T5K 2E1.

BRITISH COLUMBIA. Sport fishing in British Columbia rates among the best in the world. You can choose between the unnumbered lakes and rivers for freshwater fishing, or the bays and inlets of the coast for saltwater efforts. Chinook and coho salmon lurk in the sheltered inlets and bays, with the best fishing in September and October. The very best coho fishing, they say, is to be found in the Queen Charlotte Islands, in Copper Bay, and the Tlell and Yakoun rivers. There are no accommodations there, and you get there by boat or plane.

Steelheads are seagoing rainbow trout. They spend their first year and a half in fresh water, then go to sea for another yecr and a half. They return to the freshwater stream to spawn, usually between November and March, and this is when fishermen most often seek them out. The steelhead is wise and wary and very difficult to hook. If you do manage to hook him, you'll have a furious battle on your hands—with a good chance that he'll throw the hook before you land him.

Lake trout, which get as large as 60 pounds, are found in most of the province's larger lakes. The coastal cutthroat occurs in all the lakes and streams along the coast; some of them migrate to sea for a while, while others are content to live their lives out in fresh water. The kokanee is a landlocked salmon always found in fresh water and can be caught in most of the larger lakes. Averaging only a pound or so in size, it is rated as the best eating fish in British Columbia.

For the most recent regulations, write: Fish and Wildlife Branch, Department of Recreation and Travel Industry, Parliament Buildings, Victoria, British Columbia.

MANITOBA. A large-scale map of Manitoba looks very much as if someone splattered it with blue paint, because of the thousands of lakes which dot its surface. When you realize that every one of those lakes is full of fish—and that some

Judging the catch at the Sun Salmon Derby, Vancouver

of them may never have been fished—the mind is boggled.

In the north, above the 53rd parallel, you'll find lake trout, brook trout, northern pike, walleye, and the Arctic grayling, among others. At Churchill, you will meet the white whale. Around the first of July each year, fishermen flock to the Flin Flon Trout Festival for fiddling, dancing, prizes for the biggest trout, and an 81-mile canoe derby. South of the 53rd parallel, pike, walleye, and rainbow trout are the biggest attractions, along with the black smallmouth bass.

For the latest hunting information, write: Renewable Resources and Transportation Services, 1495 James Street, Winnipeg, Manitoba.

NEW BRUNSWICK. The inland lakes of New Brunswick yield up the landlocked salmon, while speckled trout ply most of the rivers. When these trout migrate to the sea, they change color, grow in size, and become sea trout. At spawning time, they turn in from the sea and rush back up their native rivers. In the southwestern part of the province, the smallmouth black bass is one of the main sport fish. And the saltwater striped bass has taken a fancy to the area around the Reversing Falls near the mouth of the Saint John River.

Deep-sea fishing is an important business in New Brunswick. You can find boats—most provide tackle—for charter by the hour, half day, or day in many villages around the Bay of Fundy, the Northumberland Strait, and Baie des Chaleurs. A day on a boat could get you a good catch of pollock—five pounds of fighting fish—mackerel, or striped bass.

For the most recent regulations, write: Fish and Wildlife Branch, Department of Natural Resources, Fredericton, New Brunswick.

NEWFOUNDLAND. Labrador, on the mainland, is a part of the Province of Newfoundland and is still chiefly in its natural undeveloped state. There has been some recent development of fishing facilities in the area. To get here, you must fly in. There are good runs of Atlantic salmon in the rivers along the coast, and the freshwater lakes have large speckled trout, lake trout, ouananiche, and pike. Sea runs of Arctic char occur in all rivers north of Nain.

On the island of Newfoundland itself, the lakes are full of pretty speckled trout. Brown trout and rainbow trout can be found only on the Avalon Peninsula. Tuna fishing is centered in Conception Bay, where you can charter boats.

For the most recent regulations, write: Area Director, Department of Fisheries, St. John's, Newfoundland.

NORTHWEST TERRITORIES. When you cross the 60th parallel going north, you enter the Northwest Territories and cross the last frontier. There are still another 1,600 miles to the north of you, but the area is wilderness, without roads and with few settlements. If there is any land that should produce trophy-sized fish, it is this—simply because there is no one here to take these fish. They have time to grow and grow.

This is a land with 20 hours of sun a day south of the Arctic Circle—and 24 hours a day north of it—during the summer. In July and early August, the days are warm, just about the right temperature for fishing. But summer is over by the last part of August, and the winter chill begins to set in.

The water in the lakes—there may be half a million of them—never warms up, so the fish stay close to the surface. You'll find Arctic char, northern pike, yellow walleye, Arctic grayling, and lake trout. Northerns have been known to reach 35 pounds, and the lake trout sometimes weigh in at 50 pounds. With that kind of promise in view, the long trip into this wilderness looks worthwhile.

For the most recent regulations, write: Fisheries Service, Environment Canada, Yellowknife, Northwest Territories.

NOVA SCOTIA. One doesn't often hear of a new fish being discovered, but it happened in Nova Scotia in 1951. That year, a fish called the tautog was found at Eel Brook, in Yarmouth County, and in the tidal river at Argyle, a few miles away. Today, tautog fishing is one of the province's favorite sports.

But the top sport of them all around is the run for the giant bluefin tuna. The tuna is a type of mackerel, but about 800 pounds larger than his prosaic cousins. In 1970, in St. George's Bay, Cape Breton Island, a tuna tipping the scales at 1,065 pounds was taken, establishing a new world record. Fish in the 700 – 800 pound class are caught fairly frequently.

To catch a bluefin tuna, you charter a boat equipped for the purpose. Special tackle is needed because tuna are fast and powerful—and may battle for eight hours or more after being hooked. More than one weary angler has collapsed over his reel and cut the line because his fish wouldn't give in.

The season for tuna runs from July through October, with the world Olympics of tuna fishing held at Cape St. Mary early in September. Teams of fishermen from all over the world compete for the Alton B. Sharpe Trophy. As many as 72 tuna have been taken during the three days of competition.

Sea trout fishing in Nova Scotia is subject to special regulations when you fish on posted salmon rivers. It is prohibited from October to the following April. But during the season, sea trout caught through fly fishing provide wonderful sport.

Charter boats for deep-sea fishing other than tuna will take you out for an hour or a day, find you a variety of saltwater fish, and get your nose sunburned. Many of the towns and villages, including Yarmouth, Shelburne, Lunenburg, Halifax, Digby, Inverness, and Victoria, along the coast have boats.

For the most recent regulations, write: Department of Fisheries, Provincial Building, Hollis Street, Halifax, Nova Scotia.

ONTARIO. Ontario is really two provinces, one urbane and civilized and the other rugged and untamed. Northern Ontario is still very much natural wilderness, with lakes which have yet to be fished and isolated fly-in fish camps. Southern

Charter fishing boats on Conception Bay, Newfoundland

Ontario, well punctuated by lakes also, offers fine resorts with every kind of amusement to go along with good fishing.

Northern pike and muskies and walleye are prime targets in Ontario lakes. If you've ever wondered how big a muskie can get—well, one weighing 110 pounds was taken in a net in Georgian Bay. The thought of hooking something like that on a bait casting line is frightening. And they've taken 100-pound sturgeon out of Lake Nipissing.

Large and smallmouth bass are important sport fish in the southern part of the province. Brook, rainbow, and brown trout hide behind rocks in the rivers and streams, while big lake trout live in the northern lakes.

The splake, an Ontario-developed cross between a female lake trout and a male brook trout, was the fish expert's answer to the lamprey eel, which invaded the Great Lakes a few years ago. The idea was to create a fish that would spawn at least once before it reached the size at which the lamprey would attack it. The lamprey has now been chemically controlled, but the splake is still planted in Lake Huron and Georgian Bay. The steelhead and coho salmon have also been planted in the Great Lakes and have created a whole new kind of sport fishing in the area.

For the most recent regulations, write: Sport Fishing Branch, Ministry of Natural Resources, Parliament Buildings, Toronto, Ontario.

PRINCE EDWARD ISLAND. There is always good sea-trout and brook-trout fishing on this lovely island. The island is dotted with fishing ponds and streams in pleasant rural settings, and this is where the brook trout hide. Sea trout can be taken in the rivers which lead to the sea—the Brudenell, the Montague, the Vernon, the Murray, and others.

Atlantic salmon are native to the island's rivers, but you won't catch any until the autumn months. Then the only trick is to find out when a "run" enters the stream, since you won't catch any fish until the run occurs.

Rainbow trout have been planted in some of the lakes and ponds. You can catch them up to seven pounds in size in Scales' Pond at Freetown, and at Glenfinnan Lake, about 15 miles from Charlottetown.

For the most recent regulations, write: Fish and Wildlife Division, Department of Fisheries, PO Box 2000, Charlottetown, Prince Edward Island.

QUEBEC. The provincial fish and wildlife people say that Quebec has more fish than any foreign country. Since the province covers nearly 600,000 square miles, this could well be true. Leading species include pike, black bass, walleye, yellow perch, rainbow trout, lake trout, and speckled trout (known also as the brook trout).

Speckled trout caught at Lake Waconichi, northern Quebec

A number of territories have been leased to outfitters, who completely control the hunting and fishing in their areas. Well-practiced in the art of catering to sportsmen, the outfitters can assure you of a successful fishing expedition. Other outfitters can guide you on unleased and provincial lands.

Northern Quebec has yet to be fully explored, and fly-in camps in this wilderness are noted for producing trophy-sized fish. Going to this area, nonresidents must have a guide.

Coastal fishing excursions have become very popular in recent years. Fishing boats put out from villages along the St. Lawrence (from Trois Pistoles downriver) and seek out cod and halibut. And fishing from the piers and docks for mackerel, sea trout, bass, and other fish has become important to tourists as well as to local residents.

In the fall, the smelt run up the St. Lawrence as far as Quebec City. At night, during the running, the river becomes alive with smelt hunters, lanterns in hand and baskets alongside. The smelt run has become so popular and colorful that the riverfront takes on a festive feeling while it lasts.

For the most recent regulations, write: Department of Tourism, Fish and Game, 150 East Blvd. Saint-Curille, Quebec, Province of Quebec, G1R 4Y3.

SASKATCHEWAN. Every once in a while, some lucky angler lands a 30-pound northern pike. If the strike occurs in the warmer waters in the south of the province, Mr. Pike will reel in without too much of a fight. But if the scene is one of the cold northern lakes, then look out! He may turn the hook into a straight pin or snap the line like thread.

The northern pike is Saskatchewan's most abundant fish, found in just about every lake. The average size runs 3 to 5 pounds—though the big ones are out there, waiting. Along with the pike, you'll find the walleye, who can be converted into lovely fillets for dinner. Go deep for them in hot weather.

The trout of the province—rainbow, brook, and brown—were all introduced and have taken to the local waters nicely. The lake trout is a native, runs between 5 and 20 pounds, and can be found at home in the big northern lakes. The Arctic grayling lives in the fast, cold streams of the north.

Other fish here, but in smaller numbers, are the perch, goldeye, sauger, whitefish, and sturgeon. Splake, coho, and kokanee salmon have recently been introduced into some waters.

For most recent regulations, write: Saskatchewan Travel and Extension Services, Department of Tourism and Renewable Resources, 1825 Lorne Street, Regina, Saskatchewan S4P 3N1.

YUKON TERRITORY. The lakes of the Yukon are clear and cold, and you'll find fish in all of them. Arctic grayling may be taken in practically every stream, while big lake trout and northern pike are found in most of the lakes. Rainbow, steelhead, and kokanee are plentiful in the Alsek River system. Arctic char and Dolly Varden trout may be found in the Mackenzie River watershed.

If you drive the Alaska Highway or the Klondike Highway, you can stop at communities along the way, engage a guide, and get some good fishing in. There are lakes and streams near all of them.

For the most recent regulations, write: Department of Fisheries, Box 2140, Whitehorse, Yukon Territory.

CANADA'S WEATHER PICTURE is as varied as the colors in a patchwork quilt. July and August are the warmest months across the nation, but they tend to be pleasantly warm rather than excessively hot. Summer evenings are delightful and generally cool enough for a light sweater or jacket—and for good, sound sleeping. Winter, in most places, is ideal for the sports lover. Snow is abundant, with the first heavy falls arriving in mid-December.

Vancouver, Victoria, and the Sunshine Coast never really see a winter, of course. The Japanese Current prevents even the January temperatures from dropping below the mid-30s. Victoria may see ten inches of snow, with perhaps twice that amount falling in Vancouver. But only twenty minutes from downtown Vancouver, after a ride on the Grouse Mountain alpine car, you can have all the snow you want for fine skiing.

Snowfall in the Rockies is prodigious, and it is ample across the rest of the nation. Oddly, Yellowknife, though a northern metropolis, averages only 34.5 inches of snow in a winter, while St. John's, Newfoundland, must dig out from under 141 inches.

If you think of the year in terms of activities rather than temperatures and precipitation, here is a thumbnail guide:

WINTER SPORTS. Generally begin in mid-December and continue to the first of April in the lower areas. In the mountain regions, you can usually ski through April.

SPRING BLOSSOM TIME. May is the month of rebirth, when the landscape greens and the flowers bloom. The tulips riot in Montreal and Ottawa. Vancouver, a lovely garden at any time of the year, is particularly colorful then.

FALL COLOR. Canadian autumns are magnificent. When the first frost touches the leaves about September 20, reds and golds in every imaginable shade begin to appear. The colors deepen and spread until about the middle of October. Color tours in Ontario, Quebec, and the Atlantic Provinces are particularly breathtaking.

Canadian highways are well kept in the winter months. If you travel in the winter, pay attention to weather reports. While the roads are plowed immediately after a snowstorm, you may find driving hazardous during the storm.

In summer the Great Plains, Ontario, and Quebec are generally sunny; the coastal areas offer a greater variety of weather. As a guide in making travel plans, check the chart below for temperature ranges in various locations.

Temperature Chart

Average daily minimum and maximum temperatures at selected points across Canada.

DEGREES FAHRENHEIT

	JAN		FEB		MAR		APR		MAY		JUNE		JULY		AUG		SEPT		OCT		NOV		DEC	
	L	H	L	H	L	H	L	H	L	H	L	H	L	H	L	H	L	H	L	H	L	H	L	H
Newfoundland																								
St. John's	21	33	20	32	23	33	29	42	35	50	42	59	51	69	53	68	45	61	37	51	32	44	23	35
Prince Edward Island																								
Charlottetown	11	26	10	25	20	34	30	44	40	57	50	67	59	74	58	74	51	66	42	55	32	43	19	31
Nova Scotia																								
Halifax	17	32	16	31	24	38	32	47	41	58	49	67	56	74	57	73	51	67	43	57	34	47	23	36
Yarmouth	21	34	21	33	27	39	34	47	42	57	49	64	54	69	55	70	50	65	43	57	36	48	26	38
New Brunswick																								
Fredericton	4	24	4	26	17	37	29	49	39	63	49	72	55	78	54	76	46	68	36	56	26	42	11	28
Saint John	12	28	12	28	22	37	32	46	41	57	48	65	54	70	55	70	49	64	41	55	31	44	17	32
Quebec																								
Gaspe	2	20	1	21	13	31	26	41	36	53	46	67	54	76	49	73	43	66	34	54	23	38	9	25
Montreal	8	23	9	24	21	35	34	50	47	64	57	74	62	79	60	76	52	67	41	55	30	41	15	27
Quebec	5	19	6	21	18	32	31	45	43	61	53	72	59	77	57	74	49	65	39	52	27	37	12	24
Ontario																								
Ottawa	3	21	3	22	17	34	31	50	43	65	53	75	58	80	55	78	48	69	37	55	26	40	10	25
Port Arthur	−2	17	0	20	12	31	26	45	37	58	47	68	52	74	51	72	44	63	34	51	20	34	6	22
Toronto	18	31	17	31	25	39	36	52	46	65	56	75	61	81	60	78	53	71	42	58	33	45	23	34
Manitoba																								
The Pas	−16	3	−12	10	1	25	21	44	36	60	46	69	53	76	50	73	40	61	29	47	9	25	−8	9
Winnipeg	−8	9	−5	14	9	28	28	48	41	64	51	73	57	80	54	78	45	66	34	52	16	30	1	15
Saskatchewan																								
Prince Albert	−11	9	−7	14	5	28	26	48	38	64	47	71	53	77	50	74	40	63	30	50	12	28	−5	14
Regina	−7	12	−5	16	9	29	27	50	38	66	47	73	52	81	49	78	39	67	29	53	13	31	0	18
Alberta																								
Banff	4	22	7	29	15	38	25	49	33	59	39	65	43	73	41	71	35	61	29	50	17	34	8	24
Calgary	5	26	6	28	16	37	27	52	37	63	44	68	49	76	46	74	39	64	30	54	18	38	9	29
Edmonton	−1	17	2	21	14	33	29	51	39	64	46	70	51	75	47	72	39	63	30	52	16	33	4	20
Jasper	4	22	8	30	17	39	26	51	34	61	41	68	45	74	43	71	37	63	30	51	18	35	8	24
British Columbia																								
Prince Rupert	31	40	31	41	33	45	37	50	42	56	47	60	50	63	51	63	48	60	43	53	37	46	33	41
Vancouver	33	42	34	46	37	51	42	58	47	65	52	70	55	74	54	74	50	67	45	58	39	49	35	44
Victoria	36	43	37	46	40	50	43	56	47	61	50	65	52	68	52	68	50	65	46	57	41	49	38	45
Yukon																								
Whitehorse	−3	13	−2	16	12	31	22	41	34	57	43	67	45	67	43	65	37	55	28	41	8	21	−4	11
Northwest Territories																								
Yellowknife	−26	−10	−24	−6	−11	10	7	29	31	49	44	61	52	69	50	65	39	52	26	36	0	14	−21	−6

TRANSPORTATION

BECAUSE OF ITS GREAT SIZE and natural barriers like the Rockies, Canada has always depended heavily on its internal transportation facilities. Its real growth as a nation couldn't begin until the completion of the transcontinental railroad in 1879. Today, Canadians are still very aware of the need for good transportation in their growth plans, so travel facilities enjoy a priority on the national schedule of things to be done.

The great Trans-Canada Highway stretches across the nation, covering nearly 5,000 miles from coast to coast. The Trans-Canada is laid out so that the majority of the population is within 75 miles of it. This gives the traveler an opportunity to move quickly from place to place and to make side trips to attractive places. In planning the Trans-Canada, the government saw to it that camping sites or facilities are located every 50 miles or so along the length of the road. At the height of the travel season, these facilities may be used heavily, so plan to occupy a site early. There are, of course, a great many camping facilities, both public and private, within easy reach of the Trans-Canada—all of which help to make camper travel a real pleasure in Canada.

The Trans-Canada Highway connects to the Yellowhead Highway west of Winnipeg. You can take Highway 10 north from Brandon to join it at Dauphin, or you can stay on the Trans-Canada to Regina, where you take Highway 11 northwest to Saskatoon to meet it. The Yellowhead is the main artery through Edmonton and Saskatoon, traveling northwest and west through northern Saskatchewan, Alberta, and British Columbia. The western terminus is at Prince Rupert.

Roads are being extended northward to give access to the wilderness. The Alaska Highway from Dawson Creek crosses the Yukon Territory to Whitehorse and beyond, to the Alaska border. If you are venturesome and would like to see some of Canada's finest mountain and forest scenery, this is a great trip. The Mackenzie route reaches up from Peace River, Alberta, to circle Great Slave Lake and take you to the new and thriving metropolis of Yellowknife in the Northwest Territories. The Alaska Marine Highway is a combination of roads and ferry routes to follow northward from Vancouver to Skagway, the Yukon Territory, and Alaska.

Much of the northern wilderness is not yet accessible by car, but you'll find a well-developed network of small airlines to take you to almost any out-of-the-way spot you might want to reach for hunting or fishing. Nearly every town in the northern parts of the provinces serves as a base for one or more of these airlines. The planes are flown by bush pilots, whose skill has become a part of the national folklore.

Rail travel is still extremely important in Canada, and passenger train service is very good. You can travel between the major cities and take excursions to the beauty spots, such as Lake Louise and Banff, by train. You can even book excursions into the wilderness. Check VIA, Canada's rail passenger agency, for schedules.

Ferryboats are an important part of travel in Canada, especially along the east and west coasts. Giant automobile ferries, carrying up to 200 cars, connect Vancouver and Victoria, for example, and tie the provinces of Newfoundland and Nova Scotia together. You can enter Canada via ferry from Seattle, Washington, and from Bar Harbor, Maine. Most of the bigger boats provide very comfortable passenger lounges, restaurants, and sun deck facilities so that ferry trips are enjoyable as well as practical. During the summer season, the ferries are heavily used, so it is wise to obtain a schedule of runs in advance and be at the dock well before sailing time.

The prize ferry trip of all is that from Kelsey Bay on Vancouver Island up to Prince Rupert, an overnight jump that is a memorable cruise.

Cruises on ocean liners can also be a part of your Canadian travel. The famous Inside Passage cruise, from Vancouver along the coast to Skagway and back, takes from six to seven days, and offers all the pleasures of an ocean voyage plus the bonus of magnificent coastal scenery. Another good cruise is that from Sydney, Nova Scotia, to St. Pierre and Miquelon—three days and three nights aboard a miniliner that serves as your hotel while you explore North America's only French colony.

Air travel in Canada is excellent. The two major lines are Air Canada and CP Air (Canadian Pacific), and between them they serve just about every inhabited spot. Feeder lines such as Eastern Provincial fill in the gaps with service that is equal to that of the big lines. Montreal, Toronto, and Vancouver are the hub cities, where you'll do most of your changing of planes. The terminals at all three cities are modern facilities.

CP Air's flight between Toronto and Vancouver is one of the most luxurious you'll find anywhere. The food and wine on this flight are equal to that in the finest restaurants and are elegantly served. No paper placemats or plastic ware here, but snowy linen table cloths, fine china, and silver.

American travelers will find Canadian highways well kept. Even the gravel roads like the Mackenzie and the Alaska are in good condition, easy to drive. Highway planners have kept the traveler in mind and have arranged lookouts and pullover points wherever there is an opportunity to view the great Canadian scenery.

YOUR CAR

Americans entering Canada will find that taking a car across the border is simple and quick. It is wise, however, to observe a few precautions. Carry your motor vehicle registration with you, or if you are driving a borrowed car, have a letter from the owner of the car authorizing you to drive it to Canada. If you are driving a rented car, carry a copy of the rental contract and be sure it stipulates that you can use the car in Canada.

Before leaving home, obtain from your insurance company a Canadian Non-Resident Interprovince Motor Vehicle Liability Insurance card. This is a pale yellow card, available only in the United States. You will not be asked to produce it to enter Canada, but you should have it in the event of accident. The provinces of Ontario, Manitoba, Alberta, and British Columbia do not require a visiting motorist to produce evidence of financial responsibility in the event of an accident. The other provinces do.

Americans should remember, too, that the Imperial gallon is used in Canada. Four of these are equal to five United States gallons. You'll be surprised, if you don't remember this, at the high cost of gasoline—and doubly surprised that your tank seems to hold less.

DAYLIGHT SAVING TIME

Daylight saving time comes to Canada on the last Sunday in April each year, and on the last Sunday in October, the clock is turned back to standard time. But there are some places which don't observe daylight saving time, and maintain standard time all year. To be on the safe side, check the local time as soon as you arrive at your destination. This is especially important if you are planning to make train, plane, or boat connections.

Canada is divided into seven time zones. Beginning in the east and progressing to the west, you pass through the Newfoundland, Atlantic, Eastern, Central, Mountain, Pacific, and Yukon time zones. Watch for those places where you must change your watch setting, especially in the Atlantic provinces. There are two additional time zones in Alaska, giving the continent a total of nine.

Motoring to Mount Robson via the Yellowhead Highway

CANADIAN MILEAGE CHART

	Banff, Alta.	Brandon, Man.	Calgary, Alta.	Charlottetown, P.E.I.	Edmonton, Alta.	Fort William, Ont.	Fredericton, N.B.	Gaspe, Que.	Halifax, N.S.	Jasper, Alta.	Kenora, Ont.	Moncton, N.B.	Montreal, Que.	North Bay, Ont.	Ottawa, Ont.	Prince Albert, Sask.	Prince George, B.C.	Quebec, Que.	Regina, Sask.	Rouyn, Que.	Saint John, N.B.	St. John's, Nfld.	Saskatoon, Sask.	Sault Ste. Marie, Ont.	Sherbrooke, Que.	Summerside, P.E.I.	Sydney, N.S.	Toronto, Ont.	Vancouver, B.C.	Winnipeg, Man.	Windsor, Ont.	Yarmouth, N.S.
Banff, Alta.		782	77	3176	260	1337	2929	3002	3257	176	1034	3035	2393	2038	2269	580	629	2560	550	1646	3022	4002	478	1772	2492	3137	3415	2180	571	904	2420	3146
Brandon, Man.	782		709	2394	733	551	2163	2241	2492	978	261	2289	1632	1278	1509	460	1369	1797	236	1183	2256	3301	397	999	1731	2371	2630	1458	1357	118	1698	2364
Calgary, Alta.	77	709		3222	183	1260	2868	2946	3197	253	970	2994	2337	1982	2213	508	706	2502	473	1887	2961	4079	401	1708	2436	3076	3338	2161	648	827	2401	3069
Charlottetown, P.E.I.	3176	2394	3222		3141	1930	247	565	165	3375	2146	121	783	1229	998	2857	3766	616	2749	1171	214	939	2800	1495	731	39	256	1128	3747	2276	1368	377
Chicoutimi, Que.	2708	1922	2631	745	2670	1358	342	422	671	2904	1677	483	297	652	421	2386	3295	132	2162	690	451	1653	2330	922	267	423	824	647	3279	1808	887	630
Dawson Creek, Alta.	634	1103	557	3510	370	1676	3273	3344	3597	540	1351	3399	2742	2387	2618	817	259	2907	867	2293	3011	4411	710	2102	2841	3481	3740	2567	741	1221	2807	3119
Edmonton, Alta.	260	733	183	3141		1307	2904	2965	3228	234	981	3030	2373	2018	2249	448	629	2538	497	1924	2997	4042	336	1732	2472	3112	3371	2198	835	851	2438	3105
Fort William, Ont.	1337	551	1260	1930	1307		1592	1653	1921	1541	303	1717	1061	706	937	1023	1932	1226	799	599	1685	2729	966	435	1160	1799	2058	887	1908	445	1127	1793
Flin Flon, Man.	1042	461	965	2863	919	1029	2626	2706	2955	1153	692	2746	2090	1740	1971	685	1544	2260	492	1646	2719	3758	578	1464	2189	2828	3087	1916	1513	562	2156	2827
Fredericton, N.B.	2929	2163	2868	247	2904	1592		456	329	3507	1911	126	542	982	688	2620	3529	380	2391	924	93	1138	2558	1156	502	208	486	982	3500	2037	1121	201
Gaspe, Que.	3002	2241	2946	565	2965	1653	456		647	3199	1972	444	611	966	735	2681	3652	446	2476	1017	549	1456	2643	1236	581	526	785	961	3573	2122	1201	657
Halifax, N.S.	3257	2492	3197	165	3228	1921	329	647		3462	2235	203	955	1310	1079	2949	3853	790	2720	1253	296	852	2887	1485	813	204	282	1310	3704	2366	1550	212
Hamilton, Ont.	2282	1502	2205	1172	2242	930	925	1005	1592	2476	1250	1051	394	264	303	1954	2867	559	1729	452	1018	2063	1897	495	493	1133	1392	44	2853	1380	196	1126
Jasper, Alta.	176	978	253	3375	234	1541	3507	3199	3462		1227	3364	2607	2252	2483	682	859	2772	742	2158	3231	4275	575	1981	2706	3446	3705	2432	713	1096	2762	3339
Kenora, Ont.	1034	261	970	2146	981	303	1911	1972	2235	1227		2037	1367	1025	1256	721	1618	1545	497	931	2004	3043	658	738	1479	2113	2378	1206	1605	130	1446	2112
Moncton, N.B.	3035	2289	2994	121	3030	1717	126	444	203	3364	2037		753	1012	877	2740	3649	495	2516	1050	93	1012	2683	1282	610	82	360	1007	3626	2168	1247	289
Montreal, Que.	2393	1632	2337	783	2373	1061	543	611	955	2607	1367	753		355	124	2089	2998	167	1865	408	624	1668	2032	625	99	739	920	355	2964	1497	590	732
North Bay, Ont.	2038	1278	1982	1229	2018	706	982	966	1310	2252	1025	1012	355		231	1734	2643	522	1510	214	979	2024	1677	266	454	1094	1275	216	2609	1156	460	1087
Ottawa, Ont.	2269	1509	2213	998	2249	937	668	735	1079	2483	1256	877	124	231		1965	2874	291	1741	328	761	1793	1908	501	223	863	1044	257	2840	1384	499	856
Port-aux-Basques, Nfld.	3475	2714	3419	352	3454	2443	551	869	378	3688	2457	425	1082	1437	1206	3166	4075	917	2942	1475	518	587	3109	1707	1035	932	FY.	1432	4046	2588	1672	604
Prince Albert, Sask.	580	460	508	2857	448	1023	2620	2681	2949	682	721	2740	2089	1734	1965		1073	2252	224	1640	2708	3752	107	1463	2188	2822	3081	1910	1151	578	2150	2816
Prince George, B.C.	629	1369	706	3766	629	1932	3529	3652	3853	859	1618	3649	2998	2643	2874	1073		3163	1133	2549	3617	4661	966	2372	3097	3731	3990	2863	482	1487	3059	3725
Quebec, Que.	2560	1797	2502	616	2538	1226	380	446	790	2772	1545	495	167	522	291	2252	3163		2030	575	459	1504	2197	790	135	574	855	515	3131	1676	755	567
Regina, Sask.	550	236	473	2749	497	799	2391	2476	2720	742	497	2516	1865	1510	1741	224	1133	2030		1416	2484	3528	167	1239	1964	2598	3284	1686	1121	354	1926	2592
Riviere-du-Loup, Que.	2677	1914	2619	499	2655	1343	252	329	578	2884	1662	375	282	637	406	2371	3280	117	2147	692	342	1387	2314	907	235	457	738	632	3248	1788	872	450
Rouyn, Que.	1646	1183	1887	1171	1924	599	924	1017	1253	2158	931	1050	408	214	328	1640	2549	575	1416		1143	2062	1583	480	492	1132	1391	430	2217	1062	648	1251
Saint John, N.B.	3022	2256	2961	214	2997	1685	93	549	296	3231	2004	93	624	979	761	2708	3617	459	2484	1143		1131	2656	1249	577	175	434	974	3593	2130	1214	108
St. John's, Nfld.	4002	3301	4079	939	4042	2729	1138	1456	852	4275	3043	1012	1668	2024	1793	3752	4661	1504	3528	2062	1131		3787	2380	1622	1519	697	2019	4573	3174	2259	1054
Saskatoon, Sask.	478	397	401	2800	336	966	2558	2643	2887	575	658	2683	2032	1677	1908	107	966	2197	167	1583	2656	3787		1406	2131	2765	3451	1853	1049	521	2093	2764
Sault Ste. Marie, Ont.	1772	999	1708	1495	1732	435	1156	1236	1485	1981	738	1282	625	266	501	1463	2372	790	1239	480	1249	2380	1406		724	1364	1623	408	2343	881	691	1357
Sherbrooke, Que.	2492	1731	2436	731	2472	1160	502	581	813	2706	1479	610	99	454	223	2188	3097	135	1964	492	577	1622	2131	724		692	951	449	3063	1610	689	685
Summerside, P.E.I.	3137	2371	3076	39	3112	1799	208	526	204	3446	2113	82	739	1094	863	2822	3731	574	2598	1132	175	1519	2765	1364	692		295	1089	3708	2250	1329	416
Sydney, N.S.	3415	2630	3338	256	3371	2058	486	785	282	3705	2378	360	920	1275	1044	3081	3990	855	3284	1391	434	697	3451	1623	951	295		1348	3986	2509	1588	494
Toronto, Ont.	2180	1458	2161	1128	2198	887	982	961	1310	2432	1206	1007	355	216	257	1910	2863	515	1686	430	974	2019	1853	408	449	1089	1348		2751	1336	240	1082
Vancouver, B.C.	571	1357	648	3747	835	1908	3500	3573	3704	713	1605	3626	2964	2609	2840	1151	482	3131	1121	2217	3593	4573	1049	2343	3063	3708	3986	2751		1475	3225	3852
Victoria, B.C.	654	1440	731	3830	918	1991	3583	3656	3911	796	1688	3709	3047	2692	2923	1234	565	3214	1204	2200	3676	4656	1132	2426	3146	3791	4069	2834	83	1558	3308	3935
Whitehorse, Yukon	1552	2031	1474	4428	1288	2594	4191	4252	4515	1521	2280	4317	3660	3305	3536	1735	1174	3825	1795	3211	4284	5350	1628	3034	3459	4399	4652	3485	1659	2149	3725	4392
Winnipeg, Man.	904	118	827	2276	851	445	2037	2122	2366	1096	130	2168	1497	1156	1384	578	1487	1676	354	1062	2130	3174	521	881	1610	2250	2509	1336	1475		1576	2238
Windsor, Ont.	2420	1698	2401	1368	2438	1127	1121	1201	1550	2762	1446	1247	590	460	499	2150	3059	755	1926	648	1214	2259	2093	691	689	1329	1588	240	3225	1576		1322
Yarmouth, N.S.	3146	2364	3069	377	3105	1793	201	657	212	3339	2112	289	732	1087	856	2816	3725	567	2592	1251	108	1054	2764	1357	685	416	494	1082	3852	2238	1322	

BOAT TRIPS

THERE'S SOMETHING ABOUT A BOAT trip that adds dimension to an automobile vacation. Wherever you go across Canada, you'll find interesting cruises to attract you. Some are ferry trips, some are harbor tours, some are lake or river excursions, and others are true cruises. Because schedules and prices are subject to considerable change, you should inquire locally about them.

BRITISH COLUMBIA

Dozens of ferries ply the waters of the Strait of Georgia—connecting Vancouver Island with the mainland of Canada and with the United States. Others taxi among the Gulf Islands and connect points along the Sunshine Coast. Each of these works chiefly to get you from one place to another, but you'll find some of the trips, up to a couple of hours in length, are small cruises in themselves. The ferries are commodious, with lounges and restaurant facilities and even deck chairs for soaking up the sun.

In addition to these local runs, there are the longer ferry trips—20 hours—from Kelsey Bay to Prince Rupert, and the luxurious cruises, lasting up to seven days, between Vancouver and Skagway via the beautiful Inner Passage. For something different, you might try a cruise from Vancouver to the Queen Charlotte Islands, a five-day round trip which takes you well off the beaten path. Another interesting ferry trip is a one-day junket which leaves Port Alberni, on Vancouver Island, to visit little ports along the west side of the island not often seen by tourists.

There's a good tour of the harbor to be had at Vancouver that requires a little over an hour and gives you a fine view of a busy international harbor at work. You'll find cruises and boat rides on many lakes. A notable ride is the two-hour cruise on Okanagan Lake aboard the *Fintry Queen* at Kelowna.

ALBERTA

Some of the most spectacular scenery in the three national parks in Alberta can be seen on lake cruises. In Banff National Park, you can take a beautiful 1½-hour cruise on Lake Minnewanka. There is a 2½-hour cruise of the Waterton Lakes in Waterton Lakes National Park, near the Alberta-United States border. One of the best known lake cruises in Canada is that on Maligne Lake in Jasper National Park. All of these cruises are scenic and provide excellent photographic opportunities.

MANITOBA

One of the best ways to round out a tour of Winnipeg is to take the three-hour cruise on the Red River. Or if you'd like to make a vacation out of a cruise, consider the boat trip up Lake Winnipeg which starts at Selkirk. You'll get all the way to Grand Rapids in the 2-to-7 days you are on the water.

ONTARIO

The lakes, rivers, and harbors throughout Ontario offer interesting sightseeing tours. You can see Georgian Bay, for example, on trips which start at Midland. Two-hour cruises of the Lake of the Woods begin at Kenora. Or you can cruise Lake Timagami and visit an old Hudson Bay post from the town of Timagami. Other lake cruises include Lake Nipissing, from North Bay; Muskoka Lakes, from Bracebridge; and Lake Muskoka, from Gravenhurst.

Harbor tours that give you a good view of lake shipping life can be made in Toronto Harbor and at Thunder Bay, where the big ore boats load. You'll get another and different look at the lake giants when you cruise the Soo Locks at Sault Ste. Marie. And no trip to Niagara Falls is complete without a ride on the *Maid of the Mist* behind the lacy mist at the base of the falls.

In Ottawa, you can spend a pleasant afternoon touring the Rideau Canal and taking a leisurely trip on the Ottawa River. You'll particularly enjoy the view of the government buildings from the water. And finally, one of Ontario's prime attractions is the Thousand Islands region. Cruises through the islands begin at Brockville, Rockport, Gananoque, and Kingston.

QUEBEC

Ferryboats cross the St. Lawrence at a number of points east of Quebec City—where the river is wide and the trips take up to two hours. Car-carrying ferries ply between Matane and Godbout, Riviere du Loup and St. Simeon, Tadoussac and Baie Ste. Catherine, and other points. The big oceangoing vessels coming and going on the Seaway will pass as you cross.

If a longer boat trip appeals to you, there's an interesting one that leaves Rimouski once a week, crosses the river to Sept Iles, and then touches at a number of villages along the north shore of the St. Lawrence. Eventually you'll go as far east as Blanc Sablon near the Strait of Belle Isle before turning back.

There are a number of ways to visit the Shrine of Ste. Anne de Beaupré from Quebec City, and one of them is by boat. The trip takes five hours and includes a two-hour stop at the Shrine, as well as a beautiful view of Montmorency Falls. Other boat trips from Quebec City take you to interesting spots on the river such as the Ile d'Orleans.

NEW BRUNSWICK

Ferries operate from Cape Tormentine across the Northumberland Strait to Prince Edward Island. You can also cross the Bay of Fundy from Saint John to Digby, Nova Scotia, in about three hours. Black's Harbour is the mainland terminus for the Grand Manan Island ferry, which operates daily all year. Ferry service on the St. John River is toll free.

A ferryboat on Lake Ontario at Toronto is used for transportation as well as sightseeing

NOVA SCOTIA

In addition to ferry service across the Bay of Fundy to New Brunswick, there also is service between Yarmouth, Nova Scotia, and Bar Harbor, Maine, and between Yarmouth and Portland, Maine. From Yarmouth to Bar Harbor is a five-hour trip, and Yarmouth to Portland is nine hours. There are cabins, dining facilities, and lounges aboard.

The great harbor at Halifax, big enough to shelter a whole navy and a fine place to see cargo ships in action, can be best seen from a harbor tour boat.

If you plan a motor trip around Cape Breton Island you can treat yourself to a change of pace and take a ferry trip from the northern end of the island. The service here is from North Sydney to the towns of Port aux Basques and Argentia, Newfoundland.

NEWFOUNDLAND

Since Newfoundland is an island, its chief connection with the mainland is by boat. The route most travelers take is the ferry from North Sydney, Nova Scotia, to Port aux Basques, Newfoundland, 108 miles that take about seven hours. But you can get an interesting view of Newfoundland's south coast on the longer boat ride between North Sydney and Argentia. This is a seventeen hour cruise that comes close to being a sea voyage. Very pleasant—and the boat lands you within easy drive of St. John's.

Finally, you can investigate St. Pierre and Miquelon, the only French colony in North America, by boat. There is ferry service from Fortune, Newfoundland, or you can make a three-day holiday by taking a small liner from North Sydney and living aboard ship while visiting the islands.

SHOPPING

ONE OF THE GREAT PLEASURES of travel is the finding of unusual and unique things to buy—items you seldom or never see back home. Poking in little shops, you'll find handmade sweaters, wood carvings, soapstone sculptures, lovely hooked rugs, laces, delectable jams, jellies, and homemade bread. The list is varied and nearly endless. What you find depends on where you are, since many of these specialties come only from a single village or a small area where some particular craft or talent has survived the centuries.

Or you may browse in fascinating import shops, where you'll see the woolens, the china, the silver, and the lavender from abroad. Or perhaps you'll go to the orchards when the fruit hangs heavy on the trees, or visit the smokehouses to see the red salmon fillets becoming delicacies.

Canada is rich in opportunities for this kind of shopping. It's really a matter of knowing where to look. In some places you'll be able to visit the artists and artisans at work. In others you just seek out the specialty shops.

The interest in Canadian arts and handicrafts has become so great in recent years that most of the big department stores now have sections dedicated to this kind of work gathered from all over the country. Thus, no matter where you are, you'll have some chance to see these beautiful items. You might note that the value of Eskimo art has been increasing lately as it becomes more available—and appreciated. It has passed from the "souvenir" stage.

The list that follows is a quick sketch of some of the items you might want to find, with an indication of where you can locate them. The list is by no means complete, but it's enough to get you started. In some cases stores are mentioned by name. These are by no means the only stores offering the item, but are cited as typical for the area.

SCOTTISH WOOLENS, TARTANS. You'll find these imported cloths available at many stores throughout Canada. Some shops specialize in Scotch woolens and can order the tartan of your clan for you if they don't already have it in stock. Nova Scotia, being New Scotland, is a particularly good place to look for these beautiful materials. You'll find specialty shops at *Antigonish, Pugwash, Sydney, Baddeck, Ingonish, Halifax, Yarmouth,* and other towns. Perhaps the best selection of all is found at the store of the Gaelic College at *St. Anns.* They carry no less than 150 tartans. (There are 840 different tartans altogether, many of which are scarce and known only to the clan that they represent.) Incidentally, the weavers of New Brunswick produce some fine tartans, which you'll see in the shops you visit.

SWEATERS & KNITWEAR. The famous Cowichan sweater, made of local wool in the Cowichan Valley on Vancouver Island can be bought in the heart of the valley at *Duncan, British Columbia,* or at stores in *Victoria* and *Vancouver.* If your travels take you to eastern Canada, shop for handmade woolen sweaters, mitts, and hooked mats in the area around *Egmont Bay, Prince Edward Island.* In *St. John's, Newfoundland,* not-for-profit shops such as the Jubilee Guild of Newfoundland and Nonia of Newfoundland (which also has shops in Corner Brook and Grand Falls) feature knitted, embroidered, and crocheted items that are the output of the province's cottage industry. *Fredericton, New Brunswick,* is an important handicraft center, and you'll find many shops in the cities and towns along New Brunswick's Fundy coast. *Yarmouth, Nova Scotia,* is famous for its shops, such as Tartan House and the Bluenose Gift Shop, while *Sydney, Nova Scotia,* has the Normaway Handcraft Shop and others. In *Halifax, Nova Scotia,* you'll find a dozen or more delightful little places that feature knitted goods from all over the province.

WOVEN GOODS. *St. Leonard, New Brunswick,* is famous for its Madawaska Weavers, who produce the wonderful woven Tissus Madawaska. You can buy the cloth, ties, stoles, skirts, rugs, and scarves in pleasing colorful designs not only in St. Leonard but in many towns throughout the Atlantic Provinces. You'll find a good many weavers in *Fredericton, New Brunswick,* too. *Gageton, New Brunswick,* is the home of Loomcrafters, who make drapery and upholstery materials and beautiful woven afghans. Weaving is done throughout Nova Scotia, New Brunswick, and Newfoundland—so watch for the little shops as you travel.

FURS. These can be a good buy for American travelers in Canada. You'll find fur shops in nearly every city, but two places where you get them almost straight from the trapper are *Prince Rupert, British Columbia,* and *Churchill, Manitoba,* on Hudson Bay.

ENGLISH BONE CHINA. The shops of Victoria are famous for their British imports, including fine china, Balleek, lavender, and woolens. Just stroll down Government Street. You'll find them elsewhere, too. Visit, for example, the amazing gift shop at *Moncton, New Brunswick,* right beside the Magnetic Hill. Here you'll find Royal Doulton ware, B & G Christmas plates, Lalique glass, Wedgwood china, Borsato and Hummel figurines, and a great collection of music boxes.

SILVER ARTICLES. You'll find beautiful imported silver items in most gift and jewelry shops and those shops specializing in British imports. *Sussex, New Brunswick,* not far from Fundy National Park, is famous for its silversmiths, for pottery, and for other handcrafted items. Good place to watch the craftsmen at work, too.

WOODENWARE. Pretty salad bowls and other woodenware are available at many places in Quebec. The town of *Lyster,* on Highway 5, 43 miles south of Lévis, is one good spot.

HOOKED RUGS. These often are works of art. You'll find superb examples in the villages along the west coast of Cape Breton Island, notably at *Cheticamp.* Or stop in The Teazer Shop (named for a famous privateer) at *Mahone Bay, Nova Scotia.* You'll also find hooked rugs in shops in New Brunswick.

ESKIMO ART. Until 1949, the art and craft work of the Eskimos was limited and known only to those who had traveled above the Arctic Circle. After that time, not-for-profit marketing organizations were set up to encourage Eskimo artists and to get their output to shops throughout Canada. Now you'll find lovely Eskimo soapstone carvings, art prints on sealskin and paper, handsewn mukluks, parkas, and other garments in leather, fur, and wool on display in department stores, in handicraft shops, and in specialty shops which show nothing but Eskimo products. The soapstone carvings, from a few inches to three feet in length, are graceful and attractive, with a charming simplicity. The subjects of these sculptures are the things the Eskimo knows best—the seal, Arctic birds, igloos, and the Eskimo himself. The art prints you see exhibit the same simplicity, and you can be sure they aren't mass produced, since each artist makes 50—or less—copies of each original work. Avid collectors of Eskimo art have sprung up, and certain of the artists have gained national reputations. Their work is anxiously awaited each year as the shipments begin to arrive from the northland in the spring.

MOCCASINS. This comfortable footwear, usually handmade, is available throughout Canada at stores and trading posts near Indian reservations, and in handicraft shops in the cities. If you'd like a pair of moosehide mocs made to order, you can have them from the Algonquin Indians near *Maniwaki, Quebec*.

TOTEM POLES. You can buy totem poles ranging from a couple of inches to a couple of feet in length, hand carved by the Indians of British Columbia. They are featured in some of the fine handicraft shops in *Vancouver*, for example, and also in stores in *Prince Rupert* and *Terrace*. If you drive the Yellowhead Highway through *Hazelton*, be sure to stop at the 'Ksan Indian Village, not only for totem poles but for all types of Indian arts and crafts.

INDIAN BASKETS. Every imaginable size and shape can be found near reservations across the country. An outstanding place to buy them is at *Pierreville*, on the south side of the St. Lawrence between Montreal and Quebec, where baskets are sold by the Indians from the Odanak Reserve.

CANOES. If you're in the market for a fine canoe, then head for *Peterborough, Ontario*, the nation's canoe-making capital. It is especially noted for the basswood canoe.

GEMSTONES. Canada is rich in semiprecious gemstones, and you can buy both rough and finished stones, as well as jewelry made with the stones, in dozens of places. Beautiful agate, for example, can be had at *Killarney, Manitoba*. Cufflinks and other jewelry of labradorite, with its pretty blue cast, are a specialty of Newfoundland shops like the Nonia. *Arnprior, Ontario*, 25 miles north of Carlton Place, is a gemstone center, as are *Princeton, British Columbia, Souris, Manitoba*, and *Bancroft, Ontario*.

GOLD. Raw gold nuggets make interesting jewelry. You can buy them in all sizes at shops in gold mine areas, and along rivers like the Fraser, noted for gold panning. *Quesnel, British Columbia*, is a particularly good place to look.

WOOD CARVINGS. Some of the world's finest wood carving is done at the town of *St. Jean Port Joli*, on the south shore of the St. Lawrence River, east of Quebec City. The town is noted for its many artisans, who also produce enamels, copper and wood mosaics, and paintings. The art of wood carving also has flourished in Nova Scotia and New Brunswick, and you'll find good work from here in most of the handicraft shops. Look for the delicately wrought seagulls from Nova Scotia.

SHIP MODELS. That fine old art of building full-rigged sailing ships in bottles is still practiced in New Brunswick and Nova Scotia. You'll see fine samples of these and of beautiful ship models of all sizes in shops in *Saint John, Halifax*, and in the coastal villages. The fine detail of some of these tiny ships will amaze you.

CAVIAR. The caviar produced at *Sturgeon Falls, Ontario*, is rated very highly in the world markets.

OYSTERS. Those succulent Malpeques come from Malpeque Bay on Prince Edward Island. You can also buy them at *Summerside*. A few miles away, across the Northumberland Strait at *Buctouche Bay, New Brunswick*, you'll find more exceptional oysters. Out west, the oysters from *Ladysmith, British Columbia*, are savored by those who know good food.

SALMON. This lovely fish abounds on both the east and west coasts. In a good many of the fishing villages you'll find places to buy fresh or smoked salmon, and you'll also find shops that specialize in shipping fish back home for you. In the west, the towns on *Vancouver Island's eastern shore* are one place to look, and another is along the banks of the rivers running into the Strait of Georgia. In the east, you'll find the Atlantic salmon and other seafood delicacies all around the *Gaspé Peninsula* and in the coastal villages of New Brunswick, Nova Scotia, Prince Edward Island, and Newfoundland.

CHEESE. There is excellent cheese to be had in many places. The renowned Oka, a Port Salud type, is made at the Trappist Monastery in *Oka, Quebec*. An outstanding Gouda comes from another Trappist monastery at *Mistassini*, a village near Lake St. John in Quebec. You'll find good aged Canadian cheddar at *Belleville, Ontario*, among other places. And the Raffine from *Ile d'Orleans* is another gourmet's delight.

BLUEBERRIES. The blueberries of Newfoundland are among the best in the world, rivaled perhaps by those found around Lake St. John in Quebec. For a special treat, try the wild blueberries picked at *Kazabazua, Quebec*, north of Hull.

FRUIT. The Okanagan and Similkameen valleys of British Columbia are famous for their fruit orchards. If you are there as the fruit ripens, you can have it shipped home from towns such as *Vernon, Armstrong, Creston, Osoyoos, Kaslo* (famous for Bing cherries), *Princeton, Penticton*, and Keremeos. Apples are another specialty of the Atlantic Provinces and Newfoundland in particular. And the fruits and vegetables found on the *Ile d'Orleans*, in the St. Lawrence River east of Quebec City, are always outstanding. Incidentally, on the island and in most fruit-growing areas check the local shops for homemade jams and jellies. You can have an enjoyable lunch with nothing more than a jar of one of these and a loaf of still-warm homemade bread—which you'll find available at many homes in the Atlantic Provinces. Watch for "fresh bread" signs.

FIDDLEHEADS. This gourmet food is the edible frond of the ostrich fern, served cold as a salad after it has been cooked until tender, or hot as a vegetable. You can buy fiddleheads at *Tidehead, New Brunswick*.

MAPLE SYRUP. The genuine undiluted maple syrup, boiled in the old-fashioned manner, comes from many parts of Ontario and Quebec. Watch for maple syrup signs as you tour Quebec's Eastern Townships or drive the Trans-Canada through New Brunswick. *Sundridge* and *Elmira* are two Ontario maple syrup centers, and *Thetford Mines, Quebec*, celebrates the running of the sap every year.

ACCOMMODATIONS RESTAURANTS

THE FOLLOWING IS a representative list of hotels, motels, and restaurants located throughout the provinces of Canada. This list is limited by the space available, and it has not been possible to list every fine establishment. Instead, the effort has been to provide facilities in different localities and price ranges.

The information in this listing has been taken from official publications of the national and provincial travel bureaus. The author and publishers are not responsible for inaccuracies or for the possibility that the listing may not be valid at the time of publication, though every effort has been made to be as accurate as possible.

HOW TO USE THE HOTEL/MOTEL LISTINGS

Each hotel is listed alphabetically, by province and city or town. To aid in the advance planning of your trip, the address and phone number, number of rooms, and a price-range indicator are shown. The rooms/price-range symbols, shown in parentheses after each hotel name, should be read as follows:

(22 *) — indicates 22 rooms, with minimum price for a double room for two people less than $30.

(600 **) — indicates 600 rooms, with minimum price for a double room for two people between $30 and $40 per night.

(1,200 ***) — indicates 1,200 rooms, with a double room for two people more than $40 per night.

The price range is based on room rates during the vacation season. This rate may be higher during special events, such as the Calgary Stampede, or lower before and after the vacation season. When calling for a reservation, make it a point to ask specifically for the current room rate.

RESERVATIONS AND DEPOSITS

To guarantee accommodations, you should make a reservation in advance, and a deposit of one night's lodging should accompany the reservation request. Many hotels prefer not to guarantee reservations over the phone without a credit card number, to which the room can be charged if you fail to honor the reservation. Most will refund any deposit if the reservation is canceled at least 48 hours before arrival time.

Most hotels and motels, particularly in urban areas, will not hold a reservation past 5 or 6 pm, unless you guarantee your late arrival.

CREDIT CARDS, CHECKS

Major credit cards—American Express, VISA, Chargex, Diners Club, Master Charge—and cards issued by major oil companies are recognized throughout Canada. Check with the hotel manager when you make your reservation to be sure the credit card you use is acceptable. If you plan to pay your bill by check, talk with the manager at the time you register to be sure your check will be accepted.

HOW TO USE THE RESTAURANT LISTINGS

This list has been prepared so the traveler can know in advance important information about each establishment's prices, cuisine, specialities, and hours. Most restaurants offer dinners in a price range (for example, from $3.50 to $6.00), and the symbol in each listing is designed to indicate the minimum price of dinner for one in each establishment. Menu prices will range upward from this minimum. The symbols should be read as follows:

(*) indicates a minimum dinner price below $4.00.

(**) indicates a minimum dinner price between $4.00 and $8.50.

(***) indicates a minimum dinner price above $8.50.

The letters following the symbol show what meals are served: breakfast (B), lunch (L), and dinner (D).

Restaurant listings begin on page 177.

ACCOMMODATIONS

ALBERTA

BANFF — BANFF NATIONAL PARK

ALPINE MOTEL (22 *), 521 Banff Ave. (403) 762-2332.

BANFF SPRINGS HOTEL (550 ***), Spray Ave. (403) 762-2211.

BOW VIEW MOTOR LODGE (57 **), Bow Ave. and Wolf St. (403) 762-2261.

CHARLTON'S CEDAR COURT (63 **), 513 Banff Ave. (403) 762-2575.

MOUNTAIN VIEW VILLAGE (54 *), PO Box 1326. May 1 – mid-Oct. (403) 762-2400.

PINEWOOD MOTEL (94 ***), 720 Banff Ave. (403) 762-2248.

RIMROCK INN (50 **), Sulphur Mountain Rd. (403) 762-3356.

SWISS VILLAGE LODGE (69 ***), 716 Banff Ave. (403) 762-2256.

BROOKS

TEL-STAR MOTEL (49 *), 1 mi south of Trans-Canada. PO Box 547. (403) 362-3466.

CALGARY

AIRLINER INN (120 *), 4804 Fourth St. NE. (403) 276-3391.

CALGARY INN (554 ***), Fourth Ave. and Third St. (403) 266-1611.

CARRIAGE HOUSE MOTOR INN (175 **), 9030 Macleod Trail S. (403) 253-1101.

CASCADE MOTEL (71 *), 16th Ave. and Crowchild Trail NW. (403) 289-2581.

CROSSROADS MOTOR HOTEL (240 *), 2120 16th Ave. NE. (403) 277-0161.

ELBOW LODGE MOTOR HOTEL (70 *), Macleod Trail and 19th Ave. SE. (403) 269-6771.

HOLIDAY INN (200 **), 708 Eighth Ave. SW. (403) 263-7600.

HOSPITALITY INN (102 **), 2369 Banff Trail NW. (403) 289-1973.

PALLISER HOTEL (412 ***) (Canadian Pacific hotel), 133 Ninth Ave. SW. (403) 266-8621.

STAMPEDER MOTOR HOTEL (47 *), 3828 Macleod Trail. (403) 243-5531.

WESTGATE MOTOR HOTEL (80 **), 1111 33rd St. SW. (403) 249-3181.

YORK HOTEL (180 *), corner Seventh Ave. and Centre St. S. (403) 262-5581.

CANMORE

A-1 MOTEL (22 *), Hwy 1A, 2½ mi east of Banff park gate. PO Box 339. (403) 678-5200.

CARDSTON

FLAMINGO MOTEL (20 *), Hwy. 2 at south entry to town. PO Box 92. (403) 653-3952.

DRUMHELLER

DINOSAUR MOTEL (15 *), in town. PO Box 730. (403) 823-3381.

DRUMHELLER MOTOR INN (35 *), in town. (403) 823-5111.

EDMONTON

BEVERLY CREST MOTOR HOTEL (42 *), 118th Ave. at 35th St. (403) 474-0456.

CHATEAU LACOMBE (330 ***), 101st St. at Bellamy Hill. (403) 428-6611.

EDMONTON INN (217 **), Kingsway Ave. at 119th St. (403) 454-9521.

HOLIDAY INN (192 **), 100th Ave. and 107th St. (403 429-2861.

KING EDWARD HOTEL (99 **), 10180 101st St. (403) 422-4161.

MACDONALD HOTEL (455 ***) (Canadian National hotel), Jasper Ave. at 100th St. (403) 426-4515.

RIVIERA MOTOR HOTEL (143 **), 5359 Calgary Trail (403) 434-3431.

SAXONY MOTOR INN (59 *), 156th St. and Stony Plain Rd. (403) 484-3331.

FORT MACLEOD

FORT MOTEL (14 *), in town, Main St. (403) 234-3606.

GRANDE PRAIRIE

STARLITE MOTEL (44 *), 10923 100 St. (403) 532-8819.

HIGH PRAIRIE

VILLA MOTEL (12 *), in town. (403) 523-3314.

JASPER

ANDREW MOTOR LODGE (99 **), in town. PO Box 850. (403) 852-3394.

ATHABASCA HOTEL (60 **), in town. PO Box 1420. (403) 852-3386.

DIAMOND MOTEL (80 **), in town. (403) 852-3143.

JASPER HOUSE BUNGALOWS (28 *), 2 mi south on Hwy 93. PO Box 817. May 1 – Sept. 30. (403) 852-4535.

JASPER PARK LODGE (364 ***) (Canadian National hotel), in the national park. (403) 852-3301.

TEKERRA LODGE (53 **), ½ mi south of Jasper on Hwy 93A. PO Box 669. May 1 – Sept. 30. (403) 852-3058.

LAKE LOUISE

CHATEAU LAKE LOUISE (360 ***) (Canadian Pacific hotel), in Banff park, on lake. (403) 522-3511.

DEER LODGE (108 **), 3 min. from Lake Louise. May 24 – Sept. 30. (403) 522-3747.

PIPESTONE LODGE (24 **), PO Box 69. (403) 522-3989.

POST HOTEL, adjacent to PIPESTONE LODGE (PO Box 69. [403] 522-3989), same rates, same mgmt.

LETHBRIDGE

EL RANCHO MOTOR HOTEL (68 *), 522 Mayor Magrath Dr. (403) 327-5701.

PARK PLAZA MOTOR HOTEL (69 *), 1009 Mayor Magrath Dr. (403) 328-2366.

LLOYDMINSTER

THUNDERBIRD BEST WESTERN MOTEL (36 *), 5610 44th St. (Yellowhead Hwy). (403) 875-3371.

MEDICINE HAT

FLAMINGO MOTEL (61 **), 722 Redcliff Dr. SW. (403) 527-2268.

HAT MOTEL (22 *), 560 Ninth St. SW, at junction of Hwys 1 and 3. (403) 527-3361.

TRAVOLITE FRONTIER MOTEL (44 *), Hwy 3, 2 blocks southwest of junction of Hwys 1 and 3. (403) 527-2266.

PEACE RIVER

PEACE VALLEY LODGE (42 *), 101st St. and 91st Ave. (403) 624-2020.

PIGEON MOUNTAIN

PIGEON MOUNTAIN MOTEL (16 *), Trans-Canada, 9 mi east of Banff park. (403) 678-5756.

PINCHER CREEK

FOOTHILLS MOTEL (20 *), in town, on Hwy 6. PO Box 806. (403) 627-3341.

RED DEER

GEMINI MOTEL (81 *), 4124 Gaetz Ave. (403) 343-6444.

GRANADA MOTOR INN (56 *), 4707 Ross St. (403) 347-5551.

RED DEER INN (63 *), 4217 Gaetz Ave. (403) 346-6671.

ROCKY MOUNTAIN HOUSE

ALPINE MOTEL (31 *), Hwy 11. PO Box 1. (403) 845-3325.

WALKING EAGLE MOTOR HOTEL (37 *), in town. (403) 845-3321.

WATERTON LAKES NATIONAL PARK

BAYSHORE MOTEL (44 **), on lake. May 1 – Oct. 1. (403) 859-2342.

EL CORTEZ MOTEL (34 *), Waterton Park. (403) 859-2366.

KILMOREY MOTOR LODGE (24 *), PO Box 124. mid-Apr. – mid-Oct. (403) 859-2334.

PONDERSOA MOTEL (16 **), in town. PO Box 64. May 1 – Oct. 1. (403) 859-2255.

PRINCE OF WALES HOTEL (82 **), June 1 – Sept. 20. (403) 859-2231.

BRITISH COLUMBIA

CACHE CREEK

BONAPARTE MOTOR HOTEL (21 *), on Hwy 97 near Trans-Canada junction. (604) 457-6265.

SAGE HILLS MOTEL (18 *), on Hwy 97 near Trans-Canada. PO Box 126. (604) 457-6451.

CAMPBELL RIVER

ABOVE TIDE MOTEL (32 *), 361 Island Hwy, Campbell River (604) 286-6231.

DISCOVERY INN (100 **) (Delta hotel), 975 Tyee Plaza. (604) 287-7155.

HAIDA INN (76 **), 1342 Island Hwy. (604) 287-7402.

CHILLIWACK

GREEN GABLES MOTEL (13 *), 610 Yale Rd. E. (Bus. Rt. 1) (604) 795-3223.

SPORTSMAN MOTOR HOTEL (24 *), on old Hwy 1, 48000 Yale Rd. E. (604) 792-2020.

STARDUST MOTEL (21 *), 45020 Yale Rd. W. Box 163. (604) 795-9174.

COURTENAY

ANCO SLUMBER LODGE (28 *), 1885 Cliffe Ave. (604) 334-2451.

SLEEPY HOLLOW MOTEL (50 *), 1190 Cliffe Ave. (604) 334-4476.

CRESTON

DOWNTOWNER MOTEL (24 *), 356 Canyon St. (604) 428-2238.

DAWSON CREEK

CEDAR LODGE MOTEL (29 *), 810 110 Ave. (604) 782-8531.

DAWSON CREEK TRAVELLODGE (40 *), 1317 Alaska Ave. (604) 782-4837.

PARK INN (70 *), 10100 Tenth St. PO Box 269. (604) 782-8515.

DUNCAN

VILLAGE GREEN INN (80 **), 141 Trans-Canada. (604) 746-5126.

THE V.I.P. MOTEL (20 *), 5867 Trans-Canada. (604) 748-8188.

FAIRMONT HOT SPRINGS

FAIRMONT HOT SPRINGS RESORT (140 **), 1 mi east of Hwy 95. PO Box 1. (604) 345-6311.

FERNIE

FERNIE MOTOR INN (30 *), east entrance to city. PO Box 10. (604) 423-6841.

FIELD

EMERALD LAKE CHALET (52 *), at Emerald Lake in Yoho National Park. (604) 343-6313.

FORT NELSON

FORT NELSON MOTOR HOTEL (82 **), in town, at Mile 300 on Alaska Hwy. PO Box 240. (604) 774-6971.

FORT ST. JOHN

ESTA VILLA MOTEL (15 *), at Mile 46.5 on Alaska Hwy. 9603 Alaska Rd. (604) 785-6777.

FORT ST. JOHN TRAVELODGE (60 *), in midtown. (604) 785-6647.

GALIANO — Gulf Islands

GALIANO LODGE (16 *), on Galiano Island. (604) 539-2233.

GLACIER NATIONAL PARK

NORTHLANDER MOTOR LODGE (50 *), 45 mi east of Revelstoke. PO Glacier National Park. (604) 837-2126.

GOLDEN

GOLDEN RIM MOTOR INN (50 *), Box 510. (604) 244-2216.

GRAND FORKS

BON AIR MOTEL (14 *), west of midtown. PO Box 986. (604) 442-8218.

JOHNNY'S MOTOR COURT (24 *), in midtown. PO Box 876. (604) 442-8242.

HARRISON HOT SPRINGS

HARRISON VILLAGE MOTEL (16 *), overlooks Harrison Lake. PO Box 115. (604) 796-2616.

THE HARRISON (284 ***), midtown, on Harrison Lake. (604) 796-2244.

HAZELTON — *see New Hazelton*

HOPE

HOPE MOTOR HOTEL (56 *), corner of Fraser and Wallace. PO Box 310. (604) 869-5641.

LAKE OF THE WOODS RESORT (18 *), 3 mi north of Hope on Trans-Canada. RR 1. (604) 869-2315.

RIVIERA MOTEL (17 *), 1½ mi west on Trans-Canada. PO Box 817. (604) 869-5573.

SWISS CHALET MOTEL (22 *), in town. PO Box 308. (604) 869-9020.

KAMLOOPS

DAVID THOMPSON MOTOR INN (100 **), in downtown section, 650 Victoria St. (604) 372-5282.

DELTA'S CANADIAN INN (100 **), 339 St. Paul St. (604) 372-5201.

KAMLOOPS TRAVELODGE (67 **), 430 Columbia St. (604) 372-8202.

SCOTT'S MOTOR INN (51 *), 552 11th Ave. (604) 372-8221.

KELOWNA

CAPRI MOTOR HOTEL (185 **), on Hwy 97. (604) 860-6060.

INN TOWNER MOTEL (46 *), 1627 Abbott St. (604) 762-2333.

STETSON VILLAGE MOTEL (87 *), 1455 Harvey Ave. (604) 860-2490.

LILLOOET

REYNOLDS HOTEL (27 *), Box 430. (604) 256-4202.

LYTTON

LYTTON PINES MOTEL (17 *), Box 87. (604) 455-2322.

MERRITT

GRASSLANDS MOTOR HOTEL (54 *), in town. PO Box 939. (604) 378-2292.

NANAIMO

EL SORRENTO MOTEL (44 *), in town, at 505 Terminal Ave. (604) 753-3421.

MALASPINA HOTEL (90 *), overlooking harbor at 33 Front St. (604) 753-1131.

NELSON

PEEBLES MOTOR INN (50 *), in town, at junction of Hwys 3 and 6, 153 Baker St. (604) 352-3525.

NEW HAZELTON

BULKLEY VALLEY MOTEL (12 *), in town. PO Box 177. (604) 842-5224.

NEW WESTMINSTER

ROYAL TOWERS MOTOR HOTEL (100 *), Sixth St. at Royal Ave. (604) 524-3777.

OSOYOOS

SAHARA MOTEL (32 **), Hwy 2, east of town. PO, RR 1. (604) 495-7211.

STARLITE MOTEL (43 **), 4 blocks south of town center. PO Box 540. (604) 495-7223.

PARKSVILLE

ARBUTUS GROVE MOTEL (10 *), south of town on Island Hwy 19. PO, RR 1. (604) 248-6422.

PENDER ISLAND

PENDER LODGE (17 *), at Port Washington. (604) 629-3221.

PENTICTON

BOWMONT MOTEL (37 *), near beach, 80 Riverside Dr. (604) 492-0112.

FLAMINGO MOTEL (26 *), between Skaha and Okanagan lakes, 2387 Skaha Lake Rd. (604) 492-8333.

PENTICTON MOTEL (51 *), ½ mi northwest of town, 890 Lakeshore Dr. (604) 492-2922.

PENTICTON TRAVELODGE (36 **), 950 Westminster Ave. (604) 492-0225.

PORT ALBERNI

GREENWOOD MOTOR HOTEL (60 *), northwest of town, Beaver Creek Rd. (604) 723-3516.

REDFORD MOTOR INN (28 *), 3723 Redford St. (604) 724-0121.

POWELL RIVER

THE INN AT WESTVIEW (50 **), 7050 Alberni St. (604) 485-6281.

PRINCE GEORGE

ANCO MOTEL (70 *), 1630 Central St., on Hwy 97 Bypass. (604) 563-3671.

CONNOUGHT MOTOR INN (60 *), 1550 Victoria St. (604) 562-4441.

SPRUCELAND INN (82 *), 1391 Central St., on Hwy 97 Bypass. (604) 563-0102.

PRINCE RUPERT

CREST MOTEL (105 **), 222 First Ave. W. PO Box 277. (604) 624-6771.

PRINCETON

COPPER TOWN MOTEL (25 *), Hwy 3 west. PO Box 404. (604) 295-3288.

VILLAGER MOTEL (26 *), at junction of Hwys 3 and 5. PO Box 160. (604) 295-3213.

QUESNEL

BILLY BARKER INN (60 *), 308 McLean St. (604) 992-8351.

RADIUM HOT SPRINGS

BIG HORN MOTEL (22 *), ½ block off hwy. PO Box 176. (604) 347-9522.

BLAKLEY'S BUNGALOWS (24 *), in Kootenay National Park. PO Box 190. (604) 347-9456.

RADIUM HOT SPRINGS LODGE (80 **), overlooking hot springs area. PO Box 70. (604) 347-9622.

REVELSTOKE

COLUMBIA SLUMBER LODGE (54 *), on Second St., west of Victoria Rd. PO Box 421. (604) 837-2191.

FRONTIER MOTEL (28 *), on eastern approach to Revelstoke. PO Box 1329. (604) 837-5119.

REGENT MOTOR INN (35 *), in town. PO Box 582. (604) 837-2107.

RICHMOND — *see Vancouver*

SALMON ARM

CAL-VAN MOTOR HOTEL (10 *), 4 mi east of Salmon Arm. RR 4, Trans-Canada. (604) 832-7233.

SALMON ARM MOTOR HOTEL (52 *), in town. PO Box 909. (604) 832-2129.

SICAMOUS

ALPINER MOTEL (12 *), on Trans-Canada at Hwy 97A junction. PO Box 288. (604) 836-2290.

LAKEWOOD MOTEL (9 *), on Hwy 97A, 1 mi south of Trans-Canada. PO Box 155. (604) 836-2326.

PARADISE MOTEL (22 *), in town. PO Box 100. (604) 836-2525.

SQUAMISH

CHIEFTAN HOTEL (50 *), in town. PO Box 100. (604) 892-5222.

GARIBALDI MOTOR HOTEL (25 *), in town center. PO Box 570. (604) 892-5051.

TERRACE

LAKELSE MOTOR HOTEL (64 *), 4620 Lakelse Ave. (604) 638-8141.

TERRACE SLUMBER LODGE (33 *), 4702 Lakelse Ave. (604) 635-6302.

TETE JAUNE CACHE

TETE JAUNE CACHE OVERLANDERS LODGE (15 *), at junction of Hwys 16 and 5. PO Box 428, Valemont. (604) 566-4666.

TRAIL

TERRA NOVA MOTOR INN (60 **), 1001 Rossland Ave. (604) 368-3355.

VANCOUVER

BAYSHORE INN (550 ***), 1601 West Georgia St. (604) 682-3377.

BLUE BOY MOTOR HOTEL (100 **), 725 Southeast Marine Dr. (604) 321-6611.

BURNABY MOTOR HOTEL (30 *), 7610 Kingsway at 14th. (604) 521-8891.

CAPILANO MOTEL (51 *), 1634 Capilano Rd., North Vancouver. (604) 987-8185.

DELTA'S VANCOUVER AIRPORT INN (258 **), 1025 St. Edwards Dr. (604) 278-9611.

DORIC HOWE MOTOR HOTEL (100 *), 1060 Howe St. (604) 682-3171.

DUFFERIN HOTEL (71 *), 900 Seymour St. (604) 683-4251.

HOLIDAY INN (210 **), 1110 Howe St. (604) 684-2151.

HOTEL GEORGIA (315 **), 801 W. Georgia St. (604) 682-5566.

HOTEL VANCOUVER (554 ***), 900 W. Georgia St. (604) 684-3131.

SKYLINE AIRPORT HOTEL (130 **), 303 No. 3 Rd., Richmond. (604) 278-5161.

2400 MOTEL (65 *), 2400 Kingsway. (604) 434-2464.

VANCOUVER CENTER TRAVELODGE (70 *), 1304 Howe St. (604) 682-2627.

VICTORIA

CANTERBURY INN (80 *), 310 Gorge Rd E. (634) 382-2151.

CREST HARBOURVIEW INN (99 **), 455 Belleville St. (604) 386-2421.

DOMINION HOTEL (108 *), 759 Yates St. (604) 384-4136.

EMPRESS HOTEL (416 ***), 721 Government St. (604) 384-8111.

EXECUTIVE HOUSE (98 **), 777 Douglas St. (604) 388-5111.

IMPERIAL INN (79 **), 1961 Douglas St. (604) 382-2111.

MAYFAIR MOTEL (23 *), 650 Speed St. (604) 388-7337.

RED LION MOTOR INN (83 **), 3366 Douglas St. (604) 385-3366.
ROYAL VICTORIAN MOTEL (80 *), 230 Gorge Rd. E. (604) 385-5771.
TALLY-HO TRAVELODGE (51 *), 3020 Douglas St. (604) 386-6141.
VICTORIA AIRPORT TRAVELODGE (50 *), 2280 Beacon Ave., Sydney. (604) 656-1176.
WESTWIND INTERNATIONAL MOTOR INN (49 *), 741 Goldstream Ave. (604) 478-8334.

WILLIAMS LAKE

WILLIAMS LAKE SLUMBER LODGE (58 *), Seventh Ave. PO Box 1864. (604) 392-7116.

YOHO NATIONAL PARK — *see Field*

MANITOBA

BRANDON

CANADIAN INN (63 *), 150 Fifth St. (204) 727-6404.

CHURCHILL

HUDSON HOTEL AND MOTEL (54 **), in town. (204) 675-8835.
POLAR HOTEL (10 **), 16 Franklin St. PO Box 82. (204) 675-2727.

DAUPHIN

HIGHLAND MOTEL (31 *), in town. PO Box 472. (204) 638-5100.

FLIN FLON

ROYAL HOTEL (39 *), in town, at 93 Main St. (204) 687-3437.

PORTAGE LA PRAIRIE

YELLOW QUILL MOTEL (10 *), ½ block south of Hwy 1A at 20th St. SW. (204) 857-3086.

RIDING MOUNTAIN NATIONAL PARK

DONER'S TA-WA-PIT LODGE (50 *), Wasagaming. (204) 848-2404.
MOOSWA MOTEL (49 *), on Hwy 10 in the park. PO Box 39. Open May 15 – Oct. 5. (204) 848-2533.

THE PAS

LA VERENDRYE MOTEL (24 *), in town. PO Box 2760. (204) 623-3431.

WHITESHELL PROVINCIAL PARK

EL NOR MOTEL (38 *), in town of Falcon Beach. (204) 349-2559.

WINNIPEG

ADAMS MOTEL (29 *), near city center, 1500 Pembina Hwy. (204) 453-8034.
AIRLINER MOTOR HOTEL (117 *), 3 mi west of city center, 1740 Ellice Ave. (204) 775-7131.
ASSINIBOINE GORDON HOTEL AND MOTOR INN (59 *), 1975 Portage Ave. (204) 888-4806.
BALMORAL MOTOR HOTEL (44 *), in city center, 621 Balmoral Ave. (204) 943-1544.
GORDON DOWNTOWNER MOTOR HOTEL (40 *), in city center, 330 Kennedy St. (204) 943-5581.
HOTEL FORT GARRY (240 ***), in city center, 222 Broadway. (204) 942-8251.
INTERNATIONAL INN (210 ***), near airport, 1808 Wellington. (204) 786-4801.
MONTCALM GORDON MOTOR HOTEL (21 *), south of city center, 2280 Pembina Hwy. (204) 269-1406.
NIAKWA MOTOR HOTEL (52 *), Trans-Canada and St. Anne's Rd. (204) 253-1301.
ST. REGIS HOTEL (112 *), in city center, 285 Smith St. (204) 942-0171.
SHERATON-CARLTON MOTOR MOTEL (107 *), in city center, 220 Carlton St. (204) 942-0881.
TOWNHOUSE MOTOR LODGE (35 *), 1844 Pembina Hwy. (204) 269-6230.

NEW BRUNSWICK

BATHURST

DANNY'S MOTEL (43 *), 4 mi north of town on Hwy 11. PO Box 180. (506) 546-6621.
GLOUCESTER MOTOR HOTEL (45 *), in town, 100 Main St. (506) 546-4431.
KENT MOTEL (45 **), 3 mi north of town on Hwy 11. (506) 546-3345.

CAMPBELLTON

CHATEAU RESTIGOUCHE INN (59 **), 122 Roseberry St. (506) 753-3341.
FIRST CANADIAN HOTEL (68 **), Box 800. (506) 753-5063.
FUNDY LINE MOTEL (80 *), at western city limits, on Hwy 11. PO Box 457. (506) 753-3395.
WANDLYN MOTEL (60 **), near city center, on Trans-Canada. PO Box 489. (506) 753-7606.

CAMPOBELLO ISLAND

FRIAR'S BAY MOTOR LODGE (10 *), PO Welchpool. Open all year. (506) 752-2056.

CAPE TORMENTINE

HASSAN'S MOTEL AND CABINS (7 *), on Hwy 16. Open summer only. (506) 538-7732.
SMALLWOOD'S TOURIST HOME (9 *), on Hwy 16. (506) 538-7736.

CARAQUET

DOMINION HOTEL (10 *), on Hwy 11. (506) 727-2876.
HOTEL PAULIN (12 *), 143 St. Pierre Blvd. (506) 727-9981.

CHATHAM

MORADA MOTEL (30 *), 64 King St. (506) 773-4491.

EDMUNDSTON

LYNN MOTEL (49 **), 30 Church St. (506) 735-8851.
WANDLYN MOTOR INN (86 **), on Trans-Canada. PO Box 68. (506) 735-5525.

FREDERICTON

KEDDY'S MOTOR INN (120 *), on Trans-Canada, at Forest Hill Exit. PO Box 1510. (506) 454-4461.
WANDLYN MOTOR INN (116 **), off Trans-Canada between Hanwell and Smythe St. exits. PO Box 214. (506) 455-8937.

FUNDY NATIONAL PARK

ALPINE CHALETS (24 *), 1 mi west of park. (506) 887-2848.
FUNDY PARK CHALETS (29 *), at park. (506) 887-2808.
FUNDY VIEW MOTEL (20 *), 1 mi west of park. (506) 887-2880.

MONCTON

BEAUSEJOUR HOTEL (212 ***) (Canadian National hotel), 750 Main St. (506) 854-4344.
HOWARD JOHNSON'S MOTOR LODGE (96 **), near Magnetic Hill, on Trans-Canada. PO Box 1092. (506) 854-1050.
HUB CITY MOTOR INN (57 *), 636 Salisbury Rd. (506) 389-3435.
PARK HOUSE INN (97 **), 434 Main St. (506) 382-1664.
WANDLYN MOTOR INN (78 **), at Magnetic Hill, on Trans-Canada. PO Box 1125. (506) 389-3554.

NEWCASTLE

FUNDY LINE MOTEL (46 *), 869 King George Hwy E. (506) 622-3650.
WANDLYN MOTOR INN (68 **), 365 Water St. (506) 622-3870.

OROMOCTO

OROMOCTO HOTEL (50 **), 100 Hersey St. (506) 357-8424.

SACKVILLE

MARSHLANDS INN (16 **), in city center, 73 Bridge St. (506) 536-0170.
MARSHLANDS MOTOR INN (20 **), at Trans-Canada and Bridge St. PO Box 1265. (506) 536-1327.

ST. ANDREWS

ALGONQUIN HOTEL (200 ***), 184 Adolphus St. Open June 1 – Sept. 15. (506) 529-8823.
BLUE MOON MOTEL (36 **), on Hwy 27. (506) 529-3245.

SAINT JOHN

ADMIRAL BEATTY MOTOR HOTEL (197 **), on King Sq. (506) 652-1212.
HOLIDAY INN (130 **), on Haymarket Sq. (506) 657-3610.
HOSPITALITY INN (100 **), 607 Rothesay Ave. (506) 696-4100.

ST. LEONARD

DAIGLE'S MOTEL (47 *), in town center, on Bridge St. PO Box 88. (506) 423-6351.

SHEDIAC

HOTEL SHEDIAC (40 *), in town, on Hwy 15. (506) 532-4405.

SUSSEX

PINE CONE MOTEL (20 *), on Hwy 2. PO, RR 1, Penobsquis. (506) 433-3958.

WOODSTOCK

WANDLYN MOTOR INN (50 **), on Trans-Canada. PO Box 1191. (506) 328-8876.

NEWFOUNDLAND

CAPE BONAVISTA

O HAPPY SIGHT MOTEL (16 *), in town of Bonavista on Hwy 230. (709) 468-7811.

CLARENVILLE

HOLIDAY INN (64 **), near junction of Hwys 1 and 1A. (709) 466-7911.

CORNER BROOK

GLYNMILL INN (66 **), 1 mi from Trans-Canada, at Cobb Lane. (709) 634-5181.
HOLIDAY INN (104 **), on West St. at Todd St. (709) 634-5381.
HOTEL CORNER BROOK (45 *), in town center, on Main St. (709) 643-8211.

DEER LAKE

DEER LAKE MOTEL (39 **), in town. (709) 635-2108.

GANDER

HOLIDAY INN (64 **), on Caldwell St. near Elizabeth Dr. (709) 256-3981.
HOTEL GANDER (115 **), on Hwy 1, Trans-Canada. (709) 256-3931.

GOOSE BAY (HAPPY VALLEY)

LABRADOR INN (44 **), (709) 896-3351.

GRAND BANK — Burin Peninsula

ANCHOR INN MOTEL (10 *), on Hwy 220. (709) 832-2180.

GRAND FALLS

CLOVER LEAF MOTEL (55 **), on Trans-Canada. PO Box 158. (709) 489-2116.
MOUNT PEYTON HOTEL (102 **), on Trans-Canada. (709) 489-2251.

LEWISPORTE

MANUEL HOTEL (20 *), in town. (709) 535-2621.

PORT AU CHOIX

FARWELL'S HOSPITALITY HOME (4 *), in town. (709) 861-3358.

PORT AUX BASQUES

HOTEL PORT-AUX-BASQUES (50 **), in town. (709) 695-2171.

PORTLAND CREEK

SEA POOL CABINS (9 *), in town, on Hwy 430. (709) 898-2533.

ST. ANTHONY

ST. ANTHONY MOTEL (23 *), in town. (709) 454-2722.
VINLAND MOTEL (25 *), in town. (709) 454-8843.

ST. JOHN'S

BATTERY INN (103 **), on Signal Hill Rd. (709) 722-0040.
HOLIDAY INN (190 **), in city, on Portugal Cove Rd. (709) 722-0506.
HOTEL NEWFOUNDLAND (130 ***), at Fort William, on Cavendish Sq. (709) 726-4980.
KENMOUNT MOTEL (37 **), on Elizabeth Ave. (709) 579-4031.
SKYLINE MOTEL (31 *), 3 mi east of city, on Trans-Canada. (709) 722-5400.
WELCOME HOTEL (43 *), 260 Duckworth St. (709) 753-9970.

STEPHENVILLE

GALLANT'S HOTEL (23 *), 75 West St. (709) 643-2406.

TERRA NOVA NATIONAL PARK

TERRA NOVA CABINS (24 *), on Trans-Canada. PO Box 231, Gloverton. Open May 24 – Oct. 15. (709) 256-3795.

NORTHWEST TERRITORIES

FORT PROVIDENCE

SNOWSHOE INN (40 **), on Hwy 3. (403) 699-3511.

FORT SIMPSON

FORT SIMPSON HOTEL (19 *), in town. PO Box 248. (403) 695-2201.

FORT SMITH

PELICAN RAPIDS INN (30 **), downtown. PO Box 52. (403) 872-2789.
PINECREST HOTEL (30 *), in town center. (403) 872-2104.

FROBISHER BAY — Baffin Island

FROBISHER INN (50 ***), in town. PO Box 610. Open all year. (403) 979-5241.

HAY RIVER

CARIBOU MOTOR INN (28 **), in new Hay River. PO Box 1114. (403) 874-6706.
HAY RIVER HOTEL (42 **), in old Hay River. PO Box 40. (403) 874-2481.
PTARMIGAN INN (44 ***), in new Hay River. PO Box 1095. (403) 874-6781.

INUVIK

ESKIMO INN (79 ***), in town. PO Box 1740. Open all year. (403) 979-2801.
MACKENZIE HOTEL (48 **), in town. PO Box 1618. Open all year. (403) 979-2861.

NORMAN WELLS

MACKENZIE MOUNTAIN LODGE (24 ***), in town. PO Box 37. Open all year. (403) 587-4511.

YELLOWKNIFE

EXPLORER HOTEL (120 **), downtown. PO Box 7000. (403) 873-3531.
GOLD RANGE HOTEL (52 *), downtown. PO Box 698. (403) 873-4441.
NORTHLAND MOTEL (11 **), on Franklin Rd. PO Box 933. (403) 873-2466.
YELLOWKNIFE INN (162 **), 50th St. and 50th Ave. PO Box 490. (403) 873-2601.

NOVA SCOTIA

AMHERST

LETCHER'S MOTEL (32 *), 1½ mi north of town, off Trans-Canada. PO Box 172. (902) 667-3881.
LORD AMHERST MOTEL (40 *), take LaPlanche St. exit from Trans-Canada. PO Box 277. (902) 667-3354.
TANTRAMAR MOTEL (16 *), at Fort Lawrence. Take LaPlanche St. exit. PO Box 488. (902) 667-3106.
VICTORIAN MOTEL (20 **), in town, 150 Victoria St. (902) 667-7211.
WANDLYN MOTOR INN (60 **), at Victoria St. exit of Trans-Canada. PO Box 275. (902) 667-3331.

ANNAPOLIS ROYAL

MARSHALL'S RANCH HOUSE MOTEL (16 *), 3 mi west, on Hwy 1. PO, RR 2. (902) 532-5473.
ROYAL ANNE MOTEL (20 *), ½ mi west, on Hwy 1. PO Box 400. (902) 532-2323.

ANTIGONISH

(Rates may increase and length of stay be limited during Highland Games, mid-July.)
ANTIGONISHER MOTOR HOTEL (35 **), 158 Main St. (902) 863-3360.
CLAYMORE MOTEL (52 *), 1720 Church St. (902) 863-1050.
DINGLE MOTEL (49 *), 4 mi east of town, on Trans-Canada. PO Box 279. (902) 863-3730.
OASIS MOTEL (12 *), 2 mi east of town, on Hwy 104. PO Box 1148. (902) 863-3557.

BADDECK

CABOT TRAIL MOTEL (20 **), on Trans-Canada. PO Box 309. (902) 295-2580.
SILVER DART MOTEL (70 **), on Trans-Canada. PO Box 238. (902) 295-2340.

BRAS D'OR

SEAL ISLAND MOTEL (36 **), on Trans-Canada at Seal Island bridge. PO, RR 1. Open June 1 – Oct. 15. (902) 674-2418.

CAPE BRETON ISLAND — *see Baddeck, Cheticamp, Ingonish, Inverness, Margaree Forks, North Sydney, Pleasant Bay, Port Hawkesbury, Sydney*

CHESTER

WINDJAMMER MOTEL (15 *), ½ mi west of town, on Hwy 3. PO Box 240. (902) 275-3567.

CHETICAMP

LAURIE'S MOTEL (21 *), in town, at 168 Main St. (902) 224-2400.
PARK VIEW MOTEL (17 **), at entrance to Cape Breton Highlands National Park. PO Box 117. (902) 224-3232.

DARTMOUTH

DARTMOUTH INN (125 **), in town. (902) 469-0331.
HOLIDAY INN (120 ***), 99 Wyse Rd., on Macdonald Bridge Plaza. (902) 463-1100.

DIGBY

MOUNTAIN GAP INN (112 **), 4 mi east on Hwy 1, at Smith's Cove. PO Box 40. Open June 1 – Oct. 15. (902) 245-2277.
PINES HOTEL (154 **), owned by the Province of Nova Scotia. On Annapolis Basin, near dock. PO Box 70. Open June – Sept. (902) 245-2511.

HALIFAX

CHATEAU HALIFAX (312 ***), 1990 Barrington St. (902) 425-6700.
CITADEL INN (189 **), 1960 Brunswick St. (902) 422-1391.
DRESDEN ARMS MOTOR HOTEL (94 **), 5530 Artillery Pl. (902) 422-1625.
HOLIDAY INN (237 **), 1980 Robie St. (902) 423-1161.
HOTEL NOVA SCOTIAN (316 ***), 1181 Hollis St. (902) 423-7231.
LORD NELSON HOTEL (355 **), 1515 South Park St. (902) 423-6331.

INGONISH

GLENGHORM RESORT (45 **), 2 mi east of national park north gate, at Ingonish Centre. PO Box 39. Open May 1 – Nov. (902) 285-2049.
INGONISH MOTEL (32 *) on Cabot Trail, 2 mi north of park headquarters. PO Box 368. Open June 1 – Thanksgiving. (902) 539-5733.
KELTIC LODGE (80 dbl. $70 – 92, Amer. Plan), owned by Province of Nova Scotia. At Ingonish Beach. PO Box 456. Open June 15 – Sept. 15. (902) 285-2880.

INVERNESS

INVERNESS LODGE AND MOTEL (27 *), on Cabot Trail. Open all year. (902) 258-2193.

LUNENBURG

BRAECO MOTEL (11 **), on Victoria St. PO Box 578. Open May – Oct. 15. (902) 634-8234.
TOPMAST MOTEL (12 *), on Mason's Beach Rd. PO Box 958. Open Apr. 1 – Dec. 31. (902) 634-4661.

MARGAREE FORKS

MARGAREE LODGE (46 *), at Cabot Trail and Hwy 19. PO Box 550. Open June 10 – Oct. 20. (902) 248-2193.

NORTH SYDNEY

CLANSMAN MOTEL (34 **), on Peppet St. Open all year. (902) 794-4749.

PEGGY'S COVE

CLIFTY COVE MOTEL (10 *), 1½ mi east of town, on Hwy 33. Open May 1 – Oct. 31. (902) 823-2281.

PICTOU

BRAESIDE INN (20 *), 80 Front St. Open all year. (902) 485-4323.

PLEASANT BAY

BONNIE DOON MOTEL (25 *), on Cabot Trail, near national park west gate. Open May 15 – Oct. 31. (902) 224-2467.

PORT HAWKESBURY

WANDLYN MOTOR INN (73 **), on Reeves St., at Hwy 4 junction. PO Box 532. (902) 625-0320.

PUGWASH

HILLCREST MOTEL AND CABINS (11 *), on Hwy 6. PO Box 263. Open all year. (902) 243-2092.

SHELBURNE

CAPE CODE COLONY MOTEL (24 *), in town, on Water St. PO Box 34. (902) 875-3411.

SYDNEY

HOLIDAY INN (122 **), 480 Kings Rd. (902) 539-6750.
ISLE ROYAL MOTEL (110 **), near harbor, on Kings Rd. PO Box 430. (902) 564-4567.
WANDLYN MOTOR INN (71 **), 100 Kings Rd. (902) 539-3700.

TRURO

GLENGARRY MOTEL (47 **), 138 Willow St. (902) 895-5388.
KEDDY'S MOTOR INN (96 **), 437 Prince St. (902) 895-1651.
RAINBOW MOTEL (35 *), at west edge of town, 341 Prince St. (902) 893-9438.
STONEHOUSE MOTEL (40 **), 165 Willow St. (902) 893-9413.
TIDEVIEW MOTEL (40 *), 2 mi south of Trans-Canada, on Tidal Bore Rd. PO Box 821. (902) 893-8951.

YARMOUTH

BRAEMAR LODGE (78 **), 10 mi on Hwy 1 from town center. PO Box 98. Open May 15 – Oct. 19. (902) 761-2010.
CAPRI MOTEL (36 *), at 8 Herbert St. (902) 742-7168.
EL RANCHO MOTEL (16 *), outside of town, on Lakeside Dr. PO, RR 1. Open Apr. 1 – Nov. 1. (902) 742-4363.
GRAND HOTEL (138 **), at Main and Grand. (902) 742-2446.
LA REINE MOTEL (23 *), 2 mi northeast of town, on Hwy 1. PO Box 950. Open May 15 – Nov. 1. (902) 742-7154.

ONTARIO

BANCROFT

RIVER BEND MOTEL (42 *), on Hwy 62. PO Box 293. (613) 332-2686.
SWORD MOTEL (40 *), on Hwy 62. PO Box 28. (613) 332-2420.

BARRIE

BROOKDALE PARK INN (50 *), 150 Dunlop St. W. (705) 728-1312.
CONTINENTAL INN (120 *), west on Hwy 90. PO Box 621. (705) 726-1834.
HOLIDAY INN (120 **), on Essa Rd. (705) 728-6191.
WHITE TOWERS MOTEL (27 *), 119 Donald St. (705) 726-0208.

BLENHEIM

QUEEN'S MOTEL (17 *), west of town center, on Hwy 3. PO, RR 1. (519) 676-5477.

BLIND RIVER

MACIVER'S MISSISSAUGA MOTEL (14 *), 3 mi west, on Trans-Canada. PO Box 502. (705) 356-7411.

BRACEBRIDGE

ASTON VILLA RESORT HOTEL (58 sgl. $20 – 24, Amer. Plan), on Hwy 118 at Lake Muskoka. Open June 15 – Oct. 15. (705) 764-1111.

BRANTFORD

BELL CITY MOTEL (20 *), at 901 Colborne St. (519) 756-5236.
HOLIDAY INN (121 **), at Hwy 403 and Park Rd. (519) 753-8651.
INN OF THE JOLLY BARON (102 *), 666 Colborne St. (519) 753-7371.

BROCKVILLE

FLYING DUTCHMAN MOTOR INN (62 *), 6 mi west of town. Take Exit 111 from Hwy 401. (613) 342-6631.
401 INN (56 **), 160 Stewart Blvd. (613) 342-6613.
SKYLINE BROCKVILLE (80 **), 100 Stewart Blvd. (613) 345-1405.
WHITE HOUSE MOTEL (46 **), 1 mi east of town, on Hwy 2. (613) 345-1622.

BURLINGTON

TOWN AND COUNTRY MOTEL (30 *), west end of town, 517 Plains Rd. E. (416) 634-2383.

CHATHAM

HOLIDAY INN (160 **), 25 Keil Dr. N. and Hwy 2. (519) 354-5030.
RAINBOW MOTEL (12 *), 1½ mi east of town, on Hwy 2. (519) 352-6610.

COBOURG

TOM'S MOTEL (22 *), on Hwy 2, 428 King St. E. (416) 372-9421.

COCHRANE

NORTHERN LIGHTS MOTEL (41 **), ¼ mi south, on Hwy 11. PO Box 1720. (705) 272-4281.

COLLINGWOOD

MARINER MOTOR HOTEL (23 *), in town, at 305 Hume St. (705) 445-3330.

CORNWALL

CENTURY MOTEL (24 *), 1209 Brookdale Ave. (613) 932-1430.
SUNSET MOTEL (24 *), 1127 Second St. (613) 933-4100.
THE PARKWAY INN (94 **), 1515 Vincent Massey Dr. (613) 932-0451.
TREETOPS MOTEL (16 *), on Hwy 2, Vincent Massey Dr. 1 mi west of bridge. (613) 932-9623.

FORT ERIE

GATEWAY MOTEL (20 **), on Hwy 3, ½ mi from Peace Bridge, 315 Garrison Rd. (416) 871-4438.

FORT FRANCES

MAKABI INN MOTEL (26 *), 325 Scott St. (807) 274-9874.
RAINY LAKE HOTEL (54 *), 235 Scott St. (807) 274-5355.

FRENCH RIVER

FRENCH RIVER TRADING POST MOTEL (10 **), on Hwy 69. PO, RR 2. Open Apr. – Nov. (705) 857-2115.

GALT

HOLIDAY INN (150 **), at Exit 36, Hwy 401. (519) 658-4601.
SATELLITE MOTEL (20 *), south of Hwy 401, 195 Hespeler Rd. (519) 621-0171.

GANANOQUE

BLINKBONNIE MOTOR INN (41 **), 50 Main St. (613) 382-3232.
COLONIAL MOTEL (52 **), west end of town, on King St. PO Box 190. Open Apr. – Nov. (613) 382-4677.
GLEN HOUSE RESORT (48 **), 6½ mi east of town, on Thousand Islands Pkwy. PO, RR 1. Open May – Nov. (613) 659-2204.

GODERICH

BEDFORD ARMS MOTEL (26 *), 242 Bayfield Rd. (519) 524-7348.
BEDFORD HOTEL (40 *), in town, at 92 The Square. (519) 524-7337.
DUNLOP MOTEL (10 *), on Hwy 2, 2 mi north of town. PO, RR 5. (519) 524-8781.

GRAVENHURST

CHURCHILL MOTEL (16 *), 1 mi south, on Hwy 11. (705) 687-3445.
MUSKOKA SANDS INN (71 dbl. $36 – 54, Amer. Plan), 3 mi north, on Lake Muskoka. (705) 687-2233.
PINE DALE INN (29 **), off Hwy 11B, on Gull Lake. PO Box 760. (705) 687-2822.

GUELPH

MOTEL BILTMORE (48 *), 785 Gordon St. (519) 822-9112.
PARKVIEW MOTEL (51 *), 721 Woolrich St. (519) 836-1410.

HALIBURTON

CHATEAU WOODLAND (72 dbl. $38 – 42, Amer. Plan), 2 mi southwest of town. PO Box 99. Open June – Sept. (705) 457-1892.

HAMILTON

CITY MOTOR HOTEL (98 *), 1620 Main St. (416) 549-1371.
HOLIDAY INN (231 ***), 150 King St. E. (416) 528-3451.
JAMESWAY MOTOR INN (51 *), 1187 Upper James St. (416) 385-3291.
MOUNTAIN VIEW MOTEL (22 *), 1870 Main St. (416) 528-7521.
ROYAL CONNAUGHT HOTEL (250 ***), 112 King St. E. (416) 527-5071.

HUNTSVILLE

HOLIDAY INN RESORT (89 **), 5 mi east, on Hwy 60. PO Box 6000. (705) 789-2301.
GRANDVIEW FARM (30 *), 3 mi east, on Hwy 60, Box 1089. (705) 789-7462.
SUNRISE MOTEL (18 *), north end of town, on Hwy 18. PO Box 539. (705) 789-5461.

KAPUSKASING

APOLLO MOTEL (42 *), ½ mi west, on Hwy 11. PO, RR 2. (705) 335-6084.
MATTAGAMI MOTEL (56 *), 25 Kolb St. (705) 335-6171.

KENORA

BEL AIRE MOTEL (11 *), 700 Eighth Ave. (807) 468-9874.
HOLIDAY INN (96 ***), in town, on Trans-Canada. (807) 468-5521.
KENRICIA HOTEL (100 *), 155 Main St. (807) 468-6461.

KINGSTON

CAPRI MOTOR HOTEL (61 **), 1217 Princess St. (613) 549-2211.
COMMODORE MOTOR INN (45 *), 840 Princess St. (613) 548-7741.
401 INN (164 **), on Division St. Use Exit 102 from Hwy 401. (613) 546-3661.
GREEN ACRES MOTEL (23 *), 2480 Princess St. PO, RR 3. (613) 546-1796.
KINGSTON MOTEL (30 *), 2467 Princess St. (613) 542-4961.
LE ROI MOTEL (39 *), 1187 Princess St. (613) 546-6646.
SEAWAY TOWN HOUSE MOTOR INN (69 **), 686 Princess St. (613) 546-6616.

KITCHENER

CENTRE VILLA MOTEL (20 *), 2933 King St. (519) 744–1125.
HOLIDAY INN (122 **), 30 Fairway Rd. (519) 744-6341.
KITCHENER MOTEL (21 *), 1221 Victoria St. N. (519) 745-1177.
RIVIERA MOTEL (46 **), 2808 King St. (519) 745-1196.

VALHALLA INN (130 **), at King and Benton sts. PO Box 4. (519) 744-4141.

LEAMINGTON

WIGLE'S COLONIAL MOTEL (24 *), 135 Talbot St. (519) 326-3265.

LONDON

AMERICAN MOTOR HOTEL (41 *), 2031 Dundas St. (519) 451-2030.
GOLDEN PHEASANT MOTEL (41 *), 5 mi northwest of town, on Hwy 22. PO, RR 5. (519) 679-8442.
HOLIDAY INN (611 ***), downtown, at 299 King St. (519) 439-1661.
HOLIDAY INN (219 **), south, at 1210 Wellington Rd. (519) 681-2020.
HOWARD JOHNSON'S MOTOR LODGE (120 **), 1150 Wellington Rd. (519) 681-0600.
SOUTH WINDS MOTEL (30 *), 1170 Wellington Rd. (519) 681-1550.

MANITOULIN ISLAND

MANITOWANING LODGE (23 dbl. $40 – 50, Amer. Plan), on Manitowaning Bay. PO Box 160. (705) 859-3136.

MEAFORD

BAY VUE MOTEL (20 *), 710 Sykes St. N. (519) 538-3490.

MIDLAND

MIDTOWN MOTEL (27 *), 519 Hugel Ave. (705) 526-2266.
PARK VILLA MOTEL (34 *), 751 Yonge St. (705) 526-2219.

MORRISBURG

PAQUIN PARK MOTEL (23 *), 4 mi east, on Hwy 2. PO, RR 1. Open May – Nov. (613) 543-2026.
RIVERSIDE MOTEL (10 *), 4 mi east, on Hwy 2. PO, RR 1. (613) 543-2162.
UPPER CANADA MOTEL (20 *), 3 mi east, on Hwy 2. (613) 543-2374.

MUSKOKA LAKES — *see Bracebridge, Gravenhurst, Port Carling*

NIAGARA FALLS

A-1 MOTEL (27 *), 7895 Lundys Lane. (416) 354-6038.
CANADIANA INN (29 *), 5435 Ferry St. Open Mar. – Dec. (416) 356-3573.
DETROIT MOTOR INN (37 *), 3 mi west, on Lundys Lane, Hwy 20. Open Apr. – Nov. (416) 227-2567.
FALLSWAY MOTOR HOTEL (173 **), 4946 Clifton Hill. (416) 358-3601.
FLAMINGO MOTEL (75 *), 7701 Lundys Lane. (416) 354-9809.
INN MOTEL (52 *), 7857 Niagara River Pkwy. Open Apr. – Oct. (416) 295-4371.
LINCOLN MOTOR INN (60 **), 6417 Portage Rd. (416) 356-1748.
MICHAEL'S INN (110 **), 5599 River Rd. (416) 354-2727.
NELSON MOTEL (29 *), 10655 Niagara Pkwy. Open Apr. – Oct. (416) 295-4754.
PAN-O-RAMA MOTEL (25 **), 6365 Buchanan Ave. (416) 354-0852.
PARK MOTOR HOTEL (180 **), 4960 Clifton Ave. (416) 358-3293.
PARKWOOD MOTEL (32 *), 8054 Lundys Lane. Open Apr. – Dec. (416) 354-3162.
PILGRIM MOTOR INN (40 ***), 4955 Clifton Hill. (416) 354-2783.
RENDEZVOUS MOTEL (40 *), 7611 Lundys Lane. Open Mar. – Nov. (416) 358-8713.
ROYAL COACHMAN MOTEL (38 *), 5284 Ferry St. (416) 354-2632.
SCOTSMAN MOTEL (18 *), 6179 Lundys Lane. (416) 356-0041.
TRAVEL INN MOTEL (54 *), 5781 Victoria Ave. (416) 356-2034.
UNIVERSAL MOTOR LODGE (40 **), 6000 Stanley Ave. (416) 358-6243.
WEDGEWOOD MOTEL (50 **), 5234 Ferry St. (416) 358-9456.

NIPIGON

CHALET LODGE (43 *), on Trans-Canada at Lake Helen. PO Box 97. Open May – Oct. (807) 887-3030.

NORTH BAY

ASCOT MOTOR HOTEL (46 *), 255 McIntyre St. W. (705) 474-4770.
DUNROVIN MOTEL (15 **), 415 Lakeshore Dr., on Lake Nipissing. (705) 474-1430.
EMPIRE MOTOR HOTEL (142 *), on McIntyre St. PO Box 140. (705) 472-8200.

ORILLIA

THE BIRCHMERE RESORT (33 **), on Lake Couchiching, 234 Bay St. (705) 326-6459.
THE CHIEFTAN MOTEL (10 *), north of town, on Hwy 11. PO, RR 3. (705) 325-7471.
THE ORILLIA MOTEL (24 *), 370 Laclie St. (705) 325-2354.

OTTAWA

BEACON ARMS HOTEL (158 **), 88 Albert St. (613) 235-1413.
CHATEAU LAURIER (500 ***), Major's Hill Park. (613) 232-6411.
EASTVIEW HOTEL (55 **), 200 Montreal Rd. (613) 746-8115.
EMBASSY WEST MOTOR HOTEL (147 **), 1400 Carling Ave. (613) 729-4331.
HOLIDAY INN (169 **), 350 Dalhousie. (613) 236-0201.
HOLIDAY INN (504 ***), Ottawa Centre. (613) 238-1122.
KING SLUMBER MOTEL (15 **), 2279 Prescott Hwy. (613) 825-2312.
LORD ELGIN HOTEL (400 **), 100 Elgin St. (613) 235-3333.
MACIES OTTAWAN MOTEL (100 *), 1274 Carling Ave. (613) 728-1951.
MOTEL LEMAY (41 *), 2200 Montreal Rd. (613) 746-4653.
SHERATON EL MIRADOR MOTOR INN (160 **), 480 Metcalfe St. (613) 237-5500.
SKYLINE HOTEL (450 ***), 101 Lyon St. (613) 237-3600.
THE BUTLER MOTOR HOTEL (95 **), 112 Montreal Rd. PO Box 7009. (613) 746-4641.
TOWN HOUSE MOTOR HOTEL (69 *), 319 Rideau St. (613) 236-0151.

OWEN SOUND

KEY MOTEL (14 *), 8 mi south, on Hwy 6/10. PO Box 92. (519) 794-2350.
SUN GARDENS MOTEL (27 *), 1½ mi west of town, on Hwy 6/21. PO, RR 5. (519) 376-2580.
TRAVELLERS MOTEL (17 *), 740 Ninth Ave. E. (519) 376-2680.

PARRY SOUND

JUNCTION MOTEL (16 *), on Hwy 69B at Hwy 69 junction. PO, RR 3. Open Apr. – Oct. (705) 746-9613.
MAPLES MOTEL (10 *), 15 mi south, on Hwy 69. PO, RR 2. (705) 378-2342.

PEMBROKE

CONTINENTAL MOTEL (15 *), on Golf Course Rd. PO, RR 6. (613) 735-0636.
EDGETOWN MOTEL (50 **), 910 Pembroke St. E. (613) 735-6868.
HILLSIDE MOTEL (15 *), 638 Pembroke St. E. (613) 732-3616.

PERTH

PERTH TAY MOTEL (13 *), 125 Dufferin St. (613) 267-3300.

PETERBOROUGH

GOLDEN NUGGET MOTEL (28 *), 4 mi west, on Hwy 28. PO, RR 3. (705) 743-4755.
HOLIDAY INN (171 **), 150 George St. N. (705) 743-1144.

PORT CARLING

ELGIN HOUSE (116 sgl. $25 – 35, Amer. Plan), 6 mi west, on Hwy 632. PO, RR 2. Open May – Nov. (705) 765-3101.
SHAMROCK LODGE (30 sgl. $56 – 70, Amer. Plan), 2 mi north, on Ferndale Rd. PO Box 218. (705) 765-3177.

PORT COLBORNE

RATHFON INN (16 *), 4 mi west of town, on Rathfon Point. PO Box 14. (416) 834-3908.

RENFREW

THE VALLEY MOTEL (39 *), on Hwy 17 west. PO Box 355. (613) 432-3636.

ST. CATHARINES

HIGHWAYMAN MOTOR INN (82 *), 420 Ontario St. (416) 688-1646.
HOLIDAY INN (158 **), Queen Elizabeth Hwy and Lake St. (416) 934-2561.
LORENZI'S MOTOR INN (21 *), at 2 Merritt St. (416) 227-1183.

ST. THOMAS

CARDINAL COURT MOTEL (15 *), 3 mi northwest, on Hwy 3. PO, RR 7. (519) 633-0740.

SARNIA

FAULDS MOTEL (25 *), 4½ mi east, 1675 London Rd. (Hwy 7) PO, RR 1. (519) 542-5566.

SAUBLE BEACH

SAUBLE LODGE MOTOR INN (33 **), 295 Second Ave. N. (519) 422-1040.

SAULT STE. MARIE

COMMODORE MOTOR HOTEL (51 **), 375 Trunk Rd. (705) 254-6417.
EMPIRE MOTOR HOTEL (122 **), 320 Bay St. PO Box 670. (705) 254-7565.
HOLIDAY MOTEL (27 *), 435 Trunk Rd. (705) 253-4381.
LAURENTIAN MOTEL (14 **), 507 Great Northern Rd. (705) 254-6481.
SHERATON-CASWELL MOTOR INN (76 **), 503 Trunk Rd. (705) 253-2327.
WINDSOR PARK HOTEL (70 **), 617 Queen St. PO Box 340. (705) 256-2211.

SMITHS FALLS

ROGERS MOTEL (16 *), on Hwy 15. PO Box 635. (613) 283-5200.

STRATFORD

MAJER'S MOTEL (32 **), 2 mi from town, on Hwy 7. PO, RR 4, (519) 271-2010.

STURGEON FALLS

MOULIN ROUGE MOTEL (10 *), 175 Front St. (705) 753-2020.

SUDBURY

COULSON HOTEL (122 *), 68 Durham St. S. (705) 675-6436.
GRAND PRIX MOTEL (31 *), 1889 Regent St. S. (705) 522-3600.
MANDARIN EMBASSY MOTOR HOTEL (40 *), 1806 Regent St. S. (705) 522-4610.
SHERATON-CASWELL MOTOR INN (111 **), 3 mi south, 1696 Regent St. S. (705) 522-3000.

TERRACE BAY
IMPERIAL MOTEL (21 *), on Hwy 17. PO Box 338. (807) 825-3226.
NORWOOD MOTEL (16 *), on Hwy 17. PO Box 248. Open May – Oct. (807) 825-3694.

THAMESVILLE
LONGWOODS MOTEL (15 *), 1 mi west on Hwy 2. PO, RR 6. (519) 692-3944.

THUNDER BAY (North)
SHORELINE MOTOR HOTEL (70 *), 61 N. Cumberland St. PO Box 1105. (807) 344-9661.
SLEEPING GIANT MOTOR HOTEL (42 *), 439 Memorial Ave. PO Box 748. (807) 345-7316.

THUNDER BAY (South)
AIRLANE MOTOR HOTEL (120 **), 1210 W. Arthur St. (807) 577-1181.
BOB'S MOTEL (33 *), 235 W. Arthur St. (807) 577-1343.
LOTUS INN MOTEL (24 **), 595 W. Arthur St. (807) 577-5761.
ROYAL EDWARD HOTEL (105 **), 114 May St. S. (807) 623-8467.

TILBURY
THOMAS MOTEL (10 *), on Hwy 2. PO Box 381. (519) 682-0200.

TOBERMORY
GRAND VIEW MOTEL (19 *), on Hwy 6. PO Box 35. Open May – Oct. (519) Tobermory 2220.

TORONTO (Central)
KING EDWARD SHERATON HOTEL (440 **), 37 King St. E. (416) 368-7474.
LORD SIMCOE HOTEL (720 **), 150 King St. W. (416) 362-1848.
MUIR PARK HOTEL (125 **), 2900 Yonge St. (416) 488-1193.
PARK PLAZA HOTEL (350 ***), 4 Avenue Rd. (416) 924-5471.
ROYAL YORK HOTEL (1600 ***), 100 Front St. W. (416) 368-2511.
SUTTON PLACE HOTEL (350 ***), 955 Bay St. (416) 924-9221.
WINDSOR ARMS HOTEL (88 **), 22 St. Thomas St. (416) 921-6141.

TORONTO (East)
HOLIDAY INN (203 **), 22 Metropolitan Rd., Scarborough. (416) 293-8171.
MERRY MACS MOTEL (20 *), 4374 Kingston Rd., West Hill. (416) 284-1691.
OLYMPIC MOTOR HOTEL (52 *), 2121 Kingston Rd., Scarborough. (416) 267-1141.

TORONTO (West)
BEACH MOTEL (40 *), 2183 Lakeshore Blvd. W. (416) 251-5591.
CAMBRIDGE MOTOR HOTEL (205 **), 600 Dixon Rd., Rexdale. (416) 249-7651.
CASA MENDOZA INN (20 *), 2161 Lakeshore Blvd. W. PO Box 14. (416) 252-6244.
HOLIDAY INN (200 **), 350 Muncipal Dr., Toronto-West. (416) 621-2121.
HOWARD JOHNSON'S AIRPORT HOTEL (260 **), 801 Dixon Rd., Rexdale. (416) 677-6100.
PLAZA MOTEL (72 **), 240 Belfield Rd., Rexdale. (416) 241-8513.
RAINBOW MOTEL (26 *), 2165 Lakeshore Blvd. W. (416) 259-7671.
SEAHORSE MOTOR HOTEL (50 **), 2095 Lakeshore Blvd. W. (416) 255-4433.
SEAWAY BEVERLY HILLS MOTOR HOTEL (101 **), 1677 Wilson Ave., Downsview. (416) 249-8171.
SEAWAY TOWERS MOTOR HOTEL (143 **), 2000 Lakeshore Blvd. (416) 763-4521.
SHERWAY INN (89 **), 5487 Dundas St. W., Islington. (416) 231-9241.
VALHALLA INN (160 **), 1 Valhalla Inn Rd., Islington. PO Box 250. (416) 239-2391.
WEST POINT MOTOR HOTEL (58 **), 2285 Lakeshore Blvd. W. (416) 259-1138.

TRENTON
PARK MOTEL (10 *), 276 Dundas St. E. (613) 392-1251.
PINES MOTOR HOTEL (20 *), 2 mi north, on Trent River. PO, RR 3. (613) 392-9294.

WAWA
AGATE ISLE MOTEL (12 *), 4 mi south, on Hwy 17. PO Box 581. Open May – Oct. (705) 856-7040.
MEL-ERE MOTOR HOTEL (32 *), 22 Mission Rd. PO Box 1187. (705) 856-2342.

WHITNEY
BEAR TRAIL LODGE (13 **), off Hwy 60 at Galeairy Lake. (705) 637-2662.

WINDERMERE
WINDERMERE HOUSE (90 sgl. $24 – 38, Amer. Plan), on Hwy 516 on Lake Rosseau. Open June – Oct. (705) 769-3611.

WINDSOR
ABC MOTEL (47 *), 3048 Dougall Rd. (519) 969-5090.
CADILLAC MOTEL (28 *), 2498 Dougall Rd. (519) 969-9340.
HOLIDAY INN (231 **), 480 Riverside Dr. W. (519) 253-4411.
MADRID MOTOR HOTEL (100 *), 2530 Ouellette Ave. (519) 966-1860.
PRINCETON MOTEL (52 *), 3032 Dougall Rd. (519) 969-2750.
RICHELIEU INN (150 ***), 430 Ouellette Ave. (519) 253-7281.

WOODSTOCK
WESTMOUNT MOTEL (32 *), 1 mi west, on Hwy 2. PO, RR 1. (519) 539-2073.
WOODSTOCK INN (33 *), on Hwy 401. PO Box 192. (519) 537-6667.

PRINCE EDWARD ISLAND

ALBERTON
THE WESTERNER MOTEL (24 *), on Hwys 151 and 172. PO Box 108. (902) 853-2215.

CAVENDISH
BAY VISTA MOTOR INN (38 **), 2 mi west, on Hwy 6. PO, RR 1. Breadalbane. Open May 15 – Oct. 1. (902) 963-2255.
CAVENDISH MOTEL (39 **), at Hwys 6 and 13. PO Box 1803. Open May 15 – Sept. 30. (902) 963-2244.
THE COUNTRY HOUSE INN (7 *), 1 mi west of Wild Life Park, on Gulf Shore Rd. PO Hunter River, RR 2. Open June 1 – Sept. 30. (902) 963-2055.
THE PINES MOTEL (11 *), at Rusticoville Bridge, 3 mi south of national park. Open May 1 – Nov. 1. (902) 963-2029.

CHARLOTTETOWN
(Rates may increase and length of stay be limited during Provincial Exhibition, which is held in August.)
CONFEDERATION INN (58 **), 1 mi west, on Trans-Canada. PO Box 631, Charlottetown. (902) 892-2481.
THE KIRKWOOD MOTOR HOTEL (69 **), 455 University Ave. (902) 892-4206.
THE RODD MOTOR INN (98 *), at Hwys 1 and 2. PO Box 432. (902) 894-8566.

MONTAGUE
BRUDENELL RESORT (50 **), 6 mi from town, on Hwy 3. PO Box 22, Cardigan. Open May 18 – Sept. 30. (902) 652-2332.

PRINCE EDWARD ISLAND NATIONAL PARK
DALVAY BY THE SEA HOTEL (28 dbl. $48, Amer. Plan), (Prince Edward Island National Park hotel). PO Box 18, Charlottetown. Open mid-June – mid-Sept. (902) 672-2048.

SOURIS
LORD ROLLO MOTEL (18 *), 2 mi from Souris, on Hwy 330. PO, Souris West. Open July 1 – Sept. 15. (902) 687-2339.

SUMMERSIDE
LINKLETTER MOTEL (56 **), 311 Market St. (902) 436-2157.
SUNNY ISLE MOTEL (12 *), on Hwy 1A, 720 Water St. Open May 1 – Oct. 31. (902) 963-2222.

TIGNISH
VILLAGE MOTEL (12 *), 191 Centennial Dr. (902) 882-2687.

WOOD ISLAND
MEADOW LODGE (20 *), 1 mi from ferry, on Trans-Canada. PO, Belle River. Open May 15 – Oct. 15. (902) 962-2022.

QUEBEC

ARVIDA
LE MANOIR DU SAGUENAY (85 **), 7 mi west of town, 865 Powell Dr. (418) 548-4641.

BAIE COMEAU
LE MANOIR (52 ***), on St. Lawrence at Eighth, Cabot. (418) 296-3391.

CHICOUTIMI
AUBERGE DES GOUVERNEURS (124 ***), 1303 Talbot Blvd. (418) 549-6244.

DRUMMONDVILLE
LE DAUPHIN (114 *), 600 Blvd. St. Joseph. (819) 478-4141.

GASPE
ADAMS MOTEL (66 **), at Jacques Cartier and Adams sts. PO Box 130. (418) 368-2244.

GASPE PENINSULA—*see Gaspé, Matane, Matapedia, Percé, Riviere Madeleine, Ste. Anne des Monts*

GRANBY
LES PINS MOTEL (14 *), 2 mi from city, on Hwy 1. PO, RR 4. (514) 378-4694.

LA TUQUE
LE GITE MOTEL (39 **), on Hwy 19. PO Box 640. (819) 523-9501.

MAGOG
CABANA LODGE AND MOTEL (30 *), ½ mi west, on Hwy 1. 1460 Main St. (819) 843-3313.

MATANE
MOTEL BELLE PLAGE (43 **), 1310 Matane-sur-mer Rd. Open May 25 – Oct. 15. (418) 562-2323.

MATAPEDIA
HOTEL-MOTEL RESTIGOUCHE (38 **), on Hwy 6, near Hwy 11 junction. (418) 865-2155.

MONTEBELLO
LE CHATEAU MONTEBELLO (204 dbl. $84 – 91,

Amer. Plan) (Canadian Pacific hotel), southwest of town, on Hwy 8. (819) 423-6341.

MONTREAL

AUBIN MOTEL (20 *), 6125 James St. W. (514) 484-5198.
BERKELEY HOTEL (100 **), 1188 Sherbrooke St. W. (514) 849-7351.
HOLIDAY INN (500 ***), 420 Sherbrooke St. W. (514) 842-6111.
HOLIDAY INN-LONGUEUIL (214 ***), 50 de Serigny St. on south shore of St. Lawrence. (514) 670-3030.
HOTEL BONAVENTURE (395 ***), 1 Bonaventure Pl. (514) 878-2332.
LE CHATEAU CHAMPLAIN (614 ***), Place du Canada. (514) 878-1688.
LOEWS LA CITE (500 ***), 3625 Ave. du Parc. (514) 288-6666.
QUALITY INN (182 **), 410 W. Sherbrooke W. (514) 844-8851.
QUATRE SEASONS (320 ***), 1050 W. Sherbrooke W. (514) 284-1110.
QUEEN ELIZABETH (1200 ***), 900 W. Dorchester W. (514) 861-3511.
RAMADA INN CENTER VILLE (205 **), 1005 Guy St. (514) 866-4611.
RUBY FOO'S (118 **), 7655 Decarie. (514) 731-7701.
SEAWAY MOTOR INN (222 **), 1155 Guy St. (514) 932-1411.
SHERATON-MOUNT ROYAL (1011 ***), 1455 Peel St. (514) 842-7777.
SKYLINE (233 *), 6600 Cote de Liesse. (514) 342-2262.

MONT TREMBLANT

MONT TREMBLANT LODGE (126 dbl. $60 – 84, Amer. Plan), off Hwy 11 at Lake Tremblant. (819) 425-2711.

PERCE

AU PIC DE L'AURORE (56 **), ½ mi north of city, on Hwy 6. PO Box 10. Open June 1 – Oct. 10. (418) 782-2050.
HOTEL-MOTEL PERCE (70 **), in city, on Hwy 6. PO Box 159. Open June 10 – Oct. 15. (418) 782-2166.

POINTE AU PIC

HOTEL LES TROIS CANARDS (39 *), off Hwy 362. (418) 665-3761.

QUEBEC CITY

(Rates may increase and length of stay be limited during Winter Carnival Week, which is held in February.)
AUBERGE DE LA COLLINE (20 **), 1 mi southwest of city center, 385 Blvd. du Pont. PO St. Nicholas. (418) 831-0848.
AUBERGE DES GOUVERNEURS (379 ***), 690 E. Boul St-Cyrille. (418) 647-1717.
HOLIDAY INN (350 **), south of city center at Hwys 2 and 9. (418) 653-4901.
HOTEL CHATEAU LAURIER (54 *), 695 Grande Allee E. (418) 522-8108.
HOTEL-MOTEL AUBERGE DES GOUVERNEUR (124 ***), 3030 Laurier Blvd. (514) 651-3030.
HOTEL-MOTEL CARILLON (46 **), 2800 Blvd. Laurier. PO Ste. Foy. (418) 653-5234.
HOTEL-MOTEL DES LAURENTIDES (102 **), 2½ mi east of Quebec city center, 350 Blvd. Ste. Anne. Beauport. (418) 663-7881.
HOTEL-MOTEL L'ARISTOCRATE (98 **), 5 mi from city center, 3235 Blvd. Laurier. (418) 653-2841.
LE CHATEAU FRONTENAC (662 ***) (Canadian Pacific hotel), 1 rue des Carrieres. (418) 522-3861.
LE CHATELET (30 **), 15 mi from Quebec city center, 7450 Blvd. Ste. Anne, in Chateau Richer. (418) 824-4224.
MOTEL L'ABITATION (146 *), 2828 Blvd. Laurier. PO Ste. Foy. (418) 653-7267.
MOTEL LE SABLIER (23 *), 2660 Hamel Blvd. W., Hwy 2C. (418) 871-8916.
MOTEL PIERRE (14 **), 1550 Hamel Blvd. W., Ste. Foy. (418) 681-6191.
PANORAMA MOTEL (18 *), 15 mi from Quebec city center, 7500 Blvd. Ste. Anne, in Chateau Richer. (418) 824-4208.
WANDLYN MOTOR INN (120 **), 2955 Blvd. Laurier, Ste. Foy. (418) 653-8721.

RIMOUSKI

AUBERGE DES GOUVERNEURS (124 ***), 155 E. Blvd. Rene Lepage. (418) 723-4422.
HOTEL ST. LOUIS (58 *), 214 Edmond St. (418) 723-1170.
MOTEL ST. LAURENT (20 *), 740 Blvd. St. Germain W. (418) 723-9217.

RIVIERE DU LOUP

AUBERGE DE LA POINTE (84 **), 1 mi northeast of town, on Hwy 122. PO Box 10. (418) 862-3514.
HOTEL ST. LOUIS (85 **), 473 Lafontaine. (418) 862-3591.
MOTEL LEVESQUE (66 **), 1 mi west of town, 171 Fraser. (418) 862-6927.

RIVIERE MADELEINE

AUBERGE DU GOLFE INN (24 *), on Hwy 6, PO Gaspé Nord. Open July 1 – Aug. 31. (418) 393-2323.
HOTEL-MOTEL MADELEINE SUR MER (34 *), on Hwy 6. PO Box 10, Gaspé Nord. Open May 20 – Oct. 20. (418) 393-2323.

ST. DONAT DE MONTCALM

HOTEL CHATEAU DU LAC (56 dbl. $38 – 58, Amer. Plan), via Hwy 30 on Lake Archambault. (819) 424-2111.

STE. ADELE

HOTEL LE CHANTICLER (149 dbl. $48 – 88, Amer. Plan), west of town center. (514) 866-6661.

STE. AGATHE DES MONTS

STE. AGATHE MOTEL (38 *), 1000 Principale, Hwy 11. (819) 326-2622.

STE. ANNE DE BEAUPRE

(Rates may increase and length of stay be limited during the Feast of Ste. Anne, late July.)
MANOIR GERARD (25 *), 9776 Blvd. Ste. Anne. (418) 827-2720.
MOTEL-HOTEL DU BOULEVARD (22 *), 9749 Blvd. Ste. Anne. Open May 15 – Oct. 10. (418) 827-2910.

STE. ANNE DES MONTS

HOTEL BEAURIVAGE (25 *), in town center. PO Box 9. Open May 1 – Nov. 1. (418) 763-2224.
MOTEL LE CHALUTIER (20 *), 2 mi from town center, on Hwy 6. PO Box 577. (418) 763-3377.

ST. JEAN PORT JOLI

AUBERGE DU FAUBOURG (98 **), 1½ mi west, on Hwy 2. (418) 598-6455.

ST. JOVITE

GRAY ROCKS INN (225 dbl. $61 – 85, Amer. Plan), 3 mi northeast of Lake Ouimet. PO Box 100. (819) 425-2771.

ST. SAUVEUR DES MONTS

MONT HABITANT (25 ***), 3 mi west of town, Exit 26 from Autoroute. (514) 861-2283.

SEPT ILES

HOTEL BRIAND (28 *), 491 Ave. Brochu. (418) 962-9401.

SHERBROOKE

LE BARON SHERBROOKE MOTOR HOTEL (127 **), 3200 King St. W. (819) 567-3941.
MOTEL LA PAYSANNE (29 *), 2¼ mi south of town, at Hwys 5 and 22. PO Lennoxville. (819) 569-5585.

TADOUSSAC

HOTEL TADOUSSAC (145 **), 2 blocks southeast of Hwy 15. (418) 235-4421.

TROIS RIVIERES

LE BARON MOTOR HOTEL (102 **), 3600 Royal Blvd. (819) 379-3232.
MOTEL COCONUT (41 *), 7531 Notre Dame. (819) 377-3221.

VAL DAVID

HOTEL LA SAPINIERRE (67 dbl. $92 – 120, Amer. Plan), 1 mi east of Hwy 11. (819) 322-2020.

VAL D'OR

HOTEL SIGMA MOTEL (31 *), 210 Centrale Ave. (819) 824-2747.

VALLEYFIELD

MOTEL DE BEAUJEU (56 **), 252 Langlois Blvd. (Hwy 3) (514) 373-9080.

VAL MORIN

FAR HILLS INN (63 dbl. $85, Amer. Plan). (819) 866-2219.

VILLE D'ESTEREL

HOTEL ESTEREL (135 dbl. $64 – 98, Amer. Plan), take Exit 43 from Autoroute. (519) 228-2571.

SASKATCHEWAN

CARONPORT

CARONPORT MOTEL (14 *), 14 mi west of Moose Jaw, on Trans-Canada. (306) 756-2226.

ESTEVAN

BEEFEATER INN (75 *), 1309 Ninth St. (306) 634-6456.

GRENFELL

HOMESTEAD MOTEL (22 *), at Trans-Canada and Hwy 47. PO Box 546. (306) 697-2555.

HUDSON BAY

NORWOOD MOTEL (30 *), in town. PO Box 549. (306) 865-2216.

HUMBOLDT

PIONEER MOTOR HOTEL (20 *), on Ninth St. PO Box 1060. (306) 682-2638.

KINDERSLEY

DOWNTOWNER MOTEL (32 *), in town. PO Box 1325. (306) 463-2639.

LA RONGE

LA RONGE MOTOR INN (68 *), in town. (306) 425-2190.

LLOYDMINSTER

VOYAGEUR MOTEL (31 *), 4724 44th St. (403) 825-2248.

MAPLE CREEK

PRAIRIE PRIDE MOTEL (23 *), in town. PO Box 109. (306) 667-2627.

MELFORT

CARRA VALLA INN (30 *), at Hwys 3 and 6. PO Box 1025. (306) 752-2828.
HIGHLAND HOUSE HOTEL (32 *), 112 Main St. PO Box 2080. (306) 752-2861.

MOOSE JAW

DREAMLAND MOTEL (21 *), 1035 Athabasca St. E. (306) 692-1878.

HARWOOD'S MOOSE JAW INN (100 *), 24 Fairford St. (306) 692-2366.
KNOWLES MOTEL (15 *), 1 mi east of city, on Hwy 1, Trans-Canada. PO Box 936. (306) 693-3601.
MAYNARD MOTEL (14 *), 1230 Main North. (306) 692-6329.
MIDTOWN MOTEL (29 *), 132 Athabasca St. W. (306) 692-7414.

NIPAWIN

TOBIN LAKE MOTEL (42 *), (306) 862-4681.

NORTH BATTLEFORD

BEAVER MOTOR HOTEL (40 *), city center, on Hwy 5 at 11th Ave. (306) 445-8115.
CAPRI MOTEL (36 *), 982 102nd St. (306) 445-8166.
NAY'S MOTEL (22 *), 1642 100th St. (306) 445-4474.

PRINCE ALBERT

IMPERIAL '400' MOTEL (100 *), south, on Hwy 2. (306) 764-6881.
SHERATON MARLBORO MOTOR INN (100 *), 67 13th St. E. (306) 763-2643.

PRINCE ALBERT NATIONAL PARK

ARMSTRONG HILLCREST CABINS (44 *), on Lakeview Dr., in Waskesiu. PO Box 155. Open May 1 – Sept. 1. (306) 663-5481.
RED DEER HOTEL-MOTEL (17 *), in Waskesiu. PO Box 52. Open May 15 – Sept. 15. (306) 663-5351.
SKYLINE MOTEL (22 *), in Waskesiu. Open May 1 – Oct. 15. (306) 663-5461.

REGINA

HOLIDAY INN (100 **), 1½ mi from downtown, 777 Albert St. (306) 527-0121.
HOTEL SASKATCHEWAN (252 **), Victoria Ave. and Scarth St. (306) 522-7691.
INTOWNER MOTEL (43 *), 1009 Albert St. (306) 525-3737.
REGINA INN (240 **), on Trans-Canada at Victoria Ave. and Broad St. (306) 525-6767.
VAGABOND MOTOR INN (104 **), 4177 Albert St. (306) 586-3443.
WESTWARD MOTOR INN (76 *), 1717 Victoria Ave. (306) 527-0663.

SASKATOON

BESSBOROUGH HOTEL (260 *), at Spadina Crescent and 21st St. (306) 244-5521.
HOLIDAY HOUSE MOTOR HOTEL (40 *), 2901 Eighth St. E. (306) 374-9111.
KING GEORGE MOTOR HOTEL (105 **), 157 Second Ave. N. (306) 244-6133.
SHERATON-CAVALIER MOTOR INN (199 **), 612 Spadina Crescent. (306) 652-6770.

SWIFT CURRENT

HORSESHOE LODGE MOTEL (50 **), 1 mi northeast, on Trans-Canada. (306) 773-4643.
TRAVELODGE (38 *), on Trans-Canada, at Hwy 4. (306) 773-3101.

WEYBURN

EL RANCHO MOTOR HOTEL (50 *), 53 Government Rd. S. (306) 842-2664.

WHITEWOOD

TRIPLE G MOTEL (20 *), on Trans-Canada, at Hwy 9. PO Box 427. (306) 735-2627.

WYNYARD

CARLSON'S MOTOR HOTEL (34 *), in town. PO Box 939. (306) 554-2451.

YORKTON

CORONA MOTOR HOTEL (85 *), 345 Broadway W. (306) 783-6571.
HOLIDAY INN (92 *), 1010 Broadway E. (306) 783-9781.
THE REDWOOD (48 *), 317 Broadway W. (306) 783-3663.
THE YORKE INN (18 *), 418 Broadway W. (306) 783-2251.

THE YUKON

BEAVER CREEK

ALAS/KON BORDER LODGE (129 ***), at Mile 1202 on Alaska Hwy. Open May 1 – Oct. 1. (403) Beaver Creek 5551. Reservations: 900 IBM Bldg., Seattle, Wash. (206) 623-1683.

DAWSON CITY

EL DORADO HOTEL (45 **), Third Ave. and Princess St. PO Box 338. (403) 993-5451.
GOLD CITY MOTOR INN (64 **), Fifth Ave. and Harper St. PO Box 420. (403) 993-5542.

HAINES JUNCTION

GATEWAY MOTEL (14 *), at Mile 1016 on Alaska Hwy. (403) 634-2371.

WATSON LAKE

BELVEDERE HOTEL-MOTEL (50 **), at Mile 635 on Alaska Hwy. PO Box 288. (403) 536-7411.

WHITEHORSE

CHILKOOT MOTEL (65 *), 4190 Fourth Ave. (403) 667-2379.
EDGEWATER HOTEL (15 **), Main St. and First Ave. PO Box 4429. (403) 667-2572.
WHITEHORSE TRAVELODGE (90 ***), Second and Wood sts. PO Box 4250. (403) 667-4211.
WHITEHORSE INN (100 *), 112 Main St. (403) 667-2531.

RESTAURANTS

ALBERTA

BANFF — BANFF NATIONAL PARK

ALPINE STEAK HOUSE (** D), Banff Ave. and Buffalo St. Italian cuisine, steak. Licensed. Open 4:30 – midnight, Apr. 1 – Oct. 20. (403) 762-2712.
BANFF BUFFETERIA (* BLD), 219 Banff Ave. Cafeteria. Open 6 am – 10 pm. (403) 762-3211.

CALGARY

CALGARY TOWER REVOLVING RESTAURANT (** LD), Ninth Ave. at Centre St. Steak, prime rib, seafood. Licensed. Open 8 am – midnight. $1.50 charge for ascent to tower. (403) 266-7171.
HY'S STEAK HOUSE (** D), 316 Fourth Ave. SW. Charcoal-broiled steak, seafood. Licensed. Open 4:30 pm – midnight. Closed Sunday. (403) 263-2222.
INN ON LAKE BONAVISTA (*** LD), 7 mi southeast via Hwy 2, 747 Lake Bonavista Dr. Canadian, continental cuisine. Licensed. Open 11 am – midnight. (403) 271-6711.
KOKO'S PANCAKE HOUSE AND DINING LOUNGE (** BLD), 7304 Macleod Trail. Steaks, roast beef, and short-order items. Pancake House, 7 am – 9 pm. Dining Room, 11:30 am – midnight. (403) 255-5808.

EDMONTON

PHIL'S STEAK AND PANCAKE HOUSE (* BLD), 5 mi south on Hwy 2, 4905 Calgary Trail. Beer and wine. Open 6:30 am – 11 pm. (403) 435-1663.
TOWER SUITE DINING LOUNGE (** LD), on fifth floor of Canadian National Tower, 104th Ave. and 100th St. Canadian, continental cuisine. Licensed. Open 11 am – midnight. Closed Sunday, holidays. $2 cover charge. (403) 424-3369.

FORT MACLEOD

THE WESTERNER FAMILY RESTAURANT (* BLD), on Hwys 2 and 3. Canadian cuisine. Prime rib. Beer and wine. Open 6 am – 10 pm. (403) 234-4066.

JASPER NATIONAL PARK

ASTORIA DINING LOUNGE (** BLD), 404 Connought Dr. Varied menu, steak. Licensed. Open 7 am – 1 am. (403) 852-3351.

LETHBRIDGE

PHIL'S RESTAURANT AND PANCAKE HOUSE (* BLD), on Hwys 4 and 5, 1303 Mayor Magrath Dr. Varied menu. Beer and wine. Open 6 am – midnight. (403) 328-5077.
SVEN ERICKSEN'S FAMILY RESTAURANT (** LD), on Hwys 4 and 5, 1715 Mayor Magrath Dr. Steak, prime rib, seafood. Licensed. Open 11 am – midnight. (403) 328-7756.

MEDICINE HAT

HEIDEL HAUS INN (** D), 502 S. Railway St. Wiener schnitzel, charcoal-broiled steak. Beer and wine. Open 6 pm – midnight. Closed Sunday, Monday. (403) 257-1484.
PHIL'S STEAK AND PANCAKE HOUSE (* BLD), 1½ mi southwest on Trans-Canada, 910 Redcliffe Dr. Varied menu. Beer and wine. Open 6:30 am – midnight. (403) 527-5855.

BRITISH COLUMBIA

CACHE CREEK

WANDER-INN RESTAURANT (** BLD), on Trans-Canada, south of Hwy 97 junction. Chinese, western cuisine. Licensed. Open 6:30 am – midnight. (604) 457-6511.

COURTENAY

CORONET DINING ROOM (** LD), in Arbutus Hotel, 275 Eighth St. Varied menu. Licensed. Open noon – 2:30 pm, 6 pm – 9 pm. (604) 334-3121.

DUNCAN

HY'S STEAK HOUSE (** LD), 141 Trans-Canada, in Village Green Inn. Varied menu, steak. Licensed. Open noon – 2 pm, 5 pm – midnight. (604) 746-5126.

KAMLOOPS

CLANCY'S (* BLD), in Kamloops Travelodge, 430 Columbia St. Beer and wine. Open 6 am – 10 pm. (604) 372-8202.
HIGHLANDER RESTAURANT (* BLD), 444 Victoria St. Varied menu, seafood. Licensed. Open 6 am – midnight. (604) 372-2121.

NANAIMO

THE DINER'S RENDEZVOUS (* LD), 489 Wallace St. Steak, seafood, various Chinese dishes. Licensed. Open 9:30 am – 1:30 am. (604) 753-4331.

NEW WESTMINSTER

KING NEPTUNE (* LD), on waterfront, at 800 Front St. Smorgasbord, seafood. Licensed. Open 11 am – midnight. (604) 521-3545.
TOP O' THE ROYAL (** LD), in Royal Towers Motor Hotel, Sixth St. at Royal Ave. Varied menu, steak, seafood. Licensed. Open noon – 2 pm, 6 – 10 pm. (604) 524-3777.

PENTICTON

THE CHALET (** D), 1425 Main St. French, continental cuisine. Licensed. Open 5 pm – 9 pm. Closed Sunday. (604) 492-0330.

PRINCE GEORGE

OUTRIGGER RESTAURANT (* LD), Dominion St. and Sixth Ave. Polynesian menu, steak. Licensed. Open noon – 2 pm, 5 pm – midnight. Closed holidays. (604) 563-1741.

VIENNA SCHNITZEL (** LD), 611 Brunswick St. Continental, Bavarian cuisine. Licensed. Open 11:30 am – 1 am. Music, dancing. (604) 563-7550.

PRINCE RUPERT

LA GONDOLA RESTAURANT AND DRIVE INN (* BLD), Sixth St. and First Ave., in Rupert Motor Inn. Italian cuisine, steak, seafood. Licensed. Open 6 am – midnight. (604) 624-2621.

REVELSTOKE

THREE VALLEY GAP DINING ROOM AND CAFETERIA (** BLD), 12 mi west on Trans-Canada, in Three Valley Gap Motel. Varied menu. Licensed. Open 7 am – 10 pm, Mar. 15 – Oct. 15. (604) 837-2109.

VANCOUVER

HY'S ENCORE (** LD), 637 Hornby St. Charcoal-broiled steak, chicken, seafood. Licensed. Open 11:30 am – 2 pm, 5:30 pm – 12:30 pm. Closed Sunday. (604) 683-7671.

THE OLD SPAGHETTI FACTORY (* LD), 53 Water St., in Gastown. Spaghetti dishes. Licensed. Open 11:30 am – 2 pm, 5 pm – 10 pm; June 1 – Sept. 1. (604) 684-1288.

THE SHIP OF THE SEVEN SEAS (*** D), floating restaurant at foot of Lansdale Ave., North Vancouver. Seafood, steak. Licensed. Open 4 pm – midnight. Closed Monday. (604) 987-8318.

THE THREE GREENHORNS (** LD), 1030 Denman St., at Comox St. International cooking. Licensed. Open noon – 3 pm, 5:30 – 11:30 pm. (604) 688-8655.

THE WHARF (* LD), under Burrard bridge, opposite planetarium in paddle-wheeler *Essington*. Seafood. Licensed. Open 11 am – 11 pm. (604) 687-9868.

VERNON

HY'S STEAK HOUSE (** D), in Village Green Inn, 4801 27th St. Varied menu, steak. Licensed. Open 11:30 am – 2, 5 pm to 11:30 pm. (604) 542-3321.

VICTORIA

CHINESE VILLAGE RESTAURANT (** LD), northeast of city, near Mayfair Shopping Center at 755 Finlayson St. Chinese, American cuisine. Licensed. Open noon – 11 pm. (604) 384-8151.

COACH AND FOUR STEAK HOUSE (** LD), 19 Bastion Sq. Prime rib, steak. Licensed. Open 11 am – 3 pm, 5 – 9 pm. (604) 382-5832.

DINGLE HOUSE (** LD), 1½ mi northwest on Hwy 1A, 137 Gorge Rd. S. Prime rib, Yorkshire pudding. Licensed. Open 5 pm – 10 pm. Closed January. (604) 382-8721.

HY'S STEAK HOUSE (** D), 777 Douglas St. Steak, seafood. Licensed. Open 5 pm – midnight. Closed Sunday, Oct. – Apr. (604) 382-7111.

THE MCPHERSON RESTAURANT (** LD), 2 Centennial Sq. Prime rib, steak, seafood. Licensed. Open 11 am – 3 pm, 5 – 9 pm. (604) 388-6023.

PRINCESS MARY RESTAURANT VESSEL (* BLD), ½ mi west via Johnson St. bridge, at 344 Harbour Rd. Seafood, steak, fresh berry pies. Licensed. Open 8 am – 9:30 pm. Closed Sunday, Sept. – June. (604) 386-3456.

MANITOBA

BRANDON

THE SUBURBAN RESTAURANT (** LD), 2604 Victoria Ave. Varied menu. Licensed. Open noon – 1 am. Closed holidays. (204) 728-3031.

DAUPHIN

LA VERENDRYE STEAK HOUSE (* LD), 26 First Ave. NW. Varied menu, steak. Licensed. Open 11:30 am – 1 am. Entertainment. (204) 638-5220.

WINNIPEG

THE FACTOR'S TABLE (** LD), 222 Broadway Ave., in Hotel Fort Garry. Canadian, continental cuisine. Licensed. Open noon – 2:30 pm, 6 – 10:30 pm. (204) 942-8251.

THE HAPPY VINEYARD (** LD), ¾ mi northwest, at 719 Ellice Ave. German cuisine. Licensed. Open noon – 1 am. Closed Sunday, holidays. (204) 783-6837.

LA VIEILLE GARE-RESTAURANT FRANCAIS. (** LD), 1½ mi east via Metro Rt. 57 at 630 Des Meurons St. Old railroad station. French cuisine. Licensed. Open noon – 11 pm. Closed Sunday. (204) 247-7072.

OLIVER'S (** LD), 185 Lombard St. International cuisine, charcoal-broiled steak. Licensed. Open noon – midnight. Closed Sunday, holidays. (204) 943-4448.

NEW BRUNSWICK

EDMUNDSTON

COFFEE MILL FAMILY RESTAURANT (** LD), at Trans-Canada and Hebert Blvd., in Brunswick Center Mall. Canadian cuisine, steak, lobster. Licensed. Open 10 am – 11 pm. Closed Easter weekend, July 1, Dec. 25. (506) 735-3114.

FREDERICTON

THE ACADIAN DINING SALON (* BLD), in Wandlyn Motor Inn, 2½ mi south, off Trans-Canada. Varied menu, Dover sole. Licensed. Open 7 am – 2:30 pm, 5 – 10 pm. (506) 455-8937.

MONCTON

COFFEE MILL FAMILY RESTAURANT (** LD), in Moncton Mall, off Trans-Canada, on Hwy 126, Mountain Rd. Steak, seafood, lobster. Open 11 am – midnight. Closed Sunday, Easter weekend, July 1, Dec. 25. (506) 854-2163.

CY'S SEAFOOD RESTAURANT (** LD), 170 E. Main St. Steak, seafood, lobster. Licensed. Open 11:30 am – 12:30 am. Closed Apr. 12, Dec. 25. (506) 382-0032.

HOUSE OF LAM (** LD), 957 Mountain Rd. Oriental, continental cuisine, seafood, steak. Licensed. Open 10 am – 2 am. (506) 389-1101.

MING GARDEN RESTAURANT (** LD), 797 Mountain Rd. Canadian, Chinese cuisine. Licensed. Open 10:30 am – 2 am. (506) 855-5433.

NEWCASTLE

FRENCH FORT RESTAURANT (** LD), 1½ mi northeast, on Hwy 8. Seafood, beef. Licensed. Open noon – 11:30 pm. Closed Dec. 20 – Jan. 3. (506) 622-3713.

SACKVILLE

MARSHLANDS INN DINING ROOM (** BLD), in Marshlands Inn, 73 Bridge St. Baked scallops, steak, kidney pie, lobster. Licensed. Open 7 am – 9:30 am, noon – 2 pm; dinner seatings at 6 and 8 pm. (506) 536-0170.

ST. ANDREWS

THE PINK SHELL DINING ROOM (** D), 335 Water St. Varied menu. Open 4:30 pm – 8 pm, June 15 – Sept. 15. Closed Monday. (506) 529-8974.

SAINT JOHN

REVERSING FALLS RESTAURANT (** BLD), on Hwy 100 at Reversing Falls. Seafood, steak. Licensed. Open 7:30 am – 11 pm. (506) 672-6853.

ST. LEONARD

ACADIA RESTAURANT (* BLD), on Hwy 17, ½ mi west of Trans-Canada. Canadian cuisine. Licensed. Open 7 am – midnight. (506) 423-6440.

NEWFOUNDLAND

ST. JOHN'S

MARTY'S (* BLD), 301 Water St. Seafood, chicken, homemade soup. Open 8 am – 1 am. Closed Sunday. (709) 722-3560.

THE STARBOARD QUARTER RESTAURANT (** LD), on Water St. in Royal Trust Bldg. Varied menu. Licensed. Open noon – 2:30 pm, 5:30 – midnight. $2 cover charge. (709) 726-5051.

NOVA SCOTIA

AMHERST

COLONIAL RESTAURANT (* BLD), 2 Lawrence St. Varied menu, lobster, steak. Licensed. Open 7:30 am – 11 pm. (902) 667-3797.

ANTIGONISH

THE GOSHEN RESTAURANT (* BLD), 4 mi east on Trans-Canada, at Hwy 316. Varied menu, steak, fresh seafood. Licensed. Open 8 am – midnight. (902) 863-3068.

THE OLD WORLD PUB AT THE GAEL (** BLD), 42 James St. Steak, seafood. Licensed. Open 7 am – 11 pm. (902) 863-3425.

CHESTER

SWORD AND ANCHOR INN (** BLD), center of town, off Hwy 3A. Seafood, steak. Licensed. Open 7:30 am – 10 am, noon – 2:30 pm, 6 – 10 pm. (902) 275-3561.

CHETICAMP

LAURIE'S RESTAURANT (** BLD), on Cabot Trail, at Laurie's Motel, 168 Main St. Acadian dishes, seafood, beef. Open for all meals, hours vary seasonally. (902) 224-2400.

DIGBY

BON-I-LASS RESTAURANT (* BLD), 7 mi east of ferry terminal, in Smith's Cove. Seafood. Open 11:30 am – 11 pm, June 1 – Sept. 15. (902) 245-2473.

FUNDY RESTAURANT (* BLD), 34 Water St. Canadian cuisine, seafood. Licensed. Open 7 am – midnight. Dinner music. (902) 245-4950.

HALIFAX

HENRY HOUSE (** LD), 1222 Barrington St. Varied menu. Open noon – 2:30 pm, 5:45 – 10:30 pm. Closed Sunday. (902) 423-1309.

SWISS CHARCOAL BAR B Q (* LD). 2 restaurants, 6273 Quinpool Rd. (902) 422-4414, and 233 Bedford Hwy. (902) 455-1569. Steak specialities. Licensed. Open 11:30 am – 12:30 am.

WHARF RESTAURANT (** LD), Duke and Barrington sts. Seafood, roast beef, steak. Licensed. Open 11:30 am – 11 pm. Closed Sunday. (902) 423-9365.

LUNENBURG

BLUENOSE LODGE DINING ROOM (** BLD), 10 Falkland St. Seafood, western beef. Licensed.

Open 8 am – 9:30 am, noon – 2 pm, 5:30 – 7:30 pm. Closed Saturday. (902) 634-8851.

PLEASANT BAY

BLACK WHALE SEAFOOD RESTAURANT (** LD), in town, on Cabot Trail. Seafood. Licensed. Open noon – midnight, May 15 – Oct. 15. (902) 224-2185.

SHELBURNE

HAMILTON HOUSE DINING ROOM AND COFFEE SHOP (* BLD), on Hwy 3 at Water St. Canadian cuisine, seafood. Licensed. Open 7 am – 11 pm. (902) 875-2957.

TRURO

PALLISER RESTAURANT (** BLD), at Tideview Motel, on Tidal Bore Rd. 2 mi south of Trans-Canada. Varied menu. Licensed. Open 8 am – 8:30 pm, June 1 – Oct. 15. (902) 893-7063.

YARMOUTH

HARRIS SEAFOOD RESTAURANT (** LD), on Hwy 1, 3 mi northeast. Seafood, steak, chicken. Licensed. Open noon – 11 pm, June 10 – Sept. 30. (902) 742-5420.

ONTARIO

BARRIE

GOURMET ROOM TAVERN (** BLD), in White Towers Motel, 119 Donald St. Prime beef. Licensed. Open 7 am – 1 am. (705) 728-0208.

BROCKVILLE

NEW YORK RESTAURANT (* LD), 19 King St. W. Chinese, Canadian dishes. Open 10 am – midnight. (613) 345-0015.

BURLINGTON

ESTAMINET RESTAURANT (** LD), 2084 Lakeshore Rd. Roast duck, roast beef, lobster. Licensed. Open noon – 9 pm. (416) 639-3344.

COBOURG

MARIE DRESSLER HOUSE AND DINING ROOM (** LD), 212 King St. W. Old family recipes, sweetbreads, duckling. Licensed. Open noon – 9 pm. (416) 372-5243.

FORT ERIE

NAN HAI RESTAURANT (** LD), on Hwy 3C, 3 mi west of Peace Bridge. Chinese, Polynesian food. Licensed. Open noon – 1:30 am. (416) 871-4672.

FORT FRANCES

RENDEZVOUS DINING LOUNGE (** BLD), 2 mi east on Hwy 11, then south to 1202 Idylwyld Rd. Steak, seafood. Licensed. Open 8 am – 1 am (in the summer), 5 pm – 1 am. (807) 274-9343.

GANANOQUE

ATHLONE VICTORIAN DINING ROOM (** D), 250 King St. W. Roast beef, seafood, steak. Open 5 pm – 10 pm. Closed Sunday, Nov. 1 – Apr. 1. (613) 382-2440.

GRAVENHURST

MUSKOKA SANDS INN (* BLD), at the inn on Lake Muskoka. Continental cuisine, beef. Licensed. Open 7:00 am – 11 pm. (705) 687-2233.

SLOAN'S RESTAURANT (** BLD), 155 Muskoka St. Beef, seafood, lamb chops. Licensed. Open 7:30 am – midnight. (705) 687-4611.

GUELPH

AMBER CUPOLA (** LD), on Hwy 6, south of town. Canadian menu, steak, seafood. Licensed. Open 11:30 am – 10 pm. (519) 824-6450.

HAMILTON

GOLDEN STEER STEAK HOUSE (** LD), 264 Dundurn St. Steak, seafood. Licensed. Open noon – 11 pm. (416) 528-2457.

KINGSTON

AUNT LUCY'S RESTAURANT (** LD), 1 mi west of town at 1399 Princess St. Steak, seafood, spaghetti. Licensed. Open 7 am – midnight. (613) 542-2729.

KITCHENER

THE CHARCOAL STEAK HOUSE (** LD), 2736 King St. E. Ribs, steak, lobster. Licensed. Open 11:30 am – midnight. (519) 744-3555.

LONDON

THE FRIAR'S CELLAR (** LD), Bathhurst St. and Wellington Rd. Varied menu. Licensed. (519) 438-2129.

LATIN QUARTER (** LD), 132 Maple St. Canadian cuisine. Licensed. (519) 433-1795.

MANITOULIN ISLAND

MANITOWANING LODGE (** BLD), in Manitowaning Lodge, on Manitowaning Bay Rd. Canadian cuisine, smorgasbord. Open 7:30 am – 9 am, 12:30 – 1:30 pm, 6:30 – 8 pm. (705) 859-3136.

NIAGARA FALLS

COLONY DINING ROOM (** BLD), in Michael's Inn, 5599 River Rd. Beef, steak, lobster. Licensed. Open 7 am – 11 pm. (416) 354-2727.

PAESANO RESTAURANT AND TAVERN (* LD), 5715 Victoria Ave. Italian cuisine. Beer and wine. Open noon – 1 am. (416) 354-8641.

VICTORIA PARK RESTAURANT (** LD), in Queen Victoria Pk. Varied menu. Licensed. Open noon – 2:45 pm, 5 – 10 pm; May 12 – Sept. 30. (416) 356-2217.

NORTH BAY

ROSEBUD RESTAURANT (* BLD), 2215 Algonquin Ave. Roast beef, chicken, seafood. Licensed. Open 9 am – midnight. (705) 472-9920.

OTTAWA

CANADIAN GRILL (** LD), in the Chateau Laurier. Steak, prime beef. Licensed. Open noon – 1 am. (613) 232-6411.

CATHAY DINING LOUNGE (** LD), 228 Albert St. Chinese cuisine, steak, chicken. Licensed. Open 11 am – 3 am. (613) 233-7705.

LA CHATEAUBRIAND (*** BLD), in Motel de Ville. French cuisine, roast beef, steak, seafood. Licensed. Open 8 am – 9:30 am, noon – 2 pm, 6 – 10 pm. (613) 745-2111.

LIDO TAVERN DINING LOUNGE (* LD), 201 Queen St. Greek, Canadian cuisine. Licensed. Open 11:30 am – 1 am. (613) 235-3633.

TIFFANY DINING SALON (** LD), 64 Queen St. Roast beef, charcoal-broiled steak, shish kebab. Open noon – 11 pm. (613) 235-0426.

PERTH

PATTERSON'S RESTAURANT (** BLD), on Hwy 7, ½ mi west of Hwy 43. Varied Canadian cuisine, prime rib. Open 7 am – 9 pm. (613) 267-1045.

ST. CATHARINES

JOLLY MILLER PANCAKE HOUSE (* BLD), in city center. Open 9 am – 8 pm. (416) 682-6561.

MARKARIAN'S STEAK HOUSE (** LD), 410 Ontario St. Charcoal-broiled steak, chicken, lobster. Licensed. Open noon – midnight. (416) 684-8755.

SAULT STE. MARIE

GUFFIN'S CHEW CHEW (* BLD), Bay St. and St. Mary's River Dr. Cafeteria, delicatessen-style food. Open 8 am – 9:30 pm. (705) 949-6038.

THE KING'S TABLE (** BLD), in the Royal Hotel, 2 Queen St. E. Steak, lobster, salad bar. Open 8 am – 2:30 and 5:30 – 9:30 pm. (705) 254-4321.

PURPLE LANTERN RESTAURANT AND TAVERN (* BLD), on Trans-Canada, 2¼ mi north, 349 Great Northern Rd. Chinese cuisine, prime rib, steak, fish. Licensed. Open 6 am – 2 am. (705) 254-2871.

THUNDER BAY (North)

CIRCLE INN DINING LOUNGE AND PANCAKE HOUSE (* BLD), 686 Memorial Ave. Varied menu. Licensed. Open 7 am – 1 am. (807) 344-5744.

THUNDER BAY (South)

UNCLE FRANK'S SUPPER CLUB (** LD), on Hwy 61, 6 mi west of city center. Chinese, western dishes; steak, seafood, spaghetti. Licensed. Open noon – 1 am. (807) 577-9141.

TORONTO (Central)

GASTHAUS SCHRADER (** LD), 120 Church St. German food. Licensed. Open noon – 2 pm, 5:30 – 10:30 pm. (416) 364-0706.

HINDQUARTER RESTAURANT (*** LD), 25 St. Thomas St. French, continental cuisine; flamed pepper steak, deviled live lobster, Dover sole. Licensed. Open noon – 10:30 pm. (416) 924-3163.

HY'S STEAK HOUSE (** LD), 73 Richmond St. W. Steak, seafood, chicken. Licensed. Open 11:30 am – 2:30 pm, 5:30 – midnight. (416) 364-3326.

LA CHAUMIERE FRENCH RESTAURANT (** D), 77 Charles St. Continental cuisine. Lobster tail, frogs' legs. Beer and wine. Open 5:30 pm – 10:30 pm. Closed Sunday. (416) 922-0500.

LA SCALA (*** LD), 1121 Bay St. Northern Italian cuisine. Licensed. Open noon – 2:30 pm, 5 to 10 pm. Closed Sunday. (416) 925-1216.

LICHEE GARDEN (** LD), 118 Elizabeth Sq. Chinese cuisine, steak. Licensed. Open 11 am – 2 am. (416) 364-3481.

L'OMELETTE SPECIALTY RESTAURANT (** LD), 48 Wellington St. French cuisine, steak, seafood. Licensed. Open 11 am – midnight. (416) 964-8220.

PRINCE ARTHUR DINING ROOM (*** BLD), in Park Plaza Hotel, 4 Avenue Rd. International cuisine. Licensed. Open 7 am – 10 pm. (416) 924-5471.

THE WALRUS AND THE CARPENTER (** LD), 136 Cumberland Ave. Oyster bar, seafood. Licensed. Open noon – 1 am. (416) 921-4744.

TORONTO (East)

THE OAKS DINING ROOM (** BLD), in the Guild Inn, on Guildwood Pkwy. off Hwy 2 E. Varied menu. Licensed. Open 7 am – 10 pm. (416) 261-3331.

TORONTO (West)

BLACK ANGUS STEAK HOUSE AND TAVERN (*** LD), 3277 Bloor St. W. Steak, roast beef. Licensed. Open noon – 10:30 pm. Closed Sunday. (416) 233-7406.

LATINA DINING ROOM AND RESTAURANT (* LD), 690 The Queensway. Italian cuisine. Licensed. Open noon – 1 am. (416) 259-9101.

OLD MILL RESTAURANT (** LD), next to Old Mill Subway Station on Bloor St. W., 21 Old Mill Rd. Varied menu. Licensed. Open noon – 1 am. (416) 236-2433.

WINDSOR

GAN'S TAVERN RESTAURANT (* LD), 33 Pitt St. Chinese, American dishes, smorgasbord. Licensed. Open noon – 1 am. (519) 254-7585.

MARIO'S OF WINDSOR (** LD), 755 Ouellette Ave. Canadian, continental cuisine; roast beef. Licensed. Open 11:30 am – 1 am. (519) 254-3392.

PRINCE EDWARD ISLAND

CAVENDISH

CAVENDISH ARMS (* BLD), at Hwys 6 and 13. Seafood. Licensed. Open 8 am – 10 pm, June 9 – Sept. 15. (902) 963-2732.

IDLE OARS RESTAURANT (* LD), on Hwy 6, west of North Rustico. Seafood. Licensed. Open 11 am – midnight, May 13 – Oct. 31. (902) 963-2534.

NEW GLASGOW LOBSTER SUPPERS (*** D), on Hwy 13 at Hwy 224. Family-style supper of lobster, ham, beef at communal tables. Open 4 pm – 8:30 pm, June 25 – Sept. 2. (902) 964-2870.

ST. ANN'S LOBSTER SUPPERS (*** D), 8 mi south via Hwys 6 and 224. Lobster, steak. Licensed. Open 4 pm – 8:30 pm, June 25 – Sept. 2. (902) 964-2351.

CHARLOTTETOWN

KIRKWOOD FLORENTINE DINING ROOM (** BLD), in Kirkwood Motor Hotel, 455 University Ave. Steak, lobster. Licensed. (902) 892-4206.

SUMMERSIDE

BROTHERS TWO RESTAURANT (** LD), 618 Water St. Lobster, seafood, steak. Licensed. Open 11 am – 10 pm. (902) 436-9654.

QUEBEC

GASPE

RESTAURANT CHEZ PLUMET (* LD), 1507 Rue Principale. French-Normandy style. Licensed. Open 11:30 am – 2:30 pm, 6 – 10 pm. Closed Monday. (514) 378-4694.

SONNENHOF RESTAURANT (** LD), on Hwy 1, 3½ mi west. Swiss cuisine, fondue, schnitzel. Open 11:30 am – 3 pm, 5 – 10 pm; Mar. 1 – Nov. 30. (514) 378-7531.

MATANE

BELLE PLAGE DINING ROOM (** BLD), 1310 Matane-sur-mer Rd. Continental cuisine, seafood. Licensed. Open 7:30 am – 9:30 am, noon – 2 pm, 6:30 – 8:30 pm; June 1 – Oct. 15. (418) 562-2323.

MONTREAL

AUBERGE LE VIEUX ST. GABRIEL (** BLD), in Old Montreal, at 442 St. Gabriel St. French-Canadian menu. Licensed. Open 7:30 am – 12:30 am. Oldest inn in North America. (514) 878-3561.

CAFE MARTIN (** LD), 2175 Mountain St. French cuisine. Licensed. Open noon – 11 pm. (514) 849-7525.

CHEZ MARCOUX BAR SUISSE (* BLD), in Motel Le Champlain, 7733 Taschereau Blvd. French, Swiss cuisine. Open 7:30 am – 11 pm. (514) 676-0341.

DESJARDINS SEA FOOD RESTAURANT (** LD), 1175 Mackay St. French, Canadian, American, Alsatian cuisine. Licensed. Open 11:30 am – 1 am. (514) 866-9741.

LE CASTILLON (*** LD), in Hotel Bonaventure. French, continental, western cuisine. Licensed. Open noon – 2:30 pm, 6 – 11 pm. (514) 878-2332.

LE FADEAU (** LD), in Old Montreal at 423 Rue St. Claude. French cuisine. Licensed. Open noon – 3 pm, 6 – midnight. (514) 878-3959.

LES FILLES DU ROY (** LD), in Old Montreal at 415 E. St. Paul Vieux. Canadian menu. Licensed. Open noon – midnight. (514) 849-3535.

MOISHE'S STEAK HOUSE (*** LD), 3961 St. Lawrence Blvd. Charcoal-broiled steak. Licensed. Open noon – 11 pm. (514) 845-3509.

RUBY FOO'S (** LD), 7815 Decarie Blvd. Chinese, French, American cuisine. Licensed. Open 11 am – 2 am. (514) 731-7701.

THE BLUENOSE (*** LD), in Place Ville-Marie complex on Dorchester Blvd. International, continental seafood. Licensed. Open noon – 3 pm, 6 – 11 pm. Closed Sunday. (514) 861-3511.

SAMBO (** LD), 5666 Sherbrooke St. E. French, Chinese cuisine. Licensed. Open 11 am – 2 am. (514) 256-1694.

TROIKA RESTAURANT (*** LD), 2171 Crescent St. Russian cuisine. Beef Stroganoff, shashlik, chicken Kiev. Licensed. Open 11:30 am – 3 am. (514) 849-9333.

PERCE

L'AUBERGE AU PIRATE DINING ROOM (** LD), on Hwy 6 at oceanfront. Continental cuisine, seafood. Licensed. Open noon – 3 pm, 6 – 9 pm. (418) 782-2894.

RESTAURANT AU MAZOT SUISSE (** LD), on Hwy 6, 2 mi west of Perce. Swiss cuisine. Onion soup, fondue. Licensed. Open noon – 3 pm, 5 – midnight; June 1 – Sept. 30. (418) 782-2804.

QUEBEC CITY

AUBERGE DE PARIS (** LD), 48 Rue Ste. Ursule. Gourmet French cuisine. Licensed. Open 11 am – 11 pm. (418) 694-9938.

CHEZ GUIDO (** LD), 13 Place Royale. French, Italian cuisine. Licensed. Open noon – 11 pm. (418) 692-3856.

LE MOULIN DE ST. LAURENT (** LD), on the Island of Orleans, 20 mi east of city via Hwys 138 and 368. 750 Ave. Royale. Gourmet candlelight dining. Licensed. Open 10 am – 1:30 am, June 1 – Oct. 31. (418) 828-2688.

RESTAURANT AUX ANCIENS CANDIENS (** LD), 34 Rue St. Louis. French-Canadian cuisine. Licensed. Open 11:30 am – 10 pm. (418) 692-1627.

RESTAURANT CARAVELLE (* BLD), 68½ Rue St. Louis. Spanish, French cuisine. Licensed. Open 7:30 am – midnight. (418) 694-9022.

RESTAURANT DANTE (** LD), 17 Rue St. Stanislaus. French cuisine. Licensed. Open 11 am – 2 pm, 5 – 11 pm. (418) 524-5803.

RESTAURANT D'EUROPE (** LD), 27 Rue Ste. Angele. European cuisine. Licensed. Open 11:30 am – 11:30 pm. (418) 692-3835.

RESTAURANT GEORGES V (** LD), in Hotel Chateau Laurier, 695 Grande-Allee E. French cuisine. Licensed. Open noon – 3 pm, 6 – 10 pm. (418) 529-3594.

RESTAURANT LA DUCHESSE DE LEVIS (* BLD), 1 mi off Trans-Canada via Exit 200 N., at Hwys 2 and 173. In Levis. Canadian, Italian cuisine. Licensed. Open 7 am – 2 am. (418) 837-0268.

RESTAURANT LA RIPAILLE (** LD), 9 Rue Buade. French, Italian cuisine; flambe dishes, seafood. Licensed. Open 11:30 am – midnight. (418) 692-2450.

RIMOUSKI

LA TERRINE DINING ROOM (** LD), 91 Rue St. Germain E. European cuisine, steak, seafood, beef dishes. Licensed. Open noon – 2 pm, 6 – 11 pm. (418) 723-4710.

RIVIERE DU LOUP

ST. LOUIS MOTOR INN RESTAURANT LA CANADIENNE (*** BLD), 473 Lafontaine. French, continental cuisine; fondue, flambe, seafood. Licensed. Open 7 am – 2 pm, 6 – 9 pm. (418) 862-3591.

STE. ANNE DES MONTS

HOTEL BEAURIVAGE DINING ROOM (** BLD), 100 First Ave. W. French-Canadian cuisine. Licensed. Open 7 am – 10 am, noon – 2 pm, 6 – 8 pm. (418) 763-2224.

ST. JEAN PORT JOLI

RESTAURANT AUBERGE DU FAUBOURG (* BLD), on Hwy 2, off Trans-Canada, at Exit 256. French-Canadian cuisine. Roast beef, seafood Licensed. Open 7 am – 9 pm, June 1 – Sept. 30. (418) 598-6455.

TROIS RIVIERES

MANOIR DES VIEILLES FORGES DINING ROOM (** LD), 10000 Blvd. des Forges, 6½ mi north off Hwy 2. Roast beef, steak. Licensed. Open noon – midnight. (819) 374-2277.

SASKATCHEWAN

NORTH BATTLEFORD

BRUNO'S CHALET (* BLD), 1621 100th St. Steak, Italian dishes. Licensed. Open 8 am – 2 am. (306) 445-4114.

HOUSE OF KWON (* LD), on Hwys 4 and 29, near junction with Yellowhead, 2 mi south of city center. Chinese, western cuisine. Licensed. Open noon – 2 am. (403) 937-2575.

REGINA

BUDDY'S STEAK RANCH (* BLD), 2 mi north on Hwy 6. 100 Albert St. Steak, spareribs. Open 6 am – 3:30 am. (306) 543-1077.

CHAMPS FOX AND HOUNDS (* BLD), Albert St. and Parliament Ave. Prime rib, steak, lobster tail. Licensed. Open 7:30 am – 11 pm. (306) 584-2440.

THE INN STEAK HOUSE (*** LD), in Regina Inn, Victoria Ave. and Broad St. Steak, seafood. Licensed. Open 11:30 am – 1:30 am. (306) 525-6767.

SASKATOON

GOLF'S STEAK HOUSE (** D), 317 21st St. E. Steak, lobster, shrimp, beef fondue. Licensed. Open 4:40 pm – midnight. (306) 652-7733.

HY'S STEAK HOUSE (** LD), 21st St. E. and First Ave. Charcoal-broiled steak, prime ribs, seafood. Open 11 am – 11:30 pm. (306) 653-3322.

SUBURBAN RESTAURANT AND NORMANDIE DINING ROOM (* LD), 5 mi north on Hwy 11. Varied menu. Licensed. Open 11 am – 1 am. (306) 653-0766.

SWIFT CURRENT

WONG'S KITCHEN (** LD), 1 mi northeast on Trans-Canada. Enter via S. Service Rd. Chinese cuisine. Buffet luncheon. Licensed. Open noon – 1 am. (306) 773-4636.

YORKTON

THE SAMOVAR (** LD), in Holiday Inn at 110 Broadway St. E. Seafood, steak, prime rib. Licensed. Open 11 am – 11 pm. (306) 783-9781.

THE YUKON

WHITEHORSE

THE CELLAR DINING LOUNGE (***D), First Ave. and Main St. Steak, Alaska king crab. Licensed. Open 6 pm – 10:30 pm. (413) 667-2573.

UNITED STATES CITIZENS CROSSING the border into Canada will find that red tape and regulations have been kept to a minimum. No passport is required—though you should have some identifying paper to show your citizenship.

There are two classes of visits to Canada—for more than 48 hours and for less than 48 hours. If your visit is for less than 48 hours, you can bring back to the United States personal or household use items up to $10 in fair retail value. Your list can include 50 cigarettes, 10 cigars, one-half pound of manufactured tobacco, 4 ounces of alcoholic perfume, or 4 ounces of alcoholic beverages. If you bring the perfume, then tobacco and alcoholic beverages cannot be included in the duty-free list. On the short trip, a family cannot combine the value of its purchases.

On a trip of more than 48 hours, each individual in your family can take back items for personal and household use up to a value of $100, and may do so every 31 days. These personal exemptions can be combined, so that a family of five could take $500 worth of such goods. The exemption includes up to 100 cigars, and one quart of liquor per person.

When you cross the border with your purchases, have them placed in your luggage so that they can be inspected easily, and have receipts for all purchases gathered together for quick review. This will save you time at the customs office.

If your travels take you back and forth across the border several times, tell the man at United States Customs your plans. He'll tell you of any special exemption requirements.

Certain goods cannot be brought into the United States. These include goods of Cuban origin, including cigars, and products of North Korea and North Vietnam. Limited quantities of Chinese goods may be brought across the border.

YOUR BAGGAGE

When you enter Canada, your clothing and personal effects are, of course, admitted free of duty. You can also carry in up to 50 cigars, 200 cigarettes, and 2 pounds of manufactured tobacco, as well as 40 ounces of spiritous liquor or wine. If you carry beer, you are allowed 28 pints.

You can bring sporting equipment such as fishing tackle, portable boats, outboard motors, snowmobiles, radios, your typewriter, your camera with a reasonable amount of film and flashbulbs, and similar equipment. If you do, have a list made out in advance to facilitate the crossing. You may be asked to make a deposit on this equipment. If so, it will be refunded when the equipment is taken out of the country.

Canada permits you to bring in sporting rifles and shotguns, but restricts the entry of weapons such as revoivers, pistols (unless you are scheduled to participate in a marksmanship competition), automatic firearms, and any firearm less than 26 inches in length. Two hundred rounds of ammunition are admitted free.

When you bring your gun, provide the customs agent with a description and serial number—and remember that the customs permission is not a hunting license. You still must obtain these from the province or territory where you will hunt. Each province and territory has its own gun regulations, which you should be familiar with before you start out. Generally speaking, your gun should be encased or broken down, and kept unloaded, while in your car.

PETS

You can take your dog along, but you must obtain a certificate from a licensed veterinarian showing that the dog has been vaccinated against rabies within the past 12 months. If the family cat travels with you, you don't need a health certificate. Canaries, finches, other cage birds, monkeys, skunks, hamsters, guinea pigs, rabbits, and other animals may enter Canada without restriction. Birds of the parrot family, including budgerigars and lovebirds, are admitted if found healthy, and you certify that you have owned the bird for more than 90 days and that it hasn't been in contact with other birds of the parrot family during that time.

CANADIANS VISITING UNITED STATES

If you visit the United States and bring purchases or gifts back to Canada the following rules apply:

Absent from Canada 48 hours or more—make a verbal declaration to claim duty-free and tax-free entry of articles valued at not more than $10. This does not include cigars, cigarettes, manufactured tobacco, or alcoholic beverages.

If the value of purchases exceeds $10 make a verbal declaration to claim duty-free and tax-free entry on goods valued up to $50. This can be done only once in each of the following periods: Jan. 1 to March 31; April 1 to June 30; July 1 to Sept. 30; and Oct. 1 to Dec. 31. You may include up to 50 cigars, 200 cigarettes and 2 pounds of manufactured tobacco, and up to 40 ounces of liquor or wine or 24 pints of beer. All articles must accompany you in hand or checked luggage.

Absent from Canada 7 days or more—make a written declaration and claim duty-free and tax-free entry of goods valued up to $150. You can do this only once in each calendar year, and the same restrictions apply to tobacco and alcoholic beverages as above. All goods must be in your possession at the time of reentry, unless they were purchased outside of continental North America.

You can use your $50 exemption only once in a calendar quarter, and your $150 exemption only once in a calendar year. Also, your exemption is personal and cannot be pooled with that of another person. You can use the $50 exemption and $150 exemption in the same quarter, but it must be on separate trips.

Children who understand the regulations may claim their own exemptions for articles designed for their exclusive use. A parent or guardian may sign a claim for a child too young to make his own declaration.

If you take valuable equipment with you have it identified at your local customs office before you leave or at the port of departure.

To confirm the length of your visit outside Canada, and to establish the value of goods acquired abroad, have receipts for purchases, accommodations, or services.

INDEX 

TOPOGRAPHIC FEATURES (lakes, mountains, rivers, etc.) are listed in italic type.

A

Abrams Village, PEI, 80
Acadians, The, 81, 100
Accommodations and Restaurants, 168–80
Agassiz, B.C., 12
Agawa Canyon, Ont., 51, 56
Agawa River, Ont., 51
Akamina Highway, Alba., 94
Alaska Highway, 8, 11, 14, 87, 88, 162
Alaska Marine Highway, 14, 162
Albany River, Ont., 47
Alberta, 7, 18, 19, 152, 158, 164
Alberta Campgrounds: listings, 105, 107–10, 112; map, 106
Alberton, PEI, 175
Alcock and Brown, 85
Alexander Graham Bell National Historic Park, N.S., 100
Alexandra Falls, NWT, 89
Alexandria Bay, New York, 102
Alf Hole Sanctuary, Man., 41
Algoma Central Railway, Ont., 51, 56
Algoma Region, Ont., 51
Algonquin Provincial Park, Ont., 47, 51
Alma, N.B., 99
Amherst, N.S., 76, 80, 172, 178
Amherstburg, Ont., 101
Amish, The, 48, 54
Annapolis Royal, N.S., 80, 100, 172
Annapolis Valley, N.S., 100
Antigonish, N.S., 76, 166, 172, 178
Arctic Circle, 87, 89, 90, 100
Arctic Ocean, 57, 87
Argentia, Newf., 77, 165
Armstrong, B.C., 167
Arnold, Benedict, 70
Arnprior, Ont., 167
Arrow Lakes, B.C., 13, 16
Arvida, Que., 175
Assiniboine River, Man., 38, 40
Astotin Lake, Alba., 94
Asulkan Glacier, B.C., 96
Athabasca Glacier, Alba., 94
Atikokan, Ont., 51
Atlantic Provinces, 75 and ff.
Aurora Borealis, 32
Avalon Peninsula, Newf., 82
Avon River, Ont., 48

B

Baddeck, N.S., 76, 80, 100, 166, 172
Badlands, The, Alba., 19
Baffin Bay, 47, 54
Baffin Island, NWT, 89, 100
Baffin Island National Park, NWT, 89, 100
Baie Comeau, Que., 175
Baie des Ha! Ha!, Que., 69
Baie Sainte Catherine, Que., 164
Baie Saint Paul, Que., 65
Baldy Mountain, Man., 38
Balfour, B.C., 14, 16
Bancroft, Ont., 51, 167, 173
Banff, Alba., 93, 161, 169, 177
Banff National Park, 8, 17, 19, 93, 164, 177
Banff-Windermere Highway, 13, 96
Bare Point, B.C., 11
Bar Harbor, Maine, 82, 162, 165
Barkerville, B.C., 8, 9
Barr, Isaac, 36
Barrie, Ont., 173, 179
Bathhurst, N.B., 171
Batoche Battlefield National Historic Site, Man., 31, 33
Batoche Rectory National Historic Park, Sask., 103
Battlefords Provincial Park, The, Sask., 36
Bay de Verde, Newf., 82
Bay of Fundy, 75, 78, 80, 81, 82, 83, 164, 165
Bay Saint Lawrence, N.S., 76, 81
Bear Island, Ont., 57
Beaufort Range, B.C., 11
Beaupre Coast, Que., 64, 65, 68
Beausejour, Man., 38
Beausoleil Island, Ont., 101, 102
Beaverbrook, Lord, 78
Beaver Creek, YT, 177
Beaver River, B.C., 15
Beisker, Alba., 19
Bell, Alexander Graham, 48, 52, 76, 80, 93
Bella Coola, B.C., 9
Belle Cote, N.S., 81
Belleville, Ont., 167
Bellevue House National Historic Park, Ont., 101
Betula Lake, Man., 41
Bienville, Sieur de, 68
Big Beaver House, Ont., 47
Big Bend Highway, 15
Big Muddy Badlands, Sask., 33
Big Muddy Lake, Sask., 33
Black Duck River, Ont., 47
Black Lake, Que., 70
Blanc Sablon, Que., 164
Blenheim, Ont., 173
Blind River, Ont., 173
Blood Indian Reserve, Alba., 20
Boat Trips, 164–65
Bonanza Creek, 88
Bonavista Bay, Newf., 82, 100
Bow Falls, Alba., 94
Bracebridge, Ont., 52, 164, 173, 174
Brandon, Man., 32, 38, 171, 178
Brantford, Ont., 48, 52, 173
Bras d'Or, N.S., 172
Bras d'Or Lake, N.S., 82
Brebeuf, Jean de, S.J., 102
British Columbia, 7, 9, 10, 152, 158
British Columbia Campgrounds: listings, 113, 116–17, 120–21; map, 111
Brock, Major General Isaac, 102
Brockville, Ont., 52, 164, 173, 179
Bromley Provincial Park, B.C., 14
Brooks, Alba., 19, 169
Broughton Island, NWT, 100
Bruce Peninsula, Ont., 48, 54, 101
Bruce Trail, Ont., 48, 52
Buctouche, N.B., 78, 167
Bulkley River, B.C., 12
Burlington, Ont., 173, 179
Burlington, PEI, 80
Burns Lake, B.C., 16
Buttle Lake, B.C., 16
Button, Thomas, 31
By, Colonel John, 59
Bytown, Ont., 49, 59

C

Cabot, John, 75, 100
Cabot's Landing, N.S., 75, 76, 81
Cabot Strait, N.S., 77
Cabot Trail, N.S., 76, 80–81, 100
Cache Creek, B.C., 9, 169, 177
Cairn, Peter, 36
Calgary, Alba., 8, 19, 27, 161, 169, 177
Calgary City Guide, 29
Campbell River, B.C., 9, 16, 17, 169
Campbellton, N.B., 76, 78, 171
Campgrounds, 105–49
Camping, 104
Campobello Island, N.B., 78, 171
Canadian Shield, 31
Canmore, Alba., 169
Canninton Manor Historic Park, Sask., 33
Canora, Sask., 33
Cap Chat, Que., 65
Cap de la Madeleine, Que., 70
Cap des Rosiers, Que., 66
Cape Bonavista, Newf., 75, 171
Cape Breton Highlands National Park, N.S., 80, 81, 100
Cape Breton Island, N.S., 75, 76, 82, 100
Cape Diamond, Que., 63, 68
Cape Egmont, PEI, 80
Cape Mortello, Corsica, 101
Cape North, N.S., 76, 81
Cape Race, Newf., 75
Cape Ray, Newf., 75
Cape Sable Island, N.S., 82
Cape Tormentine, N.B., 76, 78, 80, 164, 171
Cap Tormente, Que., 65
Caraquet, N.B., 76, 78, 171
Cardigan Bay, PEI, 80
Cardston, Alba., 19, 169
Caribou, N.S., 76, 81
Caribou Country, B.C., 9
Carleton, Que., 66
Carleton Martello Tower National Historic Park, N.B., 99
Carmack, George, 88
Caronport, Sask., 176
Cartier, Jacques, 63, 65, 66, 68, 102
Cartier-Brebeuf National Historic Park, Que., 102
Cascade Mountain, Alba., 93
Castle Mountain, B.C., 97
Cathedral Grove, B.C., 14
Cavendish, PEI, 80, 102, 175, 180
Cawston, B.C., 16
Cedarvale, B.C., 12
Celista, B.C., 15
Chaleur Bay, Que., 65, 76
Chambly, Captain Jacques de, 103
Chambly, Que., 103
Champlain, Samuel de, 48, 63, 80
Charlie Lake, B.C., 11
Charlottetown, PEI, 80, 102, 163, 175, 180
Chase, B.C., 15
Chatham, N.B., 171
Chatham, Ont., 173
Cheam View, B.C., 12
Chemainus, B.C., 9
Chester, N.S., 81, 172, 178
Cheticamp, N.S., 81, 166, 172, 178
Chicoutimi, Que., 65, 175
Chilliwack, B.C., 169
Chomedey, Paul de, sieur de Maisonneuve, 63
Churchill, Sir Winston, 78
Churchill, Man., 32, 38, 43, 98, 166, 171
Clarenville, Newf., 171
Clearwater Provincial Park, Man., 38
Clearwater River, 17, 94
Clearwater Station, B.C., 17
Clinton, B.C., 9
Cobalt, Ont., 57
Cobourg, Ont., 173, 179
Cochrane, Ont., 47, 52, 173
Collingwood, Ont., 173
Coleman, PEI, 80
Columbia Icefield, 19
Columbia River, 13, 15, 97
Comox, B.C., 11, 17
Confederation of Canada, 7, 80
Cook, Captain James, 7

Corner Brook, Newf., 82, 171
Cornwall, Ont., 173
Cornwallis, Lord, 84
Cortes Island, B.C., 12
Coteau du Lac National Historic Park, Que., 102
Courtenay, B.C., 11, 17, 169, 177
Cowichan Valley, B.C., 164
Crescent Lake, Man., 40
Creston, B.C., 167, 169
Crofton, B.C., 11
Crysler Farm, Morrisburg, Ontario, 55
Cypress Hills Provincial Park, Alba., 21
Cypress Hills Provincial Park, Sask., 33

D

Dalvay, PEI, 102
Daly Glacier, B.C., 97
Dartmouth, N.S., 172
Dauphin, Man., 38, 43, 171, 178
Davis, Twelve-Foot, 21
Dawson Bay, Man., 38
Dawson City, YT, 14, 88, 103, 177
Dawson Creek, B.C., 8, 11, 87, 169
Dawson Trail, Ont., 56
Deer Island, N.B., 78
Deer Lake, Newf., 82, 171
de la Jonquiere, Governor Marquis, 99
de la Mauricie National Park, Que., 65, 102
DeMonts, 80
Denman Island, B.C., 11, 12
Detroit River, Ont., 57, 101
Digby, N.S., 75, 81, 172, 178
Discovery Passage, B.C., 9
Distant Early Warning Line, 89
Dominion Bay, B.C., 11
Doukhobors, 35
Drake, Sir Francis, 7
Drumheller, Alba., 8, 19, 20, 169
Drummondville, Que., 175
Dryden, Ont., 52
Duck Mountain, Man., 40
Duck Mountain Provincial Park, Man., 38
Duck Mountain Provincial Park, Sask., 33
Duncan, B.C., 11, 17, 166, 169, 177
Dunvegan, Alba., 20

E

Earls Cove, B.C., 14, 16
Eastern Townships, Que., 69, 70, 167
Edmonton, Alba., 8, 20, 27, 169, 177
Edmonton City Guide, 27–28
Edmundston, N.B., 75, 78, 171, 178
Egmont Bay, PEI, 166
El Dorado Creek, YT, 88
Elk Island National Park, Alba., 20, 94
Elmira, Ont., 52, 167
Emerald Lake, B.C., 97
Enderby, B.C., 15
Englehart, Ont., 57
Englishman River Falls, B.C., 14
Estevan, Sask., 176

F

Fairbanks, Alaska, 11
Fairmont Hot Springs, B.C., 169
Fergus, Ont., 52
Fernie, B.C., 169
Field, B.C., 169
Flin Flon, Man., 32, 38, 40, 43, 171
Flower Pot Island, Ont., 101
Forbidden Plateau, B.C., 11, 16
Forestry Trunk Road, Alba., 20
Forillon National Park, Que., 65, 66, 103
Fort Albany, Ont., 47
Fort Amherst National Historic Park, PEI, 80, 102
Fort Battleford National Historic Park, Sask., 33, 103
Fort Beausejour National Historic Park, N.B., 76, 78, 99
Fort Brandon, Man., 38
Fort Chambly National Historic Park, Que., 65, 103
Fort Cumberland, N.B. See Fort Beausejour
Fort Dunvegan, Alba., 20
Fort Erie, Ont., 173, 179
Fort Frances, Ont., 52, 173, 179
Fort George National Historic Park, Ont., 56, 101
Fort Henry, Ont., 49, 52, 54
Fort Langley National Historic Park, B.C., 12, 96
Fort La Reine, Man., 40
Fort Lennox National Historic Park, Que., 65, 103
Fort Livingston, Sask., 36
Fort Macleod, Alba., 20, 169, 177
Fort Malden National Historic Park, Ont., 57, 101
Fort Nelson, B.C., 11, 169
Fort Norman, NWT, 89
Fort Pelly, Sask., 36
Fort-Prevel, Que., 66
Fort Prince of Wales, Man., 40, 41
Fort Providence, NWT, 172
Fort Qu' Appelle, Sask., 33
Fortress of Louisbourg, N.S., 76, 93, 100
Fort Rodd Hill National Historic Park, B.C., 96
Fort Rouge, Man., 42
Fort Rouille, Ont., 58
Fort Saint Jean, Que., 70
Fort Saint John, B.C., 11, 170
Fort Simpson, NWT, 172
Fort Smith, NWT, 89, 90
Fort Victoria, B.C., 7
Fort Walsh, Sask., 35, 103
Fort Wellington National Historic Park, Ont., 101
Fort Whoop-Up, Alba., 20, 21
Fort William, Ont., 47
Fort York, Ont., 58
Fortune, Newf., 77, 165
Found Lake, Ont., 51
Frame Lake, NWT, 91
Franey Mountain, N.S., 100
Frank, Alba., 20, 21
Fraser River, B.C., 8, 9, 11, 12, 14, 96
Fredericton, N.B., 76, 78, 166, 171, 178
French Lake, Ont., 47, 56
French River, Ont., 173
Friar's Head, N.S., 81
Frobisher, Sir Martin, 89
Frobisher Bay, NWT, 89, 172
Frobisher Bay, NWT, 89
Fundy National Park, N.B., 76, 78, 99, 164, 171

G

Gageton, N.B., 166
Galiano Island, B.C., 12, 170
Galt, Sir Alexander, 21
Galt, Ont., 173
Gananoque, Ont., 49, 52, 102, 164, 173, 179
Gander, Newf., 82, 171
Garden River Reserve, Ont., 56
Garibaldi Provincial Park, B.C., 12, 16
Gaspe, Que., 65, 66, 175, 180
Gaspe Peninsula, Que., 64, 65, 66, 78, 80, 102, 167, 175
Gaspesian Provincial Park, Que., 65
Gatineau National Park, Que., 49, 63, 66, 68
Gatineau River, Que., 64, 68
Georgian Bay, Ont., 47, 48, 54, 57, 164
Georgian Bay Islands National Park, Ont., 53, 101–2
Gibsons, B.C., 16
Gimli, Man., 31, 40
Glace Bay, N.S., 81
Glacier National Park, B.C., 8, 12, 15, 94, 96, 170
Glacier National Park, Montana, 22, 94
Godbout, Que., 69, 164
Goderich, Ont., 173
Golden, B.C., 15, 170
Golden Horseshoe, The, Ont., 48
Gold River, B.C., 16
Goldstream Provincial Park, B.C., 12
Goose Bay, Newf. (Labrador), 171
Gore Bay, Ont., 54
Granby, Que., 66, 175
Grand Bank, Newf., 171
Grand Bend, Ont., 53
Grande Mere, Que., 66
Grande Prairie, Alba., 20, 169
Grand Falls, Newf., 172
Grand Forks, B.C., 170
Grand Greve, Que., 66
Grand Manon Island, N.B., 78
Grand Metis, Que., 65
Grand Pre National Historic Park, N.S., 81, 100
Grand Rapids, Man., 40, 164
Grand Remous, Que., 68
Grand Riviere, Que., 66
Grand Vallee, Que., 66
Gravelbourg, Sask., 35
Gravenhurst, Ont., 48, 52, 53, 164, 173, 174, 179
Great Bear Lake, NWT, 31, 89
Great Bear River, NWT, 89
Great Bog, The, Man., 38
Great Mont Louis Lake, Que., 66
Great River Road, 53
Great Slave Lake, NWT, 87, 89, 91, 95
Greenland, 75
Grenfell Mission, St. Anthony, Newf., 82
Grenfell, Sask., 176
Gros Morne, Que., 66
Gros Morne Mountain, Newf., 99
Gros Morne National Park, Newf., 82, 99
Grouard, Father Emile, 20
Grouse Mountain, B.C., 8, 24
Guelph, Ont., 53, 173, 179
Gulf Islands, B.C., 12, 162
Gulf of St. Lawrence, 65, 100, 102

H

Habitation of Champlain, N.S., 76, 80
Haines, B.C., 14, 87
Haines Highway, 87, 88
Haines Junction, YT, 14, 88, 177
Halfmoon Bay, B.C., 16, 170
Half Moon Bay, Ont., 52
Haliburton, Ont., 53, 173
Halifax, N.S., 75, 76, 81, 83, 165, 166, 167, 172, 178
Halifax City Guide, 84
Halifax Citadel National Historic Park, N.S., 84, 100
Hamilton, Ont., 48, 53, 59, 173, 179
Hamilton City Guide, 61
Haney, B.C., 12
Happy Adventure, Newf., 82
Harrison Hot Springs, B.C., 12, 170
Harrison Mills, B.C., 12
Hartland, N.B., 78
Hart Mountain, Man., 40
Hay River, NWT, 89, 172
Hay River, NWT, 89
Hazelton, B.C., 12, 167, 170
Hearst, Ont., 53
Hebertville, Que., 68
Hell's Gate, B.C., 12
Helmcken Falls, B.C., 17
Henday, Anthony, 7
Henderson Lake, Alba., 21
High Falls, Ont., 57
High Prairie, Alba., 169
Hochelaga, Que., 63
Holyrood, Newf., 82
Honey Harbour, Ont., 101
Hope, B.C., 12, 170
Hopewell Cape, N.B., 78
Hopewell Rocks, N.B., 78
Horseshoe Bay, B.C., 12, 16
Howe Sound, B.C., 12
Howe Sound District, B.C., 16
Hudson Bay, Sask., 176
Hudson, Henry, 31, 89
Hudson's Bay Company, 7, 31
Huguenots, 81
Hull, General William, 57
Hull, Que., 68, 175
Humboldt, Sask., 176
Huntsville, Ont., 53, 173
Huronia, Ont., 54
Hyatt, Gilbert, 70

I

Iberville, Sieur de, 68
Icefield Highway, 21, 94
Iceland, 75
Ile d'Orleans, Que., 68, 164, 167
Ile Sainte Helene, Que., 63
Illecillewaet River, 15
Inhoff, Count Berthold, 36, 37
Indian Battle Park, Alba., 21
Indian Brook, N.S., 81
Ingonish, N.S., 81, 100, 166, 172
Ingstad, Helge, 75
Inside Passage, 8, 12, 164
International Falls, Minnesota, 52
International Peace Garden, Man., 41
Inuvik, NWT, 90, 172
Inverness, Cape Breton Island, N.S., 172
Iona Village, N.S., 81
Ipperwash Provincial Park, Ont., 53

J

James Bay, Ont., 47
Jasper, Alba., 169
Jasper Place, Alba., 21
Jasper National Park, Alba., 8, 21, 94, 164, 177
Juneau, Alaska, 14

K

Kakabeka Falls, Ont., 53
Kalamalka Lake, B.C., 17
Kamloops, B.C., 8, 12, 170, 177
Kamsack, Sask., 35
Kap-Kig-Iwan Provincial Park, Ont., 57
Kapuskasing, Ont., 53, 173
Kaslo, B.C., 16, 167
Kawartha Lakes Region, Ont., 48
Kazabazua, Que., 167
Kejimkujik National Park, N.S., 81, 100
Kelowna, B.C., 12, 14, 170
Kelsey Bay, B.C., 8, 12, 17, 87, 88, 164, 170
Kennedy, President John F., 89
Kennedy, Senator Robert, 89
Keno, S.S., YT, 88, 103
Kenora, Ont., 47, 164, 173
Kentville, N.S., 81
Keremeos, B.C., 13, 16, 167
Ketchikan, Alaska, 14
Kicking Horse River, B.C., 97
Killarney, Man., 167
Kinbrook Provincial Park, Alba., 19
Kindersley, Sask., 176
King, William Lyon Mackenzie, 54, 66, 102
Kingdom of the Saguenay, Que., 64, 68
Kingston, Ont., 49, 53, 101, 164, 173, 179
Kitchener, Ont., 48, 54, 173, 179
Klaenza Creek Provincial Park, B.C., 16
Kleinburg, Ont., 54
Klondike River, YT, 88
Klondike, S.S., YT, 103
Kluane National Park, YT, 88, 103
Kokanee Glacier Park, B.C., 13
Kootenay Boundary Region, B.C., 13
Kootenay Lake, B.C., 13
Kootenay National Park, B.C., 13, 96–97
Kouchibouguac National Park, N.B., 78, 99

L

La Baie, Que., 68
Labrador, 70, 77, 82
Labrador Sea, 89
Lac a Claude, Que., 65
Lac Beauvert, Alba., 94
Lac des Loups, Que., 68
Lac La Ronge, Sask., 35
Lac La Ronge Provincial Park, Sask., 35
Lac St. Jean. See *Lake Saint John*
Lady Slipper Drive, PEI, 80
Ladysmith, B.C., 17, 166
Lairet River, Que., 102
Lake Agassiz, Ont., 47
Lake Atikameg, Man., 38
Lake Belle Riviere, Que., 68
Lake Cameron, Alba., 94
Lake Erie, 48
Lake Fushimi, Ont., 53
Lake Hanlan, Ont., 53
Lake Huron, 48
Lake Lebarge, YT, 88
Lake Levette, B.C., 16
Lake Louise, Alba., 169
Lake Louise, Alba., 93
Lakelse Lake Provincial Park, B.C., 16
Lake Manitoba, Man., 40
Lake Minnewanka, Alba., 164
Lake Muskoka, Ont., 48, 52, 53, 164
Lake Newell, Alba., 19
Lake Nipigon, Ont., 47
Lake Nipissing, Ont., 47, 164
Lake of Bays Area, Ont., 53
Lake of the Woods, Ont., 47, 53, 162
Lake of the Woods Region, Man., 41
Lake Ontario, 48
Lake Pivabiska, Ont., 53
Lake Sainte Anne, Que., 65
Lake Saint John, Que., 64, 65, 167
Lake Sainte Therese, Ont., 53
Lake Simcoe, Ont., 48
Lake Superior, 47
Lake Superior Provincial Park, Ont., 54
Lake Timagami, Ont., 57, 164
Lake Winnipeg, Man., 32, 40, 164
Lalemant, Charles, S.J., 102
La Malbaie, Que., 65
Lambertville, N.B., 78
Langdale, B.C., 12, 16
Langdon Crossing, Alba., 19
L'Anse au Meadow, Newf., 75, 82
La Ronge, Sask., 176
Last Mountain Lake, Sask., 35
La Tuque, Que., 68, 175
Laughing Falls, B.C., 97
Laurentians, The, Que., 64, 68, 70, 103
Laurentian Autoroute, Que., 68
Laurentides Provincial Park, Que., 64, 65, 68
Laurier, Sir Wilfrid, 93, 103
La Verendrye, Pierre, 31, 40, 41, 42, 52, 70
La Verendrye Provincial Reserve, Que., 64, 68, 69
Leamington, Ont., 174
Leduc Oil Fields, Alba., 48, 56
Le Gite, Que., 65
LeMoyne, Charles, 68
Lesser Slave Lake Provincial Park, Alba., 21
Lethbridge, Alba., 21, 169, 177
Levis, Que., 63, 68
Lewisporte, Newf., 82, 172
Lillooet, B.C., 13, 170
Little Qualicum Falls, B.C., 14
Lloyd, Reverend G. E., 36
Lloydminster, Alba., Sask., 35, 169, 176
London, Ont., 54, 174, 179
Longfellow, Henry Wadsworth, 81, 100
Long Range Mountains, Newf., 99
Longueuil, Que., 68
Louise Falls, NWT, 89
Louvicourt, Que., 68
Lower Fort Garry, Man., 40
Lund, B.C., 16
Luenburg, N.S., 81, 172, 178
Lyster, Que., 166
Lytton, B.C., 9, 12, 170

M

McCrae, Colonel John, 53
Macdonald-Cartier Freeway, Ont., 48
Macdonald, Sir John A., 101
Mackenzie, Sir Alexander, 7, 16, 87, 89
Mackenzie River, 87, 89, 90
Mackenzie Highway, 87, 154, 162
Macmillan Park, B.C., 14
Magdalen Islands, 66, 69, 80
Magog, Que., 69, 175
Marten River, Ont., 57
Mahone Bay, N.S., 166
Mahood Falls, B.C., 17
Maison Laurier National Historic Site, 103
Maisonneuve, sieur de. See Chomedey, Paul de
Malaspina Strait, 14
Maligne Lake, Alba., 94, 164
Mallorytown, Ont., 102
Malpeque Bay, PEI, 75, 80, 166
Manitoba, 31, 38, 39, 98, 153, 158, 164
Manitoba Campgrounds: listings, 123–25; map, 114
Manitoba, national parks in, 98
Manitoulin Island, Ont., 54, 174, 179
Manitowaning, Ont., 54
Maniwaki, Que., 69, 167
Manning Provincial Park, B.C., 13
Maple Creek, Sask., 176
Marconi, Guglielmo, 85, 100
Margaree Forks, N.S., 81, 172
Margaree Valley, N.S., 80
Marten River, Ont., 57
Masse, Ennemond, S.J., 102
Matane, Que., 64, 65, 69, 175, 180
Matapedia, Que., 66, 175
Meaford, Ont., 174
Medicine Hat, Alba., 21, 169, 177
Medicine Lake, Alba., 94
Melfort, Sask., 176
Mennonites, 31, 41, 48
Merritt, B.C., 170
Metis sur Mer, Que., 65
Midland, Ont., 48, 54, 101, 164, 174
Miette Hot Springs, Alba., 94
Mileage Chart, 163
Miscouche, PEI, 80
Mistassini, Que., 167
Moncton, Lieutenant Colonel Robert, 99
Moncton, N.B., 76, 78, 166, 171, 178
Montague, PEI, 80, 175
Montague River, PEI, 80
Mont Albert, Que., 65
Montcalm, General, 71
Montebello, Quebec, 175
Montgomery, General, 70
Montgomery, Lucy Maud, 80, 102
Mont Jacques Cartier, Que., 65
Mont Laurier, Que., 69
Mont Louis, Que., 66
Montmorency, Que., 68
Montmorency Falls, Que., 64, 65, 68, 69, 162
Montreal, Que., 63, 69, 71, 176, 180
Montreal City Guide, 72
Mont Sainte-Anne Park, Que., 69
Mont Saint Pierre, Que., 66
Mont Tremblant, Que., 176
Mont Tremblant Provincial Park, Que., 69
Moonbeam, Ont., 54
Moore, Henry J., 41
Moose Jaw, Sask., 36, 176
Moose Mountain Provincial Park, Sask., 33
Moosomin, Sask., 36
Moosonee, Ont., 47, 54
Moraine Lake, Alba., 94
Morrisburg, Ont., 49, 55, 174
Mount Carleton Provincial Park, N.B., 99
Mount Eagle, B.C., 96
Mount Edith Cavell, Alba., 94
Mount Garibaldi, B.C., 12
Mount Jacques Cartier, Que., 65
Mount Logan, Que., 65
Mount Logan, YT, 87
Mount Norquay, Alba., 94
Mount Orford, Que., 69
Mount Revelstoke, B.C., 15, 97
Mount Revelstoke National Park, B.C., 13, 97
Mount Royal, Que., 63
Mount Sir Donald, B.C., 96
Mount Uto, B.C., 96
Mount Whitehorn, Alba., 94
Mundare, Alba., 21
Muskoka Lakes, Ont., 174
Muskoka River, Ont., 53

N

Nahanni National Park, NWT, 90, 100
Nanaimo, B.C., 13, 170, 177
Nancy Greene Recreational Reserve, B.C., 16